Families As They Really Are

Recent Sociology Titles from W. W. Norton

Code of the Streets by Elijah Anderson
Social Problems by Joel Best
You May Ask Yourself: An Introduction to Thinking Like a Sociologist by
    Dalton Conley
The Real World: An Introduction to Sociology, 2nd Edition by Kerry Ferris and
    Jill Stein
Introduction to Sociology, 7th Edition by Anthony Giddens, Mitchell Duneier,
    Richard P. Appelbaum, and Deborah Carr
Essentials of Sociology, 2nd Edition by Anthony Giddens, Mitchell Duneier,
    Richard P. Appelbaum, and Deborah Carr
The Contexts Reader edited by Jeff Goodwin and James M. Jasper
Mix it Up: Popular Culture, Mass Media, and Society by David Grazian
When Sex Goes to School by Kristin Luker
Inequality and Society by Jeff Manza and Michael Sauder
Readings for Sociology, 6th Edition edited by Garth Massey
Sociology of Globalization by Saskia Sassen
The Sociology of News by Michael Schudson
The Social Construction of Sexuality, 2nd Edition by Steven Seidman
The Corrosion of Character by Richard Sennett
Biography and the Sociological Imagination by Michael J. Shanahan and
    Ross Macmillan
Social Movements: A Primer by David Snow and Sarah Soule
Six Degrees by Duncan J. Watts
More than Just Race by William Julius Wilson

Norton Critical Editions

The Souls of Black Folk by W. E. B. Du Bois, edited by Henry Louis Gates Jr.
    and Terri Hume Oliver
The Communist Manifesto by Karl Marx, edited by Frederic L. Bender
Protestant Ethic and the Spirit of Capitalism by Max Weber, translated by
    Talcott Parsons and edited by Richard Swedberg

**For more information on our publications in sociology, please visit
wwnorton.com**

Families As They Really Are

EDITED BY

BARBARA J. RISMAN

University of Illinois at Chicago

W. W. Norton & Company ▪ New York ▪ London

W. W. NORTON & COMPANY has been independent since its founding in 1923, when William Warder Norton and Mary D. Herter Norton first published lectures delivered at the People's Institute, the adult education division of New York City's Cooper Union. The firm soon expanded its program beyond the Institute, publishing books by celebrated academics from America and abroad. By mid-century, the two major pillars of Norton's publishing program—trade books and college texts—were firmly established. In the 1950s, the Norton family transferred control of the company to its employees, and today—with a staff of four hundred and a comparable number of trade, college, and professional titles published each year—W. W. Norton & Company stands as the largest and oldest publishing house owned wholly by its employees.

Editor: Karl Bakeman
Managing editor, College: Marian Johnson
Project editor: Kate Feighery
Editorial assistants: Rebecca Charney and Sarah Johnson
Production manager: Eric Pier-Hocking
Copy editor: Sandy Lifland
Design director: Rubina Yeh
Book design: Hope Miller Goodell
Composition: TexTech, Inc.
Manufacturing: Maple-Vail Book Manufacturing Group

Library of Congress Cataloging-in-Publication Data

Families as they really are / edited by Barbara J. Risman. — 1st ed.
     p. cm.
   Includes bibliographical references.
   ISBN 978-0-393-93278-2 (pbk.)
   1. Families—United States—History.   I. Risman, Barbara J., 1956-
HQ535.F354 2010
306.850973—dc22

                                        2009032684

W. W. Norton & Company, Inc., 500 Fifth Avenue, New York, NY 10110
WWNORTON.COM

W. W. Norton & Company, Ltd., Castle House, 75/76 Wells Street, London W1T3QT

3 4 5 6 7 8 9 0

Contents

Part Three: Intimate Relationships in the Twenty-First Century

Conclusion

PART ONE

How We Know What We Know about Families

1

Springing Forward from the Past:
An Introduction

Barbara J. Risman

This anthology is written by members of the Council on Contemporary Families (CCF), an interdisciplinary community of experts who study and work with families. Our organizational mission is to provide accurate information about how families really are to the public at large. Most but not all of us are university faculty. What we all share is a commitment to using research and clinical expertise to enhance the national conversation about what contemporary families need and how these needs can best be met. The Council is nonpartisan and our members support a wide variety of social policies, but we all strongly believe that social science should be used for the public good and that research should be used to support the diversity of families, since families of all kinds provide people with their most intimate relationships. One of the Council's unique contributions is to provide journalists with accurate information about today's families. We act as a referral system to find the best experts for journalists when they research a story. We also publish *Briefing Papers* and press releases to highlight what should be getting coverage, what you should be learning about in the newspapers, but are not. In some of these *Briefing Papers* we identify and highlight the most important new studies just coming out, and in others we integrate findings that have begun to accumulate to provide strong empirical evidence about important issues facing families today. We provide this same kind of information to policy makers at the local and national level. Our members write Op-Eds for newspapers. With this anthology, we bring our contributions to students as well.

Every article in this book is a new contribution to the research and theory about families. Beyond this initial part on evaluating research, the four other parts focus on how families got to where they are today, families and relationships in the twenty-first century, youth and social class in the twenty-first century, and the current state of the gender revolution. The articles aren't reprints; you won't find them anywhere else. A unique feature of this book is that we incorporate CCF *Briefing Papers*, press releases, and the newspaper articles that follow from them. The articles titled *Briefing Papers* were prepared and released by CCF for the press. They concisely summarize the latest research findings for a general audience, to help people make informed decision about issues that matter to them. Most were widely covered by newspapers across America. We show you not only the newest work of the leading scholars in the field, but also how their work contributes to the coverage and understanding of families that you, your friends, and your family read about in newspapers and magazines. This is a textbook example of how academic and clinical experts make a difference outside the ivory tower. It is a prime example of why intellectual work, studying and writing about people, matters. Our goal is to bring cutting-edge research and clinical expertise to all Americans so that people understand their own lives and the lives of those around them more fully. We provide information that could lead to better social policy, built more on a clear and fair reading of the evidence than on passion and stereotypes. Interspersed in each section of this book are new articles, CCF *Briefing Papers*, press releases, and the actual newspaper articles that result from them. After each part I have provided questions for students to apply, interpret, integrate, and discuss the readings.

Part One includes, beyond this brief introduction to the volume, three other essays designed to challenge each and every reader to be skeptical of all research, including the studies provided in this book. These essays were originally presented at the CCF Tenth Anniversary Symposium in a session on how to assess contemporary knowledge about families. They were then released as *Briefing Papers* in the winter of 2010, as this book was going into press. Andrew Cherlin tackles the paradox of twenty-first-century science, articulating both the reality that all science is a cultural product (as the categories scientists choose reflect their worldviews, including values), while at the same time noting that empirical research does indeed help to explain what's happening around us and in our own lives. Cherlin concludes that all readers must critically assess scientific claims in light of the biases the researcher might bring to the table. Philip Cowan clarifies an error often made when interpreting social science—in particular, the confusion of correlation with causation. He cautions all readers to question *why* something happens and not simply to presume that because two social trends begin simultaneously, one has caused the other. Linda Burton discusses the kind of information we can only learn from longitudinal ethnography, explaining how we need to go beyond survey data to uncover the full story of people's lives and relationships. Burton shows how research based on interviews and observations provides essential evidence for social policy. The introductory section ends with an Op-Ed by Stephanie Coontz that shows us why we can't believe everything we read about the census.

Let me outline how the rest of the book is organized. In Part Two, *How We Got Here*, several leading historians and social scientists provide clear and compelling evidence that what we think of as the *traditional* family has changed over the course of history. Stephanie Coontz provides a sweeping overview of the dramatic changes in how families operate, and she discusses who is even considered kin from the earliest moments of history. Steven Mintz follows a similar strategy, but he focuses specifically on the fate of American children in the last three centuries. Mintz provides convincing evidence that while some parts of childhood might be harder today, many of America's children are better off now than ever before. Mintz's paper on childhood is followed by examples of how Mintz's work was covered in the national press. Donna Franklin's research suggests that professional-class African-American couples pioneered the modern marriage. The African-American community was the first American community to accept that women could have both serious intellectual lives and careers while also being wives and mothers. Franklin argues that while white women were forced to choose between marriage and career into the twentieth century, college-educated African-American women and their husbands were inventing the contemporary marriage of equals. Karen Streuning shows how the legal system often lags behind the reality of how people live their lives. Streuning provides concrete examples about same-sex marriage and technology-assisted reproduction showing how the law seems to be in flux, with state decisions at odds with each other and often with the federal courts as well. Following the Streuning piece is a CCF *Briefing Paper* by Lee Badgett on same-sex marriage, and then a news article showing how it was covered in the press. Kerry Rockquemore and Loren Henderson then take us on a historical ride from the days when interracial marriage was illegal to the Civil Rights era, and they conclude with information about today's interracial couples and their children. Their topic, interracial marriage, was also highlighted in a CCF *Briefing Paper* that focused on a new book on the same topic by Michael Rosenfeld. That *Briefing Paper* and a newspaper article based on it follow the Rockquemore and Henderson article. As in every section, questions at the end of the part help students integrate and apply the concepts.

Part Three begins with a passionate argument from Pepper Schwartz in which she writes that, despite all the sexual imagery in our society, we are still deeply afraid of sex. Schwartz identifies several social policies that result from this fear. For example, some states make women's sexual pleasure illegal if it involves the use of vibrators. Another example of our cultural fear of sex is a federal government that has supported abstinence education, even when more than half of all teenagers in high school are having sex. Schwartz concludes by examining why we are so afraid of something so natural. In their article, Pamela Smock and Wendy Manning write about the "cohabitation revolution" and trace the change from cohabitation being seen as "living in sin" to being seen as simply a stage of courtship. They show us how quickly change can happen: one generation's sin is the next one's transition to marriage. While parents in the twentieth century were upset when their adult children cohabited, today's parents were likely to have done so themselves. In his paper, Joshua Coleman offers us another view of parenting, and one that we often ignore. He reminds us that parenting doesn't end when children graduate high school, college, or even marry. Inter-generational relationships and parenting are lifetime concerns.

We move on to a discussion of a topic that worries much of America, the effect of divorce in today's world. Virginia Rutter provides a methodological critique of the studies that purport to show that divorce hurts everyone—those who end their marriages and their kids. Rutter shares her personal life history to illustrate the argument. If Rutter's parents had been happily married, she might have been better off if they'd stayed together. But that wasn't one of the options. Her parents were not happily married, and their divorce was better than what came before it for all concerned. In a CCF *Briefing Paper*, Naomi Gerstel and Natalia Sarkisian suggest that, at the moment, marriage actually reduces social ties to others. The Gerstel and Sarkisian report was covered widely in the popular press, and we provide an example of that coverage. Yet, despite the now common experience of divorce, and the reality that marriage may reduce other social ties, more and more people seem to want to marry. In an Op-Ed article, Stephanie Coontz suggests that one way to help people stay together in their marriages is to take the pressure off the marriage by encouraging strong relationships with family and friends beyond the marriage itself. Two CCF *Briefing Papers*, one by Allen Li and one by Patrick Heuveline, focus more attention on divorce. Heuveline explains how divorce rates are measured and what they mean, while Li provides cutting-edge research that suggests that divorce, per se, doesn't significantly affect children much at all, as children of divorce have already had different life experiences before their parents split up. Two news articles present Li's findings in the national press.

Stephanie Coontz and Nancy Folbre's *Briefing Paper* shows us that the federal government, at least in the past, wanted poor people to marry as part of a poverty reduction policy. But Coontz and Folbre conclude that marriage alone is unlikely to reduce poverty in America. Included after the Coontz and Folbre paper is a news article showing how the topic was covered in the popular press. Robert-Jay Green shows how same-sex couples want to marry and how their experiences have changed in the last few decades from being stigmatized and marginalized by relatives to being married (at least in a few states) with in-laws. Mignon Moore offers an in-depth look at how African-American lesbian couples think about the fairness and equality in their relationships. Moore's article is followed by a CCF Fact Sheet, a press release that helps identify some myths and realities about same-sex couples. Etiony Aldarondo and Edward Ameen review the research on contemporary immigrants, and they show how immigrant families struggle to become part of the American mosaic without losing their own cultural heritage. No matter who marries, or why, gay or straight, from the middle of the country or some other country, one thing is for sure: there is no picture-perfect, typical American family anymore. This chapter is followed by Andrew Cherlin's Op-Ed piece, which describes the diversity of American families today.

Part Four of the book focuses on children and social class in the twenty-first century. There has long been concern that changes in the family, from the effects produced by the gender revolution to the common experience of parental divorce, would hurt future generations. But the articles in this part suggest that perhaps the most important issues to consider when we worry about tomorrow's children are poverty and the impact of unequal beginnings on future possibilities. Philip and Carolyn Cowan begin this section with an article that clarifies the distinction between family process—what actually happens in homes—and simple family structure—the legal and formal relationships between members. The Cowans argue that what matters is what's actually going on between parents and children, not whether those parents are married. In an opinion piece, Valerie Adrian discusses the need for affordable and high-quality child care, and a CCF Fact Sheet discusses how child care for the children of active-duty women and men has high standards and is affordable. The rest of the articles in this part focus on how children growing up in households with few economic resources struggle to be able to even imagine their place in the American dream. Frank Furstenberg shows clearly how social class sets the parameters for the daily life experience of today's children. Annette Laureau describes how parents from different social classes hold different child-rearing philosophies, with the consequence that children from the middle-class are brought up with strategies that enable them to develop the kinds of skills and attitudes valued for good jobs in twenty-first-century America. Her paper is followed by a news article that also describes her findings. Kevin Roy and Natasha Cabrera focus attention on low-income families by tracing the kinds of involvement of fathers in such families. They offer a model of father involvement that moves far beyond the notion of fathers simply as income providers. Also included in this part is a *Briefing Paper* by Paula England and Kathryn Edin that provides a picture of low-income unmarried couples with children. The authors suggest that simply because couples are not married does not mean that men are not around. This chapter then includes several examples of how the popular press covers issues of children's poverty. This part ends with an article by Andraé Brown, Melina Demitriou, and Lisa Dressner in which they describe how young men from poor minority neighborhoods are over-represented in the criminal justice system, and in which the authors provide an innovative therapeutic technique that involves a community ritual designed to help rehabilitate young men, so that they can ease their way both into prison, and back out again, with the prospect of re-entering the community as contributing and valued members.

The final part of this book is devoted to understanding how the changes in women's and men's lives have changed families. It was only a few generations ago that a child born with a penis would have had an entirely different future than one born with a vagina. The penis-holder would have been expected to learn a trade or get an education, earn a living, and spend most of his time supporting his family. His contributions to child rearing would have primarily been his paycheck. The vagina-holder would have been expected to find a husband (who would support her economically, if possible) and spend most of her time and attention on kin-keeping, raising children, caring for aging parents, and supporting her man. While it is beyond the space limits here to provide a full discussion of just why we have seen a gender revolution, I will offer just a few possibilities. Surely the ability of women to control if and when to have a baby, by effective birth control and access to abortion, has allowed us to think about and plan for roles beyond the family. And, of course, the feminist movement helped to point out the inequity of limiting women's lives to the family when they were educated and capable of challenges beyond the domes-tic. The simple assumption that a penis-holder and a vagina-holder should neces-sarily have different life opportunities seems vaguely quaint now, but was taken for granted as the natural order of things not very long ago. Clearly, the gender revolution has had an impact on families. If women are not primarily focused on creating and managing the domestic sphere, what will happen to the children, home-cooked meals, and the warmth of the hearth? If women are expecting men to treat them as equals, and not as helpmates, will marriage thrive, or whither away? And what about sex? Has equality come to that part of men and women's lives? The chapters in this section address these important issues.

The first chapter by myself and my colleague Elizabeth Seale asks how far the gender revolution has come for today's children. We report that girls have benefited much from the feminist-inspired changes of the twentieth century, but that boys seem sadly stuck with gender expectations that keep them tightly con-strained within narrow stereotypes of masculinity. Girls still worry very much about how they look, but not too much about acting feminine. Boys who don't act very much like all the other boys live in fear of being viciously teased. In the next chapter, Elizabeth Armstrong, Paula England, and Alison Fogarty look at the kinds of sexual pleasure older adolescents and young adults experience before marriage. In a world in which college students are more likely to "hook up" than to date, what does that mean for sexuality? Does this new form of sex indicate gender equality? Are orgasm rates equal for men and women in hook-ups? The authors show us that—for women—orgasm rates seem to increase when there is greater familiarity with sexual partners, but this is less true for men. The authors suggest that the gender revolution has yet to reach its full flowering in the distribution of sexual pleasure, at least in casual heterosexual sex. Kathleen Gerson's research focuses on twenty- and thirty-somethings just beyond the college hookup scene as they talk about their goals for balancing work and family. Young adults today are children of the gender revolution, as their baby-boom parents were the first to move into uncharted territory, with feminist mothers, frequent parental divorces, and blended families. What Gerson finds is that today's young adults, both women and men, want to balance work that matters with time left for investing in their relationships and often in parenting. But she also finds that if they have trouble with such a balancing act, men and women have starkly different fall-back plans. Oriel Sullivan provides quantitative evidence that men's contribution to the household, or what used to be called "women's work," has increased over the last few decades of the twentieth century. But while the trends are in the right direction, the pace of change is slow. There are several *Briefing Papers* about gender convergence in employment, household work, and child care. The *Briefing Papers* were widely covered by the press, both in the United States and across the world. How to move toward equality marriage continues to be a hot button issue, as shown by coverage of these *Briefing Papers* in the *New York Times*, on national evening news, and morning news shows. This part ends with a chapter about gender and violence. Despite progress toward a gender revolution, women are still much more likely to be battered than are men. Rhea Almeida offers some explanations for gendered violence, and on a more hopeful note, she also offers a novel therapeutic method for working with couples experiencing violence. In this new therapeutic model, which is designed to move families and communities toward social justice, the community becomes involved, not only in trying to stop the batterer's blows, but also in reestablishing a more egalitarian relationship.

This anthology owes much to all the members of the Council on Contemporary Families who have contributed to it. But it also owes a great deal to three of my graduate assistants who have contributed to the editorial work and the intellectual endeavor. The classroom questions at the end of each section were created by Rachel Allison, Amy Brainer, and Kelly Underman. I also owe a huge debt to Wilfrid Reissner and Stephanie Coontz for their extremely helpful editorial work on many of the articles and their unending support for this project. Thanks also go to my editor at Norton, Karl Bakeman, who originally conceived the idea for this anthology. I hope this is everything he hoped it would be. I'd like to dedicate this book to my own family, siblings, nieces, nephews, and cousins, and most importantly, to my daughter, Leah KaneRisman, with the hope that the world in which she comes of age will value and accept whatever kind of family she chooses for herself.

The Council on Contemporary Families was created over a decade ago because our founding members saw the press misinterpreting good science, sometimes naively, and sometimes because they had been misinformed by ideological right-wing think tanks. The Council is dedicated to providing good scientific research and clinical expertise to the public and policy makers alike. We invite you to read the articles in this anthology with the critical lenses provided by Cherlin, Cowan, and Burton in their articles on evaluating research. Science is always becoming, and these articles are offered in the spirit of contributing the best information we have now to the body of knowledge available to us all. Each of the authors has contributed their time and effort to this volume, and all proceeds will help CCF in our mission to diffuse the best new knowledge we have on families, with the firm belief that knowledge is power.

2

One Thousand and Forty-nine Reasons Why It's Hard to Know When a Fact Is a Fact

Andrew J. Cherlin

When is a fact a fact? If you are a postmodernist, the answer is clear: never. Postmodern critics of standard social science argue that the conclusions we draw are not, and cannot be, genuinely objective. Rather, they say, our findings are contaminated in several ways. First, the questions we ask and the point of view we take often reflect our values, whether those are an enthusiasm for feminist or civil-rights-inspired activism or a belief in the importance of marriage and premarital chastity. Even the categories and labels we use often reflect values-based assumptions.

Here is an example from my field, family demography: In 1941, Paul Glick, the Bureau of the Census demographer who virtually created the field, wrote a pioneering article entitled "Types of Families: An Analysis of Census Data."[1] Glick divided American families into three groups: (1) normal families, a category that consisted of all two-parent families; (2) other male-headed families; and (3) other female-headed families. The implication, of course, was that all single-parent families were abnormal.

Or consider contemporary debates over immigration, which may be shaped by whether one uses the term "illegal alien" or "undocumented immigrant." The first conjures up an image of a law-breaking invader from outer space; the second conveys an image of a striving newcomer who merely lacks the right papers.

Recognizing that most researchers draw upon particular values when they choose what categories to use and what questions to ask does not mean that all data are suspect or that all interpretations of data are equally valid. But it does drive home the importance of treating so-called facts critically and of questioning their origins and purposes. When we read facts, we should ask ourselves a few key questions: Who produced this fact? Was it a person or an organization that promotes a particular point of view? What was the purpose of making this fact known? What do we know about the relationship of this fact to other facts or trends?

Consider familyfacts.org, a website operated by the Heritage Foundation. It publicizes findings from social scientific research on family life. On its home page (www.familyfacts.org), familyfacts.org presents itself as a neutral clearing-house for family research: "The Heritage Foundation's familyfacts.org catalogs social science findings on the family, society and religion gleaned from peer-reviewed journals, books and government surveys. Serving policymakers, journalists, scholars and the general public, familyfacts.org makes social science research easily accessible to the non-specialist."

In 2008, this site featured a "top ten" list of findings about how children in different kinds of families fare in school. According to each finding, children living with two parents were doing better than children living with one parent or with stepparents. Here are two of the findings: "Kindergartners in intact families have higher average reading scores than peers in stepfamilies or cohabiting families" and "First-graders whose mothers were married when they were born are less likely to engage in disruptive behavior with peers and teachers than those whose mothers were single or cohabiting." In fact, virtually all of the thousands of findings on the site support the view that marriage is best for children and that religion improves family outcomes.

These findings are not falsified. They are taken from reputable studies published in well-regarded journals such as the *Journal of Marriage and Family* and, by and large, are described accurately. A naive user might think that this is all social scientists know. But the facts reported on this site have been selected to support a particular conclusion, while facts that modify, complicate, or challenge that conclusion are not reported.

For example, the site quotes a 1998 article that I co-wrote about a study showing that children whose parents had divorced had a higher risk of emotional problems in adulthood.[2] Yet that same article also showed that some of the emotional problems had been visible in childhood before the parents even divorced, but this additional finding was not mentioned. Nor does the site mention a 1991 article that I co-wrote that also suggested that some of the problems experienced by children from divorced families might have occurred even had the parents stayed together.[3] This is not a fact that familyfacts.org thinks you need to know.

Which findings are included and which are excluded make sense if one knows that the Heritage Foundation, a conservative think tank, promotes the values of institutions such as "traditional" marriage and religion. This is not to say that one should disregard the findings on familyfacts.org; in fact, much evidence does suggest that growing up with two parents is beneficial to children. But the informed reader will know that it is necessary to go elsewhere to see whether the kinds of findings that are cataloged at familyfacts.org tell the whole story.

Conservatives are not the only ones who use facts in ways that reflect their values. In the 1980s, when homelessness was first being recognized as a social problem, many news stories included the information that 2 to 3 million Americans were homeless. Soon this figure became an accepted fact. Yet it subsequently came to light that this fact had been provided by a leading advocate for the homeless, Mitch Snyder, who basically made a guess. He said in a television interview:

> Everybody demanded it. Everybody said we want a number. . . . We got on the phone, we made a lot of calls, we talked to a lot of people, and we said, "Okay, here are some numbers."[4]

Snyder was just doing what advocates usually do: providing the largest credible estimate of how many people are affected by the problem they want to alleviate or by the disease they would like to cure or by the injustice they want to remedy. In counting the homeless, as in estimating the number of women who have been raped or who experience eating disorders, advocates often take the most expansive definition of the problem and adjust for underreporting. But such estimates are especially susceptible to manipulation for dramatic effect.

More recently, we have heard much in debates over same-sex partnerships about the 1,049 federal benefits and rights that marriage supposedly confers on husbands and wives. This number appeared in the late 1990s and was soon cited everywhere as a fact about the legal benefits of marriage. In 1999, advocates of same-sex marriage, while welcoming the Vermont legislation that created the nation's first civil unions, noted that state-level recognition of gay unions would not provide the partners with the federal benefits of marriage. Hanna Rosin reported in the *Washington Post*:

> The plaintiffs in the Vermont case documented a long list of benefits granted to married couples but denied to gay ones. The 300 state and 1,049 federal laws cover such matters as the right to pay taxes jointly, and social security benefits.[5]

Ever since, reputable newspapers around the country and politicians on both sides of the political spectrum have accepted this claim as fact, derived from a federal study conducted by the General Accounting Office. The precision of this fact—not 1,048 or 1,050 but exactly 1,049—gave it such verisimilitude that no one challenged it. And its magnitude suggested an overwhelming bias in favor of marriage, making it an attractive "fact" that could be used by proponents of same-sex marriage, just as the people who constructed the Heritage website were attracted to only some of the "facts" reported by family researchers on divorce. But in hindsight, its precision and size are the very factors that should have suggested caution in using this fact.

The source of this "fact" was indeed a federal study, but the study did not establish what these and many other news reports have since claimed. In 1996, when Congress enacted the Defense of Marriage Act, Represantative Henry Hyde requested that the General Accounting Office identify all federal laws that involved benefits, rights, and privileges that depend on being married. As the GAO staff discussed this request with Hyde's staff, they agreed to broaden the scope of the study to include "all those laws in the United States Code in which marital status is a factor, even though some of those laws may not directly create benefits, rights, or privileges."[6] In other words, the GAO counted all laws that involved marriage, including those that *penalized* married couples.

One of the 1,049 laws, for example, is a statute that limits the amount of certain crop support payments that one person can receive. For this purpose, a married couple is considered to be one person. But an unmarried couple can apparently escape this restriction and each receive the maximum amount. Another law mandates that a candidate may not spend more than $50,000 of his or her own money, or the money of his or her immediate family, on a political campaign and still be eligible for federal funding; but there's nothing to prevent the candidate's unmarried partner from kicking in additional funds.

Many of the so-called benefits of marriage, furthermore, are trivial. It is true that one law discriminates against cohabiting couples by making it a federal crime to try to influence United States officials by threatening to kill their spouses, whereas it seems not to be a federal crime to threaten to kill their cohabiting partners. But this "benefit" of marriage applies to very few couples.

It did not take weeks of research in dusty government archives to get to the bottom of this; rather, I found the information on the Internet in less than an hour. That so many people had quoted the number without checking it shows how easily a "fact" can become part of the dialogue about social and political issues.

What happens to a fact of this kind is that it becomes a symbol of the issue in dispute. Clearly, marriage does provide some important federal benefits. Only married couples can file their federal tax returns jointly; and only married people can continue to receive part of their partner's Social Security benefits after the partner dies. But the figure of 1,049 benefits became a dramatic, and at first glance convincing, stand-in for the general privilege of being married in American society. It was this general privilege that really was the point of the debate. This was the reasoning of the Massachusetts Supreme Court in ruling that restricting marriage to heterosexuals was unacceptable even if same-sex partners were given the same legal status. Marriage, the judges wrote, is more than a collection of benefits; rather, it is a "status that is specially recognized in society." Denying same-sex couples that special status, the justices argued would create a "stigma of exclusion."[7]

Debating the abstract notion of social status is, however, more difficult than debating legal benefits. Advocates therefore focused on the 1,049 benefits as a way of building support for their more general position. Many debates over social and political issues revolve around symbols such as this one, and it is in the interest of each side to define the symbol in the largest or the smallest terms possible to bolster their case.

Whether everyone knows where the supposed facts come from, as is the case with the findings displayed on the familyfacts.org website, or whether no one seems to know, as with the apocryphal 1,049 benefits, the careful user of facts will not take them at face value. At the least, the user must examine (or uncover) the source and determine its position on the issues. Even your most trusted friends probably care about the social and political issues they discuss, which makes it difficult for them to be truly balanced in the facts they tell you about. And as a rule, no organization that takes sides in a public debate will provide facts that should be considered fully objective and balanced. To be sure, some organizations may be more transparent and balanced, and others more opaque and one-sided, in their use of facts. But even the fairest will have made choices about what questions to ask, what counts as good research, and on what basis one draws conclusions. Unless you understand where the source is coming from, it's hard to evaluate the information it provides. And that's a fact.

3

When Is a Relationship between
Facts a Causal One?

Philip A. Cowan

After checking the accuracy of facts, as Cherlin's paper urges us to do, the next step is to examine critically the way people interpret the relationship of one fact to another. It is a fact, for example, that substantial numbers of children are growing up in single-parent families. Or, more precisely, it is a fact that many children are growing up in households that do not contain two parents who are married to each other. Some of these families have only one parent in the home, while others may have two parents who are cohabiting. It is also a fact that, in general, children and couples in nonmarried families are not faring as well as those in married families. Members of such families have less income and lower levels of physical and mental health, and the children have more emotional problems and behavior problems.[1] It is tempting to conclude from these facts that living in a single parent household is the *cause* of these difficulties.

But when we look at all people who live in single-parent households, we find a larger number of people with preexisting financial, health, or emotional disadvantages than we find in the married-couple population. It may be these characteristics of the adults in the family, rather than single-parenthood per se, that make them less likely to get or stay married and more likely to raise children who exhibit behavior problems. If so, it would be inaccurate to say that divorce or unwed behavior *causes* problems in children. In many cases, the problems seen in children raised by these individuals might develop even if the parents were able—or were forced—to stay together.

The problem of overstating causal conclusions from correlational data is not the sole property of the political left or political right. Both sides are too quick to draw support from social science research when the correlations support their cherished conclusions. Supporters of the political right tend to select studies that show correlations between divorce and negative outcomes for children. Supporters of the political left tend to select studies that show correlations between poverty and negative outcomes for children. The point here is not that these claims are wrong, but that most studies do not provide evidence for the causal assertions and policy conclusions that are made on both sides of the political spectrum.

We need to make a slight digression here. It is always legitimate and possible to make policy arguments on moral or value grounds. That is, if one's values lead to the conclusion that cohabitation is a sin, and that having children compounds that sin, it is part of the bedrock of democracy that one can argue strongly on moral grounds that laws should be made to prevent cohabitation and foster marriage. What we're concerned with here are cases in which reporters or politicians buttress their arguments with conclusions drawn from social science research. The key is for us to be explicit about when we are making arguments from a values perspective and when we are arguing based on social science research.

BASIC PROBLEMS IN THE INTERPRETATION OF RESEARCH FACTS

1. Causal facts always imply a direction of effects—the cause, A, comes before the effect, B. But statements based on statistical correlations can *never* tell us about the direction of effects. For example, it is a fact that there is a correlation between being married and having better-functioning lives and between non-marriage and financial or emotional difficulties. But we do not know whether marriage produces the partners' better functioning or whether better-functioning partners tend to marry. That is, selection effects that guide who gets married may influence the results.

2. An important corollary of point 1 is that when two social trends vary together, it is not possible to conclude that one causes the other. Increases in the proportion of mothers of young children in the workforce occurred in the mid-twentieth century around the same time that the divorce rate went up. On the basis of these two facts alone we cannot point to women's working as a cause of the increase in divorce. Why not? First, we don't know from these two statistics whether the divorces occurred more often in the families of women who went to work. And second, we do not know whether these two trends are associated with other factors that may plausibly have caused the increase in divorce.

3. Reasoning backwards about causality produces backward thinking. Most newspaper and magazine articles on family issues rely on research that starts with outcomes of interest right now and look backwards for potential explanations, because that's what most research does. For example, investigators take two groups of couples, one in which there are high levels of domestic violence, and another in which there has never been any domestic violence. They look at their histories, and find that the couples with domestic violence are much more likely to have been abused by their parents than the harmonious couples. Does this demonstrate that early abuse is a cause of domestic violence? No. What's missing from the picture is information from studies that follow families forward. These studies usually find that even if some of the abused children grow up to form violent relationships with a spouse, the majority of children who experience early abuse do not wind up in violent relationships. That is, you can't generalize with any degree of certainty from looking backwards that abused children are highly likely to establish distressing relationships.

    In this example, even if early abuse were found to be a cause of domestic violence, we might try to change each partner's understanding of the past through psychotherapy, but we could not reverse the early abuse. Other examples, though, seem to suggest that if we can identify the cause, a quick fix is possible. We know, for example, that there is a correlation between cohabitation and higher rates of domestic violence, but it would be dangerous to conclude that a causal relation exists and recommend that cohabiters should marry. Rather than their failure to marry producing domestic violence, it may have been their stormy relationship that led them not to marry in the first place. If this were the case, a policy that created incentives to marry could result in creating more harm to both the couple and their children.

4. Correlations can result from a third variable that produces the association between them. It is a fact that children whose parents are divorced, or who live with a single parent who never married, tend to have more emotional, behavioral, and academic difficulties than children whose parents are married. It is possible, though, that some of the negative effects of divorce and single parenthood come from the fact that these households have lower incomes, and that the consequences of low income in terms of reduced resources are responsible, at least in part, for children's difficulties.

5. Many studies of families focus on family status and not on family processes or relationship quality. Most studies of marriage and divorce, especially in Sociology and Social Welfare, attempt to link couple status (married, cohabiting, divorced, single) with child and family outcomes. For example, in Waite

and Gallagher's "The Case for Marriage," almost all of the studies they cite contrast married couples with cohabiting couples or single adults. In each chapter, they present evidence that the strongest positive findings occur for *happily married* couples. But in the policy summary at the end of the book, the authors revert to the argument that "married is better," ignoring the issue of quality altogether.

What the advocates for marriage ignore or dismiss are the hundreds of studies showing that high unresolved marital conflict erodes couple relationships and affects children negatively.[2] Unless we are talking about "good" marriages, getting couples to marry will not provide a solution to social problems of poverty and less effective child rearing.

THE IMPORTANCE OF SYSTEMATIC STUDIES THAT INCLUDE RANDOMIZED CLINICAL TRIALS WITH CONTROL GROUPS

Every day, the popular press, TV, government websites, and self-help books make new claims that a particular program proposed for families, or one already in operation, is effective. What is surprising is that most of these programs have no systematic evaluations at all. In order to assert that individuals, couples, and families are better off *because* of a program than they were before, what do we need?

First, we need to be able to determine that whoever is providing the information does not have an interest in consciously or unconsciously skewing the results. For example, if the intervention staff is providing the data, it is easy to see how they might be motivated or self-deluded to make higher ratings of the participants on the post-intervention assessments. When program evaluations include data from outside observers, as well as from therapists and clients, the inclusion of multiple perspectives makes statements about improvement more credible.

Second, even with a study that contains the most objective, unbiased assessments of outcome, a control group is still needed. You can't simply claim that the program is a success if the participants show positive changes. What if the average participant in a job-training program has a statistically significantly higher income a year after the program ends? How can we rule out the possibility that these results come from an economic boom in which most families have higher incomes a year later? That is, the fact of increased income does not support a causal interpretation about the impact of the intervention until we know what happens to a comparable *untreated* group.

Similarly, what if a group of children become less aggressive with their peers after their parents take a class on managing children's aggression? Again, we need to know whether children whose parents did not take such a class also became less aggressive as they grew older or whether we can show that the declines in aggression are associated with parents' more effective parenting strategies.

We know that it is not always possible to do controlled experiments. To test the hypothesis that married parents provide a better environment for children's development, we cannot assign some single parents to the "get married" group and others to the "remain single" controls. In this case, there are responsible ways of gathering data to rule out alternative hypotheses so that we can come to a more informed decision about the impact of marriage on children's adaptation. One method is to measure a number of variables that could possibly influence A and B groups differently and "subtract them" from the outcome to see if any effect of the intervention remains. This method is only as powerful as the resourcefulness of the investigator in thinking about what else outside of the intervention could have created the results. A second, more powerful method is to conduct a longitudinal study (e.g., before and after divorce) and determine whether, on the average, any change in the children can be identified from before to after their parents' divorce.

CONCLUSIONS

Both the political left and the political right have jumped to conclusions in the debate about marriage, based on the erroneous assumption that correlations support causal inferences. From the right we hear: "Married families do better; let's get those single moms married or make it harder for couples to divorce." From the left we hear: "Unmarried mothers are poor, and poor families have difficulty; let's give them money and jobs."

What we need to remember is that explanations of how two facts are connected can seem simple, but they are often exceedingly complex. At the same time that women started to work outside the home in greater numbers than they had following World War II, the incidence of divorce increased sharply. This correlation cannot be interpreted to mean that working women destroy marital life. Unpacking the causal connection requires very thoughtful systematic research, accompanied by interventions, if possible, that test hypotheses about the direction of effects. I am aware that this kind of rigorous exploration takes time, and that policy decisions must often be made in the absence of scientific proof that the proposed action will have the desired effects. What I want to convey to social service providers and policy makers is that causality is extremely difficult to nail down. We must all read accounts of research with a critical eye. The kind of complexity hidden within a "simple" correlation cannot be communicated or understood in simple sound bites.

4

Uncovering Hidden Facts That Matter in Interpreting Individuals' Behaviors: An Ethnographic Lens

Linda M. Burton

A s a social scientist who has conducted ethnographic research on low-income families for over two decades, I would argue that longitudinal ethnography moves us closer than most data collection methods to uncovering hidden facts that shape individuals' behaviors. Ethnographic research is a method of gathering data about individuals' thoughts, behaviors, and experiences in the context of their everyday lives. In ethnography, researchers engage systematically with those they are studying, participating in multiple domains of their lives and asking in-depth questions about the information they are learning.

Ethnographic research differs from surveys of human behaviors in several important ways. While surveys typically ask an individual a series of questions with fixed-option responses, usually at one point in time, ethnographers record *over time* both what individuals say about their own behaviors and what they actually do. In the process, ethnographers build trusting relationships with those they study by listening without judgment and keeping promises of confidentiality. Ethnographers are typically able to uncover hidden data about respondents through long engagement with them and by *being there* when research participants are ready to reveal previously concealed information, on their own terms. In settings in which those studied are concerned about revealing too much of themselves, it is not until a long-term comfortable relationship has been established that research participants will share information that exposes potentially disparaging knowledge about them or important others in their social worlds.

In addition to uncovering hidden information, ethnography can also offer a check against exaggeration of such information. In the course of observing participants and doing informal, yet in-depth questioning, ethnographers are able to gather many perspectives on the issue in question—and, hence, they can provide reliability checks on statements made by informants. Occasions can arise in which ethnographers experience contradictions between what people tell them and what ethnographers actually observe them doing or hear reported from others. By being there over time and participating in the social world being studied, ethnographers gain opportunities to uncover new, contradictory, and verifiable forms of data as they occur.

As a result, ethnographers' assessments of respondents usually go well beyond the "public face" and socially appropriate façades individuals tend to put on their responses to general questions. They also typically uncover patterns of behavior or experiences that informants are either ashamed to admit or that they may not even initially regard as relevant to helping ethnographers understand and interpret their lives. Such was the case in the Three-City Study ethnography of economically disadvantaged families in Boston, Chicago, and San Antonio.[1] This multiyear team ethnography was designed to examine the impact of welfare reform in the lives of low-income African-American, Latino, Hispanic, and non-Hispanic white families and revealed, beyond the ethnographers' initial estimates, that domestic violence and sexual abuse were far more central to understanding low-income women's day-to-day life experiences and vulnerability than most researchers had recognized.

More than two-thirds of the mothers who participated in the ethnography (N=256) eventually disclosed that they had been sexually abused or had experienced domestic violence as children and/or as adults. Yet in most cases, it took more than six months of in-depth interviews with and participant observations of respondents for this information to come out, and in almost 20 percent of the cases, the information emerged only after ten to twenty-four months of ethnographer's "being there" with the mothers and their families. Three patterns of disclosing sexual abuse and domestic violence were identified in the ethnographic data: trigger topics disclosure, crisis or recent event disclosure, and ethnographer prompted disclosure.

The *trigger topics* disclosure pattern occurred when mothers unexpectedly revealed sexual abuse and domestic violence histories to ethnographers when they were asked about topics such as health, intimate relationships, transportation, work history, and intergenerational caregiving. Seventy-one percent of disclosures conformed to this trigger topics pattern. For example, during an interview about her general health, a thirty-seven-year-old African-American mother of three commented that "My pregnancy with Dante was hard because

I was sick." The ethnographer neutrally asked for more information: "You were sick?"

> Yeah, he had been sleeping around and gave me gonorrhea. I'm still embarrassed talking about it. Sometimes I didn't want to sleep with him but he'd rape me. I told him I was gonna' call the police and he said, "Go ahead. Ain't nobody gonna' arrest me for wanting to be with my woman."

A different informant revealed experiences with abuse when the ethnographer asked how she had met her husband. Liza stated that this was a "funny story" and noted that she had met her husband just after ending a relationship with a man who had broken her nose. Yet another example of such unprompted disclosure was one that occurred during the twenty-third visit to the home of Delilah, a forty-year-old European-American divorcée and mother of four children. The ethnographer was conducting a follow-up interview concerning Delilah's past and current work experiences, because Delilah had failed to mention particulars about her work history over the previous two years of interviews. At this point, Delilah finally told the ethnographer that she had once worked at a bank as a switchboard operator, but quit when her former husband physically injured her. Delilah stated: "I went to work with a black eye. People at the bank noticed. When it happened a second time, I felt embarrassed coming to work, so I quit like cold turkey."

The second most common pattern of disclosure, accounting for almost 20 percent of the reports, was the *crisis* or *recent event* disclosure pattern. This pattern occurred when the ethnographer unexpectedly "walked in" on a domestic violence situation when she was visiting the participant, or when the participant experienced a sexual abuse or domestic violence episode a few days or weeks prior to the ethnographer's regularly scheduled visit. In both instances, the abuse situation was "fresh" in the minds of mothers, and they chose to discuss it with their ethnographers in great detail. In most of these cases, the ethnographers had suspected abuse (as indicated in ethnographers' field notes and in discussions with their supervisors and team members), but they hadn't felt that they could directly ask the participant about it. For example, Janine, the ethnographer for Patrice, a twenty-eight-year-old European mother of two, describes the circumstances that led to Patrice's crisis-prompted disclosure:

> I arrived at Patrice's house 10 minutes before the interview only to find the streets covered with cops, patrol cars, and an ambulance. . . . Patrice was on the porch screaming, her face bloody and cut. The kids were running around everywhere screaming and crying. . . . I feared that my worst suspicions about the prevalence of

domestic violence in Patrice's life were about to be confirmed. . . . When I visited Patrice three weeks later, the flood gates opened without me asking. I listened as she told me everything about the incident and about other incidents of physical and sexual abuse that she had experienced since childhood.

The third pattern, *ethnographer prompted* disclosure, occurred when ethnographers directly asked mothers about their past and current experiences with sexual abuse or domestic violence. Ethnographers usually asked direct but open-ended questions about these topics in an interview if they noticed a behavioral reaction from mothers when discussing their intimate relationships with their partners. Only 10 percent of all disclosures came from such prompts.

It is also important to note that only 12 percent of the mothers who revealed sexual abuse and domestic violence experiences to the ethnographers did so during visits or participant observations that occurred in the first three months of their involvement in the study. Twenty-nine percent disclosed sexual abuse and domestic violence experiences after four to six months of visits with the ethnographers, 40 percent after seven to nine months of visits, and 19 percent after ten to twenty-four months of visits.

The prolonged wait before most informants revealed their history of sexual abuse and/or domestic violence reveals the importance of ethnographers' investing enough time and participation in the mothers' lives to reach "turning points" in their relationships. A turning point is the moment when participants trust ethnographers enough to share intimate, sensitive, and sometimes highly painful information. That such revelations often occurred almost accidentally or unintentionally suggests that ethnographic studies may capture much more of the actual incidence of violence in poor women's lives than official police reports or surveys, thus uncovering vital, yet hidden facts that matter for accurately interpreting individuals' behaviors.

In the News

NOT MUCH SENSE IN THOSE CENSUS STORIES

Washington Post, July 13, 2001

Stephanie Coontz

Nearly every week, the U.S. Census Bureau releases a new set of figures on American families and the living arrangements they have been creating in the past decade. And each time, as the media liaison for a national association of family researchers, I'm bombarded with telephone calls from radio and television producers seeking a talking head to confirm the wildly differing—and usually wrong—conclusions they've jumped to about what those figures say about the evolving nature of family life in America.

In April, for example, Census officials announced that 56 percent of American children were living in "traditional" nuclear families in 1996, up from 51 percent in 1991. Several prime time television shows excitedly reported this "good news" about the American family, and I heard one radio commentator declare that young couples were finally rejecting the "divorce culture" of their parents' generation.

But this supposedly dramatic reversal of a 30-year trend was based on a peculiarly narrow definition of a traditional family: a two-parent household with children under 18 and no other relatives in the home. If a grandchild, grandparent or other relative were living in the house, the family was "nontraditional." (There's an obvious irony here, given that nothing is quite so traditional as an extended nuclear family that includes a grandparent!)

Evidently, the definition itself was largely responsible for this "trend": Enough such relatives moved to separate households during the first half of the 1990s to increase the proportion of "traditional families," even though the percentage of children living with both biological parents had stayed steady at about 62 percent, and the percentage of married couples had continued its 30-year slide. In other words, the initial reports of resurgence in traditional families were the result of wishful thinking and a misunderstanding of the terms being used by the census.

But hope springs eternal among talk show producers desperate for a new angle. In mid-May, expanding on its earlier study, the Census Bureau reported that the absolute numbers of married couples with children at home had grown in 2000 after falling in two previous head counts (although the proportion of such families in the total population was still shrinking). TV producers jumped on the story, apparently ready to trumpet the return of the "Ozzie and Harriet" family of the '50s. I soon heard from several talk show hosts in the West who, state-by-state printouts in hand, were agog about the exceptionally large increase of such families in *their* regions. They wanted me to find them an expert to comment on the heartening return to traditional values.

Their enthusiasm dimmed, however, when I told them that this regional increase in married-couple households with children was due largely to the well-reported influx of Asian and Hispanic immigrants. Their interest evaporated entirely when I reminded them that, as immigrants assimilate, their family patterns tend to match those of the preexisting population.

A week later, the Census Bureau reported that the number of unmarried women with children had increased by 25 percent, dwarfing the 7 percent growth in married-couple families. This time we moved into the "bad news" cycle: Media pundits called to confirm their worst fears, looking for more figures to prove that the explosion of single motherhood was creating an ever-deepening social and cultural crisis in the land.

In fact, most of the growth in "single" motherhood during the 1990s was due to an increase in births to women who, while not married, were living with the child's father. So, much of the recent increase in single motherhood simply reflected the 71 percent increase in cohabitation between 1990 and 2000. But the fact that many "single mother" families actually had fathers present didn't faze the talk show hosts who called seeking confirmation that the sky was falling because of the "collapse of marriage." This time around, they weren't the least bit interested in any good news— such as the figures, also released in May, that showed a 20 percent drop in births to teenagers over the decade.

Then, last month, the Census Bureau reported that the number of households headed by single fathers had increased fivefold, from 393,000 in 1970 to 2 million in 2000. I got two calls from TV producers that day, each rushing to air a show on this new trend. One asked me to explain how this reflected the increasing equality of men and women in their commitment to parenting, while the other wanted some- one to tell her viewers why it represented a backlash against working mothers, who were obviously losing custody to unwed and divorced fathers.

Both producers were crushed when I told them our researchers couldn't confirm either claim, and that we have no way of even knowing how many of these so-called single fathers are in fact living with the mother of their child outside of marriage, and how many are divorced dads who simply happened to have their children with them for the weekend on the day they filled out the form. When I called a Census

Bureau researcher to see if he could help straighten this out, he said my guess was as good as his.

It's not that the census researchers are doing a bad job. The problem is that they're asked to compress America's increasingly fluid family arrangements into one-dimensional categories that were established at a time when most single-parent households were created by death rather than by divorce, and when most people made things easy for data collectors by lying rather than admitting to "living in sin."

People's new candor about their lifestyles, combined with the undeniable changes in family arrangements that have occurred over the past 40 years, makes it increasingly hard to capture new family realities in old census categories. And using such categories to talk about families has consequences.

Labeling people single parents, for example, when they may in fact be co-parenting—either with an unmarried other parent in the home or with an ex-spouse in a joint custody situation—stigmatizes their children as the products of "single parenthood" and makes the uncounted parent invisible to society. This can lead teachers, school officials, neighbors and other family members to exclude the uncounted parents from activities and interactions into which they might otherwise be drawn. In fear of such marginalization, some separated parents find it hard to agree on a custody arrangement that's in the best interests of the child, because each wants to be the socially recognized parent.

In the past, many "intact" families had fathers who were AWOL from their children's lives. Today, conversely, many "broken" families have fathers who remain active parents. Harvard fellow Constance Ahrons, who has conducted a 20-year study of post-divorce families and their children, has certainly seen plenty of cases where the nonresident parent, usually the father, stops doing any parenting. But she has found many instances where nonresidential fathers became *more* active in their children's lives after divorce than they were during the marriage. These men need to be recognized for their support, rather than relegated to the same state of nonbeing as the deadbeat dad.

It's not only parents who are marginalized by outdated household categories. When I speak on work-family issues to audiences around the country, some of the biggest complaints I hear come from individuals who are described by the census as living in "non-family households." They resent the fact that their family responsibilities literally don't "count," either for society or for their employers. There is no category, for instance, for individuals who spend several days a week caring for an aging parent in the parent's separate residence. Yet one in four households in America today is providing substantial time and care to an aging relative, and more than half of all households say they expect to do so within the next 10 years.

It's time for our discussion of family trends to better reflect the complexities of today's family commitments. Perhaps, as Larry McCallum, a therapist who directs the family life program at Augustana College in Rock Island, Ill., suggests, we should do for parents what we have begun to do with racial categories in the census—provide several alternative ways for people to express their overlapping identities. At the very least, we need to drop the idea that we can predict how a family functions solely by its form.

The place where we keep our clothes isn't always the only place where we keep our commitments. ■

PART TWO

How We
Got Here

5

The Evolution of American Families

Stephanie Coontz

This article begins by surveying the historical and cross-cultural diversity in family arrangements, definitions of the ideal family, and the socio-emotional meanings attached to marriage and parent-child relationships. It then describes the three very different family systems that collided and interacted in sixteenth- and seventeenth-century America: those of Native American kinship societies, the conquering Europeans, and the Africans brought as captives by the Europeans. Finally, the essay traces the evolution of American families from the American Revolution through the early years of the twenty-first century.

What is a family? An Internet search of dictionaries yielded the following definitions: "parents and children, whether living together or not"; "any group of persons closely related by blood"; "a group of persons who form a household under one head"; and "the basic unit of society consisting of two or more adults joined by marriage and cooperating in the care and rearing of their children." But of course these definitions refer to very different residential and relational arrangements, and through most of history, few people would have accepted the idea that more than one of these definitions could count as a family.[1]

From the early Middle Ages to the eighteenth century, the European nobility generally used the term "family" not to refer to married parents and their children but rather to the larger kinship group from which they derived their claims to privilege and property. By contrast, most middle-class Europeans and North Americans defined family on the basis of common residence under the authority of a household head rather than on blood relatedness, a definition that included boarders or servants as family members. Samuel Pepys began his famous seventeenth-century English diary with the words: "I lived in Axe Yard, having my wife, and servant Jane, and no more in family than us three." In 1820, the publisher Everard Peck and his wife, childless newlyweds, established a new household in Rochester, New York, and wrote home: "We collected our family together which consists of seven persons and we think ourselves pleasantly situated."

Not until the mid-nineteenth century did the word "family" commonly come to refer just to a married couple with their co-resident children, excluding household residents or more distant kin. This more limited definition spread widely during the 1800s, and by the end of that century, the restriction of the word to the immediate, co-residential family was so prevalent that the adjective "extended" had to be added when people referred to kin beyond the household.

In some societies, even the simple biological definition of family can get complicated. When a woman of the Toda people of southern India gets married, she marries all her husband's brothers, even those not yet born. Each child she bears is assigned an individual father, but the assignment is based on social rather than biological criteria. Among some African and Native American groups a woman could traditionally become a "female husband" by taking a wife. The children the wife brought to the marriage or bore by various lovers were considered part of the family of the female husband, who was entitled to their labor and loyalty and from whom they derived their status and roles.

In kinship societies that trace descent exclusively through the maternal or paternal line, rather than through both parents, children are considered part of the family of only one spouse, and spouses themselves often do not count as family. In ancient China, it was said that "you have only one family, but you can always get another wife." In the late seventeenth century, some European writers also used the word "family" to refer exclusively to a man's offspring rather than his spouse, as in the phrase "his family and wife."

In some societies, a child's biological relation to a parent is only recognized when the parents are in a socially sanctioned marriage. The Lakher of Southeast Asia view a child as linked to his or her mother solely through the mother's relationship to the father. If the parents divorce, the mother is no longer considered to have any relationship to her children. She could, theoretically, even marry her son, since the group's incest taboos would not be considered applicable.

Through much of European history, a child born outside an approved marriage was a "filius nullus"—literally a child of no one, with a claim on no one. Not until 1968 did the United States Supreme Court rule that children born out of wedlock had the right to collect debts owed to their parents, sue for the wrongful death of a parent, and inherit family holdings.

By contrast, the indigenous societies of northeastern North America seldom distinguished between "legitimate" and "illegitimate" children. When a Jesuit missionary told a Montagnais-Naskapi Indian living in what is now Canada that he should keep tighter control over his wife in order to ensure that the children she bore were "his," the man replied: "You French people love only your own children; but we love all the children of our tribe."

In one society, the Mosuo or Na of China, family arrangements do not include marriage at all. In this society, brothers and sisters form the central family unit. Brothers and sisters do not have sex together—indeed, the incest taboo is so strong that it even prohibits siblings from having intense emotional discussions. But the children that the women bear by lovers who usually only visit them at night are raised by the sibling group, not the biological parents.

The eminent anthropologist J. P. Murdock once defined the family as a social unit that shares common residence, economic cooperation, and reproduction. But among the Yoruba of Africa, the family is not a unit of production or consumption, as husbands and wives do not even share a common budget. Men of the Gururumba people of New Guinea sleep in separate houses and work separate plots of land from their wives. In the southern colonies of early America, the families of indentured servants were broken up, with husbands, wives, and even very young children living in different households for many years at a time.

Prohibitions against incest among family members are nearly universal. But the definition of what family relations are close enough to constitute incest varies considerably. In traditional Islamic societies, marriage between the children of two sisters is considered a form of incest. So is marriage between two people who shared the same milk as infants, even if it was from a wet nurse not related to either of them. Marriage between the children of two brothers, however, is a favored pattern. Among the aristocracy in ancient Egypt, brother-sister marriages, especially between half-brothers and sisters, were common. The medieval church in Europe, by contrast, prohibited marriage between cousins up to seven degrees removed.

The historical and cross-cultural diversity of family life extends also to the emotional meanings attached to families and the psychological dynamics within them. For example, what is now considered healthy parent-child bonding in our society (see Coleman in Chapter 14 of this volume) may be viewed as selfishness, narcissism, or pathological isolation by cultures that stress child exchange and fostering as ways of cementing social ties. In Polynesia, eastern Oceania, the Caribbean, and the West Indies (and also in sixteenth-century Europe and colonial America) offering your child to friends, neighbors, or other kin for adoption or prolonged co-residence was not considered abandonment but was rather a mark of parental responsibility, ensuring that the child developed access to support systems and social knowledge beyond what the immediate family could provide.

Modern Americans often focus on the need for strong mother-daughter and father-son identification. But in matrilineal societies, where descent is traced through the female line, a man usually has much closer ties with his nephews than with his sons. Among the Trobriand Islanders, where a child's biological father is considered merely a "relation by marriage," the strongest legal and emotional bonds are between children and their maternal uncle. Among the patrilineal Cheyenne, by contrast, at least after the rise of the fur trade with Europeans made women's traditional work of tanning hides more onerous, mother-daughter relations were expected to be tense or even hostile, and girls tended to establish their closest relationships with paternal aunts.

These examples show that there is no universal definition of family that fits the reality of all cultural groups and historical periods. Yet almost all societies use the term to endow certain sexual relations and biological connections (or fictive biological connections) with special privileges and obligations. Within the same society, groups with different positions in the rank or class structure may have to organize their reproduction, caregiving, and interpersonal obligations in distinctive ways, and therefore several different family arrangements may coexist in the same culture. But the family that is codified as "normal" in law and ideology tends to represent the interests and ideals of the dominant members of society. Often, however, that ideal family coexists with, or even depends upon, a very different set of family arrangements among members of less powerful social groups.

FAMILY SYSTEMS OF EARLY AMERICA

In sixteenth- and seventeenth-century America, three very different systems of social and personal reproduction were practiced respectively by Native American kinship societies, the conquering Europeans, and the Africans brought as captives by the Europeans. At the time of European exploration of the New World, North American native societies used family ties to organize nearly all the political, military, and economic transactions that in Europe were becoming regulated by the state. Kinship rules and marital alliances regulated an individual's place in the overall social network, establishing who owed what to whom in terms of producing and sharing resources and conducting interpersonal relationships.[2]

When society is organized through a state system, sharp distinctions are made between family duties and civil duties, domestic functions and political ones. But prior to sustained contact with Europeans, North American indigenous peoples had few institutions organized on any basis other than kinship. Some groups, such as the Cherokee, had a special governing body for times of war (and the influence of such groups grew once Native Americans engaged in regular conflicts with settlers), but most of the time village elders, representing different kin groups, made decisions. The indigenous peoples of North America, unlike some groups in South America, had no institutionalized courts, police, army, or agencies to tax or coerce labor. Kin obligations organized not just the production and distribution of goods, but also the negotiation of conflicts and the administration of justice. Murder, for example, was an offense not against the state but against the kin group, and it was therefore the responsibility and right of kin to punish the perpetrator.

The nuclear family did not own productive property, such as land or animals, and could not, therefore, sell such resources or lose them to debt. Subsistence tools and their products were made and owned by individuals rather than families. Hunting and gathering grounds and other resources were either available to all or were controlled by the larger kin group, and even there property rights were not absolute. Indians had no concept that land could be permanently sold and access to it monopolized, although they gladly accepted gifts in exchange for the right to use land. This led to many misunderstandings and much hostility between settlers and natives, who were astonished when Europeans they had allowed to settle somewhere then fenced off traditional hunting grounds.

The nuclear family's lack of private property meant that Indian families had less economic autonomy than European households vis-à-vis other families. On the other hand, the lack of a state gave Indian families more political autonomy, because people were not bound to follow a leader for any longer than they cared to do so.

The European families that came to North America were products of a developing market economy and international mercantile system. The way they organized production, exchange, land ownership, and social control put Europeans on a collision course with Indian patterns of existence. Europeans also operated within the framework of a centralized state apparatus whose claims to political authority and whose notion of territorial boundaries and national interests had no counterpart among Native Americans.[3] Colonial families had far more extensive property and inheritance rights than Indian families, but they were also subject to stringent controls by state and church institutions. Wealthy colonial families had much more limited obligations to share surpluses than Native Americans, so right from the beginning there were substantial differences in wealth and resources among colonial families and among the indigenous peoples.[4]

Yet we cannot understand colonial families if we project back onto them modern notions of individualism and nuclear family self-sufficiency. Colonial society was based on a system of agrarian household production, sustained by a patriarchal political and ideological structure that greatly constrained the individual freedom of action of individual households. The property-owning nuclear family was the basis of the social hierarchy, but poor people tended to be brought into propertied households as apprentices, servants, or temporary lodgers. Colonial authorities tried to ensure that everyone was a member of a family. The man or woman outside a family hierarchy was a threat to the social order. A household head exerted authority over all household members, and little distinction was made between a biological child and an unrelated household member of about the same age.

The colonists' insistence that people be members of families and accept the authority of the household head might suggest that the family was the most important institution of colonial society. Yet we need to distinguish between the importance of families as an institution in colonial life and the importance of the individual family. The biological family was less sacrosanct, and less sentimentalized, than it would become in the nineteenth century. Colonial society demanded membership in a *properly ordered* family, and subordinated actual blood or marital family ties to that end.

The lower classes often lived, either together or separately, in the households of their employers. A child might be removed from his or her biological family and placed in another family if his or her parents were deemed unworthy by authorities. Many families voluntarily sent their children to live in another household at a relatively young age to work as a servant or apprentice or simply to develop wider social connections. At home, the nuclear family did not retreat into an oasis of privacy. Parents and children ate—and often slept in the same room—with other household members, whether they were related or not.

Marriage, too, was much less sentimentalized than it became in the nineteenth century. Men often married because they needed someone to help them on the farm or in their business, or because a woman came with a handsome dowry. Women married for similar economic and social reasons. It was hoped that love would develop (in moderation) after marriage, but prior to the late eighteenth century, love was not supposed to be the primary motive for marriage, and children were expected to be guided by their parents' wishes in their matches.

Contact with the European colonists was devastating to the Native American family system. Having no domestic animals such as pigs, chickens, or cattle, the Indians had no acquired immunities to the diseases associated with such animals. Massive epidemics sometimes killed more than half a group's members, decimating kin networks and tearing apart the social fabric of life. Many Indian groups were either exterminated or driven onto marginal land that did not support traditional methods of social organization and subsistence. Even where native societies successfully defended themselves, armed conflict with the settlers elevated the role of young males at the expense of elders and women. Traders, colonial political officials, and Christian missionaries deliberately undermined the authority of extended kinship and community groups.

But Indian collective traditions were surprisingly resilient, and Euro-Americans spent the entire nineteenth century trying to extinguish them. They passed laws requiring Indians to hold property as individuals or nuclear families rather than as larger kinship groups. They tried to impose European gender roles on the organization of work and social life. And Indian children were often forced into boarding schools where teachers tried to wipe out all the cultural traditions the children had learned from their elders.

The Africans who were captured and taken to the New World to serve the white settlers also came from kinship-based societies, although some of those societies had more complex political institutions and larger status differences than were found among the indigenous people of North America. The family arrangements of African slaves and their descendants varied depending on whether they lived in great cotton or tobacco plantations utilizing gang labor, small backwoods farms where one or two slaves lived and worked under a master's close supervision, colonial villages where there were just a few personal slaves or servants, or the free black settlements that gradually emerged in some areas. But in all these settings, Africans had to deal with their involuntary relocation to America, the loss of their languages, the brutality of slavery, and the gradual hardening of racial attitudes over the first two centuries of colonization.[5]

Gender imbalance on large plantations and small farms meant that many slaves remained single, and married couples often could not reside together. Slave families were constantly broken up by routine sales, as punishment for misbehavior, and when owners died, paid off debts, or reallocated their labor force between often far-flung properties. So slave families were not usually nuclear, nor were slave households organized around long-term monogamous married couples. Within the constraints of the slave trade and the plantation system, slaves adapted African cultural traditions to their new realities, using child-centered rather than marriage-centered family systems, adoptive and fictive kin ties, ritual co-parenting or godparenting, and complex naming patterns designed to maintain or recreate extended kin.

Slave families were shaped by the strategies they had to develop to accommodate as well as to resist their masters' world. But slaveowning families were also changed by the experience of slavery. Anxieties about racial/sexual hierarchies created high levels of sexual hypocrisy among Southern planters. Fears that blacks and poor whites might make common cause fostered pervasive patterns of violence against other whites as well as against slaves. And attempts to legitimize the "honor" of slave society in the face of growing Northern antislavery sentiment led to elaborate displays of patriarchy and deference, both in family life and in the community at large.

THE RISE OF THE DOMESTIC FAMILY IDEAL

During the second half of the eighteenth century, especially in the northern colonies, economic, political, and religious forces began to undermine the patriarchal and hierarchical social order that had prevailed in the seventeenth century. The power of elders to dictate to the young and of elites to control the daily life of the lower classes weakened. But economic dependence and social inequality increased as many farmers fell into debt and lost their farms, while some merchants and manufacturers became very wealthy.

From about the 1820s, the spread of a market economy led to the gradual separation of home and work, market production and household production.[6] This created new tensions between family activities and "economic" activities. Households could no longer get by, as they had traditionally, mostly consuming things they made, grew, or bartered in the community. Diaries of the day increasingly complain about the need to earn cash. But in the era before cheap mass production, families could not yet rely on ready-made purchased goods even when they could raise a cash income. Even in middle-class homes, an immense amount of labor was required to make purchased goods usable. Families no longer had to spin their own cotton and grind their own grain, but someone still had to sew factory-produced cloth into clothes and painstakingly sift store-bought flour to rid it of impurities.

Many families responded by reorganizing their division of labor by age and gender. Men (and children, too, in working-class families) began to specialize in paid work outside the home. Unmarried women also started to work outside the home to bring in cash by doing women's traditional work in factories or as household help, or filling the multiplying jobs in teaching. (Among the impoverished lower classes in the growing cities, some women also turned to prostitution.)

But wives, who had once played a vital role in producing for the household and marketing their surpluses, and who had often delegated housework and child care to servants or older children, now began to devote the bulk of their attention to housework, sewing, and child rearing. Once referred to as yoke-mates and meet-helps, wives increasingly were seen as being responsible for the family comfort rather than co-producers of the family's subsistence.

As a market economy supplanted self-sufficient farms and household businesses, middle-class sons were less likely to inherit the family farm or assume their father's occupation. So parents had to prepare their male children for new kinds of employment in the wage economy, and their daughters for a new form of domestic life. The middle classes began to keep their children at home longer and concentrate their resources on fewer children, often subsidizing their children's schooling or work training rather than utilizing their labor to augment family finances. While in the past, children had started work in the family farm or business at an early age, or had been sent out to work in other people's homes, they were now seen as little innocents who needed to be protected within the family circle. A new middle-class ideal of parenting placed mothers at the emotional center of family life and gave them the task of inculcating in their children ideals of sexual restraint, temperance, family solidarity, conservative business habits, diligence, prolonged education, and delayed marriage. This became the new "norm" for family life as popularized in the advice books and novels that proliferated in the early nineteenth century.

Yet middle-class white mothers were able to focus on child rearing and "ladylike" domestic tasks only because they could rely on a pool of individuals who had no option but to engage in paid labor outside their own homes. The extension of childhood for the middle class required the foreshortening of childhood and the denial of private family life for the slaves who provided cotton to the new textile mills, the working-class women and children who worked long hours in factories or tenement workshops to produce store-bought cloth, and the immigrant or African-American mothers and daughters who left their own homes to clean and do the laundry for their middle-class mistresses.[7] (We see a similar pattern today, with many egalitarian dual-earner families depending on the low-paid housework and child-care services of women who do what used to be the middle-class wife's domestic tasks but whose wages offer them no opportunity to achieve the economic and personal independence that the middle-class woman gains from her paid labor.)

For all the sexual prudery of nineteenth-century middle-class families, their urgent need for fertility restriction so that resources could be concentrated on fewer children led to interesting contradictions. By the time of the Civil War, the typical client of an abortionist in mid-nineteenth-century America was not a desperate unwed woman, but a respectable middle-class wife. By the end of the nineteenth century, there was a backlash in the form of laws criminalizing abortion and prohibiting the dissemination of contraceptive information or devices, but also a growing movement to defy those laws and extend women's access to birth control.[8]

As Americans adapted family life to the demands of an industrializing society during the nineteenth century, American families took on many of the characteristics associated with "the modern family." They became smaller, with fewer children. They focused more tightly around the nuclear core, putting greater distance between blood relatives and servants or boarders. Parents became more emotionally involved in child rearing and for a longer period. Marriage came to be seen as primarily about love, although the law continued to support men's legal and economic authority in the home. The distinction between home and work, both physically and conceptually, sharpened.

Average trends, however, obscure tremendous differences among and within the rapidly changing ethnic groups and classes of the industrializing United States. New professions opened up for middle-class and skilled workers, and during the Gilded Age, some entrepreneurs made vast fortunes, but job insecurity became more pronounced for laborers. More than 10 million immigrants arrived from Europe between 1830 and 1882, and each wave successively filled the lowest rungs of the industrial job ladder. Their distinctive cultural and class traditions interacted with the ways they developed to cope with the particular occupations they entered, and the housing conditions and social prejudices they met, to create new variations in family life and gender relations.

After the Civil War, African Americans who moved North found it hard to get a foothold on those rungs at all, and they were relegated to unskilled laboring jobs and segregated sections of the city, compelling new family adaptations. In the South, African-American families eked out a tenuous living as sharecroppers, domestics, or agricultural wage workers. After the end of Radical Reconstruction, they also had to cope with an upsurge of mob violence and the passage of Jim Crow laws designed to restore white supremacy.

The result was that at the same time as the new ideal of the domestic middle-class family became enshrined in the dominant culture, diversity in family life actually increased. Middle-class children were now exempted from the farm work or household tasks that all children traditionally had done. But working-class youth streamed out of the home into mines and mills, where they faced a much longer and more dangerous workday than in the past. Class differences in family arrangements, home furnishings, consumption patterns, and household organization *widened* in the second half of the nineteenth century.

There was also much more variation in the life course of individuals than would be seen through most of the twentieth century. There were greater differences among young people in the nineteenth century in the age at which they left school and home, married and set up households than among their counterparts in the first seventy years of the twentieth century. There was also more mixing of age groups than we see today, with less segregation of youth into specialized grades at school.

Although there has been a long-term trend toward restriction of household membership to the nuclear family, this was slowed down between 1870 and 1890 as some groups saw an increase in temporary co-residence with other kin, while others took in boarders or lodgers. On average, birthrates fell by nearly 40 percent between 1855 and 1915, but the fertility of some unskilled and semiskilled workers actually *rose* during this period.

The changes that helped produce more "modern" family forms, then, started at different times in different classes, meant different things to families occupying different positions in the industrial order, and did not proceed in a straight line. Family "modernization" was not the result of some general, steady evolution of "the" family, as early family sociologists suggested, but was the outcome of *diverging* and *contradictory* responses that occurred in different areas and classes at various times.

Michael Katz, Michael Doucet, and Mark Stern list five major changes in family organization that accompanied industrialization: (1) the separation of home and work, (2) the reduction of household membership to its nuclear core, (3) the fall in marital fertility, (4) the more extended residence of children in their parents' home, and (5) the lengthened time that husbands and wives lived together after their children left home. "The first two began among the working class and among the wage-earning segment of the business class (clerks and kindred workers). The third started among the business class, particularly among its least affluent, most specialized, and most mobile sectors. The fourth began at about the same time in both the working and business class, though the children of the former usually went to work and the latter to school."[9]

The fifth change—the longer period that husband and wives live together after the children are gone—did not occur until the twentieth century, and represented a reversal of nineteenth-century trends. So did a sixth major change that created more convergence among families over the course of the twentieth century: the reintegration of women into productive work, especially the entry of mothers into paid work outside the home.

THE REGULATION OF MARRIAGE

Another change in family life that did not proceed in a linear way involved the state's regulation of marriage. From the time of the American Revolution until after the Civil War, American authorities did not inquire too closely as to whether a couple had taken out a valid license. If a couple acted as if they were married, they were treated as such. Until the 1860s, state Supreme Courts routinely ruled that cohabitation, especially if accompanied by a couple's acceptance in their local community, was sufficient evidence of a valid marriage. In consequence, informal marriage and self-divorce were quite common in this era, and interracial marriage was more frequent in the first three-quarters of the nineteenth century than it became from the 1880s to the 1930s, when the government began to exert stricter control over who could marry and who could not.[10]

The United States began to invalidate common-law and informal marriages in the late nineteenth century as part of a broader attempt to exert more government control over private behavior. By the 1920s, thirty-eight states had laws prohibiting whites from marrying blacks, mulattoes, Japanese, Chinese, Indians, Mongolians, Malays, or Filipinos. Twelve states forbade marriage to a "drunk" or a "mental defective."[11]

After the 1920s, however, this restrictive trend began to be reversed, and the right to marry was gradually extended to almost all heterosexuals over a certain age. In the Civil Rights era of the 1960s, this was to culminate in Supreme Court rulings that invalidated laws against interracial marriage and overturned the right of prison officials or employers to prohibit inmates or workers from marrying.

THE FAMILY CONSUMER ECONOMY

Around the beginning of the twentieth century, a national system of mass production and mass communication replaced the decentralized production of goods and culture that had prevailed until the 1890s. Some huge new trends—the standardization of economic production, the development of schooling into the teenage years, the abolition of child labor, the spread of a national radio and film industry (and later television), and the growth of a consumer economy—created new similarities and new differences in people's experience of family life.

By the 1920s, for the first time, a slight majority of children came to live in families where the father was the breadwinner, the mother did not have paid employment outside the home, and the children were in school rather than at work. Numerous immigrant families, however, continued to pull their children out of school to go to work. African-American families kept their children in school longer than almost all immigrant groups, but their wives were much more likely than either native-born or immigrant women to work outside the home.

The early twentieth century saw a breakdown of the nineteenth-century system of sexual segregation. Single women entered new occupations and exercised new social freedoms. Women finally won the right to vote. An autonomous and increasingly sexualized youth culture emerged, as youth from many different class backgrounds interacted in high schools and middle-class youth adopted the new institution of "dating" pioneered by working-class youth and a newly visible African-American urban culture. Dating replaced the nineteenth-century middle-class courting system of "calling," where the girl and her family invited a young man to call and the couple socialized on the porch or in the living room under the watchful eyes of parents. By contrast, dating took place away from home, and since the male typically paid for a date, the initiative shifted to him. Young people—especially girls—gained more independence from parental oversight, but girls also incurred more responsibility for preventing their dates from going "too far."[12]

There was a profound change at this time in the dominant ideological portrayal of family life. In the nineteenth century, ties to siblings, parents, and close same-sex friends had been as emotionally intense as the ties between spouses. Women often called their husbands "Mr. so-and so," but wrote passionately in their diaries about their pet names and physically affectionate interactions with female friends. Men and women alike had waxed as sentimental about their love for siblings and parents as they did for their intended marital partner.

Now, however, the center of emotional life shifted to the husband-wife bond and to the immediate nuclear family. Young adults were encouraged to cut "the silver cord" that bound them to their mother. The same-sex "crushes" that had been viewed indulgently in the late nineteenth century came to be seen as threats to the primacy of heterosexual love ties.

The growing emphasis on companionship and mutual sexual satisfaction in marriage brought new intimacy to married life. But it also encouraged premarital sexual experimentation. For the first time, a majority of the boys who had sex before marriage did so with girls they had dated rather than with prostitutes. And it is not surprising that the higher standards for marriage also created an unwillingness to settle for what used to be considered adequate relationships. "Great expectations," as historian Elaine Tyler May points out, could also generate great disappointments.[13] The divorce rate more than tripled in the 1920s.

All these changes created a sense of panic about "the future of the family" that was every bit as intense as the family values debates of the 1980s and 1990s. Commentators in the 1920s hearkened back to the "good old days," bemoaning the sexual revolution, the fragility of nuclear family ties, women's "selfish" use of contraception, decline of respect for elders, the loss of extended kin ties, and the threat of the "Emancipated Woman." "Is Marriage on the Skids?" asked one magazine article of the day. Another asked despairingly, "What Is the Family Still Good For?"

The challenges of the Great Depression and World War II in the 1930s and 1940s put these concerns on the back burner. But disturbing family changes continued. During the Depression, divorce rates fell, but so did marriage rates. Desertion and domestic violence rose sharply. Economic stress often led to punitive parenting that left children with scars still visible to researchers decades later. Birthrates plummeted. Many wives had to go to work to make ends meet, but disapproval of working wives increased, with many observers complaining that they were stealing jobs from unemployed men.

World War II stimulated a marriage boom, as couples rushed to wed before the men shipped off to war. Wives who worked in the war industries while the men were away garnered social approval—as long as they were willing to quit their jobs when the men came home. But by the end of the war, most women workers in the war industry were telling pollsters they did not want to quit their jobs. Rates of unwed motherhood soared during the war, and by 1947 one in every three marriages was ending in divorce.

So as the war ended, the fears about family life that had troubled observers during "the roaring twenties" reemerged. But several factors soon combined to assuage those fears. Couples who had postponed having children because of the war now rushed to have them. The enormous deferred consumption of the war years, as well as the sense that people's family lives had been put on hold, led to a huge demand for new houses and other consumer goods. This was reinforced by a concerted campaign by businesses, advertisers, therapists, the new profession of marriage counselors, and the mass media to convince people that they could find happiness through nuclear-family consumerism.

There was a renewed emphasis on female domesticity in the postwar years. Women were told that they could help the veterans readjust to civilian life by giving up the independent decision making they had engaged in while the men were gone. They were urged to forego the challenges of the work world and seek fulfillment in domestic chores. Politicians rewrote the tax code to favor male breadwinner families over dual-earner families, explicitly to discourage wives from working. Psychiatrists—who had largely replaced ministers as the source of advice for families—claimed that any woman who desired anything other than marriage, motherhood, and domesticity was deeply neurotic.[14]

The home-centered life was supported by an unprecedented postwar economic boom. Family wage jobs became more plentiful for blue-collar workers, especially when the Eisenhower administration embarked on a massive highway-building project. And the government handed out unprecedented subsidies for family formation, home ownership, and higher education. Forty percent of the young men starting families at the end of World War II were eligible for veterans' benefits, which were much more generous than they are today. The government encouraged banks to accept lower down payments and offer longer payment terms to young men, and veterans could sometimes put down just one dollar to sign a mortgage on a new home. The National Defense Education Act subsidized individuals who majored in fields such as engineering that were considered vital to national security.

Such government subsidies, combined with high rates of unionization, rapid economic expansion, and an explosion of housing construction and financing options, gave young families a tremendous economic jump start, created predictable paths out of poverty, and led to unprecedented increases in real wages. White male workers had a degree of job security that is increasingly elusive in the modern economy. Between 1947 and 1973, real wages rose, on average, by 81 percent, and the gap between the rich and poor declined significantly. The income of the bottom 80 percent of the population grew faster than the income of the richest 1 percent, with the most rapid gains of all made by the poorest 20 percent of the population.

The result was a boom in family life, so that by the early 1950s it appeared that the threat of women's emancipation and family instability had been turned back. For the first time in sixty years, the age of marriage and parenthood fell, the proportion of marriages ending in divorce dropped, and the birthrate soared. The percentage of women remaining single reached a hundred-year low. The proportion of children who were raised by a breadwinner father and a homemaker mother and who stayed in school until graduation from high school reached an all-time high. Although more women attended college than before the war, they graduated at much lower rates than men, with more and more opting to get an MRS degree rather than a B.A. degree. And the powerful new medium of television broadcast nightly pictures of suburban families where homemaker moms had dinner on the table every night and raised healthy children who never talked back or got into any trouble that couldn't be solved by a fatherly lecture.

We now know, of course, that the experience of many families with problems such as battering, alcoholism, and incest was swept under the rug in the 1950s. So was the rampant discrimination against African Americans and Hispanics, women, elders, gay men, lesbians, political dissidents, religious minorities, and the handicapped. Despite rising real wages, 30 percent of American children lived in poverty during the fifties, a higher figure than today. African-American married-couple families had a poverty rate of nearly 50 percent. Institutionalized racism was the law in the South, and in the North there was daily violence in the cities against African Americans who attempted to move into white neighborhoods or use public parks and swim areas.

Meanwhile, underneath the surface stability of the era, the temporary triumph of nuclear-family domesticity was already being eroded. The expansion of the service and retail sections of the economy required new workers, and employers were especially eager to hire women, who were seen as less likely to join unions and were thought to be easier to move in and out of the labor market than men. But because the average age of marriage had fallen to about twenty years old, there were not enough single women to fill the demand for workers, so employers began to make changes in hiring practices to recruit married women.

Despite the dominance of full-time homemakers on TV sitcoms, the employment of women soared in the 1950s, quickly topping its wartime peak. And the fastest growing segment of this female labor force was married women with school-age children. Indeed, economists later found that the labor force participation of wives played a central role in the spread of upward mobility and the reduction of poverty during the 1950s, and it paved the way for new work aspirations among the daughters of these women.

At the dawn of the 1960s, a national poll of American housewives found that although most declared that they were happier in their marriages than their own parents were, 90 percent of them also said that they did not want their daughters to follow in their footsteps. Instead, they hoped their daughters would postpone marriage longer and get more education and work experience.[15]

As early as 1957, the divorce rate had started to climb once more. And during the 1960s, the age of marriage also began to rise, especially as more women postponed marriage for education. As the "baby-boom generation" grew up, there was a huge increase in the percentage of singles in the population, accelerating the acceptance of premarital sex that had begun to spread as early as the 1920s. The women's liberation movement helped expose the complex varieties of family experience that lay beneath the Ozzie and Harriet images of the time.[16] By the end of the 1960s, family diversity had begun to accelerate and had become more visible.

For the most part, middle-class wives and mothers entered the labor force in the 1950s and 1960s in response to new opportunities, but as the prolonged postwar expansion of real wages and social benefits came to an end in the 1970s, ever more wives and mothers of all social classes and racial-ethnic groups soon found that paid work had become a matter of economic necessity. By 1973, real wages were falling, especially for young families. Housing inflation made it less possible for a single breadwinner to afford a home. By the late 1970s, cuts in government services had gutted the antipoverty programs that in 1970 had brought child poverty to an all-time low (a low not equaled since). Still, despite these threats to families, the success of the women's movement in combating hiring and pay discrimination gave many women more economic independence than they had previously enjoyed.

The combination of expanding social freedoms for women and youth and contracting economic opportunities for blue-collar men made the 1970s and 1980s a time of turmoil. Real wages fell for workers without a college degree, and economic inequality increased, making it harder to form and maintain families. Old marital norms came into conflict with new family work patterns, leading to tensions between husbands and wives over housework. From a different angle, new social freedoms encouraged more people to feel free to leave a marriage they deemed unsatisfactory. Divorce rates reached an all-time high in 1979–1980 — and it was women who initiated most divorces. As courts began to protect the rights of children born out of wedlock, fewer women felt compelled to enter a shotgun marriage if they became pregnant.[17]

Women's workforce participation continued to mount. In 1950, only a quarter of all wives were in the paid labor force, and just 16 percent of all children had mothers who worked outside the home. By 1991, nearly two-thirds of all married women with children were in the labor force. Fifty-nine percent of children, including a majority of preschoolers, had mothers who worked outside the home (see Cotter, England, and Hermsen in Chapter 36 of this volume for more recent figures).

Meanwhile, new waves of immigrants began to arrive, the majority now coming from Asia, Latin America, and the Carribbean, rather than from Europe, as had been true in the early twentieth century when the United States had experienced its previous high point of immigration. By the 1990s, racial and ethnic diversity had reached historic highs, creating a new acceptance of family diversity and intermarriage but also fanning new racial and ethnic tensions, especially as growing socioeconomic inequality threatened the American assumption that each generation would live better than its parents.[18]

In the past fifteen years, some of the trends that undermined family stability in the late twentieth century have leveled off or decreased. Divorce rates have come down since their peak in 1979–1980, especially for college-educated couples. When divorce does occur, fewer couples engage in prolonged, bitter battles, and fewer men lose contact with their children. Teen birthrates have dropped sharply. Although the entry of women into the workforce in the 1970s initially resulted in a small decline in the amount of time that mothers spent with their children, the continued expansion of time that women spend in paid labor has since been accompanied by an increase in time with children. Mothers in both two-earner and one-earner families now spend more time with their children than they did in 1960, and fathers have also dramatically increased their time with their children.[19]

But family diversification continues apace. There has been a dramatic increase in the number of couples who live together outside marriage. Gay and lesbian couples are permanently out of the closet and seek the same legal rights as heterosexual couples. While teen births have gone down, more unwed women in their twenties and thirties are having children. And, as described in other articles in this volume, family arrangements and values continue to differ by social class, religion, race, and ethnicity.

The lessons from history are both positive and negative. American families have always been in flux, and many different family arrangements and values have worked for various groups at different times. We should not assume that recent changes in family forms and practices are inevitably destructive (see Rutter in Chapter 16 and Li in Chapter 17 of this volume). But it is also true that families have always been fragile, vulnerable to economic stress, and needful of practical and emotional support from beyond the nuclear family. And new opportunities for individuals and families to succeed have also brought new ways for them to fail.

Still, it would be a terrible mistake to delude people into believing that if we could only restore the family values and forms of the past we would not have to confront the sweeping changes America is experiencing in gender and age relations, racial and ethnic patterns, the distribution of jobs and income, and even our experience of time and space. There are many historical precedents of families and communities successfully reorganizing themselves in response to social change. But these examples should inspire us to construct *new* family values and social-support institutions rather than trying to recreate some (largely mythical) "traditional" family of the past.

6

American Childhood As a Social and Cultural Construct

Steven Mintz

Not an unchanging, biologically determined stage of life, childhood is a social and cultural construct that varies by region, class, and historical era. Over the past four centuries, every aspect of childhood, including methods of child rearing, the nature of children's play, the duration of schooling, the participation of young people in work, and the demarcation points between childhood, adolescence, and adulthood have shifted significantly. This history provides an essential perspective on the questions of whether children's well-being has declined in recent years, whether children are growing up faster than in the past, and whether the United States is a particularly child-friendly country.

Today, Americans have a firm, although somewhat contradictory, conception of childhood. On the one hand, childhood is romanticized as a time of carefree innocence, when children should play freely, untouched by the cares of the adult world. But at the same time, many middle-class mothers and fathers engage in intensive parenting designed to stimulate their children's development. They buy them educational toys, involve them in a host of organized enrichment activities, and intensively read and talk to their children, in hopes of cultivating their talents and skills. Schools, too, now place greater emphasis on early academic achievement, and marketers are targeting children with an intensity previously reserved for adult consumers. Some observers fear that our society is taking the playfulness out of childhood.[1]

Childhood is not some unchanging, biologically determined stage of life. The whole concept of childhood is a social and cultural construct that varies by region, class, and historical era.[2] Over the past four centuries, almost all aspects of childhood—including children's relationships with their parents and peers, their proportion in the population, and their paths toward adulthood—have changed dramatically. Societal views about methods of child rearing, the nature of children's play, the ideal duration of schooling, the participation of young people in work, and the demarcation points between childhood, adolescence, and adulthood have shifted significantly. In this article, I trace the changing concepts of childhood from early colonial America until today. I conclude by comparing the status of today's children with the status of those from the past.

Two centuries ago, the experience of youth was very different from what it is today. Segregation by age was far less prevalent, and chronological age played a smaller role in determining status. Adults were also far less likely to sentimentalize children as special creatures who were more innocent and vulnerable than adults.

Language itself illustrates how perceptions of childhood differed from those today. Two hundred years ago, the words used to describe stages of childhood were far less precise than those we now use. "Infancy" referred not to the first months after birth, but to the whole period when children were dependent on their mother, typically until the age of five or six. The words "childhood" and "youth" could refer to someone as young as five or as old as the early twenties.

In that era, Americans did not have a category for "adolescent" or "teenager." The vagueness of the broader term "youth" reflected how fluidly the stages of life were viewed in that era. Chronological age mattered less than physical strength, size, and maturity. Young people were not automatically granted full adult status upon reaching a certain societally agreed upon age. They became full adults only when they married and set up their own farm or entered a full-time trade or profession. In some cases that might be as early as the mid- or late teens, but usually it did not occur until the late twenties or even the early thirties.[3]

Although there were important regional differences in children's experiences, depending on the prevalence or paucity of slavery and indentured servitude in a given area, most seventeenth-century American colonists regarded children as "adults-in-training." It was recognized that children differed from adults in their mental, moral, and physical capabilities, and the colonists distinguished between childhood, an intermediate stage they called youth, and adulthood. But in colonial America, a parent's duty was to hurry the child toward adult status. Infants, being unable to stand or speak, were thought to lack two essential attributes of full humanity, and infancy was therefore regarded as a state of deficiency to be rushed through as quickly as possible. Parents discouraged infants from crawling, and placed them in "walking stools" to get them on their feet. Rods were affixed along the spines of very young children to encourage adult posture.

The goal was to get children speaking, reading, reasoning, and contributing to their family's economic well-being as quickly as possible. A key element in this process was early involvement in work, either within the parental home or outside as a servant or apprentice. Before the mid-eighteenth century, most adults exhibited surprisingly little interest in their children's very first years of life. Children's play was commonly dismissed as trivial and insignificant. In that era, adults rarely looked back on their childhood with nostalgia or fondness.

During the eighteenth century, a shift in parental attitudes took place. Fewer parents expected children to act as miniature adults, to bow or doff their hats in their parents' presence, or to stand during meals. Instead of addressing parents as "sir" and "madam," children began calling them "papa" and "mama."

By the end of the eighteenth century, furniture specifically designed for children was being widely produced. Painted in pastel colors and decorated with pictures of animals or figures from nursery rhymes, the new furniture reflected a growing popular notion of childhood as a time of innocence and playfulness.

Parents began to regard children, not as incomplete adults, but as innocent, malleable, and fragile creatures who needed to be sheltered from contamination. Childhood came to be seen not simply as a prelude to adulthood but as a separate stage of life that required special care and institutions to protect it.

By the early nineteenth century, mothers in the rapidly expanding middle class in the northeastern states were embracing an amalgam of child-rearing ideas. From Jean-Jacques Rousseau and the Romantic poets, middle-class parents acquired the idea that childhood was a special stage of life, intimately connected with nature, and purer and morally superior to adulthood. From the philosopher John Locke, they took the notion that children were highly malleable creatures and that a republican form of government required parents to instill a capacity for self-government in their offspring. From evangelical Protestants, the middle class adopted the idea that parents must implant proper moral character in children and insulate them from the corruptions of the adult world.

Behind these developments was a growing belief that childhood should be devoted to education and building character as well as play. Middle-class children were no longer sent out to work at an early age, but parents began to believe that their children's play should foster their moral growth. Because parents in the emerging middle class could not automatically transfer their societal status to their children through bequests of family lands, transmission of craft skills, or selection of a marriage partner, they adopted new strategies to give their children a boost by limiting the number of their offspring through birth control and prolonging the transition to adulthood through intensive maternal nurturing and extended schooling.

Over time, the concept of childhood became divided into much more precise, uniform, and prescriptive stages. Adults began to hold much more rigid views about what was appropriate at each stage. By the mid-nineteenth century, informal patterns of child rearing were being supplanted by more structured forms. Schools began to follow prescribed grade-specific curricula. Adult-sponsored and adult-organized activities began replacing activities that young people organized informally on their own.

The dramatic reduction in the birthrate over the past two centuries also altered the concept of childhood. In the mid-nineteenth century, children made up fully one-half of the population. By 1900 their proportion had declined to one-third of the population. As parents had fewer children and had them over a shorter time span, families became more clearly divided into distinct generations, and parents had the opportunity to lavish more time, attention, and resources on each child.

Yet until the early twentieth century, there was still a high degree of diversity in the experience of childhood, based on social class, gender, and race, and accentuated by the rapid and uneven expansion of industrial capitalism. The children of the urban middle class, prosperous commercial farmers, and southern planters enjoyed increasingly long childhoods and were free from major household or work responsibilities until their late teens or twenties. But the offspring of urban workers, frontier farmers, and blacks, both slave and free, had briefer childhoods and became involved in work inside or outside the home before they reached their teens.

Urban working-class children often contributed to the family economy through scavenging, collecting coal, wood, and other items that could be used at home or sold, or by taking part in the street trades, selling gum, peanuts, newspapers, and the like. In industrial towns, young people under the age of fifteen contributed on average about 20 percent of their family's income. In mining areas, boys as young as ten began working in the pits as breakers, separating coal from slate and wood, and then graduated into full-fledged miners in their mid- or late teens.

On farms, children as young as five might pull weeds or keep birds and cattle away from crops. By the age of eight, many were tending the livestock, and as they grew older they milked cows, churned butter, fed chickens, collected eggs, hauled water, scrubbed laundry, and harvested crops. A blurring of gender duties among children and youth was especially common on frontier farms.

Schooling in the nineteenth century varied as widely as did work routines. In the rural North, the Midwest, and the Far West, most mid- and late-nineteenth-century students attended one-room schools for three to six months a year. But city children spent nine months a year attending age-graded classes, taught by professional teachers. In rural and urban areas, girls generally received more schooling than boys.[4]

As the nineteenth century drew to an end, middle-class parents were starting to embrace the idea that child rearing should be scientific. Through the Child Study movement, teachers and mothers, under the direction of psychologists, identified a series of stages of child development, culminating in the "discovery"—more accurately the invention—of adolescence, a period marked by emotional and psychological turmoil tied to the biological changes associated with puberty. Within the middle class, acceptance of the concept of scientific parenting was reflected in young people's remaining longer within the parental home and spending longer periods in formal schooling.

The attempt to apply scientific principles to the care of children produced new kinds of child-rearing manuals, now written by doctors and psychologists rather than ministers, as had previously been the case. The most influential manual was Dr. Luther Emmett Holt's *The Care and Feeding of Children*, first published in 1894. In an era when a well-adjusted adult was viewed as a creature of habit and self-control, Holt stressed the importance of imposing regular habits on infants by rigidly scheduling a child's feeding, bathing, sleeping, and bowel movements. He also advised mothers to guard vigilantly against germs and to avoid undue stimulation of infants—for example, by kissing their babies. Holt also advised parents to ignore their baby's crying and to break such habits as thumb sucking.[5]

At about the same time, self-described "child-savers" launched a concerted campaign to universalize the middle-class model of childhood, in which childhood was defined as a period during which young people should be insulated from the stresses and corrupting influences of the adult world and free from adult-like responsibilities. Trying to universalize the modern ideal of a sheltered childhood without regard to a child's class, ethnicity, gender, and race was a highly uneven process and to this day has never encompassed all American children.

But by the early twentieth century, the middle-class conception of "modern childhood" had generally been accepted as the societal norm, although progress was slow and bitterly resisted. Child labor was not finally outlawed until the 1930s and not until the 1950s did high school attendance become a universal experience.

During the 1920s and 1930s, the field of child psychology exerted a growing influence on middle-class parenting. It provided a new language to describe children's emotional problems. Concepts like sibling rivalry, inferiority complexes, phobias, maladjustment, and Oedipus complexes gained wide acceptance. Child psychology also offered new insights into the effects of different styles of parenting, such as demanding and permissive forms. It categorized the stages and milestones of children's development and the characteristics of children at particular ages. This was when, for example, the phrase "terrible twos" was coined.

The growing prosperity of the 1920s made the late-nineteenth-century emphasis on rigid self-control and regularity seem outmoded. The new model for a well-adjusted adult was a more easygoing figure who was capable of enjoying leisure. There was a reaction against the mechanistic and behaviorist notion that children's behavior should and could be molded by scientific control. Popular dispensers of advice now advocated a more relaxed approach to child rearing, emphasizing the importance of meeting the emotional needs of babies. The title of a 1936 book by pediatrician C. Anderson Aldrich—*Babies Are Human Beings*—summed up the new attitude.[6]

The stresses and uncertainties of the Great Depression of the 1930s and World War II made parents much more anxious about child rearing. In the postwar era, many psychologists asserted that faulty mothering was the cause of lasting psychological problems in children. Leading psychologists such as Theodore Lidz, Irving Bieber, and Erik Erikson linked schizophrenia, homosexuality, and identity diffusion to mothers who displaced their frustrations and their needs for independence onto their children.

Many psychologists worried that boys, being raised almost exclusively by women, might fail to develop an appropriate sex-role identity. In retrospect, these fears reflected the fact that mothers were playing a much more exclusive role in raising their children than ever before in American history.[7]

By the 1950s, developments were already under way that would bring down the curtain on "modern childhood" and replace it with something we might call "post-modern childhood." Post-modern childhood is a product of radical changes in society that led in the space of just over thirty years to the breakdown of dominant norms regarding the family, gender expectations, age, and even reproduction (see Coontz in Chapter 5 of this volume).

Children today grow up under different circumstances than their immediate predecessors. They are more likely to experience their parents' divorce. They are more likely to have a working mother and to spend significant amounts of time unsupervised by adults. They are more likely to grow up without siblings. They are more likely to hold a job during high school.

Age norms once considered "natural" have been thrown into question. Even the bedrock biological process of sexual maturation has accelerated. Adolescent girls today, for example, enter puberty at an earlier age and are much more likely to have sexual relations during their mid-teens than their peers did a half century ago.[8]

While society still assumes that the young are fundamentally different from adults—that they should spend their first eighteen years in the parental home and should devote their time to education in age-graded schools—it is also clear that basic aspects of the ideal of a protected childhood, in which the young are kept isolated from adult realities, have broken down.[9] Post-modern children are independent consumers and participate in a separate, semiautonomous youth culture. Adults quite rightly assume that even preadolescents know a great deal about the realities of the adult world.

Since the early 1970s, a variety of factors have contributed to a surge in the scope and intensity of parental anxieties about child rearing. As parents had fewer children, they invested more emotional energy in each child. Greater professional expertise about children, coupled with a proliferation of research and advocacy organizations, media outlets, and government agencies responsible for children's health and safety made parents more aware of threats to children's well-being. Many middle-class parents responded by trying to protect their children from every imaginable harm by baby-proofing their homes, using car seats, requiring bicycle helmets, and the like, things unknown a generation earlier.

Middle-class parents also worried that their offspring might underperform compared to peers and looked for ways to maximize their children's physical, social, and intellectual development. The goal of postwar parents had been to raise normal children who fit in. Middle-class parents now try to give their child a competitive advantage, a trend spurred by fears of downward mobility and anxiety that parents may not be able to pass on their status and social class to their children (see Coleman in Chapter 14 of this volume).

Today we no longer see early childhood as a stage to be rushed through. Early childhood is viewed as the formative stage for later life. Society believes that children's experiences during the first two or three years of life mold their personality, lay the foundation for future cognitive and psychological development, and leave a lasting imprint on their emotional life. We also assume that children's development proceeds through a series of physical, psychological, social, and cognitive stages. It is accepted that even very young children have a capacity to learn, that play serves valuable developmental functions, and that growing up requires children to separate emotionally and psychologically from their parents.

There are, however, significant class differences in contemporary parenting practices, as sociologist Annette Lareau has shown (see Chapter 26 of this volume). Working-class and poor mothers and fathers are much more likely to believe that child development occurs naturally and spontaneously. Unlike their middle-class counterparts, many working-class parents reject the notion that successful child rearing requires parents to actively stimulate their children's development by organizing their leisure activities, chauffeuring their children to lessons, or supervising their homework.

Lareau has shown that middle-class parents spend more time in conversation with their children, read to them more often, employ a larger vocabulary, and are more likely to try to reason with their children rather than simply enforce rules. Middle-class parents are also more likely to place their children in adult-supervised enrichment activities, while children in working-class and poor families spend more time in free, unstructured play and are more likely to socialize with extended family.[10]

Although the middle-class ideal of child rearing has become the societal norm, social class remains a primary determinant of children's well-being.[11] In recent years, social conservatives have argued that family structure is a primary source of inequality in children's well-being, while political liberals tend to focus on ethnicity, race, and gender. But the most powerful predictor of children's welfare is, in fact, social and economic class. Economic distress contributes to family instability, inadequate health care, high degrees of mobility, and elevated levels of stress and depression.

As in the nineteenth century, social class significantly differentiates contemporary American childhoods. There is a vast difference between the highly pressured, hyperorganized, fast-track childhoods of affluent children and the very different kind of stressed childhoods experienced by children who live in poverty at some point before the age of eighteen (one-third of all children).

In many affluent families, the boundaries between parental work and family life have blurred. Parents often try to cope by tightly organizing their children's lives. But most affluent children are unsupervised by their parents for large portions of the day and have their own television and computer, which gives them unmediated access to information. Many affluent families swing back and forth between parental distance from children caused by work pressures and parental indulgence as fathers and mothers try to compensate for parenting too little.

Meanwhile, one-sixth of all children live in poverty at any given time, including 36 percent of black children and 34 percent of Hispanic children. Children who live in poverty generally experience limited adult supervision, inferior schooling, and a lack of easy access to productive diversions and activities.

How does the status of children today compare with the past? Are children better off or worse off? This question has been of importance to every generation.

One of this country's oldest convictions is a belief in the decline of the younger generation. For more than three centuries, American adults have worried that children are growing ever more disobedient and disrespectful. In 1657, a Puritan minister, Ezekiel Rogers, lamented: "I find the greatest trouble and grief about the rising generation. . . . Much ado I have with my own family . . . the young breed doth much afflict me."[12]

But wistfulness about a golden age of childhood is invariably misleading. There has never been a golden age of childhood, when the overwhelming majority of American children have been well cared for and had idyllic lives. Nostalgia typically represents a yearning not for the past as it really was but rather for a white-washed fantasy about the past.

In 1820, children constituted about half of the workers in the early factories. As recently as the 1940s, fewer than half of all high school students graduated. More than half a century ago, Alfred Kinsey's studies found rates of sexual abuse similar to those reported today. His interviews indicated that 12 percent of pre-adolescent girls had been the victims of exhibitionists and that 9 percent of girls had had their genitals fondled.

We also forget that the introduction of every new form of entertainment over the past century has been accompanied by dire warnings about its impact on children. The anxiety over video games and the Internet are only the latest in a long line of supposed threats to children that included television, movies, radio, and comic books.[13]

The danger of nostalgia is that it creates unrealistic expectations, guilt, and anger.[14] If we cling to a fantasy that once upon a time childhood and youth were years of carefree adventure, we have to ignore the fact that for most children in the past, growing up was anything but easy. Disease, death of a parent, family disruption, and early entry into the world of work were integral parts of family life. The notion of a long childhood, devoted to education and free from adult-like responsibilities, is a very recent invention, a product of the past century and a half, and one that only became a reality for a majority of children after World War II.

Another problem with nostalgia about childhood in the past is that it assumes that the family home was traditionally a haven and bastion of stability in an ever-changing world. Throughout American history, however, family stability has been the exception, not the norm. As late as the beginning of the twentieth century, fully one-third of all American children spent at least part of their childhood in a single-parent home, and as recently as 1940, one child in ten did not live with either parent—compared to one in twenty-five today.[15]

There have been genuine gains achieved in children's lives, such as the out-lawing of child labor, the expansion of schooling, the growing awareness about the evils of child abuse. But the history of childhood has not been a story of steady, linear progress.

Each generation of children has had to wrestle with the specific social, political, and economic constraints of its own historical period. In our own time, the young have had to struggle with high rates of family instability, a growing disconnection from adults, and the expectation that all children should pursue the same academic path at the same pace, even as the attainment of full adulthood recedes ever further into the future.

Profound class differences in children's experience persist and have even grown in salience over the past thirty years. Poor children grow up in an "ecology of poverty," characterized by substandard housing, inadequate schooling, deficient health care, unstable living arrangements, and limited access to decent child care. Many poor children are exposed to violence and have parents who suffer from depression stemming from erratic incomes and demanding work hours. In recent years, the gap between poor and working-class and affluent children in rates of attending four-year colleges has widened.[16]

Even for children of the middle class and the stably employed working class, American society is not as child-friendly as we might hope. Literary critic Daniel Kline persuasively suggests that contemporary American society subjects the young to three forms of psychological violence that we tend to ignore. First is the violence of expectations, in which children are pushed beyond their social, physical, and academic capabilities, largely as an expression of their parents' needs. Then there is the violence of labeling normal childish behavior (for example, childhood exuberance or interest in sex) as pathological. Third is the violence of representation, in which children and adolescents are exploited by advertisers, marketers, purveyors of popular culture, and politicians, who exploit parental anxieties as well as young peoples' desire to be stylish, independent, and defiant, and eroticize teenage and preadolescent girls.[17]

I believe there is a fourth form of psychological abuse: seeing children as objects to be shaped and molded for their own good. Contemporary American society is much more controlling of young people in an institutional and ideological sense than its predecessors. And as the baby-boom generation ages, American society has become increasingly adult-oriented, with fewer "free" spaces for the young, a society in which youth are primarily valued as service workers and consumers.

For more than three centuries, despite massive evidence to the contrary, America has considered itself to be an especially child-centered society. Yet in no other advanced country do so many young people grow up in poverty or without health care, nor does any other Western society provide so few resources for child care or restrict paid parental leave so stringently.

This paradox is not new. Since the early nineteenth century, the United States has developed a host of institutions specifically aimed at the young: the common school, the Sunday school, the orphanage, the house of refuge, the reformatory, the children's hospital, the juvenile court, and a wide variety of youth organizations. All were envisioned as caring, developmental, and educational institutions that would serve children's interests. In practice, however, they frequently end up being primarily custodial and disciplinary.

Many of the reforms that were supposed to help children were adopted in part because they served the needs, interests, and convenience of adults. The abolition of child labor removed competition from an overcrowded labor market. Separating children by age-based grades not only made it easier to handle children within schools, it also divided the young into convenient market segments.

The most important lesson that grows out of understanding the history of childhood is the simplest. While many fear that American society has changed too much, the sad fact is that it has changed too little. Americans have failed to adapt social institutions to new realities, to the fact that the young mature more rapidly than they did in the past, that most mothers of preschoolers now participate in the paid workforce, and that a near majority of children will spend substantial parts of their childhood in a single-parent, cohabitating-parent, or stepparent household.

As we navigate a new century of childhood we need to pose new questions. How can we provide better care for the young, especially the one-sixth who are growing up in poverty? How can we better connect the worlds of adults and the young? How can we give the young more ways to demonstrate their growing competence and maturity? How can we tame a violence-laced, sex-saturated popular culture without undercutting a commitment to freedom and a respect for the free-floating world of fantasy?

In the News

A "GOLDEN AGE" OF CHILDHOOD?

Christian Science Monitor, April 28, 2005

Steven Mintz

Many of America's 78 million baby boomers may feel a bit older when they realize that this year marks the 50th anniversary of Play-Doh, the fried-chicken TV dinner, and the air-powered Burp gun. The LEGO "system of play"—28 sets and 8 vehicles—was launched in 1955. And it's the year McDonald's Corp. was founded.

Today, we look back nostalgically to the 1950s as a time of a more innocent childhood. Life was safer as well as simpler then, we sigh. We worry that modern mass culture has undermined the influence of parents, and that aggressive advertising is distorting children's diet, their body image, and their attitude toward material possessions.

But by placing '50s culture on such a lofty pedestal, we fail to appreciate the huge advances that have made childhood, in many ways, a safer and more sheltered time today. What's more, such attitudes overlook the fact that much of what troubles parents today dated from that era.

For instance, the modern commercialization of childhood is in fact a direct outcome of forces that were set in motion during the 1950s. The first baby-boomer fad—the Davy Crockett coonskin cap, introduced in 1955—revealed the huge commercial potential of marketing directly to children. With products like Matchbox cars (launched in England in 1953), Trix cereal (1954), "Mad" (which changed from a comic book into a magazine in 1955), and Barbie (1959), marketers discovered that it was possible to target kids as consumers, separate and apart from their parents.

Television provided the ideal medium for reaching child consumers. ABC introduced one of the first children's television shows, "Disneyland," in 1954, and "The Mickey Mouse Club" the next year. "Disneyland" was the forerunner of modern infomercials: a program-length advertisement for Walt Disney's about-to-open theme park. Shows like "Captain Kangaroo," which debuted on CBS in 1955, contributed to the emergence of an insular world of childhood wholly separate from that of adults.

Today, we look back to the 1950s as a safer, more orderly time for raising children. But that's not how it seemed to many parents then. At the end of the decade, the infant and child mortality rate was four times as high as it is today—the scourge of polio had claimed the lives of 3,000 children annually until the Salk vaccine was developed in 1955.

Two-thirds of black children and more than a fifth of their white counterparts lived in poverty as recently as 1955. By contrast, 34 percent of African-American children and 14 percent of white children lived in poverty as of 2003. And even though the Supreme Court ruled school segregation unconstitutional in 1954, by 1960 just 1 percent of black children in the South attended integrated schools. Meanwhile, nearly a million children with disabilities were denied public schooling as uneducable. And 40 percent of kids dropped out of school before graduating high school.

Happy sitcom reruns to the contrary, the parents of 50 years ago were not insulated from fears about youth violence and children's poor academic achievement. In 1955, several Congressional hearings investigated the link between television and children's violence, while others warned of the corrupting effects of comic books. In 1955 alone, Congress considered nearly 200 bills aimed at combating what was seen as an epidemic of juvenile delinquency. Rudolph Flesch's 1955 bestseller, "Why Johnny Can't Read," announced that "3,500 years of civilization" were being lost due to bad schools and incompetent teachers. (This prompted publisher Houghton Mifflin to ask Theodor Geisel, aka Dr. Seuss, to write and illustrate an easy-read that would become "The Cat in the Hat.") The anxieties that obsess parents today—children's safety, morals, and international competitiveness—took root in the seemingly tranquil 1950s.

Nor were 1950s children protected from sexual and physical abuse or exploitation. In 1955, Vladimir Nabokov published "Lolita," with its shocking depiction of a middle-aged man's "affair" with a 12-year-old girl. The book broke a taboo on that subject in what may well have been the first high-profile commercialization of the eroticization of pre- and pubescent girls that is now standard commercial fare.

Certainly parents face new challenges today, as they grapple with expanding work pressures, changing family forms, and an accelerating commercialization of private life. But romanticizing the 1950s as the supposed golden age of American childhood ignores the fact that many of today's problems actually took root then and obscures real gains made in child welfare since then. Who knows whether 50 years from now, this may be the platinum age of childhood? ▄

In the News

HOW WE TOOK THE CHILD OUT OF CHILDHOOD

New York Times, January 8, 2006

Peter Applebome

Danny Bernstein and Robin Winter don't know each other. They both live in pricey Westchester suburbs (he's in Scarsdale, she's in Chappaqua), but their concerns aren't necessarily similar.

He is passionate about youth sports and has just started a company, Backyard Sports, that's dedicated to making the games kids play just fun for kids, rather than an achievement arms race for parents. She would just like to make it easier for her seventh grader to ride his bicycle to school, something almost no suburban child gets to do anymore. But she can't seem to get anyone in a position of influence in her town interested in even trying to tap a new government program that provides money to make it safer for children to go to school on their own.

We'll pass over the slightly incongruous premise in both cases. Kids need parents to organize sports events in a way that will let kids be kids? And it takes a government program for kids to be able to safely ride bicycles or walk to school on their own? (The answers are maybe and probably.)

But both Mr. Bernstein and Ms. Winter, in their own ways, are on to one of the great mysteries of suburban life in America. How did we get to the point where few kids ever get to play with friends outside of a play date, to walk to a neighbor's house without parental escort or to have free, unsupervised time in which they're not tethered to a television set, computer or Xbox? How is it that Mr. Bernstein's friends in their 40's go out to play soccer every Saturday but their children wouldn't know how to organize a game on their own without parents around?

How come long, long ago I got to play football in the street every day after school with Sammy Brett and Howie Kavaler and the rest of the neighborhood kids on Long Island, or to ride my bike as far out along the service road of the Long Island Expressway as I cared to, but children now live in permanent lockdown, their every moment planned, organized, monitored and measured? How did this happen?

One person who thinks he knows is Steven Mintz, a history professor at the University of Houston and the author of "Huck's Raft: A History of American Childhood," who has watched as a new model of childhood—one of a long succession of new models, it must be added—has taken hold over the past three decades or so.

He starts with three big changes.

First is an explosion in parental anxiety over child abductions, sexual abuse, and crime, a panic almost entirely due to the saturation of news media coverage and not, he says, to any glaring increase in whatever dangers lurk beyond your crab-grass. Once, the child abduction in California was a local story in California. Now, it's constant fodder for national cable news stations.

Second is the parental panic over the transmission of class status, in which grades, achievement and, of course, getting into the right college (never too early to start worrying!) are seen as part of a Darwinian struggle for economic success and social esteem. So Kumon math, si; foraging for frogs, no.

Third is guilt. Parents, often two parents, are working so hard and such long hours that they figure they owe their kids a designer childhood every bit as up-to-date as that plasma TV in the living room. And since their model of life is being busy all the time, no sense having the kids just hanging out doing nothing.

Worry, competition, guilt—what a combination. "We're all Jewish mothers now, but my mother was never as invested in the way I am with my kids," Dr. Mintz said.

You can go on from there. There's technology, which has made being alone in your room the most interesting place in the universe, just as long as the computer is on. There's the living large syndrome, in which ever bigger houses mean less prox-imity to neighbors. And with smaller families, chances are there aren't many kids down the road anyway. Throw in, for good measure, fear of being sued over almost anything.

As Dr. Mintz notes in his book, our notion of childhood changes all the time, and often it's been a pretty grim one—in the Puritan era, children as imperfect adults in need of moral uplift; or for much of the 19th century, children as fodder for sweat-shops and mines.

That said, who could have imagined that today's suburbs, with children their prime reason for being, would end up excising the one thing kids always had before: a sense of freedom, room to explore, time to wander around to see what you could find? Who could have imagined today's fortresslike homes and grand green lawns as quiet as an empty church?

This can't really be what we had in mind. Which brings us back to Mr. Bernstein and Ms. Winter, who in their small ways seem to be looking for ways to tip things back a bit, in getting parents to back off from their kids' games, in finding a way to give children the freedom to be children. Maybe good ideas, maybe bad ones. But surely there's a way out of this. If you have thoughts, please pass them along. ◼

7

African Americans and the Birth of the Modern Marriage

Donna L. Franklin

A long tradition of dual-career partnerships has defined most marriages among African-American professionals at least since the late nineteenth century. This model, which is relatively new for whites, has been overlooked by many family historians and social scientists. This chapter will explore two fundamental questions related to these revolutionary marriages: why marriage conventions differed for professional whites and blacks, and how distinct cultural values regarding women emerged in the African-American community.

We can trace the roots of dual-career marriages in the black professional community to the late nineteenth and early twentieth centuries. In an era when very few married white women worked outside the home, married black females were combining care for their families with employment responsibilities.

But as industrial capitalism developed, with its low wages, obstacles to upward mobility, and poor working conditions, marriage became an attractive alternative to working for many white women. And hand in hand with that, in the culture as a whole a new ideal took hold—the image of women as fragile, delicate, and economically dependent, needing to be sheltered and supported.

The different conventions regarding work and marriage in the white and black communities were reflected in a letter that the leading women's suffragist, Susan B. Anthony, wrote to her black friend and fellow activist, Ida B. Wells-Barnett, in 1890. Anthony had never married and doubted that women could combine marriage with a career. She lamented that Wells-Barnett's activism was suffering since she married and began having children:

> Women like you who have a special call for work should never marry. I know of no one in all this country better fitted to do the work you had in hand. Since you've gotten married, agitation practically seems to have ceased. Besides, you're trying to help in the formation of this league and your baby needs your attention at home. You're distracted over the thought that he's not being looked after as he would be if you were there, and that makes for divided duty.

When Ida B. Wells moved to Chicago and married Ferdinand Barnett she was thirty-two and her antilynching campaign was in full swing. Their marriage was a union of two black professionals. He was a prominent Chicago attorney and founder and publisher of the *Conservator*, Chicago's first black newspaper.

Barnett never expected Wells to stay home and be a housewife after their marriage. He employed household help, and he personally did most of the cooking for the family. Their temperaments complemented each other. Their daughter, Alfreda Duster, remembered that her "father was a very mild mannered man; he was not aggressive . . . or outspoken like my mother."[1] With the support of her husband, Ida B. Wells-Barnett remained a force to be reckoned with both inside and outside the home.

But even with such a supportive husband, Wells struggled with the conflicting demands of activism and her maternal role. She had her first child during an election year and was asked to campaign throughout Illinois for the Women's State Central Committee, a Republican political organization. She agreed on the condition that a nurse be provided to help with her six-month-old son. Wells-Barnett recalled, "I honestly believe that I am the only woman in the United States who ever traveled throughout the country with a nursing baby to make political speeches."

A year later she was pregnant again. By then her husband had been appointed assistant state's attorney. She resigned from the presidency of the Ida B. Wells Club and announced that she was retiring from public life to devote more time to her family. The "retirement" lasted five months.

Black women seemed to have an easier time juggling the role of activist with the role of mother and wife. This was reflected in the dramatic differences in the marital status of white and black women activists at the end of the nineteenth century. Historian Linda Gordon found that 85 percent of black women activists were married, compared to only 34 percent of white women activists.

Another factor in the difference between marriage rates for black and white women activists is that the pool of marriageable males was much smaller for white women during this historical period. More Americans were killed during the Civil War than during any other war the nation has fought. Hundreds of thousands of husbands, fathers, sons, and lovers were killed, and many more were disabled, resulting in a generation of white women who had limited prospects for marriage. In a culture in which women were defined by their relationship to men, many white women would for the first time be forced to discover their independence from men.[2]

Black women did not suffer the same deficit of marriageable men because although black men rushed to enlist in the Union army when they were finally allowed to join, they suffered far fewer casualties because they were rarely allowed to actually bear arms.[3]

Yet although barely one-third of the white activists had married, Gordon reports that "the white women, with few exceptions, tended to view married women's economic dependence on men as desirable and their employment as a misfortune."

Anna Julia Cooper, the fourth black woman to receive a doctorate, offered an alternative perspective. She married and was widowed at an early age and advised black women to seek egalitarian marriages. Cooper also believed that all married women should earn a livelihood because it "renders women less dependent on marriage for physical support (which by the way does not always accompany it)."

In Cooper's opinion, the question was not "How shall I so cramp, stunt, simplify, and nullify myself as to make me eligible to the honor of being swallowed up by some little man? But the problem rests with the man as to how he can so develop . . . to reach the ideal of a generation of women who demand the noblest, grandest, and best achievement of which he is capable."[4]

In general, black female activists were viewed more favorably within their own community than were their white counterparts because they were seen as fighting for the greater good of all black people and did not pose a threat to the political objectives of black men. Slavery, having rendered black men and women equally powerless, had leveled the gender "playing field" within the black community. In contrast, much of white women's activism, such as the fight for female suffrage, posed a direct challenge to the privileges of white men and patriarchy.

When historian Stephanie J. Shaw examined the lives of professional black women from the 1870s through the 1950s, she found that 74 percent were married at least once in their lifetime. In addition to being more likely than their white activist counterparts to be married, 51 percent of them had professional husbands. Among the more affluent black women who emerged as leaders, marriage to prominent black men often gave them a distinct advantage in that it gave them greater access to the network of powerful black men. Shaw notes that many of the women in her study had been socialized in such a way that "the model of womanhood held before [them] was one of achievement in *both* the public and private spheres. Parents cast domesticity as a complement rather than a contradiction to the public arenas."

Ida B. Wells made a similar point when speaking about balancing motherhood with her activism. Although she did not have the "longing for children that so many women have," she was glad that she had them nonetheless, adding that not having children robbed women "of one of the most glorious advantages in the development of their own womanhood."[5]

The lives of white activists Alice Freeman Palmer and Antoinette Louisa Brown Blackwell are indicative of a different convention. In 1881, twenty-six-year-old Alice Freeman became president of Wellesley College, the first female to head a nationally known institution of higher education. During her tenure as president, she met George Palmer, a Harvard professor, and in 1887, upon announcing her engagement to him, she resigned as Wellesley's president.

Antoinette Louisa Brown Blackwell, a women's rights activist and social reformer, was the first American woman to become an ordained minister. She married Samuel Charles Blackwell, an abolitionist businessman. After her marriage, even though she had a sympathetic husband, she struggled to combine marriage and her "intellectual work." They had seven children, two of whom died in infancy. While she was raising her children, Brown Blackwell for the most part gave up public speaking. She continued, however, to study and, as her children got older, she wrote and published many books on science and philosophy. Although she was more in favor of marriage than Susan B. Anthony, she had doubts about a woman's ability to juggle marriage, a family, and a career. She advocated part-time work for married women, with their husbands helping out with child care and housework.[6]

Free at Last

The defeat of the Confederacy in the Civil War and the abolition of slavery brought profound changes to black family life, altering the economic, social, and legal arrangements within which the former slaves lived. Freed slaves began creating communities, establishing networks of institutions, churches, schools, and mutual aid societies. When they were slaves, blacks had established secret churches and families, and after emancipation these institutions provided an important sense of community. With their newfound freedom, black men and women shared a common dream of living as free people.

The freed slaves particularly welcomed the opportunity to marry, a right that had been denied to them. In 1850, escaped slave Henry Bibb had written that "there are no class of people in the United States who so highly appreciate the legality of marriage as those persons who have been held and treated as property." When laws were passed requiring marriages among former slaves to be registered, some whites were "astonished by the eagerness with which former slaves legalized their marriage bonds."[7]

THE CLUB WOMEN'S MOVEMENT

The efforts of Ida B. Wells-Barnett to build a broad campaign against lynching by lecturing to groups in the United States and internationally, despite her increasing family responsibilities, had the side effect of fostering the growth of black women's clubs.

In response to a letter from an Englishwoman who had become interested in the issue of lynching after hearing Wells-Barnett give a speech in Britain,[8] John W. Jacks, president of the Missouri Press Association, published an open letter asserting that:

> Out of some 200 [Negroes] in this vicinity it is doubtful if there are a dozen virtuous women or that number who are not daily thieving from white people. To illustrate how they regard virtue in a woman, one of them, a negro woman, who asked who a certain negro woman who had lately moved into the neighborhood was. She turned up her nose and said, "The negroes will have nothing to do with "dat nigger," she won't let any man except her husband sleep with her, and we don't 'sociate with her."[9]

Josephine St. Pierre Ruffin, editor of The Woman's Era, the first American magazine owned and managed by black women, widely circulated Jacks's letter to prominent black women around the country, and the ensuing indignation led to organizing the first national conference to discuss black women's social concerns. In July 1895, 100 women from ten states convened to formulate plans for a national federation of black women.

The following year, Ruffin, who was president of the Women's Club of Boston, called the first Conference of Negro Women, which launched the National Association of Colored Women (NACW) under the motto "lifting as we climb."

These club women, primarily northerners, were reformers and activists who subscribed to the class values of Victorian America. The NACW's goal was to uplift poor women by emphasizing respectable behavior and introducing alternate images of black females. Ruffin saw it as "fitting" for the women of the race to take the lead in the movement, while recognizing "the necessity of the sympathy of our husbands, brothers, and fathers." She emphasized that our movement "is led and directed by women for the good of women and men, for the benefit of all humanity."

The club women's movement enabled black women to take a leadership role in their communities and to participate with black men in "uplifting" the race. African-American Studies professor Paula Giddings notes that at a time when patriarchal notions of men's roles were dominant, "there was a greater acceptance among black men of women in activist roles than there was in the broader society."[10]

A BLACK WOMAN'S ERA

Although black women faced many challenges, the emergence of black female leaders and the conscious efforts to improve the education of black women bore significant fruit around the turn of the century. Novelist Francis Harper, whose writings focused on the political struggles of African-American people, characterized this period as a "woman's era." Chicago activist Fannie Barrier Williams declared that although "the colored man and the colored woman started even, the achievements of black women during this period eclipsed black men."[11]

From 1890 to 1910, the number of professional black women increased by 219 percent, compared to a 51 percent rise for black men. In 1890, about 25 percent of all black professionals were women. By 1910, that number had risen to 43 percent. The growing achievement of women was reflected in the fact that in 1910 female graduates outnumbered male graduates by two to one at Dunbar High School, the leading black high school in Washington, D.C.[12]

In her study of black women's education, Jeanne Noble argued that black women had higher levels of educational achievement than men because the

> social system of the Negro rewarded the enterprising, clever, ambitious woman. Later, when attitudes that challenged the women's right to college education emerged, missionaries and earlier college founders were able to overcome these attitudes partly because of the need for teachers to educate the masses of ignorant Negroes.[13]

The perceived limitations in job opportunities for black men also contributed to the disparity between male and female academic achievement. Benjamin Mays, who received a Ph.D. from the University of Chicago and become president of Morehouse College, faced great opposition to his education from his father, who believed the only occupations for black men were preaching and farming.

Two additional factors encouraged black women's academic achievements. The first was the high probability that even married black women would need to find employment outside the home. In addition, many black women sought to avoid the degradation of domestic service, seen as a continuation of the oppression they had experienced during slavery.

The growth in black women's quest for education during this period can be seen in the enrollment trends at the thirteen schools of higher education run by the Baptist Home Mission. In 1880, male enrollment in these schools was twice as high as female enrollment. But by 1892, female students outnumbered males nearly three to two, and 120 of the 202 teachers were women. Most of the female students specialized in teacher training.

Not only were black women going to school in increasing numbers, they were also providing leadership by founding new schools specifically to train black women. Lucy C. Laney, Nannie Helen Burroughs, Charlotte Hawkins Brown, and Mary McLeod Bethune all founded training institutions.

In addition, black women actively challenged the authority of black men. Charlotte Hawkins Brown, for example, declared that her own work and writings were just as important as those of Booker T. Washington. Nannie Burroughs defied the male-dominated leadership so forcibly that she nearly lost church financial support for the National Training School for Women. Burroughs also cancelled a speech before the National Christian Mission when administrators insisted on censoring her remarks.

THE COMMITMENT TO MARRIAGE

Studying black middle- and upper-income women in Illinois at the turn of the century historian Shirley Carlson found that:

> The black community did not regard intelligence and femininity as conflicting values, as the larger society did. That society often expressed the fear that intelligent women would develop masculine characteristics. . . . Blacks seemed to have no such trepidations, or at least they were willing to have their women take these risks.[14]

Many prominent black women were married to professional black men. In addition to Wells and Barnett, there were figures like Shirley Graham DuBois, an author, composer, playwright, and activist, who was married to W. E. B. DuBois, a scholar, visionary, activist, and author. Teacher and social worker Sadie Grey Mays was the wife of Benjamin Mays, mentor to Martin Luther King, Jr., and president of Morehouse College. Eslanda Goode Robeson was a writer and social anthropologist, and was business manager for her husband Paul Robeson, the athlete, lawyer, author, activist, actor, and singer.

Margaret Murray Washington was president of the National Federation of Afro-American Women and was the wife of Booker T. Washington, president of Tuskegee Institute. Lugenia Hope Burns had a distinguished career as a social work reformer and was married to John Hope, the first black president of Atlanta University. Josephine Wilson Bruce, the first African-American principal of a Cleveland public school, was married to the first African-American to serve a full term in the United States Senate, Blanche K. Bruce.

Josephine St. Pierre Ruffin, the editor and publisher of *The Women's Era*, the first magazine in the United State owned and managed by black women, was married to George L. Ruffin, a member of the Boston City Council and Boston's first black judge. Madam C. J. Walker, owner of a beauty products company, was the first self-made female millionaire (black or white) and was married to a newspaperman, Charles J. Walker. Mary Terrell was a distinguished educator, suffragette, and civil rights activist, whose husband, Robert Terrell, was a Harvard graduate and principal of the M Street High School and the first African-American judge on the D.C. Municipal Court.

In that era, prominent black women tended to have experienced greater upward mobility than their white counterparts. About 90 percent of the black women who were classified as middle to upper class had been born into working-class families, compared to 35 percent of white women. The difference owed in part to the fact that blacks had been emancipated for only a relatively short time and higher education was the vehicle for social mobility for African Americans. Surveys conducted during that period found that black women were going to college for two primary reasons: to train for a vocation and to prepare for marriage and family life.[15]

Many educated black males were also enthusiastic about marriage and family life with an educated woman. Lugenia Burns and John Hope were both University of Chicago graduate students during their courtship. John, eager to marry and start a family, proposed after Lugenia received her degree. But she had been looking forward to a life of service and declined John's first proposal. Lugenia had four other men also vying for her hand in marriage. But John had an advantage over her other suitors because of his commitment to marital equality. He wrote her a letter saying that when they marry "neither of us [is] to be the servant, yet both of us gladly serve each other in love and patience."[16]

In writing about these marriages, Dr. Marion Cuthbert described them as a "deference of comradeship" by the men to their wives.[17] Anna Julia Cooper described the wives as having a "partnership with husbands on a plane of intellectual equality."[18]

CHANGES IN AFRICAN-AMERICAN MARRIAGE

The strong tradition of black women's education and professional employment that began during the club women's movement continued through the twentieth century. Jessie Bernard documented the higher levels of professional achievement found among black women, noting that in 1960 black women constituted 60.8 percent of black professionals, while white women constituted only 37.2 percent of the white professional class.[19]

One reason for the lower professional involvement of white women was the persistence of the nineteenth-century ethos that a woman's place was in the home. When Adlai Stevenson addressed the graduating class of Smith College (ironically the alma mater of both Gloria Steinem and Betty Friedan) in 1955, he told the students that their role in life was to "restore valid, meaningful purpose to life in your home."[20]

Three decades after Jessie Bernard's study of black and white females in the professions, Andrew Hacker found that black women made up 65.1 percent of black professionals, a rise of less than 5 percent, while white women had increased 15 points to 52.6 percent of white professionals.[21] The women's movement had been a catalyst for white women to move into the professional arena. An analysis conducted since Hacker's has found that despite gains in educational attainment and occupational status between 1975 and 2000, the median earnings of white women grew by 32 percent while the median earnings of black women grew by only 22 percent. In addition, although the proportion of black women with college degrees increased, a racial gap in education has endured. In 2007, 19 percent of black women 25 and older had college degrees compared with over 30 percent of white and non-Hispanic women.[22] This gap is even wider between white and black men.

In the three decades between the Bernard and Hacker studies, the black community has undergone what demographers describe as a "marriage squeeze," where a decrease in the availability of eligible partners leads to lower marriage rates, especially among women.

Using the College and Beyond (C&B) database, which contains the records of more than 80,000 undergraduate students who matriculated at twenty-eight academically selective colleges and universities in 1951, 1976, and 1989, we can compare the marriage and divorce patterns of black and white college-educated men and women. The "marriage squeeze" is reflected in the marriage rates of black graduates of these academically selective institutions roughly twenty years after they entered these schools. Blacks in the database were less likely to be married and more likely to be divorced or separated than their white counterparts. Whereas 77 percent of white women were married, 51 percent of black women were. For male graduates, these figures were 79 percent and 61 percent respectively. Some 14 percent of the black women were divorced or separated, compared to 6 percent of the white female graduates. For males, the differences in divorce and separation rates were miniscule, 6 percent for black men and 5 percent for white men. Of the four groups, black women had by far the highest rates of marital breakups.[23]

Although the marriage squeeze and/or the mate availability perspectives were first used to explain trends among blacks in lower economic strata, it also affects higher educated black women in that there are fewer black men with equivalent education who are available for them to marry. Social scientists and policy analysts have not paid enough attention to the challenges faced by professional black women in this regard.

For African-American women, the marriage squeeze has been exacerbated by the marriage of some of the most eligible black men to either white or Hispanic women. The C&B database didn't indicate the race of a graduate's spouse, but there is reason to believe that many of the black male graduates are not married to black women. In the three decades since the *Loving v. Virginia* decision was declared unconstitutional, ending all race-based legal restrictions on marriage, mixed couples tripled from 2 percent to 6 percent of all marriages. Black/white interracial married couples have increased from 51,000 in 1960 to 363,000 in 2000, a seven-fold increase. The majority of these marriages were of professional black men to white or Hispanic women. In view of this, it is not surprising that well-educated black women have fewer marriage options than their black male counterparts.

Black women are also more likely to be married to men who earn less money than they do. Data from the C&B studies show that white married women's *household* incomes were higher than those of black married female graduates, even though the *personal* incomes of the black women were 6 percent higher. This is because the husbands of white women graduates made substantially more money than the husbands of the black women. In fact, black women graduates also earned considerably *more* money than their husbands—exactly the opposite of the pattern for the white women graduates. This was because many of the black women graduates were married to men with less education than they had.

My analysis of the data indicates that the black women graduates, on average, contributed 63 percent of the household income, while white women graduates earned 40 percent of the total household income. Not surprisingly, the income of both black and white male graduates was substantially higher than it was for female graduates. What is more interesting is that the white and black male graduates, on average, earned 78 and 75 percent of the household income respectively.[24] This suggests that the male graduates may have entered more traditional marriages, in terms of gender, than either the white or black female graduates.

In classic exchange theory, traditional marriage has been described as an exchange of a male's economic resources for a female's social and domestic services. As American couples make the transition from more traditional to modern marriages, these marital exchanges are changing, which can be a source of tension and conflict. A wealth of research suggests that when couples get married, they bring with them a mixture of the "good things" and "bad things" from earlier generations, making the transition from traditional to modern marriages a challenging one. On the whole, both black and white male graduates, with their substantially higher incomes than those of their wives, are in more traditional marriages than female graduates. This may help explain their lower divorce rates and the fact that differences between the divorce rates of black and white males were infinitesimal.

The tensions and pressures in college-educated professional black women's marriages, however, are reflected in their much higher rates of divorce and separation. As noted earlier, household income for white women graduates was higher than for black women, even though their own earnings were, on average, 6 percent lower than those of the black women and considerably lower than their husbands' earnings. This seems to indicate that white women graduates may "downsize" their careers as they perform more family functions than their husbands, who focus on increasing their incomes. Black woman had less opportunity or pressure to downsize their careers.

Some black wives may harbor anger and resentment that they earn more than their husbands, and some husbands may be resentful that they do not earn enough money to have wives who can downsize their careers, and that anger may be displaced or misdirected at spouses. This may help explain the higher divorce and separation rates of African-American female graduates.

Bart Landry analyzed data from the National Survey of Families and Households (NSFH), which was first conducted in 1987–1988, and he found that black husbands contributed somewhat more to household chores than white husbands. According to Landry, black husbands spent on average 22.2 hours on household tasks, whereas white husbands spent 18.4 hours.[25] Other studies have supported Landry's findings and suggest that the greater involvement of black husbands in household chores may be one way of compensating for their smaller incomes relative to their wives.

The late C. Wright Mills, in *The Sociological Imagination*, distinguished between an individual's personal troubles, such as being unable to find a job or being involved in a divorce, and public issues, such as patterns of widespread joblessness or high rates of marital disruption. Mills argued that the "sociological imagination" allows us to see the interconnection between an individual's troubles and broader patterns in society.[26]

Marriage in the African-American community is a case in point. The historical analysis of black marriage over the past 100 years demonstrates that African Americans were in the vanguard of creating the modern egalitarian marriage. Marriage has both public and private domains, and the evolution of the institution is determined both by the individual emotions, cultural ideals, practices that couples bring to their unions, and by the values and constraints of any given historical moment. African Americans have helped shape modern marriage, and now they must adapt to economic circumstances where wives are not only equal partners, but often out-earn their husbands. The complex reality that couples must pave new paths but also feel pressure to adapt to current conditions must be addressed as we create public policy to support marriage as an institution.

8

Families "In Law" and Families "In Practice":
Does the Law Recognize Families
As They Really Are?

Karen Struening

This chapter will explore how families formed through the use of fertility technologies and families headed by same-sex couples have challenged legal definitions of family and parenthood. In many custody and support cases, courts have shown a willingness to recognize as parents individuals who have no biological relationship to the child and no martial relationship to the child's legal parent. These judicial decisions have undermined the law's historic emphasis on marriage and biology as the basis of family and have allowed social, rather than biological, factors to play a greater role in determining parenthood. At the same time, policies begun under the Bush administration and continued under the Obama administration have reasserted the superiority of the marital family. In addition, in same-sex marriage cases, some judges have argued for a biological understanding of the family. Consequently, family law is beset by tensions; some court decisions and government policies are making it easier for families to be recognized as they really are, while others are reasserting more conventional conceptions of family.[1]

As the chapters in this book make clear, contemporary families in the United States take many different forms. The question I address in this chapter is how well does the law respond to such variety? Why is this an important question? The overall purpose of family law, in the words of political theorist Mary Shanley, is to "create conditions under which people are best able to make deep commitments of emotional and material support to one another."[2] Families are associations in which unilateral and mutual dependencies develop.[3] It is the law's role to provide family members with a certain degree of predictability regarding their rights and responsibilities toward other family members. But when new family forms emerge, judges and legislators do not always resolve disputes equitably or protect the welfare and interests of vulnerable family members. This is because new family forms do not easily fit into old legal categories. The law cannot perform its function if judges and legislators fail to recognize families as they really are.

Historically, the law has used marriage and biology to define the family. The traditional model of family, as constructed by law, has been a different-sex couple with their own biological children. Until recently, the legal basis of motherhood was the biological connection between gestational mother and child, and fatherhood was based on marriage to the gestational mother. The emergence of new family forms, including but not limited to families headed by same-sex couples and families formed through the use of new fertility technologies and surrogacy contracts, has undermined the biological and marital bases of family law. Judges have been forced to consider whether an individual who has functioned as a parent but has neither a marital connection to the child's legal parent nor a biological connection to the child herself should be accorded parenting rights. Faced with these challenges, some judges have responded by reforming and stretching legal principles to recognize families that do not fit the traditional model. However, at the same time that some courts and state legislators have made rulings and written statutes recognizing new family forms, other judges, state and federal legislatures, and the American public through the use of ballot measures, have acted to reassert the traditional model. This can be seen in state statutes and constitutional amendments that prohibit the recognition of same-sex marriage and, in some cases, go so far as to prohibit civil unions and domestic partnerships between different-sex and same-sex couples.[4] It also can be seen in efforts on the part of federal and state governments to reassert the marital basis of family by promoting marriage, particularly among low-income couples receiving public benefits.[5] And, in a striking exception to the general trend of extending greater legal protections to gay and lesbian parents, voters recently passed a ballot measure in Arkansas that prohibits the fostering or adoption of children by unmarried adults and couples.[6] This conflict between accepting and rejecting new family forms indicates that judges and legislators, as well as the American public, are ambivalent about moving beyond the traditional definition of family. Unfortunately, failing to recognize families as they really are makes it difficult for the law to facilitate and protect relationships of mutual and unilateral dependency.

A Note on Family Law

The United States has two parallel court systems: one at the federal level and the other at the state level. Family law, which includes areas such as marriage, divorce, child custody, child support, and state regulation of parent-child relations, is primarily a matter of state law. It is largely written by state legislatures, and interpreted and applied by state courts. Consequently, family law differs from state to state. Consider the fact that six states (Massachusetts, Connecticut, Iowa, Vermont, New Hampshire, and Maine) protect the right of same-sex couples to marry and six states and the District of Columbia provide same-sex couples with legal arrangements that are equivalent to or similar to marriage, such as civil unions and domestic partnerships.[7] However, twenty-nine states have constitutional amendments restricting marriage to one man and one woman and twelve states have state laws that do the same.[8]

The federal government is able to exercise considerable influence over family law in part because states are not eligible for federal funds if they do not comply with federal statutes. For example, in 1996 Congress passed the Personal Responsibility and Work Opportunity Reconciliation Act (PRWORA), which replaced a federal entitlement to public assistance for eligible families with a block grant to states. According to PRWORA, states cannot receive federal Temporary Assistance for Needy Families (TANF) funds unless they adopt the Uniform Interstate Family Support Act, which requires states to identify the fathers of children born to women receiving public assistance.[9] As a result, under PRWORA, paternity and child support responsibilities are based on the unmarried father's genetic tie to his child.

Beginning with its decision prohibiting polygamy in 1878, the U.S. Supreme Court has created a constitutional framework for family law.[10] Under the due process clause of the Fourteenth Amendment, the Supreme Court has affirmed parental autonomy in regard to the raising of children,[11] the right to marry the person of one's choice without regard to race,[12] the right to marry,[13] the right to live in an extended family,[14] the right to use birth control,[15] the right to end a pregnancy,[16] and has decriminalized private same-sex sexual context.[17] The Court also has invoked the equal protection clause of the Fourteenth Amendment to prohibit the differential treatment of children born to unmarried parents[18] and has protected the right of unmarried fathers to the custody of their children.[19] These rulings have limited the ability of the state to arbitrarily interfere with the choices individuals make about their intimate associations and increased, to some extent, the range of family forms that are considered legitimate. By ruling that states must treat individuals born within and outside of marriage equally and by protecting an unmarried father's rights to his children, the Court decreased the power of marital status to determine how rights and benefits are distributed. And by recognizing a right of privacy that includes both the right to use birth control and the right to terminate a pregnancy (subject to certain circumstances) the Court made marriage more of a choice and less of a necessity.

THE TRADITIONAL LEGAL DEFINITION OF FAMILY

As noted above, until recently the legal definition of family has been based on marriage and biology. In practice this has meant that the law protected and indeed privileged the marital relationship, drawing a sharp boundary around the married couple and their children. Until the development of surrogacy contracts, legal motherhood was defined almost exclusively by biology: a woman was considered a child's legal mother if she gave birth to that child.[20] In contrast to biologically based motherhood, the legal definition of fatherhood was founded on marital status.[21] What mattered for men was not whether they were the biological father of a child, but whether they were married to the child's mother. If they were, men incurred all the responsibilities of fatherhood; if they were not, they incurred none. This definition of legal fatherhood served two purposes: (1) it protected a married man and his estate from the consequences of his out-of-wedlock sexual activity,[22] and (2) it gave children conceived through a wife's adulterous affair the opportunity to be considered legitimate and to inherit from the husband of their mother. The consequences of basing paternity on marriage were dire for unmarried women and their children. In addition to being treated as social outcasts, children born to an unmarried mother did not have standing to seek support from their biological father nor to inherit from his estate.

Prior to the 1970s, unwed fathers were not consulted when their children were given up for adoption and were unlikely to receive custody of their children over the objections of the mother. In 1972, the Supreme Court acted in *Stanley v. Illinois* to protect the rights of unmarried fathers.[23] The state of Illinois had placed the children of an unmarried, cohabiting couple into foster care, following the death of their mother, despite the fact that their biological father had lived with and cared for them all of their lives. The Court found that under these circumstances, at least, the biological father had a right to petition the court for custody of his children. As cohabitation and nonmarital birth have increased, federal and state law has affirmed both the rights and responsibilities of unmarried fathers. As already noted, the federal Family Support Act requires states to identify the biological fathers of children born to low-income unmarried mothers in order to recoup public dollars spent on the mother and her children. The Uniform Parentage Act, first promulgated in 1973 by the National Conference of Commissioners on Uniform State Laws and revised in 2000 and 2002, outlines how an unmarried father can establish a legal connection with his child.[24] It includes signing a paternity registry, signing the child's birth certificate, or residing with the child and holding the child out to the world as his own.

Originally, the justification for the legal principle that any child born to a married woman must be considered her husband's offspring was to protect the child from the stigma of illegitimacy. Despite the elimination of disabilities associated with being born outside of a marital relationship, the law has continued in some cases to guard the privacy of the marital family against unmarried men making paternity claims. The case of *Michael H. v. Gerald D.* involves a woman, who, while married to Gerald D., had an affair with Michael H., and lived with him and their biological child intermittently before reuniting with her husband.[25] The Supreme Court held that neither Michael H., who had held the child out to the world as his own, nor his daughter through her legal guardian, had standing to petition the court for visitation rights. In this case, the Court allowed the privileged status of marriage to trump an established relationship between father and child. However, as noted by legal theorist David Meyer, in a growing number of states, unmarried men are being allowed to use DNA testing to prove paternity despite the objections of the mother's husband.[26]

When families dissolve or take forms other than two married (different-sex) parents with biological children, the law often acts to reconstitute families so that they come as close as possible to the traditional model. For example, until recently, the law held that adoption could only occur if the biological mother gave up all legal rights to her child. This rule grew out of the traditional adoption scenario in which every effort was made to simulate a biological family, including "matching" the child's ethnic and religious background to that of her adoptive parents. A similar example can be seen in the case of children who have been taken by the state from their biological mothers because of abuse or neglect. According to the 1997 Adoption and Safe Families Act (ASFA), terminating the rights of the biological mother and placing the child up for adoption with nonrelatives is preferable to allowing children to live indefinitely in kinship care with a grandmother or aunt. Kinship care allows children to retain a relationship both with their mother and with their extended family and does not require that the biological mother's rights be terminated. It breaks with the traditional model by allowing a child to have more than one parental figure in his or her life and by locating parental authority in someone who is neither the biological nor adoptive parent of the child. According to ASFA, it is preferable to sever all of a child's existing caretaking bonds in order to reconstitute the exclusivity of the bounded, marriage-based, nuclear family.[27]

The bounded nature of the traditional model and its emphasis on family privacy also has made it difficult for the law to recognize families as they really are. Privacy and parental autonomy are positive values because they protect the parent-child bond from arbitrary action on the part of the state and other third parties. But some legal theorists have suggested that the exclusivity of parental rights goes too far and is based on the idea that children are little more than their parents' possessions. This view was expressed by Justice John Paul Stevens in a dissent to a case that denied visitation rights to grandparents: "At a minimum, our prior cases recognizing that children are, generally speaking, constitutionally protected actors require that this Court reject any suggestion that when it comes to parental rights, children are so much chattel."[28] Stevens's point was that parental autonomy and the privacy of the parent-child bond should not be used to separate children from adults with whom they have developed significant relationships. This point becomes particularly salient during a period in which emerging forms of relationship have not yet received social recognition. Judges, particularly those who adhere to the traditional model, may not believe that individuals who are actually functioning as parents in children's lives fit the legal definition of parent. As a result, they will not act to preserve the relationship between adult and child over the objections of someone whom the law recognizes as a legal parent.

COURTS CONFRONT LESBIAN CO-PARENTS

Cases involving nonbiological lesbian co-parents have required courts to find a basis for parentage that is neither biology nor marriage. In the early nineties, when cases involving the dissolution of a parenting lesbian couple reached the courts, nonbiological mothers were frequently treated as legal strangers to their children and were denied standing to petition for custody or visitation rights.[29] If they had been unmarried males, simply living with their children and holding them out to the world as their own would have sufficed to earn them parental status. But because family law regarding mothers asserted that (1) biology determines maternity, (2) a child can only have one mother, and (3) the legal parent is given exclusive rights to her child, the courts did not initially recognize the parental status of nonbiological mothers.

In the mid-nineties, some courts on both coasts and in the Mid-Atlantic and Great Lakes regions began to recognize the visitation and custodial petitions of nonbiological mothers. The legal principles of de facto parentage (the court recognizes that an individual is playing a parent-like role in a child's life) and parenthood by estoppel (the court recognizes that an individual through word or deed has created the expectation that she or he will carry out the duties of a parent), were initially developed in response to the requests of stepparents whose marriage had dissolved and who wanted to maintain a relationship with the children of their ex-spouse.[30] In several cases, courts ruled that state statutes were sufficiently flexible to allow individuals who stood *in loco parentis* (in the place of a parent) to a child to petition for custodial or visitation rights. These courts argued that individuals who had lived with a child and fulfilled the duties of a parent without receiving compensation constituted de facto or psychological parents. For example, a New Jersey review court, while affirming the biological mother's contention that as the legal mother she has a constitutionally protected right to the "care, custody and nurture of her child," went on to argue that "[A]t the heart of the psychological parent cases is a recognition that children have a strong interest in maintaining the ties that connect them to adults who love and provide for them. That interest, for constitutional reasons as well as social purposes, lies in the emotional bonds that develop between family members as a result of shared daily life."[31] Summarizing a Wisconsin ruling[32] that had established a test for when a third party qualifies as a psychological parent, the court stated: "the legal parent must consent to and foster the relationship between the third party and the child; the third party must have lived with the child; the third party must perform parental functions for the child to a significant degree; and most important, a parent-child bond must be forged."[33] The first factor shows that the legal parent and the third party intended to create a family together and that the legal parent encouraged a relationship between the third party and the child. The second shows that the third party was a part of the child's daily life and the third that she performed routine acts of care. The fourth requires expert testimony on the strength of the parent-child bond that emerged out of these daily acts of care. The New Jersey court went on to state that a person who is determined to be a psychological parent "stands in parity" with the legal parent in regards to visitation or custody rights. However, the court concluded that since the legal principle determining custody between two parties with equal claims (such as a husband and wife who are divorcing) is the best interest of the child, courts should give greater weight to the biological parent's claim. While the New Jersey court took significant steps toward the view that biology is not the sole determinant of parenthood, in the end biology was allowed to be the decisive factor. The court reasoned that children have a stronger interest in maintaining their connection with their biological parent than with their nonbiological parent because only the former can satisfy the child's desire for knowledge of her or his biological roots. In general, most psychological parenthood cases have awarded visitation rights but stopped short of transferring legal custody from the biological mother to the psychological parent.

Courts also have recognized parenthood by estoppel in cases where it can be shown through a contract, verbal agreement, and/or the conduct of the parties, that the couple intended to raise a child or children jointly as co-parents. In the case of *Elisa B. v. Superior Court*, the court concluded that Elisa, who had been the primary earner in a same-sex-headed family, owed child support.[34] After the relationship between Elisa and Emily dissolved, Elisa, the nonbiological parent, denied that she was the legal parent of her ex-partner's biological children. The court reasoned that by planning and carrying out the pregnancy and childbirth with her partner, and by caring for and financially supporting their children, Elisa created certain expectations on her partner's part, which in turn determined the actions that Emily took. Emily would not have sought out artificial insemination and become pregnant if Elisa had not made certain commitments to her. Importantly, the court ruled in *Elisa B.* and its sister case, *Kristine H. v. Lisa R.*, that a child can have two mothers. The court's decision was based, in part, on a domestic partnership law in California that provided registered domestic partners with the same rights as married couples.

Parenthood by estoppel has been used to recognize the parental status of lesbian mothers, and it therefore provides nonbiological mothers and their children with greater protection than de facto parenthood, which as noted has been mostly used to gain visitation rights. Perhaps the optimal legal mechanism for protecting the parenting rights of nonbiological parents is second-parent adoption.[35] Recently, through legislative reforms and court decisions, more than half of all states have allowed the nonbiological mother in a same-sex couple to adopt her child (second-parent adoption) without requiring the biological mother to give up her parenting rights.[36] Gay men also have been able to adopt their partner's child or children.[37] Second-parent adoption gives the nonbiological or second parent greater security and ensures that if the biological or first parent dies, the second parent will automatically receive custody of the child.

Same-sex couples that live in states that recognize their right to marry or form a civil union enjoy the same parenting rights as different-sex couples *in their home states*. But for both pragmatic and normative reasons, Nancy Polikoff argues that marriage may not be the best path to protecting the parenting rights of nonbiological, unmarried parents.[38] First, neither the federal government nor a majority of states recognize civil unions or marriages between partners of the same sex. This means the nonbiological or second parent would best be advised to adopt her child even if her home state allows same-sex couples to marry or register their civil unions. In contrast, all states and the federal government recognize the second-parent adoptions of other states. Second, giving marriage a central role in establishing parentage reinforces the special status of marriage and may increase the difficulties unmarried individuals face in establishing their parenting rights. In contrast, de facto parentage, parenthood by estoppel, and second-parent adoption protect parent-child relationships in all families and not just in those headed by married parents.

The cases discussed above show that judges have had to stretch existing family law in order to recognize families as they really are. Going beyond biology forces judges to ask difficult questions concerning how to allocate parenting rights. Is it the couple's agreement to parent a child together that makes the nonbiological mother a parent? Or, is parental status a byproduct of the daily acts of care that the nonbiological mother performs? Should the key emphasis be placed on the parent-child bond, as emphasized by the New Jersey court?

Political theorist Mary Shanley argues for a child-centered understanding of how we determine parental rights. She claims that focusing on either the intent of the couple or the conduct of the nonbiological mother places too much emphasis on adults at the expense of children. Shanley states:

> A theory of parental rights must begin not with adults, but with children, and not with volition but with need. While we may use mechanisms of consent or agreement, or look at what the adults have in fact done (or not done) to care for the child as evidence that they have assumed or relinquished parental rights and responsibilities, law and language must make it clear that the needs of the child, not adults' acts of will, create those rights and responsibilities.[39]

Shanley endorses what Barbara Woodhouse calls the generist position—the idea that parenting rights should be based on the needs of the child.[40] This child-centered approach charges courts with preserving the child's network of relationships. The advantage of this position, according to Shanley, is that "respecting networks of care would validate relationship rights based on care and leave room for different degrees of connectedness between a child and the adults in her life."[41] By placing its emphasis on the child's need for care, the generist position avoids what Justice Stevens identified in *Troxel* as a propensity within the law to treat children as if they are their parents' chattel. It encourages judges to allow individuals who in the past would not have been recognized as legal parents to petition the court for visitation rights. Like de facto parenthood and parenthood by estoppel, it provides criteria for parenting rights other than marriage and biology.

COURTS CONFRONT ASSISTED CONCEPTION

The use of fertility technologies and surrogacy arrangements demonstrates the appeal of the biologically based family while at the same time upending it. Until recently, family law has been built around the assumption that families are created through natural, meaning unassisted, procreation and that children are genetically related to both of their parents. This model of family assumes that sexual intercourse, the provision of genetic material, the conception of the child-to-be, and birth, are all one seamless process involving one man and one woman. Fertility technologies and surrogacy arrangements disrupt this assumption. Assisted conception allows for genetic contributions to come from individuals who will never have a social or legal relationship to the children their genes helped to create. In addition, while it is true that procreation continues to require gametes from both a man and a woman, cases involving fertility technologies and surrogacy arrangements show us that conception is more than a biological process: it also has an intentional, social dimension. It is the decision to bring a child into the world, and not just the contribution of genetic material or gestational capacity that makes someone a parent.

Prior to the development of artificial insemination (AI) in the 1940s, couples who lacked the ability to procreate "naturally" had only one alternative to childlessness: adoption. For some couples, assisted conception is attractive because it allows for at least one individual to have a biological connection to the resulting children. Indeed, the use of artificial insemination was at first shrouded in secrecy because the married heterosexual couples that originally had access to it wanted to appear as if they fit the biological model.[42]

An essentially unregulated practice, artificial insemination is now available to single women, lesbian couples, and unmarried heterosexual couples. When used by single women and lesbian couples, AI no longer functions to support the illusion that all families are composed of two different-sex parents and their own biological children. Instead, it opens up the jarring prospect that procreation, as a social, as opposed to a biological, phenomenon can be separated from the different-sex couple. Consider the fact that most states deny parenting rights to anonymous sperm donors.[43] This means that children born to lesbian couples with the use of AI (provided the donor was unknown to the recipient and the procedure was carried out by a doctor) do not have legal fathers.[44] This kind of scenario suggests that a lesbian couple can procreate if we take procreation to mean the intention to have a child (with the help of an anonymous donor) and raise it together.

In vitro fertilization, a more medically intrusive and complex procedure than AI, involves the use of donated eggs, which are then fertilized in a test tube, before becoming implanted in the intended mother's womb. The market in genetic material that makes artificial insemination and in vitro fertilization possible is largely unregulated.[45] When a heterosexual couple uses this procedure, access to another woman's egg allows the intended mother to give birth to a child that is genetically related to her male partner. Under such circumstances, a couple may feel that both partners have contributed to the birth of the child.

Lesbian couples, with the assistance of a sperm donor, can do the same if one partner donates her egg to the other, who then bears the resulting child.[46] Gay male couples also can take part in the biological process of birth, by fertilizing a donated egg with a mixture of their sperm and arranging for the services of a gestational surrogate.

The use of artificial insemination and in vitro fertilization is a testament to the desire of individuals and couples to have a genetic connection to their children. In this sense, it reveals that biological connections continue to shape how we think about family and the parent-child relationship. But it also sharply reduces the importance of biology by separating parenthood from the contribution of genetic material. The role of the biological "parent" is reduced to that of anonymous donor of genetic material. Factors such as intent, relationship to the gestational parent, pre-birth planning, and pre-birth investment in the child-to-be, play a greater part in determining parenting rights.

Gestational contracts refer to an agreement between a woman and a couple in which the woman agrees to bear a child that she then turns over to the commissioning couple. Twelve states, including New York and New Jersey, refuse to recognize gestational contracts.[47] Eleven states, including California, permit gestational agreements by statute or case law.[48] It is not known how many surrogacy agreements take place in the United States each year, as no organization tracks agreements and many are never formalized, but experts suspect it is at least in the hundreds.[49] Unlike AI and in vitro fertilization, which separate gestation from genetic material, surrogacy can separate the decision to bring a child into the world and to become a parent from pregnancy and birth. It therefore suggests the need for a definition of parenthood based on neither genetic nor gestational connections between parent and child.

In an early and atypical case that reached a New Jersey court in 1986, Mary Beth Whitehead, who had agreed in exchange for a fee to bear a child using her own egg and sperm belonging to the husband of the commissioning couple (Elizabeth and William Stern), refused to relinquish the child.[50] While the trial court ruled in favor of upholding the surrogacy contract and would have terminated Whitehead's parenting rights, the Supreme Court of New Jersey reversed the lower court's decision, declared the contract invalid, and ruled that Whitehead was the child's legal mother and that William Stern was the child's legal father. It gave custody to William Stern and his wife, who was now prohibited from adopting her husband's child, and gave Whitehead visitation rights. This arrangement was based, in part, on a biological theory of parenting rights. Although it had voided the surrogacy contract, the court nonetheless did not think of Mr. Stern as a mere sperm donor, with legally weak grounds to claim parentage.[51] He was given full parenting rights, while his wife was declared a legal stranger to her husband's child. Despite the fact that it was the Sterns who decided to have a child, planned for its birth, and initiated the pregnancy, Ms. Whitehead best fit the biologically based legal definition of a mother: she had contributed her genetic material, carried to term, and given birth to the child. Like Elizabeth Stern, Whitehead's husband was considered a legal stranger to the child.

To avoid the fate of the Sterns, most commissioning couples now combine in vitro fertilization, using the wife's egg or a donated egg, with surrogacy arrangements. While this method is more complicated and expensive than artificially inseminating the woman contracted to carry out the pregnancy, it has been successfully used to protect commissioning couples from parenthood claims brought by surrogate mothers. In *Johnson v. Calvert*, the court faced a disputed surrogacy case in which one woman, the wife in the commissioning couple, provided genetic material and another, the surrogate, provided gestational capacity. Because the biological bases of motherhood were perfectly split, the court adopted an intent-based theory of parentage.[52] This means the court looked at conception, pregnancy, and birth not simply as biological processes but as activities emanating from a conscious, deliberate intention to have a child. The court emphasized the fact that it was the commissioning couple who had sought and initiated the birth of the child. Its decision gave exclusive parenting rights to the commissioning couple, whose actions, the court reasoned, had actually caused the child to be born.

The court's decision in *Johnson* is significant because it recognizes that parenting rights can rest on nonbiological factors. In *Johnson*, the court granted custody to a woman who claimed parentage based on both intention and genetics, but in another case, *In re marriage of Buzzanca*, California awarded custody to a commissioning mother who had no genetic connection to the child.[53] The intent to have a child is essential to creating a pre-birth investment in the baby yet to be born. While historically this pre-birth investment has been entwined with contributing genetic material and/or undergoing pregnancy and giving birth to a child, surrogacy arrangements allow for nonbiological pre-birth investments. Decisions such as *Johnson* and *In re marriage of Buzzanca* demonstrate the ability of courts to conceptualize parenthood as arising out of consciously and often jointly made decisions, and not solely out of genetic material or gestation.

Like the families of co-parenting lesbian couples, various kinds of families created through assisted conception have required courts to rethink how the law approaches parenting rights. Both of these sorts of cases have pushed courts to consider how much weight should be given to biology and how much weight should be given to social factors such as intention, conduct, the parent-child bond, the child's interest in preserving her web of caretaking relationships, and agreements between co-parenting couples. Recognizing these social factors has allowed courts to preserve and protect families as they really are. Indeed, the above cases suggest that family law is going through an odd phase during which some judges are struggling to reform and stretch legal principles to accommodate nontraditional families. Their decisions demonstrate that the law does have the conceptual resources to respond to emerging family forms. Unfortunately, a reverse trend is also evident; some judges and policy makers are acting to reaffirm the marital and biological conception of family.

ATTEMPTS TO REASSERT THE TRADITIONAL MODEL

Public opinion is often divided about the direction of family law and policy, with individuals expressing ambivalence about divorce rates, nonmarital childbearing by unmarried heterosexual couples or single mothers, surrogacy contracts, and gay and lesbian families. During the 1970s, a backlash began against the women's and LGBT movements that eventually morphed into the 1980s crusade for traditional family values and the 1990s marriage movement. The leaders of these successive movements have all argued that the development of new family forms constitutes a national crisis and is the cause of numerous social ills. At times they have been partially successful in enlisting policy makers, as well as broad swaths of the American public, to their side. Traditionalists argue that (1) marriage is the foundation of the family, and (2) the marital relationship is rooted in biological (gender) difference. Supporters of this position claim that when the law recognizes nonmarital forms of family it undermines the traditional model by indicating that the state has no clear preference for it. Alternatively, when the state establishes benefits and rights exclusively for those who are married, while making it difficult or risky to create new family forms, it actively discourages the latter. As believers in the power of law to channel individuals into state-preferred behavior patterns, advocates of the traditional model are strongly opposed to recognizing existing nontraditional families.[54] Not only do they promote traditional different-sex marriage, they actively oppose efforts to facilitate adult and parent-child relationships that are not rooted in marriage and biological difference.[55]

Efforts to reassert the traditional model have met with some success. In 2002, under the banner of the Healthy Marriage Initiative, the Bush Administration began to develop programs designed to strengthen marriage and increase marriage rates among low-income couples. Initially, the U.S. Department of Health and Human Services, through one of its agencies, the Administration for Families and Children, used grants to encourage states and nonprofits to establish marriage skills programs for couples accessing social services.[56] The Obama administration has continued to fund these programs. In 2006, as part the Deficit

Reduction Act of 2005, Congress reauthorized the Personal Responsibility and Work Opportunity and Reconciliation Act (PRWPRA) and appropriated $150 million a year for marriage promotion and responsible fatherhood programs, with the stipulation that not more than $50 million could be spent on fatherhood programs each year.[57] Three states are currently spending significant portions of their Temporary Assistance for Needy Families (TANF) block grant on marriage initiatives. The Oklahoma Marriage Initiative began in 2000 with an allocation of $10 million. In 2007, Ohio and Utah set aside 1 percent of their TANF funds for marriage-strengthening programs.[58]

Attempts to strengthen the marital and biological bases of the family also can be seen in states that have prohibited same-sex marriage through statute or constitutional amendment. Some of these laws have been written so broadly that courts have read them as prohibiting all recognition of marriage-like relationships. For example, in May 2008, state employees in Michigan lost domestic partner benefits after the Michigan Supreme Court ruled on an amendment to the state constitution prohibiting same-sex marriage that had been passed in 2004.[59] These broadly written amendments and laws demonstrate that the goals of the marriage movement include eliminating official recognition of all non-marital intimate relationships.

State Supreme Court justices have contributed to the reassertion of the traditional family by adopting biologically based conceptions of marriage in their decisions on the constitionality of exclusive marriage laws. While the high courts in Massachusetts, Maine, Vermont, New Hampshire, Iowa, and Connecticut have legalized same-sex marriage, courts in New York, Washington, Maryland, Indiana, and Arizona have ruled that exclusive marriage laws do not violate their state constitutions.[60] Typically, courts that rule against the constitutionality of same-sex marriage employ a procreation based argument to exclude same-sex couples from the institution of marriage. For example, according to the court of highest jurisdiction in the state of New York, the Court of Appeals, the purpose of marriage is to channel potential procreators into a state-sponsored union. Consequently, the state acts within its mandate to provide for the public health and, in particular, the welfare of children, when it offers potential procreators incentives to marry. The odd part of New York's argument is that only unmediated, "natural" sexual intercourse qualifies as procreation. According to the Court, same-sex couples are legitimately excluded from the state's bargain with potential procreators because they require fertility technologies and surrogacy arrangements in order to have children.[61] Writing about same-sex couples, the court explains: "These couples can become parents by adoption, or by artificial insemination or other *technological marvels*, but they do not become parents as a result of accident or impulse."[62] The difference between unassisted and assisted conception is held to be relevant by the court because different-sex couples are in danger of reproducing spontaneously without forming stable and committed relationships; same-sex couples, who must visit fertility clinics together and negotiate contracts with surrogates, are not. While this may sound like a strange sort of backhanded compliment—same-sex couples are responsible procreators, different-sex couples are not—it betrays a preference for unmediated conception and a biologically based form of family. The majority opinion's emphasis on the natural and biological is taken even further by the concurring opinion. Justifying the limitation of marriage to different-sex couples, Justice Graffeo explains: "The binary nature of marriage—its inclusion of one man and one woman—reflects the biological fact that human procreation cannot be accomplished without the genetic contribution of both a male and a female."[63] According to Justice Graffeo, the biological phenomenon of procreation is the foundation of the legal relationship of marriage. If procreation requires one man and one woman, marriage does too.

But given the existence of a large and unregulated market in genetic material, Justice Graffeo's assertion falls flat. While procreation continues to require the genetic contribution of one man and one woman, the intention to have a child together may be formed and carried out by two women. In addition, court decisions such as *Johnson* and *In re marriage of Buzzanca*, in which the court resolved surrogacy disputes by awarding sole custody of the child to the commissioning couple, suggest procreation is a social as well as a biological phenomenon. It is difficult to see how the right to marry can be based on unassissted procreation when fertility technologies have effectively severed the intention to procreate from both the provision of genetic material and sexual intercourse.

In addition, as Vanessa Lavely has argued, New York courts use different definitions of marriage when they are deciding same-sex marriage and same-sex adoption cases. The majority on the Court of Appeals used a procreation-based definition of marriage in its same-sex marriage case, thus excluding same-sex couples from marriage. However, in deciding adoption cases, New York courts have stressed the similarity between same-sex partnerships and different-sex marriages. Lavely concludes: "By granting same-sex adoptions, courts have effectively approved of creating families by means other than procreation."[64]

Attempts to strengthen the marital and biological bases of the family are bound to disadvantage emerging family forms. Government-supported marriage programs such as the Healthy Marriage Initiative reinforce the idea that marriage is the dividing line between real families, entitled to official recognition and the rights and benefits that follow, and all others. As Nancy Polikoff has forcefully argued, marital status is all too frequently the determining factor in the allocation of workers' compensation benefits and inheritance rights, the authority to make medical decisions for others, child custody and parenting rights, and medical leave and health-care benefits.[65] Likewise, perpetuating the idea that real families consist of two different-sex parents and their own biological children makes the legal recognition of families in which biological ties are absent more difficult. And, as in the New York Court of Appeals case discussed above, it also serves to justify the exclusion of same-sex couples from a fundamental civil right—the right to marry.

THE FUTURE OF FAMILY LAW

Historically, family law has exercised a channeling, or if you prefer, disciplinary function. By this I mean that the law has been used to mold families so that they meet the needs of the state and reflect the majority's morality. In more recent years, as greater weight has been given to individual liberty, gender equality, and the interests of children, family law has begun to accommodate the choices individuals make in regard to forming families. As a result, it has done a better job recognizing and protecting families as they really are.

At the same time, opposition to recognizing families as they really are is strong. As noted, proponents of the marriage movement believe that recognizing nontraditional family forms will increase the number of parents who are unwilling or unable to provide their children with stable homes. This belief is based on the assumption that marriage and biology are the foundations of the family and that no other way of defining or thinking about the family can be found. The decisions of judges who have had to grapple with rendering judgments about real families shows that this belief is groundless. In many of the cases discussed above, judges were able to articulate criteria that help to define parenthood without relying on marriage or biology. They looked instead at other factors such as daily acts of care on the part of a nonbiological parent, parent-child bonding, verbal agreements between same-sex partners, and the intent of an infertile different-sex couple to bring a child into the world. As this chapter suggests, family law varies in its ability to protect nontraditional families from state to state and even from court to court. But this does not mean that the law lacks resources for arriving at new definitions of family. If it is to fulfill its purpose of facilitating deep commitments of emotional and material support properly, the law must move beyond a purely marital and biological conception of family.

9

Briefing Paper: Will Providing Marriage Rights to Same-Sex Couples Undermine Heterosexual Marriage? Evidence from Scandinavia

M. V. Lee Badgett

Since the November 2003 court ruling allowing same-sex couples to marry in Massachusetts, a new debate on the consequences of expanding the right to marry has exploded across the United States. While the debate involves many issues, one particularly controversial question is whether heterosexual people would change their marriage behavior if same-sex couples were given the same marital rights and obligations.

As a way to understand what might happen, some writers have looked to the experience of those Scandinavian countries that pioneered giving a marriage-like status to gay and lesbian couples.[1] Denmark adopted such a law in 1989, Norway in 1993, Sweden in 1994, and Iceland in 1996. Since then, three other countries (France, Germany, and Finland) have also created a new status for same-sex couples, and two (the Netherlands and Belgium) opened marriage to same-sex couples.

What can we learn from the experience of these countries about how giving gay couples the right to marry affects heterosexual marriage patterns? On the one hand, the fact that Danish marriage rates increased slightly after the passage of partner recognition laws has led some observers to conclude that gay couples are saving the institution of marriage.[2] On the other hand, Stanley Kurtz of the Hoover Institution claims that allowing gay couples to marry or have marital rights has undermined the institution of heterosexual marriage in Scandinavia.[3] In this paper, I show that this argument, which has been widely reprinted and quoted around the country, is based on the consistent misuse and misinterpretation of data.

The argument that same-sex partnerships undermine heterosexual marriage rests on four claims:

1. In the European countries that allow same-sex couples to register as partners, marriage and parenthood have become separated, and married parenthood has become a minority occurrence.

2. The separation of marriage and parenthood in those countries is disastrous for children because of higher rates of breakup among cohabitors.

3. Allowing gay marriage is both an effect and a cause of the separation of parenthood and marriage.

4. If the U.S. allows gay couples to marry, heterosexual people in the United States will adopt European-style family dynamics.

In fact, none of these claims fits the actual evidence of the Scandinavian experience:

1. Divorce rates have not risen since the passage of partnership laws, and marriage rates have remained stable or actually increased.

2. The average Scandinavian child spends more than 80 percent of his or her life with both parents—more time than the average American child! Norwegian children spend, on average, 89 percent of their youth living with both parents. American children spend, on average, just 67 percent of their youth living with both parents.

3. Nonmarital birthrates have not risen faster in Scandinavia since the passage of same-sex partnership laws. Although there has been a long-term trend toward the separation of sex, reproduction, and marriage in the industrialized West, nonmarital birthrates changed just as much in countries without partnership laws as in countries that legally recognize same-sex partnerships.

Married Parents Are Still the Majority in Scandinavia

Marriage and childbearing have become less directly connected over time in many European countries, including Scandinavia.[4] But as we shall see, this separation hardly qualifies as the death of marriage, and it cannot be blamed on the passage of same-sex partner laws. In fact, Denmark's long-term decline in marriage rates turned around in the early 1980s, and the upward trend in heterosexual marriage has continued since the 1989 passage of the registered partner law. Today Danish heterosexual marriage rates are the highest they have been since the early 1970s. The most recent marriage rates in Sweden, Norway, and Iceland are also all higher today than they were in the years before the partner laws were passed.

No research suggests that recognizing same-sex couple relationships caused the increase in marriage rates. But heterosexual couples in those countries were clearly not deterred from marrying by the legalization of same-sex partnerships. And couples who do marry in these countries did not become more likely to divorce after the introduction of same-sex partner registration.

Cohabitation rates are indeed on the rise in Scandinavia and other European countries, as is the likelihood that an unmarried cohabiting couple will have children. In Denmark, the number of cohabiting couples with children rose by 25 percent in the 1990s. Roughly half of all births in Norway, Sweden, and Denmark, and almost two-thirds in Iceland, are to parents who are not married. From these figures, Kurtz concludes that "married parenthood has become a minority phenomenon."[5]

In fact, however, the majority of families with children in Scandinavia are still headed by married parents. In 2000, for instance, 78 percent of couples with children were married couples in Denmark. Even if we also include single-parent families in the calculation, almost two-thirds of all families with children were headed by a married couple. In Norway, 79 percent of couples with children are married.

How can this fact coexist with high nonmarital birthrates and cohabitation rates? The main reason is that most cohabiting couples marry after they start having children. In Sweden, for instance, 70 percent of cohabitors marry after the birth of their first child, most of them within five years. As a result, high rates of married-couple parenting and rising marriage rates in Scandinavia are not incompatible with high nonmarital birthrates.

THE IMPACT ON CHILDREN

Kurtz claims that the rise in nonmarital births hurts children because unmarried couples are more likely to break up than married couples. It is true that unmarried cohabitors' unions are more likely to dissolve than are marriages, even when children are present. But when cohabiting parents marry in Scandinavian countries, as most eventually do, they are not more likely to divorce than are couples who were married when they first had their children.[6]

As a result, children in Scandinavian countries still spend most of their lives with their parents living together. In fact, they spend more time than children in the United States do! Gunnar Andersson has calculated how much time the average child in Europe and America spends living with both parents in the same household.[7] Of the countries he examined, the lowest average is in the United States, where the time spent with both parents is 67 percent. The highest is in Italy, where it is 97 percent. In Sweden the average is 81 percent, in Finland it is 88 percent, and in Norway it is 89 percent. In other words, combining the time that parents have cohabited with the time they have been married demonstrates that Scandinavian children are spending the vast majority of their young lives with their parents.

Did Gay Marriage Widen the Split Between Parenthood and Marriage?

No one would argue that marriage plays the same role in Scandinavia and in other parts of Europe that it once did. And to his credit, Kurtz himself recognizes that changes in marriage in Scandinavia were in many ways cause rather than effect of the legal recognition extended to gay couples. He acknowledges that high rates of cohabitation and the changing role of marriage in Scandinavia made it more likely that those countries would be the innovators in giving marriage-like rights to gay people. The decline of religious practice and belief, the rise of the welfare state, advances in contraception and abortion, and the improving economic status of women—all long-term trends in Scandinavia—probably contributed both to the rise in cohabitation and to the equalizing of rights for gay and lesbian people.

But Kurtz claims that registered partnerships "further undermined the institution" of marriage and that gay marriage "widened the separation" between marriage and parenthood. In other words, things were already bad, but gay marriage made it worse.

This argument does not hold up either, however, since the nonmarital birthrate began rising in the 1970s, long before any legal recognition of same-sex couples. From 1970 to 1980, the Danish nonmarital birthrate tripled, from 11 percent to 33 percent. It rose again in the following decade, but by a much smaller amount, reaching 46 percent in 1990, but then leveled off. Denmark's nonmarital birthrate did not increase at all when the Danish partnership law was passed in 1989. In fact, it actually decreased a bit after that date!

From 1980 to 1989, before Denmark passed the registered partner law, the number of cohabiting couples with children rose by 70 percent. Between 1989 and 2000, the figure rose by only 28 percent, and between 2000 to 2003, the number increased by a barely perceptible 0.3 percent. This will appear to the average reader to contradict the previous claim. Do we need it? If so, it needs to be framed better.

Norway's big surge in nonmarital births also occurred well before the passage of same-sex partnership recognition in 1993. In the 1980s, the percentage of births to unmarried parents rose from 16 percent to 39 percent. In the first half of the 1990s, the nonmarital birthrate rose more slowly, leveling off at 50 percent in the mid-1990s. If the partnership law had "further" encouraged nonmarital births, the rate should have increased faster, but in Norway, as in Denmark, the increase in nonmarital childbearing actually slowed down or stopped after the passage of registered partnership laws.

The Netherlands show a slightly different pattern, but here too there is no correlation between recognition of same-sex partnerships and rising rates of nonmarital births. The Dutch lagged well behind Scandinavia in births by unmarried couples, with rates remaining below 10 percent until 1988.[8] Sometime around 1992, the nonmarital birthrate started increasing at a somewhat faster rate, but this acceleration began well before the Netherlands implemented registered same-sex partnerships in 1998 and gave same-sex couples the right to marry in 2001.

It is also instructive to compare the trends of countries that have a partner registration law with those that do not. If recognizing gay couples contributed to the increase in nonmarital births, then we should see a bigger change in countries with those laws than in countries without them. Data from Eurostat shows that in the 1990s, the eight countries that recognized registered partners at some point in that decade saw an increase of eight percentage points in the average nonmarital birthrate—from 36 percent in 1991 to 44 percent in 2000. In the EU countries (plus Switzerland) that didn't recognize partners, the nonmarital birthrate rose by exactly the same percentage, though it started from a lower base. In this case, the increase was from 15 percent to 23 percent.

Only one piece of evidence supports Kurtz's argument that same-sex partnerships created a new wedge between parenthood and marriage—and that piece of evidence directly contradicts Kurtz's ideas about the cause of such a separation. Contrary to what many observers believe, Scandinavian parliaments did not give same-sex couples the exact same rights as heterosexual ones. Quite deliberately, the various Scandinavian parliaments chose to provide legal ties for same-sex couples through a special new legal relationship, not by the simpler path of extending the right to marry to same-sex couples. And they denied same-sex couples the right to adopt children (including their nonbiological children raised from birth) or to gain access to reproductive technologies.

Thus, Scandinavian governments did create a wedge between marriage and reproduction—but they did so by design and for same-sex couples only. Despite some loosening of those prohibitions over time, registered partners who want to have children still face legal hurdles that heterosexual married couples do not.[9]

THE IMPACT OF GAY MARRIAGE IN THE UNITED STATES

In the end, the Scandinavian experience suggests that those who worry that heterosexual people will flee marriage if gay people get the same rights do not have a basis for their concerns. This is especially true in the United States, where couples have many more tangible incentives to marry. Scholars of social welfare programs have noted that our country relies heavily on the labor market and families to provide income and support for individuals.[10] In the United States, unlike Scandinavia, marriage is often the only route to survivor coverage in pensions and Social Security, and many people have access to health care only through their spouse's employment. Scandinavian states are much more financially supportive of families and individuals, regardless of their family or marital status.[11] The lack of support alternatives plus the tangible benefits of marriage all lead to one conclusion: if and when same-sex couples are allowed to marry, heterosexual couples will continue to marry in the United States.

CONCLUSION

Overall, there is no evidence that giving partnership rights to same-sex couples had any impact on heterosexual marriage in Scandinavia. Marriage rates, divorce rates, and nonmarital birthrates have been changing in Scandinavia, Europe, and the United States for the past thirty years. But those changes have occurred in all countries, regardless of whether or not they adopted same-sex partnership laws. Furthermore, the legal and cultural context in the United States gives many more incentives for heterosexual couples to marry than in Europe, and those incentives will still exist even if same-sex couples can marry. Giving same-sex couples marriage or marriage-like rights has not undermined heterosexual marriage in Europe, and it is not likely to do so in the United States.

In the News

EXPERTS QUESTION EUROPEAN STUDIES CITED IN FMA DEBATE

Washington Blade, July 30, 2004

Joe Crea

To buttress their arguments against gay marriage, Federal Marriage Amendment proponents during the recent Senate debate cited studies from European countries showing a decline in marriages and high out-of-wedlock birth rates after those countries recognized gay unions.

But some experts say the studies referenced during the Senate debate are deeply flawed and are not accurate depictions of what may be contributing to the decline in marriage abroad.

In a recent letter, five Dutch scholars asserted that until the late 1980s, the number of marriages in the Netherlands was high, illegitimate births were down and divorce rates were low, compared to other Western countries. But social experiments in the 1990s have adversely affected marriage, they claim.

While they claim there is "no definitive scientific evidence" that the legalization of gay marriage is solely responsible for the decline in marriage in the Netherlands, the scholars note that a "successful campaign to persuade Dutch citizens that marriage is not connected to parenthood and that marriage and cohabitation are equally valid 'lifestyle choices' has not had serious social consequences."

Sen. Sam Brownback (R-Kan.) reported during the FMA debate that one of the signatories to the letter, Dutch law professor M. Van Mourik, said, "The decision to legalize gay marriage should certainly have never happened, . . . [and] that has been an important contributing factor to the decline in the reputation of marriage."

And another signatory, Dr. Joost Van Loon, according to Brownback, "believes gay marriage has contributed to a decline in the reputation of Dutch marriage."

In an interview in the Dutch paper, Reformatorisch Dagblad, Van Loon said he did not want to discuss a "clear causal connection" between gay marriage and the decline or devaluation of marriage in the Netherlands but said he did "see a strong correlation."

"Both developments have a common source," said Van Loon, a professor in contract law at Nijmegen University who also runs a legal practice as a notary.

"It's no coincidence both take place at the same time. It's a consequence of the rejection of normative schemes that are based on eternal values—whether they are connected to the natural law or to God—and the adoption of a different approach, one that says that we are quite capable of redesigning society based on our own fashionable preferences."

But less than a year ago, Van Loon says, he completed research comparing English and Dutch statistics on marriage and relationships that showed that the Netherlands "still scores better on marital fidelity and stable caring relationships but that we are busy copying the bad British family habits."

Only two countries in Europe, the Netherlands and Belgium, have legalized gay marriage. The Netherlands legalized same-sex marriage in April 2001 and Belgium did so in January 2003, according to Paula Ettelbrick, executive director of the International Gay & Lesbian Human Rights Commission.

Ettelbrick said that because the changes in the Netherlands and Belgium law are relatively new, there is no scientific proof that gay marriage has contributed to high divorce rates or a lack of interest in marriage.

M. V. Lee Badgett, research director of the Institute for Gay & Lesbian Strategic Studies, criticized the scholars' letter, saying it appears to have been written by "legal scholars and philosophers, not demographers, sociologists, economists, or any other kind of social scientist who's made a systematic, credible study of these questions."

Criticizing "marriage-lite"

Other Scandinavian countries, according to Stanley Kurtz, a research fellow at the Hoover Institution, have been weakening marriage because of the debate over whether or not to recognize same-sex unions. But Scandinavia does not recognize gay marriage. It has a registered partnership for same-sex couples.

Van Loon does think that the debate over gay marriage has contributed to devaluation of the marriage institution.

"Supporters of gay marriage often based their argument for legalization on the separation of marriage and the raising of children," Van Loon told the Reformatorisch Dagblad newspaper. "Those two things were supposed to be completely unconnected. It's difficult to imagine that an intensive media campaign based on the claim that marriage and parenthood are unrelated and that marriage is just one among a number of morally equivalent cohabiting relationships did not have any serious social consequences."

Van Mourik said that a "national debate about the question of how we can restore marriage to its original special, protected status" is imperative, adding that the Netherlands should have simply allowed gays to register as domestic partners instead of marrying.

Some, like Ettelbrick, contend that these "marriage-lite" alternatives—open to heterosexual couples as well—might be doing more to undermine traditional marriage than granting gay couples full marital rights.

10

Interracial Families in Post-Civil Rights America

Kerry Ann Rockquemore and Loren Henderson

In the four decades since the U.S. Supreme Court declared laws prohibiting interracial marriage unconstitutional, the number of interracial families in America has rapidly increased. But interracial families continue to face unique external pressures and internal relational dynamics due to the persistence of racism in America. While formal structural barriers have been reduced, interracial dating on campuses has increased, and attitudes toward acceptance of interracial marriage have improved, interracial couplings continue to be the rare exception (and not the rule) when it comes to new marriages. This chapter explores why interracial families continue to be so uncommon in the United States, and it describes the challenges interracial families face in dealing with individual and institutional racism, responding to the disapproval of family members, and raising mixed-race children in what is still not a "color-blind" world.

June 12, 2007, marked the fortieth anniversary of the historic Supreme Court decision (*Loving v. Virginia*) that struck down state laws prohibiting interracial marriage. Reporters celebrated the fourfold increase in interracial marriage rates since 1970 and the corresponding decline in opposition to interracial marriage in opinion polls. The concurrent rise of political superstar Barack Obama and a proliferation of multiracial celebrities, athletes, and writers have further focused national attention on interracial families and reframed their mixed-race offspring from "tragic mulattoes" to "Generation E.A.: Ethnically Ambiguous."[1] Indeed, the message repeatedly put forward in the media and in popular discourse is that in post–Civil Rights America, love, marriage and child rearing are all color-blind.

Less well reported is that interracial marriages represent a tiny sliver of all marriages in the United States. In 1970, less than 1 percent of marriages were interracial, and by 2005 that number increased to 7.5 percent of all marriages. Stated differently, over 92 percent of all marriages today are between people of the same race. Interestingly, of the 7.5 percent of marriages that are interracial, marriages between blacks and whites remain the least likely combination. While it is true that more young people today are dating and living with someone of a different race, those interracial relationships are far less likely than same-race relationships to lead to marriage.[2] Many argue that race is declining in significance, but the fact that interracial marriages continue to hover in the single digits—and are least likely between blacks and whites—suggests that the color-blind rhetoric may be ahead of reality.

The disconnection between Americans' attitudes toward interracial marriage and their behavior illustrates the awkward historical moment that we currently inhabit. On the one hand, in the four decades since the U.S. Supreme Court declared laws prohibiting interracial marriage unconstitutional, the number of interracial families in the United States has rapidly increased, interracial dating on college campuses has become more common, and attitudes toward interracial marriage have improved.[3] On the other hand, interracial families continue to report unique external pressures due to the persistence of racism and negotiations over the classification of their mixed-race children. As a result, interracial couplings continue to be the rare exception (and certainly not the rule) when it comes to marriage in the United States.

At a deeper level, the discrepancy between attitudes and behavior mirrors the changing nature of race relations in the United States. Several decades after the passage of Civil Rights legislation, structurally rooted racial inequalities continue to persist in our social institutions, ranging from public schools, to health care, to the criminal justice system. Yet, despite these racial inequalities, Americans increasingly believe that race is declining in significance, and many have adopted a "color-blind" ideology in which racism and discrimination are viewed as relics of the past, inequalities are understood to be class-based (as opposed to race-based), and where institutions and individuals are assumed to act in race-neutral ways. This simultaneous denial of racial inequalities and widespread desire to move "beyond race" stand in stark contrast to the persistence of race as a determining factor in life chances, opportunities, and mate selection.[4]

In this chapter, we examine the disconnection between beliefs and behavior by exploring the distinctive challenges that interracial families face in a simultaneously "color-blind" and racialized world. We focus specifically on interracial relationships between blacks and whites because they are the two groups that have the greatest social distance, their coupling carries the greatest social stigma, and the relative rarity of intermarriage between the two groups best illustrates the influence that structural patterns hold over our seemingly individual decisions about whom we have sex with, date, and marry.[5] We also explore the challenges associated with raising mixed-race children and how those challenges have changed over time. Our central goal is to make visible the invisible racial structures to better understand why interracial families continue to be so uncommon in the United States in spite of the widespread perception that we live in a post-racial and "color-blind" society.

THE HISTORY OF BLACK/WHITE COUPLING

Interracial relationships, marriages, and children are of great interest to family researchers because they exist outside the "normal" patterns of mate selection. In other words, when individuals date and marry across the color line, they are defying long-standing patterns of racial endogamy (i.e., marrying someone within your own racial group). The historical norm in American families has been to date, marry, and have children with someone of the same race. As a result, when people partner cross-racially, it not only seems "different" or "unusual," but depending on the time period, it may also have been unimaginable, illegal, nonconsensual, and/or dangerous. Every historical moment has its own specific racial stratification system at work. That system not only outlines the rules of behavior between races, but it also shapes how we understand our own race, the relative position of racial groups, and our individual expectations about the race of our sexual, dating, and marital partners.

Throughout U.S. history, black sexuality and marriage have been the subject of legal, cultural, and political regulation because of the flawed beliefs that (1) black people are fundamentally and biologically *different* from whites, and that (2) blacks are intellectually, culturally, and genetically *inferior* to whites.[6] During various historical periods, racial stratification systems (grounded in beliefs of white superiority) have supported elaborate mechanisms of separation and necessitated endogamy so that blacks and whites were not only expected, but *required* to create families within their own racial groups. Social norms and laws prohibiting interracial marriage emerged to support racial stratification systems (such as slavery or segregation) so that interracial sex and marriage were institutionally restricted through the legal system and individually regulated through interpersonal violence, rape, and intimidation.[7]

As a system of stratification, slavery relied upon ideas of racial difference and black inferiority to rationalize the domination and exploitation of Africans in America. As slaves, blacks were considered subhuman property of their slave owners. In order to control slaves and maintain white supremacy, interracial coupling was strictly prohibited, and the one-drop rule was used to determine who was "black."[8]

Miscegenation (or racial mixing) was strictly regulated so that "black blood" would not taint the purity of the white race. In spite of formal prohibitions against miscegenation, however, black female slaves were regularly sexually assaulted and raped by white slave owners. Because of the one-drop rule and the slave system, their mixed-race children were considered black, became part of the slave population, and were counted as the property of their biological fathers. In contrast, white women were protected from the specter of black male sexuality because while a mixed-race child in the slave quarters may have been socially tolerated and considered a financial asset, a mixed-race child born to a white woman directly threatened the purity of the white race and the logic of the slave system. Because of this unequal sense of threat, the mere hint of sexual contact between black men and white women was punishable by public beating, castration, and/or death.

After the Civil War, slavery was replaced by a new system of racial stratification: segregation. While the system changed, the core beliefs of racial difference and black inferiority stayed the same. Blacks were no longer slaves, but they were still believed to be biologically *different* from whites, and intellectually *inferior* to whites. Segregation required the formalization of antimiscegenation laws and explicit legal definitions of who belonged in the category "black." In this historical context, the norm of racial endogamy, firmly rooted in the ideology of white supremacy, was a powerful mechanism shaping an individual's mate selection options. Blacks and whites were legally and socially prohibited from cross-racial contact, and blacks were terrorized by widespread lynchings and brutal violence. Blacks and whites were "separate but equal" in law, and separate and grossly unequal in reality. Interracial marriages were illegal, mixed-race children were considered black, and any form of cross-racial coupling was the ultimate cultural taboo.

The Civil Rights Movement challenged the ideology of white supremacy, institutional inequalities, and individual racism. Activists and intellectuals fought fiercely against the social system of segregation and the ideological belief in black inferiority that it rested upon. In the process, progressives denounced the institutional policies and procedures that inhibited black people's mobility, and they sought to alter black individuals' self-perceptions so that they would value blackness. In this historical period of social change, formal prohibitions against interracial marriage were targeted, and in 1967, the Supreme Court ruled that all state-level antimiscegenation laws were unconstitutional. But while legal and institutional victories had been won, interracial marriages remained rare in the landscape of American families.[9]

When we consider the link between racial stratification systems, racial ideology, and the history of interracial sex and marriage between blacks and whites, we can better understand the stigma attached to interracial marriage and how that stigma is connected to a fundamentally flawed set of beliefs about race (as a biological category) and racial groups (as both different and unequal to one another). The ideas of racial difference and white superiority were historically constructed by the dominant group to support existing racial stratification systems and shaped what is considered a "normal" American family by determining whether (or not) individuals could marry cross-racially. In addition, the elaborate rules of racial categorization that were designed to keep people apart, also mandated that mixed-race children were "black" (and black only) irrespective of their mixed ancestry and physical appearance. Because the one-drop rule and the norm of racial endogamy have been uniquely constructed and enforced for blacks and because they are inseparable from the history of slavery and segregation, they allow a particularly clear illustration of the link between structure and mate selection. Throughout American history, black sexuality and marriage have been the subject of legal, cultural, and political control and regulation shaping what we typically consider an individual choice. While the *Loving v. Virginia* decision terminated state laws against interracial marriage, the norm of racial endogamy and lingering biological notions of race, resulted in a social landscape where blacks and whites were expected to marry within their own racial groups.

In post–Civil Rights America, the legal barriers against interracial marriages no longer exist and attitudes toward interracial dating and marriage have steadily improved in opinion polls. Given the widespread contention that Americans are "color-blind" and that racism is a relic of the past, we would expect that interracial couples would face few interpersonal or institutional obstacles. But researchers have repeatedly documented the myriad ways that interracial couples face covert discrimination and overt racism from family members, friends, and strangers in public places. Additionally, interracial families continue to face subtle institutional and structural forces that marginalize their existence and diminish their quality of life. Below we explain the common external pressures that interracial families face, describe the coping strategies used in the context of such marriages, explore how such couples raise their mixed-race children, and consider what the totality of their lived experiences tell us about the changing nature of race relations in the United States.

EXTERNAL PRESSURES: BORDER PATROLLING IN BLACK AND WHITE

While attitudes toward interracial relationships in national opinion surveys continue to trend in the positive direction of acceptance (for both blacks and whites), the story is a bit more complicated on the ground. Sociologist Erica Childs found that blacks and whites tend to lean in opposite directions in terms of differentiating their *general attitudes* about interracial relationships from their assessment of *specific family members* who are interracially married.[10] Blacks tend to disapprove of interracial relationships generally, but they are tolerant and make exceptions for their family and friends. By contrast, whites tend to express approval of interracial relationships generally, but they disapprove of those relationships for their immediate family or friends.

Heather Dalmage argues that the discrepancy between the attitudes of blacks and whites lies in differential conceptions of same-race relationships. For blacks, marrying within one's racial group is perceived as strengthening the black family and supporting unification in a group struggling for survival and liberation. By contrast, whites tend to support same-race relationships, but they do so unreflectively.[11] These differential views of race and marriage affect how individuals interpret and construct the consequences of interracial coupling. Irrespective of race, class, or gender, those within interracial relationships find themselves regularly faced with insulting questions and forced to legitimize their relationships as loving and consensual in ways that mono-racial couples never consider. These daily experiences, and the harsh realities that interracial couples face, create unique stressors that put additional strains on such relationships and may explain the higher divorce rate among interracial marriages and may also contribute to the decision of many interracial couples to cohabitate instead of marry.[12]

Both black and white partners in interracial relationships commonly report experiencing a particular form of racial hostility that Heather Dalmage describes as *border patrolling.*[13] Dalmage details various behaviors and attitudes expressed by white family members, friends, peers, and strangers that communicate a consistent and clear message: same-race dating and marriage are "normal" and interracial coupling is "different" and "problematic." When individuals date or marry cross-racially, previously unarticulated boundaries between blacks and whites break out into the open, shifting the way that they are perceived by others, changing their relationships with friends and family, and making them the targets of hostility by strangers. Border patrolling occurs for both black and white partners, although the way it manifests is differentiated by race and gender.

White women who marry black men describe being verbally harassed, socially ostracized, and/or excommunicated from family and friendship networks. As a result, some feel they have been re-categorized as inherently "flawed" or "polluted" by other whites, and they describe themselves as "no longer white" or "symbolically black" because of the wholesale rejection and ostracism they experience in their social network. One of Erica Childs' white respondents (named Kayla) described the response of her white family and friends when she started dating a black man:

I lost every friend I had. My friends stopped calling me, whenever I would ask them to do something they would be busy, and my ex-boyfriend said I had lost it and was dating someone black to embarrass him.[14]

Kayla experienced a common type of resistance to interracial dating: rejection by her friends and shaming by her former white boyfriend. Her friends' rejection of her because she is dating a black man lies in their (conscious or unconscious) belief that same-race dating is "normal" and that dating a black man is deviant behavior because blacks are *different* from whites. Kayla's ex-boyfriend goes a step beyond ignoring her by openly stating his belief that she was dating someone black to embarrass him. This further illustrates his assumption that blacks are not just different, but *inferior to* whites (i.e., he's embarrassed because she's done something wrong by dating a black man and that reflects negatively on him).

While white women who date interracially face resistance, marriage is considered a far more serious border crossing because of the implicit long-term commitment and prospect of raising mixed-race children. Interracially married white women, particularly those with mixed-race children, experience more intense and consistent forms of border patrolling, in response to which they may need to protect themselves and their children from overtly racist insults, haggle over how their children will be racially categorized, or deal with nuanced slights, glares, and inappropriate questions that people ask in order to make sense of their family.[15]

White male partners in interracial marriages also experience border patrolling, but it is distinctly different in form and content from that experienced by interracially married white women and is tied to the historical legacy of interracial intimacy. Unlike white women who report being policed and/or openly harassed (by both blacks and whites), white men who are partnered with black women describe resistance to their interracial coupling as expressions of curiosity, confusion, or concern. They are less likely to experience direct and open hostility from whites, but they do report experiencing it from black men. For example, Warren (one of Amy Steinbugler's white male respondents) described the way black men responded to his interracial relationship:

They'd be like, "Whoa, sister what are you doing with this guy?" I mean it has never—on occasion once or twice was it black women. At least not outspoken, it wasn't white people. The most outspoken were black men who did not like the fact that you could—a white man could have one of their black sisters. They definitely did not like that. It wouldn't be a problem for a black man, if a brother has a white woman. That's cool. The other way it doesn't work.[16]

Black spouses in interracial marriages also experience border patrolling, but it differs from that experienced by their white partners. While all border patrolling rests on the assumption that interracial relationships are "deviant," "disruptive," and "wrong," black partners describe the disapproving responses they receive from other blacks as attacks on their racial identity, group loyalty, and self-worth as a black person.[17] Black partners report negative character judgments, ostracism, speculation about their authenticity as black, and accusations that they are suffering from internalized racism. Often, black partners feel forced to legitimize their relationship to family and friends as a loving partnership, as opposed to a wholesale rejection of members of their own racial group. Daily negotiations over how to present an interracial relationship as loving and healthy can be challenging for many couples, particularly at the outset of their relationship.

The border patrolling that black women and men experience in response to their choice of a white marital partner not only differs in content from that experienced by whites, but it is also distinctly gendered. Black men in interracial relationships may be perceived as "weak," a "sell-out," or disconnected from the black community, and they may face the verbal attacks of other blacks who perceive their coupling as "treachery," "betrayal," and a weakening of the black family. They must also continually negotiate public space, and expend energy calculating their safety when accompanying their white partner. While all black men must negotiate public space around police, security guards, and others holding negative stereotypical views, being a black man and coded as having a sexual relationship with a white woman provides an additional layer of vulnerability to harassment.

Like interracially married black men, black women face social consequences such as being seen as a "sell-out" or "wanting to be white." But black women may also be viewed by those in the black community as "disloyal" for "giving their bodies" to white men, and this is particularly problematic because of the history of exploitative sexual relations between white men and black women. Family members sometimes suspect and fear that black women in interracial relationships will be exposed to racist verbal abuse when arguing with their partners, or explicit racism by their partner's family members. Black women also report being accused of social climbing or attempting to raise their social or economic status by marrying a white male.

LOOKING BEHIND THE STEREOTYPE OF THE "ANGRY BLACK WOMAN"

Using survey data, researchers have found that black women hold the least favorable attitudes toward interracial relationships. Qualitative interview studies of black male/ white female couples often feature narrative descriptions of mistreatment, hostility, and/or experiences of such couples being openly and publicly challenged about their relationships by black women. Indeed, the "angry black woman" is a persistent image in discussions of interracial intimacy.[18] But few researchers go further to ask why this pattern might exist, what relationship it has to historical trends, and what factors fuel the lack of support for interracial coupling that is expressed by black women.

Notably, researcher Erica Childs interviewed black women to better understand their perspective. She concluded that their responses to interracial relationships are shaped by both white supremacy and structural inequalities that influence who black women perceive they can and should marry.[19] Specifically, black women feel limited by Eurocentric standards of beauty that prize blond hair, blue eyes, and white skin, thereby reducing black women's attractiveness to both black and white partners.[20] As a result, some black women see interracial dating as black men's internalization of racism in which they devalue and reject black women as beautiful and/or preferable partners. Such feelings are compounded by a unique demographic reality: the limited pool of marriageable black men due to disproportionately high incarceration rates, drug abuse, homicide, and unemployment.[21] The cumulative effect of these factors is a large pool of single black women competing for a small number of marriageable black men and feeling their value as potential mates weighed against a white beauty standard. As a result, black women often describe feeling "put down," "left out" and/or "disrespected" by black men who choose to date white women. As Childs' respondent described: "As a black woman, it is difficult enough to have to deal with whites who [act] as if [black] is inferior, but it is even harder to have your own men act like white is better and systematically choose white women over you; it is hard not to get angry because it feels as if no one values your worth as a woman."[22]

COPING STRATEGIES: FROM COLOR-BLINDNESS TO RACIAL LITERACY

The emotionally charged and hostile reactions toward interracial relationships can be painful for those who are interracially married, even if it's clear how differing social locations, histories, and beliefs shape those responses. The problem faced by many interracial families is that unlike the invisible forces of institutional racism (such as differential incarceration rates), interracial coupling is highly visible and easily targeted. Through social sanctions, isolation, and disapproval, interracial dating is far easier to target and resist than any of the structural factors that influence mate selection.

Facing the daily realities of border patrolling, individual partners within interracial families are forced to develop coping strategies that range from denial to resistance. Coping strategies tend to evolve from an individual's racial worldview. The sheer act of marrying cross-racially challenges racial borders and yet some individuals rely on color-blind discourse to interpret the responses of others to their relationship. For them, daily negotiations involve patterns of systematic denial of racist actions against their relationship, particularly when they come from close friends and family. White partners who have been socialized not to talk about race often want to avoid conflict in order to protect their family and friends from being characterized as racist. When explicitly racist incidents occur, they work to forget, ignore, reconstruct, cover up, and deny the problematic actions of their loved ones. This denial can lead to complications within their marital relationships because the black partner may feel as if the white partner is not defending him/her while the white partner may feel torn between his/her family and partner. The white partner may also feel ashamed and confused when parents who profess to be "color-blind"—and have raised them to treat everyone equally—suddenly resist their relationship with someone of a different race.[23]

Alternatively, some whites are personally transformed by their intimate relationships with a black partner and cope in ways that are similar to those of blacks who have been racially socialized to recognize and resist racism and racial inequalities. Interracially married whites may never have thought about being white and/or they may have been blind to discrimination prior to their relationship, but once coupled with a black partner these same individuals describe being forced to contend with the ambiguities, contradictions, and racism that are triggered by their relationship. Being exposed to the everyday experiences of racism faced by their black partners and/or their mixed-race children can be a transformative and painful process for white partners.[24] If they were previously shielded from the negative effects of racism, they may be forced to rethink their previous understanding of race relations, confront white privilege, and reexamine their own beliefs about race, as well as those of their immediate family and friends. In other words, experiencing negative sanctions for partnering with a person of color can transform interracial intimacy into a micro-level political site that leads some (not all) white partners to shift their stance from one of *color-blindness* to *racial cognizance* or *racial literacy*.[25] France Winddance Twine and Amy Steinbugler describe racial literacy as a set of everyday analytic practices that include:

(1) a recognition of the symbolic and material value of Whiteness; (2) the definition of *racism* as a current social problem rather than a historical legacy; (3) an understanding that racial identities are *learned* and an outcome of social practices; (4) the possession of racial grammar and a vocabulary that facilitates a discussion of

race, racism, and antiracism; (5) the ability to translate (interpret) racial codes and racialized practices; and (6) an analysis of the ways that racism is mediated by class inequalities, gender hierarchies, and heteronormativity.[26]

This rethinking of race, racism, and racial identity helps white partners to cultivate a critical analysis to understand how larger socio-political and historical forces shape the different types of resistance to their interracial relationship that they experience from whites and blacks.

In terms of coping with external pressure and border patrolling, racial literacy leads individuals to reorganize their social networks and reorient their behaviors. For example, Glenn was an interracially married, white male respondent of Twine and Steinbugler. He described how the development of racial literacy increased his awareness of "everyday racism" and racial practices using the following example:

> Now having spent time with [my wife], I realize that I am a bit [racist] in terms of . . . preconceptions and ideas that you have [about black people] . . . There were jokes abut the length of a black man's penis. . . . My attitude then was, "Well, I'd quite like somebody to make a joke about . . . how big mine was." And [my wife] sort of explained to me . . . , and once it had been explained to me, I thought, "You're right." I used to tell jokes like that, but I've avoided those now. . . . As soon as somebody starts to tell a joke that's got any mention of the race of whatever the person, I tend to frown. And then afterwards I dissect the joke.[27]

Glenn's wife helped him to understand how the common social practice of joking about black men's penises was degrading to black people. Glenn's new understanding about racism and how it is reproduced in the everyday practice of joke telling has altered his behavior. Instead of telling these jokes, he now resists their telling and has the mental tools to deconstruct them to the joke teller. His emergent racial literacy enables such daily acts of resistance to the racism and border patrolling that he experiences as a white man married to a black woman.

WHAT ABOUT THE CHILDREN?

One of the most common concerns that interracial couples face is "what about the children?" Implicit in this question is the idea that mixed-race children will be social misfits ("neither fish nor fowl") who will be rejected by both blacks and whites and will be plagued by various pathologies, including depression, identity confusion, and double rejection. In addition to issues of psychological adjustment and racial identity development, "what about the children?" is also a literal question in terms of how mixed-race children will be racially socialized by their parents, as well as classified by the state, institutional bureaucracies, and on various government forms. These "tragic mulatto" stereotypes are not surprising given that throughout American history, racial group membership has been understood as mutually exclusive so that individuals can belong to one (and only one) race. The one-drop rule mandated that mixed-race children be categorized as black and develop a black identity. Only recently have multiracial groups and parents of mixed-race children begun to question and push back against the one-drop rule and the logic underlying it.

While it is true that raising mixed-race children presents particular challenges for parents, the stereotypes of identity confusion are not supported by recent research. Instead, mixed-race adolescents and young adults are creating identities that reflect their particular social context. For example, Kerry Ann Rockquemore and David Brunsma studied mixed-race college students (with one black and one white parent) and found that individuals chose between five different racial identities.[28] Some mixed-race students identified exclusively with the race of one of their parents, self-identifying as "black" (or less commonly as "white"). Others blended the ancestry of both their parents to create a hybrid identity as "biracial," "multiracial," or "mixed." Others shifted between several different identities ("black," "white," and/or "biracial"), depending on where they were and whom they were interacting with in any given environment. Still others refused any racial categorization whatsoever and instead identified themselves as "human."[29] In this way, they were neither constrained by the one-drop rule nor disallowed from the development of an identity that reflects their ancestry, physical appearance, and childhood socialization.

The second important and consistently documented fact about mixed-race children is that, in addition to *variation* in how they racially self-identify, their racial identity may change over their lifetime. This differs from conceptualizations of single-race identity because identity development for mixed-race individuals neither occurs in a predictable linear fashion, nor does it have a single endpoint. Numerous researchers have documented how racial identity is dynamic and changing as their mixed-race respondents move through their lives, shifting and changing as they are linked to social, material, cultural, economic, and institutional forces.[30] For example, Steven Hitlin, Scott Brown, and Glen Elder demonstrate how mixed-race adolescents follow various "pathways of racial self-identification" over time and are four times more likely to switch their racial identity than to consistently report the same identification over time.[31] While change occurs, it varies between diversifying, consolidating, or maintaining "multiracial" self-identification.

Certainly, mixed-race children and adolescents face situations in which they are literally forced into self-designating as a member of just one racial group (e.g., on government forms, applications, and school admission forms). Yet, even describing their racial identity as a "choice" obfuscates the reality that such choices are constrained by physical appearance, the broader context and history of American race relations, and institutional mandates of identification. Raising healthy mixed-race children and navigating the reality of race and racism in their children's lives creates an additional layer of complexity that is utterly unique to interracial families.

FAMILIES AS THEY REALLY ARE: RACIALLY HOMOGENEOUS

Considering families *as they really are* involves asking critical questions about why dominant patterns in marriages exist, what historical factors underlie those dominant patterns, and what prevents those dominant patterns from changing. In this chapter, we have asked why interracial marriages remain the rare exception in the United States, what happens to individuals who dare to break out of the dominant pattern of marrying someone of the same race, and why racial patterns of endogamy for blacks and whites have been so very slow to change. In that process, it's clear that the seemingly individual decision about whom you find attractive, desire sexually, hook up with, date, live with, marry, divorce, and/or have children with are all "choices" that are fundamentally shaped by race relations and racial ideology in your particular historical moment. In the United States, our rhetoric and thinking may encourage a color-blind worldview, but those who cross the color line experience border patrolling that works against—and fundamentally contradicts—the color-blind ideas that racism is a relic of the past and that race no longer matters in our intimate relationships.

The discrepancy between color-blind beliefs and the reality of resistance to interracial marriages helps us to better understand the slow pace of change in interracial intimacy. When we consider the history of separation and social distance between blacks and whites, as well as the deep well of ideological beliefs about the differences between groups, it is unsurprising that interracial families today continue to face hostility, ostracism, and concern over the fate of their children. And yet, ironically, it is the children of interracial unions who may just force a reconciliation of color-blind attitudes and racist behavior by openly challenging the logic of white supremacy, recognizing the social construction of racial groups, and pushing our country into a new and honest dialogue about the reality of race in America.

11

Briefing Paper: The Steady Rise of Nontraditional Romantic Unions

The Case of Interracial and Intercultural Marriage

Michael Rosenfeld

Prior to 1970, the overwhelming majority of all couples were same-race married couples. Couples who lived together outside of marriage, whether heterosexual or same-sex, were practically invisible. Interracial marriages were extremely rare. In fact, until 1967, many states in the United States had laws against interracial marriage. In Virginia, for example, all nonwhite groups, including blacks, Native Americans, and Asians, were prohibited from marrying whites. Even in states that never had laws against racial intermarriage, such as Illinois and New York, racial intermarriage was rare before the end of the 1960s.

Since 1970, there has been a steady increase in all types of nontraditional romantic unions. The number of same-sex couples living together openly has climbed significantly, while the number of heterosexual unmarried cohabiting couples has soared, from 3.1 million in 1990 to 4.6 million in 2000 to 5.2 million in 2005. This paper, however, focuses on the rise of interracial or intercultural marriages between whites and Asians, non-Hispanic whites and Hispanics, and between whites and African Americans, the kinds of marriage that were illegal in many states prior to 1967.

State laws prohibiting interracial marriages were finally struck down in the Supreme Court's 1967 *Loving v. Virginia* decision. Yet such marriages continued to be very uncommon well into the 1970s. In 1970, less than 2 percent of married couples in the United States were interracial. By 2005, the number of such marriages had risen almost fourfold, with interracial couples representing

7.5 percent of all married couples. Although this percentage may seem small, it is a dramatic increase over several decades, and many signs point to it accelerating in the future.

Why Are We Seeing More Interracial and Intercultural Marriages? The Role of Immigration

Some of the rise in racial intermarriage since 1970 is due to immigration, which has increased the racial diversity of the United States since 1965. Hispanics and Asians are the predominant groups among the new immigrants, and because neither Asians nor Hispanics have been residentially segregated to the extent that blacks in the United States historically have been, Asians and Hispanics have had substantial opportunities to socialize with members of other racial groups. The increased numbers of these immigrants have contributed to the rise in intermarriage between Hispanics and non-Hispanic whites, and the rise in intermarriage between Asians and whites.

Greater Acceptance of Diversity

The rise in black-white marriages cannot be due to immigration. One cause of the increase is improvement in race relations. Despite continued residential segregation and enduring prejudices, the post-Civil Rights era has led to more socializing between blacks and whites, and to more intermarriage. Polls show that the percentage of Americans who want interracial marriage to be illegal has declined precipitously since the early 1970s, and there is much higher acceptance of interracial unions than at any time in the past 200 years.

Rising Age of Marriage As a Cause of Increased Interracial Marriages

A second factor in the increase in interracial marriages is the rising age at which people marry. Age at first marriage is substantially later than it ever has been in U.S. history. In the 2005 American Community Survey (ACS), half of U.S.-born women age 26.5 and half of U.S.-born men age 28.2 had never been married. This is considerably higher than in any other historical period.

As young adults postpone settling down to start their own families, they have greater exposure to different kinds of potential partners. Young adults in their twenties spend time going to college, traveling, working, and encountering a broader diversity of potential mates. Later age at marriage also makes it more difficult for parents to veto or even influence their children's choice of mates. Sure enough, among people married in the same calendar year, later age at marriage is associated with higher rates of interracial marriage. And second marriages are more likely to be interracial than first marriages.

WHAT NONTRADITIONAL UNIONS TELL US ABOUT AMERICAN SOCIETY

The rise of intermarriage in the United States means that racial barriers no longer have quite the strength and power they used to have. Race continues to be a powerful division in American life, however. Racial intermarriage remains far less common than intermarriage between high school dropouts and people with college degrees, or intermarriage between Catholics and Protestants, or intermarriage between northerners and southerners.

Although the number of black-white marriages has grown from 55,000 in 1960 to 440,000 in 2005, black-white marriage remains the most unlikely racial combination in the United States, given the sizes of the black and white populations. Hispanics only slightly outnumber blacks among American adults, but the number of Hispanic marriages to non-Hispanic whites (1.75 million) was four times larger than the number of black-white marriages in 2005. There were fewer than half as many Asians as blacks in the United States in 2005, but the number of Asian-white marriages (755,000) was substantially larger than the number of black-white marriages. In the marriage market, as in the residential housing market, blacks continue to be the most socially isolated group in the United States.

Nevertheless, it is clear that acceptance of interracial unions is on the rise. In 1972, five years after all laws in the United States against interracial marriage had been declared unconstitutional, 39 percent of Americans still favored laws against racial intermarriage. This percentage has steadily dropped over time, so that by 2002 only 10 percent of Americans surveyed in the General Social Survey said they favored laws against interracial marriage. Young adults are more favorably disposed to interracial marriage than their elders: only 4 percent of young adults surveyed in 2002 favored laws against interracial marriage. Another sign of changing times: Barack Obama's parents were married in Hawaii in 1960, and at that time their marriage would have been illegal in more than a quarter of U.S. states, because they were an interracial couple. Today, such a marriage is legal in all U.S. states.

In the News

INTERRACIAL MARRIAGE
A CULTURAL TABOO FADES

Chicago Tribune, March 15, 2007

Kayce T. Ataivero and Bonnie Miller Rubin

When Mary Hughes, a white woman from Minnesota, married her husband Millard, a black man from Houston, she knew they would have to make compromises to navigate a society still largely segregated in 1965. A simple road trip to an Ohio wedding became a delicate dance to avoid stopping in Indiana, a state that banned such unions.

Today, the Homewood, Ill., couple have traveled all over the country, a freedom afforded to them by a landmark Supreme Court case that 40 years ago this summer repealed state bans on interracial marriages. Suddenly, those trips got a whole lot safer.

"I read about (the case) in *Time* magazine and I thought OK, the United States is finally getting it," Hughes said, recalling how she reacted to the 1967 high court decision. "This whole idea that people of different races couldn't be married, it should not have been an issue."

Affirming the right to love and marry without regard to race swept aside one of the last vestiges of state-sanctioned segregation.

Since then, there has been an almost fourfold increase in interracial marriages, according to a report released last week by the Council on Contemporary Families, though such unions still make up only 7.5 percent of all married couples.

A host of societal factors—marrying later, immigration, more non-traditional unions of all kinds—have contributed to the rising numbers, the council reported. However, even more telling than the number of interracial marriages is the nation's shifting attitude toward them. In 1972, 39 percent of Americans still favored laws banning them. Thirty years later, that figure had shrunk to 10 percent—and even less among young people, according to the report by the council, a non-profit organization based in Chicago.

But in 1967—13 years after Brown vs. Board of Education declared school segregation unconstitutional—interracial marriage was still taboo nationwide and illegal in 27 states. It was in that hostile climate that the Loving case started in rural Caroline County, Va. Mildred Jeter, 18 and black, fell in love with Richard Loving, 24, a white man whom she had known all her life.

They married in 1958, in Washington, D.C., then returned to their home. At 2 the next morning, they were rousted from bed by deputies and later sentenced to 1 year in jail. Caroline County Judge Leon Bazile suspended the sentence, providing the couple left Virginia.

"Almighty God created the races, white, black and yellow . . . and placed them on separate continents, and but for the interference with his arrangement there would be no cause for such marriages," Bazile said from the bench.

The Lovings moved to Washington—and then sued. The Supreme Court decided the case on June 12, 1967, wiping the laws off the books.

That same year, the once scandalous debate was prompting discussion everywhere. "Star Trek" aired the first interracial kiss on national TV. "Guess Who's Coming to Dinner" hit movie theaters, reminding Americans that it was still considered courageous to wed across color lines—even with a groom as elegant as Sidney Poitier.

And when the daughter of Secretary of State Dean Rusk married a black man in 1967, the private decision was considered so politically risky that *Time* magazine gave it cover treatment.

Stanford University sociology professor Michael J. Rosenfeld, who wrote the council's report, said that while race continues to be a major fault line in America, the findings suggest it is becoming less relevant.

"(Interracial marriage) was such a controversial topic, almost untouchable and now for most Americans it is a non-issue," Rosenfeld said.

That's what Kimberly Adami-Hasegawa, 28, a white woman from central Illinois, found last year when she married her husband, Naoto, who is Japanese. Adami-Hasegawa sees her marriage as a sign of society's growth. From the moment the couple met in a coffee shop, race was never a concern, she said.

"When people (back home) meet Naoto, they are like, 'Oh, he's an Oriental guy,'" she said, laughing. "It was never something that would hold me back. My parents were very accepting."

Hasegawa, 33, said he is rarely reminded of the racial difference between him and his wife.

"One day, we were walking around and holding hands and she was like, 'Did you notice that people are doing double takes?'" he said. "I was oblivious to it."

A more diverse country has created more opportunities to meet a melting pot of potential mates, experts say. Additionally, as couples delay marriage, parents have less influence over the choice of their children's spouses. The push to recognize same-sex relationships also has chipped away at racial intolerance. In 1967, gay marriage wasn't a blip on the radar screen. Yet the two issues became inextricably intertwined when same-sex advocates held up this last vestige of Jim Crow as an example of past discrimination, providing historical perspective, explained Brian Powell, a sociology professor at Indiana University.

When he interviewed 1,500 Americans on gay marriage, opponents sounded "eerily similar" to those who once justified laws that banned race mixing, he said.

Still, social barriers remain, especially among blacks and whites, according to Rosenfeld, who said attitudes that gave birth to anti-miscegenation laws linger.

In fact, black-white marriages remain the most unlikely interracial unions. In 2005, there were 440,000 such marriages, compared with 1.75 million white-Hispanic marriages and 755,000 white-Asian marriages, according to the council report.

Unions between white men and black women comprise just 3 percent of all interracial marriages. That might explain why despite meeting in 1980, Gary and Pat Bryan didn't exchange vows until 2001, when she was 46 and he was 51.

They first met as colleagues at Northeastern Illinois University—she was in human resources, he was an architect in the facilities management department. "I just thought he was a cute little redhead who was easy to talk to—not someone I would date," Pat Bryan said.

Besides race, the couple also wrestled with issues of religion. She's Christian, he's Jewish. But all their baggage, they said, paled in comparison to what they shared: a love of the outdoors, movies, friends and a deep spiritual connection.

Questions of culture, race and religion often get blurred. While Pat Bryan has not converted, the couple were married by a rabbi, surrounded by family and friends, and celebrate all the Jewish holidays, including hosting Passover seders in their Skokie, Ill., home. "In the end, we got together because we wanted to love and be loved," she said. "That was the driving force."

That force also has helped Mary and Millard Hughes. It wasn't always easy. There was the time the couple attended church in her hometown of Northfield, Minn., and one disapproving neighbor spent the entire mass "turned around, just staring at us." And there was another incident in a St. Joseph, Mich., parking lot, when they had car trouble and endured racial taunts.

But after 42 years and three children, they take almost everything in stride. Certainly, the initial reservations that troubled some members of her family have waned, as has social resistance to her marriage.

What hasn't changed is her attitude on interracial marriage.

"I was living in a world that was not typical for 1965," she said. "In my world it was never a big deal." ▰

For Review

1. Imagine that a friend of yours has made the argument that America is a "color-blind" society. How would you respond to this argument? Draw on evidence provided by Rockquemore and Henderson to formulate your response.

2. Coontz and Mintz both use historical analyses to show how notions of the "traditional" family and childhood have changed over time. How might these changes be related? Do changing ideas about the family change our ideas about childhood? Do changes in childhood change our ideas about families?

3. Describe some of the ways that interracial couples use "racial literacy," as described by Rockquemore and Henderson, to resist racism and border patrolling. What are some other ways that couples resist racism? Are African-American dual-career partnerships, as described by Franklin, a form of resistance to racism? Why or why not?

4. Struening writes about some of the social and legal challenges faced by same-sex couples and families. What unique challenges might African-American same-sex couples face? What about interracial same-sex couples? What cultural, legal, or other tools might these families use to resist discrimination on multiple fronts?

5. Activity: Imagine that it is 100 years in the future, and you have found this book in the archives of your local e-library. Using what you have learned about how families change over time, write a journal entry from the future, reflecting on how family life and family law have changed since the publication of this book. What is different? What has stayed the same? In your opinion, what changes are still needed?

6. Activity: Ask at least five people, "What is a family?" and compare their answers to one another and to the readings. What are some similarities and differences in the ways people respond to this question? How do their answers reflect or refute what Coontz calls the "largely mythical 'traditional' family"? Do you notice differences in the ways people respond based on age, race, gender, or other characteristics?

PART THREE

Intimate Relationships in the Twenty-First Century

12

Why Is Everyone Afraid of Sex?

Pepper Schwartz

In spite of the visibility of sex in the media and popular culture, despite a widespread acceptance of a variety of sexual practices, Americans still hold a deep-rooted fear of sex. In this article, I argue Americans are more sexually constrained than liberated, more miserable than happy, and more misinformed than informed in American society than it appears. The acceptance of abstinence-only sexual education and laws outlawing sexual toys designed for women's sexual pleasure point to the existence of a cultural fear of sex. The reasons for this fear and suggestions to overcome it are the topic of this chapter.

We all know that sexuality is a part of courtship and marriage. It goes without saying (I hope) to say it is critical, although I suppose not absolutely necessary, for reproduction. Eggs can be fertilized in a laboratory and inserted into a uterus, but most of us, if we can, prefer to become pregnant in the old-fashioned way. We flirt, we seduce, we touch, we make love in various ways, or sometimes we see sexuality as an appetite, which can be used merely to satisfy an urge. Most people think sex is most fulfilling when it is part of an expression of profound love. To put it another way, sexuality is an elemental aspect of being attracted to someone, choosing a partner, establishing or maintaining a relationship, and creating a family. It is part of our lives from childhood to old age. That said, *I believe sex is also something we are deeply afraid of. Why is that so?*

Before I begin my argument to support that statement and answer that question, I should admit that there is evidence to the contrary. Perhaps you think so too. You could, fairly, offer the following arguments.

First, look at popular culture. The media, print, Internet, movies, and television are saturated with sex. The Internet pushes the tolerance of community standards with access to exotic pornography and also allows smaller communities of people with specific sexual preferences (such as foot fetishists or swingers) to find and mingle with one another. Television titillates in almost every show, whether it is an adventure story, a soap opera ("is Brad *really* the long lost adopted brother of his lover?"), or just dancing (take a look at the costumes of the women competitors on *Dancing with the Stars*, for example). Advertising and marketing use sex both subliminally (such as showing a gorgeous woman stroking a car) or blatantly, such as Calvin Klein ads where sultry teenagers have their jeans unbuttoned to show just a little bit more of their long, lean torsos. And if that doesn't convince, you might remember the ads for Viagra and Cialis, where famous men endorse the erectile dysfunction product, or silver-haired men and women are able to be "ready when the time is right." The media doesn't seem too fearful, does it?

Second, what about actual behavior among young people? The statistics on premarital sexuality would seem to belie the title of this paper. A number of studies talk about the "decoupling of relationship status and sex" and the earlier entrance of young women into sexual intercourse, resulting in more sexual partners over a lifetime. Multiple short-term relationships and transitory cohabiting relationships[1] also help increase the number of sexual encounters in men's and women's premarital or nonmarital lives. Proponents of sexual freedom rather than restriction could also point out the relatively new phenomenon of "hooking up," a term adolescents and young adults use to describe brief and spontaneous interaction in noncommitted encounters that could encompass everything from just hanging out together to intercourse.[2]

Third, but isn't everyone doing everything? Yes, that's true too. There is a widening acceptance of different sexual behaviors, and a decrease in racial, age, class, and gender differences in terms of who is doing what.[3] There are many taboos that have been broached, not the least of which is the appearance of proudly "out" lesbians and gay men on national television, their relationships and sexual preferences interwoven into the story line of prime-time television (i.e., *Will and Grace*) and some indication that bisexual behavior is more acceptable and more common than it might ever have been, at least among young people.[4]

Still, while I agree with all these points, I still believe that we are more sexually constrained than liberated, more miserable than happy, and more misinformed than informed in American society than it would appear. And here are the issues and circumstances that support my position: (1) a national policy that underfunds or ignores comprehensive sex education and supports abstinence education, (2) a number of laws across our country that specifically outlaw sexual pleasure, and (3) our continued queasiness about homosexuality and continued insistence on a dichotomous view of sexuality.

ABSTINENCE EDUCATION

With any luck, this will change, but at the present time, Congress has systematically increased funding for programs and for a philosophy that is not supported by any credible research. Funding for abstinence started in 1997 at the cost of $9 million. At the time of this writing, the government has spent over $1 billion chasing a horse that left the barn so long ago that the manure has turned to topsoil.[5]

Complaints about the government's abstinence programs have come from Planned Parenthood, SIECUS (the Sexuality Information and Education Council of the United States), individual sex educators, state governments that resisted taking abstinence money but needed funding for sex education, and parents who want their children to hear more than "just say no." In 2004, Henry Waxman, a congressman from California, chaired congressional hearings on the efficacy of abstinence programs that, by definition, do not give any information on contraception, on sexual decision making once sexual behavior exists, or is desired, or in fact, accurate information on the consequences of sexual behavior. After reviewing the abstinence materials gathered from many states, Waxman concluded, "Over 80% of the Abstinence Only curricula used by 2/3 of federally funded programs contain false, misleading or distorted information about reproductive health."

Waxman relied on some excellent research to come to his other conclusion: that the programs didn't accomplish their own goal—to keep young men and women (indeed, all men and women) abstinent until marriage. A well-done and well-publicized 2001 study by Bearman and Brückner looked at data on 20,000 students who had taken abstinence pledges and found that only 12 percent kept their promise. They did wait longer to have intercourse, but since they were significantly less likely than people who had had a comprehensive sex education to use condoms when they did have sex, they were as likely to get a sexually transmitted infection as people who had not made virginity pledges or had abstinence education.[6]

So here we have a paradox. The majority of unmarried people are having intercourse or some kind of genital sexuality before marriage. Only a small number of people intend to wait until marriage for sex, and most of them do not accomplish that goal. Still, legislators vote for programs that have been found to be ineffective because, I imagine, they believe this is the safest course for them to pursue. Why would they do this when there is a tidal wave of research indicating that abstinence education doesn't work? Why would they fund programs whose material is full of falsehoods such as teaching that premarital sexuality is likely to cause psychological and physical problems and that abstinence from sexual activity before marriage is the expected standard for all males and females in the United States!?

My answer is that *American parents are extremely uneasy with the idea of young people being sexual and acting sexually.* Even though the parents of teenagers were unlikely to have been sexually abstinent themselves, they are uneasy about endorsing any kind of sexual behavior for their children. If this were not true, they would be fighting tooth and nail to get their kids really good sex education that included the proper use of contraception. I think adults in America still think that sex is dangerous for youth—emotionally, physically, and morally. While they "handled it" (or not) themselves, they do not feel their sixteen-year-old is capable of good sexual choices. Meanwhile, of course, their sixteen-year-old is making sexual choices anyhow (about half of them will already have had intercourse) but without proper education about what kinds of information and self-knowledge should go into decision making or physical and mental safety. While there is a lot of sexiness on television (some of which is directed at *very* young people; for example, the 2008 singing group called Cliz, girls aged eleven to fourteen, sexily clad and coiffed, appearing on the *Today Show*, June 17, 2008), no network at this time will accept condom ads! Does this sound like a sexually sane or comfortable nation to you?

LAWS OUTLAWING SEXUAL PLEASURE

It is amazing that in this period that allows so much sexual license and freedom of choice, that there are laws that prohibit the way we become sexually excited. There are a number of ridiculous laws in this category, but for purposes of discussion, let me refer to the one that I find the most ludicrous. At present, though this may fluctuate since some of these laws are under attack, about six states outlaw the sale of vibrators. I know this is hard to believe, but legislators in the states of Alabama, Georgia, Texas, Mississippi, Arkansas, and Kansas have decided that vibrators are dangerous to American morality. I was an expert witness in cases in Alabama and Georgia, and I have followed the Texas case. Legislators denounced vibrators (or any nonhuman device used for sexual stimulation) as obscene and passed legislation to outlaw their sale. In these states, owners of small businesses that sold erotic toys, books, and lotions were persecuted and prosecuted. The

Texas law was recently overturned, and after many twists and turns in court it looks like the Alabama law has also been overturned. (It is hard to know because some of these results are either under appeal or an appeal is being considered.) But the fact is that legally elected officials in these states felt that prosecuting sex shops would be a popular stance and legislators that disagreed (or were afraid to come out in favor of vibrators) were in the minority.

Isn't this more than a bit odd? When I testified in favor of vibrators, I could not base my testimony on the mere fact that vibrating devices felt great or that women deserved to have better or quicker orgasms any way they wanted to as long as their sexual pleasure was not endangering minors or pressuring an unwilling adult. No, the astute legal team felt the best approach was to defend vibrators as medical devices because they were useful for nonorgasmic women who had to learn how to have an orgasm. We took that approach and ultimately, had success with it. But it struck me, why would a sexually liberated society tolerate the control— and criminalization—of the lowly vibrator? Surely, this is in direct contradiction to other kinds of sexual license as portrayed in the media and as illustrated by sexual behavior. I could only come up with one hypothesis that seemed powerful enough to explain all the money and legal maneuvering that took place—a continuing fear of women's sexuality unless it related to either reproduction or men.

The idea of unpartnered sex is deeply frightening to many sectors of American society. Pleasurable sex is allowed if it is in the service of reproduction—or the attainment or maintenance of marriage. But when it allows women to have alternatives to men (or any partner) and, indeed, when there is the fear that the vibrator may not only be equivalent but perhaps superior to the pleasure produced by intercourse or other kinds of stimulation, then it becomes a public menace. We seem to believe in love and union, but not pleasure for its own sake. This prudish stance stands in the face of the obvious natural tendency of humans to masturbate and small children to touch themselves, unconsciously, and happily, unless criticized. Most boys and a significant number of girls teach themselves how to masturbate to orgasm, often before puberty.[7] And yet this has long been a tabooed activity. Even in the history of the last 100 years of Western civilization, children have had their hands tied to prevent touching themselves and, at the turn of the century, clitorectomies (surgical removal of the clitoris) were recommended by doctors who feared that masturbation or sexual interest by young women was a form of insanity.[8] One would think we had progressed far from those days, but perhaps we have not come as far as it would seem. Not so long ago, Joycelyn Elders, surgeon general under President Bill Clinton, was dismissed by Clinton because she said that she thought children should be taught about masturbation so that they would delay the complications that could ensue from precocious intercourse. Do you think the outcome would be different if a current surgeon general said the same thing?[9]

ATTITUDES TOWARD HOMOSEXUALITY

While there is much more acceptance of homosexuality and homosexuals than there has ever been, opinion is still split over whether or not homosexual relations between consenting adults should be legal. More encouraging is the fact that a clear majority of the public is comfortable with a gay doctor or teacher.[10] Debate has been particularly acrimonious, however, when it comes to the issue of gay marriage and gay union, though somewhat less bitter for domestic partnerships, since rights for domestic partnership are not exactly the same as rights for heterosexual marriage and it is not called "marriage."[11] After decades of political activism by gay rights leaders and civil libertarians of various sexual orientations, there has been some political movement, such as fair housing and employment laws for homosexuals in various cities and states in the United States, and most recently, the legal right to get married in Massachusetts, Connecticut, Iowa, Vermont, and Maine. The Supreme Court of California had also ruled in favor of legalizing same-sex marriage, but this right was rescinded in California in November 2008 after the "yes" vote on Proposition 8 changed the state constitution to restrict marriage to opposite-sex couples. Personal feelings about homosexuality retain a kind of fear far beyond expectation, particularly as stereotypes about homosexual predatory behavior have been dismissed or diminished. One of the interesting ways we deal with this fear is to ignore what we know to be true about the extent of casual or intermittent attraction to members of our own sex and instead create a dichotomous category (either homosexual or heterosexual) of sexual orientation, regardless of this information to the contrary. In the late 1940s, the famous study by Alfred Kinsey[12] created the Kinsey scale, a 0 to 6 scale of sexual orientation, with 0 being people who had absolutely no experience with homosexual relations and 6 being people who had absolutely no heterosexual experience. Later academic books (for example, McWhirter, Sanders, Reinisch, 1990) have examined the scale and shown additional systematic ways to look at the breadth of same-sex experience (fantasy, love, identity). Still, the original contribution is important as created because it shows that there is a wide variety of homosexual experience that is not encapsulated in dichotomous terms. For example, Kinsey found that about a third of his male population had some kind of genital sexual experience with another man and about a fifth of the women had some kind of same-sex sexual contact.

Because homosexuality is stigmatized and used as a way of defaming individuals, it is not surprising that few men or women claim a middle place on the Kinsey continuum. Some women, particularly of late, have celebrated their bisexuality,[13] but few men feel safe in doing so. The politics of desire seems to offer some cover for female bisexuality but almost none for males. While females are conceived of being sexually labile, that is they can move back and forth between homosexuality and heterosexuality without having the latter impugned, men have quite the opposite situation. A man who has had one homosexual experience and fifty heterosexual ones is perceived to be in denial of his homosexuality. He is rarely seen as a bisexual or free sexual spirit.

The place of homosexuals in our society is still politically and personally unsafe; it can even be a life and death circumstance since strong fears and hatred of homosexuals have spawned violence and homicide. How can we begin to think of ourselves as a sexually secure nation when the mere mention of homosexuality or homosexual marriage ignites a firestorm of commentary, denial, or outrage?

SOURCES OF FEAR ABOUT SEXUALITY

These points lead me to turn to the bigger question: Why are so many individuals in the United States sexually frightened? I will discuss five of what I think are the main sources of fear: (1) religious indoctrination and tradition, (2) the double standard and patriarchal norms, (3) sexual transmission of disease, (4) cultural expectations about appearance and sexual competence, and (5) ostracism for not being masculine enough.

Religious Indoctrination and Tradition

Whatever the Bible says, (and scholars differ on their interpretations), the teachings of most religious institutions vary from conservative to extremely conservative views about sexual behavior.[14] Sex outside of marriage is often condemned, even if it is almost universal. Masturbation is not mentioned, or if it is, it is seen as sick or weak. The best most parishioners can hope for vis-à-vis homosexuality is a policy of tolerance and compassion. Usually any kind of same-sex sexual contact, or even just desire, is immediately condemned as immoral. The result of this generally negative or hushed approach toward sexuality is widespread guilt, shame, blame, horror, and anger at various populations of "sinners." At the individual level, many people trace their inhibitions, and inability to enjoy sexuality, to their religious training or background.[15]

While some religions are somewhat more supportive of marital sexuality (for example, orthodox Judaism clearly sees marital sexuality as a mitzvah, a blessing), there is still no toleration in ancient religious books for masturbation or homosexuality.

Double Standard and Patriarchal Norms

Our society has watched women's sexuality change to mirror men's sexuality. Women are now more likely to buy sex toys, to have sex before marriage, to "hook up," and to be overtly sexual in their presentation of self.[16] This drives a lot of people wild with apprehension and anger. To some, it puts the family, and even the nation, in jeopardy. Sexual freedom that includes sexual freedom for women is desired by men in the particular (i.e., personal access to sexually willing women), but it is decried in the general (social policy or public approval). In the United States, women are still threatened with the words "slut" or the amorphous "bad" reputation.[17] The double standard, greatly changed, still exists.[18]

In some parts of the world (particularly the Middle East), women are killed for sexuality outside of wedlock. These are called "honor killings" because the belief is that a woman who has had sex outside of marriage, even a woman who is raped against her will, creates a blot on the family name that can only be erased by her death. While this is not the practice in most of the world, it exists in Jordan, Egypt, Syria, Lebanon, Yemen, Iraq, Iran, Saudia Arabia, and a number of other countries, as well as among Israeli Arabs. For example, one 1995 government report in Egypt counted 52 honor killings out of a total of 819 murders. Yemen reported 400 such killings in 1997.[19] Until the mid-twentieth century in Texas, it was not illegal for a husband to kill his wife if he found her in bed with another man. No one suggested a reciprocal allowance for women. The idea of a free sexual life for women, equal to the privileges given to men, is still a very new, and to many people, troubling idea.

Association of Sexuality, Disease, and Death

Sexuality does require a certain amount of physical as well as emotional vulnerability. There is a sad history of sexually transmitted diseases.[20] Without prophylactic measures that could prevent transmission, centuries of sexually active men and women have suffered from debilitating and often fatal infections. Even when those prophylactic measures became more effective, availability, promotion, and consistent use of them has been limited.[21] When AIDS first emerged as a modern-day plague in the early 1980s, all the fears and hysteria of earlier periods of contagion reemerged, and frightened, angry moralists and policy makers reacted by blaming sex, gay men, and modern immorality for the deaths.[22] Influenza has also killed many people in its time, but when sexual transmission is added to a contagion, sex itself becomes the villain. Instead of concentrating on helping people avoid infection, policy makers, some religious leaders, and multiple moral entrepreneurs go on the attack, using the medical crisis to create a moral one. Instead of using the circumstances to create good public health initiatives such as helping sexually active people understand how to prevent most disease transmission, moral conservatives attack sex itself and condemn the very health practices that would make sex safer. Thus, in the very midst of an AIDS epidemic, government figures, religious leaders, and conservative action groups have condemned condoms, exaggerating their failure rate (which is actually quite small) and promoting the idea that condoms actually increase vulnerability to disease because they allow unmarried and gay people to have sex. Conservative forces do not want anyone but married, monogamous heterosexuals to have sex, and they refuse to accept the fact that teenagers, single adults, and gay and lesbian individuals are having sex, will continue to have sex, and need the best health protections they can get. The fact that sex is so obviously not restricted to the monogamously married anymore (if it ever was) has deepened the backlash of these morality police against all kinds of premarital and nonmonogamous sexuality.

Fear about Sexual Acceptability and Competence

We pretend that because sexuality is biological that it is easily accomplished. While some lucky people get sex education and, at a deeper level, advice and information about their own sexual quandaries and challenges, most of us learn, through trial and error, how to be what we hope is a good lover. At first it is just our attractiveness and acceptability that we worry about. Each period of recorded history has had normative evocations of what is beautiful, what is masculine or feminine, what is sexy or what is not.[23] The imagery is idealized, even iconic, rather than representative. Most female stars in movie scenes are tall, beautiful, and slim. Most male teenagers in ads have a "six pack," the name these days for chest and abdominal muscle definition. It is hard for the average person, however, to fit the media and model standard for sexual attractiveness, and a huge industry has grown up trying to make us recognize our imperfections so that we can buy goods and services to correct them. An enormous number of young men and women, and many people throughout the life cycle loathe their bodies, feel unlovable, and have no faith in their ability to make someone else sexually satisfied and emotionally faithful. As a result, there is often anger at all the sexual imagery—anger at how it makes us feel, anger at the standards we are oppressed by, and anxiety about whether or not we are sexually acceptable and whether or not we have a sex life that is "normal." As a result, we vacillate from condemning sex-saturated advertising and media content, to trying desperately to have a harder penis, more perfect breasts, or more instant orgasms.[24] So many people feel that cultural expectations about appearance and behavior are beyond their capacity or desire that many act out their fear by condemning the sexual behavior of others or personally retreating from sexual or romantic engagement.

Fears about Sexual Orientation

People have a variety of fantasies, sexual experiences, and crushes before they settle on a primary sexual identity. Because we are given only two categories of sexual being—heterosexual and homosexual—the presence of anything indicating homosexuality is extremely scary to people, particularly to men. Men are not only punished for anything that indicates femininity; they are also punished for not being heroically heterosexual (dating a lot, having sex with a succession of women, sporting a "six pack" chest, etc).[25] Anything, from being bad at athletics, to choosing not to have premarital sex with a girlfriend, could cause a man to be called a "fag" or some other nasty put-down. A teen does not have to be homosexual to be called a "fag." Rather, the word is often thrown at boys who are believed to be heterosexual but who are not enacting culturally adequate portrayals of masculine behavior in the way the peer group thinks "maleness" should look. Young men who not only fail at being heterosexual enough, but who are also believed to be homosexual, or who have stated that they are indeed homosexual, can still be in grave danger of ostracism.[26] Homophobic statements, and the fear that one might not be heterosexual, and the absence of any vision of another acceptable place on the Kinsey scale, creates a huge fear about one's sexual identity and performance of that identity. The literature on lesbians and gay men is consistent about how hard it is for young people with homosexual feelings to feel good about themselves and how much adult therapeutic work they often have to do to embrace their sexual selves. Fear about homosexuality and fear about any homosexual fantasies or experience creates fear in general about sexual identity, sexual preference, and sexual behavior.

CONCLUSION

For all the sexual imagery in American society, it seems clear that we are not at ease with our sexuality at either the policy or personal level. There are mixed signals in every realm. We sell everything from cars to toothpaste on television with sexual innuendo, but we cannot sell condoms during these same time slots. Women are now having almost as much sex as men before marriage, yet there is still a double standard. We have sex earlier, and it is normative to have sex before marriage, yet there is still guilt and shame and inadequate preparation for physical or emotional safety. We still have more trouble talking about sex than we do about doing it. We have a policy that does not fund comprehensive sexual education, even though half of all American teenagers are having intercourse by age sixteen and most parents are in favor of comprehensive sex education.[27] Fear, not comfort, lies only a few centimeters under our bravado and long lists of sexual partners.

The answer to all of this confusion and irrationality is clear but still oddly out of reach. We need to reduce sexual anxiety and ignorance through education. We can do that by using well-trained sex educators, researchers, and teachers to distribute scientific data and reassuring counsel to both children and their parents. This does not mean a sexual free-for-all. Far from it. It means giving valid sexual information and help in sexual decision making throughout the life cycle. It means recognizing that sexual desire is natural and that people of all ages need information and support to feel good enough about themselves, their bodies, and their sexual behavior, and to act responsibly and comfortably on their own behalf. It means legitimizing pleasure and giving people information about how to give it to themselves and others in honorable, honest, and safe ways. It means that we have to stop snickering about sex, or pontificating about it, and we need to make it part of our mental and social health curriculum from early childhood to late adulthood. This is not a new or brilliant idea; it is merely a rational one. Our culture is still afraid of sex, and it is in our individual interest, our family interests, and the interests of public health, to quash the toxic tactics that are aimed at creating sexual fears and instead to help make sexuality a source of happiness in our own life and in our intimate relationships.

13

New Couples, New Families: The Cohabitation Revolution in the United States

Pamela J. Smock and Wendy Manning

Living in sin, playing house, shacking up, living together, cohabitation—what was a rare phenomenon just three decades ago has now become a typical experience in many people's lives. This chapter will explore the "cohabitation revolution" and address several important questions: Who cohabits? Why? Does cohabitation usually lead to marriage among heterosexual couples? How often are children a part of cohabiting households? Do men and women think about and experience cohabitation in similar ways? Do cohabiting couples divide housework more equally than married couples? How common is cohabitation for lesbians and gays? What does the "cohabitation revolution" imply for the future of families and marriage? This essay will also discuss whether and how the meaning and role of living together differs by social class, race, and ethnicity.

INTRODUCTION

Living in sin, playing house, shacking up, living together, cohabitation—what was a rare phenomenon just three decades ago has now become a typical experience in many people's lives. In 2002, over 60 percent of women ages twenty-five to thirty-nine had cohabited at least once.[1] Just seven years earlier, this percentage was roughly 48 percent.[2] A change of this magnitude in such a short period of time is striking. Indeed, cohabitation has become an integral part of the courtship process, and even adolescents are expressing an interest in cohabiting at some point in the future.[3]

This chapter explores the "cohabitation revolution," a phenomenon that is changing the way Americans date, enter marriage, and form families. We address a series of questions: Who cohabits? Why? Does cohabitation usually lead to marriage among heterosexual couples? What are cohabiting relationships like? How often are children a part of cohabiting households? Do cohabiting couples divide household chores more equally than married couples?

We summarize social science knowledge about these questions, focusing on heterosexual cohabitation. We review research done by others and interweave findings from in-depth interviews we have done with over 350 young adults to find out how people today are thinking about, and experiencing, cohabiting relationships. These men and women are from diverse racial and ethnic backgrounds, and they represent a range of social classes (from the near-poor to the middle class).

WHO COHABITS?

Currently, there are over 5 million households in the United States headed by a cohabiting couple;[4] indeed, cohabiting has become increasingly common in all demographic groups. Consider the following: Cohabitation, rather than marriage, has become the most common way coresidential romantic relationships are now being formed. Among couples who began such relationships between 1997 and 2001, 68 percent of them began by cohabiting, and just 32 percent began by marrying.

Further, the percentage of marriages that start as cohabitations continues to climb. About forty years ago (1965–1974) only 10 percent of marriages were preceded by cohabitation. About half (57 percent) of first marriages between 1990 and 1994 were preceded by cohabitation, increasing to 62 percent for those marrying between 1997 and 2001.[5]

The flip side is that the percentage of marriages begun *without* first living together has dropped from 43 percent to 38 percent between 1990 and 2001. That is, marrying "directly," without living together first, has become the rarer phenomenon.

There are some differences in the characteristics of people who are more or less likely to live together. First, education matters. The most highly educated are somewhat less likely to cohabit. Recent national data show that 45 percent of nineteen- to forty-four-year-old women who are college graduates have cohabited compared with 64 percent of women who have not completed high school.[6] These differences in educational attainment correspond with the relative educational advantage that married couples enjoy compared to heterosexual cohabiting couples. In 2000, 30 percent of husbands and 25 percent of wives were college graduates compared to 18 percent and 17 percent of cohabiting men and women.[7]

Closely related to this, cohabiting couples tend to have lower incomes than married couples. In the year 2000, approximately 27 percent of married men had earnings over $50,000 compared to 15 percent of cohabiting men. Just 6 percent of married men had earnings of $10,000 or less compared to 12 percent of cohabiting men. Also, cohabitors' levels of unemployment are more than twice as high as those of married men and women, and cohabiting families with children also experience higher poverty rates than married families with children.[8]

These educational and income differences are consistent with a large number of studies that show that being well-off financially and having high levels of education increase the chances of marriage both for people who are living together and those who are not.[9] This pattern is termed by scholars as "selection"—that is, marriage tends to be "selective" of those with better economic prospects and more financial security.[10]

In our own conversations with cohabiting young adults, we find that many (about 70 percent) believe their money situation must be solid before they will feel ready for marriage.[11] We asked cohabitors what needs to be "in place" for them to decide to marry, because many report that they would like to marry. The following excerpts from our interviews are illustrative:

I don't really know 'cause the love is there uh . . . trust is there. Everything's there except money.

—Black male, recently unemployed, age 29

I: OK. What would have had to [have] been in place for you to have gotten married?
R: Money.
I: OK. Tell me a little bit about what that means.
R: Money means um . . . stability. I don't want to struggle. . . . and income-wise we were still both struggling.

—Black female store supervisor and college student, age 36

Ah. School was not finished, but I never really considered that an impediment, but the financial situation certainly was one.

—White male information systems manager, age 33

I: What are the kinds of things that needed to be in place for you to get married?
R: Um, we wanted one of our educations to be done at least. Basically just trying to get caught up on some bills . . . and be able to afford a wedding.

—White male assistant production supervisor, age 27

A third factor that seems to distinguish people who decide to live together versus those who do not can loosely be understood under the rubric of "traditional" versus "liberal." Cohabitation tends to be less common among those who hold strong religious convictions against cohabitation, who are more conservative, and who are less supportive of equality between men and women.[12] These traditional people, particularly those who consider cohabitation to be inconsistent with their religious beliefs, constitute a subgroup that is more likely to marry directly, without living together first.

It should be noted there are few racial-ethnic differences in terms of "who cohabits." Blacks, non-Hispanic whites, foreign-born and U.S.-born Hispanics have similar chances of cohabiting. Further, the fraction of those who had ever cohabited increased for all groups between 1995 and 2002.[13]

All in all, cohabitation is becoming much more common in the United States, making it important to underscore that any existing differences are only tendencies that, arguably, may narrow in future years as cohabitation becomes even more popular. We might do well to invert the framing of much past research on "who cohabits?" Rather, we might ask "who does not cohabit?"

WHY MOVE IN TOGETHER?

For heterosexual couples who have the option to marry, an important question that has sparked much speculation is: Why are people living together? Why not just get married?

Our interviews suggest that young adults perceive cohabitation to be an obvious and sensible thing to do. They articulate several motives for living together.

One motive is a combination of wanting to spend more time together and more pragmatic considerations such as logistics. That is, if a couple is *already* spending several nights together, why not just move in together? As one man told us: "I was going to be there more, we might as well live together . . . instead of driving to see each other all the time." Indeed, we have found that, for many couples, the "decision" to cohabit is not really a decision at all. It is a gradual process as couples spend more and more nights together and just "end up" having moved in; they often cannot even state the date their cohabitation began. We term this phenomenon a "slide" into cohabitation.[14] As twenty-three-year-old Daniela told us, her boyfriend just never went home:

> Um, he had come over, and we had talked and we had, he had spent the night and then from then on he had stayed the night, so basically he ended up staying there, he just never went home, he just honestly never went home. I guess he had just got

out of a relationship, the person he was living with before, he was staying with an uncle and then once we met, it was like love at first sight or whatever and um, he never went home, he stayed with me.

Similarly, Steve, a computer consultant, recounts:

[S]he stayed at my house more and more from spending the night once to not going home to her parents' house for a week at a time and then you know . . . so there was no official starting date. I did take note when the frilly fufu soaps showed up in my bathroom that she'd probably moved in at that point.

A second motive for cohabitation concerns finances. Most of our interviewees talked about how living together allows couples to save money by pooling resources and sharing in a variety of expenses, such as rent, gas, electricity, and groceries. Again and again, we heard statements like: "Most people do it because of the bills." "Why are we paying for two apartments? Let's move in . . ." or "Two's cheaper than one" or "I mean we spent the majority of our time together, but yet we were both paying at two separate places and it just made more sense for us to live together."

Third, young adults perceive cohabitation as an important way to evaluate compatibility for marriage; this theme was highly dominant in our interviews. It's a way of learning about one another, finding out about the other person's habits (and deciding if one can tolerate them), and figuring out whether the relationship is strong or can become strong. As one woman put it, cohabitation allows "partners to work through issues or habits before marriage."

Fear of divorce is very much intertwined with the motive of checking compatibility. The young adults we interviewed were quite sensitive to high divorce rates, often mentioning that one out of two marriages ends in divorce, and high proportions of them had experienced their parents' or close friends' or relatives' divorces. They expressed concerns about not rushing into marriage, believing it essential to do everything possible to learn enough about the other person and the relationship to avoid divorce. For them, moving in together just makes sense and reduces the risk of eventual divorce; they think that not living together first would be foolish.

What Are Cohabiting Relationships Like?

Cohabiting relationships are not all the same. Scientists have studied various dimensions of cohabiting relationships; we focus on several that have received the most attention. Specifically, they vary in terms of relationship quality and stability (e.g., whether the couple breaks up or, in the case of heterosexual couples, marries), the presence of children, and the division of unpaid household labor.

Relationship Quality and Stability

Studies of cohabiting couples suggest that, overall, they experience slightly lower relationship quality and levels of commitment than do married couples.[15] But the "overall" here is very important. Many cohabiting couples, especially those with plans to marry, are just as satisfied and committed to their relationships as married couples.[16] They also enjoy relationship quality on a par with that of married couples.

What are the chances that such a couple will go on to marry rather than ending their relationship or continuing to cohabit? Information gathered about cohabitations begun between 1997 and 2001 tells us that about one-half got married. Within five years of the start of a cohabiting relationship, 49 percent headed to the altar, 37 percent broke up, and about 14 percent continued to cohabit.[17] These break-up rates are higher than those for married couples; only about 20 percent of marriages dissolve within five years.[18] When thinking about these numbers, it is important to keep in mind that while most cohabiting couples want or expect to marry, not all hold such intentions. One-quarter of cohabiting women living with a boyfriend explicitly stated that they did *not* expect to marry him.[19]

A commonly asked question is whether marriages preceded by cohabitation last as long as marriages begun without living together first. Many people believe that living together first makes a couple much more likely to divorce, despite what our interviewees believed about living together as a way to protect a relationship from divorce. Scientists studying this issue reach different conclusions, depending on the information they use, how old that information is, and the factors they consider.

The general answer, especially from new studies using more recent data (with some of these finding no effect), is that marriages begun by cohabitation may be *slightly* more prone to divorce than those that begin without living together, but this is not the case for all couples because couples who marry without living together first may have traditional values that also make it less likely for them to divorce. It is also possible that any effect may disappear altogether as more and more people live together before going to the altar.

Children and Cohabiting Families

The popular image of cohabitation as revolving solely around two romantically involved people increasingly distorts reality. Many cohabiting relationships include children—about 40 percent of the relationships.[20] About half of these children are born to the cohabiting couple, while the rest of the children find themselves in cohabiting families because their biological parent enters a cohabiting relationship.[21]

Scholars agree that cohabitation is increasingly becoming a context for childbearing and child rearing; it is estimated that two-fifths to one-half of children born in the early 1990s will spend time in a cohabiting-parent family. While it is well-known that a substantial proportion of children in the United States are born outside of marriage (nearly 40 percent), what is less well-known is that many of these children, about 40 percent to 50 percent, are being born to couples who are living together. Broken down into broad racial and ethnic categories, this translates into 50 percent among non-Hispanic white and Hispanic women, and 25 percent among African-American women.[22]

Notably, these births are not all occurring among the young and never-married either. Roughly 20 percent of births after marital separation or divorce are occurring in cohabiting unions.[23]

Trends over time can provide us with clues about possible futures. The percentage of children born in cohabiting unions doubled between 1980–1984 and 1990–1994. Further, the share of births to cohabiting mothers increased substantially more during this time period than did the share to single mothers not living with a partner. It is also noteworthy that children born to cohabiting couples are less likely to be reported as "unplanned" than those born to single women.[24] "Unplanned" means that a mother states that she didn't want a(nother) baby or that the pregnancy came too soon. Overall, the percentage of women stating their child was planned was 54 percent for cohabiting women compared with 39 percent for single women.[25]

Certainly, "planning" measures have been criticized. This is because they ask a woman to reflect back after her baby has already been born, likely coloring her response in a favorable direction and underestimating the percentage deemed as "unplanned." But these numbers are useful in that they indicate a gap between single and cohabiting women, with the latter substantially more likely to state that the birth was planned. This lends credence to the idea that cohabitation is increasingly considered an appropriate family context for childbearing and parenting.

As noted above, children may also experience living in a cohabiting family, full-time or part-time, depending on custody arrangements, if their biological mother or father starts living with her or his romantic partner. This family can be considered a type of stepfamily. In fact, if we include cohabitation in addition to marriage, approximately *one-half* of all stepfamilies in the United States are now formed through cohabitation rather than through marriage.[26]

The Division of Household Labor

Who does what in terms of everyday chores in cohabiting households? Such labor, often also termed domestic labor, includes unpaid activities such as cleaning, cooking, laundry, child care, shopping, paying bills, and many other kinds of work necessary to keep the lives of individuals and families running.

Research on married couples is clear on this point. While husbands have increased the amount of time they spend taking care of children and, to some extent, doing housework, wives still do the bulk of this labor.[27] Even counting what we might think of as "men's tasks" (yard work, taking out the garbage, household repairs, car maintenance) and despite the massive entrance of wives into paid employment, most marriages are still characterized by gender inequality in the amount of household labor performed.[28]

Research on cohabiting couples also suggests a gender divide, despite such couples holding more egalitarian gender attitudes than married couples. One study reports that cohabiting men do the same amount of household labor per week as married men (nineteen and eighteen hours, respectively), while cohabiting women perform thirty-one hours of household labor per week compared to thirty-seven hours for married women.[29]

Another study tracked *changes* in men's and women's housework hours as they entered and exited cohabiting and marital unions.[30] The key finding is telling: Men substantially reduce their housework time both when they enter *either* marriage or cohabitation, whereas women increase theirs under the same circumstances. As the author of the study concludes: ". . . the results show that entry into cohabitation induces changes in housework behavior that are no less gender-typical than does entry into marriage . . . the fact of entry into a coresidential union is of greater consequence for housework time than the form of that union."[31]

These findings echo what we learned in our interviews. Cohabiting young adults described their domestic lives in a way that suggests a relatively traditional division of labor. Cohabiting women appear to do most of the cleaning, cooking, and daily household tasks, while cohabiting men tend to focus on the traditionally male tasks described above. While there are exceptions, this generalization tends to hold for most of the cohabitors we interviewed.

THE COHABITATION REVOLUTION: CONCLUDING THOUGHTS

Workers in family agencies sometimes meet the couple or family which exists without benefit of marriage. No one knows how many such families there are in the general population, but those which come to light when their problems bring them to our agencies for assistance suggest that the average city contains a considerable number of them.[32]

What a long way we've come since social scientist Raymond Stevens wrote the above words nearly seventy years ago about cases of unmarried couples coming to the attention of urban social service agencies. From today's vantage point, it is clear that cohabitation has evolved to dramatically alter the ways that people form romantic relationships, live in them, parent, and marry. For most adults marrying for the first time, cohabitation comes first; for divorced adults, cohabitation before *remarriage* is even more commonplace.[33]

We would argue that cohabitation is indeed a "revolution." It is broad-based, affecting nearly all population subgroups, which suggests that state and religious structures are not dictating the parameters of adult relationships. At the same time, we would also call attention to the point that, in many ways, such as the presence of children and the division of household labor, cohabiting families are not all that different from married-couple families. Inequality in household labor, for example, mirrors what we have known for years about inequality in marriage, demonstrating how even dramatic change can coexist with continuity.

The cohabitation revolution is not, in our view, a transitory blip. While the pace of growth in cohabiting households appears to have slowed during the 1990s,[34] it is still growing, it has become the typical path to marriage and remarriage, and the majority of young to middle-aged adults have cohabited at one time or another.

The cohabitation revolution serves as an example of how an initially novel idea or solution about how to "do" relationships has diffused within a culture and then taken on a life of its own. We would argue that high levels of cohabitation will be sustained, and further accelerated, in this way. An important aspect of this process is that new generations of young adults are coming of age within a social milieu (e.g., society, media, parents, relatives, neighbors, siblings, peers) in which large proportions of people have experienced and accept cohabitation. Moreover, increasing numbers of children will be coming of age having been *born* into a cohabiting family. Such patterns will reinforce the idea of cohabitation as a regular and quite predictable feature of family life, even as it adds flux and new complexities to our lives.

In the end, we are reminded of comments made by some of the young adults we interviewed. To paraphrase them, but preserving their essence: "That's really interesting. Why would you want to ask about cohabitation?? It's, well, it's just so normal!"

14

Parenting Adult Children
in the Twenty-First Century

Joshua Coleman

The past century has witnessed a profound change in our perception of children and how they should be parented. Prior to the twentieth century, parents viewed children as resilient and robust, and they also believed that the rigors of life would make children stronger and more capable. For a variety of reasons, including smaller family size, the prevalence of divorce, the advent of parenting experts, a decrease in opportunities after college, and a perception of an increasingly dangerous world, today's parents believe that children are fragile and vulnerable, requiring a close and carefully managed childhood in order to succeed. Since the 1960s, there has been a gradual blurring of the boundaries between parents and children as families moved to a more democratic structure where the child's opinions and feelings became far more valued. Parents' expectations of what they wanted from their children also underwent an enormous change.

This chapter discusses the changes in the relationships between parents and children and the lengthening of intergenerational interdependence—both economic and emotional. I argue that the emotional intensification of parents' investment in their children has the potential to create deeper and closer ties than in the past, but also to create more disappointment and more bitterness when high expectations of love are not met.

When I was growing up, my friends and I couldn't stand our parents' music, clothing, and more than a few of their friends. We would have no sooner put on a Bing Crosby record than they would have worn a tie-dyed T-shirt, smoked a bong, or waxed poetic about the intensity of a Jimi Hendrix solo. They were the ADULTS—foreign, unfathomable, living in a world we scarcely deigned to penetrate except to get the keys to their cars.[1]

In addition, our parents had little interest in our music and weren't terribly concerned with what we thought about their taste in clothing. They expected us to respect them and didn't spend a lot of time worrying whether or not their parenting mistakes would ruin our love for them. They also didn't spend endless hours reading parenting books or watching experts on television, and they weren't terribly concerned about respecting our rights or infringing on our autonomy.

While these generational boundaries still exist in poor and working-class families, a very different world greets today's middle-class children and their parents.[2] In many ways, the generational markers that were common as recently as three or four decades ago have largely disappeared. While the twentieth century has seen unprecedented improvements in the quality of children's lives, today's middle-class parents are freaked out. They obsess over the slightest error in parenting and worry that they may have forever blighted their child's life with a comment made in anger or exhaustion. The constant broadcast of parenting advice causes new mothers to feel as though they and their husbands are practically committing child abuse if they don't obsessively read every available book on pregnancy, early childhood development, and acing the SATs. Both parents worry that if they don't closely monitor the academic implications of every grade from preschool through high school, their child will get crowded out of the increasingly tight bottleneck of colleges and the ever-shrinking opportunities for employment.[3] They are terrified of doing something to turn their child against them or of losing their love for good. Parents of all classes worry about drug and alcohol addiction, Internet porn, ADD, sexual predators, and a whole slew of psychiatric disorders.[4]

While prior generations of parents felt that their job was finished once children left home, many of today's parents continue to worry long afterwards. As a psychologist in private practice, I see a large number of parents struggling to understand their adult children and many are fighting to find ways to keep them in their lives. The confusion about how to remain close to adult children has spawned an explosion of new self-help books in just the past few years with titles such as *Walking on Eggshells, You're Wearing That?, Don't Bite Your Tongue, Setting Boundaries with Your Adult Children*, and my own book, *When Parents Hurt*.

FROM RESILIENCE TO FRAGILITY

In prior generations, the task of children was to prepare themselves for adult work by following the instructions appropriate to their class, race, and gender. As Steven Mintz points out (in Chapter 6 of this volume), at the end of the nineteenth century Americans began to see children as independent beings with their own needs and rhythms of development. In addition, American began to shift from believing that it was the obligation of children to meet the family's needs to believing that the family should meet the children's needs.[5]

From the 1920s to the 1970s, Americans steadily changed their child-rearing emphasis from valuing conformity, church attendance, loyalty, and obedience, to focusing on children's autonomy, tolerance, and the ability to think for themselves.[6] This change was accompanied by a transformation in the family climate of the middle class from being authoritarian to being more democratic and permissive. Children went from being quietly kept in the background to being loudly and proudly paraded into the foreground. In many households, children became the axis upon which the household turned.[7]

Freud and the experts who followed him popularized the idea that parents could be a corrupting influence on the fragile psychological development of the child. According to Freud, children could be easily led into neurosis, if not psychosis, by parents who failed to adequately address the challenges posed by each stage of development.[8] This perspective put an enormous amount of pressure on parents and made them worry that a small mistake would forever consign their child to a life spent in a therapist's office, or worse.

Nevertheless, for the first half of the twentieth century, parents continued to believe that children could not only handle the stresses created by struggle, adversity, and competition, but that these would strengthen and prepare them for the challenges they would later face.[9] Phrases such as "building backbone," "strengthening character," and "improving moral fiber" were all used to characterize the outcome of a childhood and adolescence exposed to these elements.

Over the past forty to fifty years, however, our view has slowly changed to perceiving children as fragile and requiring a kind of "hothouse parenting" in order to thrive.[10] Sociologist Annette Lareau describes this type of middle-class parenting as "concerted cultivation." It is characterized by the parents' active organization of children's leisure activities and the frequent engagement of verbally intensive interactions geared to increase a sense of entitlement and mutuality with adults. One of the goals of concerted cultivation is helping children understand the parents' decisions and assisting children to understand their own inner worlds.[11]

This angle on parenting is new. Historian Steven Mintz writes that with the notable exceptions of the Quakers and Native Americans, strategies that relied on guilt, shame, or pain dominated American parenting up through the Victorian era. During the twentieth century, these strategies gradually gave way to approaches that emphasized negotiating with children to help them understand their behavior and motivation.[12]

As a result of this shift, parents began to feel tremendous pressure to produce a child who was self-aware, but who was not unduly fettered by the corrosive effects of guilt, self-consciousness, and the burdens of "codependency" (the inclination to worry so much about the well-being of the other that you consistently put their needs above your own).

PARENTS AS PROBLEMS

This new focus on raising self-aware children created a slew of relational and parenting experts to help people overcome the guilt, anxiety, and fear that came as they began to wrestle with this new kind of identity. One of the central obstacles to this individualistic perspective became the problematic parent. Parents began to be viewed as potential baggage to be contained, if not eliminated, in the quest for self-esteem, psychological health, and personal fulfillment. A visit to any bookstore shows the success of this enterprise.

In fact, the field of psychology has probably done more to create parental, especially maternal, anxiety and guilt than any other institution. For example, in the 1960s, the influential child psychologist Bruno Bettelheim wrote that childhood autism was caused by mothers who couldn't relate to their children.[13] Psychologist Jay Haley and colleagues, along with anthropologist Gregory Bateson, argued that schizophrenia resulted from mothers who communicated in contradictory, "double-binding" fashions with their children.[14] Both theories, popular at their time, have been disproved, or shown to be highly flawed.

Parents' capacity to provide their children with entertainment became an effective and guilt-inducing tool to market products to parents. In addition, it became another way that children could later fault their parents. The statement "I'm bored" grew to be a statement that reflected on the parents' adequacy and worth. Children could now judge parents by how well they provided opportunities and, therefore, how deserving they were of the child's love and respect. Children could later, rightly or wrongly, blame parents for the ways that they turned out, or failed to turn out.[15] They could attribute the failure to provide "formative opportunities" as being far more central than they may have been.

For example, in Steven Spielberg's movie, *Hook*, a remake of *Peter Pan*, Captain Hook attempts to curry favor with Michael by arranging a baseball game. When Michael is up to bat, Hook motivates him by saying, "This is for all of the baseball games that your father never attended!" The child snarls in righteous anger and hits a home run.

This is a major reversal in polarities. Where prior generations of children were expected to earn the *parents'* love and respect, today's parents are worried that they won't have their *children's* love and respect because they're not good *enough*: not psychological enough, not sensitive enough, not fun enough, not "there" enough.[16] They're worried, often correctly, that their real or imagined mistakes in parenting may one day come back to haunt them. And in comparison to the past, parents have far fewer support systems of kin and neighbors to help them strike the right balance in their child raising.

THE ISOLATED FAMILY

In the past few decades, the financial and emotional resources that were once exchanged with extended kin, neighbors, religious institutions, and friends have become increasingly concentrated in the nuclear family. Only half as many people said that they had four to five confidants in 2004 compared with those who had that number of confidants in 1985, and the number of people stating that there is *no one* with whom they discuss important matters has tripled in that same time frame.[17]

Whereas the family and the identity of its members once existed in a rich ecosystem fed and nourished by a community of supports, American families have more and more begun to stand alone. Much of the time and energy that once went into socializing with neighbors and kin has been transferred into parenting. According to sociologists Suzanne Bianchi, John Robinson, and Melissa Milke, today's mothers spend twice as much time with their children and fathers three times as much time as they did in the supposedly halcyon days of the mid-1960s. Parents, especially mothers, achieve this by giving up time for themselves, sacrificing sleep, friendships, and time with their spouses.[18] At the same time, there has been a 40 percent reduction in the amount of time that children play outside, leaving parents with much more time under the same roof with their children.[19] These changes, combined with smaller family sizes, have increased the demands on parents to play the emotional, educational, and socializing roles that siblings, neighbors, and friends once filled.

On the one hand, these changes have benefited some families. A greater amount of time spent between parent and child offers the potential for more intimacy, understanding, and shared meaning. Many of today's parents are able to have long-term friendships with their children after they leave home that are enriched by the close and involved years that they spent together before the children moved out.[20]

Yet, this intensive parenting environment may test the limits of what couples can reasonably ask of each other and may place an undue burden on the parent-child relationship. When parents spend less time with their friends and communities, many of them may turn to their offspring for fulfillment, intimacy, and long-term security. More time and more involvement create the possibility for more conflict, resentment, and disappointment on the part of both parent and child. In addition, a close, intimate relationship with a parent may make it harder to separate from that parent and, as a result, may tempt the adult child to push away more aggressively in order to launch her own adult life.

While parents are expected to provide an even greater investment in child care, entertainment, protection, college, and after-college care than prior generations of parents, there are few guidelines for what they might expect in return. Parents may feel betrayed if they do not get the love and gratitude they look forward to and believe that they deserve. But children can also review their childhoods from the calculus of how supportive or affectionate their parents were and may declare the relationship null and void if they evaluate it as something less than they needed or deserved.

SOUL-MATE PARENT

The combination of the democratization of the family form, fewer opportunities after children leave home, a culture that blames parents for child outcomes, a more dangerous world, and an increase in parental guilt and anxiety have together created an environment where parents believe that they have to be everything for their children. From this perspective, the modern middle-class parent has much in common with another cultural icon, the soul mate. For example, in soul-mate ideology, one's future spouse is supposed to be sexy (though not insatiable), independent (but not too independent), intimate (but not cloying), funny (but not obnoxious), well-educated (but not arrogant), and sensitive (but not wimpy).

In the ideology of the soul-mate parent, Mom or Dad is supposed to be sensitive (but not intrusive), tolerant (though not neglectful), forgiving (though not weak), current on child development (though not a pedant), a good playmate (but not trying to live their life through the child), and a good mentor (without using the word "mentor"). Parents are also supposed to be an enthusiastic fan of whatever artistic, sporting, or academic endeavor is pursued by the child.

Both the ideology of the romantic soul mate and the soul-mate parent suffer from fundamental problems: (1) most individuals don't have the bounty of traits, attitudes, and attributes to bring to any one relationship, (2) what we want and need from a person at one point in time is often quite different from what we may need from him at another, and (3) our own character flaws, genetics, and moods may cause us to wittingly or unwittingly shut down or greatly inhibit the other's capacity to provide the interaction that we may so desperately crave.

WHEN THE CHILD REJECTS THE PARENT

In the past decade, I have seen an explosion in my clinical practice of parents who have come to me because they were cut off by their grown children. While some of these parents made terrible mistakes, many of them were loving and reasonable. If there is an increase in the rejecting of parents, why is it occurring?

Divorce seems to be one common factor. The ideology of family life now places affectionate choice at the center of family relationships, and the voluntary nature of relating as the central governing principle. Parents are more concerned than in the past about their children's individual happiness, but they are also looking out for their own. As a result, they increasingly feel free to leave marriages that are insufficiently supportive, meaningful, or affectionate.

In some circumstances, a divorce creates the ability to be a more involved, less distracted parent.[21] Numerous studies show that children are benefited by a divorce if their parents had a high-conflict marriage.[22] In this situation, a divorce may allow the children to have better relationships with their parents if the divorce ends their conflict. Constance Ahrons found that many adult children felt that their relationships with their fathers had either improved or remained stable over time after a divorce.[23]

But divorce also offers a variety of ways for parents and children to become distant or estranged. Numerous studies show that the relationship between father and daughter is more at risk than the mother-daughter relationship after a divorce.[24] These feelings may become especially inflamed after a parent remarries, or with increased interparental conflict, early father remarriage, or low father involvement in the early post-divorce years. And in their old age, divorced fathers usually get much less care and attention from their daughters than do mothers.[25] Divorce increases fathers' vulnerability to anxiety and depression.[26] Mothers or fathers who feel angry or hurt by the divorce and who use their children as a way to punish the other parent, often alienate adult children. Mentally ill parents may successfully cause the adult child to believe that closeness with the other parent is a selfish or disloyal act.[27]

But divorce is not the only source of tension between parents and their adult children. Many of the causes, as the previous discussion has shown, are built into today's high expectations of parent-child relations and the greater isolation of nuclear families. Both high expectations and greater isolation create more possibilities for disappointment and fewer places to turn to compensate for problems in the parent-adult relationship. These tensions have been exacerbated in the past thirty years by a decline in the prospects for youthful economic independence. Adult children have become more economically dependent upon parents, and parents are less able to understand the lives and decisions of their young adult children.

"When I Was Your Age . . ."

Prior to the 1970s, a young man could reasonably expect to leave high school and, even without a college degree, marry and support a family. College grads were likely to get permanent work shortly after graduation, and could expect to send their kids to an even better university. Women did not have the same opportunities, but they expected to marry and, for most, marriage seemed the best economic investment in their future.

As historian Stephanie Coontz notes (see Chapter 5 of this volume) many of the young men starting families after World War II were eligible for veterans' benefits that allowed an unprecedented number of them to enter the middle class. The federal government was also active in helping families by underwriting low down payments and long-term mortgages to boost home ownership. This, in combination with well-paid union jobs, allowed many working-class families to gain entry into the middle class. Women and minorities also began to believe that they might claim their fair share as a result of the women's movement and the civil rights struggle of the 1950s and 1960s.[28]

This is radically different from the opportunities that greet today's high school and college graduates. Deindustrialization and economic restructuring during the past thirty years have altered the educational and vocational requirements needed to support a family. Whereas a high school degree was once the basic requirement for successful employment, now a college degree is considered the baseline.[29] But, even a college degree may not be enough to manage the vagaries of today's changing economic market.

These recent economic changes may strain the relationship between parents and their adult children because many parents fail to understand or sympathize with the very different social and economic world that greets their newly minted adults. They may believe that the economic problems of their young adult children stem more from a lack of character than a new social reality. A *New Yorker* cartoon illustrated this dynamic. It showed two parents standing over their twenty-something who was watching television in their living room. The caption, addressed to the reclining son, read, "When I was your age, I was an adult." The cartoon reflects the sentiment that many parents feel and often express to their adult children.

Yet, many of today's parents are unaware of the extent that the job market has changed. While prior generations of children could assume they would one day outearn their parents, this opportunity appears to be dwindling except around a fortunate few. An article in the satirical paper, *The Onion*, says it all with the headline, "Most Americans Falling For 'Get Rich Slowly Over a Lifetime of Hard Work' Schemes."[30] Prior generations of parents could rely on their children's higher earnings to help provide for those parents in old age. But due to skyrocketing costs for health care, housing, low pay for entry-level jobs, and the erosion of job benefits, many of today's young adults find themselves barely able to support themselves, let alone having the ability to help support their parents. These changes in the economy have also removed an important way that adult children shared a sense of obligation and connection to their parents over the life span of both.

Of course, many young people do go on to earn very good wages, but the lengthening transition to adulthood means that their ability to do so often depends on their parents' willingness and ability to subsidize them. A study by the Institute for Social Research at the University of Michigan found that 34 percent of young adults between the ages of eighteen and thirty-four receive financial assistance on a regular basis from their parents. According to government statistics gathered in 2005, middle-income parents can expect to spend $190,980 on each child through the age of seventeen. But parents can anticipate spending an additional 25 percent of that amount again over the next seventeen years—an average of $1,556 yearly on children as old as thirty-three and thirty-four. Even parents who cannot afford these expenditures are helping out more than in the past. Today's parents spend nine weeks of their time each year helping adult children aged eighteen to thirty-four with babysitting, transportation, and laundry.[31]

So just as tensions may rise when parents are not able to understand why their kids aren't self-supporting, young adults may resent their parents, either because they can't help, or because they feel that there are strings attached to the help their parents give. They may also be tempted to blame parents for their difficult circumstances because they were raised in a culture that views parents as the most important causal agent in child development.

INDIVIDUALISM AND DEPRESSION

Less than one-fifth of Americans see class, race, or gender as important in getting ahead in life. The majority believe that what matters most is individual initiative.[32] But what happens when individual initiative is insufficient to support a family? Psychologist Martin Seligman has shown that individualistic attributions of causality that focus on enduring, personal traits can be useful in creating feelings of optimism and happiness when events go well. But they can generate feelings of depression and pessimism when events turn out poorly because of the self-blame that they engender.[33]

One of the strategies to defend against feelings of self-blame is to blame someone else—what psychologists refer to as externalization. Externalization can be a healthy defense mechanism and, as a result, most therapists work hard to help their clients find reasonable explanations that direct blame away from the self. Unfortunately, in today's culture, this often occurs by blaming the parents.

While parents are clearly important in how children turn out, they are less so than our current culture leads us to believe. As historian Stephanie Coontz writes, we live in a culture "that expects us single-handedly, or at most two-parently to counter all the comic ups and downs, social pressures, personal choices, and competing demands of a highly unequal, consumption-oriented culture dominated by deteriorating working conditions, interest-group politics, and self-serving advertisements for everything from toothpaste to moral values."[34]

An overemphasis on parental responsibility ignores compelling evidence that children are also affected by peer group, neighborhood, class, genetics, and siblings.[35] Yet, most of the stories that end up in the media feature parents who are (or were) selfish, abusive, neglectful, alcoholic, drug addicted, intrusive, or weak.

While the system of psychotherapy provides a way to externalize blame onto parents, there are fewer culturally prescribed ways for parents to externalize their feelings of guilt and inadequacy when they feel, rightly or wrongly, that they have caused their child to suffer or to fail. This is probably why so many parents suffer from depression when their children don't thrive as adults, or when they cut off contact with them.[36] While a certain level of selfless devotion comes with the job of being a parent, we need a more accurate lens for people to evaluate the outcomes of their adulthoods other than whether Mom or Dad did a good-enough job. Perspectives that blame child outcomes on parents are especially problematic when applied to the poor since the social dynamics of poverty make it harder for parents to protect their children and provide them with the assortment of educational, enrichment, and therapeutic opportunities that are available to parents with greater resources.[37]

INCREASING THE UNDERSTANDING

It is unlikely that the social foundation of the tensions between parents and their adult children will become part of the public dialogue anytime soon. For this reason, I advise parents who have been cut off or consistently criticized by their adult children to work toward not being defensive, to try to understand their children's complaints, to take responsibility for their parenting mistakes (large and small), and to continue to reach out to their adult children.

Many parents feel challenged by these suggestions. For example, I recently worked with a sixty-three-year-old mother who was frustrated by her thirty-five-year-old daughter's complaints that she wasn't encouraging enough of her when she was growing up. "When I was a child, you got what you got and you were glad for it," she told me. "I wouldn't have even *thought* about my mother not encouraging me enough." Many older parents feel confused and resentful, like this mother, when their parenting is held to the ideal of today's much more intensive parenting standard.

They struggle not to say any one of the following to their complaining adult child:

"Your childhood was a dream compared to mine."

"After everything that I sacrificed for you, this is what I get in response?"

"I didn't have all of the information about parenting that you have these days. It's unfair to have expected me to have known things that weren't part of the culture at the time."

"You had your own contributions to make to our relationship. You weren't an easy child."

I discourage parents from saying any of these statements because they sound defensive. As with marriage, communication is the most effective when people work to understand, reflect what was said, and empathize. I also let parents know that even if it feels as though an adult child has all of the power, the parent is still a powerful figure in the adult child's mind, even if the parent feels impotent.

There are many reasons why an adult child might cut off or criticize a parent. As with marriage, it is now a game negotiated between equals, and as such, it requires more patience, more respect, and less reliance on the invocations of parental authority. From adult children, it requires an understanding that much more is being asked of today's parents than was asked in prior generations. In the same way that there are numerous forces that affect a child's development, there are many forces affecting an individual's capacity to parent. The more that parents and their adult children can empathize with the separate realities of the other, the more that closeness and shared understanding can occur going forward.

15

Briefing Paper: Marriage Reduces Social Ties

Naomi Gerstel and Natalia Sarkisian

We know that partners in a good marriage are, on average, happier and healthier than single or divorced people. But do happy marriages guarantee a happy and healthy society? Not necessarily.

Many people believe that marriage is the fundamental building block of society, an institution that broadens social ties and ensures that individuals will not grow old in isolation. Perhaps that was true in the past, when marriage was a central unit of economic production and political organization. But today, despite the benefits that a good marriage delivers to the couple and their children, marriage actually tends to isolate partners from other people in ways that pose potential long-term problems both for the couple and for society as a whole.

Our research, based on national data from 1994 and 2004, indicates that married couples (both women and men) have fewer ties to relatives than the unmarried. The married are less likely to visit, call, have intimate talks with, or help out their parents, brothers and sisters, or other relatives. And the married are also considerably less likely to take care of their aging parents than unmarried adult children.

Marriage often reduces a couple's ties to the larger community. Married people are less likely than single individuals to socialize with neighbors or friends. It is the unmarried who are more likely to offer a hand or an ear—to give either practical help or emotional support to their neighbors and friends.

Marriage even lessens political involvement, especially for women. Single women are more likely than their married counterparts to attend political meetings or rallies, sign petitions, and raise money for political causes.

Does Marriage Isolate People?

Can it really be true that marriage—usually touted as the best answer to loneliness—actually isolates people? Some people might try to explain away these findings by arguing that people who are married are likely to be either older or younger than those who are not (or no longer) married, and it is their stage of life, not their marital state, that explains their lack of wider social ties. Others suggest that married people tend to have more money or better health than unmarried, people, so they just don't need other people as much. Some posit that married people simply have less available time because they have children who keep them occupied.

But none of these explanations works. Even when the married and unmarried are the same sex and age, have the same amount of money and the same overall health, the married still have fewer connections to family, neighbors, and friends. This pattern exists for those with children and those without. The plain truth is that marriage as it is practiced today often isolates couples from wider ties.

Why Does It Matter?

There are some cases in which the isolating effects of marriage may be beneficial, as when marriage causes a person to turn away from antisocial friends, such as gang members. But in most other cases, this effect has troublesome social implications. As the population ages, this effect of marriage deprives more elderly parents—who, ironically, have often pressed their children to marry—of the help and support that they want and need. Marriage can also generate excessive burdens on those who are single, as they are expected to provide the care that their married siblings do not. It also isolates neighbors from neighbors, and it narrows people's circles of friends. In addition, it puts a strain on marriage itself, when spouses become the only source of support and comfort. The increased expectations that emerge when one depends entirely on a spouse for emotional support can make marriages more fragile. And in the absence of wider support networks, individuals are especially vulnerable if the marriage ends, whether by death or by divorce.

Are There Alternatives?

The isolating effects of marriage are far from universal. The expectation that married couples should retreat from other interactions into private self-sufficiency is particularly characteristic of contemporary Western societies, especially of marriages in the United States. Americans believe that couples should be able to make it on their own—both practically and emotionally. Spouses are expected to rely on each other for all day-to-day needs. They are also supposed to be each other's confidants and main source of emotional support. In fact, the percentage of Americans who rely on their spouses as their *only* confidants has nearly doubled over the last twenty years. As we increasingly expect our partners, and only our partners, to be our soul mates, we become less involved with other people.

In contrast, anthropologists and historians find that other societies have often used marriage as a way to expand rather than shrink community ties. Historian Stephanie Coontz argues that, even in the United States, the emphasis on seeing spouses as best friends and confidants is a modern invention. So when it comes to marriage and community, another world is possible.

What Can We Do?

It is hard to find the time nowadays to include friends and neighbors, political involvement, and even contact with extended kin in our hectic lives. Sometimes people blame the schedules of their children—they are too busy running their kids to soccer practice to spend time with friends or get involved in civic life. Frequently, and with better reason, they blame the demands of their jobs and the lack of work-life balance in an increasingly speeded-up, competitive workplace, in which more and more couples are dual earners, spend long hours at the job, and often have to take work home. But rarely do they consider the isolating effects of marriage itself as it is practiced in the United States today.

There is growing advocacy for marriage-friendly social policies, from both the right and the left of the political spectrum—including initiatives to strengthen heterosexual marriages as well as movements to allow gay and lesbian marriages.

But our research suggests that we should pay equal attention to encouraging community-friendly families and partnerships. Both married and single individuals—and our society as a whole—would benefit if we paid more attention to adjusting the expectations associated with marriage, restructuring household schedules, and welcoming friends, neighbors, and relatives into our circles of care.

In the News

THE GREEDY MARRIAGE
TWO SCHOLARS ARGUE THAT GOOD
SPOUSES CAN MAKE BAD NEIGHBORS

Boston Globe, September 16, 2007

Chris Berdik

The wedding season is wrapping up, and many of the newly joined were no doubt advised that love is patient and kind. But now two Massachusetts sociologists say love can also be greedy.

More precisely, marriage can be greedy, according to Naomi Gerstel of the University of Massachusetts at Amherst and Natalia Sarkisian of Boston College, who have written a paper called "Marriage: The Good, the Bad, and the Greedy." Analyzing two nationwide social surveys, they found that married couples spend less time than singles calling, writing, and visiting with their friends, neighbors, and extended family. According to their research, married people are also less likely to give friends and neighbors emotional support and practical help, such as with household chores.

Gerstel and Sarkisian's research flies in the face of recent academic studies and political speeches arguing that marriage is the endangered cornerstone of a healthy society, benefiting the mental, physical, and financial well-being of children and adults, and, ultimately, their fellow citizens. They argue that marriage may actually, albeit unwittingly, have just the opposite effect—sapping the strength of American communities and diminishing our ability to think and act for the common good.

"Many, bemoaning the retreat from marriage, also mourn the loss of community," they wrote in the Fall 2006 issue of Contexts, a journal of the American Sociological Association. "What these nostalgic discussions do not recognize, ironically, is that marriage and community are often at odds with one another."

While some sociologists have applauded Gerstel and Sarkisian's questioning of conventional wisdom, critics dismiss the "greedy marriage" research, countering the findings with statistics that indicate a greater social involvement among married people. Others say Sarkisian and Gerstel ignore what really supports communities in the long term—the health and welfare of children.

"The purpose of marriage is to raise the next generation," says Kay Hymowitz, a fellow at the Manhattan Institute. "And to call that greedy is just an astounding use of the term."

Gerstel and Sarkisian say that they have nothing against marriage. They argue that the nature of the institution in America has changed—in ways that can endanger both society and the marriages themselves. And on this point, it turns out, even their critics agree.

Over the last century, Americans have become more romantic about marriage, and that's not always a good thing, according to some scholars.

Through the mid-20th century, husbands and wives were expected to fulfill the culturally defined roles as breadwinners and homemakers, what sociologists call the "institutional marriage." But today, as a recent Gallup poll finds, 94 percent of young, unmarried women and men say their primary goal in marriage is finding a soul mate.

One marker of the rise of soul-mate marriage is honeymoons, according to Stephanie Coontz, a sociologist with the Council on Contemporary Families, a nonprofit family research and advocacy group based in Chicago. The now nearly ubiquitous private adventures for newlyweds were nearly unheard of until the late 19th century. And even then, Coontz notes, the happy couples often took along relatives and friends for company.

"Over the past 100 years, we've made marriage much more precious," she says. "And the same things that have made it more passionate and beneficial for its members have also made it more isolating."

This notion is supported by a 2006 study by sociologists from Duke and the University of Arizona, which found that the number of people with whom Americans said they discussed important matters from 1985 to 2004 dropped by one-third. The only relationship that saw an increase in such discussions was marriage.

To conduct their own investigation, Gerstel and Sarkisian analyzed answers from the 1992–94 National Survey of Families and Households and 2004 General Social Survey, large surveys that asked thousands of Americans questions about things like closeness with extended family, attitudes about raising kids, and family routines.

They found that married respondents were significantly less likely than the unmarried to contact or see their parents and siblings, or to give them emotional or "practical" support, such as help with chores or babysitting. The married also less frequently spent time with or helped friends and neighbors. For instance, more than 80 percent of never-married individuals said they'd called or written to their parents in the last month, compared with just 60 percent of married people. Likewise, around 70 percent of unmarried people but only 30 percent of the married had socialized with friends in the last month.

There were two interesting exceptions. First, when it came to helping friends, the marriage gap showed up only with white couples, not among African-Americans or Hispanics. The researchers don't offer any explanation for this. But they do have ideas about what's behind a second wrinkle in their findings: When married couples had children it erased the gap in the amount of emotional and practical support they gave to friends and neighbors. Married couples with children gave just as much support as single parents or childless singles. The researchers surmise that while raising kids eats up lots of time and emotional energy, married parents rebuild their social networks while finding playmates, caretakers, and activity partners for their children.

"It really is marriage, not children, that's responsible for cutting off ties to people in the community," Gerstel says.

But Hymowitz of the Manhattan Institute says Gerstel and Sarkisian ignored important measures of community involvement. She points out that the article doesn't discuss volunteering, which is more prevalent among the married than those who have never married (32 percent vs. 20 percent) according to a 2006 Bureau of Labor Statistics tabulation. Nor does it mention voting rates: Sixty-seven percent of married people vote compared with just 44 percent of those who have never been married, according to the Census Bureau.

"What is this community the authors are talking about?" she asks.

It is a somewhat muddled portrait. Gerstel and Sarkisian note that married men are more likely than their single counterparts to sign petitions, but also that single women are more likely than married women to attend political meetings, sign petitions, and raise money for political causes. They also find that marriage increases men's participation in religious life—but not women's.

Gerstel and Sarkisian stress that their main objective was not to attack marriage, but to argue for a broader conception of what marriage is and should be.

"Finding a soul mate means turning inward—pushing aside other relationships," they write. They put forth several alternative models for marriage as less insular and more supportive of community, including pre-industrial societies in which "weddings are clearly community events [that] celebrate newly formed kin alliances." Sarkisian is also studying data from China to see if similar isolation occurs with married couples in that country.

But it's not just community that is hurt by the ideal of a self-sufficient soul-mate marriage, she and Gerstel contend.

"If you see marriage as the only place where you can get support and companionship, it can make marriage itself more fragile," says Sarkisian. "If you have your expectations too high, it's kind of setting yourself up for failure."

And here, it turns out, Gerstel and Sarkisian's harshest critics agree with them, up to a point.

But rather than arguing for a model of marriage in which husbands and wives cultivate ties beyond their spouse and children, some marriage promoters extol the virtues of the more traditional marriage, which emphasizes a person's responsibility as a husband, wife, or parent.

The lack of commitment to these roles, says Hymowitz, is "the reason for so many divorces and out-of-wedlock childbirths."

It is also important to realize that marriage can be difficult, adds Elizabeth Marquardt, a scholar at the Institute for American Values in New York.

"If you're in a bad period," Marquardt says, "it doesn't mean you're going from bad to worse and you need to get out as fast as you can."

Gerstel and Sarkisian's research suggests another lesson: try calling a friend.

"My sense is that there are people out there who have read our article, and it resonates with their feelings about their life," Sarkisian says. "They feel like something's missing." ▰■

16

The Case for Divorce

Virginia E. Rutter

Frequently in public and academic debates about the costs and benefits of marriage and divorce, evidence about health or economic consequences is used to support various perspectives. The book The Case for Marriage is a familiar example of this, and so we consider here "The Case for Divorce." This chapter offers evidence about when divorce leads to health benefits, rather than to more often reported negative health consequences. In particular, research shows that there are negative health consequences to remaining in a distressed marriage. The chapter also offers advice about the three things any reader of marriage and divorce research should look out for when trying to understand how useful or generalizable the claims are. Readers should consider whether marital quality has been considered—and how it has been measured; whether domestic violence and other pathologies have been examined; and whether "selection effects," or forces that occurred prior to marriage and that don't have anything to do with the marriage or the divorce itself but that make people more likely to divorce, have been tested. Finally, the chapter asks how we can explicitly—rather than implicitly—express values and beliefs when talking about the case for divorce.

Starting in 1880, when U.S. divorce statistics began to be recorded, the rate of divorce increased steadily for eighty years and then increased dramatically from 1960 to 1980.[1] By the end of that period, about half of all marriages ended in divorce. Since then, our 50 percent divorce rate has leveled off, and we haven't seen much change.[2]

Divorce policy has changed in that time. In the 1970s, there was a shift in divorce laws to allow unilateral divorce ("no-fault divorce") in the United States.

Since that time, rates of wife's suicide, domestic violence, and spousal homicide have declined.[3] Meanwhile, the number of children involved in any given divorce has gone from 1.34 children to less than 1 child per divorce[4] because of the declining birthrate.

Increases in divorce have made it a fixture in family life—and a "problem" to be understood, interpreted, analyzed, and fixed.[5] But what exactly is the problem? A better understanding of divorce—and divorce research—clarifies the case for divorce, and by extension informs us about life as it really is in contemporary families. The case for divorce asks: Are there some cases where divorce is a *better* outcome than remaining married would be? Three decades of research on the impact on adults and children points to yes.

Researching the Impact of Divorce

While discussion of research methods leaves some people cold or in wish of a nap, the consistent hallmark of the best research on the impact of divorce is that it makes a logical and reasonable comparison. Some studies do this. But some don't. It is as simple as this: if my now-divorced parents had been happily married, life would have been different, and a divorce would have been a big loss to them, me, my brothers, and the community. But that wasn't the case. They treated each other with contempt, led parallel lives, lived through their children (and also did a lot of good things). Then they were divorced.

The logical comparison for divorce versus not divorce in my own biography is a comparison between having unhappily married parents or divorced parents who moved on. My parents' post-divorce lives were up and down, but ultimately a lot more sensible for all involved, and (crucially) better than the life that preceded the divorce. Research that asks "compared to what" is designed to do a what-if exercise—not just with one person's story—but with the stories of many.

When researchers carefully examine, "divorce compared to what?" sometimes they are searching for *selection bias*—a particular kind of problem that shows there is something about the people who get divorced that happened before they got into the current situation that makes them more likely to divorce. Some attributes that existed before the marriage may affect who divorces. So when we compare divorced people to people who stayed married, the question is whether selection bias has influenced the results. There is selection bias if the divorced group was already different from the stably married group. For example, younger age at first marriage, living in poverty, not having a college degree are all associated with divorce. Already, we see that selection bias plays a role in divorce. But how have researchers answered the question about how or whether divorce *causes* problems for adults or their children? Selection bias may explain some, but certainly not all, of today's divorce.

The case for divorce includes research on children as well as research on adults. In the first section below, "Resilient Children of Divorce," I show how the research on the impact of divorce on children teaches us two important lessons. First, most children of divorce do well. And second, children who remain in high-conflict families, where the parents have a distressed marriage, are at greater risk for problems. When parents divorce, children have already been subject to their distressed marriages, and that is what puts these children at greater risk for problems. In the second section, "Does Divorce Make You Happy?," I discuss how research on the impact of divorce on adults follows a similar pattern: the consequences of a harsh or conflictual marriage exceed the consequences of divorce. In the third section, "Measuring Divorce's Impact with and without a Comparison Group," I show new evidence about how neutral the impact of divorce really is on children. At the same time, I remind you of the problems of research that fails to have a logical comparison group. As the research shows us, the case for divorce is straightforward. The consequences of remaining in a distressed marriage for children as well as for adults are myriad and long-lived. In those cases, perhaps the line shouldn't be "stay together for the kids," but "get divorced for the kids," not to mention for the health and well-being of the parents, on whom the children depend.

RESILIENT CHILDREN OF DIVORCE

In 1989, psychologist Mavis Hetherington presented her research at the American Association for Marriage and Family Therapy, showing that most children of divorce fare just as well as children from intact families. She had established a comparative rate of distress among children: while 10 percent of children in the general population have behavioral or school-related problems. 20–25 percent of children from divorced families have these problems (but about 80 percent of the children of divorce do not have such problems). Numerous research papers provided more detail and supported the finding in her research.

Hetherington reported on specific kinds of distress that parents and children experience with divorce. She found a "crisis period" of about two years surrounding the divorce. She learned that, depending upon the timing of divorce, boys and girls have different responses: when boys have problems, they tend to "act out"; when girls have problems, they are more likely to become depressed. But what Hetherington saw overall was the *resilience* of children of divorce.[6] Most children did fine. They were able to use personal resources and social networks in their family and community to cope.

Another study came out that year that refuted these findings, but also differed in terms of how the research was conducted. Psychologist Judith Wallerstein reported her research finding that children of divorce experienced more mental health problems than children who came from nondivorced, married families. She found that these children sometimes suffered a "sleeper effect": their difficulty emerged as adults—hence the phrase "adult children of divorce" that could keep us ever vigilant for some lurking form of damage that could pop up like a dormant cancer.

To judge between these two pieces of research, we need to look at how these psychologists collected their information.

Wallerstein's methods: She studied a *clinical* sample of young, white, upper-middle-class teenagers whose parents had been divorced and who sought treatment at a mental health center in northern California.[7] A clinical sample involves people who want help. They are a sample of folks who are, by definition, troubled. While a clinical sample can teach us much about the course of mental disturbances or adjustment problems, it cannot inform us about the prevalence or origins of a problem in the population, or reveal why some people end up doing well in the face of adversity, while others do not. Wallerstein provided cases full of rich detail, but they were not *representative*. Her study has the strength of being *longitudinal* (that is, she tracked her subjects over time), but her evidence couldn't tell us whether these problems occur consistently in the population, or if they were due to selection bias. Children of divorce who are troubled are, by definition, the ones who seek therapy.

Hetherington's methods: Researchers obtained a population-based sample of stably married families with a four-year-old and followed them over time. It was a *prospective*, longitudinal study. *Prospective* means that the study started before any divorces happened. Using a series of observations, parental reports, and teacher reports, Hetherington tracked these children in their everyday lives. Some children's parents went on to divorce; others remained together. We can't do experiments where we randomly assign some children to divorced parents and others to married parents, but this gives us a quasi-experimental design that helps us evaluate the impact of divorce compared to no divorce. In the comparison, all the children started off the same in the sense that they weren't showing up in the study because they already had "problems." Not only did this design allow researchers to compare children whose parents divorced versus those whose parents stayed together, it also enabled the researchers to see how children fared before the divorce versus how they were doing after the divorce. Hetherington had built-in comparisons.[8]

As research progressed, Hetherington learned more about divorce and children. Because she had detailed information about both kinds of families, she was able to compare married with divorced families. Sometimes the married families were extremely distressed; sometimes they were civil. Hetherington was able to analyze the well-being of children in extremely distressed married families versus children of divorce and children in harmoniously married families. By adding comparisons about the level of distress in all the families, she observed that children in harmonious married families fared better than children in divorced families *and* in distressed married families. Here's the punch line: The worst kind of family for a child to be raised in, in terms of mental health and behavior, was a *distressed, married* family.[9]

Several key pieces of research extended Hetherington's results by using comparison groups and a prospective design. In 1991, demographer Andrew Cherlin and his colleagues wrote about longitudinal studies in Great Britain and the United States in the journal *Science*. The studies included data from parents, children, and teachers over time. At the first time point, age seven, all the children's parents were married. Over the study period, some went on to divorce, and some did not. Cherlin confirmed Hetherington's findings: while about 10 percent of children overall are at risk for adjustment and mental health problems, children of divorce are about 20–25 percent at risk for problems. Seventy-five to 80 percent of the children are fine.[10]

Cherlin also found that the difference between the children of divorce versus children in stable marriages existed *prior* to the divorce. These were *predisruption effects*, and here's how it makes sense: parents who end up divorcing are different from parents who don't end up divorcing. They relate to each other differently; they relate to their children differently; and their children relate to them differently. Cherlin had identified selection bias, or a case of selection for who divorces.

In 1998, Cherlin and his colleagues offered an update on their continuing research.[11] Respondents analyzed in the 1991 study had gotten older, so he had more information. While the 1991 paper highlighted predisruption effects, this one reported that in addition, there were *postdisruption* effects (negative effects after the divorce) that accumulated and made life more difficult for children of divorce. Financial hardship and the loss of paternal involvement were key culprits. He called this phenomenon the "cascade of negative life events," and emphasized, as he had back in 1991, the importance of social and institutional supports for children in disrupted and remarried families.

A similar longitudinal study by Paul Amato and Juliana Sobolewski replicated these results in 2001.[12] They studied stably married, distressed but married, and divorced families over the course of seventeen years. They observed that grown children whose parents had divorced during their childhood had more adjustment problems. Although these adjustment problems were associated with predisruption effects—in other words, trouble in the family that preceded the divorce—postdisruption effects accumulated, too. Finally, the researchers found that children who grew up with married parents in distressed unions were more likely to experience psychological distress in later life, in contrast to their counterparts with nondistressed, stably married parents.

Starting with Hetherington in the 1980s, and following through Cherlin's parallel work in the 1990s, research designs that included comparison groups helped bring to light three points. First, using a population-based rather than a clinical sample provided a rate of distress among children of divorce that exemplified their *resilience*: approximately 80 percent were doing well versus 90 percent of children in the general population who were doing well. Second, difficulties—*predisruption effects*—found in longitudinal, prospective studies, indicated that children in families where their parents were headed for divorce were having troubles prior to the breakup. *Postdisruption effects*—and the cascade of negative life events—also played a role. Third, distressed marriages were harder on children than divorces. This last point foreshadowed the results in the studies of adults that I describe next.

DOES DIVORCE MAKE YOU HAPPY?

People who divorce do not go through such a costly and difficult process just to "feel good" or in some casual way to be happy. As you'll see below, research shows us just how difficult living in a distressed marriage is. The research shows us that divorce makes people feel better in the same way that the cessation of pain or illness makes them feel better.

In 2002, Linda Waite, a demographer at the University of Chicago, and several of her colleagues, released a study titled, "Does Divorce Make People Happy?" At the same time, I was completing research at the University of Washington for a paper that would be entitled "The Case for Divorce: Under What Conditions Is Divorce Beneficial and for Whom?"[13]

Our results were completely divergent. We both asked: How does people's level of well-being change when they divorce (versus when they stay married)? Both projects relied on the same data set; they both used a longitudinal design where all the people were married at the first time point, and some of them went on to divorce by the second time point. I found that adults who exited unhappy marriages were less depressed than those who stayed. According to Waite, there were no differences in happiness between those who stayed in their marriage and those who divorced.

What is the point? Should we throw up our hands and claim that research is merely a Rorschach test, a projective test that displays and reveals our deep-seated values and biases? For goodness' sake, no!

Instead, ask: "Divorce, compared to what?" Were people who divorced compared to those who stayed in a happy marriage, or compared to those who stayed in a stressed-out marriage? One difference between Waite's study and mine was that I used a more stringent measure of marital distress. I was able to detect the people who were in seriously distressed marriages. (I also took severe domestic violence into account, and I measured depression rather than "happiness.") The contrast makes all the difference. When comparing how markedly unhappily married people fare compared to people who divorced, the divorcing people were less depressed, and the unhappily married people were more depressed. My additional statistical tests ("fixed effects," discussed below) confirmed that marital distress, not other factors, accounted for the differences between the unhappily married and divorced groups. In other words, what made the married people in distressed marriages more depressed was *being in a distressed marriage*, not their risk of depression.

Other longitudinal studies, including a study by Daniel Hawkins and Alan Booth,[14] found similar results regarding marital distress: the more carefully marital distress was measured, the more pronounced were the psychological advantages of leaving over staying. Again, a better comparison between married and divorced people was accomplished by using a thoughtful measurement of marital quality. A study by Pamela Smock and her colleagues assessed the economic costs of divorcing and also used methods that took into account selection bias. Smock and her colleagues found that divorced women experience economic disadvantages but that some of that economic disadvantage would have existed even if they had remained married.[15] With psychological distress, as with economic distress, people who divorced were different for reasons *other* than divorcing, not *because* of divorcing.

More recent research has examined how the accumulation of marital transitions—a divorce, a cohabitation, a breakup, perhaps a remarriage—may be an additional important way to examine the impact of divorce. The approach is to examine "relationship trajectories." Sarah Meadows and her colleagues[16] examined the consequence of such multiple transitions for women who started as single mothers, and found that for women who face continuous instability—rather than a single transition—their health was negatively affected. Such research allows for even more complexity, and requires that we compare higher levels of disruption with lower levels of disruption, including divorce, in the story.

Why Marital Quality Matters

Marital quality makes a difference when we ask whether divorce is better than staying married. The benefits of marriage accrue only to people in happy and well-functioning marriages; the benefits of happy marriages are, indeed, robust. The same is not true for people in distressed marriages, and we save those marriages at our—and our partners'—peril. For example, studies on the "psychophysiology of marriage" show that when men and women are in distressed marriages—where they may experience contempt, criticism, defensiveness, and stonewalling—their immune systems decline over time.[17] These people are less healthy and less happy. Troubled marriages have immediate costs; they also have downstream health costs as the years of distress accumulate.

Research has demonstrated how high those costs are: Weissman used community mental health samples to assess the impact of marriage and marital distress on rates of major depression.[18] While the study found that depression was reduced for people in happy marriages, depression for men *and* women in unhappy marriages was *twenty-five* times more likely than for people in happy marriages. Another study found that marital dissatisfaction a year earlier is associated with a 2.7 times greater depression risk for women and with an elevated rate of depression for men. Even more alarming is a study that showed that, among married women who were more depressed than average, by far the most common explanation was domestic violence. In my research, women who were victims of domestic violence—severe enough to have been injured in the past year—were different in their response to distress and divorce from those in nonviolent distressed marriages, likely because the problems domestic violence victims have to solve are different from the problems of those who are in distressed but nonviolent marriages. This suggests that clear research on divorce should always seek to identify victims of abuse because these cases follow a different story line.[19]

When researchers measure marital distress in terms of level of conflict, or they use multiple measures of distress and find high conflict and distress, they find that divorce is a relief to those couples. This parallels what Hetherington found for children: that divorce is better than living in a high-conflict family. It is easy enough to ask, "how was marital distress measured?," in order to learn whether a measure of general happiness that merely captures transient feelings of satisfaction was used, or whether a measure of serious distress or conflict, which tends to identify which couples are "candidates" for divorce, was used.

On Happiness

Other measures matter, too: My study and the Waite study both looked at the personal costs of divorcing. While Waite measured "happiness," I measured "depression." It matters how we measure "personal well-being." While van Hemert and colleagues have found that happiness and depression are correlated, there's a big difference between them. Out of hundreds of correlational studies catalogued by Veenhoven in the World Database of Happiness, there are scarcely any gender differences in happiness. Nor does happiness have the major correlates to race or poverty that have been well-established for depression.[20]

All these differences suggest that "happiness" is measuring something psychologically different from "distress" or "depression." The societal implications are quite different between these two measures. Greenberg and colleagues have found that unhappy people are not usually functionally impaired, but that depression involves costs in terms of lost wages, productivity, and negative impact on children.[21] The lesson of these studies is that what we measure, as well as whether we include a good comparison, will help us better understand when and how divorce has consequences.

MEASURING DIVORCE'S IMPACT WITH AND WITHOUT A COMPARISON GROUP

In April 2008 the questions about the impact of divorce and its costs continued to be alive and well. Two studies were released the very same week on the topic. These studies asked: What is the impact of divorce? A release from the Council on Contemporary Families was based on demographer Allen Li's research. The other paper by economist Ben Scafidi was released by the Institute for American Values. Li's paper pertained to the emotional impact of divorce on children, while Scafidi's paper addressed the economic impact of divorce across America.[22]

The results in the two papers were completely divergent. Li asked: What is the impact of divorce on children? He found that divorce itself does not explain the differences between children with divorced and married parents. He did find differences between the two groups (on average)—just as researchers have been finding since the 1980s. With increasingly refined research techniques, however, Li was able to show that *selection bias*—or a case of improper comparisons—is what accounts for the differences.

Li's technique included testing for "fixed effects"—a statistical tool used in economics and biomedical research with longitudinal data. Fixed effects models tell us if there are aspects of the individuals that are not measured explicitly but that account for results. The children in Li's study whose parents ended up divorcing were getting a different kind of parenting all along the way from the children whose parents stayed married.

Meanwhile, Scafidi asked: What does divorce cost the general public? Hold on to your hats. By his calculations, divorce—plus single parenthood—costs taxpayers $112 billion a year. To calculate this, he assumed that divorce and single parenthood *cause* poverty. In other words, he neglected the notion that selection bias could play a role in who ends up as a single parent or who gets divorced. In a 2002 report, historian Stephanie Coontz and economist Nancy Folbre examined the problems with assuming that divorce and single parenthood cause poverty by taking into account selection bias.[23] While there is a correlation between single parenthood and poverty, the correlation does not mean that single parenthood *causes* poverty. *Causation* is complex and challenging to establish, but the evidence that causality flows in the other direction—that poverty often *causes* or precedes single parenthood—is to many analysts a lot stronger. As Stevenson and Wolfers point out, Scafidi neglected comparisons in another way as well: while some women end up losing financially following divorce, others actually *gain*.[24] Scafidi did not include these economic gains in his equations.

The results were divergent because of their fundamental differences in thinking about "what causes what?" While Li's article asks, "divorce, *compared to what?*," Scafidi did not assess the costs of divorce relative to, for example, remaining in a distressed, tumultuous, or violent family situation. Scafidi didn't test the premise that divorce (and single parenthood) causes economic problems. He assumed that it did.

Meanwhile, other researchers continue to find that selection bias accounts for some if not all of the differences between children whose parents divorce and children whose parents remain married to each other. For example, in 2007 Fomby and Cherlin found that the characteristics of the mother that precede the divorce helped explain the reduced cognitive outcomes for children of divorce.[25] In their study, they also found that postdisruption effects of the divorce, rather than just selection bias or predisruption effects, also were associated with behavioral problems sometimes seen in children of divorce. Just as research on relationship trajectories may help us understand more details about how and when divorce is difficult on adults, this same promising line of research may further explain the postdisruption effects of divorce on children. It turns out that children exposed to multiple transitions—a divorce, then a cohabitation and breakup, then perhaps another marriage—may be at elevated risk relative to children exposed to only one transition. In a 2007 study that focuses on single parents, Osborne and McLanahan[26] found that the accumulation of a mother's relationship transitions leads to the hardship for her children.

Lessons Learned

Divorce researchers who use comparison groups and control for selection bias, who measure marital quality carefully, and who take domestic violence into account may still disagree about just how different children of divorce are from children of married parents (Are 20 percent affected? Are 25 percent affected?). But they agree about the resilience of children in the face of divorce. Researchers may disagree about whether the impact of divorce is neutral, as Allen Li argues, or whether some of the impact of divorce is due to preexisting factors, or whether some of the impact of divorce should be attributed to postdisruption factors, or whether relationship trajectory research is an important piece of the puzzle about the circumstances under which divorce is harder on children. Scientists agree, however, that comparing married families to divorced families without taking selection bias into account is a case of comparing apples to oranges, and will get us nowhere in terms of helping families. As Rutter, Hawkins, and Hetherington all show, failing to take the quality of the marriages seriously is like ignoring the elephant in the room! The distressed marriage is where most people considering divorce start. And this distress is highly costly to the health and mental health of parents and their children.

If you are reading research on marriage and divorce—or listening to someone's conclusions about it—always remember to ask, "did this study include a comparison group and take selection bias into account?" and "did the researchers measure things—especially marital distress—carefully?"

When I ask these questions—and when I look at the role of divorce in U.S. history—I see a complicated story. Above all, I have discovered that there is a case for divorce. There are times and situations when divorce is beneficial to the people who divorce and to their children.

In the News

HOW TO STAY MARRIED

Times of London, November 30, 2006

Stephanie Coontz

As married couples become a minority, our correspondent argues that the best way to keep a marriage strong and healthy is to retain a close network of friends.

Now, for the first time, married-couple households are a minority in both the UK and the US, outnumbered by single-person households and cohabiting couples. In the US 49 percent of all households contain married couples. In the UK it is even fewer—45 percent in 2005, a drop from 54 percent in 1996. This has caused consternation among people who believe that we could restore the primacy of marriage in modern life if we could just get couples to invest more energy in their marriages. But the idea that a romantic partner can meet all our needs is a very recent invention. Through most of history, marriage was only one of many places where people cultivated long-term commitments. Neighbours, family and friends have been equally important sources of emotional and practical support.

Today, we expect much more intimacy and support from our partners than in the past, but much less from everyone else. This puts a huge strain on the institution of marriage. When a couple's relationship is strong, a marriage can be more fulfilling than ever. But we often overload marriage by asking our partner to satisfy more needs than any one individual can possibly meet, and if our marriage falters, we have few emotional support systems to fall back on.

Men are especially vulnerable after divorce, because they pay less attention to maintaining social ties outside marriage. But women also fall prey to the fantasy that once they find their "soul-mate" they can retreat to an isolated island of marital bliss.

Even the best-matched couples need to find gratification and support from sources other than their partner. When they don't, notes Joshua Coleman, a therapist and author of *The Marriage Makeover*, they have less to offer each other and fewer ways to replenish their relationship. Often the marriage buckles under the weight of the partners' expectations that each will fulfill all the other's needs.

For almost 20 years, Richard Lucas has been studying the self-reported happiness of more than 30,000 individuals. He finds that feelings of happiness increase around the time of marriage, but after a few years people return to their original happiness "set point". People who marry and stay married are slightly happier, on average, than people who never marry, and significantly happier than most people who marry and then divorce. But such individuals already reported higher-than-average happiness before they married. They didn't depend on marriage to make them happy—and that's one reason why they didn't become discontented once the honeymoon wore off. Couples who expect to find the greatest happiness from marriage are prone to the greatest disappointments.

Putting all our emotional eggs in the basket of marriage is a particular problem now that people live unmarried for longer periods of their lives than in the past. When we make romantic love our only source of commitment and obligation, we neglect the wider interpersonal ties that knit society together. This impoverishes the social lives of single and married individuals alike.

Several studies in the US reveal how couples ask love and marriage to meet too many of their interpersonal needs. Over the past two decades, according to research by three American sociologists, the percentage of people who said their spouse was a close confidante rose from 30 to 38 percent. It's good news that more couples are now close friends. But the flip side of this trend is more disturbing. Using US national data from 1992 to 2004, the sociologists Naomi Gerstel and Natalia Sarkisian found that modern married couples are less likely to visit, call, or offer support to parents and siblings than their single counterparts.

Apart from activities with other families when their children are young, married couples are also less likely to hang out with friends and socialise with neighbours. They often distance themselves from single or divorced individuals, even if they were once close to these people. This pattern can come back to haunt them if their own marriage breaks up.

Even as more spouses reported being each other's close confidantes over the past two decades, the number of neighbours, co-workers, club or church members, and extended family with whom Americans discussed important matters dropped sharply. The number of people who reported having four to five confidantes was halved between 1985 and 2004, falling to just 15 percent of the population. And almost half of all Americans now say that there is just one person, or no one at all, with whom they discuss important matters.

In the UK a British social attitudes survey in 1996 found that almost two thirds of married people or those living together said that their first port of call when depressed was their spouse or partner. Thirteen percent said they would turn to a friend first. Roughly the same number said they would turn to extended family.

Popular culture is full of advice on how to take our romantic relationships to a deeper level. One common warning is to avoid letting ties to friends or family "interfere" with the time we spend with our spouse. But trying to be everything to one another is part of the problem, not part of the solution, to the tensions of modern marriage.

Through most of history, it was considered dangerously antisocial to be too emotionally attached to one's spouse, because that diluted loyalties to family, neighbours, and society at large. Until the mid-19th-century, the word "love" was used more frequently to describe feelings for neighbours, relatives and fellow church members than spouses.

The emotional lives of Victorian middle-class women revolved around passionate female bonds that overshadowed the "respectful affection" they felt for their husbands. Men, too, sought intimacy outside the family circle. A man could write a letter to his betrothed recounting his pleasure at falling asleep on the bosom of his best friend without fearing that she might think him gay. When couples first began to go on honeymoons in the 19th century they often took family and friends along for company.

But as modern economic and political trends eroded traditional dependencies on neighbours and local institutions, people began to focus more of their emotions on love and marriage. Society came to view intense same-sex ties with suspicion. Psychologists urged people to rebuff family and neighbours who might compete with the nuclear family for attention. In the postwar "Golden Age of Marriage" people began expecting their spouse to meet more and more of their needs.

The weaknesses of this marriage model soon became apparent. Housewives discovered that they could not find complete fulfillment in domesticity. Many men also felt diminished when they gave up older patterns of socialising to cocoon in the nuclear family.

The women's movement of the 1960s offered a better balance—fairer, more intimate marriages combined with social engagement outside the home. But in the past few decades, our speeded-up global economy has made balance harder and harder to attain, leading us to seek ever more meaning and satisfaction in love and marriage.

I am not suggesting that we lower our expectations of intimacy and friendship in marriage. Instead, I propose that we raise our expectations of other relationships. Emotional obligations to people outside the family can enrich, not diminish, our marital commitments. Society needs to respect and encourage social ties that extend beyond the couple, including those of unmarried individuals, as well as ties between the married and the unmarried.

Taking the emotional pressure off marriage is a win-win situation. The happiest couples are those who have interests, confidantes and support networks extending beyond the twosome. And such networks also make single and divorced people better off.

The best protection against the atomisation of modern life is to structure our workplaces and communities in ways that allow people, whatever their marital status, to sustain commitments beyond the couple relationship and the nuclear family. As Coleman notes, "having friendships and social activities other than marriage is not only good for the self and for society, it's also good for the marriage." ▄

17

Briefing Paper: The Impact of Divorce on Children's Behavior Problems

Jui-Chung Allen Li

M any research studies have shown that, on average, children of divorce have more behavior problems than children growing up in two-parent families. But the question for social scientists is whether the problems seen in the children of divorced parents were caused by the divorce, or whether something else caused *both* the divorce and the children's problems.

Researchers wonder, in particular, whether some couples have personal characteristics and/or parenting patterns that increase the chance that their children will have behavior problems *and also* increase the chance that the couple will be unable to resolve marital issues. If this "something else" causes both divorce and behavior problems, then it is likely that children would still have had problems even if their parents had somehow managed to remain married.

How do we look for that "something else"? We know that it is a mistake to compare children of divorced parents with children of continuously married parents without taking into account differences between divorcing families and continuously married families *prior* to the marital disruption. Parents who are more likely to divorce may also be more likely to be impoverished, to live in disadvantaged neighborhoods, to be less educated, to have been raised in divorced families themselves, or to have more children than average. These factors may impair a child's well-being whether the parents stay together or not, but they may also be more likely to produce a marital disruption.

To test the effect of preexisting family characteristics versus the effect of divorce itself, prior studies have used statistical analysis to "control" for the differences we can see between divorced and continuously married families prior to the disruption. This is done by taking into account the socioeconomic status of the parents, their race or ethnicity, and other "variables" that can be determined by having respondents fill out a paper or computerized questionnaire. Some studies also take into account prior differences in children's well-being in the two types of families prior to the disruption. The old consensus is that taking these preexisting factors into account helps explain some of the association between parental divorce and children's behavior problems—but not all. It reduces the average difference between the two groups but still leaves some average deficits for children of divorce, deficits that are not explained by controlling for these observed differences.

But what about the unique characteristics of each family that we do not as yet have the tools to measure? Things such as personality, parenting strategies, and detailed aspects of a person's biography all affect children, but researchers haven't been able to measure many of these constructs, far less to include them in large-scale studies. Therefore, many studies end up comparing apples and oranges. The proper test of the impact of divorce on children is not to compare the children of divorced parents to the children of continuously married families, and thus risk ignoring all the unobservable factors that may lead both to greater behavior problems and to higher chances of divorce. It works better to compare the behavior problems of the same child before and after divorce. So, traditional methods often do not adequately estimate the impact on children of being in a family that is headed for divorce.

Several recent studies, including one of my own, which use more advanced and sophisticated research methods, present a powerful challenge to the old consensus that the average impact of divorce on children is negative. These studies are able to eliminate the impact of both "observable" and "unobservable" family differences that result in variations in child outcome, independent of divorce, and this provides a more accurate estimate of the "true" impact of divorce.

All these new studies have discovered the same thing: The average impact of divorce in society at large is to neither increase nor decrease the behavior problems of children. They suggest that divorce, in and of itself, is not the cause of the elevated behavior problems we see in children of divorce. These studies include Aughinbaugh, Pierret, and Rothstein (2005), Foster and Kalil (2007), and Li (2007).

My Study

While previous studies have compared the outcomes of children whose parents divorced to those of children whose parents remained together, I use a longitudinal study that measures changes in the behavior of children whose parents were not divorced at the beginning of the study but who divorced later. This allows me to investigate the counterfactual question, "What would have happened to the children's behavior if their parents had remained married?" For an example of how this method works, and why other methods tend to overestimate the impact of divorce on children's behavior problems, see the Appendix at the end of this report.

The data I used included all children born to a national representative sample of American women who themselves had been born between 1958 and 1965. These women had been surveyed repeatedly since 1979, and their children had been surveyed since 1988. Forty-seven percent of these mothers in my sample had been divorced by 2002. I used a twenty-eight-item checklist to measure behavior problems for children between four and fifteen years of age. Mothers in each of the biennial surveys filled out a questionnaire about whether their child engaged in behaviors such as cheating, deliberately breaking things, crying or arguing frequently, and so forth. The mother of an average boy reported 8.7 items and the mother of an average girl reported 7.8 items that were often or sometimes true.

My study included a national sample of 6,332 children. It revealed that the estimated effect of a parental divorce on children's behavior problems is so small that fewer than half of the divorced mothers would observe a one-item increase in the twenty-eight-item BPI checklist of their child. This is not a statistically significant effect.

Why would I get this result when other carefully constructed studies, which controlled for observed differences, found larger, and statistically significant effects of divorce? The kind of observed differences that show up in surveys may fail to catch subtle differences between families in which the parents eventually divorce and those in which they do not. For example, certain aspects of child temperament and behavior are associated with parental personality traits that may be hereditary. If a child has parents with difficult temperaments and divorce-prone personality traits, the child will likely exhibit greater behavior problems whether or not the parents divorce, but the child will also be exposed to a higher risk of parental divorce. Or take the fact that the resources parents are able and willing to provide for their children may vary dramatically across marriages and across divorces. If so, there may be "good" parents and "bad" parents, as well as "good" spouses and "bad" spouses. It is plausible that a "bad" spouse may well have been a "bad" parent prior to marital disruption (and may, thus, have been a factor in causing the disruption).

Disengaged or unloving parents are detrimental to children's emotional well-being and behavior. The lack of love on the part of one or both parents may increase the chance that the parents will divorce, but it may also create behavior problems in children, whether or not their parents divorce. If so, we should not attribute the worse behavior of their children to the divorce itself, but to the impact of the unloving parent or parents. The point is that "bad" marriages are more likely to harm children's well-being than good ones *and* more likely to lead to divorce, and a marriage can be "bad" in many unobserved ways.

I am not saying that divorce doesn't increase the behavior problems of some children, because I have focused only on the "average effect of divorce for the divorced." It is possible that the dissolution of some marriages decreases some children's behavior problems and the dissolution of others increases children's behavior problems, so that they cancel each other out, creating the zero effect that I found when I totaled the average effect of divorce. But for this to be true, one must admit that while certain divorces harm children, others benefit them. My findings contradict the widely accepted claim that *most* divorces increase children's behavior problems and that only a tiny minority of divorces do *not*.

It should be noted that my findings are only relevant to the kind of marriages where parents have qualities that make them likely to divorce. They should not be interpreted to imply that breaking up a randomly selected marriage in society would not lead to increased behavior problems for the children. But these findings do imply that to help children of divorce, social scientists and policy makers should seek to understand and intervene in the processes both before and after a marriage comes apart, rather than seeking to simply prevent the divorce from occurring.

APPENDIX: HOW DID I GET MY RESULTS?

Fixed-effects modeling, which is often used by economists, also helps us to understand the complex behavior of people in families.

To understand my method, consider two children of divorced parents, where the divorces occurred when they were both age nine. Suppose we measure their behavior problems once every two years, as I in fact did with a much larger sample. Here is a stylized example to illustrate conceptually how my method and the traditional method would yield different results in assessing the impact of divorce on children's behavior problems:

Age	4	6	8	10	12	14	
Kid A	7	7	7	9	9	9	(parents divorced at age 9)
Kid B	8	8	8	8	8	8	(parents divorced at age 9)

For Kid A, the effect of divorce is a two-item increase on the behavior problem index; for Kid B, the effect is 0.

Now consider two more children whose parents are continuously married:

Age	4	6	8	10	12	14	
Kid C	6	6	6	6	6	6	(parents not divorced, up to age 14+)
Kid D	4	4	4	4	4	4	(parents not divorced, up to age 14+)

The traditional estimate of the effect of divorce would take the average behavior problems of Kids A and B (which is eight), and the average of Kids C and D (which is five), and then calculate the difference between the two averages. The difference between the kids in the divorcing group and the kids in the nondivorcing group would then be a three-item increase.

The new way of looking at this is called a fixed-effects estimate. Instead of comparing the divorced kids to the kids from married families, I compare them to themselves, before and after parental divorce. I do this by averaging the pre- and post-divorce differences for Kids A $(9 - 7 = 2)$ and B $(8 - 8 = 0)$. Hence, the fixed-effects estimate of the effect is a one-item increase in behavior problems, a much lower estimate of the impact of divorce.

Or consider another child, whose behavior began to deteriorate before the divorce (again at age nine) and continued to do so afterwards:

Age	4	6	8	10	12	14
Kid E	6	7	8	9	10	11

Notice that between ages four and eight, prior to the divorce, the child's behavior problem went up by one every two years. Had the parents avoided the divorce, we would have expected that the child's behavior problems would have continued to increase at the same rate. In other words, if the trajectory of a child's behavior problems stayed at its predisruption course after the divorce, we should not claim that there is any impact of divorce because that is what would have happened had the parents remained married. This example also illustrates another subtle point that even the previous fixed-effects estimate may overstate the impact of divorce if the unobserved factors operate in a way that changes the level of child well-being but does not alter the trajectory in child well-being. Consider how we calculate the fixed-effects estimate by taking the difference between the pre- and post-divorce averages: The estimated effect will be $(9 + 10 + 11)/3 - (6 + 7 + 8)/3 = 10 - 7 = 3$ under the fixed-effects specification, whereas under the "random-trends" specification, controlling for dynamic selection [ugh, technical], the estimated effect is 0.

In the News

DIVORCE MAY NOT CAUSE KIDS' BAD BEHAVIOR

USA Today, April 24, 2008

Sharon Jayson

Divorce often gets blamed for a host of troubles faced by children whose parents split, and much past research has focused on the damage to children's well-being.

But new research suggests that at least in one segment of overall well-being—bad behavior—divorce doesn't appear to be the reason for some behavior problems.

"It really depends on the individual marriages and the family," says Allen Li, associate director of the Population Research Center at the RAND Corporation in Santa Monica, Calif. "My conclusion is that divorce is neither bad nor good."

His findings, to be presented Saturday in Chicago at a meeting of the non-profit Council on Contemporary Families, contrast with a body of research about divorce's effect on children that some researchers say has overestimated the difficulty that parents' divorce causes for children.

A review of marriage research released in a 2005 journal published by the Brookings Institution and Princeton University suggested that children from two-parent families are better off emotionally, socially and economically. Other research, released the same year in a book by Elizabeth Marquardt, a vice president at the conservative Institute for American Values in New York, found that an unhappy marriage without a lot of conflict is better for children than divorce.

Others, including Robert Emery of the University of Virginia at Charlottesville, agree that much past research has been overly simplistic in assuming divorce causes the behavior problems. But he adds that he believes Li's conclusions "are too strong."

"Divorce still does have consequences for kids," he says.

Li's study of 6,332 children is significant for its large sample, as well as a new statistical model used in the analysis. Also, unlike many previous studies on the effect of divorce on children, Li doesn't compare the children of married parents with the children of divorced parents. Rather, he took a longitudinal approach and examined children's behavior before and after their parents split.

His 28-item checklist measured behavior problems, such as crying, cheating or arguing frequently, from ages 4 to 15. He found a slight post-divorce increase in bad behavior that he says is so small it is not statistically significant. The trajectory of misbehavior that started before the divorce might well have continued, even if the parents had not divorced, he says.

By contrast, Marquardt compared the children of divorced families with those of married parents. She defends that approach as valid. "What he's doing is controlling for so many things he's making the effects of divorce disappear," she says. "People like me have some real qualms about that."

In the early 1990s, research by social demographer Andrew Cherlin of Johns Hopkins University in Baltimore looked at children before and after parents divorced and compared them with children with married parents. He found that some of the problems children showed after the divorce were apparent before the split.

"Some of the problems we attribute to divorce are present before a child's parents divorce. The implication is they might have happened anyway," he says. "Not all of the problems children of divorce show are due to divorce."

But he says that's not the whole story.

"My line on this is that most children are not seriously affected by divorce in the long-term, but divorce raises the risk that a child will have problems," Cherlin says.

In the News

THE GOOD, BAD, AND UGLY OF DIVORCE

Washington Times, June 29, 2008

Cheryl Wetzstein

Few people, if any, would call themselves pro-divorce, at least in polite company. But are you anti-divorce? Or anti-anti-divorce?

Consider some recent studies about divorce and its impact on wallets, children and adult relationships.

On April 15–"tax day"–leaders of the Institute for American Values (IAV) and three conservative groups released a study that said divorce and unwed childbearing cost taxpayers $112 billion a year in welfare, criminal justice, health care and lost tax revenue.

Their public-policy recommendations? Reduce the number of divorces and increase the number of married, two-parent families.

A few days later, the Council on Contemporary Families highlighted a study by Rand Corp. researcher Jui-Chung Allen Li called, "The Kids Are OK: Divorce and Children's Behavior Problems."

Mr. Li crunched a lot of numbers and found that divorce exacerbates problem behaviors in some children, but reduces them in other children. Because these outcomes "cancel each other out," he said, the average effect of divorce on children's behavior problems is zero. "Divorce is neither harmful nor helpful for this measure of children's well-being," he concluded.

Mr. Li's public-policy recommendation? Stop worrying so much about preventing divorce per se, and give families some help before–or after–the deed is done. Government also should become "neutral" on marital status and base neither penalties nor incentives on it.

If Mr. Li's paper is anti-anti-divorce, so is research conducted by Betsey Stevenson and Justin Wolfers, assistant professors at the Wharton School at the University of Pennsylvania.

The professors disputed the IAV study's findings about the costs of divorce, saying IAV failed to account for the financial benefits that some women experience after divorce. Moreover, the professors said, no-fault divorce is associated with other positive benefits, such as an 8 percent decline in the suicide rate for women, 30 percent decline in domestic violence and 10 percent decline in the number of women murdered by their partners.

So I ask you, the reading public, which is it? Is divorce a mostly good thing or a mostly bad thing for couples, children and the country?

One thing's for sure: Without a public consensus on even a basic question like is divorce mostly good or bad, there's little political will to change divorce laws.

Certainly, many readers will have their personal answers about divorce. About 23 million American men and 27 million American women have experienced divorce, and each one has an answer to the famous "Dear Abby" question, "Are you better off with him or without him?" (Or her.)

U.S. divorce rates have edged down to the same level as in 1970, which is a good thing. But young adults' skittishness about marriage is causing them to delay marriage—or skip it entirely, in favor of cohabiting, which is another subject.

My question is what do you, the reading public, want to do about divorce?

Do you want to hear more about the "upsides" of divorce, i.e., how it provides essential relief for marital meltdown?

Do you want to hear more about the need for a stronger "good divorce" industry with support groups, mental-health counselors and move-on tools to speed recovery? If this is your view, please speak up.

Or, have you seen enough about divorce to conclude that it's mostly bad for adults, children and society. If that's the case, what do you want to do about it? Do you want no-fault divorce laws changed? Do you want to hear more about what divorce actually has meant to people's lives?

Do you think divorce rates can be "greatly" reduced, or do you think that's just a nostalgic pipe dream?

Please consider this column as the first in a long discussion. A lot of people already are talking about the future of divorce, but are you part of the conversation? Please speak up. ▰

18

Briefing Paper: How Do They Do That?

Estimating the Proportion of Marriages That End in Divorce

Patrick Heuveline

One of the most frequently cited statistics about divorce in the United States is that half of all marriages end in divorce. Often this proportion is then used to predict the chance that any given ("average") marriage will end in divorce.

At first glance it may seem easy to measure the proportion of marriages that will end in divorce. After all, all marriages must eventually end, either in death or divorce. So the proportion of marriages that end in divorce is simply the ratio of divorces to the total number of marriages that have ended. But the problem arises when you try to determine what will happen to people marrying today by using a measure derived from the past, from marriages that have all already ended, especially when the phenomenon you are trying to measure is changing over time. And as regards divorce, times have been changing.

Take the following assertion from the March 5, 2005, issue of *The Economist*: "Unlike marriage, divorce shows no sign of going out of style" in England and Wales. The article goes on to state that "for every 100 weddings [in 2003] there were 57 divorces." Many observers yield to the same temptation to compute the ratio of divorces in a given year to weddings in that year because it is easy to access from vital statistics and can be based on marriages and divorces in a recent year, which skirts all the problems of having to examine marital events from the past. But this ratio is not very useful because it divides apples by oranges. Except perhaps in Hollywood, the people who divorce in a given year are rarely the same people who married that year. Even if the risk of divorce were constant, and a doubling in the number of marriages one year would result in a doubling of the number of divorces, the rise in divorces would not take place in the same year as the rise in marriages.

For example, if there is a big rise in marriages in a given year, that will make the ratio of divorces to marriages for that year drop significantly. Similarly, if the annual rate of marriages is dropping, as it has been in England and Wales, then the ratio of divorces per weddings in a given year is going to rise and will overestimate the chance that any particular marriage will end in divorce.

Demographers use a very different measure to determine from recent marital data the chance that any given marriage will end in divorce. That tool is the life table. Using the life table to compute the likelihood of divorce is more difficult than simply dividing divorces in a given year by marriages that same year, but the underlying idea is relatively simple. The life table builds on the observation that the risk of divorce varies strongly by marriage duration. The divorce rate typically increases after marriage to a high about three years later, and then decreases with the duration of the marriage. So we begin by examining the data on marriages and divorces by duration. We can calculate the proportions of marriages that ended in divorce in a given year for marriages contracted that same year, the year before, two years before, ten years before, and so on. The life table then splices together all these proportions to represent how many marriages are still likely to remain intact after "n" years of marriage. In practice, life table estimates are most often based on sample surveys, with the respondents reporting on their own experiences.

A survey-based life table study of the net risk of divorce for fifteen- to forty-four-year-old women in 1995 found that the proportion of first marriages having ended in divorce was 20 percent five years after marriage, 33 percent after ten years, and 43 percent after fifteen years. Since the risk of divorce in the next year decreases the longer a marriage has survived, the fact that the rate was 43 percent within fifteen years suggests that the 50 percent figure is roughly correct for the total life span of recent cohorts. For second marriages, the likelihood of divorce was higher, already reaching 39 percent after ten years of marriage.

The life table is the widely accepted approach to estimating the proportion of marriages that end in divorce. But when we project into the future, we have to bear in mind that the table only tells us the proportion of marriages that will end in divorce if marriages were subjected throughout their duration to the risk of divorce observed during the most recent year for which there is data. In that sense, it functions like a car speedometer. It only indicates how many miles will be driven in the next hour if a constant miles-per-hour speed is maintained. An experienced driver knows she must wait until her speed has stabilized before making any mileage inferences from her speedometer. So too demographers know that estimations can be greatly distorted when conditions are rapidly changing.

For instance, the introduction of laws making divorce easier to obtain may result in people getting divorced earlier than they otherwise would have, even if it doesn't affect the total proportion getting divorced. We must take this "timing" bias into account or we may misread the life table estimates computed just after the change takes effect. Just after divorce becomes easier to obtain, we are likely to see a greater incidence of divorce among long-married people who were previously forced to stay together. So there will be a temporary spike in the divorce rate among people married for longer durations. But people married more recently won't face the same obstacles to divorce in the future and will therefore be less likely to divorce after a long period of marriage.

In retrospect, life table estimates of the proportion of marriages ending in divorce based on data from the 1970s and early 1980s seem to have slightly overestimated the divorce rate to be expected. But the life table estimates were still more useful than the alternatives discussed at the outset of this paper. Moreover, in the 1990s, the proportion of a marriage cohort getting a divorce and the timing of that divorce appear to have stabilized, correcting that earlier slight overestimation of the divorce rate. Today, the proportion of first marriages that will eventually end in divorce appears to be very close to one-half, while it is slightly higher for second and other marriages, and slightly lower for marriages with children.

19

Briefing Paper: Marriage, Poverty, and Public Policy

Stephanie Coontz and Nancy Folbre

One of the stated objectives of welfare legislation passed in 1996 was "to end dependence by promoting marriage." With this legislation coming up for reauthorization, many policy makers want to devote more public resources to this goal, even if it requires cutting spending on cash benefits, child care, or job training. Some states, such as West Virginia, already use their funds to provide a special bonus to couples on public assistance who get married.[1] In December 2001, more than fifty state legislators asked Congress to divert funds from existing programs into marriage education and incentive policies, earmarking dollars to encourage welfare recipients to marry and giving bonus money to states that increase marriage rates. On February 26, 2002, President Bush called for spending up to $300 million a year to promote marriage among poor people.[2]

Such proposals reflect the widespread assumption that failure to marry, rather than unemployment, poor education, and lack of affordable child care, is the primary cause of child poverty. Voices from both sides of the political spectrum urge us to get more women to the altar. Journalist Jonathan Rauch argues that "marriage is displacing both income and race as the great class divide of the new century."[3] Robert Rector of the Heritage Foundation claims that "the sole reason that welfare exists is the collapse of marriage."[4] In this briefing paper, we question both this explanation of poverty and the policy prescriptions that derive from it.

Marriage offers important social and economic benefits. Children who grow up with married parents generally enjoy a higher standard of living than those living in single-parent households. Two parents are usually better than one not only because they can bring home two paychecks, but also because they can share responsibilities for child care. Marriage often leads to higher levels of paternal involvement than divorce, non-marriage, or cohabitation. Long-term commitments to provide love and support to one another are beneficial for adults, as well as children.

Public policies toward marriage could and should be improved.[5] Taxes or benefit reductions that impose a marriage penalty on low-income couples are inappropriate and should be eliminated. Well-designed public policies could play a constructive role in helping couples develop the skills they need to develop healthy and sustainable relationships with each other and their children. It does not follow, however, that marriage promotion should be a significant component of antipoverty policy, or that public policies should provide a "bonus" to couples who marry.

The current pro-marriage agenda in antipoverty policy is misguided for at least four reasons:

- Non-marriage is often a result of poverty and economic insecurity rather than the other way around.

- The quality and stability of marriages matters. Prodding couples into matrimony without helping them solve problems that make relationships precarious could leave them worse off.

- Two-parent families are not immune from the economic stresses that put children at risk. More than one-third of all impoverished young children in the United States today live with two parents.

- Single parenthood does not inevitably lead to poverty. In countries with a more adequate social safety net than the United States, single-parent families are much less likely to live in poverty. Even within the United States, single mothers with high levels of education fare relatively well.

In this briefing paper, we summarize recent empirical evidence concerning the relationship between marriage and poverty, and we develop the four points above in more detail. We also emphasize the need to develop a larger antipoverty program that provides the jobs, education, and child care that poor families need in order to move toward self-sufficiency.

THE ECONOMIC CONTEXT

Children living with married parents generally fare better than others in terms of family income. In 2000, 6 percent of married couple families with children lived in poverty, compared with 33 percent of female householders with children.[6] Mothers who never marry are more vulnerable to poverty than virtually any other group, including those who have been divorced.[7]

But the low income associated with single parenthood reflects many interrelated factors. Income is distributed far more unequally in the United States than in most other developed countries, making it difficult for low-wage workers (male or female) to support a family without a second income. Women who become single mothers are especially likely to have inadequate wages, both because of preexisting disadvantages such as low educational attainment and work experience and because the shortage of publicly subsidized child care makes it difficult for them to work full time. In 2000, only 1.2 percent of children of single mothers with a college degree who worked full-time year-round lived in poverty.[8] For single mothers with some college who were working full-time, the poverty rate was less than 8 percent.[9]

Whether single or married, working parents face high child-care costs that are seldom factored into calculations of poverty and income. Consider the situation of a single mother with two children working full-time, year-round at the minimum wage of $5.15 an hour, for a yearly income of $10,712. If she files for and receives the maximum Earned Income Tax Credit (EITC), she can receive as much as $3,816 in public assistance. But the EITC phases out quickly if she earns much more than the minimum wage and if her child-care costs are very high. Unless she is lucky enough to have a family member who can provide free child care, or to find a federally subsidized child-care slot, more than 20 percent of her income will go to pay for child care.[10] Federally subsidized child care remains quite limited. Most families who made a transition from welfare to employment in the 1990s did not receive a subsidy.[11]

The high cost of child care helps explain why the economic position of single parents has improved little in recent years despite significant increases in their hours of market work.[12] It may also explain why single parents are likely to live in households with other adults who can share expenses with them. About 40 percent of births to single mothers take place among cohabitors, and much of the increase in nonmarital childbearing in recent years reflects this trend rather than an increase among women living without a partner.[13] The economic stress associated with reductions in welfare benefits over the past six years may have increased the pressure on single mothers to cohabit, often with partners who are unwilling or unlikely to marry.[14]

On both a symbolic and a practical level, marriage facilitates the income pooling and task sharing that allows parents to accommodate family needs.[15] Not surprisingly, many low-income families consider marriage the ideal arrangement for child rearing.[16] The Fragile Families and Child Welfare project currently underway in about twenty cities shows that about 50 percent of unmarried parents of newborns live together and hope to marry at some point.[17] Lower expectations among some couples were associated not with disinterest in marriage but with reports of drug or alcohol problems, physical violence, conflict, and mistrust.[18]

The advantages of marriage, however, do not derive simply from having two names on a marriage certificate, and they cannot be acquired merely by going through a formality. Rather, they grow out of a long-term and economically sustainable commitment that many people feel is beyond their reach.

CAUSALITY WORKS BOTH WAYS

Liking the abstract idea of marriage and being able to put together a stable marriage in real life are two very different things. Unemployment, low wages, and poverty discourage family formation and erode family stability, making it less likely that individuals will marry in the first place and more likely that their marriages will deteriorate. These economic factors have long-term as well as short-term effects, contributing to changes in social norms regarding marriage and family formation and exacerbating distrust between men and women. These long-term effects help explain why African Americans marry at much lower rates than other groups within the U.S. population. Poverty is a cause as well as a consequence of non-marriage and of marital disruption.[19]

Dan Lichter of Ohio State University puts it this way: "Marriage can be a pathway from poverty, but only if women are 'marriageable,' stay married, and marry well."[20] Precisely because marriage offers economic advantages, individuals tend to seek potential spouses who have good earnings potential and to avoid marriage when they do not feel they or their potential mates can comfortably support a family. Ethnographic research shows that low-income women see economic stability on the part of a prospective partner as a necessary precondition for marriage.[21] Not surprisingly, men increasingly use the same calculus. Rather than looking for someone they can "rescue" from poverty, employed men are much more likely to marry women who themselves have good employment prospects.[22]

Poor mothers who lack a high school degree and any regular employment history are not likely to fare very well in the so-called "marriage market." Teenage girls who live in areas of high unemployment and inferior schools are five to seven times more likely to become unwed parents than more fortunately situated teens.[23] A study of the National Longitudinal Survey of Youth confirms that poor women, whatever their age, and regardless of whether or not they are or have ever been on welfare, are less likely to marry than women who are not poor. Among poor women, those who do not have jobs are less likely to marry than those who do.[24]

It is easy to spin a hypothetical scenario in which marrying off single mothers to an average male would raise family incomes and reduce poverty. But unmarried males, and especially unmarried males in impoverished neighborhoods, are not average. That is often the reason they are not married. Researchers from the Center for Research on Child Well-Being at Princeton University report results from the Fragile Families Survey showing that unmarried fathers were twice as likely as married ones to have a physical or psychological problem that interfered with their ability to find or keep a job, and several times more likely to abuse drugs or alcohol. More than 25 percent of unmarried fathers were not employed when their child was born, compared to fewer than 10 percent of married fathers.[25]

Poor mothers tend to live in neighborhoods in which their potential marriage partners are also likely to be poorly educated and irregularly employed. Low-earning men are less likely to get married and more likely to divorce than men with higher earnings.[26] Over the past thirty years, labor market opportunities for men with low levels of education have declined substantially.[27] Several studies suggest that the decrease in real wages for low-income men during the 1980s and early 1990s contributed significantly to lower marriage rates in those years.[28]

This trend has been exacerbated by the high incarceration rates for men convicted of nonviolent crimes, such as drug use. While in jail, these men are not available for women to marry, and their diminished job prospects after release permanently impair their marriageability. High rates of incarceration among black males, combined with high rates of mortality, have led to a decidedly tilted sex ratio within the African-American population, and a resulting scarcity of marriageable men.[29] One study of the marriage market in the 1980s found that at age twenty-five there were three unmarried black women for every black man who had adequate earnings.[30] As Ron Mincy of Columbia University emphasizes, simple pro-marriage policies are likely to offer less benefit to African-American families than policies encouraging responsible fatherhood and paternal engagement.[31]

In short, the notion that we could end child poverty by marrying off impoverished women does not take into account the realities of life among the population most likely to be poor. It is based on abstract scenarios that ignore the many ways in which poverty diminishes people's ability to build and sustain stable family relationships.

QUALITY MATTERS

Happy, healthy, stable marriages offer important benefits to adults and children. But not all marriages fit this description. Marital distress leads to harsh and inconsistent parenting, whether or not parents stay together. Studies show that a marriage marked by conflict, jealousy, and anger is often worse for children's well-being than divorce or residence from birth in a stable single-parent family.[32] For instance, research shows that while children born to teenagers who were already married do better than children born to never-married teens, children born to teen parents who married *after* the birth do worse on some measures, probably because of the high conflict that accompanies marriages entered into with ambivalence or under pressure. Some research suggests that, among low-income African-American families, children from single-parent homes show higher educational achievement than their counterparts from two-parent homes.[33]

The idea that marriage can solve the problems of children in impoverished families ignores the complex realities of these families. The Fragile Families study shows that many low-income parents of newborn children already have children from previous relationships. Thus, their marriages would not create idealized biological families, but rather blended families in which child support enforcement and negotiation among stepparents would complicate relationships.[34] A recent study of families in poor neighborhoods in Boston, Chicago, and San Antonio also reveals complex patterns of cohabitation and co-parenting.[35]

Marriage to a stepfather may improve a mother's economic situation, but it does not necessarily improve outcomes for children and in some cases leads to more problems than continued residence in a stable single-parent family. Even if programs succeed in getting first-time parents married, there is no guarantee that the couples will stay married. Research shows that marriages contracted in the 1960s in order to "legitimate" a child were highly likely to end in divorce.[36] Multiple transitions in and out of marriage are worse for children psychologically than residence in the same kind of family, whatever its form, over long periods of time.[37]

Women and children in economically precarious situations are particularly vulnerable to domestic violence.[38] While it may be true that cohabiting couples are more prone to violence than married couples, this is probably because of what social scientists call a "selection effect": People in nonabusive relationships are more likely to get married. Encouraging women in an unstable cohabiting relationship to marry their partners would not necessarily protect them or their children. Indeed, the first serious violent episode in an unstable relationship sometimes occurs only after the couple has made a formal commitment.[39]

Even when it does not take a violent form, bad fathering can be worse than no fathering. For instance, the National Center on Addiction and Substance Abuse at Columbia University found that while teens in two-parent families are, on average, much less likely to abuse drugs or alcohol than teens in one-parent ones, teens in two-parent families who have a poor to fair relationship with their father are *more* likely to do so than teens in the average one-parent family.[40]

Furthermore, even good marriages are vulnerable to dissolution. The current risks of a marriage ending in divorce are quite high, although they have come down from their peak in 1979–1981. It is now estimated that approximately 40 percent of marriages will end in divorce, and the risk of divorce is elevated among people with low income and insecure jobs. Sociologist Scott South calculates that every time the unemployment rate rises by 1 percent, approximately 10,000 additional divorces occur.[41] Comparing the income of single-parent families and married-couple families in any particular year leads to an overly optimistic assessment of the benefits of marriage, because it ignores the possibility of marital dissolution.

Marriage may provide a temporary improvement in a woman's economic prospects without conferring any secure, long-term protection for her children. Indeed, if marriage encourages mothers to withdraw from paid employment for a time, this can lower their future earnings and increase the wage penalty that they incur from motherhood itself.[42]

TWO-PARENT FAMILIES ARE ALSO UNDER STRESS

Poverty among children is not confined to single-parent families. In 2000, about 38 percent of all poor young children lived in two-parent homes.[43] These families have been largely overlooked in the debates over antipoverty programs and marriage. Indeed, the campaign to increase marriage has overlooked one of the most important public policy issues facing the United States: the growing economic gap between parents, whether married or unmarried, and non-parents.

The costs of raising children have increased in recent years, partly because of the expansion of opportunities for women in the labor market and partly because of the longer time children spend in school. The lack of public support for parenting has also contributed to a worsening of the economic position of parents relative to non-parents.[44] Unlike other advanced industrial countries, the United States fails to provide paid family leaves for parents, and levels of publicly subsidized support for child care remain comparatively low. Most employment practices penalize workers who take time away from paid responsibilities to provide family care.[45] The high cost of parenting in this country helps explain many of the economic disadvantages that women face relative to men.[46] It may also help explain why many men are reluctant to embrace paternal responsibilities.

THE NEED FOR A BETTER SOCIAL SAFETY NET

The association of single parenthood with poverty is not inevitable. In Canada and France, single mothers—and children in general—are far less likely to live in poverty. Sweden and Denmark, which have higher rates of out-of-wedlock births, have much lower rates of child poverty and hunger than does the United States. The reason for the difference is simple: These countries devote a greater percentage of their resources to assisting families with children than we do.[47] Similarly, dramatic differences in child poverty rates within our country reflect differences in tax, child care, and income assistance policies across states.[48]

Fans of the 1996 welfare reform law point to a dramatic decline in the welfare rolls since its enactment. Much of this decline is attributable to the economic boom and resulting low unemployment rates of the late 1990s. Despite promises that work requirements and time limits would lead to a more generous package of assistance for those who "followed the rules," cash benefits have declined. Between 1994 and 1999, the real value of maximum benefits fell in most states, with an overall decline in inflation-adjusted value of about 11 percent.[49] Average benefits declined even more, as recipients increased their earnings. Indeed, the declining value of benefits is another reason why caseloads have fallen.[50]

Punitive attitudes, as well as time limits, have discouraged many eligible families from applying for assistance. The Census Bureau estimates that less than 30 percent of children in poverty resided in a family that received cash public assistance in 1998.[51] Take-up rates for Food Stamps and Medicaid have declined in recent years.[52] The implementation of the new Children's Health Insurance program has been quite uneven. As a result, states have saved money, but many children have gone without the food or medical care they needed. Public support for child care increased on both the federal and the state level. Still, most families who made a transition from welfare to work in the late 1990s did not receive a subsidy.[53]

During the economic boom of the late 1990s, increases in earnings among single parents helped make up for declining welfare benefits. As a result, poverty rates among children declined from a high of about 21 percent in 1996 to about 16 percent in 2000.[54] But these figures do not take into account the costs of child care and other work-related expenses, and they offer little hope for the future of children in low-income families as unemployment rates once again begin to climb.[55]

The most important federal policy promoting the welfare of low-income families is currently the Earned Income Tax Credit (EITC), a fully refundable tax credit aimed at low-income families with children. Because benefits are closely tied to earnings, and phase out steeply after family income reaches $12,460, the EITC imposes a significant penalty on two-earner married couples, who are less likely to benefit from it than either single-parent families or married couples with a spouse at home. This penalty is unfair and should be eliminated.

Other problems with the EITC, however, should be addressed at the same time. Families with two children receive the maximum benefit, which means that low-income families with three or more children do not receive any additional assistance. More than a third of all children in the country live in families with three or more children. Partly as a result of limited EITC coverage, these families are prone to significantly higher poverty rates.[56] Furthermore, the EITC is phased out in ways that penalize middle-income families, who currently enjoy less public support for child rearing than the affluent.[57] An expanded unified tax credit for families with children could address this problem.[58]

Given the pressing need for improvements in basic social safety net programs and the threat of rising unemployment, it is unconscionable to reallocate already inadequate. Temporary Assistance to Needy Families (TANF) funds to policies designed to promote marriage or provide a "marriage bonus." There is little evidence that such policies would in fact increase marriage rates or reduce poverty among children. Indeed, the main effect of marriage bonuses would probably be to impose a "non-marriage" penalty that would have a particularly negative impact on African-American children, who are significantly less likely to live with married parents than either whites or Hispanics.[59] As Julianne Malveaux points out in her discussion of the Bush marriage bonus proposal, "a mere $100 million can be considered chump change. But the chump who could have been changed is the unemployed worker who misses out on job training because some folks find those programs—but not marriage-promotion programs—a waste."[60]

Well-designed programs to help individuals develop and improve family relationships may be a good idea. However, they should be integrated into a larger provision of public health services, or built into existing health insurance programs (mandating, for instance, that both public and private health insurance cover family counseling). Such programs also should not be limited to couples who are married or planning to marry. Fathers and stepfathers who are not living with their biological children also need guidance and encouragement to develop healthy, nurturing relationships with their children. Gay and lesbian families— who are currently legally prohibited from marriage—also merit assistance.

Public policies should not penalize marriage. Neither should they provide an economic bonus or financial incentive to individuals to marry, especially at the cost of lowering the resources available to children living with single mothers. Such a diversion of resources from public assistance programs penalizes the children of unmarried parents without guaranteeing good outcomes for the children of people who *are* married. A variety of public policies could help strengthen families and reduce poverty among all children, including a broadening of the Earned Income Tax Credit, expansion of publicly subsidized child care, efforts to promote responsible fatherhood, improvements in public education and job training, and efforts to reduce income inequality and pay discrimination. Unlike some of the pro-marriage policies now under consideration, these policies would benefit couples who wish to marry but would not pressure women to enter or remain in intimate relationships they would not otherwise choose.

In the News

A POOR EXCUSE FOR MARRIAGE

Washington Post, March 26, 2002

Abigail Trafford

The woman is doing everything in reverse. She is divorcing the father of her 7-month-old baby and going from work to welfare.

This is the opposite of what Washington wants poor young women to do. The Bush administration is proposing a $300 million program to encourage women on welfare to get married. Meanwhile it wants more of the moms to hold jobs and work longer hours.

But this woman, 22, who lives in Staunton, Va., is doing neither because she wants to do what's best for herself and her baby.

She is getting a divorce because her husband is an alcoholic and he beat her. "She had to leave the marriage," says her case manager, Ginger Sharrer, who works for a private company that provides employment services for government agencies. "It's not realistic to push people into a marital situation when there's a potential for domestic abuse."

The woman is quitting her 40-hour-a-week job at a food processing plant because she can't earn enough at $7 an hour to cover child care. Day care costs alone run $85 a week.

So welfare is her best option. Besides, with no income, she would be eligible for a federal grant to go to college. She is bright, ambitious. Chances are that with more education, she'll be able to get a better job—and a better husband.

"This is the smartest thing she could do," says Sharrer.

Smart women, few choices. This is the reality that many poor mothers face. It's why promoting marriage as an anti-poverty measure is doomed to fail.

"The notion that we could end child poverty by marrying off impoverished women does not take into account the realities of life among the population most likely to be poor," conclude family researchers Stephanie Coontz and Nancy Folbre in a report to the Council on Contemporary Families. "Such proposals reflect the widespread assumption that failure to marry, rather than unemployment, poor education and lack of affordable child care, is the primary cause of child poverty."

Everyone wants a good marriage. Children are more likely to thrive in a good home with two stable, nurturing parents. There are obvious economic benefits to growing up in a dual-income family. In 2000, only 6 percent of married couples with children were poor, compared with 33 percent of unmarried women with children.

Unfortunately these statistics have given rise to several myths about the marriage-poverty link. The first myth is that marriage protects against poverty the way a vaccination prevents measles—as though non-marriage were a social virus that causes poverty. In fact, it's the other way around. Being unmarried is often a consequence of being poor.

"Poor mothers who lack a high school degree and any regular employment history are not likely to fare very well in the so-called 'marriage market,'" point out Coontz and Folbre in their report, "Marriage, Poverty, and Public Policy." Because of the economic advantages of marriage, people seek out prospective mates who have good earning potential. Poor men and women are both at a disadvantage. They are less likely to marry—and more likely to divorce—than those who aren't poor.

The second myth is that single motherhood is a ticket to poverty. For women with a good education, that's not so. Only a little over 1 percent of single mothers with a college education and a full-time job live in poverty. Education can do more to improve the economic outlook for a single woman and her children than a marriage license.

The third myth is that some kind of marriage is better than no marriage at all. But research shows that children do worse in marriages that are scarred by conflict and anger than in single-parent families that are stable and loving.

Perhaps this Cinderella myth is the hardest one to give up. Who in the dark of night has not drifted into the rescue fantasy of "Some Day My Prince Will Come"? But the princes who are likely to marry welfare Cinderellas are not necessarily going to lift them out of poverty to improve their lives.

The Bush administration is absolutely right to try and eliminate bureaucratic marital penalties in the welfare system. A second income can put families in economic limbo, where they don't earn enough to cover expenses such as child care but earn too much to qualify for supplemental assistance. That's what happened to the woman in Staunton. The court-ordered child support payments from her ex of $60 a week helped put her over the cutoff for getting food stamps and subsidized child care.

The Bush administration is also right to look for ways to strengthen couples with children. By all means, set aside funds for parenting classes and couples therapy. At the Institute of Human Development at the University of California, Berkeley, psychologists Philip and Carolyn Cowan are testing programs to help stabilize high-risk families.

Roughly 40 percent of single mothers live with a partner. In one study, many hoped to get married but were not confident a marriage would last. Perhaps with counseling and other support, some would tie the knot. Others might end a destructive relationship. The hope is that whatever their destiny as a couple, they would become better parents.

It takes more than wedding bells to improve the lives of American women and their children. ▀

20

From Outlaws to In-Laws: Gay and Lesbian Couples in Contemporary Society

Robert-Jay Green

In 2003, the U.S. Supreme Court overturned all remaining state laws that criminalized homosexual behavior between consenting adults. In the following year (2004), the first same-sex marriages in the United States were performed in Massachusetts following a ruling by the Massachusetts Supreme Court. Thus, in the span of eleven months, same-sex partners who literally had been *outlaws* in some states could legally become *in-laws* to one another's families in Massachusetts. The enormous societal shifts represented in these legal decisions and the psychological implications for same-sex couples, their families, and their communities are the focus of the present chapter.

A THOUGHT EXPERIMENT

To set the stage for what follows, I invite you to engage in a little thought experiment. Imagine for a moment that you were asked to write a chapter on "heterosexual married couples" for this book. Where would you begin? Thinking of all the heterosexual couples you have ever known, what do heterosexual married couples as a group have in common beyond the most obvious facts that they are composed of a woman and a man? What general statements might you make about heterosexual married couples in the United States? How about these:

- Heterosexual married couples in the United States are a high-risk group for separation and dissolution of relationships. Their instability generally results from heterosexual attempts to resolve conflicts by using escalating anger or avoidance/withdrawal strategies, both of which fail to solve couple problems. In fact, almost half of heterosexual marriages end in divorce.

- The heterosexual married lifestyle is characterized by a distinctive division of household labor such that women do a significantly larger share of household work, child rearing, and caring for aging relatives, even when wives work outside the home as many hours as their husbands. Greater inequities in this regard are associated with higher levels of distress in wives and lower levels of marital satisfaction for both spouses. Given the negative effects of such unequal divisions of household and child-care labor, one wonders why heterosexual couples have maintained and sometimes extolled these imbalances for centuries.

- Heterosexuals are known for being preoccupied with sex and insufficiently consistent in their use of birth control before and after marriage, casually producing offspring at such high rates that overpopulation is becoming a grave concern. One is forced to conclude that heterosexual couples are sorely lacking in impulse control and must be uncontrollably driven to engage in their distinctive manner of sexual relations.

- A significant portion of the married population partakes in a centuries-old heterosexual practice called *extramarital affairs*. Although commonplace, other people's affairs seem to be a source of endless curiosity and highly animated gossip among heterosexuals. Even some of the most prominent and esteemed members of the heterosexual married community, including their highest-ranking politicians and leaders of their conservative religious groups, are notorious for grand acts of deception and hypocrisy when it comes to extramarital sexual behavior. Social scientists, who rarely have sex, remain perplexed as to why.

As these semi-humorous generalizations illustrate, it is prejudicial to imply that a few of a target group's characteristics are a sign of overall dysfunction. It is even more arrogant to ascribe malevolent or pathological motivations to that group for having evolved certain patterns of behavior over the course of history. Lastly, in the absence of a known causal link, there is no justification for attributing some group members' dysfunctional actions solely or mostly to their sexual orientations rather than to other factors.

Yet, an equivalent kind of negative stereotyping has been so commonplace in the public discourse about same-sex couples that it been given its own label in the social sciences, *heterocentrism*. This term may be defined as "viewing and evaluating the behavior of lesbian, gay, and bisexual people out of cultural and historical context and using heterosexual relations as the presumptive ideal."

Thus, our little experiment highlights a central point about the public debates concerning same-sex couples. In this domain of inquiry perhaps more than any other, one should actively counter the human tendency to engage in selective perception, categorical ("either/or") thinking, or the attribution of all things problematic to a group's differentness from the mainstream. *Heterosexuality and homosexuality are* not *logical opposites.* Counterpoising one against the other inevitably exaggerates their differences and minimizes their commonalities. Thus, heterosexuality and homosexuality are most accurately viewed as variations on a common theme about attractions and the human capacity for enduring love relationships.

SIMILARITIES AND DIFFERENCES BETWEEN SAME-SEX AND HETEROSEXUAL COUPLES

There is as much demographic and psychological diversity *within* these two types of couples as there is *between* them. In general, knowing a person's sexual orientation gives us much less information about that person than is often assumed. In many respects, same-sex couples may be more like heterosexual couples of their same social class, religious, racial/ethnic, or occupational group than they are like same-sex couples from markedly different demographic groups.

Research directly comparing same-sex and heterosexual couples reveals they are remarkably similar to each other on most dimensions.[1] For example, regardless of the partners' sexual orientations, the same set of factors tends to predict relationship quality and relationship longevity across all types of couples: (1) partners' placing more value on security, permanence, shared activities, and togetherness; (2) partners' placing lower value on having separate activities and on personal autonomy; (3) higher expressiveness; (4) more perceived intrinsic rewards for being in the relationship; (5) fewer perceived attractive alternatives to the relationship; (6) more perceived barriers to ending the relationship; (7) less belief that disagreement is destructive; (8) higher trust in partner—viewing partner as dependable; (9) greater closeness and flexibility; (10) better problem-solving and conflict-negotiation skills; (11) higher shared/egalitarian decision making; and (12) greater perceived social support from sources outside the relationship.

But group comparison studies also suggest that same-sex couples (especially lesbian couples) have an advantage in escaping the traditional gender role divisions that make for power imbalances and dissatisfaction in many heterosexual relationships. For example, in research by Green, Bettinger, and Zacks, lesbian couples described themselves as emotionally closer than gay male couples who, in turn, described themselves as emotionally closer than heterosexual married couples.[2] Lesbian couples also reported the most flexibility in the way they handled rules and roles in the relationship, whereas heterosexual couples reported the least flexibility. It was noteworthy that higher levels of closeness and flexibility were associated with lesbian couples staying together versus breaking up over a two-year follow-up period. Overall, high levels of closeness and flexibility were reported by 79 percent of lesbian couples and 56 percent of gay male couples, but by only 8 percent of heterosexual married couples.

Same-sex couples' greater equality also was confirmed in studies by Gottman, Levinson, and colleagues.[3] Based on observations of couples interacting in conflict situations, these scientists found that same-sex couples were better at resolving disagreements. They approached problems from a position of peer equality, using "softer" (less aggressive and accusatorial) starts in the initiation of conflict discussions and using more humor during the discussion to avoid escalation of hostilities. With married heterosexual couples, the researchers observed that there was much more of a power struggle with one partner being invalidated by the other.

SPECIAL CHALLENGES FOR SAME-SEX COUPLES

Despite the evidence above that same-sex couples may be functioning better than heterosexual couples in terms of closeness and equality within the relationship, it also is important to recognize that same-sex relationships tend not to last as long as heterosexual marriages. One explanation for this difference may be that because same-sex couples are less likely to be raising children together, they can more easily walk away from their relationships during periods of conflict. But same-sex couples also face three specific challenges unique to their position in society, which renders their relationships more vulnerable to breaking up:

- *Antigay Prejudice:* Partners in same-sex couples are subjected to, and must continually cope with, antigay prejudice and discrimination from their families, communities, and/or the larger society.
- *Relational Ambiguity:* Because of the historical absence of social norms and legalized statuses for same-sex couples, these partners typically go through much more uncertainty about what it means to commit to a relationship. Also, in the thirty-eight states where legalized statuses are not available for same-sex couples, the partners face barriers to protecting and providing for one another in times of financial need, illness, disability, and in terms of inheritance.

- *Social Network Fragmentation:* Same-sex couples typically have more difficulty creating cohesive and lasting systems of social support because their families-of-origin, work settings, religious groups, and other community members tend to be less accepting and supportive of their relationships and because the gay and straight worlds are somewhat segregated.

These three stresses are detrimental to many gay and lesbian relationships, and I will focus on them in the next sections of this chapter.

ANTIGAY DISCRIMINATION

The overarching difference in the lives of same-sex versus heterosexual couples is that the former must continually cope with the special risks of claiming a socially stigmatized identity.[4] In this section, I will examine the historical and contemporary sociopolitical contexts in which same-sex relationships have been shaped. Then I will discuss the psychological implications of these factors for the functioning of same-sex partners.

The Historical Context

For much of U.S. history, love and sexual behavior between two consenting adult women or men was against the law.[5] Depending on local norms and statutes, homosexual acts were punishable by fines, imprisonment, consignment to mental hospitals, dismissal from jobs, and extreme social ostracism of the individual and sometimes of other family members as well. In the 1950s, for example, unjustified police raids on bars serving gay and lesbian patrons were common, and newspapers frequently published photographs designed to shame the people who were arrested in these police sweeps. Careers and lives were ruined, and suicide rates were high. Lesbian and gay people feared being revealed or even blackmailed by vengeful former same-sex partners, confidants, or others who discovered their sexual orientation.

As a consequence, committed relationships between two men or two women were extremely dangerous because their ongoing nature made it more difficult to hide one's sexual orientation. This was especially true for men. Although two "single" women could live together seemingly as "just friends" in order to share household expenses and companionship (and might even elicit the sympathy of the community for never having married), two men living together after the age of thirty immediately raised suspicion.[6]

As a result, lesbians and gay men typically married heterosexual partners or lived alone, engaging in same-sex romantic encounters briefly and clandestinely.

They remained closeted to almost all heterosexuals, living in fear of familial, social, economic, and legal consequences of being "found out." The alternative of forming a continuing love relationship with a same-sex partner was too fraught with the danger of being exposed and becoming a social pariah.

In this way, throughout American history, the "closet" worked against ongoing same-sex love relationships and favored anonymous short ones. Such is still the case for most lesbian, gay, and bisexual people in most places in the world, including throughout all of Asia, most of Africa, most of Latin America, many parts of Eastern Europe, in many U.S. rural communities, and in enclaves of recent immigrants in large U.S. metropolitan areas. Homosexual behavior is still punishable by torture and death in some countries.

A paradoxical effect of this history is that having been precluded from forming committed same-sex relationships, lesbian and gay people simultaneously have been accused of not being capable of creating and sustaining them. Imagine what shape heterosexual relationships might have taken over the last 100 years if heterosexuals had been socially and legally prevented from forming *any* kind of love relationships, let alone marriages, during that time period.

Although a complete account of how same sex-couples went from being outlaws to in-laws over the last century is beyond the scope of this chapter, it is important to keep the above history in mind during any discussion of contemporary same-sex couples. As we will see, even within the current population, there are marked generational differences in worldviews and life goals as a function of when in history the partners grew up. The different historical contexts in which these individuals came out to themselves and others helped shape their couple and family relationships and their political priorities for the future.

Contemporary Discrimination

A surprising number of Americans seem to believe that discrimination against lesbian and gay people is largely a thing of the past. According to an NBC/*Wall Street Journal* poll conducted in August 2008 (using a sample of 1,075 likely voters), 23 percent of respondents said they believe gay and lesbian people are "receiving too many special advantages," and 28 percent said they believe gays/lesbians are "receiving fair treatment." By contrast, 40 percent of respondents in the survey believe that gay and lesbian people are being discriminated against. Thus, a majority of voters (51 percent) think gay and lesbian people do not face any discrimination in America.

Unfortunately, the majority's beliefs are contradicted by what gays and lesbians report about their own experiences. For example, based on an interview study of 528 New York metropolitan area (urban and suburban) youths ages fifteen to nineteen, D'Augelli and colleagues found that 80 percent reported receiving verbal taunts related to being gay or lesbian. Fourteen percent reported physical attacks. Overall, 70 percent of verbal victimization incidents and 56 percent of physical victimization occurred in schools. Nine percent of these youths (especially those who had experienced more physical victimization for being gay) met the formal psychiatric criteria for a diagnosis of Post-Traumatic Stress Disorder.[7] In this context, it is noteworthy that more than three-quarters of U.S. states (thirty-eight of them) still provide *no* legal protection from discrimination for gay and lesbian youth in public schools.

Examining workplace discrimination, Ragins, Singh, and Cornwell surveyed 500 U.S. adults who self-identified as gay or lesbian.[8] The data showed that 37 percent of workers reported having faced discrimination on the job because others suspected or assumed they were gay or lesbian. More than 10 percent said they had been physically harassed because they were perceived to be gay or lesbian. More than 22 percent said they had been verbally harassed. Nearly 31 percent said they had resigned from a job, been fired from a job, or left a job because they had encountered gay/lesbian-related discrimination. Surprisingly, most heterosexual Americans seem to think that gay and lesbian people are protected against such discrimination everywhere in the United States, but in fact a majority of U.S. states (thirty of them) do not have any laws that prevent employers from firing or not hiring employees simply for being gay or lesbian.

Most relevant for the topic of same-sex couples, as of July 2009, only twelve states and the District of Columbia currently provide any legalized status for same-sex couples. Domestic partnerships are available to same-sex couples in five states (California, Hawaii, Nevada, Oregon, and Washington) and the District of Columbia. Civil unions are provided by New Jersey. Same-sex marriages are now possible in Connecticut, Iowa, Maine, Massachusetts, New Hampshire, and Vermont. New York, New Mexico, Rhode Island, and the District of Columbia recognize marriages performed in other states but do not themselves provide same-sex marriage to couples. For a little less than five months, California also permitted same-sex marriages until a constitutional amendment on November 4, 2008, eliminated the right of same-sex couples to marry there. Approximately 18,000 same-sex marriages were performed in California during that period.[9]

In contrast to these twelve states and the District of Columbia, the remaining states and the federal government do not offer any legal recognition for same-sex couples. As of April 2009, twenty-nine states have constitutional amendments banning same-sex marriage and another thirteen states and the federal government have Defense of Marriage Acts (DOMAs) prohibiting them from recognizing same-sex marriages from other states or countries. The national DOMA prevents same-sex partners from receiving any of the federal benefits of marriage given to heterosexual spouses (most notably, Social Security income for surviving spouses, immigration rights for international spouses married to U.S. citizens, and tax-exempt portions of inheritance left to surviving spouses).

Not coincidentally, the state and federal DOMAs and constitutional amendments described above have paralleled the rise of well-funded antigay groups in America—groups that seek to prevent the equal treatment of lesbian or gay people and their relationships. For example, People for the American Way lists on its website fifty-five national organizations that have unabashedly antigay mission statements, official policies, or action agendas, and some of these organizations have state and local chapters or affiliates.[10] Most prominent among these groups is Focus on the Family, which is headquartered in Colorado Springs.

Founded in 1977 by James Dobson, Focus on the Family employs 1,300 people, gets 10,000 e-mails, 50,000 phone calls, and 173,000 letters a month; has its own zip code; maintains a mailing list of 6 million names; and has an estimated annual budget of approximately $145 million. Focus on the Family also spawned a well-funded Washington-based think tank (the Family Research Council) and dozens of Family Policy Councils in states across the country, all of which are engaged in openly antigay propaganda and antigay legislative and policy activities.

In terms of media activity alone, Focus on the Family is said to have 2.3 million subscribers to ten monthly magazines and publishes a wide variety of books, tapes, films and videos. James Dobson is heard daily on more than 3,400 radio facilities in North America, in fifteen languages, on approximately 6,300 facilities in 164 countries. His estimated listening audience is over 220 million people daily, including a program translation carried on all state-owned radio stations in China. In the United States, Dobson appears on eighty television stations daily.

Same-sex couples are daily confronted with media statements by antigay groups openly denigrating gay and lesbian people. Many of their public statements contain outright distortions of the social science findings on gay and lesbian issues. A typical example appeared in an invited commentary for *Time* magazine in 2008, following the birth of a son to Mary Cheney (the former vice-president's daughter) and her partner. In Dobson's essay titled "Two Mommies Is One Too Many," he wrote:

> With all due respect to Cheney and her partner, Heather Poe, the majority of more than 30 years of social-science evidence indicates that children do best on every measure of well-being when raised by their married mother and father. . . . We should not enter into yet another untested and far-reaching social experiment. . . . (*Time*, December 12, 2006)

However, there is not a shred of social science evidence that children raised by heterosexual mothers and fathers do better on any measure of well-being than children raised by lesbian or gay parents. All of the social science studies actually converge on the conclusion that there are no statistically significant differences in mental health outcomes, peer relations, academic achievement, and gender identity between children raised by lesbian or gay parents compared with hetero-sexual parents.[11] In fact, some researchers have found very small but statistically significant differences on a few dimensions that seem to favor children of lesbian and gay parents. For example, daughters of lesbian mothers seem to be somewhat more career-oriented, sons of lesbian mothers seem to be less objectifying in their approach to romantic partners, and lesbian parents report being closer to their child.[12]

EFFECTS OF ANTIGAY ATTITUDES ON SAME-SEX PARTNERS

Although same-sex couples do not encounter intolerance at every turn, they experience enough of it personally, vicariously (by identification with other les-bian and gay victims of discrimination), and through antigay political initiatives and media advertisements to remain constantly vigilant for its occurrence. It is impossible for a lesbian or gay person to grow up in this society without inter-nalizing some negative attitudes and fears about homosexual feelings and the dangers of discrimination.[13]

Most relevant for formation of same-sex couple relationships, the difficulty accepting one's homosexuality (termed "internalized homophobia") and/or the fear of negative social and economic consequences of coming out still discour-age many lesbian and gay people from forming lasting couple bonds. In many parts of the United States, it still remains safer for gay and lesbian people to be closeted and to restrict their sexual/romantic involvements to brief encounters. To reach the level of "outness" necessary to form a same-sex couple relationship, lesbian and gay partners must have successfully challenged in their own minds the negative views they were taught about homosexuality and overcome their fears of being seriously harmed by discrimination.

Successfully countering internalized antigay attitudes requires attributing them to societal ignorance, prejudice, fear, and the human tendency to conform to dominant norms. It also requires exposure to, and social support from, other lesbian and gay people whose behavior counteracts negative stereotypes about homosexuality. Thus, when partners participate actively in lesbian and gay com-munity organizations, whatever stereotypes they may have held about lesbian and gay people and relationships tend to fall apart because of the enormous diversity within the community.

Equally important, partners in same-sex relationships sometimes have to engage in much self-reflection and questioning in order to be able to step outside of traditional gender norms and accept the reality of their own love for one another. Typically, this involves a personal review of the many antigay social influences that pressure them to regard their capacity for same-sex love as bad, sinful, mentally disturbed, inferior, and so on. All of the negative messages they have received about homosexuality over a lifetime have to be considered against their own personal experience of self, their observations of other lesbian and gay people, and sometimes the extensive social science evidence showing that the majority of lesbian and gay people lead happy, fulfilling lives despite the discrimination they may encounter. Ultimately, in order to function well, lesbian or gay partners must come to view their love as a normal human variation—one that has always existed among a small percentage of the population in all societies, and always will.

In many cases, partners are at different levels of comfort about their sexual orientations or may face very different levels of acceptance at work or in their families. These discrepancies may create couple conflicts over whether or how safe it is to be "out" in various situations. Couples that successfully manage these conflicts tend to maximize their participation in situations where they can be safely out as a couple.

Depending on the kind of discrimination same-sex partners face, coping resiliently with antigay prejudice may require (1) working actively for change in one's current social environment; (2) changing to a different social environment (literally relocating geographically or quitting one's job to escape an intransigent or dangerously antigay situation); (3) reattributing the cause of one's distress to different factors (e.g., attributing one's distress to external prejudice and ignorance rather than to personal inadequacy); or (4) recognizing that some discriminatory situations cannot be changed, and then instead focusing on other areas in one's life that are meaningful.

LACK OF A NORMATIVE AND LEGAL TEMPLATE FOR SAME-SEX COUPLEHOOD

In contrast to heterosexual couples for whom there is a traditionally prescribed way of being a couple with explicit and implicit rules, there is no prescribed way of being a same-sex couple. For example, some of the socially prescribed rules of heterosexual marriage include expectations of monogamy, sharing responsibility for each other's aging relatives, combining financial assets, dividing instrumental/expressive and household roles somewhat along gender lines, relocating for one another's career advancement, and taking care of one another in times of serious disability. Because until very recently same-sex partners could not marry anywhere in the United States, it has been unclear whether or at what turning point these traditional expectations of couples might apply to same-sex relationships. Elsewhere, I have termed this kind of uncertainty *relational ambiguity*, and it tends to play a central role in same-sex couple relationships, especially in the early years of couple formation.

For example, committed heterosexual couples (typically within one to three years of starting to date) take a wedding vow to stay together "in sickness and in health till death do us part." This vow to take care of each other is also a promise to family members, friends, and other witnesses, including in most cases to "God as a witness."

By contrast, it is unclear when or if most same-sex partners can have the same expectations of their relationship. Do same-sex partners implicitly make this vow when they move in together? After being together for two years or ten years? Can there be equivalent vow-making for same-sex couples when they cannot get legally married or be married in the eyes of the federal government or some religious denominations? Is a vow made in private the same psychologically as one made in public? Is a promise made in a public "commitment ceremony" that is not recognized by the state and/or federal government the same as a promise made against the backdrop of legally enforceable marriage laws? Do domestic partnerships or civil unions convey the same sense of transition to a greater level of commitment as is implied by getting legally married?

Lacking a preordained prescription for what being a same-sex couple means, lesbian and gay partners must develop their own basic ideals of themselves as a couple. Inevitably, they will rely to some extent on earlier observations of successful and unsuccessful heterosexual marriages. But the same-sex composition of the couple and the unusual position of lesbians and gays in society throws into doubt how relevant these heterosexual models might be.

Furthermore, the greater variety of relationship arrangements that are acceptable within the gay community (e.g., many such couples never live together, others have nonmonogamous relationships by agreement, shorter relationships are normative, fewer same-sex couples are raising children) leaves open the possibility that a same-sex couple's commitment could be either quite similar to or quite different from that of most married heterosexual couples. Compared with the fixed expectations of marriage in the heterosexual community, the broader acceptance of varied couple arrangements in the lesbian and gay community seems to thrust each same-sex couple into a longer period of uncertainty and negotiation regarding its definition of personal couplehood.

The advent of domestic partnerships and/or civil unions in some states, and legal marriage in a few states, may help reduce the relational ambiguity for couples who obtain these legalized statuses. But the fact remains that in the vast majority of states, there is no legal status available to help anchor same-sex relationships. As a result, many same-sex couples, their families, and their state governments seem to be experiencing heightened ambiguity.[14] Even the partners that make up a couple may be at differing points on a continuum of commitment clarity and relationship definition because of the rapid social changes in the last five years. Same-sex couples are confronted nowadays with the ubiquitous question so familiar to heterosexuals—"Are you going to get married soon and have children?"—and many of these couples are ill-prepared to answer because they never conceived of either possibility until recently.

There are no simple solutions for resolving these ambiguities in same-sex couple relationships. Nor will their resolution necessarily look like heterosexual marriages, in which many of these uncertainties are settled by law and tradition. In general, however, a couple tends to function best when there are clear agreements about their commitment and boundaries and when the couple's relationship is made a higher priority than any other relationships (in terms of emotional involvement, caregiving, honesty, time, and influence over major decisions).

For couples who view their relationships as entailing a lifetime commitment but who are unable to get married or to obtain other legal couple statuses in their states, it is possible to create appropriate legal documents, especially health-care power of attorney and wills and trusts that help clarify partners' legal and financial commitment to one another.[15] If it is in keeping with their wishes, couples can have a commitment ceremony and a formal exchange of vows covering some of these issues, even if their states will not recognize their relationships.

When same-sex partners are able to clarify their expectations and create agreements in contested areas or in areas that have never been discussed (such as finances or monogamy), it helps reduce relational ambiguity. This, in turn, increases partners' feelings of secure attachment and belief in the permanence of their bond, grounding their relationship in tangible definitions of what it means for them to be couple.

FRAGMENTED SOCIAL SUPPORT SYSTEMS

Unlike members of racial, ethnic, and religious minority groups in which parents and children usually share their minority status, children who become lesbian and gay only rarely have parents who share their same sexual minority status. Being different from other family members in this way has profound consequences for the development of almost every lesbian and gay person. For example, because heterosexual parents have never suffered sexual orientation discrimination themselves, even the most well-meaning among them is not able to offer the kind of insight and socialization experiences that would buffer their child against antigay prejudice and its internalization.

By contrast, when children and parents mutually identify as members of the same minority group (for example, African Americans, Jews, Muslims), the children are explicitly taught—and parents implicitly model—ways to counter society's prejudice against their group. Typically, such parents and children are involved together in community institutions (religious, social) that are instrumental in supporting the child's development of a positive minority identity, and parents take a protective stance toward their children's experiences of oppression.

Parents of lesbian or gay children are typically unaware of their child's minority status, however, and therefore they are unlikely to seek out community groups that would support the development of a positive lesbian or gay identity in their child. In fact, rather than protecting their child against prejudice, parents often show subtle or not-so-subtle signs of antigay prejudice themselves. Instead of being on the same side as their child against the external dangers, the parents' own antigay attitudes and behavior may be the greatest external dangers of all for the child.

Large numbers of lesbian and gay adults in the United States, especially members of conservative religious families or of immigrant families with traditional values, still remain closeted from one or both parents if they perceive their parents as being antigay. In terms of couple relationships, this secrecy requires either distancing from the family of origin members lest the secret be revealed, or it requires forgoing couple commitments in order to stay connected with the family of origin.

Although most parents do not completely reject their lesbian and gay children after the disclosure, the level of acceptance that offspring receive is highly variable and usually somewhat qualified.[16] As a result, same-sex couples frequently turn to their lesbian and gay friends for greater levels of mutual support and identification. Ideally, these friendships and selected family members are woven together into a so-called "family of choice"—an interconnected system of emotional and instrumental support over time.[17]

In general, same-sex couples tend to have less interconnected social networks than heterosexual couples. The tendency toward social segregation of the straight and gay worlds generally—and between the straight and gay segments of an individual's social network—usually requires that same-sex couples have to expend more deliberate effort to create an integrated social support system that has family-like qualities. This is especially true for same-sex couples of color, interracial couples, or couples in which one or both members are bisexual or transgender.[18] Such same-sex couples often are subject to much higher levels of antigay discrimination from their families and their original communities and usually experience significantly more difficulty integrating their more segregated social networks into a coherent whole.

When a young adult or older lesbian or gay individual can accept his or her own sexual orientation and choice of partner, dealing with the family is emotionally much easier, and parents' antigay sentiments can be dealt with more dispassionately, assertively, and with fewer setbacks to the couple's functioning. In building a "family of choice," couples must take a very proactive stance toward the goal of developing an ongoing social support system consisting of about eight to ten individuals or couples. There are two basic steps the couple has to take in building a personal support system: first, developing or maintaining a reciprocally supportive relationship with each individual who would be a member of the couple's support system; and second, "knitting" these individuals together into an integrated system of support.

The best strategy is for the partners to become very active in a well-established organization together, attend its events regularly in order to become familiar fixtures in the organization, and take on positions of leadership or active committee involvement that require repeated interaction with the same people frequently and over months or years. In smaller or rural communities with fewer lesbian and gay organizations, the Internet may be the best venue for starting friendship networks.

The great advantage of meeting new people through existing lesbian and gay organizations is that those organizations already will have some degree of "groupness" to them, so that the couple may be able to become an integral part of an already existing social support system. If the couple's closest relationships arose at different times from different settings, more effort has to go into knitting these disparate relationships into a more cohesive unit. The only way to increase the cohesiveness of a fragmented support system is for the couple to actively, frequently, and persistently take the lead in physically bringing together the disconnected individuals or subgroups. It generally takes about one to two years to link a disconnected collection of about eight to ten individual relationships into a functional social support system with family-like properties (a family of choice), but same-sex couples invariably find the effort worthwhile.

THE FUTURE OF SAME-SEX RELATIONSHIPS: A TALE OF TWO GENERATIONS

The American Community Survey of 2005 revealed that there were approximately 776,943 same-sex-couple households in the United States.[19] Among these cohabiting couples, approximately 20 percent were raising children. Moreover, many observers suspect that the number of same-sex couples in the United States may be much higher because respondents (especially those in more conservative areas of the country) may be reluctant to reveal information about their sexual orientation to the U.S. Bureau of the Census. There already is some evidence for serious undercounts of same-sex couples in the census because the number of reporting same-sex households jumped 30 percent from 2000 to 2005, suggesting that a large number of couples had become more willing to self-report over that five-year period.

What in general do lesbian and gay people want in terms of their couple and family relationships as well as public policies toward them in the future? In a survey of the legal and political priorities of 768 lesbian, gay, and bisexual people, Egan, Edelman, and Sherrill[20] found interesting generational differences. For adults age sixty-five and older, highest priorities were *Laws against hate crimes*, followed by *Workplace discrimination protections*. But for those ages eighteen to twenty-five, highest priorities were *Marriage rights*, followed by *Parental and adoption rights*. These findings seem to reflect the two age groups' different experiences historically.

When lesbian and gay people who now are over sixty-five first came out, it was inconceivable that marriage or parenting would be available to them, and their major concerns revolved around being physically harmed or fired from their jobs for being gay or lesbian. The younger generation, by contrast, seems to have taken a giant leap forward in terms of rising expectations for equality, striving for same-sex marriage rights and for the same opportunities to adopt or conceive children (via alternative insemination or surrogacy) that heterosexual married couples enjoy.

For example, in a study of youths, D'Augelli, Grossman, and Rendina[21] individually interviewed 133 self-identified gay or lesbian urban and suburban young people (50 females, 83 males in the New York metropolitan area) about their aspirations for couple relationships and parenting in the future. The participants were ages sixteen to twenty-two (average age was nineteen); 42 percent were Hispanic, 39 percent were people of color, and the rest were white non-Hispanic. In this sample, 92 percent of the lesbian youths and 82 percent of gay male youths reported that they wanted to be in a long-term monogamous relationship within ten years. Furthermore, 78 percent of the lesbian youths and 61 percent of gay male youths said it was "very" or "extremely" likely they would marry a same-sex partner if legally possible. In terms of parenting, 66 percent of lesbian youths and 52 percent of gay male youths said it was "very" or "extremely" likely they would be raising children in the future. These high percentages of gay and lesbian youths aspiring to marriage and parenthood are astonishing to older gay and lesbian adults, who could not in their wildest dreams have imagined a time where such equal freedoms would be available to them.

Moreover, despite indications of continuing prejudice and discrimination against lesbian and gay people, there is abundant evidence of change in the direction of greater acceptance. Illustrative of these trends, the Gallup polling organization, which has tracked public attitudes toward homosexuality for over twenty-five years, recently summarized these changes as follows:

> Americans have shifted from frowning on homosexuality as an alternative lifestyle and being divided over whether it should be legal, to now supporting gay rights on both fronts. At the same time, the country remains highly ambivalent about the morality of homosexual relations, and as a result, support for legalizing gay marriage lags far behind the less culturally sensitive matter of gays having equal job rights.[22]

Based on telephone interviews with 1,017 adults age eighteen and over, Gallop's latest poll showed that 89 percent of respondents were in favor of equal job opportunities for lesbian and gay people; 55 percent believed homosexual relations should be legal; and 57 percent viewed homosexuality as an "acceptable alternative lifestyle." But participants were equally divided (48 percent for and against) in their opinions about whether same-sex relations are morally acceptable. Only 40 percent agreed (compared to 56 percent who disagreed) that same-sex marriages should be legal.[23]

Another national poll revealed that given three choices, 32 percent of American voters favor same-sex marriage; 33 percent favor civil unions; and 29 percent favor no legal recognition for same-sex couples.[24] Other recent national polls have yielded similar results. It thus seems that about two-thirds of the American public endorses some kind of legalized status for same-sex couples (either marriage or civil unions), and another third is against any such legal recognition.

In the recent California ballot initiative (Proposition 8) that amended the state's constitution so that it would prohibit same-sex marriage, 52 percent voted against same-sex marriage, whereas 48 percent voted in favor of it. Most revealing is that exit polls in California showed a strong effect of age, with 61 percent of voters age eighteen to twenty-nine in favor of same-sex marriage versus 61 percent of voters sixty-five and older against.[25] This age cohort effect has now been found in several national opinion polls, suggesting that it is just a matter of time until a majority of the electorate favors same-sex marriage—unless, of course, the younger cohorts become markedly more socially conservative as they age.

Recently about 42 percent of people in the United States say they are close to someone who is lesbian or gay as a friend or family member.[26] Being close to someone lesbian or gay is strongly associated with more favorable attitudes. For example, 81 percent of respondents who said they have a close gay friend or family member were against schools being able to fire gay teachers, but only 55 percent of respondents who did *not* have a close gay friend or family member were against such firings (a spread of 26 percentage points). Similarly, 55 percent of those who had a close gay friend or family member were in favor of same-sex marriage, but only 25 percent of those without a close gay friend or family member were in favor.

Thus, to the extent that younger lesbian and gay people create the kind of long-lasting couple and family relationships to which they aspire and then become friends with heterosexuals, we are likely to witness more favorable public attitudes and policies affecting lesbian and gay citizens. Heterosexuals' acceptance of same-sex relationships is clearly a case in which familiarity seems to breed favorable impressions, and absence of familiarity is associated with contempt. To know thy neighborhood same-sex couple is tantamount to losing thy stereotypes.

21

Independent Women: Equality in African-American Lesbian Relationships

Mignon R. Moore

The familial expectations that women with same-sex partners have for one another are not well understood. Where there is research, it largely references the experiences of white, middle- and upper-income lesbians who tend to develop relationships with feminist goals. This chapter presents results from a three-year, mixed-methods study of households headed by gay women of color to explore how family background and other life experiences influence subjective feelings of equality in lesbian relationships. I find that African-American women place a high value on economic independence and see self-sufficiency as much more important than the distribution of household chores when determining their satisfaction with the level of fairness in their relationships. Social class and family background influence why self-sufficiency is the more important measure of relationship satisfaction. For those who grew up in extreme poverty, economic independence protects them against homelessness and other negative conditions they may have experienced in childhood. Women raised in working-class families encourage economic independence because they tend to see everyone in the household as having an equal responsibility to bring in financial resources in order for the family to get ahead. Respondents in both of these income groups also value economic self-sufficiency because it gives them the resources necessary to escape unstable or unhealthy relationships. Women raised in middle-class families tend to view economic independence as important in their relationships because they have seen how the presence or absence of their own mother's employment facilitated or hindered her personal growth and self-actualization. Middle- and upper-middle-class black women view employment as a means toward self-fulfillment and activity necessary for upward mobility and leadership in larger society. I show how experiences around race, class, and family background importantly influence the expectations women have for their partners in intimate relationships.

R esearchers on lesbian and gay populations have tended to generalize the experiences of lesbian practice and gay sexuality from past research on white, middle-class, feminist women. But alternative histories and experiences of women from other racial and socioeconomic groups offer new information on the relationship between race, class, gender, and homosexual relationships. The present study covers three years in the lives of a population of gay women who are not often visible in public life—lesbians of color who are creating families. In this article, I offer an examination of the ways black gay women evaluate the concept of equality or egalitarianism in same-sex unions.

This research is drawn from a forthcoming book project titled *Invisible Families: Gay Identities, Relationships, and Motherhood among Black Women*, which argues that previously formed identification statuses such as those based on race or class influence how individuals perceive and enact later group memberships like those based on sexuality. It does this through the analysis of a group of women who, because of year of birth, geographic location, socioeconomic status, and other characteristics, came of age during periods of heavy racial segregation and entered into their gay identities with firmly entrenched black racial identities. The larger project from which this essay is drawn suggests there is value in analyzing the ways past experiences in families of origin influence the expectations individuals have for their own relationships, regardless of sexual preference.

In this essay, I examine the concept of equality in lesbian relationships by looking closely at the two primary aspects of egalitarianism: equal responsibility for paid work and housework. Past studies of lesbian households have emphasized the egalitarian nature of these couples vis-à-vis their division of family labor, which includes household chores such as cooking and cleaning, as well as child care and supervision. This body of literature has had little to say about the other aspect of egalitarianism: how lesbian couples distribute paid work, evaluate its importance in their relationship, and construct ideologies about economic independence. These studies have also tended to understate the experiences of women of color, working-class, and poor women.[1] In this work, I examine the relative importance of both components of egalitarianism for black lesbians, looking at differences across socioeconomic background as one explanation for how women come to make decisions about what they value in their relationships.

EGALITARIANISM: ECONOMIC INDEPENDENCE AND AN EQUITABLE DIVISION OF HOUSEHOLD LABOR

Since the 1970s, feminist research on the division of household labor has conceptualized the gender specialization model of husband as primary wage earner and wife as primary caretaker as an indicator of gender stratification. This research generally defines egalitarianism as "joint responsibility for paid work, housework, and childrearing."[2] From 1989 onward, the social science literature on household decision making in lesbian-led families has tended to measure egalitarianism and equality in relationships by focusing on the ways couples distribute household chores and child care. It has not paid close attention to how much lesbian partners value, or the extent to which they enact, the other component of egalitarianism—economic independence and financial contributions from both partners in the relationship.[3]

Part of the problem has been the way research on lesbian-headed households has been conducted. Scholars who study lesbian families have been interested in addressing the literature on heterosexual couples that measured the distribution of and time spent on household chores by husbands and wives. Studies of gender in the heterosexual division of labor sought and revealed explanations for the greater responsibility of wives for household chores.[4] Studies of the division of labor among lesbian and gay couples sought to illuminate how these same issues played out in the absence of sex differences between partners.[5] After 1989, the emphasis in the family literature focused heavily on the domestic realm and researchers of lesbian-headed households tended to follow suit.

Lesbian subjects have also persisted in emphasizing the egalitarian nature of their unions because of deep-rooted concerns about the public image of gay communities. Carrington's 1999 study of the ways gay couples assign various aspects of domesticity revealed this tendency. Even though the subjects of more recent scholarship on lesbian families may not take on a dominant identity as feminist, they hold significant ideological commitment to egalitarianism and form unions with the principles of egalitarian feminism in mind.

Recent studies show evidence that lesbian couples tend to distribute housework, paid work, and child-care duties across the couple using an "ethic of equality" that is drawn from lesbian-feminist ideologies.[6] Much of the research has focused on one component of this notion of equality—the distribution of housework. But as far back as 1983, Blumstein and Schwartz revealed that for lesbian couples, equal responsibility for household financial responsibilities was also a very important measure of equality. Partners' interest in each individual's economic independence was linked to an effort to avoid the breadwinner/homemaker patriarchy found in some heterosexual relationships.[7] In drawing attention toward domestic matters and away from the economic sphere, contemporary lesbian family scholars may have inadvertently shifted the definition of egalitarian ideologies too far in the other direction. I draw from a sample of women who do not use a lesbian-feminist framework to measure equality in their same-sex relationships, and I examine how experiences in the families they were reared in influence the expectations they have for their same-sex partners.

African-American Gay Women and Equality in Lesbian Relationships

There are several reasons why African-American women are the focus of this inquiry. First, the family studies literature identifies several household patterns that are more common among black than white heterosexual couples, such as the greater importance black women place on their partner's economic contributions when they choose and evaluate a mate, more traditional gender ideologies among black wives and husbands relative to white wives and husbands, and a greater tendency for separate rather than joint financial bank accounts in black heterosexual unions.[8] It is instructive to see if these patterns of family life are also more likely to occur in a population where sexuality is experienced differently.

Black lesbians are also a useful population for studying the division of household labor because historically as a group they developed a gay culture outside the ideology of lesbian feminism. While middle-class white women largely came to understand lesbian sexuality in the context of consciousness-raising meetings in the women's movement or women's studies classes on college campuses,[9] racial segregation in housing, education, occupations, as well as the very fabric of social life limited black women's involvements in these groups. Instead, black women were entering the lesbian world through parties and social events taking place in informal environments that were more distant from lesbian-feminist ideals. The racial segregation of these social and political environments influenced whether and in what form egalitarian ideologies would be incorporated into their self-images.[10]

A final benefit in analyzing household organization and feminist ideologies among black women in same-sex unions is that it grants us the opportunity to examine how past experiences connected to race and class background relate to the patterns of social organization lesbians use in the families they form. Analyses of unmarried partner households in the 2000 Census suggest significant differences between black and white female same-sex couples, including lower median household incomes, lower rates of home-ownership, and lower rates of employment for black women. Black female same-sex couples are also significantly more likely to have children living with them in the home.[11]

INVISIBLE FAMILIES STUDY AND ASSESSING EGALITARIAN ATTITUDES

The Invisible Family data consist of 100 women who identify as lesbian, gay, bisexual, in the Life, or women-loving-women. It includes women in committed relationships with other women as well as unpartnered mothers. To be eligible for the study, one person in the relationship had to identify as black. There are four types of data: participant-observation field notes collected over approximately thirty months, four focus groups, fifty-eight in-depth interviews, and a mail-in survey. I used participant-observation methods at predominantly black lesbian social events to recruit women. Sixty percent of survey respondents were recruited directly through my attendance and participation in these social activities, 11 percent were recruited through announcements and presentations made at these events, 25 percent were obtained through referrals from those who were in the study (using a snowball sampling method of data collection), and 4 percent were recruited through referrals from nongay people. In total, 131 surveys were mailed and 100 were returned, giving the study a response rate of 76 percent.

The mean age of the sample in 2004 was 36.7 years, with a range of 24 to 61 years of age. Sixty-four percent of the sample identified as black American, 21 percent as West Indian or African, 10 percent as Latina, and 5 percent as white. Thirty-four percent completed high school and 62 percent received a four-year college degree or advanced degree. At the time of the interview, 45 percent were in working-class occupations, including construction worker, security guard, and administrative assistant.[12] Forty-two percent were considered middle class, in jobs that included teacher and human resources administrator. Thirteen percent of the sample were upper middle class, in occupations such as attorney and physician.[13]

The survey asked respondents to evaluate three statements that measured the strength of egalitarian attitudes: "Both mates in a relationship should divide evenly the household tasks (washing dishes, preparing meals, doing laundry, etc.)," "If both mates work full time, both of their career plans should be considered equally in determining where they will live," and "It is better if one person in the relationship takes the major financial responsibility and the other person takes the major responsibility of caring for the home." Responses to all three of these statements show that the majority of respondents profess views that are consistent with feminist measures of equality or egalitarianism in relationships. Eight-four percent agreed or strongly agreed that both mates should divide household tasks evenly, 89 percent agreed or strongly agreed that both partners' career plans should be equally considered when making decisions about where to live, and 84 percent disagreed or strongly disagreed with the specialization model of one person taking on the major financial responsibility and the other person primarily caring for the home.

Despite their ideological agreement with feminist egalitarian principles, however, survey, participant-observation, focus group, and in-depth interview data all suggest that respondents tend not to behave in egalitarian ways. In most households, one person spends much more time performing household chores. But while this is sometimes a source of frustration for the partner who does more housework, it is not the primary source of conflict in their relationships, it is not the primary measure of whether respondents believe their relationships are fair, and it is not related to the balance of power in the home.[14] Instead, the focus group, participant-observation, and in-depth interviews reveal that self-sufficiency and autonomy are highly valued, and respondents place a premium on economic independence rather than the division of family labor as a value and a behavior that is critical for relationship satisfaction. This importance is expressed through the belief that each partner should contribute her own financial resources to the relationship.

Class backgrounds and experiences growing up provide different explanations for why self-sufficiency is so important. Many of these background experiences relate to the socioeconomic status of respondents' families and their experiences around race and gender. These analyses focus on how family backgrounds of black women who grew up poor, working class, or middle class and who were interviewed in depth for the study influence their ideologies regarding the importance of women's economic independence in relationships. Thirty-two percent of these women grew up in poverty, 33 percent were raised in working-class families, and 35 percent lived in middle-class or upper-middle-class households during their childhoods.

Poor and Working-Class Family Background: Economic Independence Tied to Personal Survival and Ability to Move Out of Bad Relationships

Karen Jabar[15] is a forty-two-year-old African-American woman and mother of three who left her husband of twenty-one years when she came out as gay. Karen is also a child of two alcoholic parents whose addictions resulted in traumatic consequences for everyone in her family origin. Under conditions of extreme poverty, homelessness, and constant instability, she and her ten brothers and sisters banded together to protect one another from the taunting and bullying they received from other children in their neighborhood. She says:

> My life was rough. We struggled. I would probably say that we were a poor family because I could remember eating sugar sandwiches, things like that. I remember mice and roaches being in the house, taking care of my brothers and sisters and not having electricity or the fact that we would plug in the TV cord or the extension cord into the hallway socket to get light into our apartment; having the door cracked and not really knowing who is coming into the building.

In 1974, when Karen was thirteen, her mother killed her father in self-defense during a fight that began after heavy drinking. After that incident, Karen and her siblings were separated from one another and placed in different homes. At that time, the New York child welfare services agency had not designed policies to keep siblings together after a family removal, so Karen found herself having to survive without the security of her brothers and sisters in a group home for girls. She describes her teenage years as a life of loneliness, vulnerability, and uncertainty about her day-to-day future.

Despite the dire circumstances of her childhood, Karen has been able to rise above some of the challenges she has faced. After several starts and stops, she received a four-year college degree and is the only one of her siblings to have achieved this level of education. Karen avoids drugs and is able to provide for herself economically. Nevertheless, she does not maintain close relationships with her family members, battles with depression and low self-esteem, and has a difficult time staying employed. She has held and lost positions in the U.S. military, New York State Department of Correctional Services, various security positions for private firms, and several civil service jobs in New York City.

While a snapshot of Karen Jabar at the time of her interview might have indicated a middle-class status (college education and a job as a supervisor for the Administration for Children's Services city agency), her family background of extreme poverty, her struggle to complete her education, and other factors in her personal life make her experience quite different from that of many of the middle-class lesbians usually studied by researchers. These background experiences have influenced several areas of her adult life, including the things she finds important in her intimate relationships. For Karen, economic independence, even through a succession of short-term jobs, allows her to maintain some type of control over her own life. She has had a series of negative, temporary relationships with women who have taken advantage of her financially and emotionally. But, regardless of the status of the women she dates, she stays employed so that she will be able to care for herself and have the resources to leave unhealthy relationships when she is ready to move on. While she has taken on more than her share of the financial responsibilities with the women she has dated, she expects "equal sharing of all of the family responsibilities" with a partner in a serious relationship, and this includes paid work. For Karen, economic self-sufficiency rather than strict equality in the division of household chores carries the most weight in her satisfaction with her mate.

Working-Class Family Background: Economic Independence Tied to Childhood Experience of Work and to Individual Survival during Times of Marital Distress

Roberta "Ro" Gaul is a licensed electrician who was born in Jamaica, West Indies, in 1966. Throughout her adult life, her intimate relationships have only been with women. Ro was raised by her mother with her siblings in Flatbush, a working-class, largely West Indian, community in Brooklyn, New York. When Ro was growing up, her mother worked as a nurse's aide and her father did not live with the family. Currently, Ro lives with her partner, Sifa Brody, and in separate interviews they both said that Sifa does the majority of the housework and that Ro does not do enough of it. But in their interviews, they each reported being very satisfied with their relationship. On separate surveys they both reported spending equal amounts of time on the relationship and having equal power in it.

Ro's feelings on the importance of each partner's financial independence stem from her own experiences with work as an adolescent. When asked about the qualities she looks for in a partner, she said:

> They have to be working because I'm extremely independent and I believe people, everybody should work. I grew up as a young child working, and I am still working. So I believe that you must have a job. If it means that the job is paying you enough for you to maintain yourself or your own independence, you have to be working.

While Ro links her opinions about work to her experiences in her family of origin and the necessity of each person's income to the well-being of the household, other working-class women draw on an ideology of independence as a means of self-empowerment and protection against poverty. They believe in economic independence for themselves and their mates, and they have created a life that assures their own survival when a partner is not able to fulfill her or his own financial responsibilities.

Shelly Jackson is a thirty-eight-year-old bus driver. She was raised by her black American parents, grandparents, and great-grandparents, who have all shared a two-family house in Crown Heights, Brooklyn, since her parents married in 1962. She says her father took care of the family financially while her mother was "the homemaker." Prior to entering into a gay relationship, Shelly had been heterosexually married twice. At the time of the interview, she was legally separated but not divorced from her second husband, and she was living with her children and her female partner, Shaunte Austin, in an East New York housing project. She is emphatic that regardless of sexuality, each partner should bring her own resources to a relationship, saying "I don't give a damn who you're with, you always need . . . to be independent and take care of yourself." She told us she learned the importance of financial independence by watching her father provide for the family, and knew she wanted to always be able to do that for herself and her children. When asked about some of the positive aspects of her life while growing up, she said:

> That my father was always there to take care and provide for us, and that's what made me who I am today. 'Cause even when I was married, I always took that role of being the provider. I was always the one to go out there and work and pay the rent and pay the bills and do this and do that. And not look for him to take care of me—I've seen what my mother went through and that's not what I wanted to go through growing up, being an adult.

Shelly's first marriage was tumultuous largely because of an abusive husband. After five years of kicking him out of the house and then letting him back in, she ended the relationship. Her second marriage was characterized by significant drug use that involved herself and her husband. Although her own illicit drug use ended once she was pregnant, her husband continued to use and that eventually caused their relationship to end. Throughout both of these marriages, Shelly continued to work. Had she not remained financially independent she would certainly have slipped into poverty. She defines a "provider" as someone who has the ability to take care of herself without the help of others.

Schwartz, in her 1994 study of egalitarian heterosexual marriages, defines the provider role or provider complex as a combination of roles that give one person the responsibility for financially supporting the family, and the other person responsibility for all of the auxiliary duties that allow the first person to devote himself or herself to his or her work.[16] Schwartz's definition is different from the way Shelly Jackson uses the term "provider," and this becomes clear as Shelly continues in her description of the financial contributions she expects from her mate. On separate surveys, Shelly and her partner, Shaunte Austin, each report that Shaunte spends more time on household chores and takes on much of the child-care responsibilities. Shelly often works the night shift or double shifts, and relies on Shaunte to feed and bathe the children, help them with their home-work, and keep the house tidy. But when asked how happy she is with the way she and her mate divide household responsibilities, Shelly says she became much happier once Shaunte found a job:

> Don't get me wrong. She [Shaunte] has always been so good to me as far as helping me out with the kids, 'cause my hours [at work] is crazy and Shaunte is somebody I could depend on. But it was hard when she wasn't working. She wasn't having no income coming in, and I was like, "I'm not your sugar mama!"

Shelly's comment draws on negative images of a woman's dependence on a male "sugar daddy" and simultaneously emphasizes her expectation that her partner will contribute economically to the family. But she has also prepared to provide for herself and her children in the event that her mate cannot or will not contribute her share, or if their relationship comes to an end. For working-class lesbians raising families, economic independence provides a financial and psychological barrier against a step backwards into poverty.[17]

Middle-Class Family Background: Economic Independence Tied to Upward Mobility and Leadership in Society

Dr. Renee Martin is a physician. Born in 1967, Renee grew up in New Orleans with her parents and younger sister in a middle-class neighborhood that bordered two racially segregated areas of the community. One might characterize Renee's family background as upper middle class. Her father was one of the first African Americans in Louisiana to receive a doctorate in mechanical engineering. After having two children, Renee's mother continued to work as a college professor until her recent retirement. Although Renee's father earned more than her mother, throughout Renee's childhood she witnessed her mother thrive in a respectable, middle-class occupation that she found personally fulfilling. Both of her parents were active members of their church and other volunteer organizations, and they played important leadership roles in their African-American community.

Renee currently lives in New York City, where she owns her own home, has considerable authority at work, and is advancing steadily in her career. Renee's partner, Naja Rhodes, has a master's degree in education. They report spending similar amounts of time on household chores, though Naja believes she spends about two additional hours per week taking care of the home. Renee also tends to perform more of the stereotypically male tasks like yardwork, household repairs, and taking out the trash. Both say they are satisfied with the way they organize their household responsibilities and invest equal amounts of time and have equal power in the relationship. Renee's discussion of economic independence does not mention economic survival or a worry about being able to provide for herself in the absence of an employed partner. These issues are not part of her current life nor are they part of her past experiences. Coming from a socioeconomically secure background and having a high status and economically lucrative occupation precludes Renee from experiencing many of the worries expressed by the working-class respondents in this study. She could easily take on the traditional provider role in her relationship, relieving Naja from any obligation to contribute financially to the household.

Instead, Renee's discussion of egalitarianism in her relationship involves ways of helping her partner achieve greater independence and fulfillment in her own career. Renee encourages Naja to build her finances and to own her own property, and she has shown Naja how to build wealth. When talking about Naja, Renee makes reference to the independence her mother has always had from her father's income. She is proud of the fact that her mother has always maintained her own financial accounts and used her income to create a mutual interdependence in her relationship with Renee's father. In turn, Renee wants to help her own partner achieve these things.

The structure and functioning of Renee and Naja's relationship has its parallel in the way Renee's parents organized their marriage, as described by Landry in his (2000) historical research on black working wives. Landry argues that for the black middle class, women's paid work was not simply a response to economic circumstances, but the fulfillment of women's rights to self-actualization. His evidence lies in the experience of black women who married men who could support them, yet continued to pursue careers throughout their marital lives.[18] For couples like Renee and Naja, egalitarianism is expressed not merely through each person's ability to contribute economic resources, but in the desire of each person to pursue a life of self-fulfillment in the economic sphere. It is reminiscent of the argument in Betty Friedan's *The Feminine Mystique* about middle-class white women in the 1950s. But Donna Franklin (Chapter 7 of this volume) shows how these beliefs were championed much earlier than the 1950s in African-American middle-class families.[19]

Katrice Webster is a thirty-six-year-old attorney. She attended Ivy League institutions for college and law school and is employed at one of the top three law firms in Manhattan. Katrice was born and raised in Romulus, Michigan, a lower-middle-class, racially integrated, small city just outside of Detroit. Her parents divorced when she was six, and she and her siblings were raised by her mother, who worked her way up from administrative assistant to office manager at her place of employment. After the divorce, the children lived with their mother, but they spent holidays and vacations with their father, who remained nearby. He was a business executive with a much higher income than Katrice's mother, and he continued to contribute financially to their household throughout her childhood. An extensive extended family also lived in the area and served as an important source of support for the family. Katrice describes her childhood as happy.

When asked about the qualities she looks for in a mate, Katrice does not emphasize a college background or particular socioeconomic status. As a corporate attorney, her salary is higher than the salaries of women she has dated, and it is higher than what her current partner earns. Her interest in economic independence is not to ensure her own survival. She has obtained the education and occupational opportunities to secure that part of her life, and she is not reliant on her partner's income for her own upward mobility. Instead, she wants a partner who is ambitious, and Katrice is willing to help that person move toward the type of financial independence she has obtained for herself. When asked what she looks for in a mate, she says "They just have to have a drive and want to be successful at something. If they own their own house-cleaning business, they just have to run it well."

Her partner, Caroline Tate, is a self-employed makeup artist. Caroline and Katrice each pay their own bills, but Katrice pays for a greater portion of their expenses and is the sole owner of the home where they live. Caroline is the mother of a seventeen-year-old daughter who was born in a prior heterosexual union. Caroline not only spends more time parenting, but she also takes on much more of the household chores like cooking and laundry. They hire a person to come in and clean. They report some disagreement over parenting and discipline, but they do not raise the issue of housework as a problem in the relationship. Katrice would like her partner to become more financially stable and to learn about different methods of building assets. She says, "I try to encourage her to save because I always like to think everybody needs to have a nest egg for a rainy day." For her, promoting self-sufficiency in her partner will not improve Katrice's economic standing, but is a way to uplift her mate and help her become more stable for her own personal gain.

Among black women born before 1970, it was uncommon to have parents whose lives represented the traditional patriarchal relationship that feminist egalitarian ideologies attempt to dismantle. Mothers and fathers both worked to provide (when they could find employment), and many households did not contain two married biological parents for a person's entire childhood. When looking at the family structures of the women in the study, we see that Katrice's single-mother household, though different in terms of its middle-class status, was quite similar to the family backgrounds of the majority in the study. Just 36 percent of respondents were raised with two married biological parents, and only two of the black women reported having a stay-at-home mother. Forty-four percent grew up in single-mother households, and 42 percent of these single-parent families were multigenerational and included a grandparent or other adult female relative. Fourteen percent of the respondents were not raised with any biological parents, and they grew up in households with their grandparents or nonrelatives. In terms of community context, more than 90 percent were raised in predominantly black or well-integrated neighborhoods. These experiences suggest that the black heterosexual family, in all of its varied forms, has been the dominant model for expectations that African-American lesbian women have for their families.

Linking the Experiences of African-American Women to Feminist Principles of Equality

I find that the way lesbians think about partner responsibilities in their relationships is influenced by the social contexts in which they were raised. The women in this study ideologically support the equal division of paid work and housework like lesbians in previous studies, but in practice they more closely emphasize economic independence in their relationships. Unlike the respondents in other research, they do not necessarily draw from egalitarian feminist ideologies in their relationships. Insights from the literature on black feminist thought can shed light on why this is so. Historical documents outlining the tenets of black feminism reveal that the equal division of housework and market labor in male/female relationships was never a dominant component of black feminist frameworks.[20] Egalitarian relationships were certainly important to black feminists, but unlike white feminists who saw inequality as rooted in relationships between men and women in home life and in economic life, black women concentrated their platform on how to reduce the gender inequality they believed was connected to inequalities based on race and socioeconomic disadvantage.[21]

Patricia Hill Collins and Bonnie Thornton Dill both argue that, relative to whites, black family structures have historically been more varied.[22] Comparatively fewer blacks have spent time in nuclear family units where there is one male primary or solitary earner. Black women have had comparatively greater labor force participation, and their male partners have had less earnings advantage relative to white men.[23] Historically, black women have experienced competing sources of oppression, based not only on gender but also on race, socioeconomic status, and blocked occupational mobility.[24] These factors combine to focus the attention of black women on other problems and issues outside of the platforms white lesbian feminists were fighting for.

The poor, working-class, and middle-class family backgrounds of the respondents in this study shape the values they bring to their lesbian relationships. Their values are consistent with egalitarian ideologies, but they also add other dimensions to our analyses of equality and fairness in relationships. These women create families using their understanding of role expectations that were learned through their socialization in black family structures. While patriarchy is something they find oppressive, it is not often directly related to how and why they organize same-sex partnerships in a particular way. Instead, economic independence, survival, and mobility are most important to them. The economic contribution of partners does not have to be equal—they grant their partners some leeway to complete their education, to recover from illness, or to deal with various other extenuating circumstances. However, what is paramount is that both partners can contribute as well as take away their own financial resources.

Fact Sheet

MYTHS AND REALITIES ABOUT SAME-SEX FAMILIES

Media images of lesbians and gay men often create the impression that most of them are white urban dwellers who have high incomes and whose main pre-occupations are shopping for expensive clothes, preparing gourmet food, or eating at upscale restaurants. As a result, a variety of stereotypes and misconceptions exist about lesbian and gay families with children. The Council on Contemporary Families recently drew up a quiz to test your knowledge of this population.

1. What percentage of same-sex couples are raising children in the United States?
    a. 3 percent
    b. 11 percent
    c. 27 percent

2. In which state are same-sex couples most likely to be raising children?
    a. California
    b. Massachusetts
    c. Mississippi
    d. South Carolina

3. What percentage of children being raised by same-sex couples are nonwhite?
    a. 10 percent
    b. 30 percent
    c. 45 percent

4. The median household income of different-sex married couples aged twenty-five to fifty-five with children in the United States is $60,700. What is the comparable figure of similarly aged same-sex couples raising children?
    a. $96,200
    b. $77,100
    c. $51,900

5. Which of the following statements are true?
    a. Most children being raised by same-sex couples are adopted.
    b. Most research finds that children raised by gay and lesbian people fare as well as children from other families on a wide variety of child well-being measures.

c. Most children being raised by same-sex couples live in states where their parents can automatically obtain joint parental rights.

d. None of the above statements is true.

Answer Key

1. Answer: c. 27 percent

   More than one in four of the nearly 600,000 same-sex couples identified in the U.S. Census have a child under the age of eighteen living in the home with them.

2. Answer: c. Mississippi

   Among the nearly 2,000 same-sex couples in Mississippi, as many as four in ten (41 percent) are raising children under age eighteen. Other states with high rates of child rearing among same-sex couples include South Dakota (40 percent), Alaska (38 percent), South Carolina (36 percent), and Louisiana (35 percent).

   Far from being an urban or coastal phenomenon, the data show that same-sex couples raising children are found in 96 percent of all counties in the United States. Three of the five large metropolitan areas with the highest rate of child rearing among same-sex couples are found in Texas. San Antonio, Houston, and Fort Worth rank first, fourth, and fifth respectively. Bergen-Passaic, New Jersey, and Memphis, Tennessee, rank second and third. In all of those areas, at least one in three same-sex couples are raising children.

3. Answer: c. 45 percent

   The children of same-sex couples are much more racially and ethnically diverse than those being raised by different-sex married couples. Among the children of same-sex couples, 55 percent are white, 23 percent are Latino/a, 15 percent are black, 3 percent are Asian/Pacific Islander, 1 percent are Native American, and the remaining 3 percent are identified as some other racial category or as multiracial. Thus, 45 percent of these children are nonwhite compared to 30 percent of the children of different-sex married parents.

   This racial and ethnic diversity among the children reflects similar diversity among their parents. While 73 percent of different-sex married couples (age twenty-five to fifty-five) with children are white, only 59 percent of their same-sex couple counterparts identify as white. Thus, same-sex parents are more racially and ethnically diverse than their different-sex counterparts, and their children are even more diverse.

4. Answer: c. $51,900

   Same-sex couples with children in the United States have fewer economic resources to provide for their children than do their different-sex married counterparts. They have lower household incomes, are less educated, are less likely
   to own a home, and live in homes of lesser value.

5. Answer: Only b. is true.

   a. False. Adoption rates are higher among same-sex couples than among
      different-sex couples (6 percent versus 4 percent), but the vast majority of
      children living with same-sex couples were identified as "natural born" in
      the U.S. Census.
   b. True Research on the impact of gay and lesbian parents on their children
      is relatively new, and studies tend to be small and focused on subjects that
      are predominantly white and of relatively high economic status. But find-
      ings across these studies are remarkably consistent in showing no negative
      consequences for children being raised by lesbian and gay parents with
      regard to standard child well-being measures.
   c. False. About two-thirds of the quarter million children being raised by
      same-sex couples counted in the 2000 U.S. Census live in states that do
      not guarantee same-sex parents the right to petition courts for a second-
      parent adoption. Such adoptions ensure that both partners have legal
      status as parents. This status is important for a variety of reasons, includ-
      ing ensuring that either parent can make needed medical decisions for
      the child in an emergency situation.

22

The Immigration Kaleidoscope: Knowing
the Immigrant Family Next Door

Etiony Aldarondo and Edward Ameen

This chapter is based on the twin premises that we are all stakeholders in the well-being of immigrant families and that we pay a high price for not having a good understanding of the facts about immigration. We use research findings to address some of the most insidious characterizations about immigrants in our country. We then focus on the immigration and acculturation processes, highlighting both the strains experienced by immigrant families and their strengths. We conclude the chapter with a description of immigrants' attitudes about the United States and how they experience life in this country.

I t is 10 a.m. I (the first author) approach the hotel counter for help in printing a copy of the presentation I will be making later that day. A young woman comes to assist me, and we begin a casual conversation which quickly turns into a conversation about what we do, where we come from, and our aspirations in life. I talked some about the work my students and I do with immigrant children and families before Jenny cuts in and says:

> You know, I worry that we are losing hope. My friends are losing hope. I see it happening a lot. We are the hard-working people and *they* think we are here to do nothing. They think we are nothing. Ever since I was a little girl I had this feeling inside telling me that something was not right. I mean, how could it be that they don't see that we are here to work and take care of our families, that we are good

people. How could it be that they don't see that we want the same things that they want—a good house, food on the table, peace, and good schools?

The printer was not working properly so we waited for the technician to fix it. In the meantime Jenny goes on to tell me about her life as a Mexican immigrant living in the United States since age five, going back and forth across the border for weddings and "quinceañeros," being scolded by teachers for speaking Spanish among friends, keeping the house in order while her mother worked two shifts, getting pregnant at the age of thirteen, raising a child while completing high school with academic honors, and so forth.

So many of us know so little about the immigrant next door. The ones we want to take care of our children; cut our lawns; grow, pick, cook, and serve our food; clean our cars; paint our homes; fix our clothes; teach our children; be at our bedside at the hospital; run the local ethnic restaurants; join our police and military forces; support the local economy; and assimilate to our preferred ways of being. Instead, slowly and passively we appropriate from media outlets and other relevant contexts in our lives (e.g., government, politicians) a narrative about immigrants as criminal, lazy, violent, and uneducated people who don't pay taxes, exploit our community resources, do not want to learn English, are here illegally, take away our jobs and drive wages down, spread epidemics like tuberculosis and AIDS, are threats to our national security, and so on.

But the immigrant next door is nothing like the demonized and toxic carica-ture many of us submissively come to endorse. We know so much about what *we want from them*—shouldn't we know more about them? After all, we are a nation of immigrants, and many of our ancestors were immigrants who came to this country looking for opportunities, freedom, and safety.

That we are a nation of immigrants can hardly be denied. In 2006, the immi-grant and children-of-immigrants population was estimated to be about 60 mil-lion or close to one-fifth of the total population of the United States.[1] Over two-thirds of the immigrants in this country are here legally. Among the estimated 12 million unauthorized immigrants in the country, two-thirds have been here for ten years or less, while 40 percent (4.4 million) of this population have been in the United States for five years or less.[2] What do we really know about the immi-grants and their families living in our neighborhoods? What is the price we pay for not having a good understanding of the immigrant family next door?

The answers to these questions are embedded in history, politics, psychol-ogy, and economics. They are worth exploring, for as we learn about immigrant families, we begin to understand why many Americans adopt a limited and nega-tive view of immigrant families in a context where state and federal goverments often favor criminalization and deportation over support for the development of immigrant families and their integration into society. In this chapter, we attempt to help you see immigrant families differently. As the eminent family therapist Salvador Minuchin said, "We live our lives like chips in a kaleidoscope, always part of patterns that are larger than ourselves and somehow more than the sum of their parts . . . when we look at human beings from this perspective whole new possibilities open up for exploring behavior and alleviating pain."[3]

We have divided the chapter into three main sections. In the first, we present research on immigration, and in doing so we address some of the most insidious characterizations about immigrants in our country. Rather than focusing on specific immigrant groups, we talk about immigration issues as they relate to foreign-born people of various ethnicities living in the United States. In the second section, we focus on the immigration and acculturation processes, highlighting some of the strains experienced by immigrant families. Closer attention to the immigration process helps us appreciate the resources and strengths of immigrant families while giving us a better idea about the conditions that promote and hinder their development. We conclude this chapter with a description of immigrants' attitudes about the United States and their experiences in this country. If we are to know the immigrant next door better, it seems prudent that we listen to what they have to say about living next to us.

RESEARCH ON IMMIGRATION

A large segment of the American public believes that there are too many immigrants in this country, that most immigrants are in this country illegally, and that the level of immigration should be reduced.[4] This perception appears to be fueled in part by the increased movement of immigrants to small towns and suburbs, where immigrants do not blend in as easily with the general population as they do in large urban areas of traditional immigration states like California, Texas, and New York.[5] The reality, however, is that the proportion of immigrants in this country is about the same as it has been for over 150 years. In 2007, there were 37.9 million immigrants in America (12.4 percent of the country's population).[6] Comparatively, immigrants made up 9.7 percent of the population in 1850 and 14.7 percent in 1910.[7] As a matter of perspective, "the rise in immigrant population from 1990 to 2000 was much less dramatic than the one from 1901 to 1910, when the population was just 92 million and the number of immigrants had jumped by 8.8 million."[8]

In terms of documentation status, over two-thirds of immigrants have proper legal documentation to work and live in this country.[9] Interestingly, documentation status is very discrepant between children and parents in immigrant families:

Under the age of six, 93 percent of children are citizens, but only 19 percent have one or both parents with citizen status.[10] Far more children are citizens than their parents.

Public preoccupation about the number of immigrants in this country is linked to an array of perceived detrimental effects of immigration on the well-being of the nation in the areas of health, mental health, civic life, work and the economy, education and language use, and crime. Not surprisingly, many in the public see immigrants as burdens to the country.[11] If there were fewer immigrants around, the logic goes the nation will be better off in these critical domains of life. However, research suggests these judgments to be based on incomplete or inaccurate information.

Health

According to health statistics, immigrants have a life span that is 3.4 years longer (80.0 compared to 76.6 years) than that of native-born people, they experience lower mortality rates, and they have better health statuses and behavioral outcomes.[12] Immigrant children are less likely than their native counterparts to experiment with illicit substances, engage in other risky behaviors, and be obese.[13]

Due to financial, cultural, linguistic, and documentation barriers (e.g. proper identification), immigrants have been shown to access health services at a lower rate. Although some see immigrant health insurance as a "taxpayer expense" because immigrant labor has "limited value," there is conclusive evidence to the contrary: Immigrant children cost $270 a year in health care, compared to $1,059 for native-born children.[14] Examination of health-care expenditures "refutes the assumption that immigrants represent a disproportionate financial burden on the US health care system."[15] For example, when immigrants made up 10 percent of the population in 1998, they only accounted for 7.9 percent of health-care costs. Additionally, immigrants without Social Security numbers contribute $8.5 billion a year in taxes toward Medicare and Social Security, which they are not eligible to redeem.

Mental Health

Researchers have yet to reach a consensus about the mental health status of immigrants compared with that of natives, especially after taking into consideration the toxic effects of poverty.[16] For both immigrant and native adults, poverty is the best predictor of mental health problems. Thus, the more financially strapped immigrants are, the more likely they are to experience mental health problems such as anxiety and depression. But data from studies of foreign-born and first-generation immigrant teenagers suggest that foreign-born youth are more psychologically sound than their native peers. Although the journey of migration is difficult, many immigrant teens have the benefit of protective factors that promote better health, including higher levels of parental supervision, lower levels of parent-child conflicts, involvement in religious practices, and greater satisfaction with the support offered to them by relatives, friends, and significant others in their social network. Unfortunately, the protective power of some of these factors fades away during the acculturation process.[17]

Civic Life

Given the disproportionate amount of airtime occupied by anti-immigrant voices in television and radio outlets, it is hardly surprising to find people who think immigrants are bad for American society and that whatever contribution they may make to the quality of our civic life is minimal next to the damage they cause. The data, again, do not support this view. Over 45,000 immigrants are serving in active or reserve capacity with the military and over 26,000 recruits have been naturalized as citizens since September 11, 2001.[18] (The immigration process for undocumented servicemen and -women has been expedited under President Bush and through the proposed DREAM Act in Congress.) "America gave these men, and their families, home and hope and they reciprocated with distinguished service, exceptional leadership, and boundless patriotism."[19]

Immigrant citizens are very motivated to participate in the democratic system of voting, and nearly half of all Hispanic registered voters are foreign-born.[20] The Democratic presidential debate that aired in 2007 on Univision, a Spanish-language television network, drew substantially more viewers than debates aired on English-speaking networks around the same time. Matthew Dowd, chief pollster for President Bush, said in the *Wall Street Journal* that the Hispanic vote has grown 400 percent in the last twenty years.[21] When the House passed the "Sensenbrenner Bill" in 2005, branding undocumented immigrants as criminals, the following spring saw a huge mobilization and some of the "largest civic demonstrations in the U.S. in more than a generation"[22] and resulted in the alienation of the Hispanic community from the Republican Party.

Contribution to civic life can also be thought of in terms of how often families access the resources in their community and participate in functions and events. Although accurate reporting of these data is hard to obtain, some figures suggest that immigrants may be less likely than their native counterparts to volunteer in a religious, school, or community organization.[23] To be sure, the relative lack of involvement of immigrants in broader community life is not surprising when considering that poverty, demands of physical labor, cultural, linguistic, and

documentation barriers are formidable obstacles to civic engagement and disproportionately affect immigrant families in this country. When thinking about the
civic engagement of immigrant families, however, it is also important to consider
that significant numbers of immigrants continue to be actively engaged civically
and politically in their native countries even years after immigrating to this country. Interestingly, research suggests that this group of immigrants often translates
the skills, commitments, and networks they developed in their native countries
into valuable resources for civic life in the United States.[24]

Work and the Economy

We are currently experiencing what researchers call a "bimodal migration wave,"
in which large numbers of immigrants have either low levels of education and
work-related skills or are highly skilled and educated. Combined, both groups contribute $50 billion a year in human capital to the U.S. economy.[25] In the workplace,
immigrants have frequently been met with barriers due, in part, to difficulties applying skills developed in their countries of origin to the working conditions in this
country. This may explain why immigrants seem to earn less than natives; nearly
2 million immigrants earn less than the minimum wage, and the average yearly
income in 2001 for a low-wage immigrant parent was $14,400,[26] almost $4 less
per hour. A family is in poverty when it makes below 200 percent of the federally
determined income level measured according to family size. In 2007, 40.1 percent
of all immigrant families and 28 percent of all native families were in poverty.[27]
Compared to native families, immigrant families are not as easily lifted from poverty by having an additional working parent in the home. In fact, there were double
the number of two-parent immigrant families in poverty compared to two-parent
native families in 1999 (22 percent and 44 percent respectively).[28] Thus, it seems
reasonable to assert that wages rather than employment levels account for much of
the income disparity between immigrant families and native families.

A second factor determining family income is education at the time of arrival.
The current discrepancies in wages are best explained by significant differences
in education levels, particularly at a time when recent waves of immigrants are
less educated than their predecessors.[29] Immigrant families, in particular those
starting at low-pay, entry-level positions, take ten to twenty years to earn good
incomes, become homeowners, and catch up to their native counterparts. The
poverty rate for given cohorts of immigrant families decreases incrementally over
time. Some argue that children who come from disadvantaged schools and live
in poor and minimally educated households—regardless of their aspirations or
English fluency—will continue to bear the consequences of this profile.[30] Fortunately for these families, there appears to be negligible to no difference in wages

between documented and undocumented immigrants,[31] as nearly 96 percent of undocumented immigrant men are in the labor force.[32]

Some immigrants move up the economic ladder by starting their own small businesses. Recent census reports indicate that "immigrant entrepreneurs are the fastest-growing segment of small business owners today,"[33] outpacing non-immigrant business owners. In Los Angeles, the number of Hispanic-owned businesses increased by 700 percent in twenty years, outpacing Hispanic population growth at 200 percent.[34] Furthermore, immigrants do not tend to concentrate in a few occupational sectors, as compared to native-born workers.[35] The popular image of immigrant men as farm workers and women as housekeepers is a poor match for the significant spread between managerial, professional, technical, sales, administrative, service, laborer, and farming occupations among the 18.9 million foreign-born workers in the United States in 2002.

Some wonder if immigrants have adverse affects on the labor markets for native job seekers. Aviva Chomsky[36] alerts us to the fact that this question is based on the assumption that there is only a fixed number of jobs. In fact, increases in population create more demand for products, and thus for workers to make them, whereas decreases cause the shutting down of businesses, stores, schools, and hospitals. Historically, unemployment rates have fluctuated independently of immigration rates, including during the Depression of the 1930s, when very few immigrants arrived in America. Rather than insinuate cause and effect from coincidence, it is important to investigate factors that are related to both changes in immigration *and* changes in employment. Writes Chomsky, "the same global economic restructuring that exacerbated inequality in the United States [where the wealthiest 5 percent control 60 percent of the money] *also* contributed to increasing immigration."[37]

Recently, the President's office released an economic impact statement indicating that working immigrants make the market more competitive, helping raise native-born wages by up to 1.8 percent since 1990, and increasing total U.S. native-born wages by $30–$80 billion annually.[38] Succinctly, immigrants help the economy now, and are expected to contribute in positive ways in the future.

Education and Language Use

Four out of five immigrant families speak a language other than English at home.[39] Nonetheless, there are still notably high levels of English language use within immigrant families. For example, California census data show that more than 71 percent of Latino families and 89 percent of Asian families speak English very well or exclusively at home.[40] In spite of differences in the use of language at home, children of immigrant parents "receive grades in school that are equal to or even higher" than non-immigrant peers.[41] In fact, children of immigrants account for a disproportionally large number of high-school valedictorians in this country.[42] Overall, the immigrant population is on a par with their native-born peers in rates of having a college degree (27.3 percent and 27.2 percent, respectively)[43] but is markedly behind in terms of high-school graduates in the workforce (64.5 percent and 92 percent, respectively).[44] Foreign-born students often have more favorable views about school than their peers and drop out of school less often—half as often in Miami and one-third as often in San Diego.[45]

Many might also be surprised to learn that, while immigrant children have lower verbal and reading achievement scores on standardized tests, these discrepancies fade away after considering factors such as the trajectory an immigrant family may have taken to arrive in the United States, language proficiency, and the quality of the schools they attend. We know that English-language proficiency is a strong predictor of scores on standardized tests, much more predictive than family factors.[46] We also know that more immigrant children compared to native-born children improve their English-language skills as they move into adolescence.[47] But higher levels of English-language proficiency do not shield immigrant children from the adverse effects of attending failing schools. Education experts argue that immigrant children often attend schools that not only obstruct learning and engagement but may be toxic to healthy learning and development, making the school itself "the single best predictor of academic achievement" for this group of children.[48] Schools have the potential to educate children in a way that complements their ethnic heritages as opposed to assuming that these heritages interfere with their learning. Additive, as opposed to subtractive schooling, can boost students' confidence and connect them with their school.[49]

Most ignored in the educational system are undocumented immigrant children. Without legal status, they can rarely complete basic schooling, apply to colleges, and find stable work. In fact, only 5 to 10 percent of undocumented high school graduates go on to college.[50] This has unintended consequences on the economy and sends a clear negative message to immigrant families about the importance of education for all in this society. Meanwhile, researchers have noted that school revenues would increase, and tax payments would go up if undocumented immigrant children were able to enter college.[51]

Crime

Analyses of crime in immigrant populations make it clear that anecdotal impressions of immigrants as criminals are not met with scientific evidence. "For every ethnic group without exception, incarceration rates among young men are lowest for immigrants, even those who are the least educated."[52] Interestingly, these findings mirror the conclusions of a study commissioned over 100 years ago that evaluated and discredited the negative stereotypes of criminal immigrants and a crime-ridden society of immigrants.[53] The available data suggest that an influx of immigrants over the last three decades may have indeed contributed to *lower* crime rates, even in cities like Los Angeles, New York, and Miami that have larger-than-average immigrant populations. Without evidence to support the view of immigrants as criminals, we must wonder if ignorance, xenophobia, and nativism—the belief that native-born people are superior and more entitled than immigrants—are the true operating forces in myths such as these.

IMMIGRATION AND ACCULTURATION PROCESSES

Immigration Process

The immigration process is one of separation, loss, dislocation, discovery, adaptation, integration, and growth. This is a process packed with excitement, ambiguity, possibility, and stress that requires a fair amount of flexibility and skill to navigate successfully. In addition to changes in socioeconomic status and cultural life, immigrant families must negotiate the differences between their native and host environments. Most often, these differences pertain to gender roles, the various expectations of multiple generations (i.e., grandparents, parents, children) in family life, differences in the pace of acculturation of various family members, and social isolation.[54] As is to be expected, immigrant families vary in their ability to meet these challenges.

Because children typically have fewer strings attached to specific cultural beliefs and practices and have greater access and opportunity to interact with their host culture, they tend to adapt more quickly to the new environment than their parents do. Often, immigrant parents respond to this discrepancy by rigidly holding on to ways of thinking and doing consistent with their cultures of origin. This causes discord and stress for family members attempting to find their way in the new culture. As youth spend time at school, develop social bonds, and undergo their own personal development, they often mirror and embrace the new while questioning and rejecting parts of the old culture. Adolescents in particular may question the utility of their parents' culture-based beliefs, values, and practices as they form individual identities and put pressure on their parents to conform to what they perceive to be the dominant ways of being in this country. Within this context, grandparents become "defenders of traditional values and preservers of the family's ethnic identity,"[55] often clashing with their acculturating grandchildren and putting additional pressure on parents to fulfill traditional cultural expectations.

Much of the discrepancy between an immigrant's new and old cultures rests on an oversimplified representation of what counts as traditional or normal family life in this country. "The use of monolithic images of the 'Normal American Family' as a stick against which all families are measured is pervasive in the family wars. . . ."[56] Inherent in this normalized image is a code regarding what the family can be—generally white, middle class, heterosexual, headed by a bread-winning dad, and a mother who cares for the children—and what values, norms and beliefs are acceptable—generally that families should be democratic, open, flexible, and forgiving. This image creates challenges for immigrant families that hold differing conceptions of family life. Problems arise when immigrant children internalize this ideal and when society isolates families who are different. The bridge between the immigrant family's lived reality and the prevailing family codes in this country consists of systems that allow immigrant families to maintain their traditions and values while experimenting and integrating new beliefs, values, and practices into their ways of being.

Often overlooked in the experience of immigrant families is their loss of major supportive social networks from their country of origin. Virtually all immigrant families are overwhelmed when they immigrate because the functions once taken on by extended family members and friends are now the work of the family and particularly the parents. "This increase in needs and reciprocal expectations takes place precisely while the [family member] is in turn most overloaded and less able to fulfill the other's need."[57] Because there are established connections between one's well-being and one's social network, it is understandable that immigrant parents and children will experience distress over this loss of network. Apart from relying on each other more, the challenge for many families is to reestablish a broader network of community participation. Moreover, support from host communities, positive attitudes toward immigrants, work opportunities, affordable housing, and a "general level of community wealth and support services" are crucial for immigrant families to successfully navigate this process.[58]

The above-mentioned pressures notwithstanding, the typical immigrant family appears to offer a supportive and caring environment for its members. Compared to native-born households, immigrants have been found to have higher marriage rates and lower divorce rates.[59] Greater marital harmony appears to be one of the reasons why children in immigrant families are 50 percent more likely than their native-born peers to be living with both parents.[60] The 2000 U.S. Census also shows that immigrant families with children tend to have larger household sizes. Grandparents, older siblings, and other relatives are commonly found in immigrant family homes. To be sure, an expanded family household offers greater opportunity for intimate bonds, social support, and adult supervision for children, but it can also lead to overcrowding, which is known to adversely affect child development. "Nearly half of children in immigrant families live in over-crowded housing, compared to only 11% of children in native-born families."[61]

Acculturation

Should we encourage immigrants to let go of their native identities and adopt a more generic set of American cultural beliefs, values, and practices? If you believe this to be the case, you share what was once a popular view of the ac-culturation and assimilation process in the United States, which was commonly referred to as "the melting pot." This notion that immigrants eventually lose their cultural identity and fully adopt American values and ways of being has been shown to be both inaccurate and unhealthy for many families. Some refer to this process as "straight-line assimilation," whereby immigrants irrespective of cultural background learn to take on dominant American values and attitudes with similar results.[62] Instead, a growing number of immigration experts are now proponents of other approaches. Portes and Rumbaut describe the concept of "segmented assimilation," leading to three profiles that can exist within contem-porary immigrant families.[63] The first is consonant acculturation, where children and their parents both become full parts of the mainstream at approximately the same pace. This is contrasted with dissonant acculturation, where the chil-dren and parents acculturate at different paces (typically the children acculturate much faster), and which may lead to intergenerational conflict. The third type is selective acculturation, where both familial generations adapt to aspects of the new culture and retain parts of their native culture. With this type of accultura-tion, there is little conflict between family members, and the children are often bilingual. Naturally, families that differ in education, age, social support, stress, income, cohesion, and other characteristics will fall into different types in this segmented model.[64] Particularly problematic is dissonant acculturation, where gaps in the family's adaptation to life in the United States can produce tensions and even put them into a trap of downward mobility.

John Berry examined the relationship between how people acculturate and how well they adapt to their host society.[65] Dividing immigrant youth into four clusters—integrated, national, ethnic, and diffuse—he found that integrated youth, who showed favorable affiliations toward their native and host societies, had the best adjustment in terms of psychological and sociocultural outcomes. On the other hand, diffuse youth—those with ambivalent and relatively weak native and host identities—had the poorest rates of adaptation. He found similar results at the family level: The soundest families were those that maintained their cultural heritage and identity and participated in the everyday life of the larger soci-ety. These findings suggest that policy makers and mental health professionals ought to consider the benefits of integration over the rejection or singular preference for any one particular cultural orientation.

Moderate levels of acculturation appear to be protective for immigrant youth in most circumstances, but both high and low levels of acculturation put them at risk for substance abuse and mental health problems.[66] Moderately acculturated youth from immigrant families often do better psychologically, physically, and academically relative to their native-born peers, even those peers with the same socioeconomic and ethnic background.[67] Thus, contemporary thinking in this area suggests that it is important for the well-being of children in immigrant families to maintain some form of integrated, bicultural identity.

Interestingly, researchers have reported that the protective effects of acculturation decline over time. Referred to as "the paradox of assimilation,"[68] "the immigration paradox,"[69] or "the healthy migrant phenomenon,"[70] the issue is that there is a powerful connection between the number of years lived in this country and the catching up of immigrants to the same levels of risk that their American peers are exposed to. These risks include health problems, crime, drug use, depression, anxiety, and other factors. For example, as immigrant children adopt the high-fat diets that are popular in this country, they experience a sharp increase in obesity.[71] Similarly, in the area of education, it has been noted that "immigrant children become less willing to work hard in school the longer they are in this country."[72] Thus, it seems that while some aspects of acculturation—including American educational attainment and English language acquisition—are import predictors of successful families, other factors of the acculturation process may have negative consequences.

IMMIGRANTS' PERCEPTIONS OF LIFE IN THE UNITED STATES

The mismatch between public perceptions about immigrants, research data on immigration, and the many challenges faced by immigrant families as they integrate into American society gives us cause to wonder how immigrants experience life in the United States. Do they feel welcome in this country? Why, in spite of the many vicissitudes they experience and the pressures of anti-immigrant forces, do they stay? What do they think about American citizens? Fortunately for us a recent national survey of over 1,000 immigrants in the United States provides answers for these and many other interesting questions.[73] Here we highlight the findings of the study most relevant for the purposes of this chapter.

It turns out that the overwhelming majority of immigrants consider the United States a special place to be (80 percent) and report being relatively happy living in this country (96 percent). They value the economic opportunities afforded to them in our society (88 percent), our commitment to promoting women's rights

(68 percent), our democratic system of government (62 percent), and having the freedom to choose how to live their lives (40 percent). They consider our legal (67 percent), health care (67 percent), and education (60 percent) systems to be better than what many of them had in their countries of origin. About three-quarters of immigrants indicate that they want to make the United States their permanent home and approximately eight out of ten say that they think of themselves as Americans or as acting like Americans outside the home while keeping their own culture and traditions at home. This bicultural identity is reflected also in the finding that many immigrants keep close contact with family and friends in their country of origin (59 percent), send money back to relatives (44 percent), keep abreast of current events in their home country (47 percent), and hold dual citizenship (32 percent).

In terms of how they are treated by others, immigrants are somewhat more guarded in their judgments—a little over half (53 percent) believe that as a group immigrants are not treated well by Americans. The majority (68 percent) indicated that Americans are not nice to each other. As indicated by the authors of this report, this last finding is consistent with data from general population studies showing that many Americans believe lack of respect and rudeness are on the rise in this country. Interestingly, most immigrants (63 percent) in this survey report having been treated well by government immigration officials.

Concerning other issues raised earlier in this chapter—for example, education, English language use, work, and civic life—reports by immigrants are fairly consistent with other research data. For example, the majority of immigrants believe that they have an obligation to learn English (65 percent) and find that learning English is essential for their personal and economic prosperity (87 percent). Nearly half (47 percent) of those coming to the United States with limited English take classes to learn the language and say they can read and communicate well (49 percent). In terms of attitudes toward work, immigrants profess a strong work ethic with a solid majority (73 percent) indicating that it is very important to work and stay off welfare. In reference to civic life, many immigrants believe that it is very important to become a citizen (68 percent), to serve in the military (49 percent), and to volunteer for community service (47 percent). "For an overwhelming majority, their connection to the U.S. is neither tenuous nor solely economic."[74]

CONCLUDING REMARKS

It is now about 11:30 a.m. I (the first author) have been talking with Jenny for over an hour. She is so articulate and clear about who she is as an immigrant and as an American that I am left hoping that more people could listen to her and wonder what it would be like if we could find ways to include the voices of immigrants in the national conversation about immigration in this country. Jenny has just been accepted to college in a city far away from her border hometown and far away from an abusive partner who did not see with good eyes her desire to go to school and become a professional. She told me that she had thought hard and long about what to study and had decided to become a lawyer.

> Frankly, I am better at the sciences. I was always good at math and science and for a while thought about studying to become a doctor or a nurse. But I see what is happening and have decided we all need more people fighting for us. I think as a lawyer I would be able to do that.

I think Jenny is right. But the fight is not only hers to fight. Now with the copies of my presentation ready, and reluctantly getting ready to go, I ask her if she would mind me sharing her story with others. She replies, "I don't know that there is anything special in my story—it is just like thousands of others. But if you think it would help someone, go ahead."

Shortly after this encounter with Jenny we received an invitation from the editor of this volume to write a chapter on immigration to be included in a book for college students. Rather than offering an academic treatise, we thought it would be better to try to loosen the grip that the current anti-immigrant climate holds on our collective imagination by providing readers with an opportunity to reflect about immigration from the interrelated perspectives of content, process, and worldview. Each of these perspectives is offered here as an antidote to myopic and demeaning characterizations of immigrants that are rampant in popular media outlets. Together, they offer us a better appreciation of the lived experience of our immigrant neighbors and their contribution to American society.

All of us are stakeholders in the well-being of immigrant families because they are part of our kaleidoscope: Together we eat in the same restaurants, work in the same offices, learn in the same schools, and worship in the same churches. If we agree to build a shared community, benefits abound: "The mastery of different languages, the ability to cross racial and ethnic boundaries, and a general resiliency associated with the ability to endure hardships and overcome obstacles will clearly be recognized as a new cultural capital that will be crucial for success in a modern diversified society, not a handicap."[75] Immigrant families do well and make significant contributions to our economic and community well-being when we offer them the minimal supports to so do. However, "[c]hoices to develop more empowering narratives are sorely limited by the larger culture's negative views of immigrants."[76] Consequences abound from these discriminatory processes as our nation's complex history of immigration has shown. Individuals who experience the greatest amounts of perceived discrimination also show the poorest psychological and cultural adaptations.[77] Additionally, immigration stigma can cause decreased performance in multiple domains and problematic social interactions.[78] The very thing we come to fault is something we've created.

If the one shared hope among all stakeholders is that immigrant families will contribute positively to American society, then conditions and attitudes must align to reach that goal. Otherwise we risk ending up blaming the victim while watching our distorted views turn into self-fulfilling prophecies. The challenge is not easy, considering that the majority of national magazine covers published in the last four decades of the twentieth century portrayed overwhelmingly alarmist depictions of immigration[79] and that immigrants themselves do not have much of a voice or presence in our national conversation about immigration. With more accurate portrayals of immigrant families, we are hopeful that ordinary citizens, policy makers, and service providers will be better equipped to promote the well-being of the immigrant family next door.

In the News

THE PICTURE-PERFECT AMERICAN FAMILY? THESE DAYS, IT DOESN'T EXIST

Washington Post, September 7, 2008

Andrew J. Cherlin

With the debut of the Palins before a nationwide audience, a presidential campaign that was supposed to be about the economy, Iraq or even race has unexpectedly become—for a little while, at least—a conversation about family. But even before the surprising news of 17-year-old Bristol Palin's pregnancy, the Obamas, Bidens and McCains had spent an inordinate amount of precious convention time introducing us to their loved ones: videos, scripted shout-outs, smiling tableaus as the confetti came down. Both parties clearly thought that it was crucial for the candidates to show how deeply they value their family lives.

But if the candidates wished to convince viewers that their families were just like ours, they were undone by a 21st-century reality: There is no typical family anymore—at least not in terms of who lives in the household and how they are related. Alaska Gov. Sarah Palin noted as much on Wednesday. While introducing her clan to a cheering crowd of the Republican faithful, the GOP vice presidential nominee said: "From the inside, no family ever seems typical. That's how it is with us."

In fact, the diversity of American households was the unspoken lesson of both conventions, as four strikingly different kinds of families came into view. First, the Obamas. The Democratic nominee's half-sister, Maya Soetoro-Ng, spoke to the Denver crowd, highlighting his biracial family background, dominated by an often single mother and a largely absent father. Obama's wife Michelle also took a powerful turn at the podium, focusing on her husband's biography but also playing up her own high-powered career and modest roots. The Bidens were introduced to a national audience that week as well, a stepfamily formed after the tragic death of the senator's first wife. With the McCains, we see another stepfamily, formed this time after the senator's divorce. Their family also includes Bridget, a daughter adopted from Bangladesh. And the Palins bring to the stage two working parents with five children, including a pregnant teenager and an infant with Down syndrome.

Divorce itself is not new to the presidential politics—Ronald Reagan and John F. Kerry both campaigned with second wives by their sides—but never has such an extraordinary range of family histories been center stage.

A half-century ago, when the two-parent, breadwinner-homemaker, first-marriage family was at its peak, all of the candidates would have conformed to the same mold. In the 1950s, iconic TV shows—the ones that you can still find while channel-surfing—celebrated the Cleavers and their ilk. Ward went to work and earned enough so that his single paycheck could keep June, Wally and the Beaver happily provided for at home. Sentiment against divorce in public life was so strong that New York Gov. Nelson Rockefeller's presidential aspirations were stymied in 1964 because he had recently divorced and remarried.

But the Cleavers are only available in reruns now, and the prominence of the breadwinner-homemaker family rapidly declined in the last third of the 20th century. Married women moved into the workforce, divorce rates rose, and more children were born outside of marriage.

That traditional family unit has been replaced by a wide variety of living arrangements. Today, only 58 percent of children live with two married, biological parents. Many others live with stepparents or with single parents. Even having a pregnant teen in the home is not that unusual: About one out of six 15-year-old girls will give birth before reaching age 20, according to the National Center for Health Statistics.

The candidates seemed to realize that none of their families is typical in the old sense. None of them tried to look like the '50s family. Instead, they focused on being "typical" in a different, 21st-century sense: They worked hard to show us how emotionally close they are.

Over the past few decades, the emotional rewards of family life have become more important to Americans, as compared to the rewards of bringing home a paycheck or raising children. In a 2001 national survey conducted by the National Marriage Project, more than 80 percent of women in their 20s agreed with the statement that it's more important "to have a husband who can communicate about his deepest feelings than to have a husband who makes a good living."

Personal satisfaction, the feeling that your family is helping you grow and develop as a person, communication, openness: These are the kinds of criteria people use in evaluating their family lives. Practical concerns still matter, but if that's all that holds your family together these days, people may view it askance. Given the demographic diversity of American families, emotional closeness, not who the Census takers find in your home, has become the new gold standard.

And so all four aspiring first and second families, despite their differences, appealed to the voters in much the same way. Each wanted to show how much support and warmth they provide to one another. What matters here is not whether your current wife is your first or second but whether you draw emotional strength from her. So Obama refers to his wife as "my rock" and McCain says of his wife, Cindy, "she's more my inspiration than I am hers." What matters is not whether your teenage daughter is pregnant but whether you provide loving support to her. So Palin and her husband issued a statement assuring the nation, "As Bristol faces the responsibilities of adulthood, she knows she has our unconditional love and support." What matters is being a loving, devoted father, even after the tragedy of losing one's spouse. So Biden's son Beau introduced his father to the Democrats in Denver as "my friend, my father, my hero."

This is not to say that the modern family is a free-for-all, choose-your-own-Thanksgiving-guest-list adventure for everyone. Social conservatives, for instance, still hold the family to stricter moral standards. In 1998, sociologist Penny Edgell asked all of the pastors in four upstate New York communities whether they agreed with the statement, "There have been all kinds of families throughout history, and God approves of many different kinds of families." Eighty-eight percent of pastors from the more liberal Protestant denominations agreed; none of the pastors from conservative denominations did. Social conservatives tend to disapprove of divorce except in cases of infidelity or desertion. They teach their children to abstain from sex until after marriage. But the religious right's reaction to the news of Bristol Palin's pregnancy shows they are willing to embrace a family that deviates from their ideals if the parents are willing to support each other and their children through difficult times. As former Baptist preacher, Arkansas governor and GOP presidential candidate Mike Huckabee said last week, "People of faith aren't people of perfection."

What is important today, in other words, is not who you live with—and how you're legally bound to them—but rather how you feel about them.

This is a barrier-breaking election in so many ways. But apart from the race and gender hurdles being trampled, the 2008 campaign has also shown that Americans, whether from red or blue states, have embraced a broad definition of what constitutes a family. Some traditionalists may lament the decline of the first-marriage, single-earner households. But diversity, in this case, has clear virtues. Would we really want to go back to an era when a divorce disqualified a person from running for president? Come November, it is unlikely to bother many voters that McCain is on his second marriage or that Michelle Obama had a demanding career or that Palin's daughter is facing what used to be called a shotgun wedding.

Of course, Americans' tolerance for family diversity still has limits; many voters, for instance, find it difficult to accept gay and lesbian unions. In 2004, Mary Cheney, the lesbian daughter of Vice President Cheney, sat in the audience with her partner as her father delivered his acceptance speech at the Republican convention. But the couple did not join the rest of the Cheney family on stage afterward and did not sit with the vice president when President Bush delivered his speech the following evening.

If the trend toward embracing greater diversity continues, however, convention stages a generation from now could easily look quite different from this year's. We could all be watching as a gay or lesbian candidate shouts out to his or her "rock" or "inspiration": a same-sex partner, smiling from the VIP box. ◼

For Review

1. How do you think the "cohabitation revolution" presented by Smock and Manning has changed or will change the way we view the formation of families? Do you think this trend will reduce the fear of sex and sexuality that Schwartz describes? For example, will our "fear of sexuality that is not heterosexual, married, and under the control of patriarchal norms" lessen in a world in which cohabitation is increasingly common?

2. Mignon R. Moore argues that the ways in which black lesbian couples espouse ideologies of relationship equality reflect the class backgrounds of her study participants. Moore's research highlights how the intersection of race, class, and gender shapes what we value in intimate relationships. How might we apply this lesson to Aldarondo and Ameen's discussion of contemporary immigrant families? How might immigration status also impact the ways intimate relationships are formed and what types of values couples espouse?

3. How have the ways in which young people become "adults" and create their own families and lives changed over time? What do you foresee this process looking like for children born today? Do you think that the historical shifts mentioned by the authors in Part Three will continue to follow the same paths, or will new patterns and processes emerge in coming decades?

4. Several of the readings compare groups (married and cohabiting couples, married and divorced couples, same-sex and opposite-sex couples, etc.). Other readings identify the similarities between groups. What are some of the advantages and disadvantages to each approach when researching and writing about stepfamilies and blended families? How might we benefit from comparing stepfamilies with non-stepfamilies? How might we benefit from identifying similarities between families?

5. Activity: Find a newspaper, magazine, or journal article or blog that discusses research on marriage or divorce. Using what you've learned in Part Three, explain what the marriage and divorce statistics mean, and whether or not the research is accurate and useful. Given Virginia Rutter and

250 | Part Three

Patrick Heuveline's discussions of the methods used to study marriage and divorce, how could this research be improved?

6. Activity: Think about some of the married couples you know, and the number and types of connections they have to friends, family members, and their community as a whole. Do your own experiences or the experiences of couples you know reflect Gerstel and Sarkisian's finding that marriage reduces social ties? If not, how are the couples you know maintaining social ties to others? Create a list of policy suggestions to "encourage community-friendly families and partnerships," as well as a list of suggestions for couples on how to create and maintain support networks.

PART FOUR

Unequal Beginnings: Social Class and America's Children

23

Beyond Family Structure: Family Process Studies Help to Reframe Debates about What's Good for Children

Philip A. Cowan and Carolyn Pape Cowan

Family policy discussions in the United States have been dominated by a focus on family structure (e.g., married, separated, divorced, single parents). We attempt to show how paying attention to the quality of family relationships—not just to family structure—provides a framework for designing successful interventions to promote family and child well-being. We present a five-domain risk model that illustrates how a combination of parents' mental health, father-child and mother-child relationships, couple relationship quality, patterns transmitted across generations, and life stress and social support outside the family affects children's adaptation. We describe the results of several preventive interventions that used this model and discuss the implications of our approach for family policy and family service providers.

Ever since 1992, when Republican vice-presidential candidate Dan Quayle criticized a fictional television character, Murphy Brown, for having a baby without being married, family values and family policies have assumed an important role in political debates between those with a liberal or conservative bent. Should single parenthood be discouraged and marriage encouraged? Should marriage between same-sex partners be legalized or forbidden? Should divorces be made more difficult or easier to obtain? Should poor families receive income supplements or tax breaks? These questions frame the discussion of family issues in terms of categories or typologies. Most often, the focus is on family structure—are the biological parents married, divorced, cohabiting, separated, or single? In this chapter, we argue that what is left out of too many contemporary family policy discussions is a concern with *family process*—the quality or pattern of the interactions among family members.

We are concerned with family policy debates, not only because government regulations affect the lives of many families, but also because the debates in themselves have the power to influence what ordinary families actually do. Conclusions about single parenthood and divorce, for example, propel at least some toward marriage and others to preserve their marriage despite misery or domestic violence. It would be well, then, to make sure that both the logic and the evidence cited on both sides of family policy questions actually support the position held by each of the advocates.

We see some difficulties with the evidence cited by both liberals and conservatives who describe families in terms of categories or types. Both sides typically justify their policy positions by pointing to social science research that purports to show that *their* view would lead to children's enhanced development and well-being, whereas the opposing view would fail to help children and might place them in harm's way. Some examples:

- Those who advocate policies to encourage marriage note that single mothers are more likely to be poor, and their children more likely to be at risk for academic difficulties and behavior problems.[1] Marriage, they argue, could bring the family out of poverty with resulting benefits to children.

- Opponents of same-sex marriage often claim that children will suffer from the absence of both male and female role models. Supporters of same-sex marriage point out that, contrary to stereotype, children of lesbian parents are not significantly different than children of heterosexual parents on a number of developmental measures.[2]

- In a book entitled *The Case for Marriage: Why Married People Are Healthier, Happier, and Better off Financially*, Waite and Gallagher summarize large numbers of studies showing that, on average, in comparison with nonmarried couples, married couples are better off.[3] Although the authors mention the fact that many of these advantages accrue to *happily married couples*, they continue to minimize that distinction throughout the book. This is an important omission because there is a good deal of evidence that they do not cite showing that married couples in high conflict are less healthy than couples who can regulate negative emotion in the course of an argument, and that the children of unhappily married couples suffer from their parents' heated or unresolved conflicts.[4]

We live in a time when polarized public discussions are the norm. The proponents of a particular view assume that they can only be right if they prove the other side wrong. In our attempt to highlight the importance of family process, we will not argue that categorical descriptions of families in terms of structure or demographics are irrelevant to discussions of family policy. There are often important differences in outcomes for children whose parents are married, divorced, or single, and these facts can help us fashion appropriate policies or interventions. But we intend to add a relatively neglected perspective to the discussion—by focusing on the *quality* of relationships within the family. Our own view is that (1) all of these ways of describing families are important in understanding children's well-being, and (2) a consideration of information about family processes will lead to policy recommendations for governments, social service agencies, and families themselves, that differ from typical conservative and liberal approaches to American family policy.

Because of the constraints of chapter length, we have chosen to focus our discussion of family process and children's well-being primarily on issues concerning the involvement of fathers in family life, and the *quality of the relationship between the parents*. This choice leads us to ignore other equally important family decision-making and policy questions such as whether both partners should work outside the home and utilize local child-care facilities, whether the government should regulate workplace practices to provide support for workers' family lives (e.g., through family leave), or whether it is the responsibility of the government to provide high-quality child care.

We begin with a very brief summary of the voluminous data on the association between categories of family structure and children's well-being. We then summarize the research on family process guided by a family systems model, which demonstrates that *a combination of data* regarding five family risk or protective factors provides the best explanations of children's level of development, adaptation, and problematic behavior. We discuss the model's implications for how both parents and social service agencies should think about the kind of interventions that can improve family environments. We then explore the implications of this family systems model for family policy. We conclude that, in contrast with conservative thinkers who advocate inducements to poor single parents to marry and liberal thinkers who advocate family income supplements to poor families, the data suggest that interventions to strengthen couple relationships and involve fathers more centrally in family life—regardless of whether the parents are married—have the potential to provide important benefits for children's social, emotional, and academic development.

Family Structure, Family Demographics, Family Values, and Children's Well-Being

As Stephanie Coontz points out in Chapter 5 of this volume, there have been a great many changes in family structure and demographics over the past century, although the amount of change depends in part on the beginning and end points of our historical search. We focus here on the fact that over the past sixty years, there have been marked increases in the rates of single parenthood and divorce *and* a decline in marriage rates and birthrates. The central question for family policy is how to interpret these changes. If they are interpreted as evidence of a decline in the quality of family life, then we should consider what kinds of family arrangements, social services, and government policies might alleviate the negative impact or reverse the effects. If the changes are interpreted as evidence of family variety, resilience, and a response to historical and economic shifts, then proposals that would affect marriage and divorce rates through government regulation or the provision of social services may not be necessary.

Controversies about the Impact of Divorce

The question of how divorce affects children remains one of the most contested areas of family research. There is not room to describe the controversy here, but the issue has been well-described elsewhere in both U.S. and U.K. publications.[5] There is no doubt that, at least in the short term, parents and children are affected when parents separate. Most children of any age are extremely upset by the divorce of their parents, and a substantial number suffer at least temporary setbacks in social and emotional development and academic achievement. In the long term, however, the negative effects dissipate for most children, so that "only" about 20 percent of children suffer in lasting ways.[6] This means that, despite the fact that some children may be suffering some consequences of their parents' divorce, it is also true that the vast majority will go on to develop healthy and productive lives. In our view, the sociologist Paul Amato has a sensible perspective on the issues surrounding divorce.[7] He suggests that the usual framing of the question—"Does divorce hurt children: yes or no?"—is misleading. He suggests a more differentiated approach: "Divorce benefits some individuals, leads others to experience temporary decrements in well-being, and forces others on a downward trajectory from which they might never recover fully. Understanding the contingencies under which divorce leads to these diverse outcomes is a priority for future research." As we will see below, some important contingencies can be found in the research on family processes, especially based on how conflict between parents both before and after divorce is handled.

Controversies about the Impact of Single Parenthood

Similar conclusions can be drawn from research on the impact of single parenthood on children. There is no doubt that if you are an actuary interested in predicting negative outcomes, you can rely on the myriad of studies showing that, on average, a large list of behavioral and school problems appear more frequently in children living with only one parent.[8] Again, the question is how to interpret the correlational finding. Some senior policy makers treat the correlational data as causal; if single parenthood increases poverty and produces risks for children, then provide incentives for single parents to get married and the lives of children will improve.[9] Of course, it is impossible to do a randomized clinical trial of this hypothesis by assigning some women randomly to a "get married group" and others to a "stay single" group. But we lack even correlational data to show that when poverty declines and single parents marry, their children's well-being increases.

Some researchers argue that the correlation between single parenthood and negative outcomes for children reflects a selection effect—parents with more financial, intellectual, and social resources are more likely to marry and less likely to divorce. In a careful summary of the literature, Cherlin concludes that even after selection effects are considered, there is a small but statistically significant effect of family structure (married vs. single) on children.[10] That is, family structure plays some role in determining outcomes for children, but the majority of children reared in single-parent homes fare quite well. It is necessary, then, to examine other factors to explain the fact that children of single parents are more likely to have cognitive, social, or emotional difficulties.

These brief accounts of research on divorce and single parenthood serve to make our main point. "Family decline" proponents who pay attention only to family categories and report only the statistically significant differences between family types overstate the magnitude of the effects; their presentation makes it appear as if nontraditional family structures account for the major proportion of social problems and psychopathology in children and youth. These overstatements are then used to justify recommendations to parents, social service providers, and policy makers: in order to protect children, we should encourage married parents to stay together, make divorces harder to obtain, and encourage single parents to marry. We will use the same data and other studies to come to a different conclusion: in order to protect children and prevent parents' divorce, we could profitably provide services to strengthen couple relationships before they become so problematic and painful that separation and divorce become reasonable options.

Are Family Values to Blame for Historical Changes in Family Life?

Most social observers who assert that families are in decline place the blame for this decline on an erosion of family *values*.[11] They argue that changes in single-parent, divorced, and dual-worker families result from individual decisions about family life that reflect a lack of investment in the importance of becoming responsible parents devoted to the care of their children. It follows from this analysis that to protect children, we need interventions that will remind parents of these important family values and convince them to reinvest in them.

There are two puzzling aspects of this argument. First, the idea that a change in family values triggered the social trends we have been discussing is not based on any data we know of that (a) assess changes in family values over time, and (b) show that values held by individual men and women are in fact correlated with the family arrangements they have constructed. One counter-example can be seen in an interview study of low-income unmarried women[12] suggesting that they hold rather traditional family values concerning the importance and desirability of marriage and of the financial responsibilities involved in making that commitment, and that these ideals lead them to be wary of entering into marriages they believe are doomed to failure.

A second response to the focus on family values as explaining negative family trends comes from newly emerging studies with quantitative data. One of the major sources of stress on contemporary families is financial.[13] Financial circumstances often affect family decisions about marriage, divorce, and whether both partners need to work outside the home. Not only is there external stress on families from lack of money and little workplace flexibility, there are also limited social service resources for direct services to families in difficulty, and even fewer resources for preventive services to offer assistance to families before their dysfunction reaches a level that is difficult to treat. From this perspective, what is needed to protect children is not an exhortation to parents to adopt more positive family values (a relatively inexpensive approach) but rather serious governmental commitment to change the economic circumstances that play havoc with the lives of mothers, fathers, and children. We return to this issue below.

FAMILY PROCESS AND CHILDREN'S WELL-BEING: A FRAMEWORK BASED ON FIVE FAMILY RISK AND PROTECTIVE FACTORS

The family structure and demographic approach represents an outsider perspective on family life. One can categorize a family as, for example, low-income or high-income, married or not married, on the basis of the kind of information gathered in the census. By contrast, the family process approach pays attention to the characteristics of each family member, and especially to how the members behave with each other. What are the central factors in a family process approach? Elsewhere, we have summarized our own research and many other studies that support a five-domain family systems risk model of children's adaptation.[14] This model demonstrates that a child's cognitive, social, and emotional development can be explained by information concerning five kinds of risk or protective factors that affect children's development:

1. the level of adaptation of each family member, his or her self-perceptions, and indicators of mental health and psychological distress;

2. the quality of both mother-child and father-child relationships;

3. the quality of the relationship between the parents, including communication styles, conflict resolution, problem-solving styles, and emotion regulation;

4. the patterns of both couple and parent-child relationships transmitted across the generations from grandparents to parents to children;

5. the balance between life stressors and social supports outside the immediate family.

Each Parent's Level of Adaptation

Beyond the questions of whether parents are married or poor, a family process approach looks at whether either or both parents are suffering from depression, anxiety, personality disorders, or serious mental illness. The task here is not to place parents in a particular diagnostic category, but to discover whether their difficulties interfere with or affect the quality of their relationships with each other and their children. Not surprisingly, evidence suggests that parents who are depressed, antisocial, or schizophrenic are less effective at solving their problems as a couple and function less effectively to provide nurturance, guidance, and limit setting appropriate to the age of their children.[15]

Parent-Child Relationships

There are many different ideas about what constitutes effective parenting. It is noteworthy that the proliferation of self-help books on parenting present widely different prescriptions for parenting behavior, most without systematic evidence to support the author's recommendations.[16] The picture brightens somewhat when we turn to systematic studies of parenting styles. There is reasonable agreement in the research literature on children's development that *authoritative* parenting—a combination of parental warmth, structure, limit setting, and appropriate demands for maturity—provides a context in which children are more likely to develop effective cognitive skills, better relationships with peers, and fewer behavior problems.[17] Other parenting styles are less effective. *Authoritarian* parenting is harsh and structured. *Permissive* parenting is warm but laissez-faire, with few if any limits. *Neglectful or uninvolved* parenting is neither warm nor structured and demanding. It is probably obvious that parental harshness and neglect are not good for children. The lesson here for modern parents who both work and tend to see their children for shorter times during their waking hours is that warmth without some form of limits and maturity demands is not helpful in stimulating children's growth or the development of social and cognitive skills and self-regulation.

A serious limitation of both the popular and social science literatures is that "parent" has generally meant "mother."[18] Only in the past few decades have there been systematic studies of father-child relationships,[19] and there is an even smaller body of information on how the combination of two parents' styles of parenting affects children's development. Yet, it should come as no surprise that systematic studies find that when fathers are more positively engaged with their children's daily lives, the children, the mothers, and the fathers themselves are more likely to be competent, to form more positive relationships with peers, and to show fewer signs of emotional distress. Furthermore, information about the quality of the father-child relationship enhances our ability to account for children's adaptation, over and above what we know about the quality of the mother-child relationship.

We should make clear what we are *not* saying here. We do not mean to imply that fathers should be encouraged to be involved with their children when they are abusive to the child or the mother. And we are not arguing, as some do,[20] that having a father is *essential* to raising a well-adjusted child.[21] We are simply stating that a second, positively engaged parent or parent figure can make an additional and unique contribution to children's cognitive, social, and emotional development.[22] So far, the research that makes this point has been done with heterosexual couples as parents; we await further study, but believe that studies of families with same-sex parents will show very similar findings.

The Couple Relationship

Another conspicuous omission from popular books on raising children is the conclusion from a growing body of recent research based on family systems principles about the effect of the parents' relationship on their children. With few exceptions,[23] the popular books focus almost entirely on how mothers relate to their children. What recent family systems research studies reveal, however, is that the quality of the relationship *between the parents*, whether they are married, separated, or divorced, is consistently correlated with how children fare. When couples are unable to resolve their disagreements and either escalate their anger or withdraw into freezing silence, their children are at risk for difficulties in every developmental domain.[24]

We describe below some intervention studies that help to answer the question of whether conflict or withdrawal in the relationship between parents plays a causal role in children's development. Here we briefly summarize two speculations to explain the correlations. First, parents' behavior can have a direct, anxiety-provoking effect on children. When parents' anger toward each other is out of control or they fail to talk with each other for hours or days, many children become increasingly frightened, anxious, and vulnerable. Second, when parents fail to provide a nurturing environment for each other, it is difficult to provide a caring environment for their child; the metaphor of "spillover"—anger overflowing from the relationship between the parents to one or both parent-child relationships—is used to explain the link between couple conflict and children's problematic outcomes.[25]

Intergenerational Transmission of Family Patterns

Substantial evidence exists to support the widespread belief that family patterns tend to be repeated from one generation to the next.[26] We are not suggesting that difficulties in our family of origin doom us to repeat the maladaptive patterns of our forebears. We are simply reporting the fact that mental illness in individuals, harsh or neglectful treatment of children, and dysfunctional couple relationships in one generation increase the risks of similar negative outcomes in the next generation.[27] Fortunately, although positive patterns do not guarantee good outcomes, they function as protective factors that raise the likelihood that they will occur.

During the transition to first-time parenthood, patterns from the parents' relationships in their families of origin become particularly salient. Each parent has some patterns he or she wishes to repeat and some he or she wishes to change in this new family. Coordinating these potentially different dreams is a challenge faced by many new parents. If neither parent has positive models, the challenge is even greater.

In raising the topic of intergenerational transmission, we are not simply playing the blame game—that is, explaining or excusing problems in current families as having been passed down from the grandparents. Rather, we are pointing to the fact that attempts to change current family relationship quality almost inevitably involve increasing the consciousness of both parents about the patterns they wish to carry over or avoid.

LIFE STRESS AND SOCIAL SUPPORT OUTSIDE THE FAMILY

What happens inside the nuclear family is affected by the external environment and the family's relationship to it. Families tend to fare better when outside stressors are few or at least balanced by adequate support from kin, friends, and social institutions. Evidence from McLoyd and colleagues' summary of research on African-American families[28] and Conger and colleagues' research on white farm families during a recession[29] indicate that poverty affects children through its corrosive effects on the quality of both couple and parent-child relationships. Stress in the workplace has a similarly disruptive spillover effect on family relationships.

THE FULL MODEL

Most studies of children's development focus on one or at most two of the five family risk and protective domains at a time. Elsewhere we have shown that each of these domains contributes uniquely to predicting children's academic and social competence as well as their internalizing and externalizing problem behaviors in early elementary school.[30] Child rearing is not simply a matter of "good parenting." Children are also affected by their parents' psychological adjustment and their ability as a couple to resolve problems and disagreements between them, by the repetition of cycles across generations, and by the availability of people and institutions to provide support when the culture, country, and neighborhood impose pressures that are difficult to avoid. Data from studies based on this model imply that family interventions that focus on only one of these aspects of families' lives may be limited in effectiveness.

For example, there is currently a large public and private industry devoted to "parenting classes." For a long while, the news was disappointing; the few evaluated programs amassed very little evidence that the classes had direct positive effects on children's behavior,[31] but more recently, parenting classes embedded in University-based research programs have shown some signs of success.[32] The importance of thinking in terms of more than one domain during a parenting intervention is supported by studies showing that therapeutic treatment for mothers of aggressive children often fails to work until fathers are involved and the relationship between the parents is addressed directly.[33]

We have only begun to test the hypothesis that family processes play a *causal* role in children's well-being. The correlational findings are suggestive but not conclusive. It can be argued that some of the links between family process and children's well-being are genetic[34] and that genetic transmission is not subject to interventions that can change family relationships. But newer formulations of the interaction of genes and the environment[35] indicate that even when personality characteristics are highly heritable, changes in the family relationship environment still affect how and whether heritability leads to negative outcomes in the children.

The correlations between marital conflict and children's outcomes suggest that interventions focusing on the relationship between the parents will be helpful to children, but we cannot use correlational studies as proof of our claim. We need to provide some data from intervention studies that have used randomized control designs to demonstrate that when the interventions were followed by more effective couple relationships, parenting effectiveness and the children's behavior were affected in positive ways.

THREE EXAMPLES OF PREVENTIVE INTERVENTION STUDIES BASED ON OUR MULTI-DOMAIN MODEL

The premise of our emphasis on couple relationships when we consider children's well-being lies in an unfortunate fact. In addition to marital dissatisfaction leading to a high divorce rate (around 50 percent of marriages), more than twenty-five studies in Western industrialized societies[36] find that, on average, men's and women's satisfaction with their relationship as a couple declines over at least the first fifteen years of marriage (we know of no longitudinal studies beyond that point). This trend is significant not only for the well-being of couples, but also for the well-being of their children, because other studies show consistent connections between marital dissatisfaction and unresolved couple conflict, and children's and adolescents' achievement, aggressive behavior, and depression. Given these links, interventions that help couples *maintain* satisfaction with their relationship would be an important goal.

Over the past thirty-five years we have conducted three studies of interventions in the form of couples groups led by clinically trained co-leaders. All three studies used randomized clinical trials in which some couples were randomly chosen to participate in the intervention while others were not. The male-female co-leaders met with the couples weekly over at least four months and assessments were made before and after the group interventions to evaluate the groups' effectiveness. The couples were not seeking family treatment but responding to an invitation to meet with our staff around a key family transition or during their children's early development. Our goal was to create a preventive intervention to enhance family relationships when the children were early in their development and to prevent small problems and strains from becoming more serious. We did not attempt to teach couples specific skills, but to help them become the kind of couples and parents they wanted to be. We hoped to do this by providing a safe environment in which they could consider issues concerning their needs as individuals and as a couple. Our interventions and assessments also focused on their ties with their parents and children, and on how to cope with stress and distress and enlist supports inside and outside the family.

Working with Couples during the Transition to Parenthood

In the Becoming a Family Project, we followed ninety-six couples regularly over a period of five years: seventy-two entered the study when pregnant with their first child, and twenty-four were not yet parents and not pregnant.[37] All ninety-six couples completed regular interviews and questionnaires until their first child had completed kindergarten. Some of the expectant couples, randomly chosen, were offered the opportunity to participate in a couples group that met with their co-leaders for twenty-four weeks (six months). Each group session included some open time to discuss personal events and concerns in their lives and a topic that addressed one of the aspects of family life in our model. Relevant to the focus of this chapter, we found that while there was a decline in satisfaction as a couple in the new parents without the intervention, as expected, the new parent couples who took part in a couples group maintained their level of satisfaction over the next five years until their children finished kindergarten. Although expectant couples in both conditions were initially quite happy, five years later, the average scores of couples in the control group had descended into the range where half of them resembled couples already in therapy. Five years after the groups for the parents ended, the quality of the couple relationships and the parent-child relationships in all the families during the pre-school period predicted the children's adaptation to kindergarten as their teachers rated it—academically, socially, and in terms of problematic behavior. This finding seemed especially strong since the teachers (in many different schools) did not know which children were participants in the study.

Couple Relationships and Children's Transition to School

A second intervention study, the Schoolchildren and Their Families Project, followed another 100 couples from the year before their first child entered kindergarten until the children were in eleventh grade.[38] There were three randomly assigned conditions—an offer to use our staff as consultants once a year (the control group), a couples group that emphasized parent-child relationships, or a couples group that focused more on the relationship between the parents during the open-ended part of the evenings. That is, we were comparing the effects of a more traditional parenting intervention (although it is unusual to have fathers attending with mothers) with a group in which leaders focused more on the relationship between the parents. The families were assessed when their children were in kindergarten and first grade. Parents who had been in a group emphasizing parent-child relationships had indeed improved in the aspects of parenting we observed in our project playroom, whereas the parenting style of parents in the control group showed no improvement.[39] By contrast, parents who had participated in a group in which the leaders focused more on couple relationships showed significantly less conflict as we observed them, *and their parenting became more effective.*

In this study, both variations of the ongoing intervention groups had an effect on the children. The children of parents in the parenting-focused groups improved in positive self-image, and they were less likely to show shy, withdrawn, and depressed behavior at school. Children of parents in the couples-focused groups were at an advantage in terms of higher scores on individually administered achievement tests and lower levels of aggressive behavior at school. The interventions continued to have a significant impact on the families over the next ten years—in terms of both self-reported and observed positive couple relationship quality and low levels of behavior problems in the students. The impact of the couples-focused groups was always equal to or greater than the impact of the parenting-focused groups.

Enhancing Father Involvement in Low-Income Families

On the basis of the results of the first two studies, we were asked by the California Department of Social Services Office of Child Abuse Prevention to design and evaluate an intervention that would enhance and maintain the positive involvement of low-income fathers with their children. Along with Marsha Kline Pruett from Smith College and Kyle Pruett from Yale University, we completed the first phase of the Supporting Father Involvement Project, in which ninety-six couples attended a single-session workshop in which material was presented about the importance of fathers in children's lives (the control group), ninety-two fathers attended a sixteen-week fathers group, and ninety-five fathers and their partners attended a sixteen-week couples group.[40] Again, the assignment was random, the groups were led by clinically trained male-female co-leaders, and the curriculum for both fathers and couples groups focused on the five domains of family life we have been describing.

At the beginning of the study, children ranged in age from in utero to age seven. The project was mounted in Family Resource Centers in four California counties; two-thirds of the participants were Mexican American and one-third were European American; 75 percent were married, 20 percent were living together; two-thirds of the households in both ethnic groups had incomes below twice the federal poverty line. Assessments at baseline (in English or Spanish), two months after the groups ended, and again one year after the groups ended revealed the positive impact of participation in one of the intervention groups. In both fathers and couples groups, fathers' involvement in the day-to-day activities of caring for their children (feeding, playing, taking to the doctor) increased significantly, and the children's level of aggressive and depressed behaviors remained stable, in comparison with the children in the control group, whose parents described them as increasingly aggressive or depressed over the same period of time. In addition to these positive effects in the fathers-group participants, fathers and mothers from the couples groups showed a significant decline in parenting stress, and they maintained their satisfaction as couples, in contrast with both controls and parents assigned to the fathers group, whose parenting stress rose and relationship satisfaction declined.

In sum, we have shown that the preventive intervention groups, especially the groups for both mothers and fathers, had positive effects on father involvement, parenting stress, couple relationship satisfaction, and children's problematic behavior. All of these aspects of life are related to children's well-being, and all function as either risk or protective factors for child abuse and neglect. On the strength of these positive findings, the Office of Child Abuse Prevention has supported an extension of the study to a broader sample of another 300 families and created an infrastructure to disseminate the project by providing technical assistance and training in the intervention to staff in family agencies beyond those in the original counties in our study.

IMPLICATIONS OF RESEARCH FOR PARENTS

What are the implications of the research on family process for parents? We emphasize what this perspective adds to current debates that have focused primarily on family structure.

Father Involvement

In our view, the current political dialogue on the risks associated with single parenthood has resulted in an unproductive conversation about the role that fathers play in children's development. Taking their cue from research on family structure, some observers argue for encouraging single mothers to marry so that fathers can be in the home providing income and setting examples, especially for young boys. And in fact, there is now substantial evidence that relationships with fathers are important for girls' well-being as well. In reaction, others argue that this goal represents a conservative position that privileges traditional heterosexual family arrangements and denies the vitality and resilience of diverse family forms. From the structural perspective, then, single parents, especially mothers, are given two choices: find a man to marry or remain confident about their single state.

A new set of findings makes the structural perspective a little more complex. The very large Fragile Families Study taking place in twenty American cities follows about 5,000 children, of whom about 75 percent were born to parents who were not married. The study found that around the time of childbirth, more than half of "single mothers" had the biological father as a romantic partner living in the home, and a large majority were in a romantic relationship with the biological father who wanted to play an active role in his child's life.[41] That is, the existing categories in the family structure perspective vastly underestimate the participation of men, at least in the early stages of family making.

The family process literature adds an important point for parents in all family structures to consider. If there is a second parent (studies here have examined only heterosexual families), positive engaged fathering can make a unique, positive contribution to children's development, regardless of whether the parents are married, unmarried, separated, or divorced. Even though cultural stereotypes about men's roles in the lives of their children have been moving toward a more egalitarian ideal of more equal participation in housework and child care, the realities are still far from this ideal. Men need to know that fathers are important. Women need to help men challenge the stereotype, and avoid the kind of "gatekeeping" that keeps men out if they engage the child in ways that are different from what mothers do.

Beyond Current Books on Parenting

Clearly, the research data and the intervention data we have cited suggest two important topics that are missing in most popular books on parenting. First, as we have noted, fathers are rarely referred to in parenting books, or they are acknowledged in a single chapter devoted to dads. This reinforces cultural stereotypes about the centrality of mothers and gives the mistaken message to fathers that they matter little to their young children's development. We need to find ways to get the word out to parents in two-parent families that both the mother and the father matter, so they can make their own decisions about how they will arrange their parenting responsibilities.

Second, how both fathers and mothers treat children is very important, both on the negative end in terms of abuse and neglect, and on the positive end in terms of providing warmth and structure. Equally important is what happens between the parents. One of the key obstacles to keeping couple relationships alive is time, especially in dual-worker families. We find that modern working parents typically feel that most nonwork time should be devoted to their children. The research findings indicate that it is not "selfish" for parents to focus on their relationship as a couple, to enjoy time together, or to make space to resolve disagreements and difficulties to both partners' satisfaction. Improvements in the quality of the relationship between the parents will have a direct payoff for the children.

Should We Stay Together for the Sake of Our Children?

Authors of a number of books and articles that draw heavily on social science research conclude that, except for situations of domestic violence or abuse, parents in unhappy marriages should attempt to stay together to avoid the negative impact of divorce on their children. Almost all the research they refer to adopts a family structure perspective, simply following children of divorce over time[42] or comparing them with similar samples of children whose parents did not divorce.[43] In both cases, stories recounting long-term distress about their parents' divorce from youngsters and teenagers imply that if only the parents had stayed together, the children would not be having problems. The voluminous data from which we have selected only several reviews and examples suggest strongly that a second comparison group is necessary—children of high-conflict parents or low-conflict but unhappy parents who stay together. Studies of families in which the parents are unhappy indicate that keeping the family structure intact without regard to the quality of the key family relationships does not guarantee children's well-being.

None of the studies of divorce can provide conclusive advice for a mother or father contemplating divorce because there are risks for children no matter which decision is made. Two major questions are important to answer: If the partners stay together, can they find help from a therapist, clergyman, family member, or friend that would help them to improve their relationship? If they separate or divorce, can they still be positive co-parents who support each other in regard to caring for the children? Clearly, including information about family process makes for a more complex but, we suggest, more nuanced discussion of how to think about parents' and children's well-being when parents are unhappy.

IMPLICATIONS OF RESEARCH FOR FAMILY SERVICE PROVIDERS

What are the implications of the research on family process for family service providers?

Making Fathers Welcome

The current interest in involving fathers more in family life is echoed by family service providers who want to include fathers, but complain that men are hard to reach and resistant to the services they offer. In our view, the problem of resistant men is exacerbated by the lack of father friendliness in many family service agencies. As we began the Supporting Father Involvement Project in California communities (see above), our visits to existing Family Resource Centers revealed few signs that fathers were wanted or welcome—in the physical environment (colors on the walls, pictures, magazines), the social environment (mostly women staff), and organization of services or programs (few services or programs for fathers, little flexibility in terms of times when they are offered, little outreach to men). We believe that the problem of resistance to services is much too easily attributed to the men, when an equal share of the problem resides in the resistance of the staff to reaching out to fathers. The Supporting Father Involvement Project has shown that "if you build it, they will come." By now more than 500 men have participated in the program over the last three years, most of them meeting in groups for eleven to sixteen weeks. Staff dedicated to changing the environment of the agency made that happen.

The Importance of Couple Relationships for Father Involvement

We have stated that one of the best predictors of whether a father will become and stay involved with his child is the quality of the father's relationship with the mother. Ronald Mincy and Hillard Pouncy observe that the few existing systematic evaluations of fathers groups composed of low-income men show disappointing outcomes.[44] Most of the fathers groups attempting to increase father involvement occur long after the parents have separated or divorced and after the fathers have lost contact with their children. Not surprisingly, the mothers of the children were not supportive of their ex-spouse or ex-partner's attempts to take an active role in their child's life. Our own family intervention study shows stronger effects for couples groups than for fathers groups. Father involvement, then, emerges not simply from men's decisions to be involved in the family but from the ways in which family relationships enhance or interfere with men's relationships with their children.

Beyond Parenting Classes: Couples-based Interventions for Parents

Both correlational studies and the intervention studies we have cited suggest that the many classes for parents offered in community colleges and social service agencies require some rethinking. First, the classes need to make stronger efforts to recruit both parents and provide experiences that will help them want to stay. Second, the classes need to pay much more attention to how the partners work together—or fail to—to deal with co-parenting and other disagreements. We recognize that this raises the issue that leaders of parenting classes rarely are trained to work with parents on their issues as a couple.

POLICY IMPLICATIONS

Father Involvement

In the Deficit Reduction Act of 2005 (which reauthorized the welfare reform law of 1996), one-third of the $150 million annual budget for family work was to be directed to promoting fathers' involvement with their children. The Promoting Responsible Fatherhood website (http://fatherhood.hhs.gov/index.shtml) recognizes that the goals of marriage promotion and father involvement are directly connected. As in the case of funds allocated to promote healthy marriage, some of the funds were to go to research institutions, but in the case of promoting father involvement, most of the money has been allocated to statewide and local secular and faith-based organizations (faith-based organizations have very detailed instructions that the content of the programs must not include religious material). As of this writing, no systematic evaluations of these programs have appeared.

Marriage Promotion versus Couple Relationship Enhancement

In its growing concern over the erosion of marriage and the problems of children whose parents dissolved their marriage, the U.S. Federal Administration for Children and Families (ACF) used research-based findings from the Fragile Families Study[45] as a rationale for government intervention. The finding that most unmarried biological fathers have an ongoing romantic relationship with the mother when their child is born but fade from their child's life over the next few years[46] was used as a justification for promoting marriage, especially among low-income populations. Starting in 2005, this policy objective was supported by more than $150 million per year for five years, with money from the Deficit Reduction ("welfare reform") Act.

While some of this money has been used in direct efforts to encourage marriage, a substantial amount has been allocated to two very large research projects funded by the Administration for Children and Families to test the effectiveness of "marriage education." Each study plans to include thousands of low-income couples, with the goals of supporting responsible fatherhood and strengthening marriage. One large intervention project, Building Strong Families, conducted by Mathematica,[47] focuses on *unmarried* low-income couples having babies. Another, Supporting Healthy Marriage, conducted by MDRC (www.mdrc.org/project_12_64.html), focuses on *married* low-income couples, most of whom are already parents. Both studies use random assignment to intervention and control groups and both have a primary focus on strengthening couple relationships, not on promoting marriage or coercing couples into making that choice.

The policy implications of these activities are complex and controversial. Some colleagues argue that these interventions are as yet untested with low-income populations; if one goal of the enterprise is to improve conditions for low-income families, why not supplement their incomes directly or at least provide job training, since unemployment is so directly linked to low income? Because we are not aware of evidence that income interventions have improved distressed couple relationships or parent-child relationships, we suggest that it seems reasonable to give relationship approaches that have been evaluated a chance to show whether they work, and for whom they could provide the most benefit. Anecdotal reports from the staff conducting these large national projects, along with our own results with both middle- and low-income couples, give at least some hope that this approach to preventive intervention by strengthening couple and parent-child relationships has promise in terms of strengthening families.

Training and Costs

Family systems research and our own intervention experiences have led us to emphasize the importance of couple relationships for children's well-being and the need to provide services to enhance those relationships. That is, we are calling for increased resources for training as well as for the provision of services that support mothers and fathers in the challenging task of balancing work and family demands during their children's formative years.

We are aware that these increased resources require funding. We are not aware of cost-benefit analyses of this kind of family work. It seems to us that the costs of providing services need to be compared with the costs of not providing services—in terms of family disruption, violence, parents' and children's psychological and physical health problems, and children's and young people's behavior problems.

Conclusions

Our goal in this paper has been to show that research on family processes can add new dimensions to current discussions about how to foster the well-being of children. We have shown that in addition to considering the structure of the family, what fosters children's healthy development and adaptation is having (at least) two parents who are positively involved in the children's lives and in maintaining a satisfying and effective relationship with each other. We believe that while children can grow up healthy in a one-parent household, they can also benefit from positive relationships with an additional co-parent or co-parenting figures.

In particular, we have highlighted how positively involved fathers and parents who nurture the quality of their relationship as a couple and as co-parents contribute to their children's emotional, social, and academic competence. Furthermore, studies of family process provide important messages for parents, family service agencies, and government policy makers about the need to go beyond attempting to persuade parents to "be responsible." If the policy makers are truly concerned with making a difference in children's well-being, they will need to provide more support for individual mothers and fathers and for the relationship between the parents or parenting figures. Rather then starting family policy discussions with attempts to influence family structure and hoping that children will benefit, we recommend starting with programs that enhance the quality of family relationships, with the expectations that improved family relationships will ultimately make family structures more stable and supportive of the development of all family members.

24

Opinion Piece: A Mother's Day Gift That Makes a Real Difference

Valerie Adrian

Here's a thought for a Mother's Day gift that would go beyond the complimentary flowers passed out by restaurants and the complementary speeches churned out by politicians every May: affordable child care that is operated in accord with high-quality national standards.

It's a gift long overdue. In 1971 the House and Senate overwhelmingly passed a Comprehensive Child Development Act to provide quality child care for working parents. The bill mandated extensive training for child-care workers and strict standards, written and enforced with extensive input from parents. But on December 9, 1971, President Nixon vetoed the bill, declaring that publicly provided child care would be "a long leap into the dark" that might weaken American families.

Since then, American families have indeed taken a "long leap" into an unanticipated world. Forty-five years ago, just 14 percent of working women who bore a child returned to work by the baby's first birthday. Today, 83 percent of working moms do, 70 percent of them at the same hours they worked before the child's birth.

Ten million families of children under fourteen pay for child care. And they often pay a lot, with no guarantee of quality care. Less than 10 percent of day care centers and 1 percent of in-home day cares in the private sector are accredited. In contrast to the child-care centers run by the military, there is no national accreditation or training standard in place for civilian child care.

In 2005, average child-care costs ranged from a low of $58 per child per week for a pre-school-aged child in Alabama to a whopping $259 per week for infant care in Massachusetts. Parents in Massachusetts spend an average of $802 per month on child care for a four-year-old, and $1,123 for infant child care. While their average monthly mortgage bill of $1,645 may seem staggering, if they have two children, the $1,926 monthly day-care bill exceeds it by nearly $300.

Meanwhile, the approximately 2.5 million day-care workers in this nation made an average of just $8.65 an hour in 2004. This totals $346 a week, an amount that would not give a child-care worker enough money to put her own child in day care in many states. Three-fourths of all child-care workers work in a home care setting, and they make even less. This doesn't leave much money for the kind of training that was envisioned by the 1971 bill.

On August 22, 1996, President Clinton, twenty-five years after the Comprehensive Child Care Act was first proposed, signed the Personal Responsibility and Work Opportunity Reconciliation Act of 1996, which allocated $14 billion dollars in funding for child-care subsidies for low-income workers. But budget cuts led to the loss of child-care funding for 200,000 children in 2003 and 2004, and President Bush has proposed another freeze on child-care funding for fiscal year 2009. This will represent a loss of benefits for an additional 200,000 children over two years. Meanwhile little progress has been made in regulating the quality of child care even for families that can afford to purchase it on the open market.

If politicians and businesses would initiate a serious discussion of how to provide quality child care to America's families, that would be one Mother's Day gift that wouldn't be tossed in the drawer with the guest soaps and tea towels of Mother's Days past.

Fact Sheet

MILITARY CHILD CARE: A GOVERNMENT SUCCESS STORY

When politicians make speeches celebrating Armed Forces Day, they seldom discuss the military child-care system. But this is an area in which the military has a lot to teach the civilian world. Indeed, the transformation of child care in the military is one of the government success stories of the past twenty years.

Thirty-eight percent of active-duty women and 44 percent of active-duty men have children. Yet, in the 1980s, the military child-care system was in shambles. The annual employee turnover rate in military child-care centers was 300 percent, exposing soldiers' children to the constant churn of new and untrained child-care workers. Many centers were in violation of health and safety standards.

In 1989, the Military Child Care Act established new standards and funding formulae for the care of children of those in our armed forces. Government spending for military child care increased from $89.9 million in 1989 to $352 million in 2000. Within fifteen years, the military went from having centers that didn't even meet basic health codes to having the highest quality child care in the United States.

Today there are 900 day-care centers and 9,000 family child-care centers serving over 200,000 military children each day. Child care is available for infants and children up to age twelve. In the civilian world, only 10 percent of all full-time employees have access to employer-provided child-care centers, a figure that falls to just 3 percent for men and women earning less than $15.00 per hour.

Ninety-eight percent of all military child development centers, before- and after-school programs, and summer child-care options are nationally accredited. This makes the child-care centers accountable for producing uniform, quality care. Child-care centers are subject to inspection at any time. All child-care workers in the military receive standardized training and support, and they must all undergo extensive background checks. In contrast, fewer than 10 percent of all day-care centers and fewer than 1 percent of in-home day-care facilities in the private sector are accredited.

One of the best predictors of quality child care is the level of wages and the rate of turnover for child-care employees. By 2001, entry level wages in military child care had risen to $8.00 per hour, compared to $7.40 an hour for civilian child-care center workers and $5.00 per hour for family-care workers. The turnover rate had plummeted from 300 percent to 30 percent annually. By comparison, the private sector child-care employee turnover rate exceeds 40 percent.

The military provides child care to all enlisted and civilian contracted employees' children. The tuition is based on a sliding scale fee chart. Families earning up to

$23,000 per year pay between $40 and $53 per week per child. The price gradually increases by pay category. A family earning between $44,001 and $55,000 pays between $74 and $86 per child per week, and families making $70,000 or more pay a maximum of $114 per child per week. These child-care benefits also extend to military reservists who are either on active duty or performing inactive duty training.

It's amazing what government can do for families when it puts its money where its mouth is.

25

Diverging Development: The Not-So-Invisible Hand of Social Class in the United States

Frank F. Furstenberg, Jr.

The advantages and disadvantages associated with social class position build up over time, creating huge developmental differences in the course of growing up. This chapter discusses how development is shaped by social class position and, how the processes associated with class position are either mitigated or amplified over the early part of the life course. By early adulthood, gaping disparities exist between children growing up in disadvantaged and advantaged families. I discuss how these trajectories pose special problems for less advantaged youth making the transition to adulthood due to the need for resources to pay for higher education.

America has never been a class-conscious society by the standards of the rest of the world. The notion that social class determines a person's life chances has always been anathema to this country's democratic ideology. Some of the earliest observers of American society, most notably Alexis de Tocqueville,[1] noted the disdain among American citizens for class distinctions compared with the acceptance of stratification in France or the rest of Europe. Although social class was far more prominent and salient in the United States when Tocqueville visited in the 1830s than it is today, from the country's very inception, the seemingly boundless possibilities of land ownership and the ideology of upward mobility softened its contours. The idea that any American by dint of good character and hard work could rise up the social ladder has long been celebrated, no more clearly than in the great American myth of Horatio Alger. That "rags to riches" parable instructed young men—and it was men—how to make their fortunes in nineteenth-century America.

Curiously, the United States, long regarded as the land of opportunity, has never entirely lived up to its billing. Studies comparing social mobility in the United States with that in our Western counterparts have failed to demonstrate that social mobility is higher here than in other industrialized nations.[2] Yet, Americans seem as oblivious to class gradations today as they have ever been. Most of us declare that we are middle class, and finer distinctions such as working class and upper middle class have all but vanished in the popular vernacular and even in social science research. Yet, as the salience of social class has declined during the past several decades, we have witnessed a huge rise in economic inequality.[3]

When I was entering academic sociology more than four decades ago, the social world was described very differently than it is today. Even while recognizing the muted notions of social class held by most Americans, social scientists were keenly attentive to, if not obsessed with, distinctions in values, lifestyle, and social practices that were inculcated in the family and linked to social mobility.[4] Indeed, the idea that parents in different social strata deliberately or unintentionally shaped their children's ambitions, goals, and habits, which in turn affected their chances of moving up the social ladder, was widely supported by a large body of literature in psychology, sociology, and economics. These studies showed how families at different rungs on the social ladder held distinctive worldviews and adhered to different ideas of development.[5] Most of all, social scientists believed that life chances were highly constrained by values and skills acquired in the family and by the structures of opportunity in the child's immediate environment that shaped his (and it usually was his) chances of economic success. Fine gradations of social class could be linked to virtually everything from toilet training to marriage practices.[6]

Social class, not so long ago the most powerful analytic category in the researcher's conceptual toolbox, has now been largely eclipsed by an emphasis on gender, race, and ethnicity. Socioeconomic status has been reduced to a variable, mostly one that is often statistically controlled, to permit researchers to focus on the effect of determinants other than social class. With relatively few exceptions, we have stopped measuring altogether the finer grade distinctions of growing up with differing resources. True, we continue to look at poverty and economic disadvantage with no less interest than before, and we certainly understand that affluence and education make a huge difference. Yet, most developmentalists view economic status as a continuum that defies qualitatively finer breakdowns. Consequently, working-class, lower-middle-class families, or even families in the middle of the income distribution are concealed rather than revealed by combining income, education, and occupation, without regard to the particulars of status combinations.[7] In short, the idea of social class has largely been collapsed into rich and poor, marked by education and earnings—above and below the poverty line. Think of the way we currently treat "single-parent families" as an example. They have become almost a proxy for poverty rather than a category of families that experience life differently than their two-parent counterparts do.

The contention that contemporary developmental research downplays the influence of social class in no way is meant to imply that professional attention to gender or race or ethnicity is unwarranted or should be diminished. Without a firm grasp of social class differences in contemporary America and how they affect men and women and people of different races and ethnicities, however, much of the current research on gender and ethnicity may not give us a full understanding of how the two shape social reality and social opportunities. Just as we have come to recognize the hazards of lumping together all Hispanics or Asians, I would suggest we need a more nuanced understanding of how individuals' levels of education, occupation, and income alter and shape their worldview and life course.

In this essay, I outline a research agenda for examining social class in greater detail. Beginning with a brief discussion of developmental theories, I point to some of the methodological obstacles to studying social class that must be attended to. Then I turn to developmental processes that expose research questions that warrant greater attention by social scientists, particularly developmental sociologists and psychologists. My work nicely complements observations put forth by Sara McLanahan[8] in her 2004 Presidential Address to the Population Association of America on inequality and children's development, although my attention is devoted primarily to how developmental *processes* are shaped by stratification. I examine a series of natural occurrences associated with social class that work in tandem to fashion a developmental course for children from birth to maturity that is pervasive, persistent, and far more powerful in the United States than Americans generally like to acknowledge.

SOCIAL CLASS: A PROBLEMATIC CONSTRUCT

One reason why attention to social class has faded can be traced to the academic controversies surrounding the very idea that social classes exist in this country. If what is meant by a social class system is a tightly bounded and largely closed hierarchical set of social strata that determines the life chances of its members, then surely most social scientists would agree that America is a classless society. But social class has been used in a different way to mark the structure of economic and social opportunities affecting individuals' behaviors and beliefs, networks and associations, and, ultimately, knowledge about and access to social institutions such as the family, education, and the labor market.

Viewed in this way, social classes are not tightly bounded categories; they are fuzzy sets created by experience and exposure to learning opportunities and selective social contacts that derive from resources that can be marshaled by individuals and their kinship networks. In this respect, the fuzzy nature of social class appears to differ from the constructs of gender or ethnicity, although in truth both of these constructs, too, have been appropriately critiqued as "socially constructed" statuses and are not naturally unambiguous. Still, there are no certain markers that identify individuals as belonging to one class or another; social class is probabilistically constructed and measured by constellations of economic and social opportunities. Thus, we might say that someone who has low education and works at a menial job that pays poorly is lower class, a term that admittedly has become virtually taboo in the United States. Nonetheless, we easily recognize that those possessing these attributes are more socially isolated, excluded from mainstream institutions, and limited in their access to mobility than their better educated and better paid counterparts. Whether we refer to such individuals as lower class, poor, disadvantaged, or socially excluded, we must still admit that their opportunities for advancement during their own lifetime or their ability to confer such opportunities to their children are far more restricted than the opportunities of their more advantaged counterparts—a classic example of a class-based world.

I will dodge the question in this paper of whether it makes sense to identify a particular number of social strata such as was common in social science a generation ago, designating four, five, or seven classes that possessed different family practices, values and beliefs, or lifestyles and cultural habits.[9] Instead, I merely want to observe how the neglect of social class has created a void in attention by developmentalists to how stratification structures the first several decades of life. I refer to "several decades" because toward the end of this paper, I report on what my colleagues and I on the MacArthur Network on Transitions to Adulthood[10] have learned about how social class shapes the transition to adulthood in myriad ways that have profound implications for the future of American society.

A DEVELOPMENTAL THEORY OF SOCIAL CLASS

Human development involves an ongoing interaction between individual-level biological potential and social processes shaped by children's multiple and changing social environments. Sometimes developmentalists make distinctions between maturation, regulated in part by biology, and socially arranged learning through institutions such as the family or school, the process that we generally refer to as socialization. One of the important legacies of late-twentieth-century developmental science was to put an end to the fruitless and misleading debate between nature and nurture. Researchers reoriented theories designed to explore ongoing interactions from birth to maturity in varying and often nested contexts— families, child-care settings, schools, communities, and the like—to investigate how social context afforded or denied opportunities for optimal development. In doing so, they understood that optimal development can vary both by children's innate abilities or biologically influenced capacities and by their varying exposure to learning environments. Indeed, it is the ongoing interaction between biology and environment that shapes the course of a child's development.

No one understood this scheme better or promoted it with more vigor than Urie Bronfenbrenner,[11] who, as it happens, was one of the pioneers in psychology to examine the influence of social class on children's development. Bronfenbrenner's theory of development located the individual in an embedded set of contexts that extended from the intimate and direct to distant and indirect as they socially impinged on and shaped the course of human development over the life span. Bronfenbrenner's ideas about development in context loosely parallel a tradition of sociological theory stemming from the work of George Herbert Mead and of Charles Cooley,[12] which has come to be known as "symbolic interaction." Like Bronfenbrenner, both Mead and Cooley conceptualized human development as an ongoing process of engagement and response to social others—that is, social exchange guided by feedback from the surrounding social system. As sociologists applied these ideas in practice, they quickly realized how sensitive children are to varying contexts and cultures, a lesson that is closely aligned with Bronfenbrenner's theory.[13]

It was, and I believe still is, just a short step from this general theory of human development to seeing the pervasive influence of social class in shaping the course of development. That step involves a careful appraisal of how learning environments such as families, schools, and neighborhoods set the stage for a socially orchestrated life course. These more distal social arrangements are carefully regulated in all modern societies by gatekeepers who exercise presumably meritocratic standards based on a combination of talent, performance, and sponsorship.[14] In modern societies, parents cede direct control of their children's fates at increasingly early ages to other agents (for example, teachers), who become instrumental in guiding children through an age-graded system of opportunities. Resourceful parents are able to train and coach their children, select and direct choices in this system, advocate when problems arise, and try to arrange for remediation when their children are not following an optimal path. As I have argued elsewhere,[15] parents' managerial skills have become increasingly important in modern societies, influencing how adeptly children navigate the institutional arrangements that affect their opportunities in later life.

Of course, parents themselves are also embedded in different opportunity structures; specifically, they are more or less privileged in the knowledge, skills, and resources they can provide to their children. Expressed in currently fashionable parlance, parents possess different amounts of human, social, cultural, and psychological "capital" to invest in their children, and hence their managerial resources and skills reflect their social position. But parents are not the only agents who matter in children's development. All caregivers of children also possess different levels of resources and, generally, the higher the status of the children, the higher the level of social and cultural resources these caregivers possess.

Of course, children possess different capacities to learn, relate, and procure support and sponsorship during childhood. These capacities influence their access to kin, friends, neighbors, teachers, and peers that can and do promote or diminish their chances of socioeconomic attainment. And even small differences in the abilities of parents and other caregivers to manage children's development can accumulate over time if they consistently are more positive or negative.

A century ago Max Weber used a powerful metaphor of loaded dice for how history operates.[16] Each throw of the dice, he imagined, is weighted by the result of the previous throw; constraints increase with repeated tosses of the dice, leading to progressively more skewed outcomes. Social class can be conceptualized as just such a mechanism, establishing a set of life chances that become more sharply pronounced as they play out over time. Micro-interactions accumulate in a patterned and successively more consequential pattern, etching a probabilistically preordained trajectory of success.

The outcome of these interactions is always affected by how the child comes to interpret and act in the immediate contexts. This might be an operational definition of resiliency or vulnerability as described by psychologists such as Rutter, Garmezy, and Werner[17]—the idea that some children are able to defy the odds. Interestingly, developmentalists in recent years have given at least as much, if not more, attention to research on beating the odds as on developing a careful understanding of how the structure of opportunities creates systematic advantage or disadvantage over time—or, we could say, why and how growing up in a certain social location establishes strong and long odds of departing from an expected pattern of success.

Recent data as shown in Figure 25.1 indicate that 42 percent of children born into the bottom fifth of the income distribution will remain there as adults. Only 7 percent will make it into the top one-fifth of the income distribution. For those born into the top one-fifth of the income distribution, 40 percent will remain there, while just 6 percent will fall into the lowest quintile.[18]

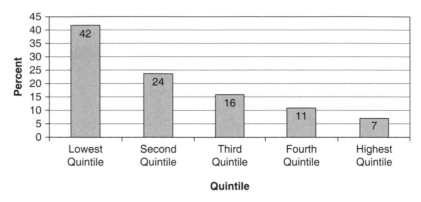

Figure 25.1 | Percent Moving from Lowest Quintile

METHODOLOGICAL OBSTACLES TO STUDY

Until very recently, we lacked the data and the methods to observe how social stratification shapes the course of human development. Longitudinal research really only became widely available in the latter decades of the last century, although pioneering studies were done on relatively small samples, such as Glen Elder's now classic work on the life course of youth in Berkeley and Oakland, California.[19] Not until the introduction of the computer could social scientists thoroughly analyze the large-scale samples necessary to examine variation in children's lives over time. Today, it is a relatively simple matter to merge and analyze multiple waves of interview data, administrative records, blood samples, and the responses to modern surveys of children that allow investigators to explore the numerous contingencies and pathways that constitute the course of children's development from conception to maturity.

Barriers based on disciplinary specialization may also have diverted attention from the potential influence of social class. Psychologists have been actively discouraged in many departments from working on large existing data sets and instructed instead to collect their own data, thus restricting the range of problems that could be examined. Beginning in the 1960s, sociologists turned away from studying children, ceding much work on socialization to psychologists. Disciplines have been organized to encourage work on specific life periods, and younger researchers have been encouraged to become specialists in infancy, early or middle childhood, or adolescence. Exceptions abound of course, and I would be remiss if I did not acknowledge those researchers such as Eleanor Maccoby, John Clausen, Doris Entwisle, Emmy Werner, and others, who broke out of the mold or, one might say, beat the odds of doing research in disciplines that discouraged such efforts.

Added to the problems stemming from data availability and disciplinary constraints are the methods themselves that are required to examine how trajectories of development unfold over time. Today, a host of novel techniques are packaged in software for analyzing and interpreting longitudinal data. No doubt, many more techniques and tools will be coming in the future as new and more powerful ways of understanding career contingencies, transitions, and the evolution of trajectories of development are invented and refined. The tools are now available to describe and explain how advantage and disadvantage along many dimensions configure and crystallize the developmental pathways from birth to maturity.[20] In fact, I would contend that data availability and methods have outpaced our theoretical and substantive understanding of how social class influences human development.

THE ORIGIN OF SOCIAL CLASS DIFFERENCES

More sensitive analytic techniques must take account of several features of social class known to influence development. *First and foremost, once set in place, early patterns of development may be difficult to surmount for several different and perhaps overlapping reasons.* At this stage, we are only beginning to learn about brain development during infancy and early childhood, but it is entirely possible that the architecture of early development could well preclude or, at least, compromise subsequent patterns of development. There is growing evidence that cognitive and emotional capacity formed early in life may be foundational, providing a template or structure for later advances.[21]

Exposure to these developmental influences begins before the child is born and is shaped in no small way by mothers' prenatal experiences—their exposure to toxins, their diet, and the quality of health care received during pregnancy—and then by the neonatal health care provided to the newborn infants. Most mothers experience a normal delivery and their children are born in good health, but steep differences exist across social classes in all of these factors.[22] Thus, children enter the world endowed unequally, even if we discount any genetic variation by social class.

The families into which they are born provide vastly different opportunities to build on that endowment. Whether children are planned or unplanned, whether they must compete for limited family resources or have enough, and whether they will receive steady and sufficient attention from parental figures are but a few of the contingencies known to vary by social class.[23] What is less understood is how these early influences combine and accumulate to create developmental divides with lasting effects on children's prospects later in life. The consequences of social attachment, for example, have not been traced long enough to understand whether or how it affects later transitions in adolescence and early adulthood.

The remarkable research by Charles Nelson and his colleagues on institutional care of children in Romania under the Communist regime provides evidence that a critical period exists for emotional development that, if breached, can lead to permanent impairment.[24] Children reared in a collective setting with little or no opportunity to develop attachments with stable emotional figures were emotionally incapacitated. Nelson and his colleagues discovered that if placed in families with emotionally engaging surrogate parents by certain ages, the pattern of emotional disfigurement could be repaired, and perhaps even reversed if the placement occurred early in life. An interesting question, relevant to the discussion here, is whether stimulation and human interaction in early childhood is dichotomous or multi-tiered—that is, whether and how much early interaction sets the parameters for later growth by establishing a critical level or by operating in a more graduated fashion that may still fall below the optimal amount. Few children in American society are impaired by lack of stimulation, but there seems little doubt that many children get less stimulation or fewer opportunities for emotional engagement than is optimal.

A series of experiments in neuropsychology conducted to determine barriers to reading reveals fascinating and perhaps parallel findings on brain development.[25] It seems that middle-class and working-class children with reading difficulties may exhibit different neural responses when faced with a task of decoding words. The researchers hypothesize that the amount of exposure to reading and remediation affects neural responses and could account for the differences by social class, suggesting that the causes and the remedies for reading problems might vary for children by social class.

Both these studies bring to mind an impressive qualitative study by Hart and Risley.[26] Home observation of family interactions among children and their families revealed gigantic variations in the range of words, expressions, and interaction styles, creating, in effect, a continuous and mounting difference in verbal environments that appeared to be linked to the vocabularies that children acquired early in life.[27] These varying cognitive contexts were later linked to reading skills and, accordingly, to school success.

This study leads to a second observation relevant to developmental trajectories of children in different social classes. *Small differences, if persistent, become larger and more consequential over time. A process of psychological and social accretion operates both at an internal and external level as children develop self-concepts, styles of thought, and habits that shape their motivation and social interactions in ways that harden over time.* If, for example, children are exposed to very modest differences in, say, language, reading practices, or interaction styles over long periods of time, the cumulative effects could be quite striking and large. Thus, if years of education, on average, are linked to small differences in parental skills or practices, they could create significant effects, on average, in children's cognitive and emotional skills. These psychological and social styles create impressions on others that are reinforced and reified in informal and formal social settings. To answer the question of how parents' educational levels affect children's development, we need stable measures of social patterns that have been established inside the home, and these patterns must be measured with sufficient frequency to permit us to examine growth curves of emotional and cognitive development that extend into middle childhood, adolescence, and early adulthood.

The cognitive and behavioral styles that emerge in the home, and which are shaped to a great degree by class differences in child-rearing practices, establish what sociologists once referred to as "anticipatory socialization," advanced training for social roles outside the home, particularly the role of student. These class-related habits of speech, thought, and behavior affect perceptions of the child and entrance into preschool programs that foreshadow and initiate placement and social tracking within the school system. Modest or perhaps not so modest differences within families are unlikely to be offset or compensated for by learning that takes place outside the home. To the contrary, these differences are greatly amplified by parents' capacities to locate, gain access to, and monitor settings outside the home and by institutional practices that selectively recruit children from families with the resources and children who exhibit the capabilities to perform well.

Parents in all social strata are well aware that beginning at an early age, children require and benefit from experiences outside the home, opportunities that can offset or reinforce patterns established in the family. We have rightly paid a good deal of attention to child-care settings,[28] but we have much less information on the impact of peer interactions[29] or experiences with skill-enhancing facilities such as recreational centers, libraries, museums, and the like. The likelihood of a steady and stable exposure to these social institutions varies tremendously by social class.[30] Qualitative studies have demonstrated large differences by social class in children's exposure both to the number and quality of these settings. The reasons why are pretty obvious. Parents with more education are both more knowledgeable of, and therefore usually more discriminating in locating high-quality settings. They also have greater resources to gain access to those settings. Finally, they have the ability to organize and take action on their children's behalf and to monitor ongoing engagements, whether they are with the right kind of peers, better classes, or high-quality teachers, coaches, or caregivers.

The other side of the coin is no less influential in channeling children from different social classes into more or less favorable settings. *Settings find and recruit children from families of different social classes with varying levels of energy and enthusiasm*. In other words, the availability of resources establishes to a large extent the social class distribution of families who participate in social institutions in American society. In many instances, settings regulate their clientele by the cost of services: the most expensive attract mostly or exclusively children from affluent families, whether they are prenatal health programs, child-care facilities, after-school programs, summer camps, or Ivy League colleges. Those who can pay the cost of admission typically can afford better teachers and can attract peers who are more motivated and prepared. We have relatively little research on the social class networks of children that emerge over time, but it is certainly plausible that most children in the United States grow up with little or no exposure to peers outside their social class. Thus, their opportunities to acquire cultural and social capital are tremendously influenced by the social class composition of kinship and peer networks. And we have every reason to believe that money and education are playing an ever larger role in regulating the level of cross-class exposure and the composition of children's social networks.

THE IMPORTANCE OF PLACE

Most parents are well aware that where one lives matters. Indeed, the primary way to manage opportunities for children is choice of the neighborhood where children are brought up. Interestingly, we have all too little information on social class and residential decision making. Given that schooling is generally determined by neighborhood, however, parents with more knowledge and resources can select neighborhoods that offer better schools, better peers, and often better recreational facilities. In the study that my colleagues and I did in Philadelphia on how families manage risk and opportunity, we discovered that parents were acutely aware of the opportunities attached to choice of neighborhood, though that awareness did not necessarily mean they were able to exercise much discretion in where to live.[31]

Most working-class families in Philadelphia could not afford to live in affluent sections of the city much less move to the suburbs, where they knew that they would find better schools and more desirable peers. They often resorted to the second-best option: sending their children to parochial schools, where children were monitored more closely, had a longer school day with more after-school activities, and attended school with like-minded peers.[32]

Schools in turn were able to select families that enabled them to produce higher test scores and hence greater academic success. A good portion of these outcomes were predetermined by the selection of parents and their children, although clearly more able, prepared, and motivated students may help schools to recruit higher-quality teachers and administrative staff. As I sometimes like to say, economists want to rule out selection as a methodological nuisance, while sociologists regard selection as a fundamental social process that must be studied as a central feature of how things happen. In any event, social life is created by multiple and interacting influences that generally come in packages rather than operating as particular or singular influences, as they are commonly studied in experimental designs.

This package of place-based influences is one of the larger lessons learned from the Moving to Opportunity Program, which gave families in public housing the chance to move to lower-poverty neighborhoods. Moving to these neighborhoods was not an event, as the researchers tended to regard it from the onset, but a succession of adaptations and interpretations. This succession affected family members differently, depending on experiences prior to moving, new and old social networks, and demographic and unmeasured psychological characteristics of the movers and those who chose to remain. The net effects, always important to policy makers, conceal a huge range of varied responses that unfortunately are only dimly understood.

SOCIAL REDUNDANCY IN MULTIPLE CONTEXTS

Perhaps what I have written thus far is leading to the impression that opportunities at the family, school, and neighborhood levels are strongly correlated—that is, that the various contexts of social class operate closely in tandem in shaping the lives of children. But important work by Tom Cook and his colleagues in their study of families in Prince George's County, Maryland, reveals that, at an individual level, most children experience a mixture of social opportunities.[33] They found that there is only a modest correlation between the quality of parental resources, school resources, and neighborhood resources—surely the opposite conclusion from the idea that children grow up in an environment of class-congruent settings.

Yet, the research by Cook and his colleagues reveals that at the population level (when family characteristics, school, and neighborhood quality are considered in the aggregate), there is a much more powerful correlation among these arenas of social stratification. On average, children from better endowed families are very likely to attend better schools and live in better neighborhoods. It is as if the playing field for families is tilted in ways that are barely visible to the naked eye. Another way of looking at the stratification of social space is to imagine that families with more resources are able to arrange the world so that their children will have to be only ordinarily motivated and talented to succeed. Those with fewer resources must make more effort or have greater talent to succeed. Those with limited or meager resources must be highly gifted and super-motivated to achieve at comparable levels. Developmentalists have often implicitly acknowledged the way the world works by valorizing the families and children who do manage to swim against the current, but we should be measuring the current as well as the swimmer's efforts, particularly when there is every reason to believe that the current has become stronger in recent years.

Opportunity structures, made up of multiple and overlapping environments shaped by social position, are not accurately perceived by individuals from different vantage points in the social system. They can only be understood by examining simultaneously what families see and respond to in their familiar settings, what they do not see but what can be seen by other observers, and most difficult of all, seeing what is *not* there. Take, for example, how much parents or children know about colleges and how they work. Most children in affluent families know more about this topic at age twelve, I would guess, than children in working-class families know when they are ready to enter college. Cultural capital—knowledge of how the world works—is acquired, like vocabulary and speech practices, in the family, schools, and from peers in the community.[34] Class differences result from a process of social redundancy that exposes children to information, ideas, expectations, and navigational tools that lead some children to know what they must do to get ahead and others merely to think they know what to do. Developmentalists have surely studied cultural knowledge of how the world works, but we have a long way to go before we have a good map of what is and is not known by parents and children about the stratification system and how this knowledge changes over time as young people's impressions of how things work run up against how they actually work. With relatively few exceptions,[35] we lack the kinds of recent cultural studies that have peered inside the family, looking at the operating culture of families.

THE SOCIAL CLASS DISTRIBUTION OF NEGATIVE EVENTS

Social class not only opens or shuts doors for advancement, it also influences the probability of negative events and circumstances in the lives of children and their families. The likelihood of bad things happening to people varies enormously by social class, although we know this more from inference and anecdote than we do from systematic studies of children's experiences in the course of growing up. Take, for example, psychological stressors, including death, poor health, accidents, family dissolution, residential changes, job loss, and so on. Virtually all of these events occur much more frequently in highly disadvantaged than moderately advantaged families, and least of all among the most privileged. Negative events are more likely to happen to families who lack educational, cultural, and social capital, which are the protective resources associated with social advantage. Lower-income families are more vulnerable than higher-income families to a host of troubles, including credit loss, health problems, transportation breakdown, criminal victimization, divorce, mental health problems, and the list goes on. They also have fewer resources to prevent problems from happening in the first place by anticipating them or nipping them in the bud (preventive and ameliorative interventions). And, when these problems do occur, social class affects a family's ability to cushion their blow.

Anyone who has studied low-income households, as I have for so many decades, cannot help but notice a steady stream of these events that constantly unsettle family functioning, requiring time, energy, and resources that often are in short supply or altogether unavailable. Life is simply harder and more brutish at the bottom, and, I suspect, it is more precarious in the middle than we ordinarily image. As developmentalists, we have not done a very good job in evaluating how such events affect the lives and life chances of children. They create wear and tear on families and often ignite a succession of subsequent difficulties. The problems may begin with job loss, which in turn results in marital strife or dissolution, and finally settles into long-term mental illness or substance abuse. Or this chain of events can just as easily be reversed. The point is that in the ordinary course of life, children at different social strata face vastly different probabilities of bad things happening to them and their parents, and these events often spiral out of control. Social scientists are accustomed to describing these behaviors as "non-normative" events, but they may only be "non-normative," at least in the statistical sense, in the lives of affluent families.

CLASS DIFFERENCES IN PROBLEM PREVENTION AND REMEDIATION

The distribution of negative events, as I have suggested above, is negatively correlated with social class, just as the distribution of means to prevent and remediate troubles is negatively related to class. Affluent families have access to a tremendous range of strategies for prevention. They purchase and practice preventive health care, they situate themselves in environments free of toxins, and their homes and streets are safer. When and if their children experience problems in school, they can take a range of actions—from changing schools to procuring help in the form of tutoring, assessments, therapy, medication, and so on. If their children happen to get in trouble in the community, they have means to minimize the consequences by tapping informal contacts or legal interventions. We know much about how families employ these preventive and remedial strategies, but we have yet to put together a comprehensive picture of how troubles are avoided and deflected for children in different social classes. If we examined a sample of problem behaviors among adolescents, what would be the likelihood of adverse outcomes occurring from a series of incidents?

The criminological literature provides ample evidence that social class (and race and ethnicity as well) accounts for much of the variation in delinquency outcomes, for example. It is not that adolescents from affluent families do not commit delinquent acts, use drugs and alcohol, and engage in risky sex. Indeed, the evidence suggests that so-called problem behaviors are fairly evenly distributed by social class. But families with greater assets and social connections can minimize the significance of troubles even when they occur, particularly the more extreme sanctions, such as going to court and being incarcerated.

Social advantage provides a form of cover from negative events when they do occur. It provides for the privileged a social airbrush that conceals mistakes and missteps that invariably occur in the course of growing up. The management of problem behavior by families, and their ability to access and use professional delegates (doctors, lawyers, tutors, social service workers) varies across different social classes and represents a neglected topic in adolescent development.

SOCIAL CLASS, SOCIAL CAPITAL, AND SPONSORSHIP

We would miss much about the use of professional and nonprofessional agents in children's lives among different social classes were we to confine our attention to their role in problem intervention and remediation. It is also important to study the role of adult sponsors in promoting children's positive behaviors, skills, and talents. This topic represents a broader exercise of what has come to be called social capital, the social resources that can be brought to bear by families, to promote children's positive development as well as to prevent or correct negative courses of action. Recently, there has been considerable interest in mentoring and the roles that mentors play in children's development, especially in helping children who have limited access to positive role models, advisers, supporters and advocates, and sponsors.[36]

Sponsors, of course, can be family members, but we generally think of them as agents outside the family who act on behalf of children. They can be gatekeepers in institutions that allocate resources and access to programs, services, and opportunities. More often, they are individuals who have connections to a range of different gatekeepers. Students of child and adolescent development should learn more about how sponsorship operates in everyday life because it undoubtedly plays an important part in channeling children into successful pathways.

We know only a little about how various adults help to cultivate skills, talents, and special abilities such as in art, music, theater, sports, and so on, and we know much less about how sponsors promote children's chances of getting ahead by nonacademic means or in combination with formal schooling. This topic merits greater attention because sponsors can play an important role in facilitating social mobility. Less visible, but perhaps equally important, is the role that sponsors play in helping to guarantee that children in the more affluent classes retain their privileged position.

Some research exists on how young people enter the world of work and the role that families play in using contacts and connections to place adolescents in training, service, and work opportunities.[37] Privileged parents understand that their children need to build portfolios of experience—résumés—to get ahead. Research in a Philadelphia study on the less advantaged and the disadvantaged suggests much less understanding on the part of these parents as to how to connect their children to select institutions.[38] Usually, it appears that sponsors identify children from less-advantaged families by dint of their good efforts in school or perhaps through community organizations. Affluent parents do not passively wait for sponsors to find their children. They actively recruit sponsors or place their children in organizations, programs, and social arenas where sponsors are present and looking for motivated and talented prospects. Schools with well-developed extracurricular programs, after-school classes and activities, summer camps, and advanced educational courses are part of the stock and trade of growing up well off. Children in affluent families become accustomed to relating to adults and appreciating what adult sponsors, mentors, and coaches can do for them in middle childhood and adolescence. Increasingly, the role of sponsors figures prominently in young people's ability to navigate successfully as they move from adolescence into early adulthood.

EARLY ADULTHOOD: THE EXTENSION OF INVESTMENT

Early adulthood, the period of life when youth enter adult roles and assume adult responsibilities (entering the labor force and becoming economically self-sufficient and forming families), has in recent decades become a less orderly and more protracted process than it was a half century ago. The driving force in this extended passage to adulthood has been the perceived need for a college education and, for the more privileged, an advanced degree often accompanied by a lengthy apprenticeship in a professional career. Related to this trend, but not wholly because of it, young people put off more permanent relationship commitments and, generally, parenthood as well. Commitments to marriage and children, public opinion tells us, have become almost a second stage of the adult transition, often put off until education has been completed and some measure of job security has been attained.[39] Social class differences are no less prominent in this new stage of life than they are during childhood or adolescence. The current demands on young adults to attain higher skills, be better prepared to enter the labor force, and postpone family formation play out quite differently in advantaged, middle-class, and disadvantaged families.

Let's begin with the obvious: the costs of higher education have become less affordable as grants and loans have not kept pace with college tuitions, much less the cost of professional education. Among low-income families, the debt taken on by parents and young adults can be crippling, even though the long-term payoff theoretically makes borrowing for education economically rational.[40] Add to these economic problems the academic liabilities from years in low-performing schools that many, if not most, youth from disadvantaged families face, and it becomes obvious that a very small proportion are academically, much less financially, prepared to tackle a lengthy period of working and attending school (usually beginning with community college). Graduation happens, but relatively rarely. Instead, other events intrude: the lack of support staff and assistance in two-year colleges makes it harder to catch up if they fall behind academically, financial crises siphon off needed resources, parents cannot or will not offer aid or require support themselves, and so on.

These hurdles are one reason for the stark differences in graduation rates by social class. As Figure 25.2 shows, among seniors in high school who are likely

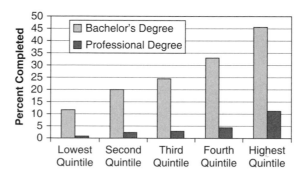

Figure 25.2 | Postsecondary Attainment of 12th Graders (1992) by Income Quintile (2000)

Source: Table 1, Postsecondary Attainment, Attendance, Curriculum and Performance: Selected Results from the NELS:88/2000 Postsecondary Education Transcript Study (PETS), 2000 (NCES 2003-394)

to go to college, approximately one in eight of those from families in the lowest income quintile completed college compared with nearly one in two of those from families in the highest quintile. Only one in four of those in the middle quintile completed college.

Among middle-class families, here the third income quintile from $43,400 to $65,832 in 2004, [41] few young adults can afford higher education without working to help pay for it. Balancing school and work commitments in early adulthood is not an easy task, often leading to high rates of school "stop out" and dropout. Thus, even when preparation for college is adequate and grants and loans can be managed, the process can be arduous and lengthy, partially accounting for the exceptionally high rates of college dropout in the United States. Many young people who enter college settle for, willingly or not, what amounts to postsecondary technical training, often restricting their mobility in their adult years.

The financial position of affluent families permits much greater latitude in helping out their children during the long period of college and professional training. The prospect of attaining a high-income job in the future, along with assistance offered by parents, more than likely sustains young adults through college and into professional careers. No doubt, too, young adults from affluent families who are generally better prepared academically are far more likely to qualify for scholarships based on academic merit and accordingly required to take on less debt.

Of course, this class-based profile is stereotypical to some degree. Talented individuals do rise from the bottom and untalented youth drift down. There may even be some disadvantages associated with the high-investment regime of child rearing more common in affluent families if children respond poorly to parental pressures for high achievement. The social class mechanisms that I have described in this paper continue to affect young adults during their twenties and thirties. The accumulation of debt, the likelihood of problematic events, the availability of social capital and sponsorship continue to tilt the playing field as youth enter institutions with different levels of selectivity or work situations that permit or thwart opportunities for attaining further human capital.

I cannot leave the topic of early adulthood without mentioning how social class exposure in childhood, adolescence, and early adulthood affects partnerships and family formation. We have always known that social class is linked to the quality and stability of marriage, though there was a time when divorce (not separation or marital unhappiness) occurred more frequently among the better off. This has not been true for some time. Lower human capital is related to lower social, cultural, and psychological capital—the skills, knowledge of the world, social networks, and sponsorship that play some part in the ability to manage and sustain emotional relationships. Striking differences emerge in marriage, its stability, and in the incidence of nonmarital childbearing by social class. [42]

These family patterns, so closely linked to class-based experiences in growing up, figure prominently in public discussions about the retreat from marriage among Americans. Curiously, the retreat has not occurred at all among the privileged, and it has occurred less often among the middle class than among the economically disadvantaged. Marriage is increasingly a luxury good attainable only by those with the social, psychological, and material goods that make it happen and make it work.

Conclusion

Social scientists have a strong interest in poverty and social disadvantage but have largely ignored gradations of disadvantage that occur beyond the least fortunate in our society. We firmly hold the view that, after all, we share a middle-class status with all but the least and most fortunate. This way of looking at the world is distorted by our own privileged circumstances that lead us to ignore relevant distinctions operating to keep most Americans in positions that are becoming economically and emotionally more precarious with each passing decade.

As social scientists and, especially as developmentalists, we must begin to ask ourselves whether we are accurately describing the social and psychological worlds of most Americans who are far less privileged than we are. Are we adequately portraying this world in our professional writings to show how the social system is arranged to allow a small number to flourish while others with equal talents and motivations never reach their human potential? To put it simply, we are not telling it like it is.

Doing a better job requires that we take advantage of the new data sources and novel techniques for analysis to tell a broader and more in-depth story of class-differentiated childhoods, adolescences, and early adulthoods. Doing a better job requires giving much more attention to opportunity differences in the so-called middle class, where most Americans see themselves. Doing a better job means doing more comparative research on social class differences and examining alternative possibilities of growing up in a less class-skewed society. It requires that we devote more attention to developing policies that restore some measure of balance and equity to our social system.

We must begin to tackle the question of why our children are not doing well (by international standards) in so many important domains of health and education, why our young adults are falling behind in college completion for the first time in American history, and how our families, wanting to do the best for their children, are unable to measure up to the task.

26

Briefing Paper: Unequal Childhoods

Inequalities in the Rhythms of Daily Life

Annette Lareau

The intersection of race and class in American life is an important but often vexing subject for sociologists. The power of social class is often obscured by the visibility of race. I wrote *Unequal Childhoods: Class, Race, and Family Life* (University of California Press, 2003) in part because I wanted to make class real by showing how it works in everyday life. I hoped that by capturing the day-to-day rhythms of life in different kinds of families—those of middle-class, working-class, and poor whites and African Americans—I could help bring the seemingly intractable problem of inequality into clearer focus.

Most of the eighty-eight families my research assistants and I interviewed during the first stage of research had children in the third or fourth grade in elementary schools in a large northeastern city and its suburbs. From this initial pool, we selected twelve families, six African American and six white, for more intensive study. Nearly every day for three weeks we spent time, usually a few hours, with each family. We went to baseball games, church services, family reunions, grocery stores, beauty parlors, and barbershops. We even stayed overnight with most of the families. We saw siblings squabble and heard parents yell. We joined kids as they sat around watching TV and as they played outside in the yard or the street. By the standards of social science research, this was an unusually intensive study.

What we found was that although all parents want their children to be happy and to thrive, social class makes a very substantial difference in how this universal goal is met. Middle-class parents promote what I call *concerted cultivation*. They actively foster their children's talents, opinions, and skills by enrolling the children in organized activities, reasoning with them, and closely monitoring their experiences in institutions such as schools. The focus is squarely on children's individual development. As a result of this pattern of concerted cultivation, children gain an *emerging sense of entitlement*. Most of the middle-class families in the study were extremely busy; this pattern held for white and African-American middle-class families. Children attend soccer games, go on Girl Scout trips, do homework, and go to birthday parties; parents need to arrange these activities as well as get children there and back. Despite the busy schedule, most parents worked full time and some had job-related overnight travel. In addition to meeting their workplace responsibilities, parents had to manage the details of family life: they had to go grocery shopping, prepare dinner, do laundry, monitor homework, oversee children's showers, and participate in bedtime rituals. I detail in the book what children's schedules mean for family life. In describing the middle class, I use the term "the frenetic family." Things are so hectic that the house sometimes seems to be little more than a holding space for the brief periods between activities.

The differences we observed between these middle-class families and those of working-class and poor families are striking. Parents in working-class and poor families promote what I call the *accomplishment of natural growth*. These parents care for their children, love them, and set limits for them, but within these boundaries, they allow the children to grow spontaneously. Children do not have organized activities. Instead, they play outside with cousins and siblings; they watch television. Parents use directives rather than reasoning with children. And children generally negotiate institutional life, including their day-to-day school experiences, on their own. The working-class and poor parents in the study often were very distrustful of contacts with "the school" and health-care facilities. They were fearful that professionals in these institutions might "come and take my kids away." Rather than an emerging sense of entitlement, children in these families developed an *emerging sense of constraint*. Working-class and poor families struggled with severe economic shortages (including lack of food in the poor families) that often led to additional labor or complexity (long bus rides, missed appointments), but the pace of their daily life was much less hectic than that of the middle-class families.

Unquestionably, the families we studied differed in terms of how they raised their children. But are these differences important—do they really matter? Neither the approach of concerted cultivation nor the accomplishment of natural growth is without flaws. Both have strengths and weaknesses. Middle-class children, for example, are often exhausted, have vicious fights with siblings, and do not have as much contact with their extended families as working-class and poor children do. But when children are in settings such as schools and health-care facilities, middle-class parents' strategy of concerted cultivation coordinates much more closely with the current standards of professionals than does the accomplishment of natural growth strategy that working-class and poor parents rely on. Middle-class parents routinely make special requests of teachers, asking, for example, that they provide their children with individualized instruction. These parents expect the institution to accommodate them, and this expectation typically is met. Middle-class children are taught to ask doctors questions and to feel that they have the right to challenge people in positions of authority. Thus, the data suggest that middle-class children gain advantages, including potential benefits in the world of work, from the experience of concerted cultivation. Working-class and poor children are not taught these life skills, and thus they do not gain the associated benefits. In short, class matters.

What about race? We found that in terms of children's time use, parents' methods of talking to children, and parents' interactions with schools and other institutions, African-American middle-class children had much more in common with white middle-class children than with African-American poor or working-class children. Still, race *does* matter in other respects: most of the children lived in racially segregated neighborhoods, middle-class African-American parents complained of race-based difficulties in the workplace, and African-American middle-class parents were very worried about their children being exposed to racial insensitivity at school. These parents also tried to promote a positive racial identity for their children (for example, by taking them to a predominantly middle-class African-American church). But in terms of the overall rhythm of children's family lives, and the ways in which parents address their own and their children's concerns, class emerged as much more important than race. Other studies also show substantial divisions between middle-class African Americans and working-class and poor African Americans.

The findings presented here, and in much greater detail in *Unequal Childhoods*, are based on an intensive study of only twelve families. Can we trust these results to tell us anything of significance? I believe that we can. The book's conclusions support established findings in social science research, which, using statistical techniques and nationally representative data, have shown important differences in how parents raise children. Rather than using numbers, *Unequal Childhoods* uses the stories of real families to highlight important social patterns. Moreover, American society is in a time of change. Children are being raised differently today than in earlier decades: middle-class children have more organized activities than in the 1950s and 1960s, for example. This shift has important implications for family life that our research helps expose by providing detailed insight into intimate details of daily life in families with young children. It gives us a chance to step back and reflect on how we are spending our time in family life as parents, and how we are choosing to raise our children. It also reminds us of the fact—all too often neglected—that there are important differences across social groups in the contours of childhood.

The arguments and evidence in *Unequal Childhoods* also point us toward new directions for social science research. The study suggests that while African-American middle-class families do face some child-rearing problems that have no counterpart in white middle-class families, African-American parents draw on a set of *generic* class resources to manage these problems. We can do better research and gain a deeper understanding of the intersection of race and class by showing how all families draw on class-based resources as they negotiate their daily lives. Put differently, we need to move beyond studying variables; it's time to focus on families.

In the News

BOTH SIDES OF INEQUALITY

New York Times, March 9, 2006

David Brooks

For the past two decades, Annette Lareau has embedded herself in American families. She and her researchers have sat on living room floors as families went about their business, ridden in back seats as families drove hither and yon.

Lareau's work is well known among sociologists, but neglected by the popular media. And that's a shame because through her close observations and careful writings—in books like "Unequal Childhoods"—Lareau has been able to capture the texture of inequality in America. She's described how radically child-rearing techniques in upper-middle-class homes differ from those in working-class and poor homes, and what this means for the prospects of the kids inside.

The thing you learn from her work is that it's wrong to say good parents raise successful kids and bad parents raise unsuccessful ones. The story is more complicated than that.

Looking at upper-middle-class homes, Lareau describes a parenting style that many of us ridicule but do not renounce. This involves enrolling kids in large numbers of adult-supervised activities and driving them from place to place. Parents are deeply involved in all aspects of their children's lives. They make concerted efforts to provide learning experiences.

Home life involves a lot of talk and verbal jousting. Parents tend to reason with their children, not give them orders. They present "choices" and then subtly influence the decisions their kids make. Kids feel free to pass judgment on adults, express themselves and even tell their siblings they hate them when they're angry.

The pace is exhausting. Fights about homework can be titanic. But children raised in this way know how to navigate the world of organized institutions. They know how to talk casually with adults, how to use words to shape how people view them, how to perform before audiences and look people in the eye to make a good first impression.

Working-class child-rearing is different, Lareau writes. In these homes, there tends to be a much starker boundary between the adult world and the children's world. Parents think that the cares of adulthood will come soon enough and that children should be left alone to organize their own playtime. When a girl asks her mother to help her build a dollhouse out of boxes, the mother says no, "casually and without guilt," because playtime is deemed to be inconsequential—a child's sphere, not an adult's.

Lareau says working-class children seem more relaxed and vibrant, and have more intimate contact with their extended families. "Whining, which was pervasive in middle-class homes, was rare in working-class and poor ones," she writes.

But these children were not as well prepared for the world of organizations and adulthood. There was much less talk in the working-class homes. Parents were more likely to issue brusque orders, not give explanations. Children, like their parents, were easily intimidated by and pushed around by verbally dexterous teachers and doctors. Middle-class kids felt entitled to individual treatment when entering the wider world, but working-class kids felt constrained and tongue-tied.

The children Lareau describes in her book were playful 10-year-olds. Now they're in their early 20's, and their destinies are as you'd have predicted. The perhaps overprogrammed middle-class kids got into good colleges and are heading for careers as doctors and other professionals. The working-class kids are not doing well. The little girl who built dollhouses had a severe drug problem from ages 12 to 17. She had a child outside wedlock, a baby she gave away because she was afraid she would hurt the child. She now cleans houses with her mother.

Lareau told me that when she was doing the book, the working-class kids seemed younger; they got more excited by things like going out for pizza. Now the working-class kids seem older; they've seen and suffered more.

But the point is that the working-class parents were not bad parents. In a perhaps more old-fashioned manner, they were attentive. They taught right from wrong. In some ways they raised their kids in a healthier atmosphere. (When presented with the schedules of the more affluent families, they thought such a life would just make kids sad.)

But they did not prepare their kids for a world in which verbal skills and the ability to thrive in organizations are so important. To help the worse-off parents, we should raise the earned-income tax credit to lessen their economic stress. But the core issue is that today's rich don't exploit the poor; they just outcompete them. ◼

27

Not Just Provide and Reside: Engaged Fathers in Low-Income Families

Kevin Roy and Natasha Cabrera

Thirty years ago, fathers were considered to be the "forgotten contributors" to children's lives.[1] Recently, however, social scientists have recognized dramatic changes in men's fathering due to shifts in cohabitation, marriage, divorce, re-marriage, and nonmarital childbearing.[2] Often these demographic changes have impacted low-income families disproportionately.[3] Low-income fathers have emerged as a diverse group of men who are engaged with children, not simply as providers and co-residers, but as caregivers who transition in and out of children's lives. In this chapter, we provide a brief overview of literature on low-income fathers' involvement with their children. We explore social and cultural contexts for men's involvement. Finally, we examine processes of fathering and patterns of change in fathering over the life course.

FATHER INVOLVEMENT AND CHILD DEVELOPMENT

We now recognize that positive father involvement with their children enhances the children's physical, cognitive, and socioemotional development.[4] Even with recent demographic shifts in the way that families organize themselves due to remarriage or cohabitation, employment, immigration, and the global economy, engaged fathers have continued to shape their children's lives in positive ways.

We have focused our attention on how fathers act as residential co-parents with mothers, although this family context may be more common for middle-class married men than for low-income minority men. However, we have shifted away from a discussion of "absent" or "deadbeat" dads and toward fathers' "presence," even if men do not live with their children. Whether or not they live with their children, unmarried and low-income fathers can positively impact their children's lives.

Recent studies show that sensitive, responsible, and accessible disadvantaged men who are engaged with their children enhance cognitive and socioemotional development in their children from the first year of birth up through pre-K.[5] Contrary to popular belief that low-income fathers are harsh disciplinarians, absent, or insensitive, fathers are often as sensitive and engaged as mothers across developmental periods.[6] Fathers and mothers both have high levels of engagement (i.e., sensitivity, positive regard, and cognitive stimulation) and low levels of negative aspects of engagement (i.e., detachment, intrusiveness, and negative regard). Moreover, low-income children with involved fathers acted out less and had fewer problems with negative social interaction. There is great diversity among low-income families in terms of education, parenting behaviors, and overall well-being. This is an important insight, because stereotypes of low-income minority families focus primarily on challenges to children rather than on the strengths in these families, which can offer a window for intervention for policies and programs.

It is also true that children living in poverty are at risk for harsh negative parenting and poor outcomes as they grow. These outcomes may be due to living in single-parent households with few resources, maternal stress, poor neighborhoods, and lack of social support. But if low-income parents are married or cohabiting, the combined effect of mother's and father's sensitivity to the children, positive regard, and cognitive stimulation lead to better cognitive development during early childhood.[7] Children in low-income families benefit from involved and caring mothers, but they benefit additionally if their fathers are also supportive of them, and if their fathers have completed years of education beyond high school. In effect, low-income fathers can contribute their own critical, additional piece of the puzzle for their children's development. For low-income children who are at risk because of poverty, two involved parents may make an important difference.

Although evidence suggests that fathers matter, we do not understand how disadvantaged fathers actually shape their children's lives.[8] Fathering studies are no longer frozen in assumptions about fathers as providers or living in residence with their children. Instead, studies have examined how fathers transition in and out of children's lives—over time and across different social contexts.[9]

Diverse Contexts for Men's Involvement

Being an involved father is not simply determined by the choices of an individual parent. How men father their children depends on men's relationship with their own parents, race and ethnicity, biological factors, demographic background and personality traits, mother's and children's own unique characteristics, community networks, mother and father's relationship, and even the economic situation in local neighborhoods.[10] With such a strong focus on co-residential, biological fathers, we often overlook the experiences of cohabiting partners, stepfathers, nonresident fathers, and grandfathers. If we carefully "break open" the assumptions of nuclear family households, we can reveal how fathers are embedded in complex family configurations that shape their parenting.

In particular, research with low-income and minority families has identified a range of flexible roles for fathers and father figures. In African-American families, biological fathers, boyfriends, godfathers, uncles, brothers, cousins, and "ol' heads" (community elders) all serve as significant father figures in communities and kin networks with flexible expectations for men's participation as caregivers of children.[11] Grandfathers affect kin relationships between generations—in particular, they influence their sons' parenting through the earlier childhood experiences their sons have had with them.[12] Paternal grandmothers have been identified as key figures in both making sure that their sons play a role as fathers (particularly for young nonresidential fathers) and caring for their sons' children.[13] Men's place as caregivers in kin networks is also clear across other racial, ethnic, and class groups in which the men serve as critical family care providers for children.[14]

Low-income men's relationships with the mothers of their children directly shape how they are involved with their children. While mothers are important contributors to men's involvement with their children, who exactly is responsible for poor men stepping up as involved fathers?[15] This is a complicated question, and we need to pay closer attention to how men and women negotiate parenting and working in their families. Over the past three decades, fathers have been doing slightly more child care and more work in the household, although this is likely due to a shift in the proportion of work that women do with children and at home, as women's work hours have increased.[16] Cooperative co-parenting is better for children, especially if it is characterized by more responsive parenting behaviors, higher-quality relationships, and more frequent contact.[17] On other hand, heightened conflict between parents, whether or not they co-reside, can threaten children's well-being in families.

Some men talk about the "package deal" for fathers—a set of expectations that society has for men to be fathers who both provide for and give care to their children.[18] Disadvantaged men try to live up to these ideals, just as middle-class or privileged fathers do. There may be a larger gap for these men, however, as they try to live up to expectations with limited opportunities and resources. For example, many would assume that men who are not breadwinners are not responsible fathers. For low-income men, however, "being there" for their children may be just as important—that is, by securing their children to a family legacy, linking them to family members, and fulfilling care obligations.[19]

Race or class-bound stereotypes about "good" fathers tend to dissolve when we look at actual paternal involvement in their children's daily lives. In studies of married or cohabiting parents across race and class, African-American and Latino fathers are often more likely to monitor and supervise their children than white fathers, and Latino fathers often spend more time with their children than white or black fathers.[20] Black fathers tend to be less engaged and less warm, but they take more control and more responsibility than white fathers, whereas Latino fathers take less control but more responsibility than white fathers, and they are as warm as white fathers. In effect, race differences in fathers' control and responsibility appear to be linked to parenting attitudes, but men's engagement and responsibility are more closely linked to economic factors, such as living in poverty.[21] Further, black and Latino nonresidential fathers are often more involved than nonresidential white fathers, a pattern explained in large part by the quality of their relationships with their children's mothers.[22]

Even within racial and ethnic contexts, men parent in very different ways.[23] For example, we acknowledge that many Latino families in low-income (and other) communities highly value family networks—a value called *familismo*.[24] But fathers and children have different experiences as they shift from one cultural context to another. They are often caught between cultures, one packed with traditional expectations of men as patriarchs and providers, and another filled with fluid and ambiguous expectations of men as friends, contributors, and co-parents. For Asian and Asian-American fathers and Native American fathers in low-income communities, making a place in American culture may be at the very heart of relationships between fathers and children.[25] Often, families move across physical contexts too, leading them to confront the challenges of immigration, even as it can alter men's roles in families.

DYNAMIC CONTEXTS FOR MEN'S INVOLVEMENT

We need to be aware of diverse settings for men's parenting in low-income families, but we also need to grow more aware of how these settings are constantly changing over time.[26] Disadvantaged men are more likely to move in and out of intimate relationships, residences, and jobs, and their fathering may become transitory and attuned to the nature and duration of such transitions. For example, mothers may both encourage and discourage men's involvement over time, and in different contexts. Men describe "babymamadrama," or conflict with mothers of their children, and how they negotiate involvement with their children even when they are incarcerated.[27] We should give more attention to the process of low-income mothers' recruitment of fathers and father figures to care for their children.[28] These mothers may call on men for their contributions of material resources and time, but they also have children's safety as their highest priority. These mothers, then, may also seek social fathers and other kin as fathers, if biological fathers present too many risks to their families over time.

Similarly, multi-partner fertility is a common status associated with poor outcomes for children in low-income families.[29] But multi-partner parenting is a complex process that unfolds over time across multiple families. Men change their behavior as fathers on a daily basis, often by sitting down at the same table with mothers of their children to rearrange contact. Instead of swapping involvement in a prior family for involvement in a subsequent family, low-income fathers often attempt to reestablish relations with older children from previous partners.[30]

It is difficult to remain involved as disadvantaged men navigate these transitions in their families. Fathers must become resilient to barriers and challenges of poor employment options, environmental risks, and changing family relationships.[31] They often rely on family members to help secure their place as fathers. It seems that "beginnings matter," as men who were engaged to the mothers of their children when the women were pregnant are likely to maintain some kind of positive involvement with the children after the birth. Continuity matters, too. Support from other family members over time can help low-income fathers to boost their involvement and to avoid the extreme effects of disruptions in work and family relationships.

Finally, fathers' involvement changes over time, as men and children age. Men's involvement changes as fathers themselves age, especially as their residential status shifts.[32] A common pattern of involvement for low-income African-American fathers is "flux"—in effect, if we take snapshots of men's residence with children, we find that a majority of men are involved with children, but they move in and out of children's households.[33] Involvement may also shift across generations. Men are socialized to being fathers when they are young themselves. Their experience with their own fathers can be a strong motivator for paternal involvement.[34]

Fathering in low-income families has changed historically as well. Globalization has transformed men's parenting as it has remade employment opportunities for families. For example, among a small group of forty low-income black fathers in Chicago, older fathers were two to three time more likely than younger fathers to find stable employment and establish co-residence with their partners and children in their early twenties.[35] More broadly speaking, across all income levels, men of child-rearing age spent 40 percent less time in families with children in 1980 than they did in 1960. In 1980, fewer young adult men lived in environments with children present.[36]

THE FUTURE OF FATHERING IN LOW-INCOME FAMILIES

Given the dramatic changes in families and men's lives that have been in the making for the past twenty-five years, where do we find fathers at the end of the first decade of the millennium? While there are large numbers of men who are increasingly disengaged from their children, there are also increasing numbers of men who are more involved than ever before. Just as American society has witnessed growing gaps in income inequality, there are growing gaps between the "highs" and "lows" of father involvement with children.

In past decades, being a low-income father was not synonymous with being disengaged from family life. But perhaps more than ever before in American history, if a father is poor in 2009, he is likely to live apart from his child as an unmarried parent. The income inequality gap has important implications for the future of these men's fathering. Even as we have expanded our notions of "new" fathers to include men's efforts to care for children—even if they live apart from children and their mothers, or are under/unemployed—we must acknowledge that men's engagement with children does not emerge solely from a change of heart or a value commitment. Families need resources—housing, health care, jobs with good wages, education—to stabilize men's involvement over time, and to stem the rapid and jarring transitions of men moving in and out of their children's lives.

28

Briefing Paper: Unmarried Couples with Children

*Why Don't They Marry? How Can Policy Makers
Promote More Stable Relationships?*

Paula England and Kathryn Edin

One-third of the babies in the United States today are born to unmarried parents, up from just 5 percent in 1960. Such births are especially common among low-income women. Yet, contrary to stereotype, most of them do not result from casual affairs, with the fathers long gone from the mothers' lives by the time of the birth. A large national survey primarily designed to study the families of children born to unmarried parents in twenty large urban areas, the Fragile Families and Child Wellbeing Study, found that more than 80 percent of the unmarried parents were romantically involved with each other when their baby was born, and about half were living together at the time of the birth. Of couples romantically involved at the birth, three-fourths of the cohabiting mothers and half of those not living with the father said there was a good or almost certain chance that the two would marry sometime in the future. Surprisingly, an even higher percentage of fathers expected to marry the mother of their child.

In reality, however, most of these couples did not marry. Five years after the baby was born, only a quarter of the cohabiting couples had married, while fully half had broken up. Among unmarried parents who were romantically involved but not cohabiting when their baby was born, only 7 percent were married to each other five years later, and more than 75 percent had broken up.

The more economically disadvantaged a couple is, the more likely they are to be unmarried when their children are born. Thus, studying the relationships of couples who have children outside of marriage helps us to understand how a large group of low-income couples organizes their family relations. We report here on a study we did involving qualitative interviews with unmarried parents who had a baby in 2000 (England and Edin, 2007).

WHY COUPLES DO NOT MARRY

Contrary to conventional wisdom, low-income couples who have children out-side of marriage value marriage very much, and they typically hope to marry in the future. When asked what it would take for them to actually marry, the most common—almost universal—response by the men and women we interviewed was that they were waiting to meet certain economic standards that they believed would offer them a better shot at a stable life.

The average household income of the cohabiting couples we interviewed was quite low, $22,500, which is just slightly more than the poverty level for a family of four. Twenty-nine percent of fathers and 26 percent of mothers had neither a G.E.D. nor a high school degree. Thus, like unmarried parents nationwide, this is a very disadvantaged group.

When we asked what their minimum economic standards were for marriage, we did not find them to be ridiculously high. What they said was usually some-thing like wanting one or both of them to have a good enough job that they didn't need family or friends or the government to give them money to pay all their bills each month and often that they'd like to be able to afford to rent or buy a house.

Given their lack of education, our respondents might have been unrealistic in expecting to meet this bar in the near future. But their standards are very main-stream, and even modest compared to those of the middle class. In any case, it is clear that the economic barriers to marriage are real for these couples, and are not just being used as an excuse not to marry. Our study classified parents into those who had met the criterion of being able to subsist without handouts four years after the baby was born and those who had not. Most of the parents in the study did not meet this economic bar by four years after the birth. But 78 percent of those who met this bar married, while only 19 percent of those who did not meet the bar did so by four years after the birth.

As liberals often argue, the inability to get decent paying jobs is a real con-straint to marriage among low-income unmarried parents. But what is interesting about today's unmarried couples is that they articulate this standard for mar-riage, even when they have already started living together and have had a child together. This suggests that, as conservatives argue, many of these couples are less deliberate about their decision to have a baby than they are about their deci-sion to marry. Why would that be true?

WHY COUPLES DO NOT USE CONTRACEPTION

Our study started by categorizing whether the pregnancies that led to the nonmarital births were planned, unplanned, or in between, based on everything the respondents told us. While a small number of the nonmarital conceptions were planned, most were not. Those that were planned—12 percent—were almost universally to couples in serious relationships, many of whom were living together, where both partners did expect to marry eventually. About a quarter (23 percent) were to couples that were using contraceptives that didn't work, or, in a few cases, had reason to think one was sterile but found out they were wrong. Roughly a quarter (22 percent) were the result of inconsistent contraception, and most of these were to couples in serious, often cohabiting, relationships. Couples often use contraception consistently and effectively when their relationship is new or still tentative, but they let their vigilance lapse when the relationship becomes more serious.

One of our most interesting findings was that another 18 percent were neither planned nor unplanned, but in between. That is, there is a continuum of how "intended" pregnancies are. Individuals characterizing the pregnancy as "in between" are almost always in a serious relationship and want children together eventually. Unsure that their current circumstances are ideal, in part because of their poor economic prospects, but wanting a child together, their ambivalence leads them to leave conception to chance.

So overall, three-quarters of the pregnancies described above did not fit the stereotype of unthinking youth or young adults who have casual sex with no contraception that leads to an unwed birth. Indeed, most nonmarital births today are not to teens.

Most of the unmarried parents we talked to subscribed to mainstream values about childbearing, in that they thought that the ideal to have a child was to be at least twenty-five years old, to have a house, and to be in a serious relationship. When the relationship was fairly serious, but having the earnings and house that they thought of as prerequisites for marriage seemed like pie in the sky, some couples, in a manner of speaking, "rolled the dice" and let chance decide.

About a quarter of the pregnancies were truly unintended, but occurred when couples were not using contraceptives. These individuals did not want—even ambivalently—to have a child now, but somehow they didn't align their use of contraceptives with their wishes. Yet, they generally knew about contraception and claimed the problem was not lack of money for birth control. These were the pregnancies where abortion was most often considered or pursued. The individuals most likely to have these pregnancies best fit the stereotype, although even here, 40 percent of these pregnancies were to couples in serious romantic relationships. Whether in a serious or casual relationship, the individuals in this group seemed to have little efficacy in achieving their own goals and some were caught up in lifestyles that were risky in many ways.

WHY COUPLES BREAK UP

We examined what issues create conflict for low-income couples with children. The four issues that came up most often were emotional attention and companionship, child discipline, housework, and money issues. Earlier studies of marriage dynamics suggested that it was only middle-class women who expected emotional intimacy and shared activities with men. But this has clearly changed. The low-income women in our study complained bitterly that their men didn't listen to them or talk to them enough, and didn't spend "quality time" with them. Women also complained about men spending time "on the street" or with male friends or kin rather than with them. It appears that in low-income as well as high-income couples, and in unmarried as well as married couples, the number one area of dissatisfaction for women is their desire for more emotional attention and companionship.

Child discipline was another hot issue. Men generally wanted a stricter regime than women. Either Dad wanted Mom to run a tighter ship while doing the child minding that they both agreed was her job, or Dad himself wanted to discipline children (especially sons) more harshly than Mom thought was appropriate.

Like other American couples, low-income couples in committed romantic relationships overwhelmingly expect sexual exclusivity regardless of their marital status, though infidelity is higher among unmarried than married couples. More than half (58 percent) of the unmarried couples in our study had experienced at least one instance of infidelity over the course of their relationship. Most of the time it was men who cheated, though some women did as well. Incidents of infidelity often occurred around events that brought the future of the relationship into question, such as the incarceration of one partner or a major argument. If there was chronic infidelity, the relationship seldom survived.

The issues that cause problems for low-income, unmarried couples, then, are quite similar to the ones that cause problems for couples at all income levels, and quite different from the ones that cause their initial reluctance to marry. Respondents who had broken up with the other parent reported infidelity, relentless arguing, verbal and physical abuse, lack of love and attention, and substance abuse as primary reasons for their breakups. Often those who broke up had multiple problems. Relationship quality is central, and men's bad behavior is key. It is almost always women who initiate the breakup, and the men who move out. Although economic problems figure prominently in why couples say they don't get married, economic problems are never central to their stories of how the breakup occurs.

What Makes for Involved Fathers, and Which Fathers Are Most Likely to Marry?

We also zeroed in on how involved fathers are in taking care of children when the couple is living together. Surprisingly, the most involved fathers—ones who did at least half the child care—were not the ones with the best relationships with their mates. The most involved dads were in couples where she was employed and he was unemployed. His non-employment was not usually based on choosing to be the one to stay home with the children, but was a result of not finding a job or being unemployable. The care work done by these fathers is appreciated by the mother, but the men often have economic and behavioral problems that strain their relationships. When men are employed, the father's primary role is typically as a "playmate" to the child, and fathers who have jobs generally do actual care only when the mothers scrutinize and supervise their work.

Many of the cohabiting couples in our study lived in a household that included not only the baby they had together but also Mom's child from a prior relationship. Often Dad also had a child from a prior relationship, although typically this child was living with his female ex-partner. Jealousy is often the cause of conflicts in these "blended" cohabiting families. When Dad goes to see his children by a previous partner, his current partner is often jealous of his time away from her and her kids, and she may worry that he will get sexually and romantically re-involved with his "ex." Dad, too, may be jealous about his new partner's dealings with her "ex" with whom she has a child—for example, when the former partner comes by to pick up children for visitation. Among couples with blended families, those who were most likely to marry each other were those in which Mom's prior partner was no longer an active father to her kids and Dad was no longer involved with any of his kids who lived with their mother. This poses policy makers with a dilemma—it appears that a good way to encourage marriage among new unmarried parents is to encourage fathers to be "deadbeat dads" to their kids by former partners, hardly a compelling public policy suggestion. Thus, what is best for a man's kids by one partner may not be best for his kids by the new partner.

Policy Implications

All too often, public debates about the lack of marriage among low-income couples resemble a food fight, with liberals shouting "it's the economy, stupid" and conservatives yelling "it's committed relationships, stupid." Policy recommendations for low-income couples often take an either-or approach to the question of improving people's economic prospects or improving their relationship skills.

Our findings suggest that some combination of the two approaches could be helpful for couples that want to stay together and raise their children. It is economic need and lack of decent job prospects that these couples see as the biggest barrier to marriage, so job training or job creation programs would probably increase marriage rates. As we showed above, when one or both partners are able to find and hold a decent job, almost 80 percent of these couples do marry. But it is relationship problems that often break these couples up, or make it impossible for them to co-parent effectively. Providing high-quality relationship skills training or other counseling interventions could also be an important component of pro-family public policy.

In the News

MARITAL MYTHOLOGY
WHY THE NEW CRISIS IN MARRIAGE ISN'T

Reason Online, June 1, 2006

Julian Sanchez

The end, as usual, is nigh. "Barring a miracle," Focus on the Family founder James Dobson writes in the April 2004 edition of his group's newsletter, "the family as it has been known for more than five millennia will crumble, presaging the fall of Western civilization itself." Dobson obviously has a knack for apocalyptic hyperbole, but some version of that sentiment haunts many a conservative mind.

It was the eschatological horror of wedding cakes adorned with pairs of little plastic men in tuxedos that prompted Dobson's prophecy. But the fear of gay marriage is only the most headline-friendly manifestation of a broader concern that the institution of marriage is in a parlous state. As conservatives look at high rates of cohabitation and divorce, especially among poor mothers, many conclude that the institution you can't disparage requires a helping hand from the federal government to stay afloat. Indeed, it's not just conservatives: Political scientist William Galston, a former adviser to President Clinton, has argued that marriage is a key component of poverty alleviation, and that government must "strengthen [two-parent] families by promoting their formation, assisting their efforts to cope with contemporary economic and social stress, and retarding their breakdown whenever possible." The most prominent recent effort in this vein is President Bush's Healthy Marriage Initiative, run by the Department of Health and Human Services and funded to the tune of $100 million annually, most of which goes to fund educational or mentoring programs in which couples learn "relationship skills," often by means of grants filtered through faith-based organizations.

If the link between gay matrimony and the "crumbling" of marriage remains something of a puzzle—for all the ink and pixels expended on the issue, no one has managed a compelling explanation of precisely how allowing more people to marry will induce fewer people to marry—concerns about the state of the family aren't groundless. A spate of studies has led to a broad consensus among social scientists that children raised by their biological parents fare significantly better than children raised by single, cohabiting, or remarried parents on a wide variety of dimensions: They're half as likely to drop out of high school or go to prison, more likely to attend college, and less likely to have behavioral problems or encounter material hardship—differences that may be reduced but do not disappear after controlling for factors such as parental income and education. These differences are apparent even in countries like Sweden, where both social norms and public policy are more hospitable toward single-parent families.

And there's a class chasm in family structure: Some 3 percent of births to college-educated women take place outside of marriage, compared to almost 40 percent among high school dropouts. The proportion of women between the ages of 18 and 24 who attend college doubled between 1967 and 2000, to more than 38 percent, and fertility rates are significantly lower for women of childbearing age who hold a bachelor's degree (an average of 1.05 offspring per mom) than for those with only a high school diploma (an average of 1.46). In short, the disadvantaged children for whom the stability marriage provides would be most helpful are also the least likely to enjoy it. "That is what government neutrality has gotten us," Sen. Rick Santorum (R-Pa.), an ardent booster of using the state to promote traditional families, told an enthusiastic audience at the 2005 Conservative Political Action Conference.

Yet two quite different recent books on marriage (and its absence) suggest there's something seriously wrong with the popular account of the American family's ills, which attributes them to a recent breakdown in values, caused perhaps by latte-sipping elites who scorn traditional matrimony. In *Marriage, a History*, Evergreen State College historian Stephanie Coontz, author of the 1992 book *The Way We Never Were: American Families and the Nostalgia Trap*, reveals that marriage has served diverse purposes through the ages, and that the really radical change in the institution was the 18th-century innovation of marrying for love. In *Promises I Can Keep*, sociologists Kathryn Edin of the University of Pennsylvania and Maria Kefalas of Saint Joseph's University take a close look at the lives of poor single mothers in Philadelphia, where they found a story much more interesting and convincing than the familiar "values" narrative.

Does marriage, as some conservatives seem to suggest, have an intrinsic nature and a deep purpose that remain constant across millennia, such that changes in its form or meaning should be considered inherently suspect, as unnatural as oceans boiling and lambs shacking up with lions? Not so much, according to Coontz, who finds that when it comes to marriage, the most reliable constant is flux.

While "one man, one woman" has become the clarion call of gay-marriage opponents, Coontz observes that the most "traditional" form of marriage adhered more closely to the rule "one man, as many women as he can afford." Many Native American groups cared about diversity of gender in marriage rather than diversity of biological sex: A couple had to comprise one person doing "man's work" and one person doing "woman's work," regardless of sex. In Tibet prior to the Chinese occupation, about a quarter of marriages involved brothers sharing one wife. To this day, the unique Na people in southwestern China live not in couples but in sibling clusters, with groups of brothers and sisters collaboratively raising children conceived by the women during evening rendezvous with visitors.

Even within the category of monogamous heterosexual unions, Coontz finds a dizzying variety of motives and meanings associated with marriage. Among early hunter-gatherer bands, trading members to other bands as spouses was, above all, a means of establishing networks of trade and economic cooperation between men. Once each group had members with loyalties and ties to both, barter became a safer bet.

That's not to say the husbands were in full control either: In ancient Rome, married sons and daughters both lived under control of the patriarch until his death, and ancient civilizations more generally regarded marital decisions as far too important to be left to the whims of the marrying couple.

In the medieval period, too, marriage might be a handy means of cementing an alliance or sealing a truce among rulers. In other times and places, marriage was seen primarily as a means of regulating inheritance or succession. Often, especially where simple market sales of land were tightly restricted, it was the primary means of transferring landed property, and that was seen as the decisive factor in marriage decisions. Such considerations were not limited to the nobility: Peasant farmers who held land in separate strips might arrange a marriage that allowed adjoining parcels to be united. And while formal state approval is regarded in America today as a sine qua non of a valid marriage, the church considered a couple married as soon as they had exchanged "words of consent," even alone and without formal trappings.

Among the working classes in later pre-industrial Europe, though a village was apt to intervene if a wedding brought a poor worker into the fold, marriage was seen as more centrally about the married couple. This view was encouraged by a church doctrine that recognized as valid any union entered by mutual consent and, later, by an emerging post-feudal economy in which young people were increasingly apt to leave extended families to seek their fortunes in cities or to work their own small plots. But husbands and wives saw each other more as business partners than as lovers. Marriage was a way of establishing an efficient division of labor, and a new widow or widower represented a job opening.

The love marriage, in which people more or less freely chose partners based on mutual affection, was really an 18th-century invention, Coontz argues. It was partly a spillover effect of new political ideologies that saw government as arising from contractual agreements designed to promote the happiness of society's members and partly a result of further increases in economic autonomy, especially the autonomy of women. As late as the mid-19th century, French wags were still bemused at the new fashion of "marriage by fascination." Opponents of gay marriage such as Maggie Gallagher sometimes identify this development as the central problem: the idea that marriage is mainly about uniting a loving couple, from which the notion that it ought to be equally available to gay couples follows.

Such critics sometimes talk as though marriage based on love is a recent innovation, rather than a transformation that's been going on for centuries. As Coontz notes, during the 1950s—the conservative's golden age for families—it was precisely the prospect of finding personal fulfillment through marriage to your soul mate that gave married life its central place in the social imagination. The vision of domestic bliss familiar from sitcoms like *Ozzie and Harriet* and *The Donna Reed Show* found its complement in a spate of self-help manuals and newspaper columns touting a successful marriage as the key to happiness, as couples' average age at first marriage reached its lowest point in half a century. "In a remarkable reversal of the past," Coontz writes, "it even became the stepping-off point for adulthood rather than a sign that adulthood had already been established. Advice columnists at the *Ladies' Home Journal* encouraged parents to help finance early marriages, even for teens, if their children seemed mature enough."

What emerges from Coontz's account is the realization that marriage has no "essence." There is no one function or purpose it serves in every time and place. This shouldn't come as any surprise to readers of F.A. Hayek, who in *The Mirage of Social Justice* spoke of evolved rules and institutions that "serve because they have become adapted to the solution of recurring problem situations. . . . Like a knife or a hammer they have been shaped not with a particular purpose or view but because in this form rather than some other form they have proved serviceable in a great variety of situations." Institutional evolution, like its biological counterpart, is opportunistic: A structure that serves one function at one stage may be co-opted for a very different function at another stage.

Coontz knows the benefits of marriage, but she's wary of attempts to stand athwart history crying "Stop!" If marriage now seems especially fragile, she argues, that's not a function of public policy mistakes subject to easy political correction. It reflects underlying economic, legal, and technological changes that are, in themselves, mostly desirable. While not opposed to attempts to help couples craft stable marriages, she warns that "just as we cannot organize modern political alliances through kinship ties . . . we can never reinstate marriage as the primary source of commitment and caregiving in the modern world. For better or worse, we must adjust our personal expectations and social support systems to this new reality."

That conclusion may seem excessively fatalistic, especially given Coontz's own chronicle of marriage's ability to adapt to changing circumstances. But it does encapsulate a core piece of Hayekian wisdom. Organic social institutions grow and evolve from the bottom up, as individuals change their behavior in light of the circumstances they perceive on the ground. Attempts to freeze or correct them in accordance with a Grand Plan—a vision of how they ought to function that views change as a dangerous deviation from an ideal—are no more likely to succeed for marriages than for markets.

Where Coontz's history gives a picture of marriage painted in broad strokes, *Promises I Can Keep* is a close-up, lapidary study of unmarried low-income mothers in eight of Philadelphia's poorest neighborhoods, culled from interviews with 162 such women over the course of five years. Several of those years were spent living in their communities. Edin and Kefalas' account makes it clear that the growth of single motherhood among poor urban women can't be chalked up to anything as simple or straightforward as a "breakdown of family values."

In a sense, the problem is an excess of family values. Women who dropped out of high school are more than five times as prone as college-educated counterparts to say they think the childless lead empty lives, and also more likely to regard motherhood as one of the most fulfilling roles for women; motherhood is so highly regarded that it becomes difficult to see even a pregnancy that comes in the mid-teens as a catastrophe to be avoided. And far from having lost interest in marriage, the authors write, the women they spoke to "revere it"—so much so that some are hesitant to marry when they become pregnant because single motherhood seems less daunting than the opprobrium they fear they'd face were they to divorce.

In a long meditation on "Marriage and Caste" in the Winter 2006 *City Journal*, the Manhattan Institute's Kay Hymowitz (who cites Edin and Kefalas) writes that the "marriage gap" between poor and middle-class mothers shows that "educated women still believe in marriage as an institution for raising children." But as Edin and Kefalas point out, high school dropouts are actually far more likely than their college-educated counterparts to believe it's important for a child to grow up in a married household and to express disapproval of childbearing outside marriage.

The crucial difference, the authors find, is not in poor women's attitudes toward marriage but in the way they approach childbearing. Middle-class couples may follow the more traditional trajectory—love, marriage, baby carriage—but they're doing it significantly later than previous generations typically did, often postponing both marriage and children until their late 20s or early 30s in order to attend college, perhaps obtain a graduate degree, and establish themselves in careers. Half a century ago, the median woman was barely 20 years old when she first married; in 2004 she was almost 26. While the average age at which women have their first child has risen across the board, the trend has been much more pronounced for those with more education. In the late 1970s, according to data from the Bureau of Labor Statistics' Current Population Survey, 15 percent of women without a college diploma were childless at age 30, compared with 40 percent of college graduates. By the early '90s, the percentages were 16 percent for the least educated and 56 percent for college graduates. Meanwhile, as noted above, the share of women attending college rose sharply. Those trends have helped change marital norms in one important way: Marriage is no longer seen as a necessary rite of passage into adulthood or, as Coontz puts it, "part of the credentialing process that people had to go through to gain adult responsibility and respectability . . . like completing high school today."

Postponing marriage has become more acceptable; both poor and middle-class couples expect to marry not in their early 20s as their careers are beginning but only once they're at least somewhat "settled" economically. Among poor women in particular, there is a fear of economic dependence, both within a marriage and in the event that it should end; marriage is regarded as a step to be taken only when both partners have significant incomes and savings of their own. But for many poor women, later marriage does not mean later childbearing. For those without realistic prospects of attending college or launching high-powered careers, Edin and Kefalas conclude, motherhood provides an alternative means of proving their worth to themselves and their peers, and an alternative identity around which to structure their lives. Many credit a child with giving them new direction and a sense of responsibility—even saving their lives by pushing them to abandon wild lifestyles. The lack of prospects makes the opportunity cost of childbearing relatively low. Poor women understand how to use birth control as well as their more affluent peers do, but they have less motivation to take every precaution against pregnancy, because they lack the high economic and academic aspirations a child might derail.

What we find, then, is not a change in marriage that can be neatly explained by changing values but a complex tangle of cultural and economic changes reinforcing each other. Women's increasing participation in the labor force resulted from a combination of factors: the internal logic of equality that has been playing out in the West for centuries, the demands of World War II, the shift to a service economy in which raw strength was a less important requirement for entry-level jobs, and labor-saving technologies that made maintaining a household less of a full-time occupation. As the economic incentives facing women—especially middle-class women with access to higher education—changed, middle-class women's marital timing adapted. That, in turn, helped to change broader norms about when, and at what stage of economic success, people of any class are expected to marry.

The reluctance of Edin and Kefalas' subjects to marry is also tied to more concrete concerns. Often the fathers of their children are in prison, have histories of violence or criminality, have become addicted to drugs, or exhibit any of a host of other serious defects that make the women reluctant to enter into what they believe should be a lifelong commitment. The women report that many men, even those who first greeted the news of a pregnancy enthusiastically, fail to change their ways when they learn a child is on the way. Some become even more wild, as if desperate to assert their youth and independence in the face of impending fatherhood. And in communities where large fractions of the young male population are incarcerated—thanks in large part to a war on drugs that disproportionately targets young African-American males—the remaining men face a buyer's market of "surplus" women, making the temptations of infidelity strong. Two-thirds of the mothers the authors interviewed described relationships that had dissolved because of alcoholism, drug dealing, infidelity, or (for almost half) chronic violence.

Kay Hymowitz finds this account, the "marriageability thesis," unsatisfactory, asking why there would be "a dearth of marriageable men when there appear to be plenty of cohabitable fathers." But women often cohabit precisely because they view marriage as different and sacred. Many of those with whom Edin and Kefalas spoke considered cohabitation a vetting period, during which they sought assurance that a partner and father had given up habits and behaviors that might make him an unsuitable husband. The woman who came home to find her apartment bare, the furniture sold to finance her live-in boyfriend's crack habit, presumably was happy not to have taken that next step. Conservatives often point out that marriages in the U.S. tend to be less stable if they're preceded by cohabitation. But if the pattern Edin and Kefalas found is common, that period of cohabitation may be a response to, rather than a cause of, that instability. And as Coontz notes, the pattern found in the U.S. is not universal: In Germany, for example, cohabitation is associated with slightly more marital stability.

Many women also voiced concerns that marriage would change their partners for the worse—make them more controlling. As one put it, "He [already] tells me I can't do nothing, I can't go out. What's gonna happen when I marry him? He's gonna say he owns me." That fear is consistent with polls finding that while lower-class women tend to share the relatively egalitarian view of gender roles common to both men and women of the middle class, lower-class men tend to subscribe to a more traditional conception of those roles—roles their partners may not be eager to fill. Among many of the women profiled in *Promises I Can Keep*, we see fragments of middle-class norms lifted from the economic context that gave rise to them and wedded with a host of other, more traditional views about marriage and family.

Yet the accounts given by the women themselves of their decisions make it difficult to say glibly that one set of values or another is wrong and needs to be corrected. By their lights, they are responding rationally to their circumstances. One says of her life before becoming a mother, for example, "There was nothing to live for other than the next day getting high. [My life had] no point, there was no joy. I had lost all my friends—my friends were totally disgusted with me—I was about to lose my job, [and] I ended up dropping out of another college. . . . Now I feel like 'I have a beautiful little girl!' I'm excited when I get up in the morning!"

In the 1980s books like Charles Murray's *Losing Ground* argued that poor women would respond to economic incentives such as welfare benefits for single mothers by bearing more children out of wedlock. But if the model was correct, the margin at which those decisions occur may have been misidentified: For many, it seems, childbearing is the default in the absence of some potent economic incentive not to have a child—some prospect for personal fulfillment other than through motherhood. What seems rational for the mother might not, of course, be in the best interests of the child. Yet neither is it obvious that once the child exists, marriage is in the best interests of the mother or child, given the quality of the available fathers.

It's true that, other things being equal, marriage seems to confer significant benefits on both parents and children—on average. But that doesn't mean all families benefit. The Penn State sociologist Paul Amato suggests, for example, that some 60 percent of children are made worse off—financially, emotionally, and in other ways—by divorce. Yet he also believes divorce at least somewhat improves the welfare of some 40 percent, in similar ways. It seems excessively sanguine to suppose that most couples who've been reluctant to marry in the first place are apt to be more like the former group than the latter. Averages, as Coontz points out, are a dangerous basis for sweeping generalizations about what is socially desirable. And while studies can control for couples' income and education, the one thing that can't be factored out, the one thing all married couples share, is a revealed preference for marriage: Given all the detailed information each particular couple had about their particular relationship, they decided to marry. Concluding that superficially similar cohabiting couples would reap similar benefits if they married is akin to concluding that everyone would benefit from a given product because those who voluntarily purchased it do. There are doubtless worse ways to spend federal dollars than on voluntary relationship counseling for poor people, but attempting to promote marriage by teaching "listening skills" is a bit like affirmative action for graduate school applicants—a superficial intervention that comes too late to help the people who presumably need it most.

The growing focus on marriage in public policy owes its resonance to two distinct themes that recur in conservative thought: anxiety about unregimented sexuality, and the belief that social problems are better solved by local groups and time-tested institutions. Those tendencies make it tempting to conclude that calls for marital reform and the genuinely distressed state of some families are part of one coherent and insidious phenomenon: the collapse of marriage. Yet as Edin and Kefalas show, the biggest problems with marriage are not first or foremost problems with marriage.

Communities grappling with dim economic prospects, violence, addiction, and high rates of incarceration are going to have trouble sustaining all sorts of valuable social institutions, marriage among them. Broader changes in marriage, meanwhile, need not herald its collapse: They're an ordinary part of the way the institution has always adapted, organically, to societies that themselves are always changing. ◼

In the News

BOOK EXAMINES TREND OF UNMARRIED PARENTS
 [Radio Transcript]

National Public Radio, *Tell Me More*, February 21, 2008

Michel Martin

MICHEL MARTIN, host: So that's unwed parenting in the movies, but what about in real life? The increase in children born out of wedlock has had serious and far-reaching consequences for families and society at large. A new book, *Unmarried Couples with Children*, is believed to be the first in-depth study of who unmarried parents are and how they're managing.

Professor Kathryn Edin of Harvard University and Professor Paula England of Stanford University are co-editors of that book, and they both join us now. Welcome. Thank you so much for speaking with us.

Professor KATHRYN EDIN: Thank you.

Professor PAULA ENGLAND: Thank you.

MARTIN: Given that you've studied this question so extensively, and there's so much sort of pop culture mythology around who these families are and what they're like, can you just give us a couple of examples in which our perceptions really differ from what you found out in your research? Professor England, if you'd start.

Prof. ENGLAND: I think the main thing, misconception, is that people think that women having a birth out of marriage don't have a partner, and usually she still is romantically involved with the father at the birth, even though the relationships often break up.

MARTIN: Professor Edin?

Prof. EDIN: Yeah, so that's really important, you know. Most of these babies enter into the world to a couple. Half of the time, that couple is living together. The second big thing that the media gets wrong is that this is not primarily a phenomenon among teenagers. Teenage pregnancy has been going down over time. Nonmarital childbearing has grown because more adults and more whites are choosing to engage in it than had been true previously.

MARTIN: In movies like *Knocked Up*, unmarried parents wind up having a cooperative relationship, end up living together. It's sort of—the movie kind of ends with the idea that they've sort of decided to commit to each other for the long haul. Is that true in real life?

Prof. EDIN: Well, it is interesting. In many ways, I think it is true that in the middle class, when we think about having a child together, you think of a child as an outgrowth of a relationship that's already there, that's a solidified relationship. It's kind of a representation of a commitment.

But we found that among these unmarried couples with children, oftentimes the relationship was kind of ad hoc. There was an accidental pregnancy. There's a sense in which there's not a whole lot to lose, by the way, among these very disadvantaged folks when they do become pregnant. And once they're pregnant, they try to get it together for the sake of the child. So the relationship is really all about the baby.

MARTIN: Given that your research shows that many of these couples consider themselves together and may wind up even living together, why don't they get married?

Prof. ENGLAND: This is Professor England. The simplest answer that they give us when we ask them is we don't have our economics together yet. In the old days, couples might say, well, we can't get married because we can't afford to get an apartment on our own, move out from our parents, and we can't afford having a baby.

But these couples oftentimes are already living together. They've already had the baby, and yet they'll still say we want to get married, and hopefully we will in the future, but we have to get our economics together first.

So it seems like what they mean is that marriage has taken on a kind of cultural meaning that you're supposed to have certain things economically in place before you get married, and they're holding marriage really to a higher standard, in a sense, than they held getting pregnant and taking a pregnancy to term.

MARTIN: Does that come from religion? Does that come from . . .

Prof. EDIN: This is Kathy. Most of the couples in the study are not extraordinarily religious, but yet you hear words like marriage is sacred. I'm not going to get married just to get divorced because that would be making a mockery of marriage.

So you hear this religious language over and over again, even among people who are not religious. And what we think that means is—what we think that refers to is this very high standard of marriage.

Sometimes people say to us well, you know, Professor England or Professor Edin, your couples just don't value marriage. And we often reply by saying, in some ways, it's almost like they value marriage too much, too much to sully this sacred, precious institution with their own less-than-perfect relationships.

They want to make sure they engage in marriages that last. The worst thing that can happen from their point of view is to get married just to get divorced. That's a bad thing to do.

MARTIN: Speaking of divorce, I mean, we do have a high divorce rate in this country, and in others. And I think it's considered kind of common wisdom or at least a sort of an assumption that the reasons that couples who marry get divorced are disagreements over money, disagreements over sex, and oftentimes, people would say disagreements over kids. What are the reasons that these couples break up?

And also, I think I'd want to ask, too, is their rate of breakup pretty much the same as for married couples?

Prof. ENGLAND: No, the rate is much higher. And one of the sad things is, you know, we told you on the one hand that 80 percent of these unmarried parents are still romantically involved at the birth, and half are even living together. But, in fact, over half break up within five years, and that is a higher rate of breakup than you would see in the average birth inside a marriage.

And here's what's interesting. It's economics that they say keeps them from getting married, but it's usually not directly economics that leads to the breakup. The breakups are usually over conflicts and oftentimes very bad behavior on the part of men—sometimes cheating, you know, sometimes involvement in crime, sometimes involvement with drugs. At some point, the women just put the man out.

Prof. EDIN: Yeah, and these relationship problems are serious and real, and they're oftentimes problems that few of us would put up with for very long. So it's not like they're breaking up sort of flippantly, because they don't feel like staying together or working hard. It usually is the result of some very serious problems, infidelity probably being the leading cause of breakup.

MARTIN: Infidelity being the leading cause of breakup? That's interesting. So one of the things that you're finding is that these couples really value children and they really value marriage. But what you're finding out is that the men in these relationships don't necessarily value fidelity, and I wonder if that's the difference between men who get married and men who don't.

Prof. ENGLAND: This is Paula. It's hard to figure this out. You know, in all groups, married and unmarried, in all social classes, I think the data show that men cheat more than women. But actually, if you ask people in surveys, you know, 95 percent of the population in all social groups say that within marriage, you're not supposed to cheat.

In these unmarried relationships, maybe people don't think the norm is quite as strong, although the fact that they'll get really upset and call it cheating if their partner does it, either the man or the woman, suggests that, you know, there is somewhat of a norm. But sometimes the situations get more ambiguous.

Prof. EDIN: Can I give you an example of one of our couples, to speak to Professor England's point?

MARTIN: Sure.

Prof. EDIN: A young couple in Chicago, a fairly stable relationship, again, cohabitating without being married. So in those situations, whether the couple is together or not is always a bit ambiguous. She one morning is called into work, and she's told she'll be doing some heavy cleaning. So she takes her engagement ring off and leaves it on the bedroom bureau.

Her boyfriend, the father of her child, wakes up, sees the ring on the table, assumes they've broken up, and by the time she gets home from work, he's already gone out and had an affair with another woman.

So it's a bit of an extreme example, but it speaks to the ambiguity of what the relationship is, because the fact that you're not married means that you're really not sure this is the right one, or you're really not sure that this relationship is suitable for marriage.

MARTIN: Do these couples want these children? Are these children planned, in a way?

(Soundbite of laughter)

MARTIN: I mean, in a way, we're used to thinking of, you know, couples saying okay, it's time. You know, we're going to start now.

Prof. ENGLAND: We struggled with the data on this question a long time and asked parents about this particular question over and over again because their answers were so confusing, and there are really two themes in the end.

First of all, there's a strong positive orientation toward children. The poor really see children as the center of meaning and identity, particularly since there are so few sources of meaning and identity available to them outside of having children. So, in some sense, the unplanned pregnancies are, in a sense, planned, or at least ambiguously wanted.

But there's another thing going on here, and that is that the poor often have a hard time aligning their behavior with their goals. It's really hard to use birth control in the meticulous sort of way that it requires to keep from having a baby. And when you're living in a chaotic environment and your circumstances are somewhat chaotic, it's hard to do that. And so we also see a behavioral part of this, that young women and young men are getting into situations they didn't intend, in part because they're not able to follow through with the kinds of behavior that lead to successful contraception.

MARTIN: Paula England is a professor of sociology at Stanford University. She joined us from their studios in Stanford. And Kathryn Edin is a professor of public policy at Harvard University. She joined us from their studios in Cambridge, Massachusetts. Thank you both so much for speaking with us.

Prof. ENGLAND: Thank you.

Prof. EDIN: Thank you, Michel.

Listen to this interview on the NPR Media Player at <www.npr.org/templates/story/story.php?storyId=19229729>.

In the News

IT TAKES A WEDDING

New York Times, November 13, 2002

Alex Kotlowitz

With the Republican victory last week, Congress now appears likely to set aside funding for programs that promote marriage among the poor. A friend who provides services for inner-city children declared this marriage push "nuts." That had been my initial reaction, as well. But now I wonder if the conservatives who are driving this effort might be on to something.

There's a shift in the winds in our inner cities. On the heels of a fatherhood movement (which, incidentally, also had conservative roots), more and more young couples are considering marriage. A long-term study of 5,000 low-income couples has found that eight of 10 who have a child together have plans to marry. "I was out in the field all of the time, interviewing low-income single mothers," Kathy Edin, a sociologist at Northwestern University, told me. "And what really struck me in those interviews was how many people talked about the desire to get married. And I would go back, you know, and talk to my friends in academia and they would say, 'Oh, they can't mean that.' But I would hear it again and again."

Might marriage be making a comeback in communities where the vast majority of children are born to single parents? A minister on Chicago's West Side told me that when he began preaching there 10 years ago, his congregation scoffed at his efforts to foster matrimony. But this year his church co-sponsored an event called "Celebrating Contentment," in which long-married couples testified to their happiness together. Last summer, there was such demand for the minister's weekly marriage enrichment workshops that he had to put some parishioners on a waiting list. In Baltimore, Joe Jones, who runs a program to promote fatherhood, is adding marriage classes to his curriculum. And the Nation of Islam, which organized the Million Man March, has now taken up the mantle of marriage, declaring it "a social institution in need of restoration."

Marriage can be treacherous terrain. In 1965, Daniel Patrick Moynihan, then a young official in the Department of Labor, issued a report titled "The Negro Family: The Case for National Action." It suggested that the breakdown of the black family—one-third of all black children at the time lived with only one parent—was keeping African-Americans from finding their way into the middle class. Mr. Moynihan was pilloried by progressives; he was accused of blaming the victim. Liberals essentially abdicated the discussion about family to the conservatives, and have had a tough time finding their way back since.

But there is now growing consensus among social scientists that, all things being equal, two parents are best for children. It would seem to follow that two-parent families are also best for a community. It may take a village to raise a child, but it takes families to build a village.

While liberals haven't done enough to emphasize the importance of marriage in reinforcing the bonds that hold society together, conservatives have put too much faith in the power of marriage alone to lift people out of poverty.

In 1988, Vince Lane, then the director of the Chicago Housing Authority, was conducting top-to-bottom searches of public housing high-rises, looking for guns and drugs. But the discovery that most dismayed him was the large number of men living with their girlfriends illegally. They weren't on the lease. In the raids, Mr. Lane found them hiding in closets and in bathtubs and in laundry baskets. At one high-rise, Mr. Lane got fed up. He told the men they could stay—if they got married. So the city hosted an all-expenses-paid (honeymoon included) eight-couple shotgun wedding.

What's happened to the couples since? Most have split up, which should come as no surprise. The stress of not having money, of living in decrepit housing, of sending children to poorly funded schools would take its toll on even the most committed relationship. So how then might we help get couples to the altar? By pushing marriage? Or by helping ease the strains in people's lives?

It would be wrongheaded to encourage marriage by stigmatizing single parenthood, a process that has already begun with the reintroduction of the word "illegitimacy" into the lexicon. After all, that's the very constituency the government is trying to reach.

Wade Horn, the Bush administration official who oversees the welfare program, has assured critics that the administration, by supporting demonstration projects that promote marriage, doesn't intend to coerce people to the altar. And, indeed, what tools government has available—like the relationship training seminars Oklahoma has begun to offer—seem benign enough, if unproven.

When it comes to social engineering, government has turned out to be a clumsy catalyst. Mr. Moynihan, whose report was in many ways prescient—the numbers he cited for black families in 1965 now apply to all families, regardless of race—has said, "If you expect government to change families, you know more about government than I do."

Even if conservatives don't know how to get there, at least they recognize that marriage, this very private institution, has very public consequences. Liberals, who have a much firmer understanding of the obstacles poor people face, need to enter that conversation. ▬

29

Rituals As Tools of Resistance:
From Survival to Liberation

Andraé L. Brown, Melina Dimitriou, and Lisa Dressner

Rituals help families mourn losses, transition through life, and mark significant moments that shape and define families over generations. During times of crisis, rituals help families restore balance, reestablish a steady pace, and recommit to shared values and goals. Rituals are used extensively to cope with family crises around the death of a loved one, chronic illness, and changes in the life cycle such as marriage, retirement, or adjustment to the empty nest. But rituals are rarely incorporated into a family's process of adjusting to the loss of a member through incarceration. The incarceration process, from the time of arrest through sentencing, does not provide adequate time and space for family rituals to occur naturally. This paper demonstrates how a community ritual that prepares a young man for incarceration may support his commitment to rehabilitation, facilitate the family's grieving process, and prepare the community for his reintegration.

FAMILY RITUALS

> Every family and every culture throughout time create, enact, alter and preserve rituals. (Imber-Black, 2002, p. 455)

We are all ritual makers. Rituals help us stay connected to the past as we move toward the future. They enable us to preserve a sense of continuity, consistency, identity and belonging, while simultaneously integrating change and marking the transitions in our lives.[1] In addition to cultivating a sense of identity and root-edness within families, rituals connect those families to a wider community.[2]

Social scientists describe rituals as formalized, symbolic performances. "Formalized" suggests that there is an accepted format for carrying out the event. "Symbolic" implies that the ritual's components might be more significant and meaningful than they appear on the surface. And "performance" indicates that the ritual's importance depends on how it is enacted by the participants. The extent to which participants follow a ritual's pre-established script is indicative of their sense of its importance.[3]

When family members participate in a ritual, it is quite common for each member to ascribe a unique meaning to the ceremony. Participation in a ritual also delivers a hidden meaning to the insiders, bolstering their sense of rightness and emotional commitment and providing members of the group with a sense of continuity and commonality across generations.[4]

Rituals frame and express family structures and relationships, reinforce roles and boundaries, and articulate family identity and belief systems. When we examine rituals critically, they can serve as a lens through which we can better understand a family's intergenerational patterns—how people relate, communicate, and articulate their needs.[5]

Often older generations are more committed to carrying on family rituals, seeing them as mechanisms that build successful families and that allow elders to demonstrate and validate their role in the family. But for traditions to be carried forward, younger family members must also become more appreciative of the rituals as they grow older and must feel that such practices are relevant to their lives.[6]

Mealtime provides an example of how rituals, viewed as patterns of interaction, can tell us a lot about family dynamics. We can deduce a great deal about how a family functions if we know how often a family eats together, how the food is prepared, who is seated at the table, and how they relate and converse at mealtime. With contemporary families spending more time sitting mutely in front of the television, the family meal may be the one time and place where members of the family share their stories and reflect on their daily experiences.[7]

Because the broader sociopolitical and cultural context influences how families organize, develop, and utilize rituals, any examination of the function of family rituals needs to take into account the social and political context of power, privilege, and oppression.[8] For example, who is allowed to participate in the ritual, who is accepted, and who is rejected? If we examine the extent to which lesbian, gay, transgendered, bisexual, queer, or unisex (LGTBQU) couples participate in family rituals, we need to know if the LGTBQU family member is invited to participate in a celebration, if her/his partner is also invited, and how they are treated during the celebration.

Because rituals can foster a sense of common identity, they can support families during difficult transitions by providing a sense of stability, which can reduce anxiety about change and incorporate it into the family system. Celebrations like birthdays, holidays, and family reunions are important in providing a sense of family togetherness, stability, and continuity. They also reinforce the family's racial, ethnic, religious, and cultural identity.[9]

TYPES OF RITUALS

Transition rituals, healing rituals, and identity-reforming rituals all have therapeutic value. Transition rituals mark changes in family relationships, membership, and boundaries that accompany exceptional life events such as marriage and birth. Family transition rituals can create unique and meaningful ways to facilitate insight and ease transformations.[10] We have also developed an additional transition ritual, explained in detail later, which we feel helps families and communities deal with impending incarceration.

Healing rituals, employed at times of profound loss, help to cope with the grieving process of survivors and promote healthy living after the loss. Healing rituals may also be created to address losses attendant to the breakup of relationships, reconciliation after an affair, losses of bodily parts or losses due to an illness, as well as losses of life roles, expectations, and dreams.

When a loss is accompanied by social stigma, such as death from AIDS or suicide, the healing process may be truncated because standard healing rituals may not address the specific circumstances of the loss. By creating their own healing rituals that address their own circumstances, families can find a safe space and time to genuinely mourn their loss, without worrying about social stigma.

Through rituals that involve redefining identity, therapists try to remove stigmatizing labels from individuals, couples, and families, especially where the larger sociopolitical context views them negatively.

RITUALS AS A MECHANISM OF RESISTANCE

> To be human is to belong to the whole community, and to do so involves participating in the beliefs, ceremonies, rituals and festivals of that community. A person cannot detach himself from the religion of his group, for to do so is to be severed from his roots, his foundation, his context of security, his kinship and the entire group of those who make him aware of his own existence. (Mbiti, 1969, p. 2)

When a family faces traumatic life-cycle events like imprisonment, sudden loss, forced migration, divorce, and hospitalization, the creation or adaptation of rituals can help it cope with the crisis. When families are experiencing multiple or constant crises, they tend to operate in survival mode, focusing solely on the basic and immediate needs of family members. Their inability to maintain rituals increases the risks of intergenerational schisms, isolation, stigma, secrecy, and shame, especially if there is a lack of social support from the larger system. Conversely, when rituals are maintained, people are better adjusted and more satisfied because they feel a heightened sense of belonging, membership, and commitment to the family.

When traditional family structures and ceremonies do not fulfill the need for connection, some groups, particularly oppressed and marginalized communities, create their own rituals to mark transitions and elevate their spirits, and sometimes to confront and resist the dominant culture.[11]

Rituals are fluid and changing. Seemingly straightforward activities may be construed in different ways in different times and places. The format of a ceremony is not the only thing that determines its impact. Equally important is the involvement and investment of the participants.

A case in point is the history of marriage ceremonies in the African-American community. Enslaved Africans in America created their own secret wedding ceremony, called "jumping the broom," to mark their committed relationships. During the marriage ceremony the new couple jumped over a broom to symbolize that they were sweeping away their past and beginning new lives together. Although this ritual took place as the participants were enslaved, subjugated, and oppressed, the participants transformed it into an occasion of joy and pride.[12] Even today many contemporary African-American marriages incorporate this tradition.

Similarly, DeSilva describes how, in the face of starvation and almost certain death, Jewish women in a Nazi concentration camp in Czechoslovakia recorded their traditional recipes as a way to maintain their dignity.[13] Through this ritual, the women stayed connected to their culture, ethnic heritage, faith, and families of origin during a time of unimaginable stress.

Establishing and participating in their own rituals can help marginalized groups increase their self-esteem and challenge values promoted by institutions that look down on them. One example is the mechanism that LGBTQU communities developed to publicly honor the loss of lovers, friends, family, and community to HIV/AIDS related deaths.

It began in San Francisco in 1985, when gay rights activist Cleve Jones established the NAMES AIDS Memorial Quilt, the largest ongoing community arts project in the world. The quilt consists of hand-sewn pieces of cloth, each memorializing a person who has died of HIV and AIDS related causes. The names are read aloud in a public ceremony to symbolize breaking the silence of shame and stigma associated with HIV/AIDS. This ritual provides relief, solace, and solidarity for mourners and advocates.[14]

Another example is the Clothesline Project, a community ritual highlighting domestic violence. Hand-painted T-shirts are hung on a clothesline, accompanied by the sound of bells and horns. The ritual symbolizes how often a woman is assaulted, raped, or murdered. This public exposure of violence against women helps these women to regain power and heal.[15]

RITUALS FOR JUSTICE-INVOLVED FAMILIES

The United States incarcerates a much higher proportion of its people, and especially minorities, than other wealthy countries. A white boy born in 2001 has a one in seventeen chance of going to prison during his lifetime. But a black boy born the same year has a one in three chance and a Latino boy has a one in six chance of going to jail! Selective prosecution and punishment accounts for much of this difference. A black youth is about five times more likely to be incarcerated after a drug offense than his white peer. Latino youths are twice as likely as whites to get jail time for a drug arrest.

Minority youth, who make up 39 percent of the juvenile population, account for 60 percent of incarcerated juveniles. The majority of poor children live in working families that play by the rules. But racial disparity influences every aspect of the life of children of color, from education to health care to employment to society's tolerance for boys "acting up."[16]

The disproportionate incarceration rate of people of color tears young adults away from their families and their communities during their most productive years, when they should be building careers and families. Communities suffer when so many of their young men and women are prevented from establishing long-term personal relationships, getting or keeping jobs, and living conventional lives.

RENAMING CEREMONY: FROM SURVIVAL TO EMPOWERMENT AND LIBERATION

Because most African names have a meaning in many parts of Africa, naming children is an important occasion marked by elaborate ceremonies and rituals, during which a name is bestowed that describes personality traits, character, or a key life event.[17] It is hoped that a positive name like "strength" or "pride" might empower an individual to live up to its essence. Receiving names is an ongoing process, and by the time a person is old, he or she might have acquired a sizeable collection, including the names of dead family members in order to continue the family legacy.

At Affinity Counseling Group[18] the therapeutic team came up with a renaming ritual for "Gaston," a young black man out on bond, pending sentencing for violating probation for a drug offense. Gaston was not gang affiliated, although many in his family were, including an uncle who had recently received a life sentence for gang-related murders.

Gangs routinely give street names to their members, typically embodying violent and subhuman personality characteristics like Monster, Money, Boss, or Killer. The counseling group developed a "Renaming Ceremony" ritual to encourage Gaston to accept accountability for his actions, to help him stay in touch with his humanity and maintain his spirit under the conditions of prison life, and to empower him to shift his personal and family life in a positive direction.

Coming up with forms and structures for the ritual was a very fluid and flexible process. The therapeutic team's goal was to get the community to decide what they wanted to see in the ritual so that it would offer an opportunity and encouragement to an adolescent to take responsibility for his own future. The therapists also hoped to foster equity in the client-therapist relationship by expanding the client's choices through a collaborative process rather than imposing their own morality.

When the session began, all members of the therapeutic community (what we call the cultural circle) stood in a circle and held hands. The participants turned off their cell phones and an adolescent member of the circle was delegated to collect them in a basket and place them on a table in the center of the room. Another member of the circle led the recitation of the opening statement: "I place my hand in yours and together we can do what I cannot do alone. Peace."

Then the participants released their hands, made the peace sign, and returned to their chairs. Once seated, all the participants introduced themselves and said what they were feeling. The therapist then began to stage the room for the "Renaming Ceremony."

Gaston sat on a chair in the center while the members of the therapeutic community sat on the floor in concentric circles. His relatives and close friends sat in the closest circle. Positioning the participants in concentric circles around him symbolized the safety, support, and boundaries that the community wanted to create around Gaston to help him survive incarceration.

The therapists began by discussing the purpose of the gathering, which was to acknowledge how Gaston's actions had led to the difficult consequences that he and his family must now bear, as well as how the larger context of the judicial system does not promote rehabilitation and destroys the human spirit. The aim of the ritual, it was explained, was to create a memory for Gaston to hold onto, one that would remind him of his true identity should prison life begin to destroy his concept of self.

Then everyone was asked to sit silently and reflect while the hip-hop/rap artist DMX's spoken word/rap "Prayer" (2001) was played. After that, a member of the group read the essay "They're Playing Your Song" by Alan Cohen (2002), which describes the process of naming children in African tribes.

The piece details how a child is given a name at birth, and how during the struggles of childhood and early adulthood a child may lose his/her way and need to be reminded of the name's significance to the community he/she belongs to. The reading notes that the ritual of remembering one's name is more effective than punishment or scolding in bringing people back to their identity and life purpose.

The tribe creates a name and a song for each newborn and is responsible for remembering it throughout the child's life. The community supports the individual and sings that song, even when the person has forgotten it and has committed actions that are not in line with the spirit of the name.

After the reading, the participants shared their feelings. Family and friends usually grieve privately for the loss of the incarcerated, but here each person was encouraged to express his or her grief and hopes for the future. This can be especially meaningful for young men who are not encouraged in this culture to express their feelings and then are punished if their anger and rage finally manifests itself in acts of violence.

A reading of the poem "Be Who You Must Be" by Diarmuid Cronin (1997) followed the group's discussion. This poem emphasizes the importance of not imposing judgment on people and instead accepting and valuing each individual for who he is.

The client, Gaston, was given the opportunity to reflect and discuss his thoughts, feelings, regrets, anticipations, and wishes for the future. The ritual ended with a member of the community standing and stating on behalf or the entire cultural circle that Gaston's new name was "Hope." Finally, the community engaged in silent reflection as Tupac Shakur's (1993) song "Keep Your Head Up" played.

Participants were then asked to reconvene the circle for the closing ritual. A member of the group, Gaston's best friend, was called upon to "blow bubbles for the circle." As he blew a continuous stream of bubbles, others expressed what they would like to do better or give up in the upcoming weeks. They also expressed their commitments to Gaston and his family.

To end the ceremony, Gaston led the "Place my hands in yours . . ." recitation and everyone shook hands and hugged.

FURTHER AIMS OF THE RENAMING CEREMONY

Every component of the ritual served multiple purposes for all members of the cultural circle. Traditional norms of masculinity emphasize toughness and are adverse to expressions of emotion and activities that are perceived as feminine or hypersensitive. Holding hands, reciting the ritual statement, hugging, and blowing bubbles are behaviors that expand definitions of manhood to include softness, vulnerability, emotional closeness, and relationships with the other men. Holding hands with other men undercuts homophobia and encourages males to create nurturing relationships with other males, while holding hands with women encourages men to relate to females in nonsexualized ways.

Another goal is to encourage emotional connections among adolescents and create a safe and violence-free space, which is especially important because the adolescent participants in the sessions are often affiliated with different street gangs. Participants in this ritual commit themselves to forsaking violent action against any other member of the group. The goal is to create strong, lasting ties of friendship and connection as a way to create community bonding rather than gang bonding.

This is reinforced when adolescents, who want to present themselves as being very tough, see each other blowing bubbles and saying what they hope to do better or give up. By engaging in a very soft activity, like blowing bubbles, the adolescents are encouraged to feel safe to express their emotions and to commit to more life-affirming choices with members of the community.

So even before Gaston started his incarceration, the Renaming Ceremony marked the beginning of his reentry process. During the ritual, the community described what Gaston's process meant to them, what changes they saw in him, and offered their encouragement and support to him and his family. They also discussed plans for him after the end of his incarceration.

In turn, Gaston reflected on his own process and what this experience meant to him. At the end of the ritual, when the community gave him the name "Hope," they indicated that they expected him to live up to the meaning, expectations, and essence of the new name. The Renaming Ceremony also aimed to break the pattern of intergenerational incarceration and create a new legacy for Gaston, his family, and his community. It marked his shift from survival to empowerment and liberation.

In addition, the Renaming Ceremony served as a healing ritual by providing a safe and manageable space for community members to express and deal with emotions associated with the violence that has become a part of everyday life. The reactions of community participants in the ritual were strong and intense. This renaming ritual forced individuals to bring their emotions to the surface and to face the pain of loss that family and friends go through when they lose a loved one.

Another very important element of this ritual was to foster accountability. Participants had to consider their own responsibility in either having deterred or promoted Gaston's criminal involvement. And by connecting with the grieving family, they became more aware of the reality of the loss their own families would feel if they were incarcerated or killed. Participants begin to take responsibility for their lives.

IMPLICATIONS AND CONSIDERATIONS

The creative and flexible use of rituals holds promise for promoting the health and well-being of families. Creating and integrating rituals into the fabric of family life can be vital in a context where American society tends to underestimate the importance of spirituality and ignores the internal need to maintain individual and family health in a chaotic and complex world.

Different types of rituals provide rich sources of information about factors contributing to family dysfunction as well as to family health. Families are often less resistant to using rituals as tools to help produce healthy change than they are to accepting assignments or tasks aimed at change. As we explore strategies to help families build resiliency around normal as well as traumatic life cycle transitions, rituals can be very helpful in acknowledging family history and strengths, and fostering positive change in family interaction. In some instances, they can also be used as tools to support social and political action.

For Review

1. How do family processes, as described by Cowan and Cowan, apply to Laureau's discussion of race and class in child-rearing strategies? What family processes may be influential to a working class white child's well-being? What family processes may affect the well-being of a middle-class African-American child? What kinds of family processes and child-rearing strategies do you observe in your own home?

2. Furstenberg makes an argument for studying social class independently of race, ethnicity, and gender. In contrast, how do some of the other authors in Part Four incorporate race, ethnicity, and gender when they write about social class? Discuss the challenges and benefits of studying class independently versus studying it in combination with race, ethnicity, and gender.

3. What are some of the social and cultural factors discussed by Roy and Cabrera and England and Edin that enable low-income fathers to develop and maintain strong ties with their children? How might these fathers and children use ritual as a "tool of resistance" in the way Brown, Dimitriou, and Dressner describe?

4. The authors in Part Four argue that social class is an important factor to consider when we discuss child care and children's well-being. How might this argument apply to a discussion about elder care and the well-being of older adults in our society? Are some of the family dynamics, social processes, and cultural factors that these authors write about applicable to elder care as well as to child care?

5. Activity: Cowan and Cowan find public policy debates problematic when the people involved in them think that they can only be right if they prove the other side wrong. Choose a public policy debate that is going on right now and find two blog or newspaper articles that represent two different sides of the debate. Are these sides polarized in the way Cowan and Cowan describe? How might the debate be different if people paid more attention to social processes? Write your own short blog or newspaper article presenting the topic you have chosen as a conversation between two or more viewpoints, rather than a polarized debate.

6. Activity: The Council on Contemporary Families Fact Sheet on Military Child Care reports that among military families, those with an annual income of up to $23,000 pay between $40 and $53 per week per child for child care. How does this compare to what families in your neighborhood pay for child care? Suppose you are a parent making $20,000 per year and cannot rely on employer-provided child care. Do some research to find out what child-care options are available near your home. Can you find full-day child care for $53 per week or less? If so, is the child-care provider you found nationally accredited? Is care provided for infants as well as for older children? If the provider you found is more expensive than military child care, calculate what percentage of your family income will be spent on child care each month (assume that you make $20,000 per year, or approximately $1,600 per month).

PART FIVE

The Unfinished Gender Revolution

30

Betwixt and Be Tween: Gender Contradictions among Middle Schoolers

Barbara J. Risman and Elizabeth Seale

This research is based on interviews with middle-school children in a southeast-ern city of the United States. In this paper, we ask whether the gender revolution has freed these children from being constrained by stereotypes. We find that both boys and girls are still punished for going beyond gender expectations, but boys much more so than girls. For girls, participation in traditionally masculine activi-ties, such as sports and academic competition, is now quite acceptable and even encouraged by both parents and peers. We find, indeed, that girls are more likely to tease each other for being too girly than for being a sports star. Girls still feel pressure, however, to be thin and to dress in feminine ways, to "do gender" in their self-presentation. Boys are quickly teased for doing any behavior that is tradition-ally considered feminine. Boys who deviate in any way from traditional masculinity are stigmatized as "gay." Whereas girls can and do participate in a wide range of activities without being teased, boys consistently avoid activities defined as female to avoid peer harassment. Homophobia, at least toward boys, is alive and well in middle school.

Today parents and educators tell children that they can be whatever they want to be. Children are taught that women and men and whites and blacks are equal.[1] Changes in gender norms have created opportunities for girls that never before existed. For instance, in school, Title IX has encouraged girls' participation in athletics. But are boys and girls actually free to construct personal identities that leave behind gen-der stereotypes, even when their parents and teachers encourage them to do so?

How free are middle-school boys and girls to form identities outside the constraining gender expectations that have traditionally disadvantaged girls in the public sphere and repressed boys from exploring their emotions? We approached this subject by interviewing forty-four middle-school children in a mid-sized southeastern city. They were not yet teenagers but were already adapting to pressures to view the world through the eyes of their peers. Middle school is a time when peers become a crucial reference group. Conformity to group norms becomes central to popularity, fitting in, and self-image.[2] What do the experiences and perceptions of these preadolescent kids (tween-agers) tell us about growing up in contemporary society? How much have their expectations and self-images transcended traditional gender norms?

Peers become centrally important as tween-agers face new and complicated situations in which they must negotiate friendships, issues of sexuality, self-image, conflict, stratification, cliques, and the like. In this so-called "tween" culture, these kids try to make sense of things in their daily lives by using new tools as well as old ones taken from "cultural tool kits." The lives of tween-agers provide a glimpse into how contemporary definitions of race and gender are shaping the next generation, and what new realities the children themselves may be creating at a time when their core identities are developing.

Our data suggest that American middle-school children, at least in the mid-sized southeastern city we examined, have adopted an ideal of equality. Nearly all the kids say that men and women are equal, and that race no longer matters, or at least that it shouldn't. These children have been raised in a society that posits the ideals of gender and racial equality, and the kids seem to accept and believe in those ideals, at least when you scratch the surface of their opinions. But that ideal of equality is not what they experience in their real lives, and at least half of them recognize and identify contradictions between what should be and what is.

Despite their acceptance of the rhetoric of gender equality, these tween-agers hold very gender-stereotypical beliefs about boys, although not about girls. Any male gender nonconformity, where boys engage in behaviors or activities traditionally considered female, is taken as evidence that the boy is "gay." As a result, boys are afraid to cross any gender boundaries for fear of having that stigma attached to them. By contrast, the lives of girls are much less constricted by stereotypes about femininity. In fact, girls are more likely to be teased for being "too girly," than for being a tomboy. Girls still police each other's behavior, but the rules of femininity that they enforce now seem to focus almost exclusively on clothes, makeup, diet, and bodily presentation. The girls in our study still "do gender,"[3] but mostly by how they look.

Research on Gender and Youth

Research on how traditional femininity constrains girls is contradictory. Some studies suggest that girls are viewed as less feminine if they participate in sports. Others argue that athleticism is no longer seen as incompatible with femininity and may indeed be part of the "ideal girlhood" package.[4]

In their study of middle-school cheerleaders, Adams and Bettis also point to fundamental contradictions in the contemporary ideal of girlhood. Traditional feminine characteristics like passivity and docility, they argue, have been replaced by independence, assertiveness, and strength, and participation in sports is considered an "essential component of girl culture today."[5] At the same time, when it comes to popularity, attractiveness trumps all other attributes. Cheerleading, in keeping up with changing gender expectations, has incorporated the new ideals of girlhood, including "confidence, rationality, risk-taking, athleticism, independence, and fearlessness."[6] But it continues to attract girls who value feminine looks and who are interested in attracting boys. Becoming a cheerleader is one way to cope with the contradictions of girlhood because it allows girls to be athletic and adopt some desired masculine traits, while retaining feminine characteristics that the girls enjoy and that make them desirable to boys.[7]

A few studies address how race and class differences among young women affect their standards of femininity. Bettie found class- and race-specific versions of femininity among high-school girls.[8] Lower-class white and nonwhite girls adopted a more sexualized style of femininity than white middle-class girls. Bettie suggested that "las chicas," the Latina girls, adapted a style of femininity that emphasized their ethnicity, preferring darker and more visible makeup and tight-fitting clothes. Working-class white girls also generally wore more makeup than middle-class students. While school officials and middle-class peers commonly interpreted these bodily expressions as evidence of "looser" sexual morals, Bettie found that these girls were less interested in romantic attachments than outsiders supposed, and that their styles of bodily presentation had more to do with incorporating racial and community markers into their gender displays. For example, working-class white girls expressed resistance to middle-class culture by "dressing down" in torn jeans, whereas Mexican-American girls, feeling that their brown skin was already perceived as a "dressed down" appearance, would dress "up" in an effort to deny any link between color and poverty. Bettie also found that although these girls presented a very sexualized version of femininity, they did not want to or expect to lead traditional lives as at-home mothers and wives and they were in favor of gender equality for adults.

Many studies of middle- and high-school girls find strong evidence of pressures to be attractive to boys.[9] Lemish finds that widely different modes of femininity are acceptable among preadolescent girls, as long as the girl is also "pretty." One of the paradoxes of contemporary girlhood is that there are confusing and conflicting messages about what a girl should be like, as well as what type of girl should be (de)valued.

There is very little latitude or tolerance for boys to behave in ways that have been traditionally labeled as girlish. Engaging in any traditionally feminine activity, from dancing well, to knitting, to playing the piano opens boys up to being taunted as "gay." Usually it is boys who tease other boys, but sometimes girls do as well. Researchers suggest that homophobia is not merely antihomosexual prejudice. It also reinforces sharp gender divisions through the deployment of fear. This is seen particularly at the high-school level, but some research suggests it is also evident in elementary school and in middle school.[10] Thorne found that by the fourth grade "fag" is sometimes used as an insult. But Plummer points out that homophobic insults used in grade school do not actually carry sexual meaning.[11] Rather they are used to tease boys who are different, including boys viewed as effeminate. The use of homophobic terms as insults, Plummer maintains, increases with adolescence. Eder and her coauthors discuss homophobic insults among middle-school boys as a ritualistic way to assert masculine dominance, as a way to insult and further isolate the lowest on the peer hierarchy, and as a self-defense mechanism in identifying oneself as heterosexual and normal.[12] Their research illustrates the intense anxiety over peer approval and acceptance, and how that fosters bullying in middle school for both girls and boys, although more so for boys. By middle school, any sign of gender boundary crossing by boys is taken as signifying homosexuality, and elicits strong homophobic teasing.

As boys grow older, the gender expectations appear to become more rigid and regulated. Among high-school youth, masculinity is defined as toughness: a potential if not an inclination for violence, lack of emotion, and sexual objectification of girls. By high school, it is a major insult for a boy to be called gay, and the label may be applied to any boy who is different from his male peers in some way, any boy who is considered feminine or unpopular, any boy who is a target for being bullied. Among young people, the word "gay" has acquired such a negative connotation that it is commonly used to describe anything that is bad, undesirable, or "lame."[13]

Pascoe (2005) identifies a "fag" discourse through which high-school boys use the term as an epithet on a daily basis. Any boy, she notes, may be temporarily labeled a "faggot," and so all boys continually struggle to avoid being stigmatized. With the possibility of being called a "faggot" only an insult away, constant work is required to be sufficiently masculine to avoid the label. In fact, the primary use of homophobia in policing the activities of boys is not to root out, expose, or punish potential homosexuals, but rather to regulate gender behavior and narrowly channel boys toward accepted activities and away from others.

It is not clear whether or how this use of homophobia to police boys' gender varies according to race. In Pascoe's (2007) study of "fag" discourse among high-school boys in a working-class California school, she found that behaviors that incur a "fag" stigma for white boys, such as attention to fashion, or dancing with another man, are accepted as normal by nonwhite boys. She suggests that the use of homophobic insults is more common among white than nonwhite teenagers.

Froyum studied an underclass African-American summer program in a large East Coast city, however, and found heavy policing of heterosexuality among both boys and girls.[14] She argues that these impoverished urban kids use heterosexuality to carve out some self-esteem from the only stratification in which they can feel superior to someone else, that they take solace in the fact that "at least they aren't gay."

METHODS

The authors and several graduate students interviewed forty-four middle-school students. We asked the children a set of questions, told them stories and solicited their responses, and had them draw pictures and write poems in order to find out what these boys and girls thought about their own lives, their friends, and their interactions with peers at school. We wanted to delve into middle-school students' expectations around gender, to examine how it feels to grow up in a society that proclaims gender equality and encourages "girl power."

We wanted to find out if children today still see limitations based on their sex, or if they really feel they live in a post-feminist world. We asked about family life, friendship, popularity, cliques, pressures to conform to stereotypes around being a boy or a girl, what "girl power" means, and attitudes regarding racial inequality. This was a diverse group of children, mostly white and African-American, and we paid careful attention to whether the answers to our questions differed by race and/or ethnicity.

The interviews took place between the fall of 2003 and the summer of 2004. They typically lasted between one and two hours and were recorded. Respondents were in the sixth, seventh, and eighth grades and ranged in age from eleven to fourteen. The children were recruited at a racially integrated magnet middle school, a diverse YWCA after-school program and summer camp, and an urban, mostly black Girls' Club. All attended public middle schools in a mid-sized city in the southeastern United States. Because we did not get data on many topics of interest from two of the middle schoolers, we reduced our sample to be discussed here to forty-two. The pseudonyms and specific demographic information for each student are listed in a chart in the appendix at the end of this chapter. Most were middle class, although a few were from working-class or upper middle-class professional families. We paid careful attention to any racial differences in the responses. But having only four nonwhite boys, two of whom were black, hampered our ability to examine racial or ethnic differences among boys. We hoped to learn something about what it is like to grow up in today's world. Interviewers asked the children many questions. How are you similar to other boys/girls? How are you different from other girls/boys? We also asked about likes and dislikes, activities, friendship groups, cliques at school, and favorite subjects. Many of our questions dealt specifically with the children's perceptions of gender. What does it mean when someone is called a "girly-girl"? What does it mean when a girl is called a tomboy? Is there a word (like "girly" for prissy boys) that refers to boys who are really tough or macho? Is there a word for a boy who is quiet and thoughtful and likes to do arts and crafts, one who likes the kinds of activities that girls more often like to do?

Using a hypothetical scenario to draw them out, we asked students to describe what their lives would be like as the opposite sex. We asked: "If an alien with supernatural powers came into your bedroom one night and turned you into a boy/girl, how would your life be different in the morning?" We also asked: "How would your life be different if an alien made you gay?"

We asked students to write a poem or paragraph beginning with "If I were a boy/girl . . ." If they preferred they could draw a picture elaborating on that theme. We also explored their acceptance of nontraditional gender behavior by using vignettes and asking how they or their peers would react to a person who crossed a gender boundary.

To understand the boundary of female behavior, we used this hypothetical story: "Pretend for a moment that there is a girl in your grade named Jasmine. Jasmine is very athletic and loves competition. She decides that she wants to start an all-girls football club at your school. She places posters all over student lockers and the hallways promoting the girls' club and asking for players. Then she approaches the principal and asks if she can start the team." For male gender nonconformity, we constructed this story: "Imagine that there is a boy in your grade named Marcus. He loves to dance. He has taken gymnastics since he was little, and is very good. Now that he is older, he wants to be a cheerleader. He knows that [Name of University] has male cheerleaders and he wants to join that squad when he goes to college." Students who seemed mature enough were asked about homosexuality, including how they and their peers would react to a gay student.

Due to time constraints, variations in maturity levels, and the occasional tape malfunction, we do not have responses to all of these questions from every student. Although we do have a wealth of information from almost every student to utilize for analysis, with such open-ended qualitative data it is very challenging to compare responses across kids for interpretation.

There were several limitations to the methods we employed. Because we did not directly observe interactions between the middle schoolers, we had to rely on what they told us, and how they explained their thoughts on boys, girls, gender non-conformity, gender expectations, homosexuality, heterosexuality, and life in general. Nonetheless, we believe the method is useful because the thoughts and feelings of these preadolescents help us understand how they experience and react to peer pressure. Moreover, in one-on-one interviews, children and adults may reveal more about their thoughts and feelings than they would if others were present.

Contradictions and Equality Rhetoric

When we asked these students questions about gender or race, their responses indicated that most have assimilated both the feminist-inspired ideology that women and men are equal and the post-civil rights ideology that all races are equal. Nine out of twelve male students and seventeen of twenty-two female students (for whom we have appropriate data) professed some belief in gender equality. For example, Molly finished the phrase "If I were a boy" in a poem that read: "If I were a boy, / Nothing should be different, / Because all people are equal." For the same exercise, another student, Marney, wrote that "I think I would be treated mainly the same by parents, friends, teachers." Brady similarly argued that "all people should be treated the same," although he felt life would be "very freaky" if he were turned into a girl. Micah told us that girl power means that girls now have every right that men do. The kids appeared to believe that males and females either were equal in reality or ought to be.

Despite this equality rhetoric, there were serious inconsistencies in their responses. For example, when the kids answered questions about what would happen if they were turned into the opposite sex, most expressed a belief that gender stereotypes were based in biology, despite earlier declarations that "we are all the same." With these questions, we found that many kids were well aware of the consequences for not conforming to gender norms.

This contradiction between the rhetoric of equality and more experience-biased appraisals of gender inequality was further revealed when we asked the children to place cards with occupations written on them under the categories "men," "women," and "both." They were first asked to place their cards according to whether men or women are more likely to hold each job, and afterward according to how they think it *should* be. This activity showed us whether students felt there was occupational segregation by sex and how they judged it. None of the boys and only five out of twenty-three girls thought that men and women were equally distributed among all occupations. Six of twelve boys and ten of twenty-two girls told us that all occupations *should* be distributed equally among men and women. The others, who believed gender segregation was appropriate, usually explained that men and women were different. In most cases, when asked how it should be versus how it really is, students put more occupations under the category of "both." Nurse, secretary, and librarian were commonly thought to be women's jobs, whereas police officer, firefighter, mechanic, and engineer were often seen as men's jobs. Sixteen out of thirty-four students expressed the belief that men and women were or should be "equal" and that girls and women should be able to do anything they want.

These children, even those consistently committed to equality in theory, however, often expressed contradictory views in other parts of the interview, displaying a belief in the essential differences between boys and girls or holding their peers to gendered expectations. In many cases, advances in ideology were not consistently guiding reported behavior.

BETWEEN TOMBOY AND GIRLY-GIRL

We asked boys and girls to answer questions about what girly-girls and tomboys are like, how girls think they are similar to and different from other girls, and what boys thought would be different if they were "turned into a girl."

Nearly all the students could describe a typical girly-girl and a tomboy. Many boys and girls alike defined girly-girls as preoccupied with appearances, in contrast to tomboys. One female student, Kay, described girly-girls in these terms: "'Oh my gosh!' totally into stuff like that. Always having their hair, you know, down like that, you know, kind of prissy. Want to wear high-heeled shoes all the time. Laughing and flirting and stuff like that." Marney, who stated that she did not consider herself a girly-girl, responded that "they're afraid to get dirty, you're obsessed with your hair, you like to wear makeup a lot." Kay indicated that girly-girl meant being obsessed with boys or talking about boys. Although this description was less common than references to appearance in characterizing girly-girls, romance-centered behavior (e.g., being "boy-crazy" or obsessed with boys, flirting, talking about boys, or gossiping about relationships) was mentioned by four girls and two boys as characterizing "girly-girls." Several more mentioned such behavior when discussing "typical" girls in general.

Nearly 80 percent of those who responded provided what we interpret as a "negative" description of a girly-girl, and the rest gave neutral responses. Of the nine males, five gave negative descriptions and four gave neutral descriptions of girly-girls. A neutral response, for instance, might refer to girly-girls as wearing pink often, without indicating that wearing a lot of pink is objectionable.

There was not a single overtly positive definition of a girly-girl. No one told us, for instance, that girly-girls are kind, looked up to, or even desirable to boys. We did not count the suggestion that girly-girls are the most popular as being positive in itself, because such comments were often paired with expressions of disdain for the "popular" kids.

Common descriptions of girly-girls included fear of getting dirty, breaking a nail, or getting sweaty. Seven girls and two boys used the word "prissy." Samantha suggested that a girly-girl is "prissy," wears makeup everyday, and is obsessed with hair. She mimics such a person: " 'Oh my gosh, it has to be perfect. I have to put hairspray in it.' Glitter, gel, whatever. Like, always running around screaming [high-pitched], 'Oh my God, a spider! Oh my gosh, my nail broke!' Just little things that are like your nail breaking. Crying over it or something. That's a girly-girl."

Girls were, overall, more censorious, but boys sometimes described girly-girls in a similarly contemptuous fashion. With a disgusted expression on his face, Jason told his interviewer that, "To me, it means makeup and a whole lot of other girlie perfumes and . . . lipstick and mascara and eye shadow and other makeup that they put on that I don't even want to mention."

At the same time, when researchers asked explicitly whether "being a girly-girl is a good or bad thing" the kids were divided. Karlin, for example, initially portrayed girly-girls in a contemptuous fashion, saying that they are girls who would say, " 'Guys are better. I don't do sports. I might get my shoes wet.' Or like, 'I can't kick a ball. I try to look good but I don't have any specific talent.' " But when asked directly whether being a girly-girl is a bad or good thing, her response was that it depends on the person. If they are selfish, that is bad, but if this is just how they were brought up, then "it's fine."

Several kids indicated that being girly made a girl popular, whereas others (and sometimes even the same respondents) suggested that it was annoying, or that they themselves did not like these people. Mona talked about the "bad preps"—girls who dye their hair blonde, wear too much makeup, wear revealing clothes, and draw their eyebrows in after waxing them. She reported that she and her friends despise this group and frequently make jokes about them. But in other parts of the interview she associated girl preps with playing a lot of sports. Girly-girls were often defined in the abstract as girls who do not play sports, but in actual references to peers, being a girly-girl and playing sports were not always incompatible.

Although students tended to associate girly-girls with being popular and being more feminine, stereotypical girls were subject to substantial ridicule by girls and boys alike in these interviews. None of the female respondents identified themselves to the interviewer as exclusively girly-girl. And all three of the girls who did say they thought of themselves as at least part girly, also described themselves as partly or occasionally tomboyish (and none of these girls considered herself a "typical girl"). This reflects the negative connotations associated with being a girly-girl, which was usually defined contemptuously or with reference to activities and concerns generally seen as narcissistic and trivial (e.g., wearing too much makeup too often, afraid of breaking a nail, excessive shopping).

These disdainful descriptions of what it means to be a girly-girl tell us that too much emphasis on femininity is looked down upon at this age level. No matter where they fell on the girly-girl/tomboy continuum, the girls saw themselves as different from the category of the prototypical feminine girl, who was seen as narcissistic, vain, and silly. They did not want to be identified as that type of girl. But in the process of rejecting this stereotype for themselves, they sometimes conferred it upon others as the prototypical teenage girl.

The girls in our study also felt that girls should display *some* level of femininity, especially when it comes to looks. Several girls, black and white, indicated that being too much of a tomboy could be a bad thing. Karlin, for instance, chastised tomboys who fail to "recognize the fact that they're a girl." According to her, playing sports should not get in the way of "being a girl."

Kerri indicated that it is okay to be girlish if one is athletic as well. She asserted that "there are a lot" of girly-girls, although she did not personally *know* very many:

> Yeah, there are a lot. I don't know a lot of girly-girls. I know I don't mind wearing skirts and I don't mind wearing makeup but I'm not a girly-girl. And I know what a girly-girl is. It's when you're all obsessed with makeup and looking good and I mean all the girls I know play at least two sports and they own makeup, and they're, I mean, my room is blue and pink and yellow but you'd have to look around and see all my soccer pictures and all my basketball trophies. And I mean if you just looked in my room, didn't see any trophies, you'd think I was a really big girly-girl.

At least five kids indicated that being a tomboy was positive in some respects, but no one indicated that tomboys were considered the popular or privileged girls. One female middle schooler suggested a tomboy might have difficulty getting a boyfriend. In the interviews, being a tomboy was associated with being athletic, although girls could be athletic without being seen as a tomboy. It is also noteworthy that only three girls identified themselves as tomboys but not at all girly, although this was more than the number who considered themselves "girly-girls."

Most girls clearly do not place themselves in either of these two extreme categories, although they often suggest that they have characteristics associated with both. These two extremes bracket the entire spectrum of gender meanings for girls, but do not represent the majority of identities. Some girls embraced the label of tomboy (often while simultaneously embracing aspects of bodily femininity) as a strategy to avoid negative associations with being female. For example, one girl told us "we've actually made up, like those ten girls, we've made up the tomboy club because we don't mind competing against the guys for stuff, and we, I mean I actually liked being called a tomboy because then I knew people didn't just look at me as a girl. That they could actually see me as doing something more than being just a ballet dancer."

Most girls do adopt some aspects of traditional femininity. They wear makeup or lip gloss, enjoy shopping for and dressing up in gendered clothes, or like talking about boys. This became apparent in the interviews where girls discussed how they were similar to other girls, what they liked to do, and how they spent their time. It was also apparent in some of the field notes written by interviewers, who noted details about how the students dressed and presented themselves.

The female middle schoolers criticized only extreme forms of this femininity, such as wearing lots of makeup everyday, dressing in too revealing a fashion, worrying about looking good all of the time, and especially having a "girly-girl" identity. Jamie, for example, said she is similar to other girls in that she likes clothes and guys, but says she is not girly like the ones who are "prim" and "afraid to get dirty, to get down and goof around."

When it comes to untangling the gender expectations that these middle schoolers hold and perceive, contradictions abound. In one part of her interview, Lola said that "there's just some traits that all girls have in common. . . . Ability to accessorize [laughs]. Just stuff. You can always tell who's a boy and who's a girl. It's different. Like boys like video games and girls like makeup. . . . Boys are rougher. Girls are more into sitting and talking. And boys are more into going outside and playing Frisbee or something." But she also asserted that girls would love to have their own football team. It is clear that girls perceive pressures both to be identifiably feminine and to take on some traditionally masculine characteristics like assertiveness, fearlessness, rationality, and independence in order to be taken seriously.

While girls face less restrictive norms for gender-appropriate behavior, there still seem to be limitations, especially in regard to ideals of beauty. Girls are still expected to demonstrate a type of femininity, although one that is no longer threatened by participation in traditionally male-dominated activities. Our story about a girl who wants to start a football team elicited a few worries that she might be teased because she did not play well, but there was little concern that Jasmine would be teased for violating norms of femininity. As Malcom pointed out in her study of softball players, girls who play sports run the risk of being seen as or teased for being incompetent as athletes rather than for displaying behavior inappropriate for girls.[15]

The girls in this study felt a girl can ignore many gender boundaries (in fact playing sports is no longer even considered a gender boundary). But in their view, girls are still expected to display some markers of traditional femininity. Put another way, appropriate femininity does not require avoidance of traditionally masculine activities, but it is accomplished through attention to how the girl displays her body. Femininity has become very body-centered and many respondents simply equate femininity with "looks." But it is interesting that even on this dimension, girls tend to look down on and avoid extreme femininity. For example, several girls criticized pop stars for dressing in tight, revealing clothing, although they also saw this as a requirement for celebrity.

We only have very suggestive data in our sample on how gender norms varied by race. But in three interviews, white girls criticized black girls for overly emphasizing the sexualized aspects of femininity—dressing in tight, revealing clothing, wearing inappropriate makeup, and engaging in inappropriate bodily display. Kerri related the following story about a black peer:

> And the girls, we won't really make fun of her but we just "why? Why is she wearing that?" Because like if she combed her hair and put on some makeup and wore pants she'd be very pretty. But she doesn't. She has to wear the tightest skirts. She never combs her hair. She'll put on makeup but she doesn't put it on right. She'll put on like this dark blue and like gold mascara and she doesn't look right and she's trying, but she's not using the right stuff. So all of us got together one recess and we, not to be mean, but to say okay we could give her a makeover and this one girl, who could really draw. We said okay, we're gonna give her—if we could give her a makeover this is what we'd do. Some girl said okay I'd pick out all her makeup and I'd tweeze her eyebrows and I'd like shave her legs or something. And one girl said, I'd get her on Slim-Fast. And all this stuff. And like she drew a picture of what she'd look like if we all worked with her and she looked kind of looked a lot like me, but kinda, it looked like all the girls had given a part of themselves to her so that was really fun and we thought if she did all of those things she'd look like that.

We also have suggestive data that African-Americans girls sometimes try to adapt "white" beauty norms. Three black or biracial girls indicated that they wished they had physical traits more often seen in Caucasian women. For example, Joleesa, an African-American sixth grader, wished she had long, soft, smooth hair and blue eyes. We do not have a large enough sample to have strong evidence of racialized femininity, but we do find suggestions that white and black girls value white markers of femininity, and that black girls are criticized by white girls if they exhibit more sexualized forms of femininity.

When boys were asked how they would be different if turned into a girl, several indicated they would act the way girly-girls are described. Four boys thought they would act "girly" in some way. Boys spoke of girls with stereotypical language. Tyrone drew a picture of a woman's makeup table and explained that "I drew a vanity, which is a mirror with bulbs around it, and it usually has makeup and perfume around it, and then I drew a little girl stretching since it's been a long day and she's about to go out to the movies with her friends. . . . I drew the vanity because they like wearing tons of makeup." By referring to an exaggerated, abstract notion of femininity when asked to imagine themselves as a girl or to describe girls in general, boys are implicitly defining masculinity as the opposite of this girly-girl femininity. Girls as well as boys distance themselves from this feminized, stereotypical "other" when they try to construct valued images of themselves.

POLICING MASCULINITY

Our respondents described preadolescent masculinity in very narrow and uniform ways. The most common response was that boys like sports (sometimes specific sports like football and basketball were emphasized). Other responses included competitiveness, hating losing to a girl, playing video games, general rowdiness, and being different from girls in that girls want to "really impress people and boys want to have their own way." When boys talked about their interests, they commonly emphasized sports, video games, and competing with male friends. But they almost never mentioned "liking" girls, flirting with girls, or talking about girls. It appears that at this age, romantic interests figure prominently among girls, but not among boys.

A boy who is perceived as too feminine is subject to much more ridicule than a girl who is seen as either overly masculine or overly feminine. If a boy tends to be quiet, shy, bookish, artistic, and/or nonassertive, his sexuality is called into question and he loses respect among other boys. We saw this in the way students made sense of our hypothetical story about Marcus, the boy who wants to be a cheerleader. We asked students whether Marcus should be allowed to join a cheerleading squad when he gets to high school, whether he would be teased by others, and whether the student her/himself would remain friends with Marcus, even if he were teased.

Many pointed out that Marcus would be the target of substantial ridicule because not many boys are cheerleaders.[16] In Lorenzo's opinion, "yeah [Marcus should be allowed to join a cheerleading squad], but um, he's probably gonna get made fun of by like a lot of boys." Asked what the boys would say, Lorenzo responded, "Like um, they're like homosexual or something." Krista told us that "people think that a male cheerleader is always gay, and, I mean, people would make fun of him. Or if he does stuff that people only think girls should do." Deirdre replied that the kids would call Marcus a sissy, and the boys especially would "call him gay." She also suggested that even if they had been friends, she would not stay "close friends" with him because "everyone [would be] calling him gay, and if I hang around him, they'd be like, ew you're gay too." Other questions also revealed the middle-schoolers' fear of peer disapproval. For instance, when we asked Samantha if she would still dance if she were turned into a boy, she responded "probably not" because she would be "made fun of."

Deviating from masculine norms inevitably led to teasing, according to student reports. While only two kids suggested that a tomboy might have her heterosexuality questioned, many suggested that a boy who liked girl-type activities would be called gay. Some of the terms the students applied to girlish boys were "wimps," "tomgirls," "weird," "geeks," "weak," and "punk." Because of the stigma associated with being considered feminine in any way, it is not surprising that some girls described themselves as tomboys, but not a single boy described himself in any way as "girly." A few female students, however, indicated that some of the girls would appreciate such a boy, even though other boys would make fun of him. The threat of being stigmatized as "gay" or a "faggot" plays a big part in policing and enforcing masculinity.

POLICING HETEROSEXUALITY

Antigay sentiment is widespread among these youth, although there was a total confusion between sexual preference and gender behavior, which led to very low tolerance for gender nonconformity among boys. Usually we broached the topic of homosexuality toward the end of the interview and only with those students who seemed relatively mature or comfortable enough with the topic. Typically the researcher asked how the student would respond if a friend revealed to him/her that he or she was gay. They were also usually asked how their own life would change or how they would feel if they woke up one morning and found out they were gay.

In all, thirty-four students answered one or both of these questions (twenty-two girls and twelve boys). Most of these children expressed opposition to homosexuality in general, although white girls were more accepting of homosexuality than others. Most of the boys who discussed homosexuality in any way were clearly homophobic, although one boy seemed unsure and another indicated some acceptance of gays. Jason was adamant that "guys should go with girls and girls should go with guys." "It shouldn't be the same sex . . . that is eeww." Micah thought "it's nasty to be gay." When Dante was asked what would happen if he found out he were gay, he replied, "It would be extremely different and I would hate myself."

None of three nonwhite boys felt comfortable about homosexuality. The two African Americans, Marc and Tyrone, told interviewers that they thought being gay was wrong and "nasty." Lorenzo, a Latino American, did not condemn homosexuality, but neither did he indicate much tolerance for it.

In many instances, a feeling of disgust was cited as a rationale for judging gays, as in Jason's interview. This was especially common among boys, somewhat common among nonwhite girls, and the least common among white girls. Marc said, "I think they would be like, 'Stay away from me, I don't want you doing this and this,' and some people, when they go to the bathroom they would always be looking over their shoulder." Cynthia claimed that teachers might "pay close attention" to a gay student "just to make sure he doesn't do anything nasty around other kids and stuff."

Several of the respondents were horrified at the suggestion of being gay. Jason claimed he would shoot himself if he woke up gay, and Micah said "I would be suicidal. I know that's wrong, but I would." Deirdre responded that if she were gay "I would like girls, which would be nasty." And Kay would be too embarrassed even to go to school. Prejudice by heterosexuals against gays appears to be very much internalized by most of the kids.

A substantial minority, however, expressed tolerant views. Katie felt that people should love who they want to love. When Jack, a seventh grader, was asked what life would be like if he were gay, he said nothing would really be different. He also claimed that he would remain friends with a gay boy, as long as the friend did not "like" him. But even the eleven tolerant youths expressed concern over the reactions of other people, especially peers, toward any indication of homosexuality. The fear of associating with gay peers was quite strong, even among the otherwise tolerant girls, who exhibited some sense of discomfort to the idea of a friend coming out as gay.

This confusion of sexuality and gender stereotypes feeds into the fear boys have about crossing gender boundaries. Responses to the hypothetical scenario about Marcus, the boy who wanted to be a cheerleader in high school, often raised doubts about his sexuality, even though there was absolutely no reference to sexuality in the scenario. All these responses were volunteered by the kids themselves.

Nearly all of the children told the interviewers that Marcus would be teased. Forty-one percent of boys and 43 percent of girls suggested that other students would call Marcus gay, but more girls voiced support for the hypothetical Marcus. None of the respondents believed that Marcus *must* be gay if he wants to be a cheerleader. Rather, responses focused on the idea that he would be called gay and would have to prove his heterosexuality.

There was a widely held conviction that Marcus' peers would verbally abuse him. Jason admitted he would directly taunt Marcus: "I'd go up to his face and say, 'You are a little fruitcake, do you know that?'" But most students seemed to want to protect Marcus from taunts and bullying, especially from *other boys*. Ten girls and three boys who discussed Marcus getting teased mentioned boys as the primary teasers. Some students recommended that Marcus should "keep it hush-hush" or even reconsider his decision, because of the negative peer reaction it would invite. Jack said "if I were him I would choose not to say anything about it or else everyone would make fun of me."

Most students acknowledged that if a boy wants to be a cheerleader in high school it does not necessarily mean he is gay, but 40 percent suggested their peers would operate on such an assumption. A few students thought that Marcus might not face much disapproval—that it would not be a big deal. But most kids told us that their peers severely tease male gender nonconformity. No one policed girls' sports behavior by insinuating girl athletes must be gay.

HOMOPHOBIC TAUNTS AND ENFORCEMENT OF MASCULINITY

The Marcus scenario was not the only part of the interview that brought out the *gender nonconformity = gay* assumption for boys. When we asked students to give us a word to describe boys who are shy, quiet, maybe artistic or creative, and who like activities that girls usually do, four students asserted that such a boy is or would be called gay or some variant thereof. Jeffrey, for example, volunteered that there is no word for boys who act like girls, the way tomboy describes girls who act like boys, but he has heard such boys called "fruit." When we asked Marshall for a term to describe boys who like to do the kinds of activities girls usually do, he responded that "a lot of people call 'em gay." Similarly, without hesitation Deidre gave us the word "fag." Other responses to this particular question indicated that such a boy would be teased in some way, even if he were not called gay.

Just as kids interpret boys' gender nonconformity as evidence of homosexuality, the flip side is that they also consistently associate homosexuality with gender nonconformity. Middle-school students assume that someone who is gay will violate gender norms. One male student told us that if he were gay, he would no longer like sports. In general, the kids assumed that gay males are more feminine than straight members of their sex. Jeffrey thought that if he were gay he "might like to hang around with girls a little more. Not like flirting, but acting like a girl or around girls."

Such presumptions lend legitimacy to the regulation of male gender nonconformity through antigay remarks. The stigmatizing of Marcus was in sharp contrast to responses to the hypothetical scenario about Jasmine, the girl who wanted to start a girls' football club. None of the students suggested that Jasmine's sexuality would be suspect, although a few suggested she might be teased or thought "weird" by other students. It seems that gender nonconformity is less policed among girls than boys, and is much less likely to be presumed as a marker of sexuality for girls.

Kids fear being labeled gay by their peers, which makes this a powerful tool for policing gender. In general, when the kids were asked "what if you found out you were gay?," their first response was to discuss the reaction of their peers, rather than their parents or family members, providing further evidence that, for preadolescents, peers form a critical reference group. In fact, eighteen of twenty-one girls referred to peer disapproval when responding to hypothetical questions about being gay themselves or having a gay friend. Seven of nine boys did the same. Boys and girls consistently suggested that their peers would react negatively to them if they came out as gay. In several cases, respondents acknowledged that they might react negatively or would apply some type of sanction to a gay student.

Being called gay is evidently the worst insult and the most effective way to shame another student. When Cynthia spoke of a male friend of hers who is frequently bullied, she claimed that "most of the time he ignores it but if somebody ends up calling him 'gay' or something, he takes it really bad." Interestingly, Cynthia and others do not consider this friend to be particularly feminine, although they describe him as "scrawny" and "short." Rather, she believes that he is called gay because it is a dependable way for his attackers to insult him.

Branding nonconformists as gay in this middle-school context constitutes a primary form of regulation as well as harassment. When a boy is labeled as gay, it is not necessarily about his sexuality, but it is rather a surefire way to insult him. The gay stigma is not primarily used to tease someone as homosexual, but to deprive a boy of the status that comes with masculinity.[17]

Paradoxically, we have some very suggestive evidence that if a person actually does embrace a gay identity, he or she is freer to cross gender boundaries and to enjoy activities usually limited to the other sex. Mallory and several of the other children told us that a male gay student they knew was taunted by peers for a while, but the bullying leveled off substantially with time. Jamie told us that she has a gay female friend who had some problems with other students, "but people kind of just got over it, and said, 'hey, so what?' " Jamie claimed that other people were initially standoffish with her gay female friend, but they forgot about it by the next year.

In some cases, when discussing other students who are openly gay or lesbian, a student would claim that the teasing was not that bad. Cynthia said that her gay male friend is called names by "like two or three" of the girls in her class, but the boys do not really make fun of him. She thought that is because although he's told all the girls, he probably has not told the boys. When asked if the boys would make fun of him if they knew, she replied: "No, I think he has told them but they probably really don't consider it something big."

In response to the story about Marcus the cheerleader, Mallory described her gay friend, Jo, as an exception to the gender rules. She said, "Now, I know for a fact that [Marcus would] be made fun of for that. Except Jo. Everybody knows Jo's going to do something like that, so nobody really cares if Jo did something like that. But if that boy is not Jo, he will probably get made fun of." When asked why people do not make fun of Jo, Mallory explained that he's friends with half of the seventh grade, even though there are *some* people who "hate him." Jo, as openly gay, seems accepted by most of his peers. Mallory indicated that Jo enjoys some girl-typed activities like dancing, but it is accepted because he is gay.

It is not possible to conclude from our data that openly gay students are not harassed precisely in ways similar to male gender nonconformists, but further research would do well to investigate the possibility. It is notable that all three examples of exempting gays and lesbians from sustained harassment in this study related to a specific person that the respondent knew, whereas most of the respondents who thought a gay person would be subject to significant harassment were dealing with an imaginary scenario. Since stereotypes about gay people being gender nonconformist were common among our respondents, it makes sense that gay peers are not harassed for gender nonconformity in the same ways that heterosexuals are. Openly gay kids, having already acknowledged they are gay, face different challenges than their peers who are anxious to avoid the taunt of being a "faggot" or gay.

The data clearly show that most middle-school children in our sample still hold stereotypical views about gay people. For boys, no distinction is made between same-sex attraction and gender nonconformity. The children expect that boys who break gender norms will be teased and called gay. But the children in this study are quite diverse in their own opinions and many feel that although harassment would occur, it should not.

DISCUSSION AND CONCLUSION: FEMININITY ON THE BODY, MASCULINITY AS THE BOY

Our findings confirm other studies about the narrow confines in which boys need to stay in order to avoid being teased by peers. What is perhaps more unexpected in our findings is that girls are now stigmatized for displaying some of the traditional markers of femininity. Girls look down on peers who are ultra-feminine, "wimpy," and afraid to get dirty or be competitive. The responses from girls in this study suggest that the way girls now "do gender" is restricted to "looks" and the body.

Girls have come to expect and take advantage of access to traditionally masculine arenas such as sports, and they display heightened expectations of academic success in all subjects, and are willing to compete with boys in those arenas. None of the girls discussed personally shying away from competition with boys, or worrying about their popularity if they did well in school, and no mention at all was made of fear of math and science. Girls in this study took for granted that they can be involved in different sports, and they rarely mentioned any constraints in their academic pursuits or their career plans.

The girls consistently expressed disdain for exaggerated notions of femininity and looked down on other girls who were seen as too passive, too prissy, or too vain. Girls who are good at sports and still exhibit a feminine bodily presentation are looked upon with favor. The traditional aspects of girlhood most related to subordination to boys are no longer revered or even accepted aspects of femininity. In a world where most mothers work for pay and all the girls expect to do so themselves, it makes sense that they've adopted the means to develop strong bodies and competitive minds.

In our view, the new concept "undoing gender" offered recently by Deutsch is the best framework for understanding contemporary girlhood.[18] These girls do not "do gender" the way generations before them did. They compete with other girls on the field and with boys in the classroom. They get dirty, and they expect to be taken seriously by teachers, parents, and boys.

While these girls have begun to "undo gender" as we knew it, they have not undone it completely. Their focus on femininity seems to have narrowed to concern and attention, even if sporadic, to their looks. For most girls, being feminine means wearing nice clothes, applying lip gloss, and paying attention to hairstyles.

While girls are allowed, and perhaps even encouraged, to "undo gender" in how they behave, they still face pressures to be attractive, to be good looking.

But the norms are contradictory. Most girls we questioned believe they should do gender with their body display. But if they concentrate too much on this aspect, they risk being looked down upon as overly feminine. They want to be seen as feminine, but not too much so.

On the other hand, boys gain no social approval by deviating from traditional definitions of masculinity. Any behavior remotely stereotyped as feminine is intensely policed by other boys and some girls. Being stigmatized as "gay" is the primary way masculinity is policed and enforced because it is a potent insult among young males. Being gay and being masculine are seen as contradictory, just as femininity and masculinity traditionally have been. The gay stigma among middle schoolers is really about deviating from gender expectations rather than about homosexuality, although it may draw upon insecurities about sexuality. It is a way of enforcing masculinity. When boys live up to those expectations, they not only establish themselves as masculine, but they also assert their superiority to girls. Boys who hesitate to participate in homophobic or gender policing activities open themselves up to teasing.

Despite the great success in boosting acceptance of gender equality and women's rights, the peer culture of these tween-agers remains incredibly resistant to any changes in defining masculinity for boys. While middle-school girls now are free to sometimes act like boys, as long as they make an effort, at least occasionally, to look feminine, the fear of being called "gay" quite effectively polices boys' gender behavior. Boys' lives seem hardly influenced by any feminist transformation except that they must now compete with girls as well as with each other, at least in the classroom.

For both girls and boys the truly feminine is looked down upon. For boys, this means that to be respected by other boys they must make continual efforts to act in masculine ways. Girls walk a different tightrope. They are strongly pressured to "do gender" with their bodies, although not so much so as to be seen as too girly. But they are free to cross gender borders in the other aspects of their lives.

Boys now have to compete with girls in nearly every realm of life, and they can no longer take for granted that because they are boys they are smarter or superior in any way to the girls they know. And yet their fear of teasing leaves boys more constrained by gender stereotypes than are girls. Perhaps the exaggerated gender difference is the last remnant of male privilege left to this generation of boys.

Boys need a "feminist revolution" of their own.

APPENDIX

Demographic Information for Middle Schoolers in the Study

Pseudonym	Sex	Race	Grade
Alison	Female	White	7
Audrey	Female	White	6
Brady	Male	White	6
Candace	Female	White	6
Cassie	Female	Black	6
Cynthia	Female	Biracial (black/white)	6
Dante	Male	White	6
Deb	Female	Asian-Indian	6
Deirdre	Female	Black	6
Eric	Male	White	6
Erica	Female	White	6
Eve	Female	White	6
Isabel	Female	Black	7
Jack	Male	White	7
Jackie	Female	Black	8
Jamie	Female	White	8
Jason	Male	White	7
Jeffrey	Male	White	7
Joleesa	Female	Black	6
Kamry	Female	White	8
Karlin	Female	White	8
Kay	Female	Black	7
Katie	Female	White	7
Kerri	Female	White	6
Kirsten	Female	White	8

APPENDIX (continued)

Demographic Information for Middle Schoolers in the Study

Pseudonym	Sex	Race	Grade
Krista	Female	White	8
Lana	Female	Biracial (black/white)	6
Lola	Female	Biracial (black/white)	6
Lorenzo	Male	Latino	6
Mallory	Female	White	7
Marc	Male	Black	6
Marney	Female	White	6
Marshall	Male	White	8
Max*	Male	White	6
Micah	Male	White	6
Molly	Female	White	6
Mona	Female	White	6
Nathan	Male	White	6
Reese	Male	White	7
Samantha	Female	White	6
Samir	Male	Asian-Indian	6
Shawn	Male	White	7
Tyrone	Male	Black	6
Wayne*	Male	White	7

*Due to missing data, not included in this study.

31

Orgasm in College Hookups and Relationships

Elizabeth A. Armstrong, Paula England, and Alison C. K. Fogarty

This report uses data from an online survey of 12,925 undergraduates at seventeen universities and qualitative in-depth interviews at two universities to describe college students' sexual experiences in hookups and relationships. We describe how rates of orgasm differ for men and women in hookups and relationships. We find a gender gap in orgasm across both hookups and relationships, with men experiencing more orgasms in both. The gender gap in orgasm is the lowest in relationships, in part because men are more likely to engage in cunnilingus—a practice strongly associated with women's orgasm—in relationships than in hookups. In contrast, women engage in fellatio at high rates across all contexts. The skewed nature of sexual reciprocity is in part a consequence of a new version of the old sexual double standard. In relationships, today's norms support women's right to sexual pleasure, whereas in hookups, especially first hookups, the double standard means that the man does not feel obligated to provide oral sex or to ensure his partner's sexual satisfaction.

I s the sex in college hookups good? How does hookup sex compare to relationship sex? How often do men and women have orgasms in hookups and in relationships? Is the sex in some situations good for men but not so good for women, or the other way around?

We describe college student sexual experiences in hookups and relationships, with a focus on gender differences. We define hookups as sexual events that occur outside of an exclusive relationship, often without a prearranged date, involving varying degrees of interest in a relationship. Hookups sometimes involve just making out, or they may involve oral sex or intercourse.[1]

This report uses data from an online survey of 12,925 undergraduates at seventeen universities and qualitative in-depth interviews at two universities. Students taking the online survey were asked fixed-response questions about their experiences with hooking up, dating, and relationships.[2] Statistics presented in this paper are from responses to the online survey, taken by students at the seventeen universities between 2005 and 2008. Quotations in the paper are from approximately fifty in-depth qualitative interviews conducted at Stanford and Indiana University between 2006 and 2008. In this article, we discuss only heterosexual hookups and relationships, leaving same-sex encounters for future research.

While most students hook up, few know what others are doing in their hookups. Thus, we begin with an overview of college student sexual behavior to provide background for a closer investigation of sexual pleasure in hookups and relationships. Using orgasm as an indicator of good sex, we then describe how rates of orgasm differ for men and women in hookups and relationships. We find a gender gap in orgasm across both hookups and relationships, with men experiencing more orgasm in both. This gender gap is not constant, however. It is largest in first hookups, smaller in repeat hookups with the same person, and the smallest in relationships. In this paper we delve into how variation in sexual reciprocity by context contributes to the varying size of the orgasm gap. To foreshadow some of our findings, women are more likely to receive oral sex in relationships than in hookups, and this is associated with women reaching orgasm. These findings suggest that both women and men have absorbed a notion that women are entitled to sexual pleasure in relationships. Women and men are, however, more ambivalent about the importance of women's sexual pleasure outside of relationships. This ambivalence, supported by a stubborn double standard that stigmatizes women who have sex outside of relationships, lets men off the hook in terms of responsibility for sexually pleasuring hookup partners and makes it more difficult for women to actively pursue sexual satisfaction in hookups.

These empirical findings inform debates about the rise of the hookup culture. Sexual conservatives often argue that hooking up is damaging, particularly for women, counseling that it is better to limit sex to serious relationships (and in extreme versions of the argument, to marriage).[3] They see changes in gender and sexuality as having gone too far, and they advocate a return to more traditional arrangements. Their position is expressed in the "Take Back the Date" movement.[4] Like sexual conservatives, a number of feminist sociologists and activists have focused on the negative aspects of sexual culture on campus—particularly on sexual assault and sexual harassment.[5] In contrast to sexual conservatives, though, feminists tend to see gender and sexual change as having not gone far enough. This position is expressed in the annual "Take Back the Night" marches organized on many campuses in protest of sexual violence. Our focus on sexual pleasure—and our finding that college women enjoy sex, albeit not as much as men, and not equally in all contexts—leads us to see the situation as less dire than these two groups. Most college students—both men and women—see women as entitled to sexual pleasure in relationships and the reciprocity required to achieve it. This is a meaningful change from prior generations, where women were seen as entitled to sexual pleasure only within marriage.[6] That these norms of reciprocity and entitlement to pleasure have not fully diffused beyond relationships leads us to sympathize with both the conservative distaste for hookups—after all, sex is better in relationships, particularly for women—and with the feminist insistence on tackling sexual double standards. Hookup sex is not usually great for women. It could be a lot better. Further extension of egalitarian norms and practices would improve women's experience of hookup sex.

SEXUAL ACTIVITY IN HOOKUPS AND RELATIONSHIPS

Seventy-four percent of respondents—both men and women—reported at least one hookup by their senior year in college. Of these, 40 percent had hooked up three times or less, 40 percent had hooked up between four and nine times, and 20 percent had hooked up ten or more times.

In addition to asking students about how many hookups they had overall, we also asked them for details about their most recent hookup, including a question on the number of times the student had previously hooked up with *this same partner*. From these questions, we learned that multiple hookups with the same person were common. About half of the hookups reported were first hookups with that partner. Eighteen percent were cases where the student had hooked up with this same person once or twice before, and in 33 percent of the cases the couple had hooked up at least three times before. Fully 16 percent of these hookups involved someone the student had hooked up with ten or more times. The media often refer to higher-order hookups as "friends with benefits" or "fuck buddies."[7] Students know and occasionally use these terms, but they are more likely to refer to them as "repeat," "regular," or "continuing" hookups, or to not label them at all.[8] When we report below on what happened in these different kinds of hookups, we'll use the term "repeat hookup" when the hookup was with someone the individual had hooked up with three or more times before.

The rise of hookups has not meant the demise of relationships among college students. By their senior year, 69 percent of heterosexual students reported that they had been in a relationship that lasted at least six months while they were in college.[9] In interviews, we learned that many more have had shorter relationships.

Our interviewees told us that, to them, relationships involved sexual exclusivity, spending time together, and frequently a talk to clarify that they had become girlfriend-boyfriend.[10] While college students still form relationships, the rise of the hookup has changed how relationships begin. Traditional dating has been largely replaced by hookups as the main pathway to relationships.[11]

The online survey asked students who had hooked up while in college to tell us about what happened on their most recent hookup. Students who had been in a relationship were asked to report on the most recent time they did something sexual more than kissing in that relationship. We classify events into four contexts: first hookups, second or third hookups (1–2 previous hookups), repeat hookups (3 or more previous hookups), and relationships. Figure 31.1 shows what happened sexually in these different contexts, categorized by the behavior that entailed going farthest, as students generally view it. For example, if a couple had oral sex and intercourse, it is classified as an intercourse event. Students did not go as far on first hookups as on higher-order hookups, and they went farther in relationships. In first hookups, 44 percent of students reported kissing and touching, but no genital contact (i.e., no stimulation of one partner's genitals with the other's hand, no oral sex, and no intercourse).[12] In contrast, the percent that only had non-genital activity was 30 percent among those who had hooked up

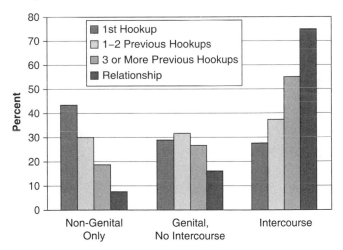

Figure 31.1 | Percent Engaging in Various Sexual Behaviors* in Four Sexual Contexts

*Respondents are classified in "Non-Genital Only" if they did not engage in oral sex, hand-genital stimulation, or intercourse; in "Genital, No Intercourse" if they did not engage in intercourse but engaged in oral sex or hand-genital stimulation (irrespective of who gave or who received it); in "Intercourse" if they had intercourse. Percents for three behaviors within one context may not add up to 100 percent because of rounding error.

one or two times before, 19 percent in repeat hookups, and 7 percent of those in relationships. The percent having intercourse was 27 percent on the first hookup, 37 percent when they had hooked up once or twice before, 54 percent in repeat hookups, and 76 percent of those in relationships.[13] In sum, most relationship events involve intercourse, while most hookups don't, but the more times people have hooked up before, they more likely they are to have intercourse.

We also asked students what sexual acts they had *ever* done. Eighty percent reported intercourse by senior year of college, so 20 percent graduated from college as virgins—a bit of information that some may find surprising. Of those who engaged in intercourse by their senior year, students reported a median of four partners and 67 percent reported having intercourse outside of a relationship.

WHO HAS ORGASMS IN HOOKUPS AND RELATIONSHIPS?

The survey asked students whether they had an orgasm on their most recent hookup and in their most recent relationship sexual event.[14] While orgasm is certainly not the only indicator of sexual pleasure, most who have experienced it find it to be extremely pleasurable.[15]

Figure 31.2 shows what percent of men and women had an orgasm in first hookups, higher-order hookups, and relationship sexual events. Both men and women experience orgasm more in repeat hookups than with a new hookup partner. And relationship sex is most likely to lead to orgasm for both men and women. This is partly a function of the fact that couples go farther sexually the more times they have hooked up, and they go the farthest in relationships. But this effect is not only driven by behavior. For both men and women, the same behaviors yield higher rates of orgasm in relationships than in hookups, and in higher-order hookups than in first hookups. Sex in relationships tends to be better in part because in any encounter one has a greater incentive to treat one's partner well if a repeat is likely.[16] Also, good sex takes practice, as, over time, partners learn what turns each other on. The importance of partner-specific sexual skills was mentioned by numerous men and women in the qualitative interviews. For example, a man, when discussing why he believed women would be more likely to orgasm in relationships, explained that, "Because a guy will already know how she likes it, where she likes it and how much she likes it." Similarly, a woman noted that in a relationship you are accustomed to communicating with your partner about everything, which means that "you're more open to talking about different things that you want out of the sex or if you want to experiment. You could explore more because you have knowledge about the other person. You trust the other person." Context matters for both men and women.

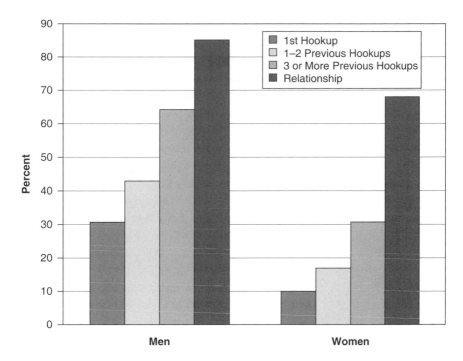

Figure 31.2 | Percent of Men and Women Having an Orgasm In Four Sexual Contexts

But, in an odd echo of the gender gap in pay, there is a gender gap in orgasm as well. This gap exists in all contexts, but it is less severe in repeat hookups than in first hookups, and least severe in relationships. If we take the percent of women having an orgasm as a ratio of the male percent, those ratios are .32 for first hookups, .39 if they've hooked up one to two previous times with this person, .49 on repeat hookups with the same person, and .79 in relationships. Comparing the two extremes, this means that women orgasm only 32 percent as often as men in first hookups, but 79 percent as often as men in relationships.

WHY IS SEXUAL PLEASURE MORE EQUAL IN RELATIONSHIPS THAN IN HOOKUPS?

Why is sexual pleasure more equal between men and women in relationships than in hookups, particularly first hookups? Some might find this a ridiculous question, viewing men's greater enjoyment of uncommitted sex as simply obvious.

Others might explain this difference by evolutionary psychology—arguing that women need commitment to enjoy sex because of a "hard-wired" need to secure male resources for any offspring produced.[17] Some might argue that gender socialization leads women to be more relationally oriented than men, in sex as well as other arenas.[18] Others might argue that partner-specific experience matters more for women than for men because women's orgasm is more difficult to achieve. Still others might attribute the difference to a sexual double standard: women may feel guilty about casual sex and thus enjoy it less. These explanations are not mutually exclusive, but our data don't allow us to judge their relative merits. We can, however, demonstrate more immediate, proximate causes of some of the gap: behaviors especially conducive to female orgasm are more likely to occur in repeat hookups and relationships. Below we document variation in rates of cunnilingus and women's genital self-simulation across contexts, and their role in boosting rates of orgasm.

WHAT MEN AND WOMEN GIVE: ORAL SEX IN HOOKUPS AND RELATIONSHIPS

Cunnilingus (the woman receiving oral sex) is more likely to produce a female orgasm than is fellatio (the man receiving oral sex). Additionally, many women need direct clitoral stimulation along with intercourse to reach orgasm. This point, sensationalized by *The Hite Report* in the 1970s, has since become well-documented empirically in sex research.[19]

Cunnilingus, effective as it is for women's orgasm, is less well-represented in college student sexual repertoires than fellatio. Figure 31.3 illustrates for four sexual contexts the percent of men and women receiving oral sex in sexual events without intercourse. If only one person received oral sex, it was more likely to be the man. But this disparity was shown less in repeat hookups and least in relationships. Men received oral sex roughly 80 percent of the time in all contexts (combining when men alone received oral sex and when both men and women mutually received it), while women received it (combining when women alone received oral sex and when both men and women mutually received it) 46 percent of the time in first hookups, 55 percent in second or third hookups, 59 percent in repeat hookups, and 68 percent in relationships.[20] Men gave oral sex to their female partners more in repeat hookups and especially in relationships. Women gave oral sex to their male partners in all contexts at higher rates than women received it in any context.

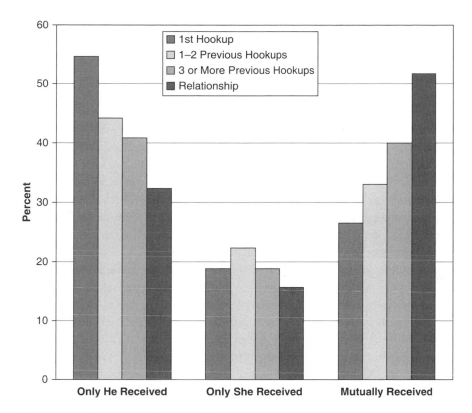

Figure 31.3 | Percent of Men and Women Receiving Oral Sex in Events Where at Least One Received Oral Sex and Intercourse Did Not Occur, in Four Sexual Contexts

What about when the couple had intercourse? Our survey showed that when they also had intercourse, men received oral sex in 77 percent of first hookups, 82 percent of second or third hookups, 88 percent of repeat hookups, and 91 percent of relationship events. Women, on the other hand, received oral sex between 60 percent and 68 percent of the time in hookups, but in 84 percent of relationship events. And, sure enough, women's orgasm rates reflect the difference. In events that included intercourse and oral sex for the woman, she was generally more likely to report an orgasm than when intercourse was not combined with oral sex.[21] In repeat hookups with intercourse, she had an orgasm 40 percent of the time if there was no oral sex but 55 percent of the time when intercourse was accompanied by oral sex. In relationships, orgasms in women increased from 55 percent when there was intercourse but no oral sex to 80 percent when oral sex was combined with intercourse. Oral sex is important for some women to have orgasms, so the fact that women are much more likely to receive it in repeat hookups and relationships is part of why they have orgasms more often in those contexts.[22]

These findings suggest that women treat hookup partners with sexual generosity—often giving oral sex even in first hookups. Men, on the other hand, appear to be comparatively sexually selfish in hookups, particularly first hookups, and more sexually generous as they become more committed. This pattern is built into gendered sexual scripts: Men feel entitled to fellatio on a first or second hookup and women obligated to provide it, while women do not similarly feel entitled to cunnilingus, nor do men feel obligated to give it.[23]

This brings us to a good news/bad news story about gender equality in sex. Our culture continues to have a double standard that judges women's and men's sexual practices differently. In the past, women were expected to be virgins before marriage, while men were not.[24] Women were evaluated negatively for premarital sex, and they were certainly not viewed as entitled to sexual satisfaction in premarital sexual relationships. Over the course of the past forty years or so, among most groups the stigma associated with premarital sex within relationships for women has almost entirely disappeared. The removal of this stigma has the added bonus of making it not just acceptable for women to have sex in premarital relationships, but acceptable for women to *enjoy* it. Men and women agree that it is normal for women to expect sexual satisfaction in relationships, to ask for what they need to get it, and to be disappointed, and perhaps even end relationships, if they do not get it. Relationships have become defined as an appropriate space for unmarried women to express sexual desire and to engage in sexual exploration. Men and women also agree that it is expected that men in a relationship attend to their partners' sexual needs as well as their own. This is the good news, and it accounts for the greater reciprocity of oral sex in relationships, as many men now care about women's pleasure in relationships.

The bad news is that sexual double standards have not disappeared. Instead, what we see now is a new double standard, in which women who seek sexual pleasure *outside* of committed relationships are judged more harshly than men who do. Men and women at both schools told us that women perceived as hooking up too much, or going too far on hookups, are called "sluts" by both men and women.[25] Along with ambivalence about women's participation in sex outside of relationships comes ambivalence about women's pleasure in these contexts. The survival of a sexual double standard may be an important reason that men tend to treat hookup and relationship partners differently—in short, some men think that that it is acceptable to be sexually selfish with hookup partners, especially first-time partners. Men's lack of respect for women who will have sex outside of a relationship seems to translate into a sense that hookup partners are not owed the same level of sexual reciprocity as girlfriends—both in terms of what sex acts are engaged in (e.g., giving her oral sex) and in the care and attention to her sexual pleasure.

In interviews, men were up-front about expressing different levels of concern for hookup and relationship partners. For example, one man, after explaining that, with his girlfriend, "definitely oral is really important [for her to orgasm], you can do it for pretty much as long as needed," told us that in a hookup, "I don't give a shit." Another noted that, "I mean like if you're just like hooking up with someone, I guess it's more of a selfish thing." A third man explained that:

> Now that I'm in a relationship, I think [her orgasm is] actually pretty important. More important than [in a] hookup. Because you have more invested in that person. You know, when you have sex, it's more a reciprocal thing. When it's a hookup you feel less investment. You still want [her to orgasm] in that, sort of, "I'm a guy who's the greatest lover in the world and I want to, you should orgasm."

This man suggested that his interest in a hookup partner having an orgasm was primarily selfish, as her pleasure reflected on his sexual performance and sense of masculinity. A number of others noted that in hookups her orgasm just did not matter. In contrast, men's comments revealed universal endorsement of the notion of women's entitlement to sexual pleasure in relationships. For example, one man explained, with pride, that:

> [In my relationship] she comes every time and that's because I know what she likes and I make sure she does. And if I have to go down on her for a longer period of time, I'll do that. I've a pretty good idea of what she likes and it's been partly through trial and error, partly through explicit instruction. She definitely likes for me to go down on her and usually it goes both ways before we have sex.

This passage suggests—and this is reflected throughout the interviews—that the importance of oral sex to women's orgasm is well understood by college men.

Some women complained about the lack of mutuality in oral sex, particularly in early hookups. One woman said, "When I . . . meet somebody and I'm gonna have a random hookup . . . from what I have seen, they're not even trying to, you know, make it a mutual thing." Another complained, "He did that thing where . . . they put their hand on the top of your head . . . and I hate that! . . . Especially 'cause there was no effort made to, like, return that favor." A third woman complained of a recent encounter, "I just was with some stupid guy at a frat party and we were in his room and I gave head. And I was kind of waiting and he fell asleep. And I was like, 'Fuck this,' and I just left. It's degrading." This woman did not consider hooking up to be degrading. What she felt was degrading was the one-sided nature of the encounter. Some women reported learning to turn the tables. For example, one assertive woman said, "(I)n my first relationship . . . it was very one way . . . and that just didn't do much for me in terms of making me feel good about myself . . . so . . . I hate it when a guy is like take your head and try and push it down, because I then just switch it around to make them go down first usually. And some guys say no and then I just say no if they say no."

Women provided descriptions of sexually attentive boyfriends, confirming men's self-reports. For example, in describing her boyfriend, one woman told us that:

> I know that he wants to make me happy. I know that he wants me to orgasm. I know that, and like just me knowing that we are connected and like we're going for the same thing and that like he cares.

In general students reported that their relationships were characterized by much greater mutuality than their hookups.[26]

WOMEN'S AGENCY: GENITAL SELF-STIMULATION AND ENTITLEMENT TO PLEASURE

It is not just men whose sexual practices may be affected by the new version of the sexual double standard. The double standard may also lead women to feel ambivalent about enjoying hookup sex, or not entitled to pleasure within it. While we typically think of the double standard as involving how men and women are differently judged for *participating* in sex, double standards also often involve gendered notions about appropriate degrees of *enthusiasm, pleasure, or initiative*. In interviews with adolescent girls, Deborah Tolman found that the expectation that it is girls' job to play the role of the "gatekeeper" interfered with girls' experience of bodily desire because they had to monitor and suppress their own physical responses in order to keep the sexual activity from going "too far."[27]

We found both quantitative and qualitative evidence that women feel less entitled to pleasure in hookup contexts than in relationships. In the survey data, the practice of women stimulating their own genitals with a hand as part of partnered sex, much as one would in masturbation, proved to be particularly interesting.

Engaging in this practice clearly shows one's interest in one's *own* pleasure, and reveals to a sex partner one's familiarity and competence with masturbatory technique. We asked students if they had done this and learned that only 4 percent of women did this in a first hookup, 6 percent in a hookup with a partner hooked up with one to two times previously, 10 percent in a repeat hookup, and 24 percent in a relationship. Examining only events where the partners had intercourse, it was also true that women were least likely to self-stimulate in first hookups and most likely in relationships. Like oral sex, self-stimulation helps women to orgasm. We found that among women having intercourse and receiving oral sex, there was still a big boost to orgasm from the addition of self-stimulation—a difference of 37 percent versus 63 percent having orgasm in first hookups, and a difference of 80 percent versus 92 percent in relationships (see Figure 31.4). In every context, the addition of self-stimulation made a difference to orgasm. But women were more likely to feel comfortable enough to self-stimulate in repeat hookups, and most likely in relationships. Women's reticence about self-stimulation in hookups is another part of the reason why women orgasm less in these contexts.

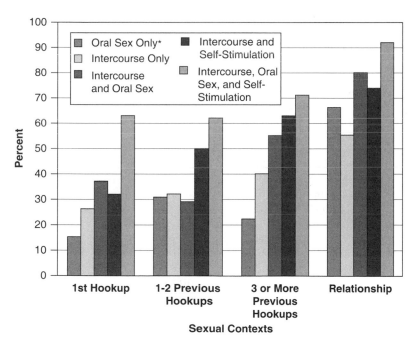

*Oral sex refers to receiving oral sex.

Figure 31.4 | Percent of Women Having an Orgasm in Four Sexual Contexts, by Occurrence of Selected Sexual Behaviors

Evidence that women feel more entitled to sexual pleasure in relationships was also present in interviews. This attitude was reflected in general discussions of rights and obligations. For example, one woman explained that, for her, "being able to communicate" about what she wanted and needed was important for good sex, but, she added, "I feel like when it's just a hookup, I just feel like I almost like don't have the right. Or not that I don't have the right but it's just not comfortable enough to be like, 'You know, hey, this isn't doing [it] for me.'" In contrast, a number of women stated their sense of entitlement to good sex within a relationship:

> I think that I'm assertive enough of a person to know what it takes for me to orgasm and like be able to communicate that. I probably would try to work it out, try to give him more practice, more lessons, before I would ultimately break off the relationship. But I I'm gonna say this very hesitatingly, I probably would end the relationship after having tried many, many things to fix it so that it's sexually pleasurable.

While she was willing to work hard with a boyfriend to improve sex to make sure she had orgasms, she viewed lack of success in this department as grounds to end the relationship. This sense of entitlement to sexual satisfaction was less evident in women's discussions of hookup sex—although there was variation on this issue. A number of women noted that they had gotten better over time about insisting on getting their needs met in hookups.

One woman, implicitly contrasting relationships with hookups, pointed to the more egalitarian nature of relationship sex:

> I think also just because in a relationship, there's much more expected as far as like equality wise, like give and take sexually. If you're gonna be in a relationship, it's expected, like more equality. . . . You can explore more, be more fun and goofy and stuff like that which I think is always fun too.

Her reference to exploring in a relationship hints at the way that relationships, by creating a zone in which sex is viewed as acceptable for women, give women license to relax (e.g., be "goofy") and experiment. One woman noted that she could imagine the conditions for good sex to be present outside of a relationship:

> But for me, I feel that to have good sex there's a few qualities that need to be present. Like the desirability and that confidence in being able to ask for what you want or what you don't want. And if you can find that outside of a relationship, I think that's

good. But I feel that [it] would be a lot more difficult to find those qualities with someone that you're not in a relationship with.

And some women did find the conditions necessary for good sex outside of relationships. The more times couples hooked up, the greater the degree of comfort and familiarity, and, consequently, the higher the rates of orgasm.

It is important, however, to emphasize that differences in rates of orgasm in hookups and relationships are not driven *solely* by the behaviors we were able to measure, such as whether the woman received oral sex or engaged in self-stimulation. We suspect that a sense of entitlement led to other behavioral changes by women in repeat hookups and relationships that our survey didn't measure—such as initiating changes in position. But as Figure 31.4 shows, at every level of sexual activity, relationship sex yields orgasm for women at higher rates than hookup sex (and repeat hookups at higher rates than first hookups). This pattern is true for men as well as for women, although both context and behavior seem to matter more for women than for men. Women's rates of orgasm become nearly universal and almost converge with men's (92 percent compared with men's 96 percent) only in one situation—in relationships when couples engaged in intercourse and the women received oral sex and engaged in self-stimulation. This convergence suggests that a gender gap in orgasm is not inevitable, but it is largely a consequence of the social organization of sexuality.

Overall, our findings suggest that women's orgasm is strongly affected by how comfortable women are seeking their own sexual pleasure, how motivated men are to provide stimulation of the sort that a particular woman finds pleasurable, and the extent to which either partner engages in behaviors that provide plentiful clitoral stimulation for women. We strongly suspect that the sexual double standard is an important factor behind why women feel less entitled to sexual pleasure in hookups. The sexual double standard also permits men not to care about their partner's pleasure in hookups. Women would orgasm more in hookups if their sexual satisfaction were considered to be as important as that of their male partners.[28]

CONCLUSION

As measured by orgasm, relationship sex is better than hookup sex for both men and women, but especially for women. Similarly, sex is better in repeat hookups than in first hookups, particularly for women. The gender gap in orgasm is the lowest in relationships, in part because men are more likely to engage in cunnilingus—a practice strongly associated with women's orgasm—in relationships than in hookups. In contrast, women engage in fellatio at high rates across all contexts. The skewed nature of sexual reciprocity is in part a consequence of a new version of the old sexual double standard. In relationships, today's norms support women's right to sexual pleasure, whereas in hookups, especially first hookups, the double standard means that the man does not feel obligated to provide oral sex or to ensure his partner's sexual satisfaction. Women's behavior varies across these contexts, too. In early hookups, women may feel they have to focus on limiting how far things go because of concerns about negative judgments if they go too far. Many don't feel comfortable enough to focus on their own pleasure through self-stimulation of their genitals, or to communicate what they want. In relationships women are more free of the effects of the double standard, and this decreases the orgasm gap between men and women.

If we think the current hookup culture doesn't foster gender equality or good sex for all women, what would be better? According to sexual conservatives, the sexual revolution has led men to have more access to sex, but it has also led women to be exploited by men who don't respect the women they have sex with and don't concern themselves with women's pleasure. In this view, women would be better off refusing to hook up, and instead holding out for relationships before they have sex.

In one sense our research supports this strategy; if college women want good sex without stigma, relationships make sense. This may help explain why college women report a stronger desire for relationships than college men.[29] Men, who are less stigmatized for having sex outside of relationships, may prefer hookups because they provide sex with orgasms, while not limiting their options to hook up with other people. Thus, one way to view gender inequality in college sex is as a gender struggle over hookups versus relationships as contexts for having sex. From this perspective, women try to form relationships while men try to avoid them. Some research suggests that women participate in lower-quality hookup sex because they can't get men to commit to relationships and in hopes that a series of hookups will turn into a relationship.[30] If this is the main reason why so much of the sex college women engage in does not lead to orgasm, perhaps a campaign to move all sex back into relationships could be seen as a move toward gender equality.

But moving college sex back into relationships would have some drawbacks. First, not all women want relationships with their hookup partners. We found that although more women than men reported an interest in a relationship with their most recent hookup partner, fewer than half of the women reported any such interest. At the same time, after a hookup, women reported high levels of enjoyment (even without orgasm) and low levels of regret.[31] These findings are inconsistent with the view that college women would prefer relationships as a context for all of their sexual activity. Second, focusing exclusively on getting sex back into relationships would not improve the treatment of those women chose to hook up. The woman who was annoyed with her partner who fell asleep after getting fellatio did not want a relationship with this man—she just wanted him to be considerate enough to return the favor. And, third, while relationships are better contexts for sex than hookups, relationships involve a lot more than sex. Sometimes relationships lead women to withdraw from college or scale back on their career ambitions; even worse, they sometimes involve physical or emotional abuse.[32]

Our research suggests a second, complementary response to the poor quality of hookup sex for women. In addition to creating conditions that facilitate college relationships, we advocate addressing factors that degrade the quality of hookup sex for women—sexual double standards and lack of reciprocity. A challenge to the contemporary sexual double standard would mean defending the position that young women and men are equally entitled to sexual pleasure and sexual respect in hookups as well as relationships. To achieve this, the attitudes and practices of both men and women need to be confronted. Men should be challenged to treat even first hookup partners generously and with the respect and consideration that they treat their girlfriends. (They might find that if they did so, more women would want to hook up with them and that the hookups would be more fun!) Women should grow into adulthood with a sense of entitlement to sex and sexual pleasure. For women, a first condition is understanding their own sexual response (e.g., learning how to masturbate). A second condition is the confidence to ask for what they want *in all contexts*. This means assertiveness to say "no" as well as to say "yes."[33] If this seems utopian at present, this is evidence of how far we have to go to achieve gender equality in premarital sexual relations.

32

Falling Back on Plan B: The Children of the Gender Revolution Face Uncharted Territory

Kathleen Gerson

Young adults today grew up with mothers who joined the workplace and parents whose relationships often departed from traditional marriage. Now facing their own choices, what do the women and men of this new generation hope and plan to do in their own lives? In contrast to popular images of twenty- and thirty-somethings returning to tradition, this chapter demonstrates that most young people want to create a lasting marriage (or a "marriage-like" relationship) and to find a personal balance between home and work. Most women and men are more alike than different in their aspirations, with both hoping to blend the traditional value of lifelong commitment with the modern value of flexible, egalitarian sharing. Yet, these children of the gender revolution are also developing strategies to prepare for "second-best" options. Fearful that they will not find the right partner to help them integrate work with family caretaking, most women see work as essential to their survival. Worried about time-greedy workplaces, most men hope to avoid the costs that equal sharing might exact on their careers. The differing fallback positions of "self-reliant" women and "neo-traditional" men may point to a growing gender divide, but they do not reflect this generation's highest aspirations.

Young adults today grew up with mothers who broke barriers in the workplace and parents who forged innovative alternatives to traditional marriage. These "children of the gender revolution" now face a world that is far different from that of their parents or grandparents. While massive changes in work and family arrangements have expanded their options, these changes also pose new challenges to crafting a marriage, rearing children, and building a career. Members of this new generation walk a fine line between their desire to achieve egalitarian, sharing relationships that can meld with satisfying work, and succumbing to the realities of gender conflict, fragile relationships, and uncertain job prospects. The choices they make will shape work and family life for decades to come.

Social forecasters have reached starkly different conclusions about what these choices will be. Some proclaim that the recent upturn in "opt-out" mothers foreshadows a wider return to tradition among younger women.[1] Others believe the rising number of single adults foretells a deepening "decline of commitment" that is threatening family life and the social fabric.[2] While there is little doubt that tumultuous changes have shaped the lives of a new generation, there is great disagreement about how. Does the diversification of families into two-earner, single-parent, and cohabiting forms represent a waning of family life or the growth of more flexible relationships? Will this new generation integrate family and work in new ways, or will older patterns inexorably pull them back?

To find out how members of the first generation to grow up in these diversifying families look back on their childhoods and forward to their own futures, I conducted in-depth, life history interviews with a carefully selected group of young people between eighteen and thirty-two. These young women and men experienced the full range of changes that have taken place in family life, and most lived in some form of "nontraditional" arrangement at some point in their childhood.[3] My interviews reveal a generation that does not conform to prevailing media stereotypes, whether they depict declining families or a return to strict gender divisions in caretaking and breadwinning.

In contrast to popular images of twenty- and thirty-somethings who wish to return to tradition or reject family life altogether, the young women and men I interviewed are more focused on *how well* their parents met the challenges of providing economic and emotional support than on *what form* their families took. Now making their own way in early adulthood, women and men share a set of lofty aspirations. Despite their varied family experiences, most hope to blend the traditional value of a lifelong relationship with the modern value of flexibly sharing work, child care, and domestic chores. In the best of all possible worlds, the majority would like to create a lasting marriage (or a "marriage-like" relationship) that allows them to balance home and work in a flexible, egalitarian way.

Yet young people are also developing strategies to prepare for "second-best" options in a world where time-demanding workplaces, a lack of child care, and fragile relationships may place their ideals out of reach. Concerned about the difficulty of finding a reliable and egalitarian partner to help them integrate work with family caretaking, most women see work as essential to their own and their children's survival, whether or not they marry. Worried about time-greedy work-places, most men feel they must place work first and will need to count on a partner at home. As they prepare for second-best options, the differing fallback positions of "self-reliant" women and "neo-traditional" men may point to a new gender divide. But this divide does not reflect a new generation's highest aspira-tions for blending lifelong commitment and flexible, egalitarian sharing in their relationships.

GROWING UP IN CHANGING FAMILIES

Even though theorists and social commentators continue to debate the merits of various family forms, my interviewees did not focus on their family's "structure."[4] Instead, I found large variation among children who grew up in apparently simi-lar family types. Those who grew up in families with a homemaking mother and breadwinning father were divided in their assessments of this arrangement. While a little more than half thought this was the best arrangement, close to half reached a different conclusion. When being a homemaker and out of the workforce appeared to undermine a mother's satisfaction, disturb the house-hold's harmony, or threaten its economic security, the children concluded that it would have been better if their mothers had pursued a sustained commitment to work.

Many of those who grew up in a single-parent home also expressed ambiva-lence about their parents' breakups. Slightly more than half wished their parents had stayed together, but close to half believed that a breakup, while not ideal, was better than continuing to live in a conflict-ridden or silently unhappy home.[5] The longer-term consequences of a breakup shaped the lessons children drew. If their parents got back on their feet and created better lives, children developed surprisingly positive outlooks on the decision to separate.

Those who grew up in a dual-earner home were the least ambivalent about their parents' arrangements. More than three-fourths believed that having two work-committed parents provided increased economic resources and also pro-moted marriages that seemed more egalitarian and satisfying.[6] If the pressures of working long hours or coping with blocked opportunities and family-unfriendly workplaces took their toll, however, some children concluded that having over-burdened, time-stressed caretakers offset these advantages.

In short, growing up in this era of diverse families led children to focus more on how well—or poorly—parents (and other caretakers) were able to meet the twin challenges of providing economic and emotional support mother than on its form. Even more important, children experienced family life as a dynamic process that changed over time. Since family life is best seen as a film, not a snapshot, the key to understanding young people's views lies in charting the diverse paths their families took.

Family Paths and Gender Flexibility

Families can take different paths from seemingly common starting points, and similar types of families can travel toward different destinations. When young adults reflect on their families, they focus on how their homes either came to provide stability and support or failed to do so. About a third of my interviewees reported growing up in a stable home, while a quarter concluded that their families grew more supportive as time passed. In contrast, just under one in ten reported living in a chronically insecure home, while a bit more than a third felt that family support eroded as they grew up. Why, then, do some children look back on families that became more supportive and secure, while others experienced a decline in their family's support?

Parents' strategies for organizing breadwinning and caretaking hold the key to understanding a family's pathway.[7] Flexible strategies, which allowed mothers, fathers, and other caretakers to transcend rigid gender boundaries, helped families prevail in the face of unexpected economic and interpersonal crises. Inflexible responses, in contrast, left families ill-equipped to cope with eroding supports for a strict division in mothers' and fathers' responsibilities.

Rising Family Fortunes

The sources of expanding support differed by family situation, but all reflected a flexible response to unexpected difficulties. Sometimes marriages became more equal as demoralized mothers went to work and pushed for change or helped overburdened fathers. Josh, for example, reported that his mother's decision to go to work gave her the courage to insist that his father tackle his drug addiction:[8]

> My parents fought almost constantly. Then my mom got a job. They separated for about five, six, seven months. Even though I was upset, I thought it was for the best. That's when (my dad) got into some kind of program and my mom took him back. That changed the whole family dynamic. We got extremely close. A whole new relationship developed with my father.

Chris recalled how his mother's job allowed his father to quit a dead-end job and train for a more satisfying career:

> Between 7th and 8th grade, my dad had a business which didn't work. It was a dead-end thing, and he came home frustrated, so my mom got him to go to school. It was hard financially, but it was good because he was actually enjoying what he was doing. He really flourished. A lot of people say, "Wow, your mom is the breadwinner, and that's strange." It's not. It is a very joint thing.

Parental breakups that relieved domestic conflict or led to the departure of an unstable parent also helped caretaking parents get back on their feet. Connie recounted how her mother was able to create a more secure home after separating from an alcoholic husband and finding a job that offered a steady income and a source of personal esteem:

> My father just sat in the corner and once in a while got angry at us, but [my mom] — I don't know if it was him or the money, but she didn't stand up for herself as much as I think she should. The tension with my dad never eased, and my mom had gotten sick with multiple bleeding ulcers. That was her real turning point. It was building inside of her to leave, 'cause she'd got a job and started to realize she had her own money . . . [She] became a much happier person. And because she was better, I was better. I had a weight taken off of me.

More stable and egalitarian remarriages could also give children the economic and emotional support they had not previously received. Having never known her biological father, Shauna recalled how her stepfather became a devoted caretaker and the "real" father she always wanted:

> At first, I was feeling it was a bad change because I wanted my mom to myself. Then my mom said, "Why don't you call him daddy?" The next thing I was saying "Daddy!" I remember the look on his face and his saying "She called me daddy!" I was so happy. After that, he's always been my dad, and there's never been any question about it. . . . [He] would get home before my mom, so he would cook the dinner and clean. My dad spoiled me for any other man, because this is the model I had.

When Isabella's parents divorced, her grandfather became a treasured caretaker:

> It's not like I didn't have a father, because my grandfather was always there. He was there to take me to after-school clubs and pick me up. I was sheltered — he had to

take me to the library, wait till I finished all my work, take me home. I call him dad. Nobody could do better.

And when Antonio's single mother lost her job, his grandparents provided essential income that kept the family afloat:

> My mom and grandparents were the type of people that even if we didn't have [money], we was gonna get it. Their ideal is, "I want to give you all the things I couldn't have when I was young." My grandparents and my mother thought like that, so no matter how much in poverty we were living, I was getting everything I wanted.

Despite their obvious differences, the common ingredient in these narratives is the ability of parents and other caretakers to reorganize child rearing and breadwinning in a more flexible, less gender-divided way. Mothers going to work, fathers becoming more involved in child rearing, and others joining in the work of family life—all of these strategies helped families overcome unexpected difficulties and create more economically secure, emotionally stable homes. Growing flexibility in how parents met the challenges of earning needed income and caring for children nourished parental morale, increased a home's financial security, and provided inspiring models of adult resilience. While children acknowledged the costs, they valued these second chances and gleaned lessons from watching parents find ways to create a better life. Looking back, they could conclude that "all's well that ends well."

DECLINING FAMILY FORTUNES

For some children, home life followed a downward slope. Here, too, the key to their experiences lay in the work and caretaking strategies of those entrusted with their care, but here gender inflexibility in the face of domestic difficulties left children with less support than they had once taken for granted. Faced with a father's abandonment or a stay-at-home mother's growing frustration, children described how their parents' resistance to more flexible strategies for apportioning paid and domestic work left them struggling to meet children's economic and emotional needs. Over time, deteriorating marriages, declining parental morale, and financial insecurity shattered a once rosy picture of family stability and contentment.

When parents became stuck in a rigid division of labor, with unhappy mothers and fathers ill-equipped to support the household, traditional marriages could deteriorate. Sarah explains how her mother became increasingly depressed and "over-involved" after relinquishing a promising career to devote all of her time to child rearing:

> When my sister was born, [my mom's] job had started up, career-wise, so she wasn't happy [but] she felt she had to be home. She had a lot of conflicts about work and home and opted to be really committed to family, but also resented it. . . . She was the supermom, but just seemed really depressed a lot of time . . . [It came] with an edge to it—"in return, I want you to be devoted to me." If we did something separate from her, that was a major problem. So I was making distance because I felt I had to protect myself from this invasion. . . . She thought she was doing something good to sacrifice for us . . . but it would have been better if my mother was happier working.

Megan recalls her father's mounting frustration as his income stagnated and he endured the complaints of a wife who expected to him to provide a "better lifestyle":

> My mother was always dissatisfied. She wanted my father to be more ambitious, and he wasn't an ambitious man. As long as he was supporting the family, it didn't matter if it was a bigger house or a bigger car. Forty years of being married to a woman saying, "Why don't we have more money?"—I think that does something to your self-esteem.

Unresolved power struggles in dual-earner marriages could also cause problems, as wives felt the weight of "doing it all" and fathers resisted egalitarian sharing. Juggling paid and domestic work left Justin's mother exhausted, while a high-pressured job running a restaurant left his father with no time to attend nightly dinners or even Little League games. Justin describes the strain his parents experienced and its effect on him:

> I was slightly disappointed that I could not see my father more—because I understood but also because it depends on the mood he's in. And it got worse as work [went] downhill . . . [So] I can't model my relationship on my parents. My mother wasn't very happy. There was a lot of strain on her.

Harmful breakups, where fathers abandoned their children and mothers could not find new ways to support the family or create an identity beyond wife and mother, also eroded family support. Nina remembers how her father's disappearance, combined with her mother's reluctance to seek a job and create a more independent life, triggered the descent from a comfortable middle-class existence to one of abiding poverty:

> My mother ended up going on welfare. We went from a nice place to living in a really cruddy building. And she's still in the same apartment. To this day, my sister will not speak to my father because of what he's done to us.

Children (and their parents) sometimes lost the support of other caretakers. Shortly after Jasmine's father left to live with another woman and her mother fell into a deep depression, she suffered the loss of a "third parent" when her beloved grandmother died. Her grandmother's loss left her feeling especially bereft after her father's departure:

> It was so great when my parents were together any my grandmother was alive, so when she died, it was really hard. I lost [the money], and I lost her just being there. We were going through a real trauma in my whole family, so when [my father] left, it was like another death. I don't think it would have been any better if they'd stayed together, but my grandmother being alive would have been much more of a difference.

The events that propelled families on a downward track—including rising financial instability, declining parental involvement and morale, and a dearth of other supportive caretakers—share a common element. Whether parents faced marital impasses or difficult breakups, resistance to more flexible gender arrangements left them unable to sustain an emotionally or economically secure home. Their children concluded that all did *not* end well.

In sum, sustained parental support and economic security were more important to my informants than the form their families took. Since any family type holds potential pitfalls if parents do not or cannot prevail over the difficulties that arise, conventional categories that see families as static "forms" cannot account for the ways that families change as children grow to adulthood. Instead, young women and men from diverse family backgrounds recounted how parents and other family members who transcended gender boundaries and developed flexible strategies for breadwinning and caretaking were better able to cope with marital crises, economic insecurities, and other unanticipated challenges.

A range of social trends—including the erosion of single-earner paychecks, the fragility of modern marriages, and the expanding options and pressures for women to work—require varied and versatile ways of earning and caring. These institutional shifts make gender flexibility increasingly desirable and even essential. Flexible approaches to work and parenting help families adapt, while inflexible ones leave them ill-prepared to cope with new economic and social realities.

CONVERGING IDEALS, DIVERGING FALLBACKS

How do young adults use the lessons of growing up in changing families to formulate their own plans for the future? Women and men from diverse family backgrounds share a set of lofty aspirations. Whether or not their parents stayed together, more than nine out of ten hope to rear children in the context of a satisfying lifelong bond. Far from rejecting the value of commitment, almost everyone wants to create a lasting marriage or "marriage-like" partnership. This does not, however, reflect a desire for a traditional relationship. Most also aspire to build a committed bond where both paid work and family caretaking are shared. Three-fourths of those who grew up in dual-earner homes want their spouse to share breadwinning and caretaking, but so do more than two-thirds of those from traditional homes, and close to nine-tenths of those with single parents. While four-fifths of women want an egalitarian relationship, so do two-thirds of men. In short, most share an ideal that stresses the value of a lasting, flexible, and egalitarian partnership with considerable room for personal autonomy. Amy, an Asian American with two working parents, thus explains that:

> I want a fifty-fifty relationship, where we both have the potential of doing everything—both of us working and dealing with kids. With regard to career, if neither has flexibility, then one of us will have to sacrifice for one period, and the other for another.

And Wayne, an African American raised by a single mother, expresses the essentially same hopes when he says that:

> I don't want the '50s type of marriage, where I come home and she's cooking. I want her to have a career of her own. I want to be able to set my goals, and she can do what she wants, too.

While most of my interviewees hope to strike a flexible breadwinning and caretaking balance with an egalitarian partner, they are also skeptical about their chances of achieving this ideal. Women and men both worry that work demands, a lack of child-rearing supports, and the fragility of modern relationships will undermine their aspirations to forge an enduring, egalitarian partnership. In the face of barriers to equality, most have concluded that they have little choice but to prepare for options that may fall substantially short of their ideals. Despite their shared aspirations, however, men and women face different institutional obstacles and cultural pressures, which are prompting divergent fallback strategies. If they cannot find a supportive partner, most women prefer self-reliance over economic dependence within a traditional marriage. Most men, if they cannot strike an equal balance between work and parenting, prefer a neo-traditional arrangement that allows them to put work first and rely on a partner for the lion's share of caregiving. In the event that Plan A proves unreachable, women and men are thus pursuing a different Plan B as insurance against their "worst case" fears. These divergent fallback strategies point toward the emergence of a new gender divide between young women, most of whom see a need for self-reliance, and young men, who are more inclined to retain a modified version of traditional expectations.

Women's Plan B

Torn between high hopes for combining work and family and worries about sustaining a lasting and satisfying partnership, young women are navigating uncertain waters. While some are falling back on domesticity, most prefer to find a more independent base than traditional marriage provides. In contrast to the media-driven message that young women are turning away from work and career in favor of domestic pursuits, the majority of my interviewees are determined to seek financial and emotional self-reliance, whether or not they also forge a committed relationship. Regardless of class, race, or ethnicity, most are reluctant to surrender their autonomy in a traditional marriage. When the bonds of marriage are so fragile, relying on a husband for economic security seems foolhardy. And if a relationship deteriorates, economic dependence on a man leaves few means of escape. Danisha, an African American who grew up in an inner-city, working-class neighborhood, and Jennifer, who was raised in a middle-class, predominantly white suburb, agree. Danisha proclaims that:

> Let's say that my marriage doesn't work. Just in case, I want to establish myself, because I don't ever want to end up, like, "What am I going to do?" I want to be able to do what I have to do and still be okay.

Jennifer concurs:

> I will have to have a job and some kind of stability before considering marriage. Too many of my mother's friends went for that—"Let him provide everything"— and they're stuck in a very unhappy relationship, but can't leave because they can't

provide for themselves or the children they now have. So it's either welfare or putting up with somebody else's c--p.

Hoping to avoid being trapped in an unhappy marriage or left by an unreliable partner without a way to survive, almost three-fourths of women plan to build a non-negotiable base of self-reliance and an independent identity in the world of paid work.[9] But they do not view this strategy as incompatible with the search for a life partner. Instead, it reflects their determination to set a high standard for a worthy relationship. Economic self-reliance and personal independence make it possible to resist "settling" for anything less than a satisfying, mutually supportive bond.

Women from all backgrounds have concluded that work provides indispensable economic, social, and emotional resources. They have drawn lessons about the rewards of self-reliance and the perils of domesticity from their mothers, other women, and their own experiences growing up. When the bonds of marriage are fragile, relying on a husband for economic security seems foolhardy. They are thus seeking alternatives to traditional marriage by establishing a firm tie to paid work, by redesigning motherhood to better fit their work aspirations, and by looking to kin and friends as a support network to enlarge and, if needed, substitute, for an intimate relationship. These strategies do not preclude finding a life partner, but they reflect a determination to set a high standard for choosing one. Maria, who grew up in a two-parent home in a predominantly white, working-class suburb, declares:

> I want to have this person to share [my] life with—[someone] that you're there for as much as they're there for you. But I can't settle.

And Rachel, whose Latino parents separated when she was young, shares this view:

> I'm not afraid of being alone, but I am afraid of being with somebody's who's a jerk. I want to get married and have children, but it has to be under the right circumstances, with the right person.

Maria and Rachel also agree that if a worthy relationship ultimately proves out of reach, then remaining single need not mean social disconnection. Kin and friends provide a support network that enlarges and, if needed, even substitutes for an intimate relationship. Maria explains:

> If I don't find [a relationship], then I cannot live in sorrow. It's not the only thing that's ultimately important. If I didn't have my family, if I didn't have a career, if

I didn't have friends, I would be equally unhappy. [A relationship] is just one slice of the pie.

And Rachel concurs:

I can spend the rest of my life on my own, and as long as I have my sisters and my friends, I'm okay.

By blending support from friends and kin with financial self-sufficiency, these young women are pursuing a strategy of autonomy rather than placing their own fate or their children's fate in the hands of a traditional relationship. Whether or not this strategy ultimately leads to marriage, it appears to offer the safest and most responsible way to prepare for the uncertainties of relationships and the barriers to men's equal sharing.

Men's Plan B

Young men face a different dilemma: Torn between women's pressures for an egalitarian partnership and their own desire to succeed—or at least survive—in time-demanding workplaces, they are more inclined to fall back on a modified traditionalism that contrasts vividly with women's search for self-reliance. While they do not want or expect to return to a 1950s model of fathers as the only breadwinner, most men prefer a modified traditionalism that recognizes a mother's right (and need) to work, but puts his own career first. Although Andrew grew up in a consistently two-income home, he distinguished between a woman's "choice" to work and a man's "responsibility" to support his family:

I would like to have it be equal—just from what I was exposed to and what attracts me—but I don't have a set definition for what that would be like. I would be fine if both of us were working, but if she thought, "At this point in my life, I don't want to work," then it would be fine.

Because equality may prove to be too costly to their careers, seven out of ten men are pursuing a strategy that positions them as the main breadwinner, even if it allows for two working spouses. When push comes to shove, and the demands of work collide with the needs of children, this approach allows men to resist equal caretaking, even in a two-earner context. Like women, men from a range of family, class, and ethnic backgrounds fall back on neo-traditionalism. They favor retaining a clear boundary between a breadwinning father and a caretaking mother, even when she holds a paid job. This neo-traditional strategy stresses women's primary status as mothers and defines equality as a woman's "choice" to add work onto mothering.

By making room for two earners, this strategy offers the financial cushion of a second income, acknowledges women's desire for a life beyond the home, and allows for more involved fatherhood. Yet, by claiming separate spheres of responsibility for women and men, it does not challenge a man's position as the primary earner or undermine the claim that his work prospects should come first. Although James's mother became too mentally ill to care for her children or herself, Josh plans to leave the lion's share of caretaking to his wife:

> All things being equal, it [caretaking] should be shared. It may sound sexist, but if somebody's going to be the breadwinner, it's going to be me. First of all, I make a better salary, and I feel the need to work, and I just think the child really needs the mother more than the father at a young age.

Men are thus more likely to favor a fallback arrangement that retains the gender boundary between breadwinning and caretaking, even when mothers hold paid jobs. From young men's perspective, this modified but still gendered household offers women the chance to earn income and establish an identity at the workplace without imposing the costs of equal parenting on men. Granting a mother's "choice" to work supports women's claims for independence, but it does not undermine men's claim that their work prospects should come first. Acknowledging men's responsibilities at home provides for more involved fatherhood, but it does not envision domestic equality. And making room for two earners provides a buffer against the difficulties of living on one income, but it does not challenge men's position as the primary earner. Modified traditionalism thus appears to be a good compromise when the career costs of equality remain so high.[10] New economic insecurities, coupled with women's growing desire for equality, are creating dilemmas for men, even if they take a different form than the ones confronting women. Ultimately, however, men's desire to protect work prerogatives collides with women's growing desire for equality and need for independence.

Across the Gender Divide

In contrast to the popular images of a generation that feels neglected by working mothers, unsettled by parental breakups, and wary of equality, these life stories show strong support for working mothers, a focus on the quality of a relationship, and a shared desire to create lasting, flexible, and egalitarian partnerships. The good news is that most young women and men had largely positive experiences with mothers who worked and parents who strove for flexibility and equality. Those who grew up with a caring support network and sufficient economic security, whether in a single- or a two-parent household, did well. Young women and men both recounted how gender flexibility in breadwinning and caretaking helped their parents (and other caretakers) overcome such increasingly prevalent family crises as the loss of a father's income or the decline of a mother's morale. By letting go of rigid patterns that once narrowly defined women's and men's "proper" places in the family and the wider world, all kinds of families were able to overcome unexpected challenges and create more financially stable and emotionally supportive homes. And most, even among those who grew up in less flexible families, hope to build on the struggles and gains of their parents' generation by seeking equality and flexibility in their own lives.

The bad news, however, is that most young adults remain skeptical about their chances of achieving their ideals. Amid their shared desire to transcend gender boundaries and achieve flexibility in their own lives, young women and men harbor strong concerns that their aspirations will prove impossible to reach. Faced with the many barriers to egalitarian relationships and fearful that they will not find the right partner to help them integrate work with family caretaking, they are also preparing for options that may fall substantially short of their ideals. Reversing the argument that women are returning to tradition, however, these divergent fallback strategies suggest that a new divide is emerging between "self-reliant" women, who see work, an independent income, and personel autonomy as essential to their survival, and "neo-traditional" men, who grant women's "choice" to work but also feel the need and pressure to be a primary breadwinner.

While women are developing more innovative strategies than are men, the underlying story is one of a resilient, but realistic generation that has changed far more than the institutions it has inherited. Whether they grew up in a flexible home or one with more rigid definitions of women's and men's proper places, their hard-won lessons about the need for new, more egalitarian options for building relationships and caring for children are outpacing their ability to implement these goals.

Yet, young men and women still hope to reach across the divide that separates them. Aware that traditional job ladders and traditional marriages are both waning, they are seeking more flexible ways to build careers, care for families, and integrate the two.[11] Convinced that the traditional career, defined by orderly steps up an organizational chart, is a relic of the past, most hope to craft a "personal career" that is not bound by a single employer or work organization. Most men as well as women are trying to redefine the "ideal worker" to accommodate the ebb and flow of family life, even if that means sacrificing some income for a more balanced life.[12] They hope to create a shared "work-family" career that interweaves breadwinning and caretaking.

Growing up in changing families and facing uncertainty in their own lives has left this generation weary of rigid, narrowly framed "family values" that moralize about their personal choices or those of others. They are searching for a morality without moralism that balances an ethic of tolerance and inclusiveness with the core values of behaving responsibly and caring for others. The clash between self-reliant women and neo-traditional men may signal a new divide, but it stems from intensifying work-family dilemmas, not from a decline of laudable values.

Since new social realities are forcing young adults to seek new ways to combine love and work, the best hope for bridging gender divides lies in creating social policies that will allow twenty-first-century Americans to pursue the flexible, egalitarian strategies they want rather than forcing them to fall back on less desirable—and ultimately less workable—options. Whether the goal is equal opportunity or a healthy family landscape, the best family values can only be achieved by creating the social supports for gender flexibility in our communities, homes, and workplaces.

33

Men's Changing Contribution to Family Work

Oriel Sullivan

While women still do most of the family work (including household tasks and child care), the balance of both quantitative and attitudinal evidence over the past forty years shows a slow but significant increase in men's contributions. In this chapter, I present some of this evidence and argue that it is the combination of these different kinds of evidence that provides the most convincing case for change. In order to continue to promote change, we must understand the processes involved both at the level of the couple (through analyzing women's efforts to negotiate change in the home) and at the institutional level (through an analysis of institutional obstacles to, and facilitations of, change).

INTRODUCTION

For twenty years, research studies concluded that men's contribution to family work barely changed at a time when women were increasingly joining the workforce. The most common argument was that even though women were working longer hours on the job and cutting back on their own housework, men were not making up for women's lost hours of domestic work. But newer research has shown that men are doing significantly more, both of domestic work and, particularly, of child care. Using large-scale data and a longer perspective, it is possible to show a slow but significant change in the direction of a more equal division, with the result that more couples are sharing more tasks. While women still continue to do more family work than their male partners, convergence has been significant, with the result that the total amount of work contributed by men and women in two-parent dual-earner families—including paid work as well as unpaid family work—is now virtually identical.[1]

In addition, there have been slow but significant changes observed over the same period in gender ideologies, as measured by attitudes to gender equality and the significance of men's domestic work performance. For example, according to national opinion polls, Americans have become slightly more conservative about marriage and divorce than they were in the 1970s and 1980s, but the belief in gender equality within families continues to gain acceptance among both men and women. A 2007 national opinion poll conducted by the Pew Research Center provides recent evidence of the increasing importance of this gender equality ideal for Americans. Sixty-two percent of respondents ranked "sharing household tasks" as very important for a successful marriage, up from 47 percent in a similar poll from 1990. The Pew Center notes that sharing household tasks was the only item showing a sharp increase from 1990–2007, taking over the number three position from the item on the importance of children for a successful marriage.[2]

In light of these various kinds of evidence, I argue that the bulk of the past literature in this area has not taken a sufficiently long view of change. Where change has been acknowledged, it has often been accompanied by the claim that the amount of change has not been meaningful. But should we have expected to see a revolutionary change since the 1960s? The question is one of emphasis: Should we see the glass as half empty (by focusing on the fact that women still perform the bulk of domestic labor and child care) or half full (by focusing on the evidence for progressive change in men's contributions)? I want to understand and promote the processes of change. Instead of concentrating on the failure to achieve absolute parity in hourly contributions, we should acknowledge the importance of a slow change that may in the end lead to significantly greater gender equality. Through an active recognition that change is occurring, albeit slowly, we can begin to develop the theoretical frameworks and the empirical tools to recognize how it happens and how it can be promoted.[3]

In the first part of this chapter, I present some of the diverse evidence for change, ranging from changes in attitudes toward gender equality to changes in actual gender practices in the domestic sphere. I address some changes in attitudes to gender equality, and changes in images of masculinity, in particular in relation to fatherhood. Such changes are indicative of shifts both in gender ideologies and practices. While evidence for change in attitudes in itself does not necessarily mean that change is occurring in the performance of family work (that is, it is not *sufficient* evidence for such change), we might well consider it a *necessary* condition for meaningful change. My general argument is that it is the combination of diverse kinds of evidence that provides the most compelling argument for change. Thus, I turn to the quantitative empirical evidence for change in the time spent by men and women on various kinds of unpaid family work over the period from the 1960s to the 1990s.

EVIDENCE FOR CHANGE: THE CHANGING SOCIAL AND POLITICAL ENVIRONMENT

The association between attitudes to gender equality and the division of family work is by now well established from research based on large-scale data. In general, those men and women whose attitudes to gender equality are more positive ("liberal" or "progressive" in other formulations) tend to share domestic work more equally.[4] With respect to change in attitudes over time, the majority of research has found that there has been a movement toward a rejection of normatively defined "gender expectations" in the home. This has taken the form of a greater acceptance of nonfamilial roles for women, particularly among younger women with higher levels of education, and a rather less clear movement toward acceptance of more familial work for men. Scott and her coauthors have provided cross-national comparisons of men's and women's attitudes from several countries in Europe on three types of gender-related beliefs and attitudes: the consequences of women working for pay, gender ideology, and the importance of paid work.[5] They found different patterns of change emerging across different countries, and they speculate as to how these differences may be related to (1) patterns of female employment, (2) the consciousness-raising effects of the women's movement, and (3) the relative emphasis on individual autonomy. Their overall conclusion is that despite inter-country and cross-time variations "traditional gender roles" are increasingly rejected, although there is evidence that the pace of change slowed in the 1990s.[6] They also note that "women have been much more prepared than men to reject traditional gender role attitudes" but, significantly for the argument about change, they also report that within-cohort changes have been more rapid recently among men. This implies a faster process of change in which individuals of the same age group ("cohort") display changing attitudes over time, as opposed to changes occurring because younger cohorts have more egalitarian attitudes than older ones.

The significance of changes in attitudes among men toward gender equality is that this finding contradicts the argument that men are taking on more household responsibilities simply as a practical requirement as their partners take on paid jobs. Further evidence of men's changing attitudes comes from the recent growth of research on changing symbolic representations of masculinity.[7]

Writers on masculinity have found changing images of masculinity and fatherhood and real changes in gender practice, particularly in relation to masculine
caring behavior.[8]

When images of men change in the media, we see the symbolic representation of the possibilty of "the new father." This new father, who bonds deeply with
and accordingly cares for his children, according to Knijn, becomes part of male
gender identification.[9] Hochschild argues for the existence of a wide diversity of
choices of fathering styles, however, rather than one simplistic media image of
the new father.[10] The point is taken further by Smart and Neale when they refer
to the image of the new father as being composed of different and often contradictory elements.[11] The question is: To what extent can the emergence of new,
diverse, and shifting images and ideals of fatherhood and masculinity be linked
to empirical changes in practice?

At the turn of the twenty-first century, there is considerable evidence for
changes in paternal behavior—in particular, evidence for a substantial increase
in paternal involvement in child care.[12] Moreover, there is now also more general
agreement in support of Coltrane's claim that "the move is towards uncoupling
gender from caring."[13] A growing body of research focuses on "involved fathers"
or even "equal caretakers"—fathers who participate to greater degrees in caring
for children, as opposed to only filling the traditional breadwinner role. Typically,
"involved fathers" do not make a distinction between mothering and fathering
in caring.[14] A number of authors have directly addressed the theoretical reasons
for such changes in the meaning and practice of fatherhood. Beck and Beck-
Gernsheim argued that the social forces of late modernity generate increasing
individualization, autonomy, and the weakening of family ties. The parent-child
bond, however, is an enduring element in the family despite high rates of marital
dissolution (Beck and Beck-Gernsheim 1995).[15] Other authors have placed more
emphasis on issues of personal identity,[16] arguing that increases in involved fatherhood are: "in line with the growing awareness of, or belief in, personal identity as a
reflexive identity."[17] Men are more likely to see themselves as choosing fatherhood,
and how to do it, than simply following traditional life-course norms.

To summarize, the overall picture suggests shifts in attitudes and representations of masculinity occurring both within and between successive generations, and somewhat slower changes in practice, particularly in fatherhood. Such
changes in attitudes and symbolic representations support the case for a change
in the environment in which men and women make their choices. And, as I have
already suggested, it is the *co-incidence* of changes in this wider context with the
growing empirical evidence for changes in gender practices in the home which
is our strongest argument for change in the direction of gender equality. These

changes in family life deserve our serious attention. I now turn to the quantitative evidence for change in men and women's contributions to family work.

EVIDENCE FOR CHANGE: THE QUANTITATIVE DATA

The longitudinal multinational quantitative empirical evidence for change is based on nationally representative data sets, and stretches in time from the 1960s to the 1990s. The importance of the quantitative evidence is about consistency: consistent measures across time can actually measure change.

There are several sources of quantitative evidence for long-term changes over time in the allocation of family work, of which time-use diary studies are by now perhaps the main source. In such diaries, people record their activities every ten or fifteen minutes throughout the day, which yields more accurate results than simply asking people how much time they spend in a particular activity per day. Researchers have analyzed time-use diaries and found growing evidence for change,[18] confirming that *both within and across* countries there have been changes in the amount of time that men and women spend in housework and child care and that these changes are in the direction of greater equity.

At the start of the twenty-first century, the average full-time employed American married man with children has increased his contribution to child care by four hours a week since the 1970s, and his contribution to other family work by two hours a week. Overall, he now does six hours a week of child care and ten hours a week of other family work. By comparison, the average full- or part-time employed American married woman with children is employed for fewer hours per week on average than her male counterpart, but she does eleven hours of child care (an increase of seven hours from the 1970s) and nineteen hours of other family work (a *decrease* of three hours from the 1970s). So, over thirty years, she has increased her total time devoted to family work and child care by four hours (all of it in child care), while the average full-time employed married man has increased his total by six hours (four hours in child care and two hours in other family work).[19] The outcome of these changes is that the percentage of family work and child care done by men in families in which both partners are employed has increased from something over 20 percent in the 1970s to nearly a third at the start of the twenty-first century. Men's relative contributions are even greater in those families where both partners are employed on a full-time basis. Here the contribution of the man has increased from just under 30 percent in 1975 to 37 percent by the start of the twenty-first century.[20]

Similar trends are evident across other Western countries. Using data from twenty industrialized countries over the period 1965–2003, Hook showed an overall cross-country increase in men's contribution to family work (i.e., including housework, child care, and shopping) from less than 20 percent to almost 35 percent.[21] Sullivan and Gershuny showed how this increase varied according to the *type* of family work for six countries of Europe and North America over a similar time period. For routine housework (cooking, cleaning, and clothes care), the time full-time employed women with children aged five to fifteen living with them spent in these activities decreased (by just under one hour per day), while the time full-time employed men with children of the same age spent went up (by around twenty minutes per day). This was reflected in an increase in these men's share of the routine housework from roughly 15 percent to 25 percent of the overall total. With respect to child care, women increased their time commitments and, to a lesser degree, so did men (this finding held for all employment statuses and ages of children). Both women and men also reported spending significantly more time doing another category of family work: shopping and travel (including driving children). The overall effect is of a trend toward convergence in the distribution of activities for men and women over time.[22] So change is by now widely reported— but the question remains, are such changes meaningful in magnitude?

It is true that the overall increase in men's contribution to core domestic work may not seem that impressive if we calculate the change over three decades (only twenty minutes more daily after more than thirty years). In addition, it is still reasonable to emphasize the ongoing discrepancy between the overall amount of time that women and men spend in domestic work tasks. But some authors continue to argue that the main effect involved in any change is that of women's reduction in hours spent doing housework. The upward trend for men as well as the downward trend for women in routine housework tasks is consistent in direction across different countries and statistically significant when controlling for other relevant variables. The fact that the trends for men and women move in opposite directions also supports the change to greater gender equality in the performance of domestic tasks. And although statistical significance in itself does not translate directly to substantive importance, these trends are not only statistically robust but also consistent, both internally (i.e., over time and space), and externally (in relation to other evidence for change).

How to Explain Change

Until now, I have focused on evidence for changes in men's contributions to family work. It is crucial to understand the processes that have been involved in such changes, in order both to attempt to understand circumstances that have enabled change and to continue to promote it. The question is, then, how might we go about explaining change?

The model that I suggest starting with emphasizes the importance of daily interaction between partners, for the couple relationship constitutes the arena for gender relations and practice within the domestic sphere. There is a message here for all of us, for through this focus on daily interaction it is possible to conceive of women's everyday struggles as a part of social processes of change. Individuals bring their own resources. These resources involve their absolute and relative levels of income, their level of education, the status of their job, and their skills at negotiation or in the management of emotions.[23] In addition, all interaction necessarily occurs within a wider structural and symbolic social context. Negotiation about household labor is embedded within wider structures of diminishing patriarchy and individualism within late modern capitalism, as well as within a local context of (changing) gender ideologies.

Within this context, individuals "do gender" in the domestic sphere. The "doing gender" perspective emphasizes processes of "situated behavior," in which gender is continuously being actively constructed in interaction.[24] According to this approach, for an individual woman or man the "accomplishment" of gender involves behaving in a way that is "accountable" to expectations of appropriate gender behavior. Thus, in general, men perform normatively masculine-defined tasks and women perform normatively feminine-defined tasks in order to be accepted as "good" men and women. But since they are social constructions, the normative guidelines that regulate appropriate gender behavior are contingent on the situation, and vary from time to time and from place to place. As such, the idea of "doing gender" in daily interaction clearly provides potential for the *production* of new gender relations, and therefore for the possibility of change.

One framework for conceptualizing such change is provided by the idea of "gender consciousness." Gerson and Peiss describe gender consciousness as the extent of consciousness or awareness of gender issues.[25] This ranges from a generalized vague awareness of gender at one end of the continuum to a full consciousness of the rights that are associated with specific genders at the other. The development of this consciousness partly arises from the recognition of rights based on information from the wider society. The rise of feminism, for example, provided new conditions for the development of gender consciousness. Critically for my argument, however, social interaction also has an influence on the recognition of, and generation of, these rights. This means that the active bargaining and negotiation that women and men engage in on a daily basis can help to develop gender consciousness by acknowledging rights (and responsibilities) in social interaction. According to Thompson, gender consciousness thus constitutes a central component of women's attempts at change.[26] The key to understanding changes in the family roles of women and men is to integrate different levels of analysis—from changing attitudes, to couple's negotiations, to observing images in the media. The model I advance is an integrative approach, which treats gender as a structure that combines individual, interactional, and institutional dimensions.[27] Thus, "actors shape the gender structure they inherit."[28] My argument is that, in order to better understand the processes of change that are occurring, we need to make connections between the wider social and political environment that affects both the public and the private spheres, and the interactions and negotiations that individuals engage in on a day-to-day basis, with the focus on gender relations and practices in the domestic sphere. It is critical to identify changes at the level of the ideologies and images that structure gendered interactions. In addition, we see how attitudes toward equality in the family have shifted across, and even within, generations. How these attitudes are shaped, and how they translate into (inter)action, is far less well researched. Empirical observations of changes in practice within the home, as measured by the time spent on different domestic tasks, are also by now well documented. But again, far less is known about the processes that have led to these changes. At this level, the key lies in the detailed analysis of processes of change as they occur in day-to-day intimate interaction. We must pay attention not just to observations of changes in practice, but also to the resources, processes, negotiations, and struggles that have led to changes, as described by the actors themselves.

CONCLUSION

I have presented an argument that change has happened in the division of family work. I have shown that (slow) change is ongoing by reference to the large-scale empirical documentation of who does what at home, and with evidence from changes in attitudes and symbolic representations of masculinity. It is the combination of evidence that provides a convincing argument.

Yet, we should not be complacent about these changes or their continuation. It is clear that changes toward gender equality have been struggled for, fought over, and hard-won over decades, not only in the public and political arena, but also during innumerable daily contestations and negotiations both in the home and outside of it. Change is *not* inevitable. Under the right conditions of changing gender ideologies and consciousness, we see the possibility for effecting change. One goal of feminist research has been women's empowerment, and by focusing on it daily as a potentially transformative process it is possible to conceive of women's everyday struggles with their male partners as part of social change. According to such a perspective, individual actors are also active agents of change, even if the process may not be a rapid or an easy one. My argument is a return to the call of early second-wave feminism that "the personal is political." We should resist the fatalistic assertion that men and women come from different planets, and are thus doomed to permanent miscommunication. Every small struggle to redefine boundaries, to open up the "marital conversation," to negotiate change in domestic gender practices can contribute in the end to gender equality in the home and outside of it.

34

Briefing Paper: Men's Changing Contribution
to Housework and Child Care

Oriel Sullivan and Scott Coltrane

For thirty years, researchers studying the changes in family dynamics since the rise of the women's movement have concluded that, despite gains in the world of education, work, and politics, women face a "stalled revolution" at home. According to many studies, men's family work has barely budged in response to women's increased employment. The typical punch line of many news stories has been that, even though women are working longer hours on the job and cutting back their own housework, men are not picking up the slack.

Our research suggests that these studies were based on unrealistic hopes for instant transformation. They underestimated the amount of change going on behind the scenes and the growing willingness of men to adapt to their wives' new behaviors and values. In fact, more couples are sharing family tasks than ever before, and the movement toward sharing has been especially significant for full-time dual-earner couples.

Most previous literature on the division of family work began with the naive assumption that the massive gender rearrangements that began in the late 1960s would, unlike any other major social transformation in history, have instantaneous results. Researchers did not take a sufficiently long view of change over time. Our ongoing studies of couple relationships reveal instead that change has been continuous and significant, not merely in younger couples who begin their relationship with more flexible ideas about gender, but also in older couples where the wife has worked long enough to change her husband's values and behaviors.[1] We believe that the transformation of marriage that has occurred in the comparatively short period of forty years is too great a break from the past to be dismissed as a slow and grudging evolution that has not fundamentally changed family dynamics. Men and women may not be fully equal yet, but the rules of the game have been profoundly and irreversibly changed.[2]

KEY EVIDENCE OF CONVERGENCE IN WORK-FAMILY BALANCING BY MEN AND WOMEN

- In the USA, men's absolute and proportionate contributions to household tasks increased substantially over the past three decades, substantially lessening the burden on women. National cross-time series of time-use diary studies show that from the 1960s to the twenty-first century, men's contribution to housework doubled, increasing from about 15 percent to over 30 percent of the total.[3] By the early twenty-first century, the average full-time or part-time employed American married woman with children was doing two hours less housework than in 1965.

- The most dramatic increase in men's contributions has been to child care. Between 1965 and 2003, men tripled the amount of time they spent in child care.[4] Fathers in two-parent households now spend more time with co-resident children than at any time since large-scale longitudinally comparable data were collected.[5] In this period, women also increased their time spent in child care and interaction with children, doubling the time over the period from 1965 to 2003. This mutual increase in child care appears to be related to higher standards for both mothers and fathers about spending time with children.

- These trends are occurring in much of the Western industrial world, suggesting a worldwide movement toward men and women sharing the responsibilities of both work life and family life. Data from twenty industrialized countries over the period 1965–2003 reveal an overall cross-country increase in men's proportional contribution to family work (including housework, child care, and shopping), from less than one-fifth in 1965 to more than a third by 2003.[6]

- Furthermore, an analysis of a couple's relative contribution to housework in Britain found a steady growth from the 1960s to the 1990s in the percentage of families where the man contributed *more* time to family work (including housework, shopping, and child care) than the woman. This trend was particularly marked among full-time employed couples.[7]

- There is, overall, a striking convergence of work-family patterns for American men and women. While the total hours of work (including both paid and family work) done by men and women have remained roughly equal since the 1960s—in particular for parents—there has been a growing convergence in the hours that both women and men spend in the broad categories of paid work, family work, and leisure.[8] Women's paid work time has significantly increased, while that of men has decreased. Correspondingly, women's time devoted to housework has decreased, while the time men spend in family work of all kinds has increased.

WILL MEN'S CONTRIBUTIONS CONTINUE TO INCREASE?

We believe that increases in men's involvement in family work are part of a continuing rather than a stalled revolution, and are likely to continue as more women join the labor force. Men share more family work if their female partners are employed more hours, earn more money, and have spent more years being educated.

In addition, whatever a man's original resistance to sharing, we have found that men's contributions to family work increase over time: The longer their female partners have been in paid employment, the more family work men are likely to do.[9]

All these trends are likely to continue for the foreseeable future. According to national opinion polls, belief in gender equality within families continues to gain acceptance among both men and women. And with greater belief in gender equality and more equal sharing of tasks comes the possibility of more equal and open negotiation about who does what in families.[10] This should have positive outcomes for the families involved, since research shows that when men do more of the housework, women's perceptions of fairness and marital satisfaction rise and the couple experiences less marital conflict.[11] Supporting the general association between sharing housework and healthier marriages, Cooke found that couples in the USA who have more equal divisions of labor are less likely to divorce than couples where one partner specializes in breadwinning and the other partner specializes in family work.[12]

CONCLUSION: NOT A CALL FOR COMPLACENCY!

American couples have made remarkable progress in working out mutually satisfying arrangements to share the responsibilities of breadwinning and family care. And polls continue to show increasing approval of such arrangements. So the revolution in gender aspirations and behaviors has not stalled. But progress in getting employers to accommodate workers' desires has been less encouraging, as high earners are forced to work ever longer hours, while less affluent earners face wage or benefit cuts and layoffs that often force them to work more than one job. Aside from winning paid parental leave laws in Washington and California (with similar bills being considered in Illinois, Massachusetts, New Jersey, and New York), families have made little headway in getting the kind of family friendly policies that are taken for granted in most other advanced industrial countries. Even as American couples' beliefs and desires about gender equity have grown to be among the highest in the world, America's work policies and social support systems for working parents are among the lowest.[13]

All in all, the "stalled revolution" in America is not taking place in families but in the highest circles of our economic and political elites.

In the News

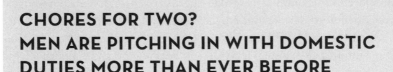

CHORES FOR TWO?
MEN ARE PITCHING IN WITH DOMESTIC
DUTIES MORE THAN EVER BEFORE

Christian Science Monitor, April 29, 2008

Marilyn Gardner

When domestic chores beckon—when there are dinners to cook, dishes to wash, diapers to change, and dust bunnies to chase—who's doing the work?

Increasingly the answer is: men. After decades of collective sighs from women that husbands and fathers aren't doing their part on the home front, old stereotypes are crumbling. More men are sharing housework and child care, and doing it not grudgingly but willingly, according to a largely optimistic study released by the Council on Contemporary Families at the University of Illinois, Chicago.

"Men and women may not be fully equal yet, but the rules of the game have been profoundly and irreversibly changed," says Scott Coltrane, a sociologist at the University of California, Riverside, and coauthor of the study. This is true not only for younger couples who begin their relationship with more flexible ideas about gender, but also for older couples where the wife has worked long enough to change her husband's values and behavior. The longer a wife is employed, the more housework her husband does.

Since the 1960s, men's contribution to housework has doubled, increasing from about 15 percent to more than 30 percent of the total, the study reports. "Women are still doing twice as much as men, but it's very much more a partnership these days," Professor Coltrane says. Between 1965 and 2003, men also tripled the amount of time they spent caring for children.

"As far as housework and chores go, my husband and I have a simple philosophy: If we see that something needs to be done, do it," says Silvana Clark, an author and professional speaker in Bellingham, Wash. "He's changed diapers, put bows in our daughter's hair for dance recitals, and scrubbed toilets. Plus he's a great cook."

The couple's equal-opportunity approach to domesticity extends outside the house as well. "I mow the lawn when I have time or take the cars in for an oil change," Mrs. Clark says. In their 31 years of marriage, she can't remember fighting over chores. "It seems common courtesy; it shouldn't be a problem."

Housework used to be a topic of dissension for Donna Maria Coles Johnson and her husband, Darryl, of Charlotte, N.C. After she explained that the house would run more smoothly if they both committed to certain chores, "We were able to sit down and come up with some processes," she says. Now they take turns cleaning up the kitchen after dinner and putting their two children to bed.

Mrs. Johnson also believes in training the next generation to help. "Our 6-year-old daughter sweeps, and our 4-year-old son takes out the recyclables," she says. "Both of the kids clean up the family room."

Another study of more than 17,000 people in 28 countries finds that married men do less housework than live-in boyfriends. "Marriage as an institution seems to have a traditionalizing effect on couples, even couples who see men and women as equal," says Shannon Davis, a sociologist at George Mason University in Fairfax, Va., and coauthor of the study.

Allison Peltz of Cleveland, who shares an apartment with her boyfriend, says he does most of the cleaning: "He's very into vacuuming, dusting, and keeping all things neat and tidy. A lot of my friends who are married or living together have husbands or boyfriends who also do a lot of the cleaning."

David Gonnerman of Northfield, Minn., divides the chores fairly equally with his wife, Kasia. Both like to cook, although she does most of it. He does the dishes and most of the laundry. He pays the bills and shuttles their two sons to activities.

But some couples still struggle. Belinda Rachman, a divorce attorney in Carlsbad, Calif., calls housework one of the few unresolved areas in her own marriage of more than 20 years.

"Neither of us wants to clean," she says. "We end up doing a big clean when we know we are going to have visitors but pretty much letting things go to pot the rest of the time."

Despite progress, nobody pretends the domestic revolution is over yet. Even when men do their fair share, women often still find themselves playing the role of household CEO. "I am the one who monitors what needs to be done and sees that it happens," says Mary Ellen Amtower of Highland, Md.

Different standards also present challenges. Paul Davis of Orlando, Fla., shares the housework but acknowledges that his wife does "a substantial bit more" than he does, in part because of his demanding workload. He adds, "My wife is quite the perfectionist, which means that even when I do household chores she may complain about how I did it and thereafter do it herself."

Then there is the tricky little matter of couples' perceptions of who does what. In a survey on changing gender roles by the Harrison Group, a large number of men say they share responsibility for certain day-to-day tasks. Their wives counter that the responsibility falls solely on them.

Whatever the reality, one thing is certain: Dust cloths, vacuums, washers, and cleaning supplies show no sign of becoming obsolete, giving couples plenty of opportunity to decide who will use them. As Clark says, "We feel we both live in this house, so we both need to work together on chores." ◾

35

Briefing Paper: A "Stalled" Revolution or a Still Unfolding One?

Molly Monahan Lang and Barbara J. Risman

After over thirty-five years of continuous change toward more egalitarian gender attitudes and behaviors, recent signs of a slowdown have led some observers to suggest that the gender revolution is coming to an end. Evidence for this claim includes a slight dip in women's labor force participation, a rise in support for traditional gender attitudes among adults, and an increase in the age of sexual initiation among the young. In the past year, the Council on Contemporary Families has received many enquiries from the press and general public about whether the transformation of men's and women's roles has now run its course.

In a review of this question prepared for the Tenth Anniversary Conference of the Council, we conclude that these short-term countertrends do not amount to a revival of traditional family roles and beliefs. Instead, we show that the evidence overwhelmingly shows an ongoing shift toward what we call "gender convergence," an ever-increasing similarity in how men and women live and what they want from their lives.

WOMEN'S EMPLOYMENT

In 1960, only 40 percent of women aged twenty-five to fifty-four years old were in the labor force. By 2000, 70 percent of women that age were employed. For married women with children aged six through seventeen, employment rates grew from 40 percent in 1960 to a peak of almost 80 percent by the new millennium.

Sixty percent of married women with children under school age now work for pay, compared with less than 20 percent in 1960. Mothers are still more likely than fathers to work part-time rather than full-time, but they are less likely to do so than they were in the past. Wives work for pay 80 percent of the hours their husbands work for pay, a huge increase since the 1960s.

During the same period, men's rates of labor force participation showed a downward trend, from just above 90 percent in 1970 to just above 80 percent in 2005. The combination of a general upward trend in women's employment and a downward trend in men's has led toward a convergence in labor force participation.

Between 2000 and 2004, there was a small dip in women's employment rates, which fell from just above 70 percent in 2000 to just below 70 percent in 2004. But, as economist Heather Boushey points out, the rate of employment fell for all workers between 2000 and 2004—not just mothers, but also childless women, fathers, and childless men. This was due more to the weak economy than to mothers' opting out of employment.

MEN'S PARTICIPATION IN HOUSEWORK AND CHILD CARE

Despite the sometimes gloomy newspaper articles about men's resistance to sharing household chores, research on families shows that, over time, each generation of men has taken on a greater share of the work involved in running a home. While men's family work has not changed nearly as much as has women's labor force participation, there is clear evidence that married men are more involved in child care and housework than in past eras.

Significantly, younger fathers spend more time with their children than older fathers do. When the Families and Work Institute compared the workday hours that Gen-X and baby boomer fathers spent caring for and doing things with their children in 2002, they found that Gen-X fathers spent more than an additional hour every day than did baby boom generation dads. After controlling for the possible effect of the children's age, the same difference remained. The baby boom generation of men was the first that had to deal with a new kind of family life, where women demanded more equality at home and at work. Generation X men may not talk as much about changing family roles as the baby boomers, but in practice they are breaking new ground in co-parenting their children.

In housework as well as child care, the tendency has been toward convergence, despite some holdovers from the past. Research by Robinson and Godbey shows that men spent more than four hours per week longer each week doing housework and child care in 1985 than they did in 1965. During the same period, women decreased their time doing such work by over nine hours per week. Some people have claimed the revolution in gender behavior "stalled" in the 1980s. But between 1985 and 2000, fathers continued to increase their time doing housework and child care, while mothers continued to decrease their time doing housework. Women still do more household labor than men, but they have been doing less in every generation and every decade. In addition, men are much more likely than in the past to tell pollsters that they desire fewer hours in the labor force and more time for their family.

Sexual Behavior

Some behaviors among the young have also prompted speculation about a resurgence of "traditional" values. Since the beginning of the 1990s, for example, all the social problems related to teen sexuality have plummeted. Rates of teen pregnancy and STDs have fallen. Age of first intercourse has actually risen. Some have interpreted this as an indication of a return to traditional sexual mores among today's young people. But a closer look reveals a different interpretation. Research by Risman and Schwartz indicates that it is actually young men who have increased their age at first intercourse. During the early sexual revolution, high school girls became more like boys, as premarital sex became more common at younger ages. In the 1990s, boys and girls became even more alike, but it was boys that were changing to behave somewhat more like girls. Risman and Schwartz suggest that, as girls became more sexually active, boys became more likely to begin their sexual lives with a girlfriend, rather than a young woman they perceived to be a "bad girl," good only for a one-night stand. Relationship sex is more likely to be safe sex, and this change may help account for the decrease in STDs and premarital pregnancy.

Attitudes toward Equality

It is not just behaviors but also women's and men's attitudes that are changing. Women consistently hold more egalitarian attitudes than do men, but the general trend has been upwards for both sexes. Research shows that since the 1970s Americans have become increasingly more accepting of women's contributions to family decisions, women's paid employment, and sharing child care with others. According to General Social Survey data, Americans' gender attitudes became steadily more egalitarian from the late 1970s to 1995.

From 1998 to 2002, there was a dip in egalitarian attitudes, but they have resumed their upward march since then, especially in people's support for mothers' employment and men's sharing of housework. This return to a rise in egalitarian attitudes in the early twenty-first century makes us skeptical of arguments that women are somehow becoming more "traditional," especially since young people continue to hold more egalitarian attitudes than older people, including baby boomers.

Conclusion

A disproportionate amount of attention has been given to a few pieces of data suggesting that women are abandoning the effort for equality. As we show here, the bulk of the evidence indicates a decades-long trend of convergence between women and men in their behaviors and in their gender attitudes. Yes, men and women continue to exhibit some differences in these respects. And among low-income groups, where economic stress and job insecurity make family life less stable, there are fewer signs of convergence. Unemployed single men, in particular, have been less likely to adopt egalitarian attitudes or to be involved in caregiving work. Without success at breadwinning, they are less likely to marry or cohabit over long periods of time, and without stable partnerships with women, much less likely to share child rearing. Overall, however, the trend is toward greater convergence in men's and women's values and behavior, in and out of the home.

Is this good for families? We think so. The children of employed parents have more time with their parents than did the average child twenty-five years ago. Among married couples with children, mothers are spending the same amount of time doing things with and taking care of their children on days when they are working today as they did twenty-five years ago—more than three hours a day—despite the increase in their paid work hours. Meanwhile, fathers' time with children has increased dramatically, from under two hours to nearly three. Women's sustained levels of attention to their children, when complemented by the growing amount of time spent by spouses or partners with the children, means that children in families headed by two parents are actually receiving more combined attention from their parents today than children did twenty-five years ago—six hours per weekday in 2002 versus five hours in 1977.

As researchers and practitioners, members of the Council on Contemporary Families are sensitive to variations and differences in people's attitudes and behaviors. Many more women than men continue to take time from paid work to raise children, and a significant minority of men and women continue to believe that it is natural for men to specialize in breadwinning and women to specialize in homemaking. But a long-range perspective shows that American women continue to show an interest in having greater autonomy in their lives, while men are increasingly interested in taking on tasks historically seen as "women's work," such as spending time with their children. The data show that the trend toward gender convergence is real, and it is not going to go away. America's economic and political institutions, along with our research agendas and practical interventions with families, all need to reflect this. It would be a disservice to the families we study and with whom we work to continue to operate on the misguided assumption that there will be any revival of the 1950s male breadwinner family, or that such a revival is desired by most American men and women.

In the News

SIGNS OF DÉTENTE IN THE BATTLE BETWEEN VENUS AND MARS

New York Times, May 31, 2007

Patricia Cohen

Like bickering relatives at the end of a long holiday dinner, women have been arguing about whether the gender revolution is over and more mothers are choosing to leave work and stay home with the children.

Now experts who shared their latest research at a conference this month say that far from reverting to more traditional sex roles, women and men are becoming more alike in their attitudes toward balancing life at home and at work.

The gender revolution is not over, they say, it has just developed into "gender convergence."

"The conventional wisdom is that 'men are from Mars and women are from Venus,' " said Molly Monahan Lang, a sociologist at Bloomsburg University of Pennsylvania. "On the contrary, we are from one small world that is getting smaller."

In one of the most comprehensive reviews of current research on families and work, Dr. Monahan Lang and Barbara J. Risman, chairwoman of the sociology department at the University of Illinois in Chicago, analyzed findings from studies based on national census data, in-depth interviews, and dozens of surveys for a conference organized by the Council on Contemporary Families, a nonpartisan group of researchers and clinicians.

What they found were more similarities than differences in men and women. "The evidence overwhelmingly shows an ongoing shift toward what we call 'gender convergence,' an ever-increasing similarity in how men and women live and what they want from their lives," Dr. Monahan Lang and Dr. Risman write.

Several other social scientists at the conference who are doing independent research have come to similar conclusions. Ellen Galinsky, president of the Family and Work Institute, said many more men were reporting feeling tension between family and work life, even if their wives stayed home. And in a report about parents at Fortune 100 companies published in December, Rosalind Chait Barnett, the director of the Community, Families and Work Program at Brandeis University, found that when it came to concern over how their children spent their time after school, fathers and mothers were virtually the same.

Of course, most people recognize that mothers are working more and doing less housework, and men are working less and doing more housework and child care than a generation ago—albeit still significantly less than women. But what much of the recent research has tried to tease out is more information on attitudes and desires.

And so far, the evidence points toward men and women having increasingly similar goals. When Teresa Aguayo and Frederick Moehn had their third child, Mr. Moehn took a six-month sabbatical from teaching music at Stony Brook University to care for the baby.

Now, the 1-year-old has a nanny, the 3-year-old is in day care and the 5-year-old is in preschool. Child care costs more than Ms. Aguayo, 34, makes as the program coordinator for the Brazilian studies program at Columbia University, but she said: "We figured it would be much harder to get back in the job market after caring for a child. I knew I wanted to go back to work, and I love my job."

Convergence shows up more in younger parents, said Kathleen Gerson, author of "Hard Choices: How Women Decide About Work, Career, and Motherhood." After conducting 120 in-depth interviews with men and women ages 18 to 32, Dr. Gerson found that Generation X fathers spent more time with their children than did baby boomer fathers, and that both sexes aspired to the same ideal: "a balance between work and family."

What would they do if they could not achieve that balance? The women, at least, said that rather than stay home with the children, they were intent on establishing "a solid economic base," Dr. Gerson said. (For men, the fall-back position is to have their wives stay home while they win the bread.)

Still, given the passions that surround this issue, the conclusions are just as likely to stir up the debate as to settle it. In recent months, women have variously argued in books and elsewhere that mothers want to work for personal fulfillment; need to work for economic security; want to raise children full time; or want all of these things at different times. Scholars, meanwhile, complain that the public discussion has been distorted by a fascination with a tiny sliver of high-income earners.

When it comes down to it, discussions about the so-called mommy wars really encompass two separate arguments: one about interpreting work-force statistics, the other about values. And how one decides the first is often determined by the second.

One prominent dispute over figures, for example, involves the slight decline in women's employment—less than 2 percent—since 2000 after four decades of steady climb. Paula England, a sociologist at Stanford University, maintains the tiny up-and-down blips are not that important.

"If you really look at the big picture, it's completely trivial," Dr. England said.

"Some resurgence of traditional values," may partly explain the slowed increase in women's employment in the 1990s, she said. But she and others argue that it is also likely that "there is a limit to how much women's employment can continue to increase unless business, the state or men take up the slack," by offering paid parental leave or flexible working times.

Similarly, Dr. Monahan Lang and Dr. Risman concede that many more women than men take time off to take care of their children. But those differences are minor, they say, compared with the large historical leaps in the number of women working.

"I think there is little doubt that men and women have become more similar over time, and that gender expectations are less rigid than they used to be," Dr. Monahan Lang said. "The controversy is really about whether to view these changes as positive or negative."

36

Briefing Paper: Moms and Jobs

Trends in Mothers' Employment and Which Mothers Stay Home

David Cotter, Paula England, and Joan Hermsen

THE FINDINGS IN BRIEF

The employment of wives and mothers rose dramatically from 1960 to about 1990, and thereafter has leveled off. There was a small dip from 2000 to 2004, but employment rates had inched back to 2000 levels by 2006, the latest figures available. Contrary to recent press accounts, there has not been an "opt-out" revolution. Rather than a strong downward trend, there has been a flattening out of the trend line, so that mothers' employment has stabilized, with a majority employed. This strong upward thrust followed by a flattening of the trend holds for most groups of women.

Well-educated women are especially likely to be employed, despite the fact that they generally have well-educated, and thus high-earning, husbands. Surprisingly, the percentage of married moms staying home doesn't go up consistently as husbands' earnings go up. In fact, it is women with the poorest husbands (in the bottom quarter of male earnings) who are most likely to stay home, followed by women with the very richest husbands (those in the top 5 percent of male earners).

WHAT'S THE TREND IN WOMEN'S EMPLOYMENT?

Recent media reports have talked about an "opt-out revolution," reporting on a real but very small downturn in women's employment rates since 2000.[1] These media reports have been misleading in two ways, as Figure 36.1 shows.

- They ignore the dramatic upsurge in mothers' employment in the 1960s, 1970s, and 1980s.

- They focus on a small downturn since 2000, but a fairer characterization of mothers' employment in the years since 1990 is that it has leveled off.

Figure 36.1 shows trends in employment for all women and men aged twenty-five to fifty-four between 1962 and 2006. (All figures in this Briefing Paper refer to whether women were in the labor force (which means employed or actively looking for work) any time in the last year, and refer exclusively to individuals between ages twenty-five and fifty-four. The data come from the U.S. government's Current Population Survey for each year.

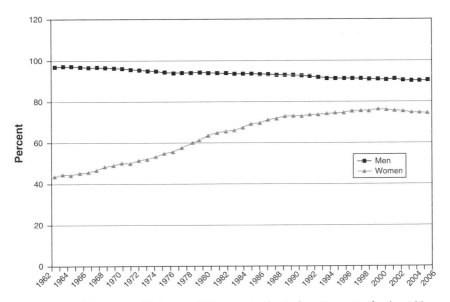

Figure 36.1 | Percent of Men and Women in the Labor Force in the Last Year, 1962-2006 (for Individuals 26-54 Years of Age)

What's the trend for women with children? As shown in Figure 36.2, there is an increase followed by a leveling off in the rate of change—a plateau. Moms with children under age five are most likely to stay home, but they are much less likely to do so than in the past. There was a tiny dip in their employment between 2000 and 2004, but it then inched back up to the 2000 level in 2006 (Figure 36.2).

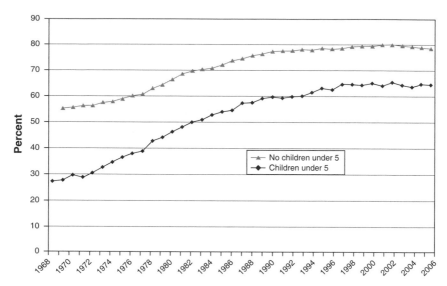

Figure 36.2 | Percent of Mothers in the Labor Force in the Last Year, 1968–2006, by Age of Their Children (for Mothers 25–54 Years of Age)

In 1970, only 30 percent of mothers of children under age five had been employed in the last year. But then huge increases ensued—from 30 percent in 1970 to 46 percent in 1980 and to 60 percent in 1990. The next decade saw just a small increase—from 60 percent in 1990 to 65 percent in 2000, a much slower rate of increase than previously. Moms' participation in paid labor then dropped a bit to 64 percent by 2004, but inched back to 65 percent by 2006. Up or down, the changes since 2000 have been tiny. As with women overall, the big picture is a dramatic increase followed by a leveling off in the rate of change—a plateau.

Moms with no preschoolers are more likely to be working for pay than are those with preschoolers (Figure 36.2). But the workforce participation rates of mothers with older children also leveled off in the late 1990s, after a substantial increase over the last several decades. The percent of these mothers employed was 56 percent in 1970, 67 percent in 1980, and 77 percent in 1990. After these big increases, the rate has hovered right around 79 percent or 80 percent from 2000 to 2006. Again, the picture is of dramatic increase in employment rates to 1990, followed by a leveling off.

This is hardly an "opt-out revolution." Sixty-five percent of mothers with pre-schoolers and 79 percent of mothers with older children were employed at least part of the time in 2006.

Why Did the Trend in Women's Employment Rates Go Up then Level Off?

What caused the big increase in women's employment in the '60s, '70s, and '80s? Many factors contributed. Women began having smaller families. The increase in the proportion of mothers who were single made more women absolutely need a job. The fall in men's real wages since 1980 increased the need for two earners even in married couple families. Probably even more important were increases in women's education, better job opportunities for women, and the "equal opportunity" ideology of the women's movement. All these things increased women's access to interesting and well-paying jobs, raising the cost of having a woman quit work and give up that extra income. All this contributed to the dramatic upsurge in women's employment.[2]

Why did the trend level off? Social scientists really aren't sure. One possibility is that women's employment, which has gotten much closer to men's, can't move all the way to parity with men's unless men take on a more equal share of child rearing, and unless employers or the state adopt policies making it easier for parents to combine work and family. Men have increased the time they spend caring for children and doing housework, but nowhere near enough to offset women's increased employment.[3] And the United States lags way behind other countries in family leave, child-care provision, and other policies that make it easier for people to be parents and workers.[4] Perhaps a cultural backlash to the women's movement is a factor as well.[5]

What does the future hold? We do not know if the trend in moms' employment will turn up again, go down a bit more, or stay stable. It is too early to tell. But it seems extremely unlikely that it will go down signficantly. What is clear is that, as in most affluent nations, women's employment in the Unites States is at high levels, with about 80 percent of all American mothers and 64 percent of women with preschoolers in the workforce in 2006.

Education Encourages Women's Employment

Which moms are working for pay and which are working as full-time homemakers? Moms are much more likely to be working for pay if they have more education. Figure 36.3 shows the labor force participation rates based on level of education for mothers with preschoolers. Figure 36.4 it shows these rates for mothers with only older kids.

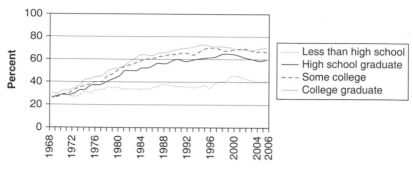

Figure 36.3 | Labor Force Participation Rates for Mothers with Children under Age 5, 1968-2006 (Includes Mothers Age 25-54)

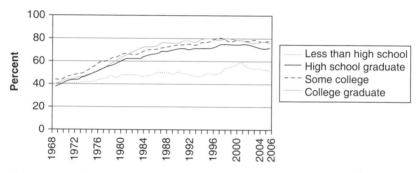

Figure 36.4 | Labor Force Participation Rates for Mothers with No Child under Age 5, 1968-2006 (Includes Mothers Age 25-54)

In 2006, among mothers with no preschoolers at home, Figure 36.4 shows that 77 percent of mothers with a college degree were employed, 71 percent of those who had only finished high school, and 51 percent of those who hadn't finished high school. The percentages are lower for moms with kids under five, but they show an even stronger relationship between education and employment. The employment gap between the most and least educated moms was smaller in the 1970s than it has been since 1980.

Why do more educated moms work for pay at higher rates than less educated moms? In one sense it isn't surprising that well-educated moms are working; after all, many of them got that education to pursue the career they are in. Education improves access to well-paying and interesting jobs that make employment more worthwhile. Women with low education may not be able to make enough to pay for the child care required when they go to work. But what makes the higher employment of well-educated women a challenge to conventional wisdom is that they tend to be married to well-educated and high-earning men.[6]

HUSBANDS' EARNINGS AND MARRIED MOTHERS' EMPLOYMENT

The conventional wisdom is that married women with kids stay home when the family can afford for them to, and work for pay mainly when the family needs the money. If this were the main factor, we'd expect that the higher their husbands' income, the lower women's employment. But Figure 36.5 shows that the conventional wisdom is wrong.

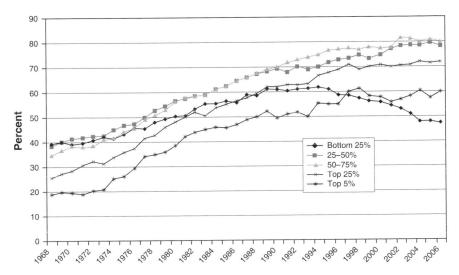

Figure 36.5 | Married Mothers' Labor Force Participation by Husband's Earnings, 1968–2006 (Includes Married Mothers Age 23–54)

As Figure 36.5 shows, the largest group of stay-at-home mothers is found among wives whose husbands are in the *lowest* 25 percent of the male earnings distribution. (Cut-off points for each quartile and the top 5 percent were established separately for each year, using the earnings distribution of married men with children for that year.) The next largest group of stay-at-home mothers is found among women married to men who are in the highest 5 percent of the income distribution. Oddly enough, then, the two groups of married moms with the lowest employment rates are those with both the poorest and the richest husbands!

If we look at what Figure 36.5 shows for the most recent year, 2006, less than half (48 percent) of mothers with husbands in the bottom quarter of the male earnings distribution were employed. Among married moms whose husbands had the very highest 5 percent of earnings, 60 percent were employed. These two groups probably have different reasons for their relatively low employment rates. Moms with the highest-earning husbands have little economic need to be employed. Moms with the poorest husbands have great economic need for a job, but they often have low education and earning potential themselves, so they may not be able to earn enough above child-care costs to make a job pay.

The highest employment rates were among mothers whose husbands had earnings toward the middle of the pack—between the 25th percentile and the 75th percentile. Approximately 80 percent of mothers married to husbands in these groups were employed in 2006.

So contrary to the idea that men's earnings predict whether their wives will stay home, the poorest men are most likely to have stay-at-home wives, the very richest men are the next most likely, and the men earning middle-range earnings are the least likely. These findings complicate our analysis of why families make the decisions they do and what social support systems they need.

APPENDIX

Below are additional figures (Figures 36.6–36.10) showing more detail on which groups of women are in the workforce, and trends in these patterns.

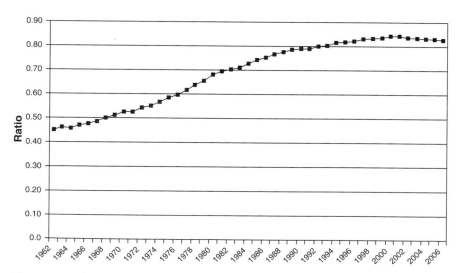

Figure 36.6 | Ratio of Women's to Men's Labor Force Participation in the Last Year, 1962-2006 (Includes Individuals 25-54 Years of Age)

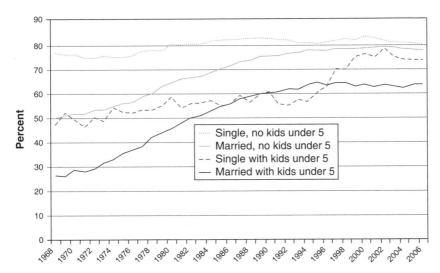

Figure 36.7 | Percent of Mothers in the Labor Force, by Marital Status, 1968-2006 (Includes Mothers 25-54 Years of Age)

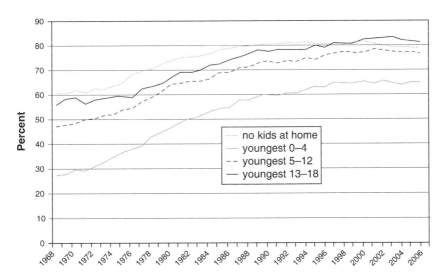

Figure 36.8 | Percent of Women In the Labor Force by Age of Youngest Child, 1968-2006 (Includes Women 25-54 Years of age)

Figure 36.9 | Percent of Women in the Labor Force, by Race/Ethnic Group, 1962–2006 (Includes Women 25–54 Years of Age)

Figure 36.10 | Ratio of Women to Men in the Labor Force by Race/Ethnic Group, 1962–2006 (Includes Individuals 25–54 Years of Age)

In the News

WORKING MOMS MORE THE NORM THAN EXCEPTION

Palo Alto Online, May 14, 2007

Don Kazak

A study by a Stanford University researcher and her colleagues has debunked the belief that mothers with college educations are opting out of working once they begin to raise families.

Instead, those mothers are continuing to work at high numbers.

Well-educated women continue to work even if their husbands have high-paying jobs that could support the family, the study found.

During the last 15 years, the largest group of stay-at-home moms has been those from the poorest families, according to Paula England, professor of sociology. The second-largest group of such moms has been those married to men in the top 5 percent income distribution.

For other mothers, working has been the norm. In 2006, 65 percent of mothers with preschool children worked at least part time and 79 percent of mothers with school-aged children worked.

Those numbers increased greatly since 1970, when only 30 percent of mothers of preschool children worked and only 56 percent of mothers with school-aged children worked.

"This is hardly an opt-out revolution" of mothers deciding to stay home once they have children, England said.

England conducted her research with David Cotter, a sociologist at Union College in Schenectady, N.Y., and Joan Hermsen, a sociologist at the University of Missouri-Columbia.

37

Briefing Paper: Women's Money Matters

Earnings and Housework in Dual-Earner Families

Sanjiv Gupta

Many researchers have found that women who contribute earnings to the family have more bargaining power in marriage than women who do not earn wages. And contrary to claims of a "stalled revolution" in gender roles, husbands have significantly increased their participation in household chores and child care over the past thirty years. The proportion of couples who divide housework equally, though still small, seems to be growing. But how far have we proceeded toward real equality? Are men and women willing to accept a relationship where the wife contributes as much or more of the household income as her husband, or does that threaten their traditional notions of masculine and feminine identity? And do husbands feel equally responsible with their wives for making sure the household work gets done?

In the past, researchers have noted that although employed wives do less housework than full-time housewives, a peculiar counter-tendency kicks in as wives approach equality in earning with their husbands or actually earn more. On average, in households where women earn as much as or more than their husbands, they actually do *more* housework, or their husbands do less. This has been interpreted as reflecting the continuing attachment of men and women to traditional gender identities. Women are seen as engaging in "gender display"— trying to demonstrate that despite their atypical earnings outside the home they are not in violation of traditional gender roles inside the home. Men are seen as engaging in "compensatory" behavior. In refusing to do housework, they are shoring up their masculine identity at home to compensate for their failure to be the main breadwinner. The implication is that when women improve their relative wages in comparison to their husbands, they may find themselves paying for that violation of gender roles by an increase in their share of housework—a discouraging prospect for women who aspire to careers.

I have found that these earlier studies, which suggest that men and women are strongly attached to preserving traditional gender roles, were based on the mistaken assumption that the factor most strongly affecting women's housework was how much money a wife earns compared to her husband. Instead, I find, it is the absolute amount of a woman's own earnings that best predicts the time she will spend on housework. The more she earns, the less time she spends on routine housework. It does not matter how much money she makes compared to her husband, or what her husband earns.

Focusing on the ratio of wives' to husbands' earnings distorts our understanding of household dynamics because, on average, the married women most likely to have high earnings compared to their husbands are married to low-earning men and are themselves relatively low earners. So if it is their low earnings that account for their inability to shed housework, rather than their relative earnings, this means that the discouraging findings of earlier research do not necessarily apply to higher-earning couples where the wife makes as much as or more than the husband.

Among married women working full time around the year, every additional $7,500 in their earnings corresponds to one less hour spent on routine chores per week, controlling for other relevant factors. Women with the highest 10 percent of earnings spent 9 fewer hours on housework per week, on average, than the women with the lowest 10 percent of earnings. That is equivalent to one and a quarter fewer hours per day. In a multivariate model controlling for other relevant differences among women, this economic gap in their housework works out to about 30 minutes per day. The difference is directly a result of the woman's own earnings, not how much she makes relative to her husband. (A similar pattern is observed when cohabiting heterosexual women are included in the calculations.)

The median annual labor market earnings of women in the United States rose from about $9,800 in 1965 to more than $16,000 in 1995 (U.S. Bureau of the Census, 1998). Over the same period, married women's time spent weekly on routine chores declined from 30.4 to 15.8 hours (Bianchi et al., 2000). The findings reported here suggest a link between these trends.

My findings highlight the importance of class differences among women in their performance of housework. Not only do women with higher earnings do less housework than women with low earnings, but the gap between how much housework high-earning women do and how much their husbands do is much narrower. Women with the lowest earnings do nearly 16 hours more housework each week than their husbands, whereas the gender gap in housework for women with the highest earnings is less than 5 hours per week. This difference is due almost entirely to the difference in time spent doing housework by women with the lowest earnings compared with women with the highest earnings, not to any substantial difference in the time spent on housework by their husbands.

The good news here is that neither men nor women are so committed to "traditional" gender roles that they feel a need to "compensate" by engaging in gender-stereotyped housework behavior if the husband and wife have nontraditional occupational or income profiles. It appears that married working women are exercising their economic autonomy to reduce the burden of the well-known "gender gap" in the performance of housework. This implies a greater degree of agency and flexibility in women's housework behavior than much earlier research generally supposed. Much of the research to date has focused on the inequity and intractability of the division of housework in heterosexual households. The new study implies that women can use their own money to make the division somewhat more balanced.

The bad news is that these findings emphasize the continued gender segregation of unpaid household labor. Not only do women spend more time on everyday housework than do their husbands, they also appear to draw only upon their own earnings to cut down on it, not their husbands'. Married women do not appear to benefit greatly from their husbands' earnings when it comes to housework. In a multivariate model that includes both their earnings and their husbands', only their own earnings have a significant relationship to their time spent doing housework. This is surprising given that the daily work of providing nutrition, clean clothing, and a sanitary environment benefits everyone in a household. It suggests that both men and women still tend to feel that it is the woman's responsibility to organize such chores, though she may use her own money to farm them out. Thus, despite profound changes in the nature of marriage over the past thirty years, the study calls into question the idea that marriage is as yet an arrangement in which spouses share their resources for the maximum benefit of each partner or the household as a whole.

The data for this study come from the second wave of the National Survey of Families and Households (NSFH), conducted in the period 1992–1994. The final analytic sample consists of 914 married women between the ages of eighteen and sixty-five and working full time, year-round.

In the News

WEALTHIER WOMEN DO LESS HOUSEWORK

Daily Collegian, November 20, 2007

Stella Cernak

As the figures on a woman's paycheck climb, the time she spends doing housework dwindles, according to a study conducted by University of Massachusetts associate professor of sociology Sanjiv Gupta.

Gupta's study emphasizes that the amount of housework that women with full-time jobs do in a family where both husband and wife are working is unaffected by her spouse's income. He points out that focusing on the ratio of earnings between husbands and wives acts as a roadblock to understanding household dynamics.

"Up to this point, people have thought that the important thing was how much money a woman makes compared to her husband. But the only thing that matters is how much money she earns," said Gupta in a Reuters interview.

Gupta's studies are based on information obtained from 918 women and data on double-income families in the United States in 1992 through 1994, and in 2000. His research reveals that for every $7,500 a woman earns annually, she performed one less hour of housework per week. Women making $10,000 or less per year spend nearly one hour more on housework each day than women making $40,000 or more, according to the National Survey of Families and Households.

His study also recognizes that the median annual labor market earnings of U.S. women rose from about $9,800 in 1965 to more than $16,000 in 1995, according to the U.S. Bureau of the Census. At the same time, the hours married women spent on weekly routine chores plummeted from 30.4 to 15.8.

Gupta's findings, recently published in the *Journal of Marriage and Family*, suggest that women can use their income to make the time they spend on household duties more balanced with their spouse.

However, the article also points out that equality still does not exist when dividing household duties between husbands and wives. Other researchers in the *Journal* support this claim, linking the reason for this gap in equality to slowly fading stereotypes and gender roles people learn at a young age.

For instance, in one study from 2005, it is pointed out that if a woman's mother took on the majority of domestic work, she will likely feel the need to take on a similar role in her marriage.

This study also suggests that men take on less domestic work to pick up the slack for their working wives than women do in a similar situation. Husbands increase their domestic work by around 2 hours per week when wives enter full-time jobs, while wives reduce their domestic work by four to eight hours per week. Husbands eventually do increase their domestic work over time, but this change is inconsistent. These gaps are believed to often lead to spousal conflict.

Gupta's article does not focus much on spousal differences in domestic work but instead concentrates on the differences between women and housework, particularly women with different incomes. He points out that the difference in time spent on domestic work between women making more money ($40,000 or greater) with women making the least amount of money ($10,000 or less) is just as great as the average difference in time spent doing housework between men and women.

"In general, especially among women who have more egalitarian-type ideas, the more equitable division of labor gives a better outcome of equality and satisfaction," said Gupta. "It's not that straightforward and there is no bottom line. Someone who does more housework isn't necessarily less happy than someone who does less housework." ▄

38

Briefing Paper: "Traditional" Marriages Now
Less Stable Than Ones Where Couples
Share Work and Household Chores

Lynn Prince Cooke

et's face it: The road to happily-ever-after is pitted with potholes. Children,
finances, and in-laws can all put stress on a marriage. But what about who
cleans the floor? This matters, too. A survey released this week by the Pew Research Center shows that most Americans now regard sharing household chores
as more vital to a good marriage than such traditional measures of marital success as having children. This does not mean couples are neglecting their kids.
Indeed, both moms and dads are now spending more time with their children
than in 1965, the heyday of the female homemaker.

But just having kids is no longer sufficient for a marriage to last. As detailed
in one study recently published in the *American Journal of Sociology*, and in
my ongoing research about the relationship between housework and divorce, I
find American couples that share employment and housework are less likely to
divorce than couples where the husband does all the earning while the wife does
all the cleaning. These findings starkly contrast with the claims of some that to
turn back high rates of divorce, we should return to the male breadwinner family
idealized during the 1950s and '60s in such television programs as *Father Knows
Best* and *Leave It to Beaver.*

One reason some people urge a return to male breadwinner marriages is that
wives' employment is associated with greater risk of divorce. Among U.S. couples,
however, I find this increase in divorce risk when the wife is employed is more
than offset when a husband takes on an equitable share of the housework. So it

is not women's employment that directly leads to divorce, but only the strain of her employment when she must still perform the housework alone as well. Using data from the Panel Study of Income Dynamics to follow couples marrying for the first time between 1985 and 1995, I found that couples where the wife earns about 40 percent of the income while the husband does about 40 percent of the housework have the lowest risk of divorce—considerably lower than the divorce risk in families where the husband earns all of the income and the wife does all of the housework. We have not yet realized perfect equality, however. The divorce risk begins to rise again when a wife starts earning as much as or more than her husband and he does more of the housework. But this risk does not exceed that of male breadwinner marriages until the woman earns more than 80 percent of the couple's income. This means neither "Mr. Mom" nor "Father Knows Best" is a stable family scenario for American couples today.

Surprisingly, although either extreme is rare, "Mr. Mom" is more common now than "Father Knows Best." Less than 1 percent of the couples I studied reported the husband earns all of the money while the wife does all of the housework. In contrast, almost 3 percent of couples claimed that the husband does all the housework while the wife earns all the money. The vast majority of couples share responsibility for the family's financial security as well as the household maintenance. Indeed, a research paper issued this May by the Council on Contemporary Families reveals that each generation of men is doing more domestic work and child care than the previous one. So couples appear to understand what many pundits do not. In today's world, it is give-and-take that makes marriage work. Returning to the days when marital tasks were divided and gendered would do the opposite of what proponents of "traditional" marriage believe; it would ring the death knell for modern American marriages.

In the News

MATRIMONIAL BLISS LIES IN THE MOP BUCKET AND BROOM

Seattle P-I, July 10, 2007

Paul Nyhan

The secret to a happy marriage isn't love, honor and respect; it's mop, vacuum and scrub, according to the Council on Contemporary Families.

It turns out parents who share the housework burden are less likely to divorce than parents who cede all the earning power to dad and all the cleaning power to mom, council research associate Lynn Prince Cooke wrote last week.

"Returning to the days when marital tasks were divided and gendered would do the opposite of what proponents of 'traditional' marriage believe; it would ring the death knell for modern American marriages," Cooke, a United Kingdom-based sociologist, wrote in a research brief.

In fact, young adults said dividing household chores was more important for a successful marriage than having kids, sharing religious beliefs or making enough money in a July 1 Pew Research Center survey cited by Cooke.

While the divorce rate rises when Mom works in the United States, the risk "is more than offset" when Dad does his fair share of cleaning and scrubbing around the house, wrote Cooke, who teaches at the University of Kent in Canterbury, England.

When Mom earns as much or more than Dad, and he does more of the housework, the divorce rate rises again.

"But this risk does not exceed that of male breadwinner marriages until the woman earns more than 80 percent of the couple's income," Cooke wrote in a research brief.

Cooke even suggests the ideal marriage:

"I found that couples where the wife earns about 40 percent of the income while the husband does about 40 percent of the housework have the lowest risk of divorce," she said.

"This means neither 'Mr. Mom' nor 'Father Knows Best' is a stable family scenario for the American couple today," Cooke wrote.

(Uh oh, what about the flip side, speaking hypothetically of course, when Mom earns 60 percent, or maybe more . . . ?)

Of course, Mom and Dad have to agree on what constitutes housework. I still don't get dusting, and I refuse to make the bed because we're just going to mess it up 15 hours later.

Cooke also offered further proof that family roles are blurring and evolving. She found less than 1 percent of couples where Hubby brought home all of the money and Mommy did all of the housework. Yet in her research 3 percent of couples were defined by a woman making all of the money and a man taking care of all the household chores. ▬

39

Domestic Violence in Heterosexual Relationships

Rhea V. Almeida

Domestic violence is perhaps one of the most studied fields, and yet its study remains controversial in terms of scholarship, protection for victims, and accountability for perpetrators. This chapter addresses the historic polarization of policy and practice for victims and perpetrators, and it presents a new paradigm for helping families to heal. Steeped in principles of social justice, the author describes her model, the Cultural Context Model, which addresses the complexity of this twenty-first century social dilemma, offering challenging notions of change to entire families and communities.

Imagine being a poverty-stricken, battered women working with a mistrained therapist who expects that positive change will come simply from engaging in conversation. The battered woman knows that these conversations will not change her life because they do not include any consequences or incentives for her batterer to change.

This chapter presents information about domestic violence, and it offers a new and cutting-edge clinical approach, grounded in feminist social-justice theory, to help families in which domestic violence has occurred become healthy and functioning.

The chapter begins by defining domestic violence. It then situates the context of domestic violence in American families today within gendered norms that support male domination. The main body of this chapter is the presentation of a model I have developed for working with couples in which domestic violence occurs.

Definition of Domestic Violence

The National Coalition Against Domestic Violence defines domestic violence as the "willful intimidation, assault, battery, sexual assault, or other abusive behavior perpetrated by an intimate partner against another." We expand this definition to include "the patterned and repeated use of coercive and controlling behavior to limit, direct, and shape a partner's thoughts, feelings, and actions."[1]

Tactics of domestic violence include

- physical abuse,
- emotional abuse,
- economic abuse,
- threats and intimidation,
- isolation and entrapment (including job relocation and language barriers),
- sexual abuse and exploitation, and
- control and abuse of children.

Factors on a broader societal level may shape violence at home, as seen by the fact that economically compromised families are at greater risk for domestic violence, as are undocumented immigrant women due to the threat of deportation. We use the pronoun "he" when referring to batterers because the majority of heterosexual violence is perpetrated by men against women.

Domestic violence continues to be a crushing problem for families, although over the past decade things have gotten considerably better. The Bureau of Justice Statistics reports that rates of family violence in this country have dropped by more than half since 1993.[2] Much of this decline is due to the efforts of people quietly working in the field, including social workers, staff at women's crisis centers, police forces, and prosecutors. The passage of the Violence Against Women Act in 1994, and amendments to it in 1998 and 2006, also played a part. But all of these efforts are part of a larger story. A web of positive, mutually reinforcing social trends has led to this decline in family violence.

In a compelling article, Deborah Weissman lays out the relationship between the economic system and domestic violence.[3] The movement against domestic violence, grounded in the U.S. civil rights movement, began as a struggle for the rights of women as victims. Unfortunately it has evolved into a movement whose main strategies are tied to the law enforcement system, which is avoided by many who need help. Weissman concedes that the legal approach has some merit, but that by its very nature the legal system is individualistic and downplays the social and historical context for patterns of behavior and ignores the role of economics, globalization, and the numerous victims of domestic violence who cannot or will not participate in the criminal justice system. That is why we need a paradigm shift in how we approach all the factors contributing to domestic violence in the twenty-first century.

The boundary that separates families from the larger world is bigger in our imaginations than in reality. In the real world, human beings live, learn, and change communally. We learn to understand ourselves and relate to others through experiences within our homes, schools, neighborhoods, workplaces, communities of faith, and organizations. Our perspectives are built from what we see on television, hear on the radio, read, and absorb from authority figures like child-care providers, teachers, employers, and community leaders. Families, communities, and the societies we live in recreate one another in an endless cycle.

In creating a different paradigm, my intention was to provide social workers, family therapists, counseling psychologists, students, and practitioners with a way to inject social-justice values into everyday clinical practice. This model for social-justice practice, which I call the Cultural Context Model, places the connection between family and society at the center of therapeutic thinking and intervention strategies. All too often, the world in which families have to function encourages values and actions that undermine health and sanity.

Because there is a dynamic interplay between families and the broader context in which they function, professional helpers have to expand their focus to look beyond the individual and beyond relationships forged by blood and household connections. Practitioners in the twenty-first century need to help clients construct couple partnerships and families governed by just values. But they must also help to build communities that sustain these values.

Although most family therapists, and therapists in general, often claim to apply a systemic perspective, the patriarchal ordering of the world keeps them from utilizing the work of sociopolitical theorists.[4] The concept of intersectionality, the idea that personal and political identities are shaped by broader societal forces, is rarely considered in the therapeutic context. This results in a one-dimensional method that focuses solely on the abuse and ignores all the aspects of one's resilience that are key to healing.

GENDER LAYS THE FOUNDATION FOR DOMESTIC VIOLENCE

Domestic violence can be described as gender norms taken to their extreme. The patriarchal definition of family as a private domain governed by men has long perpetuated unequal power relationships between the genders, as well as a separation between community and home life.[5] Accordingly, most societies have tolerated husbands' oppression of their wives as a normal pattern. "What goes on behind closed doors is private" and "a man's home is his castle." Less than 100 years ago, a man would be criminally prosecuted for beating a stranger, but he could legally beat his wife.[6]

While violence occurs at all stages of the life cycle, the most vulnerable are teens, pregnant women, and the elderly. I recommend using the teenage wheel at the end of this chapter to assess for levels of violence among teens.

The intersection of gender, race, and class conspire to silence victims so that many crimes committed within the home evade public scrutiny. Men of all colors still hold power over women and children when there is no community oversight. But because racism disproportionately relegates people of color to the lower socioeconomic strata, and because masculinity is often defined in terms of a man's earning power, men of color and men of lower socioeconomic classes disproportionately suffer in their self-definition as adequate males.[7] When men in economically depressed communities feel severely challenged about their masculinity, this places women and children at higher risk of abuse.[8]

Historically, in most cultures men have promoted group solidarity by devaluing women. "Being men" involves verbally objectifying or degrading women (e.g., pornography), bragging about sexual exploits, and defining "feminine" characteristics as antithetical to being male.[9] Devaluing women sometimes escalates into activities such as gang rape ("wilding," and men on the "down low"), or men/boys going to brothels together. These acts join sexuality and violence with domination of females.

While this article focuses on heterosexual violence, gay, lesbian, bisexual, and transsexual (GLBT) violence can rise to the same level, which ultimately raises many questions about the binary definitions of gender that elude the main discourse on intimate violence.

WOMEN AS CULTURAL PURVEYORS OF PATRIARCHY

Women uphold patriarchal practices and structures in many ways. A white mother from a fundamentalist church might justify violence toward her children, arguing that it is done calmly and teaches respect. An Asian Indian woman might argue that in her culture it is important to support the dowry system, keep her daughter-in-law in check, ignore a father-in-law's sexual harassment of his daughter-in-law, and accept a son's violence toward his wife.[10] Practices such as dowries, foot-binding, genital mutilation, and Western medicalization of women's bodies are all examples of patriarchal practices that women accept and pass on as part of the "culture."

The acceptance of abusive mothers-in-law and women who physically discipline their children also needs to be challenged.[11]

OVERVIEW OF THE CULTURAL CONTEXT MODEL

Feminist scholarship greatly advanced the therapeutic field by opening pathways to address inequities linked to sexism. But the inequities of racism, homophobia, and culture were left out of the discourse. Most practice methods do not address how power, privilege,[12] and oppression interconnect and intersect. What was missing was a social-justice approach that would weave all these threads into therapeutic practice.

The model I describe transforms therapeutic convention to include the pursuit of justice at every level, using the following tools and techniques:

- Initiating clients' critical awareness of diversity and power.
- Emphasizing how "normal" hierarchies of power, privilege, and oppression perpetuate suffering.
- Experientially demonstrating the link between fairness and relational healing.
- Expanding the therapeutic encounter to include a community with critical consciousness rather than focusing just on one family at a time.
- Defining *empowerment* in collective rather than individual terms.
- Encouraging social action as a means for empowering communities, families, and self.
- Providing *accountability* for all participants, including therapists.
- Creating a basis for developing authentic relationships and diverse communities.
- Helping people think about ways to connect past, present, and future legacies within the matrix of critical consciousness, empowerment, and accountability. (At the end of this chapter we provide tools that offer language and structure to bring these ideas into therapeutic practice).
- Applying these tools and techniques—which boil down to critical consciousness, empowerment, and accountability—are crucial in any social-justice approach and lead to a radically different kind of practice.

CRITICAL CONSCIOUSNESS

The first element of this approach is "critical consciousness," which refers to awareness of the political and economic foundations that underlie relationship patterns. The Cultural Context Model (CCM) works to develop critical consciousness as a catalyst and a map for positive change. To develop critical consciousness among clients and staff, we employ social education through the use of film, dialogue, and inquiry.[13]

The groundbreaking Brazilian educator Paulo Freire originated the term "critical consciousness" to describe how his literacy students came to understand the impact of social class dynamics on their own life circumstances.[14] As we develop critical consciousness, we stop accepting current reality as "the unquestioned and unchangeable nature of things." Instead, we see options for change. For example, those who view men as genetically programmed for aggression also accept war and domestic violence as the natural order of things. But those who view men's aggression as a learned tactic of domination see possibilities for peace on all societal levels.

EMPOWERMENT

Liberation theorists and feminists assert that the personal is political. Social injustices—poverty, racism, colonialism, sexism, homophobia, discrimination against the physically disabled—permeate personal lives. Unless we break down the broader social dimensions in the course of the therapeutic process, we become complicit with practices of domination.

Social-justice-based empowerment promotes "power with" rather than "power over." An Asian Indian woman would be encouraged to pursue an education not solely to be marketable as a bride, but to fulfill a lifelong dream while also contributing financially to her family. An orthodox Jewish man would gain empowerment by acknowledging that he has harmed his family through violence, that he accepts responsibility for his acts, and that he will make things right for them. He, and those on the receiving end of his previous violence, are empowered through this action to bring justice to the situation.

ACCOUNTABILITY

Accountability begins with accepting responsibility for one's actions and for the impact those actions have on others. But real accountability goes beyond blame and guilt. It requires action that makes amends for the wrongs done and demonstrates empathic concern for others by making changes that enhance the quality of life for all involved parties.

Conventional practice calls for perpetrators of domestic violence to attend a fifty-two-week social education program in a group setting. Most of the curriculum focuses on power and control along gender lines. There is no examination of family legacies or community relationships that might illuminate areas for future focus. Most importantly, the criminal justice system—rather than other informal systems of influence—exacts retribution and determines the punishment.

But with the Critical Consciousness Movement, accountability comes about with the help of sponsors and others in the therapeutic community. Sponsors are men and women who have themselves taken part in this therapeutic endeavor and who then link up with new clients to raise critical consciousness, support empowerment, and ensure accountability.[15]

At the end of the process, an abuser writes a document that acknowledges the details of the harm caused to the victim, and outlines reparations that offer some element of justice.

CULTURE CIRCLES

Culture circles, another term borrowed from Freire, are heterogeneous helping communities that are made up of members of families seeking treatment, helpers from the community who volunteer to work with the families, and a team of therapists. In Freire's view, collective discussions within culture circles prompt critical reflection and dialogue about the life circumstances of the participants. Freire believed that individuals could develop a "critical consciousness of their own being in the world" through reflective dialogue combined with social action.

In the Cultural Context Model, culture circles promote healing by developing critical consciousness and resistance to societal norms that maintain hierarchies of power, privilege, and oppression. During culture circle sessions, victims talk about and read from documents that describe the harm they have experienced. Community members and sponsors are present on a regular basis and encourage the victims to give voice to their experiences while embracing their new or recovered goals. The perpetrators of violence also speak and read their own testimonies about the harm they brought to their loved ones. Many months are spent on these letters/documents, during which time ideas for making reparation are forged.

Employing a Social-Justice Model to Domestic Violence Intervention

A social-justice model examines all the problems that compromise the safety and health of families and communities (including domestic violence), from a perspective that takes power, privilege, and oppression into account. A social-justice perspective transforms the assessment questions that guide intervention. It takes a question like "what kind of individual pathologies cause abuse to occur?," and reframes it by asking "how do those who exert power and privilege over others abuse that power and privilege?"

The mainstream domestic violence movement has made enormous gains in legally securing protection for battered women and changing the social climate in favor of rights for battered women. Most states now mandate that perpetrators of domestic violence go through treatment programs, and there are certified specialists who offer these services in partnership with battered women's organizations. But victims and perpetrators from socially marginalized communities, as well as undocumented immigrants and those who do not hold green cards, are more likely to avoid the criminal justice system. While it is true that many women of color and immigrant women are served by this system, many more are not.[16]

The social-justice perspective, working outside the criminal justice system, approaches batterer intervention from a different trajectory. Men who have used violence and are court-mandated to seek treatment are not separated from other men seeking services. Court-mandated people and people who voluntarily seek treatment have much to learn from one another. In the course of therapy, men who have used violence may develop friendships with men who do not support abusiveness. They often get better at parenting their children, negotiating school and medical systems, evaluating the way they manage finances (including the support of dependents), examining their understanding of love, and focusing on the value of housework and other after-work activities. Just as importantly, they learn to expand their range of emotional expressiveness.[17]

When men who have not used violence against their intimates find themselves next to men who have, it is easier for them to confront similarities in their own thinking, as well as the choices they have made regarding violence. Sponsors have an enormously powerful role in probing what makes for masculinity, and sorting out choices that lead to domination versus those that create equity in relationships.

When men who have not committed acts of physical violence discuss their patterns with men who have taken control to the extreme, they find it easier to see where their own actions lie along the continuum of power and control (see the power and control wheels at the end of this chapter). Violence is no longer an abstraction involving "others," but is a reality demonstrated by the actions of real men, sitting in the very same room, men who seem unremarkable, approachable, and undeniably human.

Couples on society's margins face additional burdens that affect women as victims and men as perpetrators:

1. **Economic:** Men and women of color are often relegated to low-paying positions offering few benefits and limited upward mobility. They are frequently the last to be hired and the first to be fired. As a result, men and women of color are less likely to speak out in support of fair labor practices for fear of losing their jobs or jeopardizing their chances for promotion. Immigrants are especially vulnerable.

2. **Sexual:** Historically, women and men of color have been objectified sexually. Men have been portrayed as animals possessing mythical and "nonhuman" sexual prowess. Women have been portrayed as "exotic" and sexually insatiable. Both stereotypes are exploited and objectified in pornography.

3. **Perceptions of Family:** Children of color are more readily perceived as delinquent and are devalued on the basis of their appearance or speech patterns. They are overrepresented in detention and other disciplinary situations, and in child abuse investigations.

4. **Physical and Psychological:** A man of color is far more likely to experience instances of police brutality and harassment. Men of color are more likely to be singled out for investigation at police road checks. Latino men are stopped as often as African-American men, and since September 11, 2001, men perceived as Arab or South Asian have also been racially targeted.

5. **Emotional Isolation:** The homes and family lives of women and men of color are frequently subject to intrusions by police, welfare workers, school personnel, and other public institutions. The dearth of positive role models and the negative representations of persons of color in the media all serve to reinforce the notion that white culture is the ideal to which other cultures must aspire.

All of these factors intensify violence in the home and should be examined and confronted. Accountability, however, must not romanticize these hardships. The goal must be to establish safety and caring in intimate life.

Thoughts for the Future of Therapy in Regard to Domestic Violence

The field of mental health is often compartmentalized, with the result that individuals, families, and communities are defined and organized along the lines of their presenting problems. Public awareness of domestic violence has focused on women as victims being battered by men, with the goal being to stress equity and nonviolence. But if the focus of responsibility were placed on men talking to men about the moral compass of domestic violence, the public narrative would be very different.

When we bring men who have engaged in domestic violence into contact with others who are seeking help, we begin to redraw the lines of a therapeutic community. The CCM model has done just that in those few centers around the country that have adopted this perspective,

Therapists and mental health providers from all areas of training routinely miss cases of domestic violence. Referring to the power and control wheels that appear at the end of this chapter can help in this regard. For example, when we use the control wheel, we might say to the individual: "Misuse of power within relationships takes many different forms. I'm going to ask you to take a look, one at a time, at the description in each section of the pie in this power and control wheel. Let me know if you (or your partner) have done or experienced any of the things mentioned, or anything similar to what's mentioned."

Many of the gendered descriptions in these categories apply to most couples, while the ones that manifest extreme coercion and violence are associated with those who have histories of domestic violence.

We still live in a patriarchal system that accepts rather than challenges traditional male roles that reinforce the misuse of power and privilege. But when a therapeutic context posits that perpetrators of violence and those who misuse power and privilege can and must change their behavior, the result is a paradigm of change.

Appendix: Goals of Assessment and Tools for Dismantling Violence

When violence is described, we thoroughly assess for danger and lethality using the following checklist:

- Determine the nature, frequency, severity, and consequences of aggression.
- Obtain a detailed behavioral description of the sequence of events in context.

- Understand the intended function of the violence and its impact.
- Evaluate the degree of fear and intimidation.
- Expand your inquiry to explore broader patterns of control and domination.
- Ensure that confidentiality is managed to prioritize safety. (Information will not be shared with the perpetrator unless the victim consents while in a safe context.)

WHEELS FOR ASSESSING MISUSE AND ABUSE OF POWER IN MULTIPLE CONTEXTS

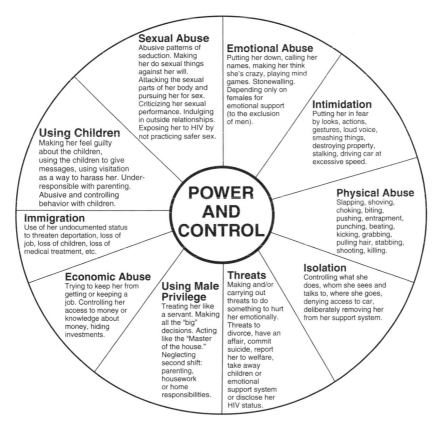

Figure 39.1 | Private Context: The Misuse and Abuse of Power within Heterosexual Relationships

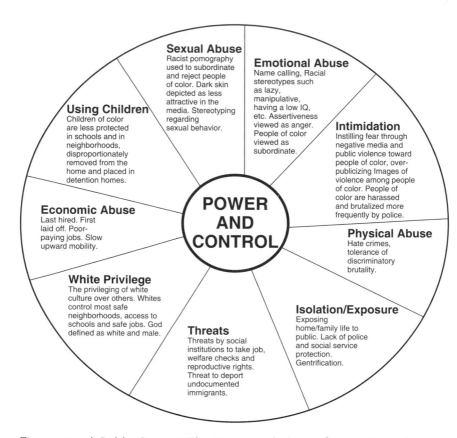

Figure 39.2 | Public Context: The Misuse and Abuse of Power Toward People of Color

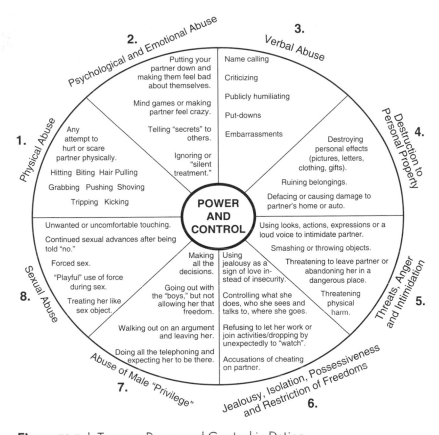

Figure 39.3 | Teenage Power and Control in Dating
How do I love thee, Let me count the ways . . .

For Review

1. Risman and Seale discuss the ways in which tween-age boys use sexual identity to police one another's masculinity. How do you think this influences the ways young men approach hooking up as described by Armstrong, England, and Fogarty? Are there elements of the "ideal girlhood package" that have developed in adulthood in the young women Armstrong, England, and Fogarty discuss?

2. There are several articles and Briefing Papers about equality in contemporary marriage. In reading Cooke, Sullivan, Lang and Risman, and Gupta, how do you see marriage "equality" being defined? What is the evidence for the argument that equality is increasingly being achieved within modern marriages? What counter-evidence can you find? Which arguments do you find most persuasive and why?

3. How might you use Almeida's "critical consciousness" to think about the ways in which the women and men Gerson studied developed their life plans? What suggestions do you think Almeida would make to couples trying to balance both paid work and caretaking responsibilities?

4. The articles in this section focus on different stages of the life cycle—from young adults to married couples. When you look at the unfinished gender revolution over the life cycle, do you see any patterns? Are there stages of life, at this historical moment, that are more or less equal for boys and girls, men and women? Do the data on young people suggest increased gender convergence in the future? Why or why not?

5. Activity: Interview one or two older friends or relatives about how their expectations and strategies for managing family responsibilities and paid employment have changed over time. How have the expectations they had as young adults changed (or not) with life circumstances? Are there differences by sex? Do you foresee similar changes in your own future? What strategies do you use, or plan to use, to manage family responsibilities and paid employment?

6. Activity: Risman and Seale find that being athletic and participating in sports are considered normative by middle-school girls. Yet, middle-school girls are expected to "do gender" largely in terms of physical appearance and bodily presentation. Do you think these findings hold for college-aged students as well? Check out your school's websites for both women's and men's sports (or the websites of a school that has varsity athletics). Describe how you see male and female athletes being portrayed, either similarly or differently. What types of messages about gender do you see? What do you think accounts for any differences you see? Try looking at the websites of schools that differ from your own along several dimensions (size, division, geographic location) to see if you see the same patterns across schools.

Conclusion

40

Families: A Great American Institution

Barbara J. Risman

Perhaps the greatest problem in American politics today is that so many people in Washington tend to think in two- and four-year cycles. We don't think long term, yet children are a long-term proposition.

—Howard Dean[1]

From the inside, no family ever seems typical.

—Sarah Palin[2]

I'll be a president that stands up for American families—all of them.

—President Barack Obama[3]

You don't ask for much. You never give up. You soldier on for your families and your communities.

—Hillary Clinton[4]

I think we all in America understand today that families have challenges and I know there's further challenges for my family, but I thank God every day for them.

—John McCain[5]

The American dream must never come at the expense of the American family.
For decades we've had politicians in Washington who talk about family values,
but we haven't had policies that value families.

—President Barack Obama[6]

From progressives to conservatives, American politicians universally proclaim "family" to be the cornerstone of American society. The diversity of families as they really are has some Americans worried that the increase in cohabitation, the frequency of divorce, and the proportion of children living outside of two-parent households means the family is being undermined, and failing us. Focus on the Family founder James Dobson, a minister, wrote in an edition of his group's newsletter, "the family as it has been known for more than five millennia will crumble, presaging the fall of Western civilization itself."[7] The government itself has acted as if it fears for the future of the American family. A key component of President Clinton's reform of welfare was an attempt to strengthen two-parent families. And President Bush's Healthy Marriage Initiative, run by the Department of Health and Human Services, spent $100 million annually, much of it to help couples learn relationship skills. Clearly, both clergy and the government sometimes worry that the family is breaking down.

Nearly all Americans seem to agree on the importance of a strong family. And yet, as we have seen, there is tremendous diversity in what people define as family and in what they see as the strengths and weaknesses of families. One reason that these debates matter is that, for all its diverse forms, a family is not just an individual choice. It is also a social institution. Sociologists identify twelve features that characterize a social institution, and I will conclude this book by showing how many of the articles in this anthology illustrate those features. I believe that the analysis below provides clear evidence that the family is as strong an institution now as it has ever been.

1. *Institutions are profoundly social.* No social institution can exist unless it includes a group of people who interact with one another often and fulfill social roles that obligate them to behave in certain ways. Families are groups composed of people who take on social roles that come in sets, with obligations that are expected between people based on their positions as parents and children, husbands and wives, in-laws—or even as former partners. Although adults choose which families to join, once they are part of a family, they assume kin connections that take on an existence of their own. Even if a couple divorces after they marry, the former partners always remain "an ex"

to each other, for better or for worse. We know that when divorced parents continue to argue or denigrate each other, children suffer. But divorced and blended families can also use their ties to construct new forms of social support, as when former in-laws or new stepparents provide resources or mentoring for children. Research on post-modern families suggests that the relationships between mothers and daughters-in law often survive even after a divorce, so that a previous mother-in-law might be a regular member of Thanksgiving celebrations every fall.[8] Adult siblings often keep in contact, and help one another out, whether or not they like each other well enough to be friends beyond their family ties. The articles by Robert-Jay Green and Karen Struening show us that one reason many same-sex partners want the chance to marry is that they desire to be part of a social institution that identifies their social role as spouse, creates public marital obligations to one another, and facilitates wider social bonds by bringing their families of origin into interaction as in-laws.

2. *Institutions endure across time and space.* We can identify groups of people that have social role obligations to one another and are defined as family in every culture, and over history. The articles by both Coontz and Mintz show that although families have changed over time, every society and subgroup within society have used their family ties to transmit values, behaviors, and obligations across generations and to maintain social ties across geographic boundaries. Coleman shows us that the norms around parenting continue long past children's coming of age.

3. *Institutions entail distinct social practices that recur.* Families throughout history have been a source of emotional support and intimacy. In some cultural systems, such support and intimacy are sought primarily from relatives of the same sex, such as sisters and mothers, or brothers and fathers. In the United States today, however, we expect the marital relationship to be the main source of support. The research by Gerstel and Sarkisian shows us that spouses today depend on one another nearly exclusively for their emotional support. Coontz argues that this over-reliance on spouses may end up being a burden too heavy for the institution of marriage to bear. Reproduction and the socialization of youth are also recurring social practices in families. Lareau shows us how the distinctive parenting practices of people with different class and educational resources help reproduce class advantages and disadvantages over time.

4. *Institutions both constrain and facilitate behavior by members.* Families provide their members with a set of expectations for entering any family role. Such expectations provide people with guidelines for organizing daily life,

so that they generally know what to do and what to expect in family interactions. They also set limits on people's freedom of action. Several articles in this book show how the historical roles for wives and husbands facilitated a division of labor in the household that made it clear whose job was whose, but that also constrained women as they began to lobby for equality. Until the 1970s, legal codes specifically defined which duties were assigned to husbands and wives. These legal codes have now been repealed, but the social norms associated with marriage are still strong, encouraging women to perform more housework when they marry than when they are single or cohabiting. Gupta suggests that when women earn money, they tend to exempt themselves from such labor without challenging the assumption that it is their responsibility to pay for it if not to do it themselves. But as Lang and I suggest, new institutional norms are arising that facilitate the more egalitarian behaviors that we call gender convergence.

5. *Institutions have social positions characterized by expected norms and behaviors.* In some historical periods, sexual pleasure has been dissociated from marriage, especially for men, who faced no sanctions for having mistresses or frequenting prostitutes. In contemporary American families, by contrast, the couple is presumed to be the major source both of emotional support and of sexual pleasure. One of the most widely expected norms for families today is that spouses will be active and mutual sexual partners. Yet, that norm often collides with older norms about women's sexual purity, as Schwartz points out. Each of the contributions on divorce, those by Rutter, Li, and Coontz, takes as a given that husbands and wives are expected to love, honor, and be faithful to one another, and divorce is what happens when those norms are flouted.

6. *Institutions are made, supported, and changed by real people.* Franklin presents interesting research to show us that African Americans pioneered modern marriage, in which husbands and wives are allowed to have serious careers, as well as children. The article by Struening is the best example of how men and women in the twenty-first century are redefining who is in a family and how you can be a family. With new technologies, there can be one family with three types of mothers, the genetically related egg donor, the surrogate birth mother, and the adopting social mother. Similarly, as same-sex couples demand to be in families, we have new legislation institutionalizing lovers into "domestic partnerships" with legal rights. And courts in states without same-sex marriage must now deal with the custodial battles of gay couples who married somewhere else and are now figuring out how to part without institutionalized guidelines. Mignon Moore's article shows lesbians

creating blended families and inventing their own norms around the household division of labor and couple power. These are real-life examples of the family as an institution being made anew in our own generation.

7. *Institutions are important to their members, and their rules and expectations become internalized as important identities and parts of selves.* Cowan and Cowan show us that what actually happens in families, the processes of everyday life, are internalized in children's self-images or expressed in their behavior. The ability to lay claim to the identity of wife or husband clearly matters very much to many Americans. Green and Struening show how same-sex couples today want to be able to say, "I do" and to call their loved one a wife or a husband, even when they share the same biological sex.

8. *Institutions have a legitimating ideology.* The norms attached to the positions of people in families wield great ideological force. Despite the reality that those norms can and do change all the time, most people believe the social norms they follow are necessary and inevitable. We live in a society that presumes marriage is between one man and one woman, and even though many polygamous cultures exist, we take it for granted that a marriage involves two people and only two people. The result is that many people cannot even recognize the love and mutual support that exist in families that do not meet those conditions. Most people yearn for public recognition and validation. Rockquemore and Henderson show us that cross-racial couples who were forbidden to marry sued to make their love formally accepted within the institution of the family. Many same-sex couples also want the public recognition that comes with marriage, even if they can claim the same legal rights through a domestic partnership.

9. *Institutions are inconsistent, contradictory, and rife with conflict.* Families are always evolving and that leads to contradictions between what used to be and what is. What was once so taken for granted as to be seen as inevitable, that marriage can only be between one man and one woman, is now being challenged state by state. Sometimes contradictions and change can create conflict between parents and children. Families may share many common interests, but different individuals within the family may have different interests in the distribution of resources, obligations, and authority, and they may openly contest or maneuver behind the scenes to further their individual interests. Gerson's research suggests that young adults, both men and women, want egalitarian relationships. But if such relationships are out of reach, men and women have contradictory solutions, with men wanting neo-traditional wives, and women preferring to go it alone rather than trading income for housekeeping services. If such men and women marry, their

different Plan B's may indeed create conflict, producing outcomes that are different from those they both originally intended.

10. *Institutions continuously change.* Families as an institution are constantly in flux. Rockquemore and Henderson, Rosenfeld, Green, Moore, and Struening show clearly that who even gets to be defined as family has recently and is even at this very moment changing. Not only is a larger cast of characters now allowed into the institution, but the norms attached to gender relations inside marriage itself are shifting, as the articles in the section on the gender revolution show clearly. Once it was assumed that marriage largely regulated a woman's entry into sexual activity. Articles by Schwartz and by Armstrong, England, and Fogarty show that Americans of both sexes become sexual actors long before they become wives and husbands, if they ever do. Smock and Manning show us how cohabitation has gone in a short period of time from being an alternative to marriage to a normal pathway into it.

11. *Institutions are organized by and permeated by power.* The most obvious way in which families are permeated by power is between generations. Parents have traditionally had the right to impose their own norms, beliefs, and rules on their children. Many social institutions—from schools to child protective agencies—as well as norms now limit some aspects of parental power. But parents still exercise power over many of the circumstances of children's lives, consciously or unconsciously. Several of the authors in this book show that parents transmit their own social class privileges or disadvantages to their children. There are also power differences between husbands and wives, as Almeida's article on domestic violence shows most clearly. Schwartz argues that women's sexuality, even in marriage, is regulated by laws making sex toys used primarily by women illegal. Armstrong, England, and Fogarty show us that hooking up privileges men, at least when it comes to sexual pleasure.

12. *Individuals must adapt to institutions, but they remake them at the same time.* This final criterion for defining an institution is the theme of this anthology, recognizing "families as they really are." Nearly every child born into the world enters a family that is an institution constrained by the criteria explained in this chapter, and each child learns the norms attached to his or her familial social roles. Every adult who enters the institution of marriage has to cope with the norms and expectations that come with being a wife or a husband. So, too, when we become parents, we face the entire institutional weight of expectations about being good mothers or fathers. Even grandparents and aunts and uncles must adapt to institutional expectations about their relationships to new babies who enter into the extended kinship group.

Some people always do exactly what they believe the norms dictate, never questioning whether they're right or wrong for them or others. But other people bend, twist, and remake those rules so that they fit their own needs and desires. In this anthology, we've seen how American families have evolved over time, with more freedom for spouses to choose one another and to treat one another as equals. Similarly, we have seen how childhood is a social and cultural construct, redefined in every age and increasingly endowed with rights that in the past were not recognized. We have also seen how access to the institution of marriage itself has increased, as women and men who loved each other across race lines sued for the right to marry and to be recognized as family. Currently, gays and lesbians are making the same argument, and in a few states they can now marry as well. None of these changes just happened. Rather, some people have always rebelled against the norms, and sometimes they have succeeded, especially when they are part of a larger social movement, in altering the institution to meet their own needs.

One reason that the family as an institution remains so strong, and so important to us, is that we have been able to change it. It is a sign of the family's strength, not its weakness, that Americans have been able to reject aspects of the institution, revise others, and invent new norms for relationships. Perhaps that is the secret of an enduring institution like the family: that it matters enough in people's lives for them to work on making it anew in every generation. Families as they really are are always works in progress. On behalf of my colleagues on the Council on Contemporary Families, I hope that you can use the new research and clinical expertise presented in this volume not only to enhance your understanding of the social context and internal dynamics of your own families, and of those that differ from yours, but also to help you build the kind of family that can deliver the support and satisfaction that you need in your intimate relationships. We hope that having accurate information will help you to preserve the family traditions that still work for you and to create the new family norms and relationships that you need, so that the family can remain a strong, thriving institution for the children of the next generation.

Contributors

Etiony Aldarondo is Associate Dean for Research and Director of the Office for Research in Educational and Community Well-Being in the School of Education at the University of Miami. The recipient of various recognitions for academic excellence and community involvement, his scholarship focuses on the positive development of ethnic minority and immigrant youth, on domestic violence, and on social-justice-oriented clinical practices. His publications include the books *Advancing Social Justice through Clinical Practice* (Routledge, 2007) and *Programs for Men Who Batter: Intervention and Prevention Strategies in a Diverse Society* (Civic Research Institute, 2003, co-edited with Fernando Mederos). Dr. Aldarondo currently serves on the Board of Directors for the National Latino Alliance for the Elimination of Domestic Violence, the Council on Contemporary Families, the Melissa Institute for Violence Prevention and Treatment, and Project Hope.

Rhea V. Almeida, founder of the Institute for Family Services, is a family therapist and graduate of Columbia University. She is the author of numerous articles and books and creator of the Cultural Context Model. Her recent book, *Transformative Family Therapy: Just Families in a Just Society* (Allyn & Bacon, 2007, co-authored with Lynn Parker and Kenneth Dolan-Del Vecchio) chronicles this work. From Ecuador to South Africa and India, she has trained professionals in the Cultural Context Model. She has been featured in the *Los Angeles Times* and *USA Today*, and on CNBC, National Public Radio, and Pure Oxygen. Dr. Almeida is a member of the Board of Directors for the Council on Contemporary Families.

Edward Ameen completed his bachelor's degree at Northwestern University and his Master's degree in mental health counseling at Boston College. He is currently receiving doctoral training in Counseling Psychology at the University of Miami. He has served as an outpatient counselor with two mental health agencies in Massachusetts. He is the Executive Director of Stand Up For Kids Miami, an all-volunteer organization that reaches out to homeless and runaway youth. His research interests include resiliency, social relationships, community engagement, and immigrant integration.

Elizabeth A. Armstrong is Associate Professor of Sociology at Indiana University. Her research interests include sexuality, gender, social movements, sociology of culture, and higher education. With Laura Hamilton and research assistants, she conducted a year of ethnographic observation on a women's floor in a college residence hall as well as five waves of in-depth interviews with more than forty residents of this floor. A paper from this project, "Sexual Assault on Campus: A Multi-level, Integrative Approach to Party Rape," co-authored with Laura Hamilton and Brian Sweeney, was published in *Social Problems*. She and Hamilton are working on a book exploring the relationship between college peer culture and social inequality. Armstrong received a National Academy of Education/Spencer Postdoctoral Fellowship and was a fellow at the Radcliffe Institute for Advanced Study at Harvard University.

Andraé L. Brown is Assistant Professor in the Graduate School of Education and Counseling at Lewis and Clark College in Oregon. He is Co-Director of Affinity Counseling Group, NJ, and secretary for the Board of Directors for the Council on Contemporary Families. His research involves development of treatment modalities that use the social ecology of families, schools, and communities to address trauma, violence, and substance abuse.

Linda M. Burton is the James B. Duke Professor of Sociology at Duke University. She earned her Ph.D. in sociology in 1985 from the University of Southern California. She is currently a member of the Board on Children, Youth, and Families, National Academy of Sciences; Co-editor of the *Journal of Research on Adolescence*; Deputy Editor for *Demography*; and a member of the Board of Directors for the Family Process Institute and the Council on Contemporary Families. She directed the ethnographic components of "Welfare, Children, and Families: A Three-City Study" and the Family Life Project. Dr. Burton is the former Director of the National Institute of Mental Health-sponsored Research Consortium on Diversity, Family Processes, and Child Adolescent Mental Health; the Consortium's Multisite Postdoctoral Training Program; and the African American Mental Health Research Scientists Consortium. She also is a recipient of the Family Research Consortium IV Legacy Award and the American Family Therapy Academy Award for Innovative Contributions to Family Research.

Natasha Cabrera received her Ph.D. in educational psychology from the University of Denver (1994) and joined the University of Maryland faculty in 2002. Dr. Cabrera arrived at the University of Maryland with several years of experience as an Expert in Child Development with the Demographic and Behavioral Sciences Branch (DBSB) of the National Institute of Child Health and Human Development (NICHD). Her current research topics include the role of father involvement with their children and its effect on children's development, paternal and maternal involvement and its effect on children, theoretical frameworks related to father involvement, and children's developmental trajectories in low-income and minority families. She has published in peer-reviewed journals on policy, methodology, theory, and the implications of father involvement on child development. She is co-editor with Catherine Tamis-LeMonda of the *Handbook of Father Involvement: Multidisciplinary Perspectives* (Erlbaum, 2002).

Andrew J. Cherlin is Griswold Professor of Sociology and Public Policy at Johns Hopkins University. In 1999, he was president of the Population Association of America. In 2003 he received the Distinguished Career Award from the Family Section of the American Sociological Association. In 2005–2006, he was a Guggenheim Foundation Fellow. His research interests include the well-being of parents and children in low-income families and the changing nature of marriage and family life over the past century. His recent articles include "The Deinstitutionalization of American Marriage" in the *Journal of Marriage and Family* and "Family

Instability and Child Well-Being" in the *American Sociological Review*. He is the author of the new book, *The Marriage-Go-Round: The State of Marriage and the Family in America Today* (Knopf, 2009).

Joshua Coleman is a psychologist in private practice in the San Francisco Bay Area specializing in couples and family issues. A frequent guest on the *Today Show*, NPR, and the BBC, he has also appeared on ABC's *20/20*, *Good Morning America*, America Online Coaches, and numerous news programs for FOX, ABC, CNN, and NBC television. He has served on the clinical faculties of the University of California at San Francisco, the Wright Institute Graduate School of Psychology, and the San Francisco Psychotherapy Research Group, and is a member of the Board of Directors for the Council on Contemporary Families. His advice has been featured in the *New York Times*, the *Times of London*, the *Chicago Tribune*, *Psychology Today*, *U.S. News and World Report*, the *San Francisco Chronicle*, *Parenting Magazine*, and many others. He is the author of four books, the most recent which is *When Parents Hurt: Compassionate Strategies When You and Your Grown Child Don't Get Along* (HarperCollins, 2007). Dr. Coleman's books have been translated into Chinese, Croatian, and Korean, and are also available in the United States, the U.K., Canada, and Australia.

Stephanie Coontz teaches history and family studies at The Evergreen State College in Olympia, Washington, and serves as Director of Research and Public Education for the Council on Contemporary Families. Her books include *Marriage, A History: How Love Conquered Marriage* (Penguin, 2006), *American Families: A Multicultural Reader* (Routledge, 1998), and *The Way We Never Were: American Families and the Nostalgia Trap* (Basic Books, 2000). Professor Coontz is a frequent contributor to the editorial pages of the *New York Times*, the *Washington Post*, and other newspapers.

Carolyn Pape Cowan is Emerita Adjunct and Clinical Professor of Psychology at the University of California, Berkeley. She co-directs the Becoming a Family Project, the Schoolchildren and Their Families Project, and the Supporting Father Involvement Project—research and preventive intervention studies with couples who are parents of young children. Dr. Cowan has published widely in the literature on family research, family transitions, and father involvement. She co-edited *Fatherhood Today: Men's Changing Role in the Family* (Wiley, 1988) and *The Family Context of Parenting in Children's Adaptation to Elementary School* (Erlbaum, 2005) and is co-author of *When Partners Become Parents: The Big Life Change for Couples* (Erlbaum, 2000). Dr. Cowan consults widely on the development and evaluation of interventions for couples, and is a member of the Board of Directors for the Council on Contemporary Families.

Philip A. Cowan is Emeritus Professor of Psychology at the University of California, Berkeley, former Director of the Institute of Human Development and the Psychology Clinic. He co-directs the Becoming a Family Project, the Schoolchildren and Their Families Project, and the Supporting Father Involvement Project—research and preventive intervention studies with couples who are parents of young children. Dr. Cowan writes about the family context of child development and adaptation. His books include *Piaget: With Feeling* (Holt, 1978); co-author of *When Partners Become Parents: The Big Life Change for Couples* (Erlbaum, 2000); and co-editor of *Family Transitions* (Erlbaum, 1993) and *The Family Context of Parenting in Children's Adaptation to Elementary School* (Erlbaum, 2005). Dr. Cowan is a member of the Board of Directors for the Council on Contemporary Families.

Melina Dimitriou is an international graduate of the School Counseling Program in the Graduate School of Education at Hunter College, NY. She is also an intern at Affinity Counseling Group, NJ, receiving training in the Cultural Context Model.

Lisa Dressner is a founding member and Co-Director of Affinity Counseling Group. Her research and clinical interests include families' experiences of trauma through domestic and community violence, creating therapeutic healing communities, antiracism and white privilege, sexual abuse, contested divorces, adoption, and juvenile justice reform.

Paula England is Professor of Sociology at Stanford University. Her teaching and research focus on the sex gap in pay, class differences in unplanned pregnancies, and youth sexuality and relationships. She is author of numerous books and articles, including *Comparable Worth: Theories and Evidence* (Aldine, 1992) and *Unmarried Couples with Children* (Russell Sage, 2007, co-edited with Kathryn Edin). Dr. England is a former editor of the *American Sociological Review*. She is a member of the Board of Directors for the Council on Contemporary Families.

Alison C. K. Fogarty is a doctoral candidate in Sociology at Stanford University. Her research interests are in gender, sexuality, and social psychology. With Paula England and Emily Shafer, she wrote "Hooking Up and Forming Romantic Relationships on Today's College Campuses" in *The Gendered Society Reader*, edited by Michael Kimmel (Oxford University Press, 2007).

Donna L. Franklin's first book, *Ensuring Inequality* (Oxford University Press, 1997), won two major awards: The American Sociological Association's William J. Goode Distinguished Book Award for "outstanding scholarship on the family" and *Choice Magazine's* award for "outstanding academic book." She was the first African-American author to win the ASA award. *Ensuring Inequality* was hailed by the *Washington Post* as one of the "most important contributions to the study of the black family in recent years." Her second book, *What's Love Got To Do With It? Understanding and Healing the Rift Between Black Men and Women* (Simon & Schuster, 2000), is one of the first books to include a historical analysis of gender relations in the African-American community. Professor Franklin has held academic appointments at the University of Chicago, Smith College, Howard University, and the University of Southern California. She was a member of the founding board of the Council on Contemporary Families and one of its National Chairs. Her commentary has been published in the *New York Times*, the *Washington Post*, and the *Atlanta-Journal Constitution*. She is currently working on a book about African Americans who have strong partnerships in marriage.

Frank F. Furstenberg, Jr. is the Zellerbach Family Professor of Sociology and Research Associate in the Population Studies Center at the University of Pennsylvania. His interest in the American family began at Columbia University, where he received his Ph.D. in 1967. His recent books include: *Destinies of the Disadvantaged: The Politics of Teen Childbearing* (Russell Sage, 2007), *On the Frontier of Adulthood: Theory, Research, and Public Policy* (University of Chicago Press, 2005, co-edited with Richard A. Settersten, Jr., and Ruben G. Rumbaut), *Managing to Make It: Urban Families in High-Risk Neighborhoods* (University of Chicago Press, 1999, with Thomas Cook, Jacquelynne Eccles, Glen Elder, and Arnold Sameroff). His current research projects focus on the family in the context of disadvantaged urban neighborhoods, adolescent sexual behavior, cross-national research on children's well-being, urban education, and the transition from adolescence to adulthood. He is current Chair of the MacArthur Foundation Research Network on Transitions to Adulthood and has received numerous honors for his contributions to research on adolescence and public policy. He was a visiting scholar at the Russell Sage Foundation, Fall 2004. Dr. Furstenberg is a past member of the Board of Directors for the Council on Contemporary Families.

Kathleen Gerson is Professor of Sociology at New York University and 2008–2009 President of the Eastern Sociological Society. She is the author or co-author of numerous books and articles on the connections among gender, work, and family change, including *Hard Choices: How Women Decide About Work, Career, and Motherhood* (University of California Press, 1985); *No Man's Land: Men's Changing Commitments to Family and Work* (Basic Books, 1993); and *The Time Divide: Work, Family, and Gender Inequality* (with Jerry A. Jacobs, Harvard University Press, 2004). Her new book, *The Unfinished Revolution: How a New Generation Is Reshaping Work, Family, and Gender in America* (Oxford University Press, 2009), examines young women's and men's strategic responses to growing up in an era of gender, work, and family transformations. She has participated in a wide range of research and policy initiatives on these issues and makes regular contributions to various print and broadcast media, including the *New York Times*, the *Washington Post*, *USA Today*, the *American Prospect*, PBS, NPR, and CNN. Dr. Gerson is a past member of the Board of Directors for the Council on Contemporary Families.

Robert-Jay Green is Executive Director of the Rockway Institute, a national center for lesbian, gay, bisexual, and transgender psychology research, education, and public policy. He is Distinguished Professor in the Clinical Psychology Ph.D. Program, California School of Professional Psychology, Alliant International University, San Francisco. Dr. Green is a past member of the Board of Directors for the Council on Contemporary Families.

Loren Henderson is a graduate student in the Ph.D. program in sociology at the University of Illinois at Chicago and a research assistant in the Institute of Government and Public Affairs at the University of Illinois at Chicago. Ms. Henderson was a Scholarship Winner of the Ronald McNair Scholars Program in 2006–2007. She was named the First Place Winner of the 2007–2008 James W. Compton Research Competition, sponsored by Chicago United. She is the co-author of "Diversity in Illinois: Changing Meanings, Demographic Trends, and Policy Preferences" in The Illinois Report, 2008. She is also the author of "Organizational Factors that

Influence Diversity in Management," as well as the author of "Between the Two: Determinants of Bisexual Identity among African Americans" in the *Journal of African American Studies*.

Wendy D. Manning is Professor of Sociology at Bowling Green State University, Director of the Center for Family and Demographic Research, and Co-director of the National Center for Marriage Research. Her research focuses on adolescents' dating and sexual relationships, transitions from adolescence to early adulthood relationships, and adult relationship formation and maintenance. She is the author of numerous journal articles, including "The Changing Institution of Marriage: Adolescents' Expectations to Cohabit and to Marry" (*Journal of Marriage and Family*, 2007, co-authored with Monica Longmore and Peggy Giordano) and "Gender and the Meanings of Adolescent Romantic Relationships: A Focus on Boys" (*American Sociological Review*, 2006, co-authored with Monica Longmore and Peggy Giordano).

Steven Mintz is a member of the History Department and Director of the Graduate School of Arts & Sciences Teaching Center at Columbia University, and a former fellow of the Center for Advanced Study at Stanford University. He is the author and editor of thirteen books, including *Huck's Raft: A History of American Childhood* (Belknap Press, 2004), which received major awards from the Association of American Publishers, the Organization of American Historians, and the Texas Institute of Letters. Dr. Mintz has served as Co-chair of the Board of Directors for the Council on Contemporary Families.

Mignon R. Moore is Assistant Professor of Sociology and African-American Studies at the University of California, Los Angeles. Her research interests are in the sociology of families, gender, race, sexuality, identity, and aging. She is completing a book manuscript titled "Invisible Families: Gay Identities, Relationships and Motherhood among Black Women." Other ongoing projects include a two-city study of social histories and physical health outcomes among African-American lesbian and gay elders. She analyzes the social context of entering into a gay sexuality for black lesbian, gay, bisexual, and transgender people during the 1960s and 1970s political movements, and this population's current experiences with health and social support as they age. Dr. Moore is a member of the Board of Directors for the Council on Contemporary Families.

Kerry Ann Rockquemore is Associate Professor of African-American Studies and Sociology at the University of Illinois at Chicago. Her scholarship focuses on racial identity development among mixed-race children, interracial family dynamics, and the politics of racial categorization. She is the author of *Beyond Black: Biracial Identity in America* (Rowman & Littlefield, 2001, 2008) and *Raising Biracial Children* (Rowman & Littlefield, 2005), as well as numerous articles and book chapters on biracial identity. Dr. Rockquemore is a member of the Board of Directors for the Council on Contemporary Families.

Kevin Roy is an associate professor in the Department of Family Science at the University of Maryland College Park School of Public Health. Through a mix of participant observation and life history interviews, he explores the intersection of policy systems, such as welfare reform and incarceration, with parents' caregiving and providing roles. His research focus is the life course of men on the margins of families and the workforce, and he has conducted research primarily in state correctional facilities and community-based fathering programs. He has received funding for his research from NICHD, the W. T. Grant Foundation, and the National Poverty Center. Dr. Roy has published articles in *Social Problems, American Journal of Community Psychology, Journal of Family Issues,* and *Family Relations,* and has co-edited a book entitled *Situated Fathering: A Focus on Physical and Social Spaces* (Rowman & Littlefield, 2005). He received a Ph.D. from the Human Development and Social Policy program at Northwestern University in 1999.

Barbara J. Risman is Professor and Head of the Department of Sociology at University of Illinois at Chicago. She was previously Distinguished Research Professor at North Carolina State University, and she has also taught at the University of Washington and the University of Pennsylvania. She is the author of *Gender Vertigo: American Families in Transition* (Yale University Press, 1998) and research articles about families and gender relations in a variety of scientific journals. The Southern Sociological Society has awarded her the Katherine Jocher–Belle Boone Beard Award for lifetime contributions to the study of gender. Sociologists for Women in Society has awarded her the Feminist Mentoring award. Professor Risman is currently the Executive Officer of the Council on Contemporary Families and is writing a book on gender structure theory.

Virginia E. Rutter is an assistant professor of sociology at Framingham State College in Framingham, MA. Previously she was a research scientist at the Battelle Centers for Public Health Research and Evaluation in Seattle and Arlington, VA, where she was a co-investigator in the NIH-funded National Couples Survey. Her work focuses on research questions that are responsive to public concerns about social problems. As a survey researcher, she studies family, gender, and sexuality. At the same time, she has worked translating social science work in these areas to general audiences via the media. Her most recent work is titled "Divorce in Research vs. Divorce in Media." She is co-author of two books, *The Gender of Sexuality* (Pine Forge Press, 1998) and *The Love Test* (Perigee, 1998), several academic book chapters, and numerous articles for general audiences. She pens the "Nice Work" column for www.girlwpen.com and is a board member of the Council on Contemporary Families.

Pepper Schwartz is Clarence and Elsa Schrag Professor in the Sociology Department at the University of Washington. She is the past president of the Society for the Scientific Study of Sex and the Pacific Sociological Association and Chairperson of the Board of the Centers for Sexuality and the National Sexuality Resource Center. She is a board member of the Council on Contemporary Families and the winner of the American Sociological Association's award for Public Understanding of Sociology. She is also the relationship expert for Perfectmatch.com and developer of their matching system, Duet. She lives on a horse farm in Snoqualmie, Washington.

Elizabeth Seale is a doctoral student at North Carolina State University. Her research interests include gender, race, and class inequality; welfare reform, poverty, and the third sector; and global change. She currently teaches courses in sociology of the family and social problems.

Pamela J. Smock is Professor of Sociology at the University of Michigan-Ann Arbor. She is also Research Professor at the Population Studies Center. Professor Smock is a family demographer and sociologist. Her scholarship focuses on the causes and consequences of family patterns and change, engaging their intersections with economic, racial/ethnic, and gender inequalities. She has published on issues including cohabitation, the economic consequences of divorce and marriage, nonresident fatherhood, child support, remarriage, and the motherhood wage penalty. Professor Smock has received funding from the Eunice Kennedy Shriver National Institute of Child Health and Human Development (NICHD) to support her research on (1) nonresident fatherhood, (2) heterosexual cohabitation, and, most recently, (3) integrating and harmonizing fifty years of family and fertility surveys. Professor Smock has served as Chair of the Section on Family of the American Sociological Association and on the National Science Foundation Sociology Advisory Panel. She is currently Chair and member of NICHD's Population Sciences Subcommittee and a board member of the Council on Contemporary Families.

Karen Struening is the Director of the Skadden, Arps Honors Program in Legal Studies at The City College of New York. She teaches constitutional law and other legal studies courses in the Department of Political Science. Professor Struening is the author of *New Family Values: Liberty, Equality and Diversity* (Rowman & Littlefield, 2002). She is currently writing about substantive due process analysis after *Lawrence v. Texas*. Professor Struening is treasurer for the Board of Directors for the Council on Contemporary Families.

Oriel Sullivan is Research Reader at the Centre for Time Use Research, Department of Sociology, University of Oxford. Her research is mainly in the area of changing gender relations in the domestic arena, with a focus on changes in the domestic division of labor. She is author of *Changing Gender Relations, Changing Families: Tracing the Pace of Change* (Gender Lens Series, Rowman & Littlefield, 2006).

Notes

Chapter 2: One Thousand and Forty-nine Reasons Why It's Hard to Know When a Fact Is a Fact, by Andrew J. Cherlin

1. Glick (1941).
2. Cherlin, Chase-Lansdale, and McRae (1998).
3. Cherlin et al. (1991).
4. Snyder in Jencks (1994).
5. Rosin (1999).
6. U.S. General Accounting Office (1997).
7. *Goodrich v. Department of Public Health* (2003).

Chapter 3: When Is a Relationship between Facts a Causal One?, by Philip A. Cowan

1. Waite and Gallagher (2000).
2. Cowan and Cowan (2002); Cummings and Davies (1994); Emery (1999); Gottman and Notarius (2002).

Chapter 4: Uncovering Hidden Facts That Matter in Interpreting Individuals' Behaviors: An Ethnographic Lens, by Linda M. Burton

1. A detailed description of the Three-City Study and a series of reports are available at www.jhu.edu/~welfare.

Chapter 5: The Evolution of American Families, by Stephanie Coontz

1. For the following section of this article, see Stephanie Coontz, *The Social Origins of Private Life: A History of American Families, 1600–1900* (New York: W. W. Norton, 1988); Barrie Thorne and Marilyn Yalom, *Rethinking the Family: Some Feminist Questions* (Boston: Northeastern University Press, 1992); Stephanie Coontz, *Marriage, A History: How Love Conquered Marriage* (New York: Penguin Books, 2006); K. Ishwaran, *Family and Marriage: Cross-Cultural Perspectives* (Toronto: Thompson Educational Publishing, 1992); Bron B. Ingoldsby and Suzanna D. Smith, *Families in Global and Multicultural Perspective*, 2nd ed. (Thousand Oaks, CA: Sage Publications, 2006); Cai Hua, *A Society Without Fathers or Husbands: The Na of China* (Cambridge, MA: MIT Press, 2001).

2. On Native American families, see Coontz, *The Social Origins of Private Life* (1988); Ward Stavig, "'Living in Offense of Our Lord': Indigenous Sexual Values and Marital Life in the Colonial Crucible," *Hispanic American Historical Review* 75 (1995): 597–622; Cynthia Kennedy, *Braided Relations, Entwined Lives: The Women of Charleston's Urban Slave Society* (Bloomington, IN: Indiana University Press, 2005); Susan Lobo, *Native American Voices: A Reader* (New York: Longman, 1998); David Wallace Adams, *Education for Extinction: American Indians and the Boarding School Experience, 1875–1928* (Lawrence, KS: University Press of Kansas, 1988); Virginia Bergman Peters, *Women of the Earth Lodges: Tribal Life on the Plains* (New Haven, CT: Archon Books, 1995).

3. On European family history, see Coontz, *Marriage, A History* (2006); Beatrice Gottlieb, *The Family in the Western World from the Black Death to the Industrial Age* (New York: Oxford University Press, 1993); Andre Burguiere et al., *A History of the Family* (Cambridge, MA: Belknap Press, 1996); Wally Seccombe, *A Millennium of Family Change* (London: Verso, 1992); Rosemary O'Day, *The Family and Family Relationships, 1500–1900* (London: Palgrave Macmillan, 1994).

4. On colonial families, see Coontz, *The Social Origins of Private Life* (1988); Steven Mintz and Susan Kellogg, *Domestic Revolutions: A Social History of American Family Life* (New York: Free Press, 1988).

5. On African-American families in slavery and freedom, see Brenda E. Stevenson, *Life in Black and White: Family and Community in the Slave South* (New York: Oxford University Press, 1996); Leith Mullings, *On Our Own Terms: Race, Class, and Gender in the Lives of African-American Women* (New York: Routledge, 1997); Stephanie McCurry, *Masters of Small Worlds: Yeoman Households, Gender Relations, and the Political Culture of the Antebellum South Carolina Low Country* (Athens, GA: University of Georgia Press, 1995); Jennifer Ritterhouse, *Growing Up Jim Crow: How Black and White Southern Children Learned Race* (Chapel Hill, NC: University of North Carolina Press, 2006); David Barry Gaspar and Darlene Clark Hine, *More Than Chattel: Black Women and Slavery in the Americas* (Bloomington, IN: Indiana University Press, 1996); Tia Miles, *Ties That Bind: The Story of an Afro-Cherokee Family in Slavery and Freedom* (Berkeley, CA: University of California Press, 2005); Harriette Pipes McAdoo, *Black Families*, 4th ed. (Thousand Oaks, CA: Sage Publications, 2007).

6. On the mutual interaction and transformation of the economy and of family life in both the middle and working classes, see Coontz, *The Social Origins of Private Life* (1988); Mary P. Ryan, *Cradle of the Middle Class: The Family in Oneida County, New York, 1790–1865* (New York: Cambridge University Press, 1983); Jeanne Boydston, *Home and Work: Housework, Wages, and the Ideology of Labor in the Early Republic* (New York: Oxford University Press, 1990).

7. On the interactions and mutual dependencies of families of different classes and racial-ethnic identities, see Stephanie Coontz, Maya Parson, and Gabrielle Raley, *American Families: A Multicultural Reader* (New York: Routledge, 2008); Theresa L. Amott and Julie A. Matthaei, *Race, Gender, and Work: A Multicultural Economic History of Women in the United States* (Boston: South End Press, 1991); Vicki Ruiz and Ellen DuBois, *Unequal Sisters: A Multicultural Reader in U.S. Women's History*, 3rd ed. (New York: Routledge, 2000).

8. John D'Emilio and Estelle B. Freedman, *Intimate Matters: A History of Sexuality in America*, 2nd ed. (Chicago: University of Chicago Press, 1997).

9. Michael B. Katz, Michael J. Doucet, and Mark J. Stern, *The Social Organization of Early Industrial Capitalism* (Cambridge, MA: Harvard University Press, 1982), p. 347.

10. Clare A. Lyons, *Sex among the Rabble: An Intimate History of Gender and Power in the Age of Revolution* (Chapel Hill, NC: University of North Carolina Press, 2006); Nancy Cott, *Public Vows: A History of Marriage and the Nation* (Cambridge, MA: Harvard University Press, 2000); Aaron Gullickson, "Black/White Interracial Marriage Trends, 1850–2000," *Journal of Family History* 31 (2006): 1–24.

11. Rachel Moran, *Interracial Intimacy: The Regulation of Race and Romance* (Chicago: University of Chicago Press, 2001); Peter Wallenstein, *Tell the Court I Love My Wife: Race, Marriage, and Law—An American History* (New York: Palgrave Macmillan, 2002).

12. On the new trends in family life and gender relations between 1900 and the end of World War II, see Beth L. Bailey, *From Front Porch to Back Seat: Courtship in Twentieth-Century America* (Baltimore: Johns Hopkins University Press, 1989) and Coontz, *Marriage, A History* (2006).

13. Elaine Tyler May, *Great Expectations: Marriage and Divorce in Post-Victorian America* (Chicago: University of Chicago Press, 1980).

14. On postwar families, see Elaine Tyler May, *Homeward Bound: American Families in the Cold War Era* (New York: Basic Books, 1988); Jessica Weiss, *To Have and to Hold: Marriage, the Baby Boom, and Social Change* (Chicago: University of Chicago Press, 2000); Stephanie Coontz, *The Way We Never Were: American Families and the Nostalgia Trap* (New York: Basic Books, 2000).

15. George Gallup and Evan Hill, "The American Woman," *The Saturday Evening Post* (December 22–29, 1962), pp. 16–26.

16. Ruth Rosen, *The World Split Open: How the Women's Movement Changed America* (New York: Penguin Books, 2000).

17. For a detailed exploration of these complicated economic and social trends in two American families, see Judith Stacey, *Brave New Families: Stories of Domestic Upheaval in Late Twentieth-Century America* (New York: Basic Books, 1990).

18. On the recent history of immigration and other sources of cultural, religious and economic family diversity, see Barbara C. Aswad and Barbara Bilge, *Family and Gender among American Muslims: Issues Facing Middle-Eastern Immigrants and Their Descendants* (Philadelphia: Temple University Press, 1996); Donna Gabaccia and Vicki L. Ruiz, *American Dreaming, Global Realities: Rethinking U.S. Immigration History* (Chicago: University of Chicago Press, 2006); Bill Ong Hing, *Making and Remaking Asian America through Immigration Policy, 1850–1990* (Stanford, CA: Stanford University Press, 1993); Jennifer S. Hirsch, *A Courtship After Marriage: Sexuality and Love in Mexican Transnational Communities* (Berkeley, CA: University of California Press, 2003); Juanita Tamayo Lott, *Common Destiny: Filipino American Generations* (Lanham, MD: Rowman & Littlefield, 2006); Mario Maffi, *Gateway to the Promised Lands: Ethnic Cultures on New York's Lower East Side* (New York: New York University Press, 1995); Mae M. Ngai, *Impossible Subjects: Illegal Aliens and the Making of Modern America* (Princeton: Princeton University Press, 2004); Mae Paomay Tung, *Chinese Americans and Their Immigrant Parents: Conflict, Identity, and Values* (Binghamton, NY: Haworth Press, 2000); Diane C. Vecchio, *Merchants, Midwives, and Laboring Women: Italian Migrants in Urban America* (Champaign, IL: University of Illinois Press, 2006);

Bernard P. Wong, *The Chinese in Silicon Valley: Globalization, Social Networks, and Ethnic Identity* (Lanham, MD: Rowman & Littlefield, 2006); Lillian B. Rubin, *Families on the Fault Line* (New York: HarperCollins, 1994); Arlene S. Skolnick and Jerome H. Skolnick, *Family in Transition*, 12th ed. (Boston: Allyn & Bacon, 2003); Maxime Baca Zinn, D. Stanley Eitzen, and Barbara Wells, *Diversity in Families*, 8th ed. (Boston: Allyn & Bacon, 2008).

19. Suzanne M. Bianchi, John P. Robinson, and Melissa A. Milke, *Changing Rhythms of Family Life* (New York: Russell Sage Foundation, 2006).

Chapter 6: American Childhood As a Social and Cultural Construct, by Steven Mintz

1. Annette Lareau, *Unequal Childhoods: Class, Race, and Family Life* (Berkeley, CA: University of California Press, 2003).

2. Colin Heywood, *A History of Childhood: Children and Childhood in the West from Medieval to Modern Times* (Cambridge, UK: Polity Press, 2001); Joseph Illick, *American Childhood* (Philadelphia: University of Pennsylvania Press, 2002); James A. Schultz, *The Knowledge of Childhood in the German Middle Ages, 1100–1350* (Philadelphia: University of Pennsylvania Press, 1995), p. 11.

3. Howard P. Chudacoff, *How Old Are You? Age Consciousness in American Society* (Princeton: Princeton University Press, 1989); Joseph F. Kett, *Rites of Passage: Adolescence in America* (New York: Basic, 1977).

4. Priscilla Clement, *Growing Pains: Children in the Industrial Age, 1850–1890* (New York: Twayne, 1997); David Nasaw, *Children in the City: At Work and at Play* (Garden City, NY: Anchor Press/Doubleday, 1985); Christine Stansell, *City of Women: Sex and Class in New York, 1789–1860* (New York: Knopf, 1986).

5. Ann Hulbert, *Raising America: Experts, Parents, and a Century of Advice about Children* (New York: Knopf, 2003); Julia Grant, *Raising Baby by the Book: The Education of American Mothers* (New Haven, CT: Yale University Press, 1998).

6. Kathleen W. Jones, *Taming the Troublesome Child* (Cambridge, MA: Harvard University Press, 1999).

7. Steven Mintz and Susan Kellogg, *Domestic Revolutions: A Social History of American Family Life* (New York: Free Press, 1988), p. 189.

8. On changes in the onset of sexual maturation, see Marcia E. Herman-Giddens et al., "Secondary Sexual Characteristics and Menses in Young Girls Seen in Office Practice: A Study from the Pediatric Research in Office Settings Network," *Pediatrics* 9(4) (April 1997): 505–512. In 1890, the average age of menarche in the United States was estimated to be 14.8 years; by the 1990s, the average age had fallen to 12.5 (12.1 for African-American girls and 12.8 for girls of northern European ancestry). According to the study, which tracked 17,000 girls to find out when they hit different markers of puberty, 15 percent of white girls and 48 percent of African-American girls showed signs of breast development or pubic hair by age 8. For conflicting views on whether the age of menarche has fallen, see Lisa Belkin, "The Making of an 8-Year-Old Woman," *New York Times*, December 24, 2000; Gina Kolata, "Doubters Fault Theory Finding Earlier

Puberty," *New York Times*," February 20, 2001; Gina Kolata, "2 Endocrinology Groups Raise Doubt on Earlier Onset of Girls' Puberty," *New York Times*, March 3, 2001.

9. Stephen Robertson, "The Disappearance of Childhood," http://teaching.arts.usyd.edu.au/history/2044/.

10. Lareau, *Unequal Childhoods* (2003).

11. David I. Macleod, *The Age of the Child: Children in America, 1890–1912* (New York: Twayne, 1998).

12. Rogers quoted in James Axtell, *School Upon a Hill: Education and Society in Colonial New England* (New Haven, CT: Yale University Press, 1974), p. 28.

13. Hard as it is to believe, in 1951 a leading television critic decried the quality of children's television. Jack Gould, radio and TV critic for the *New York Times* from the late 1940s to 1972, complained that there was "nothing on science, seldom anything on the country's cultural heritage, no introduction to fine books, scant emphasis on the people of other lands, and little concern over hobbies and other things for children to do themselves besides watch television." *Chicago Sun Times*, August 9, 1998, p. 35.

14. Phil Scraton, ed., *"Childhood" in "Crisis"?* (London: University College of London Press, 1997), pp. 161, 164.

15. Richard Weissbourd, *The Vulnerable Child: What Really Hurts America's Children and What We Can Do About It* (Reading, MA: Addison-Wesley., 1996), p. 48.

16. Ibid.

17. Daniel T. Kline, "Holding Therapy," March 7, 1998, History-Child-Family Listserv (history-child-family@mailbase.ac.uk).

Chapter 7: African Americans and the Birth of the Modern Marriage, by Donna L. Franklin

1. Wells and Duster (1970), p. 101.

2. Gordon (1991), p. 583.

3. Wells and Duster (1970), p. 244.

4. Cooper in Loewenberg and Bogin (1976), p. 325.

5. Wells and Duster (1970), p. 251.

6. Harris (1978).

7. Foner (1988), p. 84.

8. See Giddings (2008).

9. Jacks in Moses (1978), p. 115.

10. Giddings (1985), p. 59.

11. Williams (1904), p. 544.

12. Higginbotham (1993), p. 41.

13. Noble (1956), p. 45.

14. Carlson (1992), p. 24.

15. Higginbotham (1993), p. 24.

16. Hope in Rouse (1989), p. 23–24.

17. Cuthbert (1936), p. 48.

18. Cooper in Carby (1987), p. 100.

19. Bernard (1966), p. 68–70.

20. Stevenson in Mintz and Kellogg (1988), p. 181.

21. Hacker (1992), p. 120.

22. Bowen and Bok (1998), pp. 175–176.

23. Bowen and Bok (1998), p. 175–176.

24. Bowen and Bok (1998), p. 176–178.

25. Landry (2000), p. 158–159.

26. Mills (1959).

Chapter 8: Families "In Law" and Families "In Practice": Does the Law Recognize Families As They Really Are?, by Karen Struening

1. Karen Struening would like to thank Derek Wikstrom for the excellent work he performed as a research assistant on this book chapter.

2. Mary Lyndon Shanley, *Making Babies, Making Families: What Matters Most in an Age of Reproductive Technologies, Surrogacy, Adoption, Same-Sex Marriage and Unwed Parents* (Boston: Beacon Press, 2001), p. 7. On the various functions that family law serves and how they sometimes conflict, see Linda C. McClain, "Love, Marriage and the Baby Carriage: Revisiting the Channeling Function of Law," 28 *Cardozo L. Rev.* 2133 (April, 2007).

3. Martha Fineman has written powerfully about how dependencies structure families and the relationships among families, civil society, and the state in *The Autonomy Myth: A Theory of Dependency* (New York: The New Press, 2004).

4. See Human Rights Campaign, "Statewide Marriage Prohibitions," last updated April 7, 2009, Washington, DC; retrieved on May 8, 2009, from wwwhrc.org/documents/marriage_prohibitions_2009.pdf.

5. Karen Struening, "Do Government Sponsored Marriage Promotion Policies Place Undue Pressure on Individual Rights," *Policy Sciences* 40 (2007): 241–259.

6. Mississippi and Utah also have laws barring adoption by unmarried couples. The only state law to specifically outlaw adoption by gays and lesbians, which has been in place in Florida since 1977, was found unconstitutional by the Miami-Dade Circuit Court in November 2008. The decision is likely to be appealed. Yolanne Almanzar, "Florida Gay Adoption Ban Is Ruled Unconstitutional," *New York Times*, November 26, 2008. Robbie Brown, "Antipathy Toward Obama Seen as Helping Arkansas Limit Adoption," *New York Times*, November 9, 2008.

7. It is likely that several additional states, for example, New York and New Jersey, will join this list soon. See Human Rights Campaign, "Marriage Equality and Other Relationship Recognition Law," last updated May 8, 2009; Washington, DC; retrieved on May 9, 2009, from www.hrc.org/documents/Relationship_Recognition_Laws_Map.pdf.

8. See Human Rights Campaign, "Statewide Marriage Prohibitions," last updated April 7, 2009, Washington, DC; retrieved on May 8, 2009, from www.hrc.org/documents/marriage_prohibitions_2009.pdf.

9. Public Law 104-193 (H.R. 3734) 10 Stat.2105 (August 22, 1996).

10. *Reynolds v. United States*, 98 U.S. 145 (1878).

11. *Meyer v. Nebraska*, 262 U.S. 390 (1923); *Prince v. Massachusetts*, 321 U.S. 158 (1944); *Pierce v. Society of Sisters*, 268 U.S. 510 (1925).

12. *Loving v. Virginia*, 388 U.S. 1 (1967). This decision was based on both the equal protection clause and the due process clause of the Fourteenth Amendment.

13. *Zablocki v. Redhail*, 434 U.S. 374 (1978). This decision struck down a Wisconsin law prohibiting individuals who owed child support from marrying.

14. *Moore v. East Cleveland*, 431 U.S. 494 (1977).

15. *Griswold v. Connecticut*, 381 U.S. 479 (1965); *Eisenstadt v. Baird*, 405 U.S. 438 (1972).

16. *Roe v. Wade*, 410 U.S. 113 (1973); *Planned Parenthood v. Casey*, 505 U.S. 833 (1992).

17. *Lawrence v. Texas*, 539 U.S. 558 (2003).

18. *Levy v. Louisiana*, 391 U.S. 68 (1968). This decision makes wrongful death suits available to both legitimate and illegitimate children.

19. *Stanley v. Illinois*, 405 U.S. 645 (1972).

20. David D. Meyer, "Parenthood in a Time of Transition: Tensions Between Legal, Biological, and Social Conceptions of Parenthood," 54 *Am. J. Comp. L.* 125 (Supplement, Fall 2006).

21. Susan E. Dalton, "From Presumed Fathers to Lesbian Mothers: Sex Discrimination and the Legal Construction of Parenthood," 9 *Mich. J. Gender & Law* 261(2003).

22. Mary Shanley summarizes the common law succinctly: "Under the common law a man had complete custodial authority over any children born to his wife, even if they were sired by another man, yet he had no legal relationship at all to children he sired out of wedlock." Shanley, *Making Babies, Making Families* (2001), p. 49.

23. *Stanley v. Illinois*, 405 U.S. 645 (1972).

24. Uniform Law Commissioners, NCCUSL, *Summary of the Uniform Parentage Act* (Revised 2002); available at www.nccusl.org/nccusl/uniformact_summaries/uniformacts-s-upa.asp.

25. *Michael H. v. Gerald D.*, 491 U.S. 110 (1989).

26. Meyer, "Parenthood in a Time of Transition" (2006), p. 139.

27. My thanks to Kathryn Krase for pointing this out to me.

28. *Troxel v. Granville*, 530 U.S. 57 (2000) (Justice John Paul Stevens, dissenting).

29. *Alison D. v. Virginia M.*, 572 N.E. 2d 27 (N.Y. 1991); *Nancy S. v. Michele G.*, 279 Cal. Rptr. 212 (Ct. App. 1991). But in 1991 in Washington, D.C., a lesbian couple was able to secure the joint adoption of their children. See *In re Adoption of Minor T.*, 17 Fam. L. Rptr. 1523 (D.C. Super Ct. 1991).

30. Nancy D. Polikoff, "This Child Does Have Two Mothers: Redefining Parenthood to Meet the Needs of Children in Lesbian Mother and Other Nontraditional Households," 78 *Geo L. R.* 459 (1990).

31. V.C. v. M.J.B., 748 A.2d 539, 550 (N.J. 2000).

32. *In re Custody of H.S. H.-K.*, 533 N.W. 2d 419 (Wis. 1995).

33. V.C. v. M.J.B., 748 A.2d 539, 551 (N.J. 2000).

34. *Elisa B. v. Superior Court*, 117 P. 3d 660 (Cal. 2005); *Kristine H. v. Lisa R.*, 117 P.3d 690 (Cal. 2005).

35. Polikoff, "This Child Does Have Two Mothers" (1990).

36. According to the National Gay and Lesbian Task Force, four states have passed laws authorizing second-parent adoption (CA, CO, CT, VT), appellate courts in six states plus the District of Columbia have ruled that state adoption laws permit second-parent adoption (IL, ID, MA, NY, NJ, PA), and trial courts in sixteen states have granted second-parent adoptions. There are twenty states in which it is unclear whether state adoption law permits second-parent adoption, and appellate courts in three states (NE, OH, WI) have ruled that their state laws do not permit second-parent adoption. See "National Gay and Lesbian Task Force, Second-Parent Adoption in the U.S."; last updated November 4, 2008; retrieved on November 24, 2008, from thetaskforce.org/downloads/reports/issue_maps/2nd_parent_adoption_5_07_color.pdf. On November 4, 2008, a ballot measure passed in Arkansas banning unmarried individuals and couples from fostering or adopting children. This will, of course, prevent lesbian or gay individuals or same-sex couples from doing so in Arkansas.

37. *In Re M.M.D. & B.H.M.*, 662 A 2nd 837 (D.C. Cir. 1995).

38. Nancy Polikoff, *Beyond (Straight and Gay) Marriage: Valuing All Families Under the Law* (Boston: Beacon Press, 2008), pp. 100–109.

39. Shanley, *Making Babies, Making Families* (2001), p. 144.

40. Barbara Bennett Woodhouse, "Hatching the Egg: A Child-Centered Perspective in Parents' Rights." 14 *Cardozo Law Review* 1747 (1993).

41. Shanley, *Making Babies, Making Families* (2001), p. 140.

42. Shanley, *Making Babies, Making Families* (2001), p. 82; Meyer, "Parenthood in a Time of Transition (2006); Naomi Cahn, "Perfect Substitutes or the Real Thing?" 52 *Duke L.J.* 1077 (2003).

43. Walter Wadlington and Raymond C. O'Brien, *Family Law in Perspective*, 2nd ed. (New York: Foundation Press, 2007), p. 113; "Developments in the Law: IV. Changing Realities of Parenthood: The Law's Response to the Evolving American Family and Emerging Reproductive Technologies," 116 *Harv. L. Rev.* 2052 (May 2003), p. 2067.

44. In cases in which the identity of the donor was known and the donor had developed a relationship with the ensuing child, the donor has (unsuccessfully) petitioned for parenting rights. *Matter of Thomas S. v. Robin Y.*, Court of Appeals of New York, 86 N.Y. 2d 779, 655 N.E. 2d 708, 631 N.Y.S. 2d 611 (July 26, 1995).

45. The most recent version of the Uniform Parentage Act treats egg donors like sperm donors, stripping them of all parenting rights and according exclusive parenting rights to the gestational mother.

46. K.M. v. E.G., 117 P.3d 673 (Cal. 2005).

47. The same is true of most European countries. The United States and India have attracted foreign couples in search of a surrogacy contract. See Lorraine Ali and Raina Kelly, "Womb for Rent: The Curious World of Surrogate Mothers," *Newsweek* (April 7, 2008), p. 47.

48. Uniform Parentage Act (Revised 2002), Article 8: Gestational Agreement, Comment.

49. Ali and Kelly, "Womb for Rent" (2008), p. 47.

50. *In the Matter of Baby M*, 537 A.2d 1227 (N.J. 1988). *Baby M* was atypical because most surrogates do not break their contracts.

51. Sperm is almost always anonymous when it is acquired through a fertility clinic. In these cases, the anonymous donor has no parenting rights or responsibilities.

52. Marjorie McGuire Schultz, "Reproductive Technology and Intent-Based Parenthood: An Opportunity for Gender Neutrality," 1990 *Wis. L. Rev.* 297. *Johnson v. Calvert* 5 Cal. 4th 84 (1993).

53. *In re marriage of Buzzanca*, 61 Cal. App. 4th 1410 (Cal. App. 1998).

54. For more on marriage and gender difference, see Linda C. McClain, "Love, Marriage, and the Baby Carriage" (2007).

55. Some of these organizations are religiously motivated, such as the Family Research Council, and others base their argument on social science research, such as the Heritage Foundation and the Institute for American Values. For critical analysis of the social movement to reassert traditional notions of family, see Karen Struening, *New Family Values: Liberty, Equality, Diversity* (Lanham, MD: Rowman & Littlefield, 2002); Fineman, *The Autonomy Myth* (2004); Linda C. McClain, *The Place of Families: Fostering Capacity, Equality and Responsibility* (Cambridge, MA: Harvard University Press, 2006); Polikoff, *Beyond (Straight and Gay) Marriage* (2008).

56. Healthy Marriage Initiative (2002), Administration for Children and Families, U.S. Department of Health and Human Services; available at: www.acf.hhs.gov/ healthymarriage/index.html; last accessed July 29, 2008. See Theodora Ooms, Stacey Bouchet, and Mary Parke, *Beyond Marriage Licenses: Efforts in States to Strengthen Marriage and Two-Parent Families* (Washington, DC: Center for Law and Social Policy, 2004); retrieved on July 29, 2008, from http://clasp.org/publications/beyond_marr.pdf. See also Struening, "Do Government Sponsored Marriage Promotion Policies Place Undue Pressure on Individual Rights" (2007).

57. Paula Roberts, *Update on the Marriage and Fatherhood Provisions of the 2006 Federal Budget and the 2007 Budget Proposal.* Washington, DC: Center for Law and Social Policy (February 10, 2006); retrieved on July 28, 2008, from http://s242739747 .onlinehome.us/publications/marriage_fatherhood_budget2006.pdf.

58. Claire Hughes, "On Heels of Success, Marriage Supporters Lobby for More Welfare Dollars" (Albany, NY: Rockefeller Institute of Government, State University of New York, The Roundtable on Religion and Social Welfare Policy, January 23, 2007).

59. A November 2, 2004, referendum amended the Michigan Constitution by adding the following text: "the union of one man and one woman in marriage shall be the only agreement recognized as marriage or similar union for any purpose" (Michigan State Constitution, Article I, Section 25). On May 7, 2008, the Michigan Supreme Court held that the amendment prohibited same-sex domestic partner benefits (Michigan Supreme Court, May 7, 2008, No. 133429).

60. The California Supreme Court's decision was reversed by a narrowly decided ballot measure on November 4, 2008. New Hampshire, legalized same-sex marriage on June 3, 2009.

61. *Hernandez v. Robles*, 855 N.E.2d 1, 7(N.Y. 2006).

62. Ibid.

63. Ibid., p. 15 (Justice Graffeo, concurring).

64. Vanessa A. Lavely, "Comment: The Path to Recognition of Same-Sex Marriage: Reconciling the Inconsistencies Between Marriage and Adoption Cases," 55 *UCLA L. Rev.* 247 (October 2007), pp. 286–287.

65. Polikoff, *Beyond (Straight and Gay) Marriage* (2008).

Chapter 9: Briefing Paper: Will Providing Marriage Rights to Same-Sex Couples Undermine Heterosexual Marriage? Evidence from Scandinavia, by M. V. Lee Badgett

1. Eskridge (2002); Sullivan (2001).

2. Eskridge (2002).

3. Kurtz (2004).

4. Kiernan (2001).

5. Kurtz (2000).

6. Kiernan (2001).

7. Andersson (2002).

8. Coleman and Garssen (2002); Sprangers and Garssen (2003).

9. Minot (2000).

10. Espring-Andersen (1999).

11. Ibid.

Chapter 10: Interracial Families In Post-Civil Rights America, by Kerry Ann Rockquemore and Loren Henderson

1. The phrase "Generation E.A." was used by Ruth La Ferla (2003) to describe the trend in advertising to use multiracial and ethnically ambiguous models because racial ambiguity is "chic" among young adults.

2. Simmons and O'Connell (2003) provide an overview of married and cohabitating couples using census data. Qian (1997) documents the differential rates of out-marriage for blacks, Asians, and Native Americans. For an overview of interracial marriage patterns in the United States, see Rosenfeld (2007).

3. Between 1958 and 1997, white approval of intermarriage with blacks rose from 4 percent to 67 percent. Approval rates are even higher among blacks, with 87 percent of blacks reporting approval of intermarriage in 1997 (Schuman, Steeh, Bobo, and Kryson, 1997).

4. Oliver and Shapiro's *Black Wealth/White Wealth* (1997) provides an overview of persistent institutional and economic inequalities between blacks and whites. Eduardo Bonilla-Silva (2001, 2003) describes the ideology of color blindness that underlies the Latin Americanization of race relations in the United States.

5. We focus explicitly on heterosexual couples in this chapter due to the dearth of empirical research on same-sex interracial couples. Steinbugler (2005) is a notable exception.

6. See Tukufu Zuberi, *Thicker Than Blood* (2001), as well as Omi and Winant (1994) for a macro-structural analysis of race, racial categories, and racism.

7. See Randall Kennedy's *Interracial Intimacies* (2003) for an historical analysis of interracial sex and coupling.

8. The "one-drop rule" mandates that anyone with one drop of "black blood" is a member of the black race. The idea is that "black blood" taints the purity of whiteness; therefore, even "one drop" deprives a person of any claim to whiteness. For an overview of the history of the one-drop rule, see F. James Davis, *Who Is Black?* (1991).

9. See Root (2001).

10. See Childs (2005b).

11. See Dalmage (2000).

12. Cohabitation can be seen as qualitatively different from legal marriage in terms of structure and interaction. Given that cohabitating couples may be seen as less stable, this may increase the perception that interracial couples are not as committed to their relationships as are same-race couples (Bratter and Eschbach, 2006).

13. See Dalmage (2000).

14. See Childs (2005b), p. 60.

15. See Dalmage (2000).

16. Steinbulger (2005), p. 433

17. See Dalmage (2000).

18. See Todd et al. (1992) and McNamara, Tempenis, and Walton (1999).

19. See Childs (2005a).

20. See Russell, Wilson, and Hall (1993).

21. Patricia Hill Collins (2004) critically examines how European notions of femininity and beauty combine with new forms of racism to disadvantage black women.

22. Childs (2005a), p. 554.

23. See Childs (2005b).

24. Some of the most powerful illustrations of the transformative power of interracial relationships appear in memoirs such as Jane Lazarre's *Beyond the Whiteness of Whiteness* (1996) and Maureen Reddy's *Crossing the Color Line* (1994).

25. Frankenberg (1993) describes the experience of secondhand experiences of discrimination and intolerance that white women in interracial couples experience as "rebound racism." Her analysis suggests that intimate relationships between whites and blacks shift white women's perspective on race relations and racism. She uses the term "racial cognizance" to describe a more advanced stage of understanding that whites evolve into as part of their development in interracial relationships.

26. See Twine and Steinbugler (2006) p. 344.

27. The excerpt is drawn from Twine and Steinbugler (2006) p. 354.

28. Rockquemore and Brunsma (2001).

29. This variation in racial identity has been replicated using various methodologies and data sets, for example, see Renn (2004) and Harris and Sim (2002).

30. See Renn (2004), and Wallace (2001).

31. See Hitlin, Brown, and Elder (2006).

Chapter 12: Why Is Everyone Afraid of Sex?, by Pepper Schwartz

1. Laumann, Mahay, and Youm (2007).

2. Bogle (2008).

3. Laumann et al. (1994).

4. Baumgardner (2007).

5. Klein and Strossen (2006).

6. Bearman and Brückner (2001); Brückner and Bearman (2005).

7. Laumann et al. (1994).

8. Schwartz and Rutter (2000).

9. Klein and Strossen (2006).

10. Rom (2007).

11. Wilcox et al. (2007).

12. Kinsey, Pomeroy, and Clyde (1948).

13. Baumgardner (2007).

14. Campbell and Robinson (2007).

15. Reiss and Reiss (2002).

16. Kamen (2000).

17. Tannenbaum (1999).

18. Carpenter (2005).

19. Jehl (1999).

20. D'Emilio and Freedman (1988).

21. Brandt (1987).

22. Shilts (1987).

23. D'Emilio and Freedman (1988).

24. Tiefer (1995).

25. Schwartz (2007).

26. Pascoe (2007).

27. Boonstra (2009).

Chapter 13: New Couples, New Families: The Cohabitation Revolution in the United States, by Pamela J. Smock and Wendy Manning

Some research discussed in this chapter was made possible from grants from the National Institutes of Health, Eunice Kennedy Shriver National Institute of Child Health and Human Development (R01 HD040910 and R03 HD039835) to the first and second authors, and to the Population Studies Center, University of Michigan and the Center for Family and Demographic Research, Bowling Green State University (R24 HD41028 and R24 HD050959).

1. See U.S. Department of Health and Human Services (2005).

2. See Bumpass and Lu (2000).

3. See Manning, Longmore, and Giordano (2007).

4. See Simmons and O'Connell (2003).

5. See Bumpass and Lu (2000), Bumpass and Sweet (1989), and Kennedy and Bumpass (2007).

6. See Kennedy and Bumpass (2007).

7. See Fields and Casper (2001).

8. See Fields and Casper (2001); Manning and Brown (2006).

9. See Smock, Manning, and Porter (2005) for a review of such studies.

10. See Smock and Manning (2004) for further discussion of the selection issue and its implications for debates about family policy.

11. See Smock, Manning, and Porter (2005).

12. See Clarkberg, Stolzenberg, and Waite (1995), Lye and Waldron (1997), and Thornton, Axinn, and Hill (1992).

13. See Kennedy and Bumpass (2007).

14. See Manning and Smock (2005).

15. See Nock (1995).

16. See Brown and Booth (1996).

17. See Kennedy and Bumpass (2007).

18. See Bumpass and Sweet (1989).

19. See Manning and Smock (2002).

20. See Fields and Casper (2001).

21. See Acs and Nelson (2002).

22. See Bumpass and Lu (2000) and Kennedy and Bumpass (2007).

23. See Brown (2000).

24. Manning (2001) and Musick (2002).

25. See Musick (2002).

26. See Bumpass, Raley, and Sweet (1995).

27. See Sullivan (2010), in Chapter 33 of this volume.

28. See Smock and Noonan (2005).

29. See South and Spitze (1994).

30. See Gupta (1999).

31. Ibid., p. 710.

32. See Stevens (1940).

33. There is even some evidence that cohabitation may be *replacing* remarriage for adults who are middle-aged or older.

34. See Casper and Bianchi (2002).

Chapter 14: Parenting Adult Children in the Twenty-First Century, by Joshua Coleman

1. Joshua Coleman, *The Lazy Husband: How to Get Men to Do More Parenting and Housework* (New York: St. Martin's Press, 2003).

2. Annette Lareau, *Unequal Childhoods: Class, Race, and Family Life* (Berkeley, CA: University of California Press, 2003).

3. Joshua Coleman, *When Parents Hurt: Compassionate Strategies When You and Your Grown Child Don't Get Along* (New York: HarperCollins, 2007).

4. Peter N. Stearns, *Anxious Parents: A History of Modern Childrearing in America* (New York: New York University Press, 2003).

5. Virgina A. Zelizer, *Pricing the Priceless Child: The Changing Social Value of Children* (Princeton: Princeton University Press, 1994).

6. Scott Coltrane, *Family Man: Fatherhood, Housework, and Gender Equity* (New York: Oxford University Press, 1996).

7. Stearns, *Anxious Parents* (2003).

8. Sigmund Freud, "Inhibitions, Symptoms, and Anxiety," in the Standard Edition of *The Complete Psychological Works*, Vol. 20, 77–175. (London: Hogarth Press, 1926).

9. Stearns, *Anxious Parents* (2003).

10. H. E. Marano, "A Nation of Wimps," *Psychology Today* (November/December, 2004).

11. Lareau, *Unequal Childhoods* (2003).

12. Steven Mintz, *Huck's Raft: A History of American Childhood* (Cambridge, MA: Harvard University Press, 2004).

13. Bruno Bettelheim, *The Empty Fortress: Infantile Autism and the Birth of the Self* (New York: Free Press, 1967).

14. Gregory Bateson, *Steps to an Ecology of Mind* (New York: Ballantine, 1980).

15. Stearns, *Anxious Parents* (2003).

16. Diane Ehrensaft, *Spoiling Childhood: How Well-Meaning Parents Are Giving Children Too Much—But Not What They Need* (New York: Guilford Press, 1997).

17. Stephanie Coontz, "How to Stay Married," *Times of London*, November 30, 2006; Robert D. Putnam, *Bowling Alone: The Collapse and Revival of American Community* (New York: Simon and Schuster, 2000).

18. Suzanne Bianchi, John Robinson, and Melissa Milke, *Changing Rhythms of American Family Life* (New York: Russell Sage Foundation, 2006); Oriel Sullivan and Scott Coltrane, *Men's Changing Contribution to Housework and Child Care*, Discussion paper prepared for the Council on Contemporary Families, 2008.

19. Steven Mintz, "How We All Became Jewish Mothers," *National Post*, February 17, 2006.

20. Pew Research Center. *Adult Children and Parents Talking More Often*, Februrary 23, 2006.

21. E. Mavis Heatherington and John Kelly, *For Better or Worse: Divorce Reconsidered* (New York: W. W. Norton, 2002).

22. Paul R. Amato and Alan Booth, *A Generation at Risk* (Cambridge, MA: Harvard University Press 1997); Hetherington and Kelly, *For Better or Worse* (2002).

23. C. Ahrons, *We're Still Family* (New York: HarperCollins, 2004); C. Ahrons and J. L. Tanner, "Adult Children and Their Fathers: Relationship Changes 20 Years After Parental Divorce," *Family Relations* 52 (2003): 340–351.

24. L. Nielsen, *Embracing Your Father: How to Build the Relationship You've Always Wanted with Your Dad* (New York: McGraw-Hill, 2004); Hetherington and Kelly, *For Better or Worse* (2002).

25. I-Fen Lin, "Consequences of Parental Divorce for Adult Children's Support of Their Frail Parents," *Journal of Marriage and Family* 70 (2008): 113–128.

26. Paul Amato and Julie Sobolewski, "The Effects of Divorce on Fathers and Children: Nonresidential Fathers and Stepfathers," pp. 341–367, in *The Role of the Father in Child Development*, 4th ed., edited by Michael Lamb (New York: Wiley, 2004); N. Baum. "Postdivorce Paternal Disengagement," *Journal of Marriage and Family Therapy* 32 (2006): 245–254.

27. Hetherington and Kelly, *For Better or Worse* (2002); Nielsen, *Embracing Your Father* (2004).

28. Stephanie Coontz, *American Families: A Multicultural Reader*, 2nd ed. (New York: Routledge, 2008).

29. Constance Flanagan, "The Changing Social Contract at the Transition to Adulthood: Implications for Individuals and the Polity," in R. Silbereisen, *Social and Political Change in Adolescent Development*. Invited paper symposium for the biennial meetings of the Society for Research on Adolescence, San Francisco, CA, March 2006; S. Danziger & P. Gottschalk, "Diverging Fortunes: Trends in Poverty and Inequality," in *The American People: Census 2000 Series*, edited by R. Farley (New York: Russell Sage Foundation and Population Reference Bureau, 2005).

30. *The Onion*, "Most Americans Falling for 'Get Rich Slowly over a Lifetime of Hard Work' Scheme," *The Onion*, Volume 41, Issue 49, December 7, 2005, p. 2.

31. Marvi Lacar, "The Bank of Mom and Dad," *New York Times*, April 9, 2006.

32. Annette Lareau, *Unequal Childhoods* (2003); Barry Schwartz, *The Paradox of Choice: Why More Is Less* (New York: Harper's Perennial, 2004).

33. Martin E. P. Seligman, *The Optimistic Child: Proven Program to Safeguard Children from Depression and Build Lifelong Resilience* (New York: Houghton Mifflin, 1996).

34. Stephanie Coontz, *The Way We Really Are: Coming to Terms with America's Changing Families* (New York: Basic Books, 1997), p. 151.

35. J. Dunn and R. Plomin, *Separate Lives: Why Siblings Are So Different* (New York: Basic Books, 1990); Judith Rich Harris, *The Nurture Assumption: Why Children Turn Out the Way They Do* (New York: Touchstone, 1999); D. Reiss, J. M. Neiderhiser, E. M. Hetherington, and R. Plomin, *The Relationship Code: Deciphering Genetic and Social Influences on Adolescent Development* (Cambridge, MA: Harvard University Press, 2000).

36. Chris Knoester, "Transitions in Young Adulthood and the Relationships Between Parent and Offspring Well-Being," *Social Forces*, 81 (2003): 1431–1458.

37. Stephanie Coontz, *The Way We Really Are* (1997).

Chapter 16: The Case for Divorce, by Virginia E. Rutter

1.   See Ruggles (1997).

2.   See Heuveline (2005).

3.   Discussed by Stevenson and Wolfers (2006).

4.   Reported by Cowen (2007).

5.   See Coltrane and Adams (2003).

6.   See Hetherington and Stanley-Hagan (1997).

7.   See Wallerstein and Blakeslee (1988).

8.   A complete, accessible review of Hetherington's longitudinal research is in Hetherington and Kelly (2002).

9.   See Hetherington (1999).

10. Cherlin et al. (1991).

11. Cherlin et al. (1998).

12. Amato and Sobolewski (2001).

13. See Waite et al. (2002); Rutter (2004).

14. Hawkins and Booth (2005).

15. See Smock, Manning, and Gupta (1999).

16. Meadows, McLanahan, and Brooks-Gunn (2008).

17. See Gottman (1994); Kiecolt-Glaser et al. (1988); and Robles and Kiecolt-Glaser (2003).

18. See Weissman (1987).

19. See Whisman (1999) on depression and Campbell (1998) on domestic violence.

20. See van Hemert, van de Vijver, and Poortinga (2002) and Veenhoven (2004) on the World Database of Happiness.

21. Greenberg et al. (1993a, 1993b).

22. See Li (2008) and Li (2007); also see Scafidi (2008).

23. See Coontz and Folbre (2002).

24. See Stevenson and Wolfers note in Li (2007) and Ananat and Michaels (2008).

25. Fomby and Cherlin (2007).

26. Osborne and McLanahan (2007).

Chapter 19: Briefing Paper: Marriage, Poverty, and Public Policy, by Stephanie Coontz and Nancy Folbre

1.   Alexandra Starr, "Shotgun Wedding by Uncle Sam?" *Business Week*, June 4, 2001.

2.   Cheryl Wetzstein, "States Want Pro-Family Funds," *Washington Times*, December 10, 2001; Robin Toner and Robert Pear, "Bush Urges Work and Marriage Programs in Welfare Plan," *New York Times*, February 27, 2002.

3.   Jonathan Rauch, "The Widening Marriage Gap: America's New Class Divide," *National Journal*, May 18, 2001.

4. Cheryl Wetzstein, "Unwed Mothers Set a Record for Births," *Washington Times*, April 18, 2001.

5. See Jared Bernstein, Irv Garfinkel, and Sara McLanahan, *A Progressive Marriage Agenda*, forthcoming from the Economic Policy Institute.

6. U.S. Bureau of the Census, "Historical Poverty Statistics—Table 4. Poverty Status of Families, by Type of Family, Presence of Related Children, Race, and Hispanic Origin: 1959–2000," available at www.census.gov. In 1999, 36 percent of single-mother households lived in poverty. *Poverty in the U.S. 1999*, Current Population Reports, P60-210 (Washington, DC: Government Printing Office, 2000).

7. Alan Guttmacher Institute, "Married Mothers Fare the Best Economically, Even If they Were Unwed at the Time They Gave Birth," *Family Planning Perspectives* 31, no. 5 (September 1999): 258–260. Ariel Halpern, *Poverty Among Children Born Outside of Marriage: Preliminary Findings from the National Survey of America's Families* (Washington, DC: Urban Institute, 1999).

8. Calculations by Arloc Sherman, Children's Defense Fund, based on the March 2001 Current Population Survey.

9. Ibid. See also Neil G. Bennett, Jiali Li, Younghwan Song, and Keming Yang, "Young Children in Poverty: A Statistical Update," released June 17, 1999 (New York: National Center for Children in Poverty), available at http://cpmcnet.columbia.edu/dept/nccp/99uptext.html

10. Linda Giannarelli and James Barsimantov, *Child Care Expenses of America's Families*, Occasional Paper Number 40 (Washington, DC: Urban Institute, 2000).

11. Rachel Schumacher and Mark Greenberg, *Child Care After Leaving Welfare: Early Evidence from State Studies* (Washington, DC: Center for Law and Social Policy, 1999).

12. Kathryn H. Porter and Allen Dupree, "Poverty Trends for Families Headed by Working Single Mothers, 1993–1999," Center on Budget and Policy Priorities, August 16, 2001. For full article, see www.cbpp.org/8-16-01wel.pdf.

13. Pamela Smock, "Cohabitation in the U.S.: An Appraisal of Research Themes, Findings, and Implications," *American Review of Sociology* 26, no.1 (2000): 1–20.

14. Gregory Acs and Sandi Nelson, "'Honey, I'm Home.' Changes in Living Arrangements in the Late 1990s," *New Federalism: National Survey of America's Families* (Washington, DC: Urban Institute, June 2001), pp. 1–7. A new study by Johns Hopkins researchers, presented on February 20, 2002, at a welfare forum in Washington, DC, however, shows that these partnerships are unstable and may not be better for children than single-parent households. See Robin Toner, "Two Parents Not Always Best for Children, Study Finds," *New York Times*, February 20, 2002.

15. Many dual-earner families with preschool-age children include a parent who works evenings and nights in order to provide care during the day while their husband or wife is at work. See Harriet Presser, "Employment Schedules Among Dual-Earner Spouses and the Division of Household Labor by Gender," *American Sociological Review* 59, no. 3 (June 1994): 348–364.

16. Kristen Harknett and Sara McLanahan, "Do Perceptions of Marriage Explain Marital Behavior? How Unmarried Parents' Assessments of the Benefits of Marriage Relate to Their Subsequent Marital Decision;" and Marcia Carlson, Sara McLanahan, and Paula

England, "Union Formation and Stability in Fragile Families," papers presented at the meetings of the Population Association of America, Washington DC, April 2001.

17. More details on the Fragile Families study are available at http://crcw.princeton.edu/fragilefamilies/nationalreport.pdf.

18. Maureen Waller, "High Hopes: Unwed Parents' Expectations About Marriage," *Children and Youth Services Review* 23 (2001): 457–484.

19. Sara McLanahan, "Parent Absence or Poverty: Which Matters More?," in *Consequences of Growing Up Poor*, edited by Greg Duncan and Jeanne Brooks-Gunn (New York: Russell Sage Foundation, 1997), pp. 35–48. On the impact of poverty in creating non-marriage and marital disruption, see Aimee Dechter, "The Effect of Women's Economic Independence on Union Dissolution," Working Paper No. 92-28 (1992), Center for Demography and Ecology, University of Wisconsin, Madison; Mark Testa et al., "Employment and Marriage among Inner-City Fathers," *Annals of the American Academy of Political and Social Science* 501 (1989): 79–91; Karen Holden and Pamela Smock, "The Economic Costs of Marital Dissolution: Why Do Women Bear a Disproportionate Cost?" *Annual Review of Sociology* 17 (1991): 51–58. On the association of low income with domestic violence, see Kristin Anderson, "Gender, Status, and Domestic Violence," *Journal of Marriage and Family* 59 (1997): 655–670; A. M. Moore, "Intimate Violence: Does Socioeconomic Status Matter?" in *Violence Between Intimate Partners*, edited by A. P. Gardarelli (Boston: Allyn & Bacon, 1997), pp. 90–100; A. J. Sedlack and D. D. Broadhurst, *Third National Incidence Study of Child Abuse and Neglect: Final Report* (Washington DC: Department of Health and Human Services, 1996).

20. Daniel T. Lichter, *Marriage As Public Policy* (Washington, DC: Progressive Policy Institute, September 2001).

21. Kathryn Edin, "A Few Good Men: Why Poor Mothers Don't Marry or Remarry?" *American Prospect*, January 3, 2000, p. 28; Kathryn Edin and Laura Lein, *Making Ends Meet: How Single Mothers Survive Welfare and Low-Wage Work* (New York: Russell Sage Foundation, 1998).

22. Valerie Oppenheimer and Vivian Lew, "American Marriage Formation in the 1980s," in *Gender and Family Change in Industrialized Countries*, edited by Karen Mason and An-Magritt Jensen (Oxford: Oxford University Press, 1994), pp. 105–138; Sharon Sassler and Robert Schoen, "The Effects of Attitudes and Economic Activity on Marriage," *Journal of Marriage and Family* 61 (1999): 148–149.

23. John Billy and David Moore, "A Multilevel Analysis of Marital and Nonmarital Fertility in the U.S.," *Social Forces* 70 (1992): 977–1011; Sara McLanahan and Irwin Garfinkel, "Welfare Is No Incentive," *New York Times*, July 29, 1994, p. A13; Elaine McCrate, "Expectations of Adult Wages and Teenage Childbearing," *International Review of Applied Economics* 6 (1992): 309–328; Ellen Coughlin, "Policy Researchers Shift the Terms of the Debate on Women's Issues," *Chronicle of Higher Education*, May 31, 1989; Marian Wright Edelman, *Families in Peril: An Agenda for Social Change* (Cambridge, MA: Harvard University Press, 1987), p. 55; Lawrence Lynn and Michael McGeary, eds., *Inner-City Poverty in the United States* (Washington, DC: National Academy Press, 1990), pp. 163–67; Jonathan Crane, "The Epidemic Theory of Ghetto and Neighborhood Effects on Dropping Out and Teenaged Childbearing," *American*

Journal of Sociology 96 (1991): 1226–1259; Sara McLanahan and Lynne Casper, "Growing Diversity and Inequality in the American Family," in *State of the Union in the 1990s*, vol. 2, edited by Reynolds Farley (New York: Russell Sage Foundation, 1995), pp. 1–46; Mike Males, "Poverty, Rape, Adult/Teen Sex: Why 'Pregnancy Prevention' Programs Don't Work," *Phi Delta Kappan*, January 1994, p. 409; Mike Males, "In Defense of Teenaged Mothers," *The Progressive*, August 1994, p. 23.

24. Diane McLaughlin and Daniel Lichter, Poverty and the Marital Behavior of Young Women," *Journal of Marriage and Family* 59, no. 3 (1997): 582–594.

25. Wendy Sigle-Rushton and Sara McLanahan, "For Richer or Poorer?" manuscript, Center for Research on Child Well-Being, Princeton University, July 2001, p. 4; Kathryn Edin, "What Do Low-Income Single Mothers Say About Marriage?" *Social Problems* 47 (2000): 112–133.

26. Robert Nakosteen and Michael Zimmer, "Man, Money, and Marriage: Are High Earners More Prone than Low Earners to Marry?" *Social Science Quarterly* 78 (1997): 66–82.

27. Francine D. Blau, Lawrence W. Kahn, and Jane Waldfogel, "Understanding Young Women's Marriage Decisions: The Role of Labor and Marriage Market Conditions," *Industrial and Labor Relations Review* 53, no. 4 (July 2000): 624–648.

28. Nakosteen and Zimmer, "Men, Money, and Marriage" (1997); Frank F. Furstenberg, Jr. "The Future of Marriage," *American Demographics* 18 (June 1996): 39–40; Blau, Kahn, and Waldfogel, "Understanding Young Women's Marriage Decisions" (2000).

29. William A. Darity, Jr., and Samuel L. Myers, Jr., "Family Structure and the Marginalization of Black Men: Policy Implications," in *The Decline in Marriage Among African Americans: Causes, Consequences, and Policy Implications*, edited by M. Belinda Tucker and Claudia Mitchell-Kernan (New York: Russell Sage Foundation, 1995), pp. 263–308.

30. Daniel T. Lichter, D. McLaughlin, F. LeClere, G. Kephart, and D. Landry, "Race and the Retreat from Marriage: A Shortage of Marriageable Men?" *American Sociological Review* 57 (December 1992): 781–799.

31. Ron Mincy, Columbia University, personal communication, February 18, 2002.

32. E. Mavis Hetherington and John Kelly, *For Better or for Worse: Divorce Reconsidered* (New York: W. W. Norton, 2002); Paul Amato and Alan Booth, "The Legacy of Parents' Marital Discord," *Journal of Personality and Social Psychology* 81 (2001): 627–638; Andrew Cherlin, "Going to Extremes: Family Structure, Children's Well-Being, and Social Science," *Demography* 36 (November 1999): 421–428.

33. Elizabeth Cooksey, "Consequences of Young Mothers' Marital Histories for Children's Cognitive Development," *Journal of Marriage and Family* 59 (May 1997): 245–262; Juan Battle, "What Beats Having Two Parents? Educational Outcomes for African American Students in Single- Versus Dual-Parent Families," *Journal of Black Studies* 28 (1998): 783–802.

34. Ron Mincy and Chen-Chung Huang, "'Just Get Me to the Church . . .': Assessing Policies to Promote Marriage among Fragile Families," manuscript prepared for the MacArthur Foundation Network on the Family and the Economy Meeting, Evanston, Illinois, November 30, 2001. Contact Ron Mincy, School of Social Work, Columbia University.

35. Research by Andrew Cherlin and Paula Fomby at Johns Hopkins University, as reported in Toner, "Two Parents Not Always Best for Children" (2002).

36. Frank Furstenberg, Jeanne Brooks-Gunn, and S. Philip Morgan, *Adolescent Mothers in Later Life* (New York: Cambridge University Press, 1987).

37. Frank Furstenberg, "Is the Modern Family a Threat to Children's Health?" *Society* 36 (1999): 35.

38. Richard Gelles, "Constraints Against Family Violence," *American Behavioral Scientist* 36 (1993): 575–586; Sedlack and Broadhurst, *Third National Incidence Study of Child Abuse and Neglect: Final Report* (1996); Anderson, "Gender, Status and Domestic Violence" (1997); Jacqueline Payne and Martha Davis, "Testimony of NOW Legal Defense and Education Fund on Child Support and Fatherhood Initiatives," submitted to the United States House Human Resources Subcommittee of the Ways and Means Committee, June 28, 2001.

39. Catherine Kenney and Sara McLanahan, "Are Cohabiting Relationships More Violent Than Marriages?" manuscript, Princeton University, 2002; E. D. Leonard, "Battered Women and Criminal Justice: A Review, 1994, doctoral dissertation cited in Todd Migliaccio, "Abused Husbands: A Narrative Analysis," *Journal of Family Issues* 23 (2002): 26–52; K. D. O'Leary et al., "Prevalence and Stability of Physical Aggression Between Spouses: A Longitudinal Analysis," *Journal of Consulting and Clinical Psychology* 57 (1989): 263–268.

40. National Center on Addiction and Substance Abuse at Columbia University, "Back to School 1999 — National Survey of American Attitudes on Substance Abuse V: Teens and Their Parents," August 1999. See also Irvin Molotsky, "Study Links Teenage Substance Abuse and Paternal Ties," *New York Times*, August 31, 1999.

41. "Census Bureau Reports Poor Two-Parent Families Are about Twice As Likely to Break Up As Two-Parent Families Not in Poverty," *New York Times*, January 15, 1993, p. A6; Don Burroughs, "Love and Money," *U.S. News & World Report*, October 19, 1992, p. 58; Scott South, Katherine Trent, and Yang Shen, "Changing Partners: Toward a Macrostructural-Opportunity Theory of Marital Dissolution," *Journal of Marriage and Family* 63, no. 3 (2001): 743–754. Also see information on Fragile Families Study at http://crew:princeton.edu/fragilefamilies/nationalreport.pdf.

42. Michelle Budig and Paula England, "The Wage Penalty for Motherhood," *American Sociological Review* 66 (2001): 204–225; Heather Joshi, Pierella Paci, and Jane Waldfogel, "The Wages of Motherhood: Better or Worse," *Cambridge Journal of Economics* 23, no. 5 (1999): pp. 543–564; Jane Waldfogel, "The Effect of Children on Women's Wages," *American Sociological Review* 62, no. 2 (1997): 209–217.

43. Bennett, Li, Song, and Yang, "Young Children in Poverty: A Statistical Update" (1999). http://cpmcnet.columbia.edu/dept/nccp/99uptext.html. Data for 2000 from CPS, http://ferret.bls.census.gov/macro/032001/pov/new01_003.htm.

44. Nancy Folbre, *Who Pays for the Kids? Gender and the Structures of Constraint* (New York: Routledge, 1994); Ann Crittenden, *The Price of Motherhood: Why the Most Important Job in the World Is the Least Valued* (New York: Metropolitan Books/Holt, 2001); Sylvia Ann Hewlett and Cornell West, *The War Against Parents* (New York: Houghton Mifflin, 1998).

45. Joan Williams, *Unbending Gender. Why Family and Work Conflict and What to Do About It.* (New York: Oxford University Press, 2000).

46. Crittenden, *The Price of Motherhood* (2001).

47. Timothy Smeeding, Barbara Boyle Torrey, and Martin Rein, "Patterns of Income and Poverty: The Economic Status of Children and the Elderly in Eight Countries," in *The Vulnerable*, edited by John L. Palmer, Timothy Smeeding, and Barbara Boyle Torrey (Washington, DC: Urban Institute Press, 1988); Sharon Houseknecht and Jaya Sastry, "Family 'Decline' and Child Well-Being: A Comparative Assessment," *Journal of Marriage and Family* 58 (1996): 726–739; Sara McLanahan and Irwin Garfinkel, "Single-Mother Families and Social Policy: Lessons for the United States from Canada, France, and Sweden," in *Poverty, Inequality, and the Future of Social Policy: Western States in the New World Order*, edited by K. McFate, R. Lawson, and W. J. Wilson (New York: Russell Sage Foundation, 1995), pp. 367–83; Michael J. Graetz and Jerry L. Mashaw, *True Security: Rethinking American Social Insurance* (New Haven: Yale University Press, 1999).

48. Marcia K. Meyers, Janet C. Gornick, and Laura R. Peck, "Packaging Support for Low-Income Families: Policy Variation Across the U.S. States," *Journal of Policy Analysis and Management* 20, no. 3 (2001): 457–483.

49. Table 7-6, *Green Book 2000*. Committee on Ways and Means, U.S. House of Representatives, 106th Congress. Available at www.access.gpo.gov/congress/wm001.html.

50. President's Council of Economic Advisors, *The Effects of Welfare Policy and the Economic Expansion of Welfare Caseloads: An Update* (Washington, DC: Council of Economic Advisors, 1999).

51. *2000 Kids Count Data Online*, www.aecf.org/kidscount/kc2000/sum_11.htm.

52. Jennifer Steinhauer, "States Proved Unpredictable in Aiding Uninsured Children," *New York Times*, September 28, 2000. See also Leighton Ku and Brian Bruen, "The Continuing Decline in Medicaid Coverage" Series A, No. A-37 (Washington, DC: Urban Institute, 1999); Sheila Zedlewski and Sarah Brauner, "Are the Steep Declines in Food Stamp Participation Linked to Falling Welfare Caseloads?" Series B, No. B-3 (Washington, DC: Urban Institute, 1999).

53. Schumacher and Greenberg, *Child Care After Leaving Welfare* (1999). On the added costs of child care and care-giving activities for low-income families, see Jody Heymann, *The Widening Gap: Why America's Working Families Are in Jeopardy and What Can Be Done about It* (New York: Basic Books, 2000).

54. Bureau of the Census, Current Population Reports, *Money Income and Poverty in the U.S.*, 1999. Figures for 2000 from ferret.bls.census.gov/macro/032001/pov/new17_008.htm.

55. Patricia Ruggles, *Drawing the Line: Alternative Poverty Measures and Their Implications for Public Policy* (Washington, DC: Urban Institute Press, 1990); Constance Citro and Robert Michael, eds. *Measuring Poverty: A New Approach* (Washington, DC: National Academy of Science, 1995); Jared Bernstein, Chauna Brocht, and Maggie Spade-Aguilar, *How Much Is Enough? Basic Family Budgets for Working Families* (Washington, DC: Economic Policy Institute, 2000).

56. Robert Greenstein, "Should EITC Benefits Be Enlarged for Families with Three or More Children?" Washington, DC: Center on Budget and Policy Priorities, 2000. Available at www.cbpp.org/3-14-tax.htm.

57. David Ellwood and Jeffrey B. Liebman, "The Middle Class Parent Penalty: Child Benefits in the U.S. Tax Code," manuscript, John F. Kennedy School of Government, Harvard University, Boston, MA., 2000.

58. Robert Cherry and Max Sawicky, "Giving Tax Credit Where Credit is Due," Briefing Paper (Washington, DC: Economic Policy Institute, April 2000). Available at www.epinet.org/briefingpapers/eitc.html.

59. Ronald B. Mincy, "Marriage, Child Poverty, and Public Policy," *American Experiment Quarterly* 4, no. 2 (Summer 2001): 68–71. See also Sigle-Rushton and McLanahan, "For Richer or Poorer?" (2001).

60. Julianne Malveaux, "More Jobs, Not More Marriages, Lift Poor," *U.S.A. Today*, February 22, 2002, p. 15A.

Chapter 20: From Outlaws to In-Laws: Gay and Lesbian Couples in Contemporary Society, by Robert-Jay Green

1. Balsam, Beauchaine, Rothblum, and Solomon (2008); Kurdek, (2004, 2005); Peplau and Fingerhut (2007); Roisman et al. (2008); Solomon, Rothblum, and Balsam (2004).

2. Green, Bettinger, and Zacks (1996).

3. Gottmon et al. (2003a, 2003b).

4. Herek (1998).

5. Emilio (1998); Katz (1992).

6. Faderman (1991).

7. D'Augelli, Grossman, and Rendina (2006); D'Augelli, Rendina, Sinclair, and Grossman, (2006/2007).

8. Ragins, Singh, and Cornwell (2007).

9. Because the legal status of same-sex marriage is changing so rapidly, readers are advised to consult the following Web site for updated information: www.freedomtomarry.org/states.php.

10. People for the American Way, www.pfaw.org

11. Crowl, Ahn, and Baker (2008); Patterson (2005); Wainright and Patterson (2008); Wainright, Russell, and Patterson (2004).

12. Crowl, Ahn, and Baker (2008); Stacey and Biblarz (2001); Tasker and Patterson (2007).

13. Meyer (2003).

14. Herek (2006); Herdt and Kertzner (2006).

15. See Clifford, Hertz, and Doskow (2007) for examples.

16. Lanutti (2008); Savin-Williams (2001).

17. Weston (1991).

18. For these topics, see especially Firestein (2007); Laird and Green (1996); and Lev (2004).

19. Romero, Baumle, Badget, and Gates (2007).

20. Egan, Edelman, and Sherrill (2008).

21. D'Augelli, Grossman, and Rendina (2006).

22. Saad (2008).

23. Ibid.

24. Quinnipiac University Polling Institute (2008).

25. CNN (2008).

26. Pew Research Center (2007).

Chapter 21: Independent Women: Equality in African-American Lesbian Relationships, by Mignon R. Moore

1. Examples include work by Patterson (1995), Kurdek (1993), Carrington (1999), Gartrell et al. (2000) and Mezey (2008). But Maureen Sullivan's 2004 study is one exception. Although her sample is almost all white and middle-class, the family backgrounds of her respondents include both working and middle-class experiences, which are reflected in the way they conceptualize their lesbian relationships.

2. Walby (1990).

3. For example, in Sullivan's 2004 study of lesbian-headed families, economic independence is not a direct concern for her respondents because they are largely middle-class, dual-earner couples with relatively secure jobs and financial resources. A portion of her sample is working class, but the author's analysis of egalitarianism in these families concerns how the partners divide housework and child care and does not focus on the association between economic independence and relationship satisfaction. Sullivan finds that self-sufficiency is a trait some women from working-class families were raised to value in their relationships, but it is not a deciding factor in their decision making about family and work responsibilities (p. 108). Nelson's 1996 study of lesbian-headed households finds conflict around parenting authority among partners in blended families, but it does not provide an analysis of the way respondents feel about economic independence and self-sufficiency in their unions.

4. See, for example, Myra Marx Ferree, "The Gender Division of Labor in Two-Earner Marriages," *Journal of Family Issues* 12 (1991): 158–180; Arlie Hochschild, *The Second Shift: Working Parents and the Revolution at Home.* (New York: Viking, 1989); Veronica Tichenor, *Earning More and Getting Less: Why Successful Wives Can't Buy Equality.* (New Brunswick, NJ: Rutgers University Press, 2005).

5. See, for example, Christopher Carrington, *No Place Like Home: Relationships and Family Life among Lesbians and Gay Men* (Chicago: University of Chicago Press, 1999); Maureen Sullivan, *The Family of Woman: Lesbian Mothers, Their Children, and the Undoing of Gender* (Berkeley, CA: University of California Press, 2004); Lawrence Kurdek "The Allocation of Household Labor in Gay, Lesbian, Heterosexual, and Married Couples," *Journal of Social Issues* 49 (1993): 127–139; Mignon R. Moore "Gendered Power Relations among Women: A Study of Household Decision-Making in Black, Lesbian Stepfamilies," *American Sociological Review* 73 (2008): 335–356.

6. See Kurdek (1993); Patterson (1995); Nelson (1996); Sullivan (2004).

7. Blumstein and Schwartz (1983), p. 60.

8. For differences between black and white heterosexual couples in the relative importance of economic contributions of partners, see Bulcroft and Bulcroft (1993). For the relationship between race and gender ideologies among women and men, see Ransford and Miller (1983); Hunter and Sellers (1998); Kamo and Cohen (1998). For understandings of married and cohabiting couples and their financial accounts, see Kenney (2006).

9. Wolf (1979).

10. I make this argument in my 2006 article, "Lipstick or Timberlands? Meanings of Gender Presentation in Black Lesbian Communities," *Signs: Journal of Women in Culture and Society* 32(1): 113–39. Even many college-educated black lesbians first came into their gay sexualities in predominantly black social circles and predominantly black college settings. See Cornwell (1983); Abdulahad et al. (1983).

11. See Dang and Frazer (2004); Gates (2008).

12. Four percent of women in the sample might be considered "working poor" because they were single mothers and their income-to-needs ratio at the time of the interview put them below the poverty line for their family size. These women have been included in the working-class socioeconomic category in this study.

13. For details on the sample recruitment and other information on these data, see Moore (2008).

14. See Moore (2008) for an analysis of the division of household labor and the importance of economic independence in the Invisible Families data.

15. All names are pseudonyms. The ages given for the respondents are their ages in the year 2004.

16. See Schwartz (1994), p. 111.

17. Sullivan (2004) reports something similar among the portion of her sample that was working class. She found that women from working-class backgrounds were taught "not to depend on anyone for material or other support but to survive and make a life for oneself, by oneself, because no one would be there to help" (p. 107).

18. Landry (2000), p. 79.

19. Landry (2000) also makes this argument in his work.

20. See Combahee River Collective (1983).

21. See King (1988) and Combahee River Collective (1983).

22. See Collins (2004); Dill (1979).

23. See Kessler-Harris (2003).

24. See Crenshaw (1995); Collins (2004).

Chapter 22: The Immigration Kaleidoscope: Knowing the Immigrant Family Next Door, by Etiony Aldarondo and Edward Ameen

1. Hirschman (2006).

2. Passel (2006).

3. Minuchin (1984), p. 3.
4. Gallup/CNN/USA *Today* (2002).
5. See Espenshade (1997).
6. Camarota (2007).
7. Briggs (2003).
8. Guskin and Wilson (2007), p. 19.
9. Camarota (2007).
10. Fix and Capps (2004).
11. Gallup Poll (2000).
12. Singh and Hiatt (2006).
13. Suárez-Orozco, Suárez-Orozco, and Todorova (2008).
14. Mohanty et al. (2005).
15. Ibid., p. 1431.
16. Hao and Johnson (2000), p. 602; Fennelly (2006).
17. Harker (2001).
18. Gonzalez (2006).
19. Ibid., p. 6.
20. New Democrat Network (2007).
21. *Wall Street Journal* (2006, April 3). Matthew Dowd, chief pollster to President Bush, quoted in "Republicans Fear 'Amnesty,' but They Should Fear Losing Hispanics," The Journal Editorial Report. Included in New Democrat Network Presentation (2007).
22. New Democrat Network (2007), p. 17.
23. Reardon-Anderson, Capps, and Fix (2002).
24. DeSipio (2008).
25. Camarota (2007).
26. Capps et al. (2003).
27. Camarota (2007).
28. Reardon-Anderson, Capps, and Fix (2002).
29. Allen (2005).
30. Koepke (2007).
31. Ibid., p. 16.
32. Passel, Capps, and Fix (2004).
33. Institute for the Future (2007).
34. Mutti (2002).
35. Migration Policy Institute (2004).
36. Chomsky (2007).
37. Ibid., p. 13.

38. Executive Office of the President (2007).

39. Greico (2002).

40. Allen (2005).

41. Fuligni (1998), p. 99.

42. Suárez-Orozco and Suárez-Orozco (2001).

43. Singh and Hiatt (2006).

44. Camarota (2007).

45. Rumbaut (2002).

46. Suárez-Orozco, Suárez-Orozco, and Todorova (2008), p. 52.

47. Levanthal, Yange, and Brooks-Gunn (2006).

48. Suárez-Orozco, Suárez-Orozco, and Todorova (2008), p. 52.

49. Allen (2005), p. 19.

50. Gonzalez (2007).

51. Ibid.

52. Rumbaut and Ewing (2007), p. 1.

53. Ibid.

54. Hernandez and McGoldrick (2005).

55. Ibid., p. 178.

56. Pyke (2000), p. 240.

57. Sluzki (1998), p. 13.

58. Chapman and Perreira (2005), p. 106.

59. Singh and Hiatt (2006).

60. Hernandez (2004a).

61. Hernandez (2004b), p. 24.

62. Portes and Rumbaut (2001).

63. Ibid.

64. Levitt, Lane, and Levitt (2005).

65. Berry (2007).

66. Chapman and Perreira (2005).

67. Fuligni (1998).

68. Portes and Rumbaut (2001).

69. Chang (2003).

70. Fennelly (2006).

71. Ibid.

72. Allen (2005), p. 20.

73. Farkas, Duffet, and Johnson (2003).

74. Ibid., p. 38.

75. Trueba (2002), p. 7.
76. Falicov (2002), p. 291.
77. Phinney, Berry, Sam, and Vedder (2006).
78. Deaux (2006), pp. 84–85.
79. Chavez (2001).

Chapter 23: Beyond Family Structure: Family Process Studies Help to Reframe Debates about What's Good for Children, by Philip A. Cowan and Carolyn Pape Cowan

1. See Fagan, Patterson, and Rector (2002).
2. See Stacey and Biblarz (2001).
3. See Waite and Gallagher (2000).
4. See Davies, Cummings, and Winter (2004).
5. For reviews of the research, see Ahrons (2004); Amato (2001); Hetherington and Kelly (2002); Pruett (2009); Rodgers and Pryor (1998); Wallerstein, Lewis, and Blakeslee (2000).
6. See Hetherington and Kelly (2002).
7. See Amato (2000).
8. See Moore, Jekielek, and Emig (2002).
9. A good example is Haskins and Sawhill (2003) of the Brookings Institute.
10. See Cherlin (2005).
11. For example, Blankenhorn, Bayme, and Elshtain (1990).
12. See Edin and Kefalus (2005).
13. See Conger et al. (1994).
14. See P. A Cowan and C. P. Cowan (2006).
15. See Belsky and Barends (2002); Seifer and Dickstein (2000) for reviews.
16. Even very good ones; see, for example, Brazelton and Sparrow (2001), Faber and Mazlish (1995).
17. See Baumrind (1980); P. A. Cowan, Powell, and Cowan (1998).
18. See Luchetti (1999).
19. For reviews of fatherhood research, see P. A. Cowan et al. (2008); Lamb (2000); Tamis-LeMonda and Cabrera (2002).
20. See Blankenhorn (1995) and Popenoe (1996).
21. Silverstein and Auerbach (1999) have a useful discussion of this issue.
22. See Bronfenbrenner and Ceci (1994).
23. Parke (1996) and Pruett (2000) are among them.
24. See Cummings, Davies, and Campbell's text (2000), which presents a family systems view of child psychopathology.

25. See P. A. Cowan and C. P. Cowan (2002) and Cui and Conger (2008).

26. See Cicchetti, Toth, and Maughan (2000).

27. See Caspi and Elder (1988).

28. See McLoyd (1990) and Mistry, Vandewater, Huston, and McLoyd (2002).

29. See Conger et al. (1994).

30. See P. A. Cowan, C. P. Cowan, and Heming (2005).

31. See review by Durlak and Wells (1997).

32. See Powell (2006).

33. An example can be seen in Dadds, Schwartz, and Sanders (1987).

34. See Plomin (2003).

35. See Tully et al. (2004) for an example of how family process and genetic vulnerability interact.

36. See C. P. Cowan and P. A. Cowan (1995) for a review.

37. The study is described in detail in C. P. Cowan and P. A. Cowan (2000).

38. The study is described in detail in P. A. Cowan et al. (2005).

39. The observers did not know which couples were in which condition.

40. C. P. Cowan, P. A. Cowan, Pruett, and Pruett (2007) for an early report.

41. McLanahan, et al. (1998).

42. Wallerstein, Lewis, and Blakelee (2000).

43. Marquardt (2005).

44. Mincy and Pouncy (2002).

45. Harknett, Hardman, Garfinkel, and McLanahan (2001).

46. Mincy and Dupree (2001).

47. Dion, Avellar, Zaveri, and Hershey (2006).

Chapter 25: Diverging Development: The Not-So-Invisible Hand of Social Class in the United States, by Frank F. Furstenberg, Jr.

1. See de Tocqueville (1835).

2. See Bendix and Lipset (1966); Goldthorpe and Erickson (1993).

3. See Danziger and Gottschalk (1995); Levy (1999); Wolff (2002, 2004).

4. See Hollingshead (1949); Lynd and Lynd (1929); Warner (1949).

5. See Bernstein and Henderson (1969); Gans (1962); Komarovsky (1987); Miller and Swanson (1958).

6. See Blood and Wolfe (1960); Mead and Wolfenstein (1955).

7. For exceptions, see Kefalas (2003); Lareau (2003).

8. See McLanahan (2004).

9. See Hollingshead (1949); Warner (1949).

10. See the MacArthur Network on Transitions to Adulthood website: www.transad.pop .upenn.edu.

11. See Bronfenbrenner (1979).

12. See Mead (1934); Cooley (1902).

13. See, for example, the work of anthropologists and sociologists such as Inkeles (1968); Kluckhohn and Murray (1948); Mead and Wolfenstein (1955); Miller and Swanson (1958).

14. See Buchmann (1989); Heinz and Marshall (2003).

15. See Furstenberg et al. (1999).

16. See Weber (1949).

17. See Rutter (1985, 2000); Garmezy (1991, 1993); Werner (1995).

18. See Hertz (2005).

19. See Elder (1974).

20. See Wagmiller et al. (2006).

21. See Danziger and Waldfogel (2000); Haggerty, Sherrod, Garmezy, and Rutter (1994); Shonkoff and Phillips (2000).

22. See Case, Fertig, and Paxton (2005); Conley and Bennett (2000).

23. See Brown and Eisenberg (1998); Joyce, Kaestner, and Korenman (2000).

24. See Nelson (2000); Nelson et al. (2005); Smyke et al. (2007).

25. See Noble, Norman, and Farah (2005).

26. See Hart and Risley (1995).

27. See Bernstein (1971); Bernstein and Henderson (1969); Farkas and Beron (2004).

28. See Chaudry (2004); Magnuson and Waldfogel (2005).

29. See Corsaro (2005).

30. See Medrich, Roizen, and Rubin (1982).

31. See Furstenberg et al. (1999).

32. Ibid.

33. See Cook, Herman, Phillips, and Settersten (2002).

34. See Bourdieu (1973, 1986); Lamont (2000); Lareau (1989, 2003).

35. See Edin and Kefalas (2005); Newman (1993); Burton and Stack (1993).

36. See Rhodes (2002).

37. See Mortimer (2008).

38. See Furstenberg et al. (1999).

39. See Furstenberg et al. (2004); Settersten, Furstenberg, and Rumbaut (2005).

40. See Rouse (2004).

41. Census Historical Income Tables, 2004, Table F-1.

42. See Ellwood and Jencks (2001); Goldstein and Kenney (2001); Wu and Wolfe (2001).

Chapter 27: Not Just Provide and Reside: Engaged Fathers in Low-Income Families, by Kevin Roy and Natasha Cabrera

1. Lamb (1975).

2. Eggebeen (2002a). LaRossa (1997) asserted that there is a culture of "new fatherhood" with expectations that men provide and care for their children. He noted, however, that men often do not live up to these emerging expectations—in effect, that there is a gap between the cultural ideal and the actual conduct of "new" fathers. Another perspective on "new" fathering was offered by Townsend (2002) with the notion of "the package deal." Again, middle-class men in his research saw that marriage, parenthood, employment, and homeownership represented a cluster of roles that went beyond traditional and outmoded sole breadwinner expectations.

3. Coley (2001).

4. Black, Dubowitz, and Starr (1999); Lamb (2004); Shannon, Tamis-LeMonda, London, and Cabrera (2002).

5. Cabrera et al. (2004); Shannon, Tamis-LeMonda, and Cabrera (2006); Tamis-LeMonda, Shannon, Cabrera, and Lamb (2004).

6. Cabrera, Shannon, and Tamis-LeMonda (2007).

7. Ibid.

8. Palkovitz (2002a).

9. Pleck and Masciadrelli (2004) confirm this redirection in father involvement research over the past five years. They write: "[This] increase in supportive evidence has been accompanied by increased awareness of methodological and conceptual complexity of association between paternal involvement and children's development. The research agenda has thus shifted from whether paternal involvement has positive consequences to questions about the *context* in which and the *processes* by which paternal effects occur" (p. 256).

10. Few models of father involvement have followed Bronfenbrenner's theoretical framework (1979) and considered human development in multiple contexts. Cabrera, Fitzgerald, Bradley, and Roggman's model (2007) is a step forward, with an explicit developmental approach to how men's involvement shapes child well-being over time.

11. Jarrett, Roy, and Burton (2002); Waller (2002).

12. Roy (2006).

13. Roy, Dyson, and Jackson (forthcoming).

14. Nelson (2005); Hansen (2005).

15. Doherty, Kouneski, and Erickson proposed a model of father involvement (1998) that placed mothers as central figures in men's involvement with children. This model was critiqued by Walker and McGraw (2000), who questioned whether we should assume that women are responsible for men's engagement with children.

16. Pleck and Masciadrelli (2004).

17. Sobolewski and King (2005). Further, couples' marital expectations and changes in status are important predictors of men's involvement with children in low-income families; see Carlson and McLanahan (2002, 2004); Waller and McLanahan (2005).

18. Townsend (2002).

19. This is relevant particularly in research with African-American fathers (Allen and Connor, 1997; Jarrett, Roy, and Burton, 2002; Roopnarine, 2004). As Cabrera and Garcia Coll (2004) argue, the "form and meaning of [father involvement] are culturally dependent and have not been explored widely."

20. Toth and Xu (1999).

21. Hofferth (2003).

22. Cabrera et al. (2007).

23. For example, Roopnarine (2004) contrasted subtle differences in parenting between African-American and African-Caribbean fathers, and argued that less emphasis on family structure would draw focus to "areas in which men from different socioeconomic backgrounds and familial arrangements mature and succeed as parents in raising socially/ intellectually competent children—and which factors are responsible (such as cultural beliefs or practices, processes and changes in paternal involvement at different stages of the life cycle with different age children, quality of coparenting relationships, extrafamilial support, education, and income)."

24. Cabrera and Garcia Coll (2004).

25. Kwon and Roy (2007); Shwalb, Nakawaza, Yamamoto, and Hyun (2004).

26. Eggebeen (2002b) suggests that "we need data that is sensitive not only to the diverse settings of fatherhood, but also to its dynamic and constantly changing nature" (p. 205). Spaces and places, social relationships and family configurations, local or national cultural contexts, and social policies and institutions all shift in ways that must be accounted for within developmental research.

27. Roy and Dyson (2005).

28. Roy and Burton (2007).

29. If men have multiple children, they are likely to see less of their children and to contribute less financially (Carlson and Furstenberg, 2006).

30. Roy, Kaye, and Fitzgerald (under review). Most low-income fathers in our study did not perceive themselves as having children across distinct family systems. Instead, they saw themselves as "pivot points" in a father-centered family system.

31. Roy, Palkovitz, and Fagan (2007); Fagan, Palkovitz, Roy, and Ferrie (in press).

32. Building on Hogan's (1981) work on early work transitions in men's lives, Palkovitz (2002b) discerned specific stages of men's involvement as they aged—and the impact that such involvement had on men as individuals. With men as the focal point of the study, Palkovitz raised the issue of reciprocal developmental effects, as children also shape men's developmental trajectories.

33. Mott (1990).

34. Hofferth et al. (under review). Roy (2006) finds that for low-income African-American men, experience with their own father—whether as a stable presence, a transitory figure, or even a complete absence—is a strong motivator for paternal involvement. In this study, low-income African-American men tied their own fathering to the barriers and dynamics that they had experienced with their own fathers.

35. Roy (2005).
36. Eggebeen and Uhlenberg (1985).

Chapter 29: Rituals As Tools of Resistance: From Survival to Liberation, by Andraé L. Brown, Melina Dimitriou, and Lisa Dressner

1. Bennett, Wolin, and McCavity (1988); Fiese et al. (2002); Imber-Black (1999).
2. Imber-Black (2002).
3. Bjork (2002); Quantz (1999).
4. Fiese (2007).
5. Laird (1984); Mackey and Grief (1994); Roberts (1988).
6. Meske, Sanders, Meredith, and Abbott (1994).
7. Fiese and Marjinsky (1999).
8. Almeida, Dolan-Del Vecchio, and Parker (2008).
9. Karenga (1998).
10. van der Hart (1983).
11. Giroux (1988).
12. Dundes (1996).
13. DeSilva (1996).
14. NAMES Project Foundation (2008).
15. Clothesline Project (2008).
16. Brown (2004); Children's Defense Fund (2007); Payne (2008); Pewewardy and Severson (2003).
17. Mbiti (1969).
18. Affinity Counseling Group (ACG) is an example of a community-based mental health center that utilizes rituals to provide family therapy to youth and families involved in the criminal justice system. The therapeutic model used, the Cultural Context Model, focuses on raising clients' critical awareness of the dynamics of power, privilege, and oppression and how they manifest in their lives and perpetuate suffering.

Chapter 30: Betwixt and Be Tween: Gender Contradictions among Middle Schoolers, by Barbara J. Risman and Elizabeth Seale

The authors' names are listed alphabetically. The authors thank other members of the research team for their collaboration with data collection. These colleagues include Rena Cornell, Carissa Froyum, Kris Macomber, Amy McClure, and Tricia McTague. We also thank Pallavi Banerjee, Stephanie Coontz, Carissa Froyum, Wilfrid Reissner, Kathleen Gerson, and Kelly Underman for their reviews of this manuscript.

1.   Researchers have looked at how multicultural education works (Talbani, 2003), as well as how education and other cultural beliefs reinforce white privilege (Wellman, 1993).

2.   Eder, Evans, and Parker (1995) examined the role of gender in the language and socialization of a group of eighth graders.

3.   "Doing gender" unlinks biological sex from gender by describing gender not as the traits of a person, but as the embedded social actions that a person takes to express socially accepted gender (West and Zimmerman, 1987).

4.   Allison (1991), Cockburn and Clarke (2002), and Krane et al. (2004) discuss female athletes and the challenge of athletics to femininity, while Broad (2001) examines queer athletes. Malcom (2003), Adams, Schmitke, and Franklin (2005), and Enke (2005), on the other hand, discuss the remaking of femininity to include athletics. Adams, Schmitke, and Franklin (2005) find that girls enjoy athleticism and take pride in being tough and competitive.

5.   Adams and Bettis (2003), pp. 74–75.

6.   Ibid., p. 80.

7.   This comes from Adams and Bettis' (2003) study on cheerleading.

8.   Bettie (2003).

9.   For an more on peer groups and cliques, both Eder, Evans, and Parker (1995) and Adler and Adler (1998) explore adolescent culture. Cockburn and Clarke (2002), Adams and Bettis (2003), and Adams, Schmitke and Franklin (2005) all examine these pressures to be attractive to boys in the context of female athletes. See also Lemish (1998) on modes of femininity and attractiveness.

10. Eder, Evans, and Parker (1995) map the gendered dynamics of teasing. Several researchers examine how this teasing functions to control boys through fear (Kehily and Nayak, 1997; Burn, 2000; Plummer, 2001; Phoenix, Frosh, and Pattman, 2003; Chambers, Tincknell, and Van Loon, 2004), including Pascoe's (2005) "Dude, You're a Fag." Thorne (1993) and Plummer (2001) describe this behavior in elementary school, and Eder, Evans, and Parker (1995), Adler and Adler (1998), and Phoenix, Frosh, and Pattman (2003) discuss it in middle school.

11. See Plummer (2001).

12. See Eder, Evans, and Parker (1995).

13. Pascoe (2003, 2007) and Phoenix, Frosh, and Pattman (2003) have written about masculinity and toughness, while Plummer (2001) and Pascoe (2005, 2007) write about teasing.

14. Froyum (2007).

15. Malcom (2003).

16. This gender-specific cheerleading is very region-specific. In some schools on the West Coat, cheerleading squads are either all-male or mixed sex. As cheerleading has become more athletically demanding, more boys are often included to lift and throw the girls.

17. For more on this, read Kehily and Nayak (1997), Plummer (2001), Pascoe (2003, 2005, 2007) and Phoenix, Frosh, and Pattman (2003).

18. See Deutsch (2007) for a description of the concept of "undoing gender." For an example of "undoing gender," in Gerson's (2002) article, she describes the process of young men an women choosing lives that are distinct from traditional gendered expectations.

Chapter 31: Orgasm in College Hookups and Relationships, by Elizabeth A. Armstrong, Paula England, and Alison C. K. Fogarty

1. Elizabeth L. Paul, Brian McManus, and Allison Hayes, "'Hookups': Characteristics and Correlates of College Students' Spontaneous and Anonymous Sexual Experiences," *Journal of Sex Research* 37 (2000); Norval Glenn and Elizabeth Marquardt, *Hooking Up, Hanging Out, and Hoping for Mr. Right: College Women on Mating and Dating Today* (New York: Institute for American Values, 2001); and Kathleen A. Bogle, "The Shift from Dating to Hooking Up in College: What Scholars have Missed," *Social Compass* 1/2 (2007), for definitions of hooking up.

2. Participating universities include University of Arizona, Indiana University, Stanford University, University of California at Santa Barbara, State University of New York at Stony Brook, Ithaca College, Evergreen College, University of Massachusetts at Amherst, Ohio State University, Whitman College, Foothill College, Harvard University, University of Illinois at Chicago, Framingham State College, Radford University, Beloit College, and the University of California at Riverside. In almost all cases, respondents were recruited through classes. We did not employ probability sampling, so our sample is not strictly representative of college students at these institutions.

3. OCSLS data collection is ongoing. This uses the June 2008 version of the data. Anonymous, M. D., *Unprotected: A Campus Psychiatrist Reveals How Political Correctness in Her Profession Endangers Every Student* (New York: Sentinel HC, 2006); Glenn and Marquardt, *Hooking Up, Hanging Out, and Hoping for Mr. Right* (2001); Leon R. Kass, "The End of Courtship," *Public Interest* 126 (1997); David Popenoe and Barbara Defoe Whitehead, *The State of Our Unions, 2000: The Social Health of Marriage in America* (New Brunswick, NJ: National Marriage Project, 2000); Laura Sessions Stepp, *Unhooked: How Young Women Pursue Sex, Delay Love, and Lose at Both* (New York: Riverhead Books, 2007); and Linda J. Waite and Maggie Gallagher, *The Case for Marriage: Why Married People Are Happier, Healthier, and Better Off Financially* (New York: Doubleday, 2000).

4. Allison Kasic, "Take Back the Date" (2008), Independent Women's Forum; available at www.iwf.org/campus/show/20122.html.

5. A. Ayres Boswell and Joan Z. Spade, "Fraternities and Collegiate Rape Culture: Why Are Some Fraternities More Dangerous Places for Women?," *Gender & Society* 10 (April 1996); Patricia Yancey Martin and Robert A. Hummer, "Fraternities and Rape on Campus," *Gender & Society* 3 (Dec. 1989); and Mindy Stombler, "'Buddies' or 'Slutties': The Collective Sexual Reputation of Fraternity Little Sisters," *Gender & Society* 8 (1994).

6. Evangelical Christians have not moved in this direction. See Donna Freitas, *Sex and the Soul: Juggling Sexuality, Spirituality, Romance, and Religion on America's College Campuses* (New York: Oxford University Press, 2008) for a discussion of the ideal of purity among conservative Christian college students. Immigrant groups may also retain ideas of premarital chastity. See Gloria González-López, *Erotic Journeys: Mexican Immigrants and Their Sex Lives* (Berkeley, CA: University of California Press, 2005), for a discussion of sexual ethics among Mexicans immigrating to the U.S.

7. Benoit Denizet-Lewis, "Friends, Friends With Benefits and the Benefits of the Local Mall," *New York Times*, May 30, 2004.

8. See also Kathleen A. Bogle, *Hooking Up: Sex, Dating, and Relationships on Campus* (New York: New York University Press, 2008); Freitas, *Sex and the Soul* (2008); and Laura Hamilton and Elizabeth A. Armstrong, "Gendered Sexuality in Emerging Adulthood: Double Binds and Flawed Options," *Gender & Society* 23 (2009), for more discussion of repeat hookups.

9. Glenn and Marquardt, *Hooking Up, Hanging Out, and Hoping for Mr. Right* (2001), also find high participation in relationships.

10. Paula England, Emily Fitzgibbons Shafer, and Alison C. K. Fogarty, "Hooking Up and Forming Romantic Relationships on Today's College Campuses," in *The Gendered Society Reader*, 3rd ed., edited by Michael Kimmel and Amy Aronson (New York: Oxford University Press, 2007).

11. For discussions of the rise and fall of dating as a social form, see Beth Bailey, *From Front Porch to Back Seat: Courtship in Twentieth-Century America* (Baltimore: Johns Hopkins University Press, 1988), and Bogle, *Hooking Up* (2008).

12. Men and women's reports of what happened in their most recent hookup differ slightly, with men reporting a bit more action. This may be a result of men's over-reporting or women's under-reporting of sexual activity and/or of women more often than men classifying "making out" as a hookup. We combine male and female respondents' reports here.

13. While 76 percent reported intercourse in the last relationship sexual event, 84 percent reported intercourse ever in this relationship.

14. If a couple had never gone beyond kissing, they were not asked the question, but only 3 percent of those in a relationship of at least six months had not.

15. Orgasm is correlated with a subjective measure of sexual satisfaction for our respondents—and, contrary to common lore, more so for women than for men.

16. See Edward O. Laumann et al., *The Social Organization of Sexuality: Sexual Practices in the United States* (Chicago: University of Chicago Press, 1994), and Linda J. Waite and Kara Joyner, "Emotional Satisfaction and Physical Pleasure in Sexual Unions: Time Horizon, Sexual Behavior, and Sexual Exclusivity," *Journal of Marriage and Family* 63 (2001), for more detailed discussions of this perspective. Laumann and his colleagues found that married people reported higher levels of sexual satisfaction than single people. Waite and Joyner found that how long women thought their relationship would last and sexual exclusivity were associated with emotional and physical satisfaction with sex.

17. David M. Buss, *The Evolution of Desire: Strategies of Human Mating* (New York: Basic Books, 1994), and J. M. Townsend, "Sex without Emotional Involvement: An Evolutionary Interpretation of Sex Differences," *Archives of Sexual Behavior* 24 (1995).

18. Nancy Chodorow, *The Reproduction of Mothering: Psychoanalysis and the Sociology of Gender* (Berkeley, CA: University of California Press, 1978).

19. Shere Hite, *The Hite Report: A Nationwide Study of Female Sexuality* (New York: Seven Stories Press, 1976); C. A. Darling, J. K. Davidson, Sr., and D. A. Jennings, "The Female Sexual Response Revisited: Understanding the Multiorgasmic Experience in Women," *Archives of Sexual Behavior* 20 (1991); Seymour Fisher, *The Female Orgasm* (New York: Basic Books, 1973); and Kenneth Mah and Yitzchak M. Binik,

"The Nature of Human Orgasm: A Critical Review of Major Trends," *Clinical Psychology Review* 21 (2001).

20. These percentages and those in the next paragraph use both men's and women's reports.

21. In these percentages, we excluded intercourse events that also included the woman self-stimulating her own genitals with her hand. Figure 31.4 shows that, in events with intercourse, when oral sex also occurred, it helped women's orgasm in three of the four contexts, but not in intercourse events in hookups where the couple had previously hooked up one to two times.

22. Juliet Richters et al., "Sexual Practices at Last Heterosexual Encounter and Occurrence of Orgasm in a National Survey," *Journal of Sex Research* 43 (2006), similarly found that the addition of oral or manual stimulation to vaginal intercourse provided a big boost to women's experience of orgasms.

23. See John H. Gagnon and William Simon, *Sexual Conduct: The Social Sources of Human Sexuality* (London: Aldine Transaction, 1974), for a discussion of the ways in which sexual scripts organize sexual behavior.

24. See Pepper Schwartz and Virginia Rutter, *The Gender of Sexuality* (Lanham, MD: Alta-Mira Press, 2000), and Mary Crawford and Danielle Popp, "Sexual Double Standards: A Review and Methodological Critique of Two Decades of Research," *Journal of Sex Research* 40 (2003), on sexual double standards.

25. See Bogle, *Hooking Up* (2008); Freitas, *Sex and the Soul* (2008); and Hamilton and Armstrong, "Gendered Sexuality in Emerging Adulthood" (2009), for discussions of the double standard among today's students. See Leora Tanenbaum, *Slut!: Growing up Female with a Bad Reputation* (New York: Seven Stories Press, 1999), and Emily White, *Fast Girls: Teenage Tribes and the Myth of the Slut* (New York: Simon and Schuster, 2001), for discussions of how girls and young women get labeled as sluts, and the consequences of such labeling for their lives.

26. See Virginia Braun, Nicola Gavey, and Kathryn McPhillips, "The 'Fair Deal?' Unpacking Accounts of Reciprocity in Heterosex," *Sexualities* 6 (2003), for a more critical view of the consequences for gender equality of the discourse of sexual reciprocity among heterosexuals.

27. Deborah L. Tolman, *Dilemmas of Desire: Teenage Girls Talk about Sexuality* (Cambridge, MA: Harvard University Press, 2002).

28. Our argument echoes that of Richters et al., "Sexual Practices at Last Heterosexual Encounter and Occurrence of Orgasm in a National Survey" (2006), who found that "the proximal cause—the sexual stimulation delivered to women in the typical, rigidly-scripted heterosexual interaction—has more to do with whether they reach orgasm (and, we suspect, enjoy sex) than with more obscure and distant causes" (p. 252).

29. See England et al., "Hooking Up and Forming Romantic Relationships on Today's College Campuses" (2007); Bogle, *Hooking Up* (2008).

30. Bogle, *Hooking Up* (2008).

31. England et al., "Hooking Up and Forming Romantic Relationships on Today's College Campuses" (2007).

32. Hamilton and Armstrong, "Gendered Sexuality in Emerging Adulthood" (2009); Dorothy C. Holland and Margaret A. Eisenhart, *Educated in Romance: Women, Achievement,*

and College Culture (Chicago: University of Chicago Press, 1990); and Shannon K. Gilmartin, "The Centrality and Costs of Heterosexual Romantic Love among First-Year College Women," *Journal of Higher Education* 76 (2005).

33. Feminist scholars often use the term "sexual subjectivity" to refer to women's feelings of ownership of their sexuality and feelings of entitlement to pleasure. See Karin Martin, *Puberty, Sexuality, and the Self: Boys and Girls at Adolescence* (New York: Routledge, 1996); Amy Schalet, "Must We Fear Adolescent Sexuality," *Medscape General Medicine* 6 (2004); Amy Schalet, "Subjectivity, Intimacy and the Empowerment Paradigm of Adolescent Sexuality," *Feminist Studies* (2009); and Tolman, *Dilemmas of Desire: Teenage Girls Talk about Sexuality* (2002).

Chapter 32: Falling Back on Plan B: The Children of the Gender Revolution Face Uncharted Territory, by Kathleen Gerson

1. Anecdotal, but high-profile stories have touted an "opt-out revolution," to use Lisa Belkin's term (2003), although a number of analysts have shown that "revolution" is a highly misleading and exaggerated term to describe the recent slight downturn in young mothers' labor force participation (Boushey, 2008; Williams, 2007). Most well-educated women are not leaving the workforce, and even though the percent of working mothers with infants has shown a small downtown from its 1995 peak, mothers with children over the age of one are still just as likely as other women to hold a paid job. Even mothers with children under age one show levels of employment that are much higher than the1960s levels, which averaged 30 percent. Moreover, Williams (2007), Stone (2007), Bennetts (2007), and Hirshman (2006) also point out that the metaphor of "opting out" obscures the powerful ways that mothers are, in Williams' words, "pushed out."

2. Recent overviews of the rise of the number of unmarried adults can be found in studies by the Pew Research Center (2007a, 2007b) and by Roberts (2007). Prominent proponents of the "family decline" perspective include Blankenhorn (1995), Popenoe (1988, 1996), Popenoe, Elshtain, and Blankenhorn (1996), and Whitehead (1997). Waite and Gallagher (2000) focus on the personal and social advantages of marriage. For rebuttals to the "family decline" perspective, see Bengtston, Biblarz, and Roberts (2002), Coontz (2005), Moore et al. (2002), Skolnick and Rosencrantz (1994), and Stacey (1996).

3. Randomly chosen from a broad range of city and suburban neighborhoods dispersed throughout the New York metropolitan region, the group includes 120 respondents from diverse race and class backgrounds and from all parts of the country. In all, 54 percent identified as non-Hispanic white, 21 percent as African American, 18 percent as Latino, and 7 percent as Asian. About 43 percent grew up in middle- and upper-middle class homes, while 43 percent lived in homes that were solidly working class, and another 15 percent lived in or on the edge of poverty. With an average age of twenty-four, they are evenly divided between women and men, and about 5 percent identified as either lesbian or gay. As a group, they reflect the demographic contours of young adults throughout metropolitan America. See Gerson (2006 and forthcoming) for a full description of my sample and methods.

4. Most research shows that diversity *within* family types, however defined, is as large as the differences *between* them. Acock and Demo (1994) argue that family type does not predict

children's well-being. Parcel and Menaghan (1994) make the same case for different forms of parental employment.

5. In the case of one-parent versus two-parent homes, children living with both biological parents do appear on average to fare better, but most of the difference disappears after taking account of the family's financial resources and the degree of parental conflict prior to a breakup (Amato and Booth, 1997; Amato and Hohmann-Marriott, 2007; Booth and Amato, 2001; Furstenberg and Cherlin,1991; Hetherington, 1999; McLanahan and Sandefur, 1994). In a recent study of the effects of divorce on children's behavior, Li (2007) shows that "while certain divorces harm children, others benefit them."

6. Decades of research have shown that children do not suffer when their mothers work outside the home. A mother's satisfaction with her situation, the quality of care a child receives, and the involvement of fathers and other caretakers are far more important factors (Galinsky, 1999; Harvey, 1999; Hoffman, 1987; Hoffman, Wladis, and Youngblade, 1999). Bianchi, Robinson, and Milkie (2006) report that parents are actually spending more time with their children. Recent research on the effects of day care have found only small, temporary differences. Barnett and Rivers (1996) demonstrate a range of advantages for two-income couples, and Springer (2007) reports significant health benefits for men whose wives work.

7. Hochschild (1989) refers to dual-earner couples' "gender strategies," although she focuses more on how these strategies reproduce gender divisions than on when, how, and why they might transcend gender distinctions. See Lorber (1994), Risman (1998), and West and Zimmerman (1987) for discussions of the social construction of gender. Zerubavel (1991) analyzes the social roots of mental flexibility.

8. All of the names have been changed to protect confidentiality, and some quotes have been shortened or lightly edited to remove extraneous phrases.

9. About a quarter of the women concluded that if work and family collide, they would rather make a more traditional compromise. These women worried about inflexible workplaces and the difficulty of finding an equal partner. Yet, they still hoped to fit work into their lives. This outlook, too, reflects the dilemmas facing young women who lack the supports to share work and caretaking equally. (See Gerson, *The Unfinished Revolution*, forthcoming, for a full analysis of the variation in women's fallback strategies.)

10. About three in ten men stress independence over traditional marriage, but autonomy has a different meaning for them than it does for women. Poor work prospects leave them determined to remain single unless they find a partner who does not expect financial support. Unlike self-reliant women, who hope to be able to support themselves and their children, autonomous men worry about their ability to earn enough to support a family. (See Gerson, *The Unfinished Revolution*, forthcoming, for a full analysis of men's varied strategies.)

11. Moen and Roehling (2005).

12. Williams (2000).

Chapter 33: Men's Changing Contribution to Family Work, by Oriel Sullivan

1. Suzanne M. Bianchi, John P. Robinson, and Melissa A. Milkie, *Changing Rhythms of American Family Life* (Rose Series in Sociology) (New York: Russell Sage Foundation, 2006).

2. Pew Research Center, "As Marriage and Parenthood Drift Apart, Public Is Concerned about Social Impact: Generation Gap in Values, Behavior," Social and Demographic Trends Report (2007); available at http://pewresearch.org/pubs/526/marriage-parenthood.

3. Oriel Sullivan, *Changing Gender Relations, Changing Families: Tracing the Pace of Change over Time* (Gender Lens Series) (Lanham, MD: Rowman & Littlefield, 2006).

4. See, for example, Frances K. Goldscheider and Linda J. Waite, *New Families, No Families? The Transformation of the American Home* (Berkeley, CA: University of California Press, 1991).

5. Jackie Scott, D. F. Alwin, and M. Brown, "Changing Sex-Role Attitudes," *Sociology* 30 (1996): 427–445.

6. Ibid., p. 489.

7. R. W. Connell, *The Men and the Boys* (Cambridge, UK: Polity Press, 2000).

8. For example see Scott Coltrane, *Gender and Families* (Thousand Oaks, CA: Pine Forge Press, 1998); Scott Coltrane, "Fathering: Paradoxes, Contradictions and Dilemmas," pp. 224–243 in *Handbook of Contemporary Families: Considering the Past, Contemplating the Future*, edited by Marilyn Coleman and Lawrence Ganong (Thousand Oaks, CA: Sage Publications, 2004); Francine M. Deutsch, *Halving It All* (Cambridge, MA: Harvard University Press, 1999).

9. T. Knijn, "Towards Post-Paternalism," in *Changing Fatherhood: An Interdisciplinary Perspective*, edited by M. C. P. van Dougen, G. A. Frinking, and M. J. Jacobs, (Amsterdam: Thesis Publishers, 1995).

10. Arlie R. Hochschild, "Understanding the Future of Fatherhood," in *Changing Fatherhood: An Interdisciplinary Perspective*, edited by M. C. P. van Dougen, G. A. Frinkiny, and M. J. Jacobs (Amsterdam: Thesis Publishers, 1995).

11. Carol Smart and Bren Neale, *Family Fragments?* (Cambridge, UK: Polity Press, 1999).

12. For example: Joseph H. Pleck and Brian P. Masciadrelli, "Paternal Involvement: Levels, Sources, and Consequences," in *The Role of the Father in Child Development*, 4th ed., edited by Michael E. Lamb (New York: Wiley, 2003); Bianchi, Robinson, and Milkie, *Changing Rhythms of American Family Life* (2006).

13. Scott Coltrane, *Gender and Families* (1998), p. 106.

14. Kathleen Gerson, "Dilemmas of Involved Fatherhood," in *Shifting the Center: Understanding Contemporary Families*, 2nd ed., edited by S. J. Ferguson (Mountain View, CA: Mayfield Publishing, 2001).

15. Ulrich Beck and E. Beck-Gernsheim, *The Normal Chaos of Love.* (Cambridge, UK: Polity Press, 1995).

16. For example: Anthony Giddens, *The Transformation of Intimacy.* (Cambridge, UK: Polity Press, 1992); Knijn, "Towards Post-Paternalism?" (1995).

17. Knijn, "Towards Post-Paternalism?" (1995).

18. For example: John. P. Robinson and Geoffrey Godbey, *Time for Life: The Surprising Ways Americans Use Their Time*, 2nd ed. (University Park, PA: Penn State University Press, 1999); Jonathan Gershuny, *Changing Times: Work and Leisure in Postindustrial Society* (Oxford, UK: Oxford University Press, 2000); Bianchi, Robinson, and Milkie, *Changing Rhythms of American Family Life* (2006).

19. Numbers taken from Bianchi, Robinson, and Milkie, *Changing Rhythms of American Family Life* (2006).

20. Kimberley Fisher, Muriel Egerton, Jonathan I. Gershuny, and John P. Robinson, "Gender Convergence in the American Heritage Time Use Study (AHTUS)," *Social Indicators Research.* 82 (2007): 1–33.

21. Jennifer L. Hook, "Care in Context: Men's Unpaid Work in 20 Countries, 1965–2003," *American Sociological Review* 71 (2006): 639–660.

22. Oriel Sullivan and Jonathan I. Gershuny, "Cross-National Changes in Time-Use: Some Sociological (Hi)stories re-examined," *British Journal of Sociology* 52 (2001): 331–347.

23. Orly Benjamin and Oriel Sullivan, "Relational Resources, Gender Consciousness and Possibilities of Change in Marital Relationships," *Sociological Review* 47 (1999): 794–820.

24. C. West and D. H. Zimmerman, "Doing Gender," *Gender & Society* 1 (1987): 125–151; Myra Marx Ferree, "Beyond Separate Spheres: Feminism and Family Research," *Journal of Marriage and Family* 52 (1990): 866–884.

25. J. M. Gerson and K. Peiss, "Boundaries, Negotiation, Consciousness: Reconceptualizing Gender Relations," *Social Problems* 32 (1985): 317–331.

26. Linda Thompson, "Conceptualising Gender in Marriage: The Case of Marital Care," *Journal of Marriage and Family* 55 (1993): 557–569.

27. Connell, *The Men and the Boys* (2000); Barbara Risman, "Gender As Social Structure: Theory Wrestling with Activism," *Gender & Society* 18 (2004): 429–450.

28. Barbara Risman, *Gender Vertigo* (New Haven: Yale University Press, 1998).

Chapter 34: Briefing Paper: Men's Changing Contribution to Housework and Child Care, by Oriel Sullivan and Scott Coltrane

1. Oriel Sullivan, *Changing Gender Relations, Changing Families: Tracing the Pace of Change over Time* (Gender Lens Series) (New York: Rowman & Littlefield, 2006).

2. Scott Coltrane, *Family Man: Fatherhood, Housework and Gender Equity* (New York: Oxford University Press, 1996); Scott Coltrane, "Research on Household Labor: Modeling and Measuring the Social Embeddedness of Routine Family Work," *Journal of Marriage and Family*, 62 (2000): 1209–1233; Scott Coltrane, "Fathering: Paradoxes, Contradictions and Dilemmas," pp. 224–243 in *Handbook of Contemporary Families: Considering the Past, Contemplating the Future*, edited by Marilyn Coleman and Lawrence Ganong. (Thousand Oaks, CA: Sage Publications, 2004); Jerry A. Jacobs and Kathleen Gerson, *The Time Divide: Work, Family and Gender Inequality.* (Cambridge, MA: Harvard University Press, 2004).

3. John P. Robinson and Geoffrey Godbey, *Time for Life: The Surprising Ways Americans Use Their Time*, 2nd ed. (University Park, PA: Penn State University Press, 1999); Kimberley Fisher, Muriel Egerton, Jonathan I. Gershuny, and John P. Robinson, "Gender Convergence in the American Heritage Time Use Study (AHTUS)." *Social Indicators Research*, 82 (2006):1–33.

4. Suzanne M. Bianchi, John P. Robinson, and Melissa A. Milkie, *Changing Rhythms of American Family Life* (Rose Series in Sociology) (New York: Russell Sage Foundation,

2006); Fisher et al., "Gender Convergence in the American Heritage Time Use Study (AHTUS) (2006).

5. Coltrane, "Fathering: Paradoxes, Contradictions and Dilemmas" (2004); Joseph H. Pleck and Brian P. Masciadrelli, "Paternal Involvement: Levels, Sources, and Consequences," in *The Role of the Father in Child Development*, 4th ed., edited by Michael E. Lamb (New York: Wiley, 2003).

6. Jennifer Hook, "Care in Context: Men's Unpaid Work in 20 Countries, 1965–2003," *American Sociological Review*, 71(2006): 639–660.

7. Sullivan, *Changing Gender Relations, Changing Families* (2006).

8. Fisher et al., "Gender Convergence in the American Heritage Time Use Study (AHTUS) (2006); Bianchi, Robinson, and Milkie, *Changing Rhythms of American Family Life* (2006).

9. Jonathan I. Gershuny, Michael Bittman, and John Brice, "Exit, Voice, and Suffering: Do Couples Adapt to Changing Employment Patterns?," *Journal of Marriage and Family*, 67 (2005): 656–665.

10. Sullivan, *Changing Gender Relations, Changing Families* (2006).

11. Coltrane, "Research on Household Labor: Modeling and Measuring the Social Embeddedness of Routine Family Work" (2000).

12. Lynne P. Cooke, "'Doing' Gender in Context: Household Bargaining and Risk of Divorce in Germany and the United States." *American Journal of Sociology* 112 (2006): 442–472.

13. See "How Does the U.S. Rank in Work Policies for Families?" (www.contemporaryfamilies. org/subtemplate.php?=briefingPapers&ext=workpolicies)

Chapter 36: Briefing Paper: Moms and Jobs: Trends in Mothers' Employment and Which Mothers Stay Home, by David Cotter, Paula England, and Joan Hermsen

1. See Joan Williams "'Opt Out' or Pushed Out? How the Press Covers Work/Family Conflict." Center on Work Life Law, University of California Hastings School of the Law (2006), available at www.uchastings.edu/site_files/WLL/OptOutPushedOut.pdf.

2. See Chinhui Juhn and Kevin M. Murphy, "Wage Inequality and Family Labor Supply," *Journal of Labor Economics* 15 (1997):72–79; Barbara Bergmann, *The Economic Emergence of Women*, 2nd ed. (New York: Basic Books, 2005).

3. See Suzanne Bianchi, John P. Robinson, and Melissa A. Milkie, *Changing Rhythms of American Family Life* (New York: Russell Sage Foundation, 2006).

4. See Williams "'Opt Out' or Pushed Out? (2006); Janet Gornick and Marcia K. Meyers, *Families That Work: Policies for Reconciling Parenthood and Employment* (New York, Russell Sage Foundation, 2005).

5. For trends in attitudes to gender issues, see David A. Cotter, Joan M. Hermsen, and Reeve Vanneman, *Gender Inequality at Work* (New York: Russell Sage Foundation and Population Reference Bureau, 2004).

6. See Robert D Mare, "Five Decades of Educational Assortative Mating," *American Sociological Review* 56 (1991):15–32.

Chapter 39: Domestic Violence in Heterosexual Relationships, by Rhea V. Almeida

1. Almeida and Durkin (1999).

2. U.S. Department of Justice (2005).

3. Weissman (2007).

4. Crenshaw (1994), Collins (1989), Almeida (1993).

5. Dobash and Dobash (1979), Bograd (1984, 1986, 1988), Avis (1992a, 1992b), Duneier (1992).

6. Coontz (2006).

7. Lui et al. (2006).

8. Weissman (2007).

9. Farley (1992), Kivel (1992).

10. Narayan (1995).

11. Almeida (1996).

12. *Privilege:* One gains an advantage, or privilege, when one possesses certain identity characteristics like white skin, maleness, heterosexuality, middle- or upper middle-class status, and able-bodied status. One loses an advantage, or privilege, when one possesses characteristics like femaleness, queerness, skin with color, and poverty-social class status (Almeida, Dolan-Del Vecchio, and Parker, 2007).

13. Almeida (1986), Almeida, Dolan-Del Vecchio, and Parker (2007).

14. Freire and Ramos (1982).

15. Almeida, Dolan-Del Vecchio, and Parker (2007), Almeida and Lockard (2005), Almeida and Bograd (1990).

16. Sokoloff (2005).

17. Almeida, Dolan-Del Vecchio, and Parker (2007), Almeida and Lockard (2005), Almeida and Hudak (2002).

Chapter 40: Families: A Great American Institution, by Barbara J. Risman

1. Howard Dean on children, from his campaign website, DeanforAmerica.com, "On the Issues," November 30, 2002; available at www.ontheissues.org/celeb/Howard_Dean_Families_+_Children.htm.

2. Sarah Palin in her 2008 National Republican Convention speech.

3. Barack Obama in a letter to Family Equality Council on August 1, 2008; available at www.familyequality.org/blog/wp-content/family-equality-council-chrisler-08-01-08.pdf.

4. Hillary Clinton during Presidential Election Season 2008, Obama Rally in Scranton, PA, October 12, 2008.

5. John McCain in interview with Charlie Gibson on September 3, 2008.

6. Barack Obama in a letter to Family Equality Council on August 1, 2008; available at www.familyequality.org/blog/wp-content/family-equality-council-chrisler-08-01-08.pdf.

7. James Dobson in April 2004 edition of the Focus on the Family Newsletter.

8. See Judith Stacey's study of post-modern families in *Brave New Families: Stories of Domestic Upheaval in Late-Twentieth Century America* (Berkeley, CA: University of California Press, 1998).

References

Chapter 2: One Thousand and Forty-nine Reasons Why It's Hard to Know When a Fact Is a Fact, by Andrew J. Cherlin

Cherlin, Andrew J., Frank F. Furstenberg, Jr., P. Lindsay Chase-Lansdale, Kathleen E. Kiernan, Philip K. Robins, Donna Ruane Morrison, and Julien O. Teitler. 1991. "Longitudinal Studies of Effects of Divorce on Children in Great Britain and the United States." *Science* 252: 1386–1389.

Cherlin, Andrew J., P. Lindsay Chase-Lansdale, and Christine McRae. 1998. "Effects of Parental Divorce on Mental Health throughout the Life Course." *American Sociological Review* 63: 239–249.

Glick, Paul C. 1941. "Types of Families: An Analysis of Census Data." *American Sociological Review* 6: 830–838.

Goodrich v. Department of Public Health. 2003. 440 Mass. 309.

Jencks, Christopher. 1994. *The Homeless*. Cambridge, MA: Harvard University Press.

Rosin, Hanna. 1999. "Same-Sex Couples Win Rights in Vermont; Gay Activists Say Ruling Is a Legal Breakthrough." *Washington Post*, December 21.

U.S. General Accounting Office. 1997 (January 31). Letter to the Honorable Henry J. Hyde, Chairman, Committee on the Judiciary, from Barry R. Bedrick, Associate General Counsel. Reference: GAO/OGC-97-16 Defense of Marriage Act.

Chapter 3: When Is a Relationship between Facts a Causal One?, by Philip A. Cowan

Cherlin, Andrew J., P. Lindsay Chase-Lansdale, and Christine McRae. 1998. "Effects of Parental Divorce on Mental Health throughout the Life Course." *American Sociological Review* 63: 239–249.

Cowan, Philip A., and Carolyn Pape Cowan. 2002. "Interventions as Tests of Family Systems Theories: Marital and Family Relationships in Children's Development, and Psychopathology." *Development and Psychopatholology, Special Issue on Interventions as Tests of Theories* 14: 731–760.

Cummings, E. Mark, and Patrick Davies. 1994. *Children and Marital Conflict: The Impact of Family Dispute and Resolution*. New York: Guilford Press.

Emery, Robert E. 1999. *Marriage, Divorce, and Children's Adjustment*, 2nd ed. Thousand Oaks, CA: Sage Publications.

Gottman, John M., and Clifford I. Notarius. 2002. "Marital Research in the 20th Century and a Research Agenda for the 21st Century." *Family Process* 41: 159–197.

Waite, Linda J., and Maggie Gallagher. 2000. *The Case for Marriage: Why Married People Are Happier, Healthier, and Better off Financially*. New York: Doubleday.

Chapter 5: The Evolution of American Families, by Stephanie Coontz

Adams, David Wallace. 1988. *Education for Extinction: American Indians and the Boarding School Experience, 1875–1928.* Lawrence, KS: University Press of Kansas.

Amott, Theresa L., and Julie M. Matthaei. 1991. *Race, Gender, and Work: A Multicultural Gender Economic History of Women in the United States.* Boston: South End Press.

Aswad, Barbara C., and Barbara Bilge. 1996. *Family and Gender among American Muslims: Issues Facing Middle-Eastern Immigrants and Their Descendants.* Philadelphia: Temple University Press.

Bailey, Beth L. 1989. *From Front Porch to Back Seat: Courtship in Twentieth-Century America.* Baltimore: John Hopkins University Press.

Bianchi, Suzanne M., John P. Robinson, and Melissa A. Milkie. 2006. *Changing Rhythms of Family Life.* New York: Russell Sage Foundation.

Boydston, Jeanne. 1990. *Home and Work: Housework, Wages, and the Ideology of Labor in the Early Republic.* New York: Oxford University Press.

Burguiere, André, et al. 1996. *A History of the Family.* Cambridge, MA: Belknap Press.

Coontz, Stephanie. 1988. *The Social Origins of Private Life: A History of American Families.* New York: W. W. Norton.

———. 2000. *The Way We Never Were: American Families and the Nostalgia Trap.* New York: Basic Books.

———. 2006. *Marriage, A History: How Love Conquered Marriage.* New York: Penguin Books.

Coontz, Stephanie, Maya Parson, and Gabrielle Raley. 2008. *American Families: A Multicultural Reader.* New York: Routledge.

Cott, Nancy. 2000. *Public Vows: A History of Marriage and the Nation.* Cambridge, MA: Harvard University Press.

D'Emilio, John, and Freedman, Estelle B. 1997. *Intimate Matters: A History of Sexuality in America,* 2nd ed. Chicago: University of Chicago Press.

Gabaccia, Danna, and Vicki L. Ruiz. 2006. *American Dreaming, Global Realities: Rethinking U.S. Immigration History.* Chicago: University of Chicago Press.

Gallup, George, and Evan Hill. 1962. "The American Woman," *The Saturday Evening Post,* December 22–29.

Gaspar, David Barry, and Darlene Clark Hine. 1996. *More than Chattel: Black Women and Slavery in the Americas.* Bloomington, IN: University of Indiana Press.

Gottlieb, Beatrice. 1993. *The Family in the Western World from the Black Death to the Industrial Age.* New York: Oxford University Press.

Gullickson, Aaron. 2006. "Black/White Interracial Marriage Trends, 1850–2000." *Journal of Family History* 31(3): 1–24.

Hing, Bill Ong. 1993. *Making and Remaking Asian America through Immigration Policy, 1850–1990.* Stanford, CA: Stanford University Press.

Hirsch, Jennifer S. 2003. *A Courtship After Marriage: Sexuality and Love in Mexican Transnational Communities.* Berkeley, CA: University of California Press.

Hua, Cai. 2001. *Society Without Fathers or Husbands: The Na of China.* Cambridge, MA: MIT Press.

Ingoldsby, Bron B., and Suzanna D. Smith. 2006. *Families in Global and Multicultural Perspective,* 2nd ed. Thousand Oaks, CA: Sage Publications.

Ishwaran, K. 1992. *Family and Marriage: Cross-Cultural Perspectives*. Toronto: Thompson Educational Publishing.

Katz, Michael J., Michael J. Doucet, and Mark J. Stern. 1982. *The Social Organization of Early Industrial Capitalism*. Cambridge, MA: Harvard University Press.

Kennedy, Cynthia. 2005. *Braided Relations, Entwined Lives: The Women of Charleston's Urban Slave Society*. Bloomington, IN: Indiana University Press.

Lobo, Susan. 1998. *Native American Voices: A Reader*. New York: Longman.

Lott, Juanita Tamayo. 2006. *Common Destiny: Filipino American Generations*. Lanham, MD: Rowman & Littlefield.

Lyons, Clare A. 2006. *Sex Among the Rabble: An Intimate History of Gender and Power in the Age of Revolution*. Chapel Hill, NC: University of North Carolina Press.

May, Elaine Tyler. 1980. *Great Expectations: Marriage and Divorce in Post-Victorian America*. Chicago: University of Chicago Press.

———. 1988. *Homeward Bound: American Families in the Cold War Era*. New York: Basic Books.

McAdoo, Harriette Pipes. 2007. *Black Families*, 4th ed. Thousand Oaks, CA: Sage Publications.

McCurry, Stephanie. 1995. *Masters of Small Worlds: Yeoman Households, Gender Relations, and the Political Culture of the Antebellum South Carolina Low Country*. Athens, GA: University of Georgia Press.

Maffi, Mario. 1995. *Gateway to the Promised Lands: Ethnic Cultures on New York's Lower East Side*. New York: New York University Press.

Miles, Tiya. 2005. *Ties That Bind: The Story of an Afro-Cherokee Family in Slavery and Freedom*. Berkeley, CA: University of California Press.

Mintz, Steven, and Susan Kellogg. 1988. *Domestic Revolutions: A Social History of American Family Life*. New York: Free Press.

Moran, Rachel. 2001. *Interracial Intimacy: The Regulation of Race and Romance*. Chicago: University of Chicago Press.

Mullings, Leith. 1997. *On Our Own Terms: Race, Class, and Gender in the Lives of African-American Women*. New York: Routledge.

Ngai, Mae M. 2004. *Impossible Subjects: Illegal Aliens and the Making of Modern America*. Princeton: Princeton University Press.

O'Day, Rosemary. 1994. *The Family and Family Relationships, 1500–1900*. London: Palgrave Macmillan.

Peters, Virginia Bergman. 1995. *Women of the Earth Lodges: Tribal Life on the Plains*. New Haven: Archon Books.

Rosen, Ruth. 2000. *The World Split Open: How the Women's Movement Changed America*. New York: Penguin Books.

Ritterhouse, Jennifer. 2006. *Growing Up Jim Crow: How Black and White Southern Children Learned Race*. Chapel Hill, NC: University of North Carolina Press.

Rubin, Lillian B. 1994. *Families on the Fault Line*. New York: HarperCollins.

Ruiz, Vicki, and Ellen Dubois. 2000. *Unequal Sisters: A Multicultural Reader in U.S. Women's History*, 3rd ed. New York: Routledge.

Ryan, Mary P. 1983. *Cradle of the Middle Class: The Family in Oneida County, New York, 1790–1865*. New York: Cambridge University Press.

Seccombe, Wally. 1992. *A Millennium of Family Change*. London: Verso.

Skolnick, Arlene S., and Jerome H. Skolnick. 2003. *Family in Transition*, 12th ed. Boston: Allyn & Bacon.

Stacey, Judith. 1990. *Brave New Families: Stories of Domestic Upheaval in Late Twentieth-Century America*. New York: Basic Books.

Stavig, Ward. 1995. "'Living in Offense of Our Lord': Indigenous Sexual Values and Marital Life in the Colonial Crucible." *Hispanic American Historical Review* 75(4): 597–622.

Stevenson, Brenda E. 1996. *Life in Black and White: Family and Community in the Slave South*. New York: Oxford University Press.

Thorne, Barrie, and Marilyn Yalom. 1992. *Rethinking the Family: Some Feminist Questions*. Boston: Northeastern University Press.

Tung, Mae Paomay. 2000. *Chinese Americans and Their Immigrant Parents: Conflict, Identity, and Values*. Binghamton, NY: Haworth Press.

Vecchio, Diane C. 2006. *Merchants, Midwives, and Laboring Women: Italian Migrants in Urban America*. Champaign, IL: University of Illinois Press.

Wallenstein, Peter. 2002. *Tell the Court I Love My Wife: Race, Marriage, and Law—An American History*. New York: Palgrave Macmillan.

Weiss, Jessica. 2000. *To Have and to Hold: Marriage, the Baby Boom, and Social Change*. Chicago: University of Chicago Press.

Wong, Bernard P. 2006. *The Chinese in Silicon Valley: Globalization, Social Networks, and Ethnic Identity*. Lanham, MD: Rowman & Littlefield.

Zinn, Maxime Baca, D. Stanley Eitzen, and Barbara Wells. 2008. *Diversity in Families*, 8th ed. Boston: Allyn & Bacon.

Chapter 6: American Childhood As a Social and Cultural Construct, by Steven Mintz

Axtell, James. 1974. *School Upon a Hill: Education and Society in Colonial New England*. New Haven, CT: Yale University Press.

Belkin, Lisa. 2000. "The Making of an 8-Year-Old Woman," *New York Times*, December 24.

Clement, Priscilla. 1997. *Growing Pains: Children in the Industrial Age, 1850–1890*. New York: Twayne.

Chudacoff, Howard P. 1989. *How Old Are You? Age Consciousness in American Society*. Princeton: Princeton University Press.

Grant, Julia. 1998. *Raising Baby by the Book: The Education of American Mothers*. New Haven, CT: Yale University Press.

Heywood, Colin. 2001. *A History of Childhood: Children and Childhood in the West from Medieval to Modern Times*. Cambridge, UK: Polity Press.

Herman-Giddens, Marcia E., et al. 1997. "Secondary Sexual Characteristics and Menses in Young Girls Seen in Office Practice: A Study from the Pediatric Research in Office Settings Network." *Pediatrics* 99(4): 505–512.

Hulbert, Ann. 2003. *Raising America: Experts, Parents, and a Century of Advice about Children*. New York: Knopf.

Illick, Joseph. 2002. *American Childhoods*. Philadelphia: University of Pennsylvania Press.

Jones, Kathleen W. 1999. *Taming the Troublesome Child*. Cambridge, MA: Harvard University Press.

Kett, Joseph F. 1977. *Rites of Passage: Adolescence in America*. New York: Basic Books.

Kline, Daniel T. 1998. "Holding Therapy," March 7, History-Child-Family Listserv (history-child-family@mailbase.ac.uk).

Kolata, Gina. 2001. "Doubters Fault Theory Finding Earlier Puberty," *New York Times*, February 20.

——. 2001. "2 Endocrinology Groups Raise Doubt on Earlier Onset of Girls' Puberty," *New York Times*, March 3.

Lareau, Annette. 2003. *Unequal Childhoods: Class, Race, and Family Life*. Berkeley, CA: University of California Press.

Macleod, David I. 1998. *The Age of the Child: Children in America, 1890–1912*. New York: Twayne.

Mintz, Steven, and Susan Kellogg. 1988. *Domestic Revolutions: A Social History of American Family Life*. New York: Free Press.

Nasaw, David. 1985. *Children in the City: At Work and at Play*. Garden City, NY: Anchor Press/Doubleday.

Robertson, Stephen. "The Disappearance of Childhood." http://teaching.arts.usyd.edu.au/history/2044/.

Schultz, James A. 1995. *The Knowledge of Childhood in the German Middle Ages, 1100–1350*. Philadelphia: University of Pennsylvania Press.

Scraton, Phil, ed. 1997. *"Childhood" in "Crisis"?* London: University College of London Press.

Stansell, Christine. 1986. *City of Women: Sex and Class in New York, 1789–1860*. New York: Knopf.

Weissbourd, Richard. 1996. *The Vulnerable Child: What Really Hurts America's Children and What We Can Do about It*. Reading, MA: Addison-Wesley.

Chapter 7: African Americans and the Birth of the Modern Marriage, by Donna L. Franklin

Bernard, Jessie. 1966. *Marriage and Family Among Negroes*. Englewood Cliffs, NJ: Prentice-Hall.

Berlin, Ira, and Leslie S. Rowland, eds. 1998. *Families and Freedom: A Documentary History of African-American Kinship in the Civil War Era*. New York: New Press.

Bird, Carol. 1979. *The Two-Paycheck Family*. New York: Rawson, Wade.

Boris, Eileen. 1993. "The Power of Motherhood: Black and White Activist Women Redefine the Political." In *Mothers of a New World*, edited by Seth Koven and Sonya Michel. New York: Routledge.

Burbridge, Lynn C. 1995. "Policy Implications for a Decline in Marriage among African-Americans." Pp. 229–260 in *The Decline in Marriage Among African Americans*, edited by M. Belinda Tucker and Claudia Mitchell-Kernan. New York: Russell Sage Foundation.

Blumstein, Phillip, and Pepper Schwartz. 1983. *American Couples*. New York: Morrow.

Bowen, William C., and Derek Bok. 1998. *The Shape of the River: Long Term Consequences of Considering Race in College and University Admissions*. Princeton: Princeton University Press.

Butterfield, Fox. 2002. "Study Finds Big Increase in Black Men as Inmates Since 1980." *New York Times*, August 29.

Carby, Hazel V. 1987. *Reconstructing Womanhood: The Emergence of the Afro-American Woman Novelist*. New York: Oxford University Press.

Carlson, Shirley J. 1992. "Black Ideals of Womanhood in the Late Victorian Era." *Journal of Negro History* 77(2): 61–73.

Clinton, Catherine, and Nina Silber, eds. 1992. *Divided Houses: Gender and the Civil War*. New York: Oxford University Press.

Conrad, Cecelia A. 2008. "Black Women: An Unfinished Agenda." *The American Prospect* 19(10): A12–A15.

Coontz, Stephanie. 2006. *Marriage, A History: How Love Conquered Marriage*. New York: Penguin Books.

Cooper, Anna Julia. 1990. *A Voice of the South*, introduction by Mary Helen Washington. New York: Oxford University Press.

Cott, Nancy F. 2000. *Public Vows: A History of Marriage and the Nation*. Cambridge, MA: Harvard University Press.

Cuthbert, Marion. 1936. "Problems Facing Negro Young Women." *Opportunity* (February 2): 48.

Davis, Elizabeth Lindsay. 1933. *Lifting As They Climb: The National Association of Colored Women*. Washington, DC: National Association of Colored Women.

DuBois, W. E. B. 1924. *The Gift of Black Folk*. Boston: Stratford Press.

Epstein, Cynthia Fuchs. 1971. "Law Partners and Marital Partners: Strains and Solutions in the Dual-Career Family Enterprise." *Human Relations* 24(6): 549–563.

Faust, Drew Gilpin. 1996. *Mothers of Invention*. Chapel Hill, NC: University of North Carolina.

Foner, Eric. 1988. *Reconstruction: America's Unfinished Revolution. 1863–77*. New York: Harper and Row.

Franklin, Donna L. 1997. *Ensuring Inequality: The Structural Transformation of the African-American Family*. New York: Oxford University Press.

———. 2000. *What's Love Got to Do With It? Understanding and Healing the Rift Between Black Men and Women*. New York: Simon and Schuster.

Freeman, Elsie, Wynell Burroughs Schamel, and Jean West. 1992. "The Fight for Equal Rights: A Recruiting Poster for Black Soldiers in the Civil War." *Social Education* 56(2): 118–120.

Giddings, Paula. 1985. *When and Where I Enter: The Impact of Black Women on Race and Sex in America*. New York: Bantam Books.

———. 2008. *Ida: A Sword Among Lions: Ida B. Wells and the Campaign Against Lynching*. New York: Amistad.

Gordon, Linda. 1991. "Black and White Visions of Welfare: Women's Welfare Activism, 1890–1943." *Journal of American History*, 78, 559–590.

Hacker, Andrew. 1992. *Two Nations: Black and White, Separate, Hostile, Unequal*. New York: Ballantine Books.

Hall, Francine S. 1979. *The Two Career Couple*. Reading, MA: Addison-Wesley.

Harley, Sharon. 1988. "Mary Church Terrell: Genteel Militant." In *Black Leaders of the Nineteenth Century*, edited by Leon F. Litwack and August Meier. Urbana, IL: University of Illinois Press.

Harris, Barbara J. 1978. *Beyond Her Sphere: Women and the Professions in American History*. Westport, CT: Greenwood Press.

Higginbotham, Evelyn Brooks. 1993. *Righteous Discontent: The Women's Movement in the Baptist Church, 1880–1920*. Cambridge, MA: Harvard University Press.

Holmstrom, Lynda Lytle. 1972. *The Two Career Family*. Cambridge, MA: Schenkman.

Jones, Jacqueline. 1985. *Labor of Love: Black Women, Work, and the Family from Slavery to Present*. New York: Basic Books.

Kennedy, Susan Estabrook. 1979. *If All We Did Was to Weep at Home: A History of White Working Class Women in America*. Bloomington, IN: Indiana University Press.

Kessler-Harris, Alice. 1982. *Out to Work: A History of Wage-Earning Women in the United States*. New York: Oxford University Press.

Landry, Bart. 2000. *Black Working Wives: Pioneers of the American Family Revolution.* Berkeley, CA: University of California Press.

Lerner, Gerda. 1972. *Black Women in White America: A Documentary History.* New York: Vintage Books.

Litwack, Leon F. 1998. *Trouble in Mind: Black Southerners in the Age of Jim Crow.* New York: Knopf.

Loewenberg, Bert James, and Ruth Bogin, eds. 1976. *Black Women in the Nineteenth-Century American Life: Their Words, Their Thoughts, Their Feelings.* University Park, PA: Pennsylvania State University Press.

Massey, Mary E. 1966. *Bonnet Brigades.* New York: Knopf.

Matthaei, Julie. 1982. *An Economic History of Women in America.* New York: Schocken Books.

McMurry, Linda O. 1998. *To Keep the Waters Troubled: The Life of Ida B. Wells.* New York: Oxford University Press.

Mills, C. Wright. 1959. *The Sociological Imagination.* New York: Oxford University Press.

Mintz, Steven, and Susan Kellogg. 1988. *Domestic Revolutions: A Social History of American Family Life.* New York: Free Press.

Moses, William Jeremiah. 1978. *The Golden Age of Black Nationalism.* New York: Oxford University Press.

Noble, Jeanne. 1956. "The Negro Woman's College Education." Ph.D. dissertation, Teachers College, Columbia University, New York.

Margaret M., and T. Neal Garland. 1971. "The Married Professional Woman: A Study in the Tolerance of Domestication." *Journal of Marriage and the Family* 33(3): 531–540.

Powdermaker, Hortense. 1939. *After Freedom: A Cultural Study in the Deep South.* New York: Viking Press.

Rapoport, Rhona, and Robert Rapoport. 1971. *Dual Career Families.* Middlesex, UK: Penguin Books.

Rouse, Jacqueline A. 1989. *Lugenia Hope Burns: Black Southerner Reformer.* Athens, GA: University of Georgia Press.

Satcher, David, et al. 2005. "What If We Were Equal? A Comparison of the Black-White Mortality Gap in 1960 and 2000?" *Health Affairs* 24(2): 459–464.

Scott, Ann Firor. 1970. *The Southern Lady from Pedestal to Politics: 1830–1930.* Chicago: University of Chicago Press.

Shaw, Stephanie J. 1996. *What a Woman Ought to Be and Do: Black Professional Women Workers during the Jim Crow Era.* Chicago: University of Chicago Press.

Smith-Rosenberg, Carol. 1985. *Disorderly Conduct: Visions of Gender in Victorian America.* New York: Knopf.

Vicinus, Martha. 1985. *Independent Women: Work and Community of Single Women, 1850–1920.* Chicago: University of Chicago Press.

Vinoskis, Maris A. 1989. "Have Social Historians Lost the Civil War? Some Preliminary Demographic Speculations." *Journal of American History* 76(1): 35–59.

Wells, Ida B. 1970. *Crusade for Justice: The Autobiography of Ida B. Wells,* edited by Alfreda M. Duster. Chicago: University of Chicago Press.

Wertheimer, Barbara M. 1977. *We Were There: The Story of Working Women in America.* New York: Pantheon Books.

Williams, Fannie Barrier. 1904. "The Women's Part in a Man's Business." *Voice* 1(11): 544.

Wilson, W. J., & Neckerman, K. M. 1987. "Poverty and family structure: The widening gap between evidence and public policy issues." Pp. 232–259 in *The Truly Disadvantaged*, edited by W. J. Wilson. Chicago: University of Chicago Press.

Chapter 8: Families "In Law" and Families "In Practice": Does the Law Recognize Families As They Really Are?, by Karen Struening

Ali, Lorraine, and Raina Kelly. 2008. "Womb for Rent: The Curious World of Surrogate Mothers," *Newsweek*, April 7.

Cahn, Naomi. 2003. "Perfect Substitutes or the Real Thing?" 52 *Duke L.J.* 1077.

Dalton, Susan E. 2003. "From Presumed Fathers to Lesbian Mothers: Sex Discrimination and the Legal Construction of Parenthood," 9 *Mich. J. Gender & Law* 261.

Fineman, Martha Albertson. 2004. *The Autonomy Myth: A Theory of Dependency*. New York: New Press.

Healthy Marriage Initiative. 2002. Administration for Children and Families, U.S. Department of Health and Human Services, Retrieved July 29, 2008, from www.acf.hhs.gov/healthymarriage/index.html.

Hughes, Claire. 2007. "On Heels of Success, Marriage Supporters Lobby for More Welfare Dollars." Albany, NY: Rockefeller Institute of Government, State University of New York: Roundtable on Religion and Social Welfare Policy, January 23.

Human Rights Campaign. 2008. "Statewide Marriage Prohibitions," Washington, DC. Last updated November 17, 2008. Retrieved November 24, 2008, from www.hrc.org/documents/marriage_prohibitions.pdf.

Lamdalegal. 2008. "Status of Same-Sex Relationships Nationwide," New York, NY. Last updated October 10, 2008. Retrieved November 24, 2008, from lambdalegal.org/publications/articles/nationwide-status-same-sex-relationships.html#9.

McClain, Linda C. 2006. *The Place of Families: Fostering Capacity, Equality and Responsibility*. Cambridge, MA: Harvard University Press.

———. 2007. "Love, Marriage and the Baby Carriage: Revisiting the Channeling Function of Law." 28 *Cardozo L. Rev.* 2133.

Meyer, David D. 2006. "Parenthood in a Time of Transition: Tensions Between Legal, Biological, and Social Conceptions of Parenthood." 54 *Am. J. Comp. L.* 125 (Supplement, Fall), National Gay and Lesbian Task Force, Second-Parent Adoption in the U.S. Last updated November 4, 2008.

Ooms, Theodora, Stacey Bouchet, and Mary Parke. (2004). *Beyond Marriage Licenses: Efforts in States to Strengthen Marriage and Two-Parent Families*. Washington, DC: Center for Law and Social Policy. Available at http://clasp.org/publications/beyond_marr.pdf.

Polikoff, Nancy D. 1990. "This Child Does Have Two Mothers: Redefining Parenthood to Meet the Needs of Children in Lesbian Mother and Other Nontraditional Households." 78 *Geo L. R.* 459.

———. 2008. *Beyond (Straight and Gay) Marriage: Valuing All Families Under the Law*. Boston: Beacon Press.

Roberts, Paula. 2006. *Update On the Marriage and Fatherhood Provisions of the 2006 Federal Budget and the 2007 Budget Proposal*. Washington, DC: Center for Law and Social Policy, February 10.

Schultz, Marjorie McGuire. 1990. "Reproductive Technology and Intent-Based Parenthood: An Opportunity for Gender Neutrality." 1990 *Wis. L. Rev.* 297.

Shanley, Mary Lyndon. 2001. *Making Babies, Making Families: What Matters Most in an Age of Reproductive Technologies, Surrogacy, Adoption, Same-Sex Marriage and Unwed Parents.* Boston: Beacon Press.

Streuning, Karen. 2002. *New Family Values: Liberty, Equality, Diversity.* Lanham, MD: Rowman & Littlefield.

——. 2007. "Do Government Sponsored Marriage Promotion Policies Place Undue Pressure on Individual Rights," *Policy Sciences* 40: 241–259.

Uniform Law Commissioners, NCCUSL. (2002). Summary of the Uniform Parentage Act. Available at www.nccusl.org/nccusl/uniformact_summaries/uniformacts-s-upa.asp. Uniform Parentage Act (Revised 2002), Article 8: Gestational Agreement, Comment.

Wadlington, Walter, and Raymond C. O'Brien. 2007. *Family Law In Perspective*, 2nd ed. New York: Foundation Press.

Woodhouse, Barbara Bennett. 1993. "Hatching the Egg: A Child-Centered Perspective in Parents' Rights." 14 *Cardozo Law Review* 1747.

Legal Cases:

Alison D. v. Virgino M., 572 N.E. 2d 27 (N.Y. 1991).

Eisenstadt v. Baird, 405 U.S. 438 (1972).

Elisa B. v. Superior Court, 117 P. 3d 660 (Cal. 2005).

Griswold v. Connecticut, 381 U.S. 479 (1965).

Hernandez v. Robles, 855 N.E. 2d 1, 7 (N.Y. 2006).

Johnson v. Calvert, 5 Cal. 4th 84 (1993).

K.M. v. E.G., 117 P. 3d 673 (Cal. 2005).

Lawrence v. Texas, 539 U.S. 558 (2003).

Levy v. Louisiana, 391 U.S. 68 (1968).

Loving v. Virginia, 388 U.S. 1 (1967).

Meyer v. Nebraska, 262 U.S. 390 (1923).

Michael H. v. Gerald D., 491 U.S. 110 (1989).

Moore v. East Cleveland, 431 U.S. 494 (1977).

Nancy S. v. Michele G., 279 Cal. Rptr. 202 (Ct. App. 1991).

Pierce v. Society of Sisters, 268 U.S. 510 (1925).

Planned Parenthood v. Casey, 505 U.S. 833 (1992).

Prince v. Massachusetts, 321 U.S. 158 (1944).

Reynolds v. United States, 98 U.S. 145 (1878).

Roe v. Wade, 410 U.S. 113 (1973).

Stanley v. Illinois, 405 U.S. 645 (1972).

Troxel v. Granville, 530 U.S. 57 (2000).

V.C. v. M.J.B., 748 A.2d 539, 550 (N.J. 2000).

Zablocki v. Redhail, 434 U.S. 374 (1978).

In re Adoption of Minor T., 17 Fam. L. Rptr. 1523 (D.C. Super Ct. 1991).

In re Custody of H.S. H.-K., 533 N.W. 2d 419 (Wis. 1995).

In re M.M.D. & B.H.M., 662 A 2nd 837 (D.C. Cir. 1995).

In re marriage of Buzzanca, 61 Cal. App. 4th 1410 (Cal. App. 1998).

In the Matter of Baby M, 537 A.2d 1227 (N.J. 1988).

In the Matter of Thomas S. v. Robin Y., Court of Appeals of New York, 86 N.Y. 2d 779, 655 N.E. 2d 708, 631 N.Y.S. 2d 611 (July 26, 1995).

Chapter 9: Briefing Paper: Will Providing Marriage Rights to Same-Sex Couples Undermine Heterosexual Marriage? Evidence from Scandinavia, by M. V. Lee Badgett

Andersson, G. (2002, August 14). "Children's experience of family disruption and family formation: Evidence from 16 FFS countries." *Demographic Research*, 7, Article 7. Retrieved March 25, 2004, from www.demographic-research.org.

Coleman, D., & Garssen, J. (2002, September 10). The Netherlands: Paradigm or exception in Western Europe's demography? *Demographic Research*, 7, Article 10. Retrieved August 28, 2004, from www.demographic-research.org.

Eskridge, W. N. (2002). *Equality Practice: Civil Unions and the Future of Gay Rights.* New York: Routledge.

Esping-Andersen, G. (1999). *Social foundations of postindustrial economics.* Oxford, UK: Oxford University Press.

Kiernan, K. (2001). "The rise of cohabitation and childbearing outside marriage in Western Europe." *International Journal of Law, Policy and the Family*, 15: 1–21.

Kurtz, Stanley. 2000. "What Is Wrong with Gay Marriage." *Commentary*, September, pp. 35–41. Available at: www.commentarymagazine.com/viewarticle.cfm/what-is-wrong-with-gay-marriage-9203.

Kurtz, Stanley. 2004. "The End of Marriage in Scandinavia: The 'Conservative Case' for Same-Sex Marriage Collapses." *The Weekly Standard*, February 2 (vol 9, issue 20), pp. 26–33. Available at: www.weeklystandard.com/Content/Public/Articles/000/000/003/660zypwj.asp.

Minot, L. (2000). *Conceiving Parenthood.* San Francisco: International Gay and Lesbian Human Rights Commission.

Sprangers, A., & Garssen, J. (2003, February 26). "Nonmarital-fertility in the European Economic Area." *Centraal Bureau voor de Statistiek.*

Sullivan, A. (2001, August 13). "Unveiled: The case against gay marriage crumbles." *The New Republic.* Retrieved August 12, 2004, from www.andrewsullivan.com/homosexuality.php?artnum=20010813

Chapter 10: Interracial Families in Post–Civil Rights America, by Kerry Ann Rockquemore and Loren Henderson

Bonilla-Silva, E. 2001. *White Supremacy and Racism in the Post-Civil Rights Era.* Boulder, CO: Lynne Reinner.

———. 2003. *Racism Without Racists: Color-Blind Racism and the Persistence of Racial Inequality in the United States.* New York: Rowman & Littlefield.

Bratter, Jenifer, and Karl Eschbach. 2006. "What About the Couple? Interracial Marriage and Psychological Distress." *Social Science Research* 35: 1025–1047.

Childs, Erica. 2005a. "Looking Behind the Stereotypes of the 'Angry Black Woman': An Exploration of Black Women's Responses to Interracial Relationships." *Gender & Society* 19(4): 544–561.

———. 2005b. *Navigating Interracial Borders: Black-White Couples and Their Social Worlds.* New Brunswick, NJ: Rutgers University Press.

Collins, Patricia Hill. 2004. *Black Sexual Politics: African Americans, Gender, and the New Racism*. New York: Routledge.

Dalmage, Heather. 2000. *Tripping on the Color Line: Black-White Multiracial Families in a Racially Divided World*. New Brunswick, NJ: Rutgers University Press.

Davis, F. James. 1991. *Who Is Black? One Nation's Definition*. University Park, PA: Pennsylvania State University Press.

Frankenberg, Ruth. 1993. *White Women, Race Matters*. Minneapolis: University of Minnesota Press.

Harris, David, and Jeremiah Sim. 2002. "Who Is Multiracial? Assessing the Complexity of Lived Race." *American Sociological Review* 67: 614–627.

Hitlin, Steven, J. Scott Brown, and Glen H. Elder, Jr. (2006). "Racial Self-Categorization in Adolescence: Multiracial Development and Social Pathways." *Child Development* 77(5): 1298–1308.

Kennedy, Randall. 2003. *Interracial Intimacies: Sex, Marriage, Identity and Adoption*. New York: Pantheon.

La Ferla, Ruth. 2003. "Generation E.A.: Ethnically Ambiguous," *New York Times*, December 28.

Lazarre, Jane. 1996. *Beyond the Whiteness of Whiteness: Memoirs of a White Mother of Black Sons*. Durham, NC: Duke University Press.

McNamara, Robert P., Maria Tempenis, and Beth Walton, 1999. *Crossing the Line: Interracial Couples in the South*. Westport, CT: Praeger.

Oliver, M., and T. Shapiro. 1997. *Black Wealth/White Wealth: A New Perspective on Racial Inequality*. New York: Routledge.

Omi, Michael, and Howard Winant. 1994. *Racial Formation in the United States: From the 1960s to the 1980s*, 2nd ed. New York: Routledge.

Qian, Zhenchou. 1997. "Breaking the Racial Barriers: Variations in Interracial Marriage between 1980 and 1990." *Demography* 34: 478–500.

Reddy, Maureen. 1994. *Crossing the Color Line: Race, Parenting and Culture*. New Brunswick, NJ: Rutgers University Press.

Renn, Kristen. 2004. *Mixed Race Students in College: The Ecology of Race, Identity, and Community on Campus*. Albany, NY: State University of New York Press.

Rockquemore, Kerry Ann, and David Brunsma. 2001. *Beyond Black: Biracial Identity in America*. Thousand Oaks, CA: Sage Publications.

Root, Maria. 2001. *Love's Revolution: Interracial Marriage*. Philadelphia: Temple University Press.

Rosenblatt, Paul, Teri Karis, and Richard Powell. 1995. *Multiracial Couples: Black and White Voices*. Thousand Oaks, CA: Sage Publications.

Rosenfeld, Michael. 2007. *The Age of Independence: Interracial Unions, Same-Sex Unions, and the Changing American Family*. Cambridge, MA: Harvard University Press.

Russell, Kathy, Midge Wilson, and Ronald Hall, 1993. *The Color Complex: The Politics of Skin Color Among African Americans*. New York: Anchor Books.

Schuman, Howard, Charlotte Steeh, Lawrence Bobo, and Maria Kryson. 1997. *Racial Attitudes in America: Trends and Interpretations*, rev. ed. Cambridge, MA: Harvard University Press.

Simmons, Tavia, and Martin O'Connell. 2003. *Married-Couple and Unmarried-Partner Households: 2000*. Washington, DC: U.S. Census Bureau.

Steinbugler, Amy. 2005. "Visibility as Privilege and Danger: Heterosexual and Same-Sex Interracial Intimacy in the 21st Century," *Sexualities* 8(4): 425–443.

Todd, Judith, Jeanice Mckinney, Raymond Harris, Ryan Chadderton, and Leslie Small. 1992. "Attitudes Toward Interracial Dating: Effects of Age, Sex, and Race." *Journal of Multicultural Counseling and Development* 21 (October): 202–208.

Twine, France Winddance, and Amy Steinbugler. 2006. "The Gap Between Whites and Whiteness: Interracial Intimacy and Racial Literacy." *DuBois Review* 3(2): 341–363.

Wallace, Kendra. 2001. "Relative/Outsider: The Art and Politics of Identity Among Mixed Heritage Students." Westport, CT: Ablex Publishing.

Zuberi, Tukufu. 2001. *Thicker Than Blood: When Racial Statistics Lie*. Minneapolis: University of Minnesota Press.

Chapter 12: Why Is Everyone Afraid of Sex?, by Pepper Schwartz

Baumgardner, Jennifer. 2007. *Look Both Ways: Bisexual Politics*. New York, Farrar, Straus, and Giroux.

Bearman, Peter S., and Hannah Brückner. 2001. "Promising the Future: Virginity Pledges and the Transition to First Intercourse." *American Journal of Sociology* 106: 859–912.

Bogle, Kathleen A. 2008. *Hooking Up: Sex Dating and Relationships on Campus*. New York: New York University Press.

Boonstra, Heather D. 2009. "Advocates Call for a New Approach after the Era of 'Abstinence Only' Sex Education." Guttmacher Policy Review 12 (Winter).

Brandt, Allan. 1987. *No Magic Bullet: A Social History of Venereal Disease in the United States since 1880*. New York: Oxford University Press.

Brückner, Hannah, and Peter S. Bearman. 2005. "After the Promise: The STD Consequences of Adolescent Virginity Pledges." *Journal of Adolescent Health* 36: 271–278.

Campbell, D., and C. Robinson. 2007. "Religious Coalitions for and against Gay Marriage: The Culture War Rages On." Pp. 131–154 in *Politics of Gay Marriage*. Chicago: University of Chicago Press.

Carpenter, Laura M. 2005. *Virginity Lost*. New York: New York University Press.

D'Emilio, John, and Estelle B. Freedman. 1988. *Intimate Matters: A History of Sexuality in America*. New York: Harper and Row.

Jehl, Douglas. 1999. "For Shame: A Special Report; Arab Honor's Price: A Woman's Blood." *New York Times*, June 20.

Kamen, Paula. 2000. *Her Way: Young Women Remake the Sexual Revolution*. New York: New York University Press.

Kinsey, Alfred C., Wardell B. Pomeroy, and Martin, Clyde E. 1948. *Sexual Behavior in the Human Male*. Philadelphia: W. B. Saunders.

Klein, Marty, and Nadine Strossen. 2006. *America's War on Sex: The Attack on Law, Lust and Liberty*. Westport, CT: Praeger.

Lauman, Edward O., John H. Gagnon, Robert T. Michael, and Stuart Michaels. 1994. *The Social Organization of Sexuality: Sexual Practices in the United States*. Chicago: University of Chicago Press.

Laumann, Edward O., Jenna Mahay, and Yoosik Youm. 2007. "Sex Intimacy, and Family Life in the United States." Pp. 165–190 in *The Sexual Self*, edited by Michael S. Kimmel. Nashville, TN: Vanderbilt University Press.

McWhirter, David P., Stephanie A. Sanders, and June M. Reinisch. 1990. *Homosexuality/Heterosexuality: Concepts of Sexual Orientation*. Kinsey Institute Series. New York: Oxford University Press.

Pascoe, C. J. 2007. *Dude, You're a Fag: Masculinity and Sexuality in High School*. Berkeley: CA: University of California Press.

Reiss, I., and H. Reiss. 2002. "The Role of Religion in Our Sexual Lives." In *Sexual Lives: A Reader on the Theories and Realities of Human Sexualities*, edited by Robert Heasley and Betsy Crane. New York: McGraw-Hill.

Rom, M. C. 2007. "Introduction." Pp. 1–38 in *The Politics of Same Sex Marriage*, edited by Craig Rimmerman and Clyde Wilcox. Chicago: University of Chicago Press.

Schwartz, Pepper. 2007. "The Social Construction of Heterosexuality." Pp. 80–92 in *The Sexual Self*, edited by Michael Kimmel. Nashville, TN: Vanderbilt University Press.

Schwartz, Pepper, and Virginia Rutter. 2000. *The Gender of Sexuality*. Lanham, MD: Alta Mira Press.

Shilts, Randy. 1987. *And the Band Played On*. New York: St. Martins Press.

Tannenbaum, Leora. 1999. *Slut! Growing Up Female With a Bad Reputation*. New York: Seven Stories Press.

Tiefer, Leonore. 1995. *Sex is Not A Natural Act and Other Essays*. Boulder, CO: Colorado Westview Press.

Wilcox, Clyde, P. Brewer, S. Shames, and C. Lake. 2007. "If I Bend This Far I Will Break? Public Opinion about Gay Marriage." Pp. 215–242 in *The Politics of Same Sex Marriage*, edited by Craig A. Rimmerman and Clyde Wilcox. Chicago: University of Chicago Press.

Chapter 13: New Couples, New Families: The Cohabitation Revolution in the United States, by Pamela J. Smock and Wendy Manning

Acs, Gregory, and Sandra Nelson. 2002. "The Kids Are Alright? Children's Well-Being and the Rise in Cohabitation." *New Federalism National Survey of America's Families*, B-48. Washington, DC: Urban Institute.

Brown, Susan. 2000. "Fertility Following Marital Dissolution: The Role of Cohabitation." *Journal of Family Issues* 21: 501–524.

Brown, Susan, and Alan Booth. 1996. "Cohabitation versus Marriage: A Comparison of Relationship Quality." *Journal of Marriage and Family* 58: 668–678.

Bumpass, Larry, and Hsien Lu. 2000. "Trends in Cohabitation and Implications for Children's Family Contexts." *Population Studies* 54: 9–41.

Bumpass, Larry, R. Kelly Raley, and James Sweet. 1995. "The Changing Character of Step-families: Implications of Cohabitation and Nonmarital Childbearing." *Demography* 32: 425–436.

Bumpass, Larry and James Sweet. 1989. "National Estimates of Cohabitation." *Demography* 26: 615–625.

Casper, Lynne, and Suzanne Bianchi. 2002. *Continuity and Change in the American Family*. Thousand Oaks, CA: Sage Publications.

Clarkberg, Marin, Ross Stolzenberg, and Linda Waite. 1995. "Attitudes, Values, and Entrance into Cohabitational versus Marital Unions." *Social Forces* 74: 609–634.

Fields, Jason, and Lynne Casper. 2001. *America's Families and Living Arrangements: Population Characteristics*. Current Population Reports, P20-537. Washington, DC: U.S. Census Bureau.

Gupta, Sanjiv. 1999. "The Effects of Transitions in Marital Status on Men's Housework Performance." *Journal of Marriage and Family* 61: 700–711.

Jepson, L., and C. Jepsen. 2002. "An Empirical Analysis of the Matching Patterns of Same-Sex and Opposite-Sex Couples." *Demography* 29: 435–453.

Kennedy, Sheela, and Larry Bumpass. 2007. "Cohabitation and Children's Living Arrangements: New Estimates from the United States." *Center for Demography and Ecology Working Paper*, 2007-20. Madison, WI: University of Wisconsin-Madison.

Lye, Diane, and Ingrid Waldron. 1997. "Attitudes Toward Cohabitation, Family, and Gender Roles: Relationships to Values and Political Ideology." *Sociological Perspectives* 40: 199–225.

Manning, Wendy. 2001. "Childbearing in Cohabiting Unions: Racial and Ethnic Differences." *Family Planning Perspectives* 33: 217–223.

Manning, Wendy, and Susan Brown. 2006. "Children's Economic Well-Being in Married and Cohabiting Parent Families." *Journal of Marriage and Family* 68: 345–362.

Manning, Wendy, Monica Longmore, and Peggy Giordano. 2007. "The Changing Institution of Marriage: Adolescents' Expectations to Cohabit and to Marry." *Journal of Marriage and Family* 69: 559–575.

Manning, Wendy, and Pamela Smock. 2002. "First Comes Cohabitation and Then Comes Marriage." *Journal of Family Issues* 23: 1065–1087.

———. 2005. "Measuring and Modeling Cohabitation: New Perspectives from Qualitative Data." *Journal of Marriage and Family* 67: 989–1002.

Musick, Kelly. 2002. "Planned and Unplanned Childbearing among Unmarried Women." *Journal of Marriage and Family* 64: 915–929.

Nock, Steven. 1995. "A Comparison of Marriages and Cohabiting Relationships." *Journal of Family Issues* 16: 53–76.

Simmons, T. and M. O'Connell. 2003. *Married-Couple and Unmarried Partner Households: 2000. Census 2000 Special Reports.* Washington, DC: U.S. Bureau of the Census.

Smock, Pamela J., and Wendy Manning. 2004. "Living Together Unmarried in the United States: Demographic Perspectives and Implications for Family Policy." *Law and Policy* 26: 87–117.

Smock, Pamela, Wendy Manning, and Meredith Porter. 2005. "'Everything's There Except Money.' How Money Shapes Decisions to Marry Among Cohabitors." *Journal of Marriage and Family* 67: 680–696.

Smock, Pamela J., and Mary Noonan. 2005. "Gender, Work, and Family Well-Being in the United States." Pp. 343–360 in *Work, Family, Health and Well-Being*, edited by Suzanne Bianchi, Lynne Casper, and Rosalind Berkowitz King. Mahwah, NJ: Lawrence Erlbaum Associates.

South, Scott, and Glenna Spitze. 1994. "Housework in Marital and Nonmarital Households." *American Sociological Review* 59: 327–347.

Stevens, Raymond. 1940. "Illegal Families Among the Clients of Family Agencies." *Social Forces* 19: 84–87.

Thornton, Arland, William Axinn, and Daniel Hill. 1992. "Reciprocal Effects of Religiosity, Cohabitation, and Marriage." *American Journal of. Sociology* 98: 628–651.

U.S. Department of Health and Human Services. 2005. *Fertility, Family Planning, and the Health of U.S. Women: Data from the 2002 National Survey of Family Growth*. Series 23–25. Hyattsville, MD: National Center for Health Statistics.

Chapter 14: Parenting Adult Children in the Twenty-First Century, by Joshua Coleman

Ahrons, C. 2004. *We're Still Family*. New York: HarperCollins.

Ahrons, C., and J. L. Tanner. 2003. "Adult Children and Their Fathers: Relationship Changes 20 Years After Parental Divorce." *Family Relations* 52: 340–351.

Amato, Paul R., and Alan Booth. 1997. *A Generation at Risk*. Cambridge, MA: Harvard University Press.

Amato, Paul, and Julie Sobolewski. 2004. "The Effects of Divorce on Fathers and Children: Nonresidential Fathers and Stepfathers." Pp. 341–367 in *The Role of the Father in Child Development*, 4th ed., edited by Michael Lamb. New York: Wiley.

Bateson, Gregory. 1980. *Steps to an Ecology of Mind*. New York: Ballantine.

Baum, N. 2006. "Postdivorce Paternal Disengagement." *Journal of Marriage and Family Therapy* 32: 245–254.

Bettelheim, Bruno. 1967. *The Empty Fortress: Infantile Autism and the Birth of the Self*. New York: Free Press.

Bianchi, Suzanne, John Robinson, and Melissa Milke. 2006. *Changing Rhythms of American Family Life*. New York: Russell Sage Foundation.

Coleman, Joshua. 2003. *The Lazy Husband: How to Get Men to Do More Parenting and Housework*. New York: St. Martin's Press.

——. 2007. *When Parents Hurt: Compassionate Strategies When You and Your Grown Child Don't Get Along*. New York: HarperCollins.

Coltrane, Scott. 1996. *Family Man: Fatherhood, Housework, and Gender Equity*. New York: Oxford University Press.

Coontz, Stephanie. 1997. *The Way We Really Are: Coming to Terms with America's Changing Families*. New York: Basic Books.

——. 2006. "How to Stay Married." *Times of London*, November 30.

——. 2008. *American Families: A Multicultural Reader*. 2nd ed. New York: Routledge.

Danziger, S., and P. Gottschalk. 2005. "Diverging Fortunes: Trends in Poverty and Inequality." In *The American People: Census 2000 Series*, edited by R. Farley. New York: Russell Sage Foundation and Population Reference Bureau.

Dunn, J., and R. Plomin. 1990. *Separate Lives: Why Siblings Are So Different*. New York: Basic Books.

Ehrensaft, Diane. 1997. *Spoiling Childhood: How Well-Meaning Parents Are Giving Children Too Much—But Not What They Need*. New York: Guilford Press.

Flanagan, Constance. 2006. "The Changing Social Contract at the Transition to Adulthood: Implications for Individuals and the Polity." In *Social and Political Change in Adolescent Development*, edited by R. Silbereisen. Invited paper symposium for the biennial meetings of the Society for Research on Adolescence, San Francisco, CA.

Freud Sigmund. 1926. "Inhibitions, Symptoms, and Anxiety." Pp. 77–175 in the *Standard Edition of the Complete Psychological Works*, vol. 20. London: Hogarth Press.

Harris, Judith Rich. 1999. *The Nurture Assumption: Why Children Turn Out the Way They Do*. New York: Touchstone.

Hetherington, E. Mavis, and John Kelly. 2002. *For Better or Worse: Divorce Reconsidered*. New York: W. W. Norton.

Knoester, Chris. 2003. "Transitions in Young Adulthood and the Relationships Between Parent and Offspring Well-Being." *Social Forces* 81: 1431–1458.

Lareau, Annette, 2003. *Unequal Childhoods: Class, Race, and Family Life*. Berkeley, CA: University of California Press.

Lacar, Marvi. 2006. "The Bank of Mom and Dad." *New York Times*, April 9.

Lin, I-Fen. 2008. "Consequences of Parental Divorce for Adult Children's Support of Their Frail Parents." *Journal of Marriage and Family* 70: 113–128.

Marano, H. E. 2004. "A Nation of Wimps." *Psychology Today*, November/December.

Mintz, Steven. 2004. *Huck's Raft: A History of American Childhood*. Cambridge, MA: Harvard University Press.

———. 2006. "How We All Became Jewish Mothers." *National Post*, February 17.

Nielsen, L. 2004. *Embracing Your Father: How to Build the Relationship You've Always Wanted with Your Dad*. New York: McGraw-Hill.

Onion, The. 2005. "Most Americans Falling for 'Get Rich Slowly Over a Lifetime of Hard Work' Schemes." Volume 41, Issue 49, December 7.

Pew Research Center. 2006. *Adult Children and Parents Talking More Often*, February 23.

Putnam, Robert D. 2000. *Bowling Alone: The Collapse and Revival of American Community*. New York: Simon and Schuster.

Reiss, David, Jenae M. Neiderhiser, E. Mavis Hetherington, and Robert Plomin. 2000. *The Relationship Code: Deciphering Genetic and Social Influences on Adolescent Development*. Cambridge, MA: Harvard University Press.

Schwartz, Barry. 2004. *The Paradox of Choice: Why More Is Less*. New York: Harper's Perennial.

Seligman, M. E. P. 1996. *The Optimistic Child: Proven Program to Safeguard Children from Depression and Build Lifelong Resilience*. New York: Houghton Mifflin.

Sullivan, Oriel, and Scott Coltrane. 2008. "Men's Changing Contribution to Housework and Child-Care." Discussion paper prepared for the Council on Contemporary Families.

Stearns, Peter N. 2003. *Anxious Parents: A History of Modern Childrearing in America*. New York: New York University Press.

Zelizer, Virginia, A. 1994. *Pricing the Priceless Child: The Changing Social Value of Children*. Princeton: Princeton University Press.

Chapter 16: The Case for Divorce, by Virginia E. Rutter

Amato, Paul R., and Juliana M. Sobolewski. 2001. "The Effects of Divorce and Marital Discord on Adult Children's Psychological Well-Being." *American Sociological Review* 66: 900–921.

Ananat, E, and G. Michaels. 2008. "The Effect of Marital Breakup on the Income Distribution of Women and Children." *Journal of Human Resources* 43(3): 611–629.

Becker, Howard S. 1973. *Outsiders: Studies in the Sociology of Deviance*. New York: Free Press.

Campbell, Jacquelyn C., ed. 1998. *Empowering Survivors of Abuse: Health Care for Battered Women and Their Children*. Thousand Oaks, CA: Sage Publications.

Cherlin Andrew J., Frank F. Furstenberg, Jr., P. Lindsay Chase-Lansdale, Kathleen E. Kiernan., Philip K. Robins., Donna Ruane Morrison, and Julien O. Teitler. 1991. "Longitudinal Studies of Effects of Divorce on Children in Great Britain and the United States." *Science* 252: 1386–1389.

Cherlin, Andrew J., P. Lindsay Chase-Lansdale, and Christine McRae. 1998. "Effects of Parental Divorce on Mental Health through the Life Course." *American Sociological Review* 63: 239–249.

Coltrane, Scott, and Michele Adams. 2003. "The Social Construction of the Divorce 'Problem': Morality, Child Victims, and the Politics of Gender." *Family Relations* 52: 363–372.

Coontz, Stephanie, and Nancy Folbre. 2002 (April). "Marriage, Poverty, and Public Policy." A Briefing Paper from the Council on Contemporary Families. Retrieved June 24, 2008, from www.contemporaryfamilies.org/public/briefing.html.

Cowen, Tyler. 2007. "Matrimony Has Its Benefits, and Divorce Has a Lot to Do with That." *New York Times*, April 19. Retrieved online on June 20, 2008.

Fomby, Paula, and Andrew Cherlin. 2007. "Family Instability and Child Well-Being." *American Sociological Review* 72(2): 181–204.

Gottman, J. M. 1994. *What Predicts Divorce?* Hillsdale, NJ: Lawrence Erlbaum Associates.

Greenberg, P. E., L. E. Stiglin, S. N. Finkelstein, and E. R. Berndt. 1993a. "Depression: A Neglected Major Illness." *Journal of Clinical Psychiatry* 54: 419–424.

———. 1993b. "The Economic Burden of Depression in 1990." *Journal of Clinical Psychiatry* 54: 405–418.

Hawkins, Daniel N., and Alan Booth. 2005. "Unhappily Ever After: Effects of Long-Term, Low-Quality Marriages on Well-Being." *Social Forces* 84(1): 451–471.

Hetherington, E. Mavis. 1999. "Should We Stay Together for the Sake of the Children?" Pp. 93–116 in *Coping with Divorce, Single Parenting, and Remarriage: A Risk and Resiliency Perspective*, edited by E. Mavis Hetherington. Mahwah, NJ: Lawrence Erlbaum Associates.

Hetherington, E. Mavis, and John Kelly. 2002. *For Better or For Worse: Divorce Reconsidered*. New York: W. W. Norton.

Hetherington, E. Mavis, and P. Stanley-Hagan. 1997. "Divorce and the Adjustment of Children: A risk and resiliency perspective." *Journal of Child Psychology & Psychiatry* 40: 129–140.

Heuveline, P. 2005. "The Tricky Business of Estimating Divorce Rates." A Briefing Paper from the Council on Contemporary Families. Last modified October 6, 2006. Retrieved June 24, 2008, from www.contemporaryfamilies.org/public/briefing.html.

Kiecolt-Glaser, J. K., S. Kennedy, S. Malkoff, L.Fisher, C. E. Speicher, and R. Glaser. 1988. "Marital Discord and Immunity in Males." *Psychosomatic Medicine* 50: 213–299.

Li, Jui-Chung Allen. 2007. "The Kids Are OK: Divorce and Children's Behavior Problems." RAND Labor and Population Working Paper No. WR-489. Santa Monica, CA: RAND.

———. 2008. "New Findings on an Old Question: Does Divorce Cause Children's Behavior Problems?" A Briefing Paper from the Council on Contemporary Families. Posted at www.contemporaryfamilies.org/public/briefing.html (April 24; retrieved online June 24, 2008).

Meadows, S.O., S. McLanahan, and J. Brooks-Gunn. 2008. "Stability and Change in Family Structure and Maternal Health Trajectories." *American Sociological Review* 73(2): 314–334.

Mintz, Steven. 2004. *Huck's Raft: A History of American Childhood*. Cambridge, MA: Harvard University Press.

Osborne, C., and S. McLanahan. 2007. "Partnership Instability and Child Well-Being." *Journal of Marriage and Family* 69(4): 1065–1083.

Robles, T. F., and J. K. Kiecolt-Glaser. 2003. "The Physiology of Marriage: Pathways to Health." *Physiology and Behavior* 79(3): 409–416.

Ruggles, Steven. 1997. "The Rise of Divorce and Separation in the United States 1880–1990. *Demography* 34(4): 455–466.

Rutter, V. E. 2004 (August). "The Case for Divorce: Under What Conditions Is Divorce Beneficial and for Whom?" Ph.D. dissertation, Department of Sociology, University of Washington.

Scafidi, B. 2008. *The Taxpayer Costs of Divorce: First-Ever Estimates for the Nation and All Fifty States*. New York: Institute for American Values.

Smock, Pamela J., Wendy D. Manning, and Sanjiv Gupta. 1999. "The Effect of Marriage and Divorce on Women's Economic Well-Being." *American Sociological Review* 64: 794–812.

Stevenson, B., and J. Wolfers. 2006. "Bargaining in the Shadow of Divorce Laws and Family Distress. *Quarterly Journal of Economics* 121(1): 267–288.

van Hemert, Dianne A., F.J.R. van de Vijver, and Ype H. Poortinga. 2002. "The Beck Depression Inventory as a Measure of Subjective Well-Being: A Cross-National Study." *Journal of Happiness Studies* 3(3): 257–286.

Veenhoven, Ruut. 2004. *World Database of Happiness: Continuous Register of Scientific Research on Subjective Appreciation of Life*. Rotterdam, The Netherlands: Erasmus University. Available at: www2.eur.nl/fsw/research/happiness/.

Waite, Linda J., Don Browning, William J. Doherty, Maggie Gallagher, Ye Luo, and Scott M. Stanley. 2002. *Does Divorce Make People Happy? Findings From a Study of Unhappy Marriages*. New York: Institute for American Values.

Wallerstein, J., and Sandra Blakeslee. 1988. *Second Chances: Men, Women, and Children a Decade after Divorce: Who Wins, Who Loses, and Why*. New York: Ticknor & Fields.

Weissman, M. M. 1987. "Advances in Psychiatric Epidemiology: Rates and Risks for Major Depression." *American Journal of Public Health* 77: 445–451.

Whisman, Mark A. 1999. "Marital Dissatisfaction and Psychiatric Disorders: Results from the National Comorbidity Survey." *Journal of Abnormal Psychology* 108: 701–706.

Chapter 17: Briefing Paper: The Impact of Divorce on Children's Behavior Problems, by Jui-Chung Allen Li

Aughinbaugh, A., C. R. Pierret, and D. S. Rothstein. 2005. "The Impact of Family Structure Transitions on Youth Achievement: Evidence from the Children of the NLSY79." *Demography* 42: 447–468.

Foster, E. M., and A. Kalil. 2007. "Living Arrangements and Children's Development in Low-Income White, Black, and Latino Families. *Child Development* 78: 657–1674.

Li, Jui-Chung Allen. 2007. "The Kids Are OK: Divorce and Children's Behavior Problems." RAND Labor and Population Working Paper, WR-489. Santa Monica, CA: RAND.

Chapter 20: From Outlaws to In-Laws: Gay and Lesbian Couples in Contemporary Society, by Robert-Jay Green

Balsam, K. F., T. P. Beauchaine, E. D. Rothblum, and S. E. Solomon. 2008. "Three-Year Follow-up of Same-Sex Couples Who Had Civil Unions in Vermont, Same-Sex Couples Not in Civil Unions, and Heterosexual Married Couples." *Developmental Psychology* 44: 102–116.

Clifford, D., F. Hertz, and E. Doskow. 2007. *A Legal Guide for Lesbian and Gay Couples*, 14th ed. Berkeley, CA: Nolo Press.

CNN 2008. Exit poll for California Proposition 8, November 4, 2008, general election, Retrieved November 8, 2008. Available at: www.cnn.com/ELECTION/2008/results/polls/#CAI01p1

Crowl, A. L., S. Ahn, and J. A. Baker. 2008. "A Meta-Analysis of Developmental Outcomes for Children of Same-Sex and Heterosexual Parents." *Journal of GLBT Family Studies* 4: 386–407.

D'Augelli, A. R., A. H. Grossman, and J. Rendina. 2006. "Lesbian, Gay, and Bisexual Youth: Marriage and Child-Rearing Aspirations." Paper presented at the Family Pride Academic Symposium, May 23. Philadelphia: University of Pennsylvania.

D'Augelli, A. R., H. J. Rendina, K. O. Sinclair, and A. H. Grossman. (2006/2007). "Lesbian and Gay Youths' Aspirations for Marriage and Raising Children." *Journal of LGBT Issues in Counseling* 1: 77–98.

Dobson, J. 2006. "Two Mommies Is One Too Many." *Time*, December 12. Retrieved December 12, 2006, from www.time.com/time/magazine/article/0,9171,1568485,00.html.

Egan, P. J., M. S. Edelman, and K. Sherrill. 2008. "Findings from the Hunter College Poll of Lesbians, Gays, and Bisexuals: New Discoveries about Identity, Political Attitudes and Civic Engagement." Retrieved November 10, 2008, www.nyu.edu/public.affairs/pdf/hunter_college_poll_report_complete.pdf

Emilio, J. D. 1998. *Sexual Politics, Sexual Communities*, 2nd ed. Chicago: University of Chicago Press.

Faderman, L. 1991. *Odd Girls and Twilight Lovers*. New York: Columbia University Press.

Firestein, B., ed. 2007. *Becoming Visible: Counseling Bisexuals across the Lifespan*. New York: Columbia University Press.

Fox, R., ed. 2006. *Affirmative Psychotherapy with Bisexual Women and Bisexual Men*. Binghamton, NY: Haworth Press.

General Accounting Office 2004. "Defense of Marriage Act: Update to Prior Report," GAO-04-353R. Retrieved October 23, 2004, from www.gao.gov/new.items/d04353r.pdf.

Gottman, J. M., R. W. Levenson, J. Gross, B. L. Frederickson, K. McCoy, L. Rosenthal, A. Ruef, and D. Yoshimoto. 2003a. "Correlates of Gay and Lesbian Couples' Relationship Satisfaction and Relationship Dissolution." *Journal of Homosexuality* 45: 23–43.

Gottman, J. M., R. W. Levenson, C. Swanson, K. Swanson, R. Tyson, and D. Yoshimoto. 2003b. "Observing Gay, Lesbian, and Heterosexual Couples' Relationships: Mathematical Modeling of Conflict Interaction." *Journal of Homosexuality* 45: 65–91.

Green, R.-J., M. Bettinger, & E. Zacks. 1996. "Are Lesbian Couples Fused and Gay Male Couples Disengaged?: Questioning Gender Straightjackets." Pp. 185–230 in *Lesbians and Gays in Couples and Families*, edited by J. Laird and R.-J. Green. San Francisco: Jossey-Bass.

Herdt, G., and R. Kertzner. 2006. "I Do, but I Can't: The Impact of Marriage Denial on the Mental Health and Sexual Citizenship of Lesbians and Gay Men in the United States." *Sexuality Research & Social Policy Journal of NSRC* 3: 33–39.

Herek, G. M., ed. 1998. *Stigma and Sexual Orientation: Understanding Prejudice against Lesbians, Gay Men, and Bisexuals*. Thousand Oaks, CA: Sage Publications.

Herek, G. M. 2006. "Legal Recognition of Same-Sex Relationships in the United States: A Social Science Perspective." *American Psychologist* 61: 607–621.

Katz, J. N. 1992. *Gay American History: Lesbians and Gay Men in the U.S.A.* (revised sub edition). New York: Plume.

Kurdek, L. A. 2004. "Are Gay and Lesbian Cohabiting Couples Really Different from Heterosexual Married Couples?" *Journal of Marriage and Family* 66: 880–900.

———. 2005. "What Do We Know about Gay and Lesbian Couples?" *Current Directions in Psychological Science* 14: 251–254.

Laird, J., and R.-J. Green, eds. 1996. *Lesbians and Gays in Couples and Families: A Handbook for Therapists*. San Francisco: Jossey-Bass.

Lanutti, P. J. 2008. "Attractions and Obstacles while Considering Legally Recognized Same-Sex Marriage Relationships." *Journal of GLBT Family Studies* 4: 245–264.

Lev, A. I. 2004. *Transgender Emergence: Therapeutic Guidelines for Working with Gender-Variant People and Their Families*. Binghamton, NY: Haworth Press.

Meyer, I. H. 2003. "Prejudice, Social Stress, and Mental Health in Lesbian, Gay, and Bisexual Populations: Conceptual Issues and Research Evidence." *Psychological Bulletin* 129: 674–697.

NBC/*Wall Street Journal*. 2008 (August). Study #6080. Retrieved November 10, 2008, from http://s.wsj.net/public/resources/documents/WSJ_NBCPoll_prtl_082108.pdf.

Patterson, C. J. 2005. *Lesbian and Gay Parenting: Summary of Research Findings*. Washington, DC: American Psychological Association. Available at www.apa.org/pi/parent.html.

Peplau, L. A., and A. W. Fingerhut. 2007. "The Close Relationships of Lesbians and Gay Men." *Annual Review of Psychology* 58: 405–424.

Pew Research Center. 2007 (May 23). Four-in-Ten Americans Have Close Friends or Relatives Who Are Gay. Retrieved August 19, 2007, from http://pewresearch.org/pubs/485/friends-who-are-gay.

Quinnipiac University Polling Institute. 2008 (July). Retrieved November 12, 2008, from www.quinnipiac.edu/images/polling/us/us07172008.doc.

Ragins, B. R., R. Singh, and J. M. Cornwell. 2007. "Making the Invisible Visible: Fear and Disclosure of Sexual Orientation at Work." *Journal of Applied Psychology* 92: 1103–1118.

Roisman, G. I., E. Clausell, A. Holland, K. Fortuna, and C. Elief. 2008. "Multimethod Comparision of Same-Sex Couples with Opposite-Sex Dating, Engaged, and Married Dyads. *Developmental Psychology* 44: 91–101.

Romero, A. P., A. Baumle, M. V. L. Badget, and G. J. Gates. 2007. "Williams Institute Census Snapshot: December 2007." Retrieved November 10, 2008, from www.law.ucla.edu/williamsinstitute/publications/USCensusSnapshot.pdf.

Saad, L. 2008. "Americans Evenly Divided on Morality of Homosexuality." Princeton, NJ: Gallup Poll. Retrieved June 18, 2008, from www.gallup.com/poll/108115/Americans-Evenly-Divided-Morality-Homosexuality.aspx.

Savin-Williams, R. C. 2001. *Mom, Dad. I'm Gay: How Families Negotiate Coming Out*. Washington, DC: American Psychological Association.

Solomon, S. E., E. D. Rothblum, and K. F. Balsam. 2004. "Pioneers in Partnership: Lesbian and Gay Male Couples in Civil Unions Compared with Those Not in Civil Unions and Married Heterosexual Siblings." *Journal of Family Psychology* 18: 275–286.

Stacey, J., and T. Biblarz. 2001. "(How) Does the Sexual Orientation of Parents Matter." *American Sociological Review* 66: 159–183.

Tasker, F., and C. J. Patterson. 2007. "Research on Gay and Lesbian Parenting: Retrospect and Prospect" *GLBT Studies* 3: 9–34.

Wainright, J. L, and C. J. Patterson. 2008. "Peer Relationships among Adolescents with Female Same-Sex Partners." *Developmental Psychology* 44: 117–126.

Wainright, J. L., S. T. Russell, and C. J. Patterson. 2004. "Psychological Adjustment, School Outcomes, and Romantic Relationships of Adolescents with Same-Sex Parents." *Child Development* 75: 1886–1898.

Weston, K. 1991. *Families We Choose: Lesbians, Gays, Kinship*. New York: Columbia University Press.

Chapter 21: Independent Women: Equality in African-American Lesbian Relationships, by Mignon R. Moore

Abdulahad, Tania, Gwendolyn Rogers, Barbara Smith, and Jameelah Waheed. 1983. "Black Lesbian/Feminist Organizing: A Conversation." Pp. 293–319 in *Home Girls: A Black Feminist Anthology*, edited by B. Smith. New York: Kitchen Table Press.

Blumstein, Philip, and Pepper Schwartz. 1983. *American Couples: Money, Work, Sex*. New York: Morrow.

Bulcroft, Richard A., and Kris A. Bulcroft. 1993. "Race Differences in Attitudinal and Motivational Factors in the Decision to Marry." *Journal of Marriage and Family* 55(92): 338–355.

Carrington, Christopher. 1999. *No Place Like Home: Relationships and Family Life among Lesbians and Gay Men*. Chicago: University of Chicago Press.

Collins, Patricia Hill. 2004. *Black Sexual Politics: African Americans, Gender and the New Racism*. New York: Routledge.

Combahee River Collective. 1983. "A Black Feminist Statement." Pp. 232–240 in *Words of Fire: An Anthology of African-American Feminist Thought*, edited by Beverly Guy-Sheftall. New York: New Press.

Cornwell, Anita. 1983. *The Black Lesbian in White America*. Tallahassee, FL: Naiad Press.

Crenshaw, Kimberlé Williams. 1995. "Race, Reform, and Retrenchment: Transformation and Legitimation in Anti-discrimination Law." Pp. 103–122 in *Critical Race Theory: The Key Writings that Formed the Movement*, edited by Kimberlé Crenshaw, Neil Gotanda, Gary Peller, and Kendall Thomas. New York: New Press.

Dang, Alain, and Somjen Frazer. 2004. "Black Same-Sex Households in the United States: A Report from the 2000 Census." New York: National Gay and Lesbian Task Force Policy Institute and the National Black Justice Coalition.

Dill, Bonnie Thornton. 1979. "The Dialectics of Black Womanhood." *Signs: Journal of Women in Culture and Society* 4: 543–555.

Esterberg, Kristin G. 1997. *Lesbian and Bisexual Identities: Constructing Communities, Constructing Selves*. Philadelphia: Temple University Press.

Ferree, Myra Marx. 1991. "The Gender Division of Labor in Two-Earner Marriages." *Journal of Family Issues* 12(2): 158–180.

Gartrell, Nanette, Amy Banks, Nancy Reed, Jean Hamilton, Carla Rodas, and Amalia Deck. 2000. "The National Lesbian Family Study: 3. Interviews with Mothers of Five-Year-Olds." *American Journal of Orthopsychiatry* 70(4): 542–548.

Gates, Gary. 2008. "Diversity among Same-Sex Couples and their Children." Pp. 394–399 in *American Families: A Multicultural Reader*, 2nd ed., edited by Stephanie Coontz, with Maya Parson and Gabrielle Raley. New York: Routledge.

Hequembourg, Amy. 2007. *Lesbian Motherhood: Stories of Becoming*. New York: Harrington Park Press.

Hochschild, Arlie Russell. 1989. *The Second Shift: Working Parents and the Revolution at Home*. New York: Viking.

Hunter, Andrea G., and Sherrill L. Sellers. 1998. "Feminist Attitudes among African-American Women and Men." *Gender and Society* 12(1): 81–99.

Kamo, Yoshimore, and Ellen L. Cohen. 1998. "Division of Household Work between Partners: A Comparison of Black and White Couples." *Journal of Comparative Family Studies* 29(1): 131–145.

Kenney, Catherine T. 2006. "The Power of the Purse: Allocative Systems and Inequality in Couple Households." *Gender and Society* 20(3): 354–381.

Kessler-Harris, Alice. 2003. *Out to Work: A History of Wage-Earning Women in the United States*. New York: Oxford University Press.

King, Deborah. 1988. "Multiple Jeopardy, Multiple Consciousness: The Context of a Black Feminist Ideology." *Signs: Journal of Women in Culture and Society* 14(1): 42–72.

Kurdek, Lawrence A. 1993. "The Allocation of Household Labor in Gay, Lesbian, Heterosexual, and Married Couples." *Journal of Social Issues* 49(3): 127–139.

Landry, Bart. 2000. *Black Working Wives: Pioneers of the American Family Revolution*. Berkeley, CA: University of California Press.

Mezey, Nancy J. 2008. *New Choices, New Families: How Lesbians Decide about Motherhood*. Baltimore, MD: Johns Hopkins University Press.

Moore, Mignon R. 2006. "Lipstick or Timberlands? Meanings of Gender Presentation in Black Lesbian Communities." *Signs: Journal of Women in Culture and Society* 31(1): 113–139.

———. 2008. "Gendered Power Relations among Women: A Study of Household Decision-Making in Black, Lesbian Stepfamilies." *American Sociological Review* 73: 335–356.

Nelson, Fiona. 1996. *Lesbian Motherhood: An Exploration of Canadian Lesbian Families*. Toronto, Canada; University of Toronto Press.

Patterson, Charlotte. 1995. "Families of the Lesbian Baby Boom: Parents' Division of Labor and Children's Adjustment." *Developmental Psychology* 31(1): 115–123.

Phelan, Shane. 1993. "(Be)Coming Out: Lesbian Identity and Politics." *Signs: Journal of Women in Culture and Society* 18(4): 765–790.

Ransford, H. Edward, and Jon Miller. 1983. "Race, Sex, and Feminist Outlooks." *American Sociological Review* 48(1): 46–59.

Schwartz, Pepper. 1994. *Peer Marriages: How Love Between Equals Really Works*. New York: Free Press.

Sullivan, Maureen. 2004. *The Family of Woman: Lesbian Mothers, Their Children, and the Undoing of Gender*. Berkeley, CA: University of California Press.

Tichenor, Veronica Jaris. 2005. *Earning More and Getting Less: Why Successful Wives Can't Buy Equality*. New Brunswick, NJ: Rutgers University Press.

Walby, Sylvia. 1990. *Theorizing Patriarchy*. Oxford, UK and Cambridge, MA: Oxford University Press.

Wolf, Deborah Goleman. 1979. *The Lesbian Community*. Berkeley, CA: University of California Press.

Chapter 22: The Immigration Kaleidoscope: Knowing the Immigrant Family Next Door, by Etiony Aldarondo and Edward Ameen

Allen, J. P. 2005. "How Successful Are Recent Immigrants to the United States and Their Children?" Presidential address at the annual meeting of the Association of Pacific Coast Geographers, Phoenix, AZ.

Berry, John. 2007. "Acculturation Strategies and Adaptation." Pp. 69–82 in *Immigrant Families in Contemporary Society*, edited by Jennifer Lansford, Kirby Deater-Deckard, and Marc Bornstein. New York: Guilford Press.

Briggs Jr., V. E. 2003. *Mass Immigration and the National Interest: Policy Directions for the New Century*, 3rd ed. Armonk, NY: M. E. Sharpe.

Camarota, S. A. 2007. "Immigrants in the United States, 2007: A Profile of America's Foreign-Born Population." Center for Immigration Studies Backgrounder. Retrieved May 1, 2008, from www.cis.org/articles/2007/back1007.pdf.

Capps, R., M. Fix, J. S. Passel, J. Ost, and D. Perez-Lopez. 2003. "A Profile of the Low-Wage Immigrant Workforce." Immigrant Families and Workers. Retrieved May 1, 2008, from www.urban.org/UploadedPDF/310880_lowwage_immig_wkfc.pdf.

Chang, H. F. 2003. "The Immigration Paradox: Poverty, Distributive Justice, and Liberal Egalitarianism." *DePaul Law Review* 52: 759–776.

Chapman, M. V., and K. M. Perreira. 2005. "The Well-Being of Immigrant Latino Youth: A Framework to Inform Practice." *Families in Society* 86: 104–111.

Chavez, L. R. 2001. *Covering Immigration: Popular Images and the Politics of the Nation.* Berkeley, CA: University of California Press.

Chomsky, A. 2007. *"They Take Our Jobs!": and 20 Other Myths about Immigration.* Boston: Beacon Press.

Deaux, K. 2006. *To Be an Immigrant.* New York: Russell Sage Foundation.

DeSipio, L. 2008. "Do Home-Country Political Ties Limit Latino Immigrant Pursuit of U.S. Civic Engagement and Citizenship?" Pp. 69–89 in *Immigration*, edited by I. Stavans. Westport, CT: Greenwood Press.

Espenshade, T. J. 1997. "New Jersey in Comparative Perspective." Pp. 19–29 in *Keys to Successful Immigration: Implications of the New Jersey Experience*, edited by T. J. Espenshade. Washington, DC: Urban Institute Press.

Executive Office of the President. 2007. "Immigration's Economic Impact: June 20, 2007." Washington, DC: Author. Retrieved March 10, 2008, from www.whitehouse.gov/cea/cea_immigration_062007.pdf.

Falicov, C. J. 2002. "Immigrant Family Processes." Pp. 280–300 in *Normal Family Processes*, 3rd ed., edited by F. Walsh. New York: Guilford Press.

Farkas, S., A. Duffett, and J. Johnson. 2003. "Now That I'm Here: What Immigrants Have to Say about Life in the U.S. Today." New York: Public Agenda. Retrieved August 1, 2008, from www.publicagenda.org/files/pdf/now_that_im_here.pdf.

Fennelly, K. 2006. "Listening to the Experts: Provider Recommendations on the Health Needs of Immigrants and Refugees." *Journal of Cultural Diversity* 13: 190–201.

Fix, M., and R. Capps. 2004. "The Health and Well-Being of Young Children of Immigrants." Presentation at the meeting of the Brookings Institution's Policies for Children in Immigrant Families, Washington, DC.

Fuligni, A. J. 1998. "The Adjustment of Children from Immigrant Families." *Current Directions in Psychological Science* 7: 99–103.

Gallup Poll. 2000 (September 11–13).

Gallup/CNN/*USA Today* Poll. 2002 (September 2–4).

Gonzalez, E. T. 2006 (July 10). "Regarding a Hearing on 'Contributions of Immigrants in the U.S. Military.'" Speech presented before the Senate Committee on Armed Services, Miami, FL.

Gonzalez, R. G. 2007. "Wasted Talent and Broken Dreams: The Lost Potential of Undocumented Students." *Immigration Policy in Focus*, 5(13): 1–11. Retrieved March 12, 2008, from www.ilw.com/articles/2007,1121-gonzales.shtm.

Greico, E. 2002 (December). "Characteristics of the Foreign Born in the United States: Results from Census 2000." Retrieved May 1, 2008, from www.migrationinformation.org/USFocus/display.cfm?ID=71.

Guskin, J., and D. L. Wilson. 2007. *The Politics of Immigration: Questions and Answers*. New York: Monthly Review Press.

Hao, L., and R. W. Johnson. 2000. "Economic, Cultural, and Social Origins of Emotional well-being." *Research on Aging* 22: 599–629.

Harker, K. 2001. "Immigrant Generation, Assimilation, and Adolescent Psychological Well-Being." *Social Forces* 79: 969–1004.

Hernandez, D. J. 2004a (December). "A Demographic Portrait of Children in Immigrant Families." Presentation at the meeting of the Brookings Institution's Policies for Children in Immigrant Families, Washington, DC.

———. 2004b. "Demographic Change and the Life Circumstances of Immigrant Families." *Future of Children* 14: 17–47. Princeton, NJ: David and Lucile Packard Foundation.

Hernandez, M., and M. McGoldrick. 2005. "Migration and the Life Cycle." Pp. 169–184 in *The Expanded Family Life Cycle: Individual, Family, and Social Perspectives*, 3rd ed., edited by B. Carter and M. McGoldrick. New York: Pearson.

Hirschman, C. 2006. "The Impact of Immigration on American Society: Looking Backward to the Future." Social Science Research Council. Retrieved March 20, 2008, from http://borderbattles.ssrc.org/Hirschman/.

Institute for the Future. 2007. Intuit Future of Small Business Report: First Installment, Demographic Trends and Small Business. Palo Alto, CA: Author.

Koepke, L. A. 2007. "A Call to Action: Five Policy Proposals on Behalf of All Families. President's Address to the 2007 Groves Conference on Marriage and Family." *Journal of Feminist Family Therapy* 19: 1–12.

Leventhal, T., X. Yange, and J. Brooks-Gunn. 2006. "Immigrant Difference in School-Age Children's Verbal Trajectories: A Look at Four Racial/Ethnic Groups." *Child Development* 77: 1359–1374.

Levitt, M. J., J. D. Lane, and J. Levitt. 2005. "Immigration Stress, Social Support, and Adjustment in the First Postmigration Year: An Intergenerational Analysis." *Research in Human Development* 24: 159–177.

Migration Policy Institute. 2004 (January). "What Kind of Work Do Immigrants Do? Occupation and Industry of Foreign-Born Workers in the United States." Immigration Facts. Retrieved May 1, 2008, from www.migrationpolicy.org/pubs/Foreign%20Born%20Occup%20and%20Industry%20in%20the%20US.pdf.

Minuchin, S. 1984. *Family Kaleidoscope*. Cambridge, MA: Harvard University Press.

Mohanty, S. A., S. Woolhandler, D. U. Himmelstein, S. Pati, O. Carrasquillo, and D. Bor. 2005. "Health Care Expenditures of Immigrants in the United States: A Nationally Representative Analysis." *American Journal of Public Health* 95: 1431–1438.

Mutti, L. 2002. "Immigrants, Welfare and Work [Electronic version]." National Center for Policy Analysis, 400, 1–2.

New Democrat Network. 2007 (September 20). "Hispanics Rising: An Overview of the Emerging Politics of America's Hispanic Population." Retrieved May 1, 2008, from www.ndn.org/hispanic/hispanics-rising.pdf.

Passel, J. S. 2006. "Size and Characteristics of the Unauthorized Migrant Population in the U.S.: Estimates Based on the March 2005 Current Population Survey." Retrieved May 1, 2008, from http://pewhispanic.org/files/reports/61.pdf.

Passel, J. S., R. Capps, and M. E. Fix. 2004. "Undocumented Immigrants: Facts and Figures." Urban Institute Fact Sheet. Retrieved May 1, 2008, from www.urban.org/url.cfm?ID=1000587.

Phinney, J. S., J. W. Berry, D. L. Sam, and P. Vedder. 2006. "Understanding Immigrant Youth: Conclusions and Implications." Pp. 211–234 In *Immigrant Youth in Cultural Transition: Acculturation, Identity and Adaptation Across National Contexts*, edited by J. W. Berry, J. S. Phinney, D. L. Sam, and P. Vedder. Mahwah, NJ: Lawrence Erlbaum Associates.

Portes, A., and R. G. Rumbaut, eds. 2001. *Legacies: The Story of the Immigrant Second Generation*. Berkeley, CA: University of California Press.

Pyke, K. D. 2000. "'The Normal American Family' as an Interpretive Structure of Family Life among Children of Korean and Vietnamese Immigrants." *Journal of Marriage and the Family* 62: 240–255.

Reardon-Anderson, J., R. Capps, and M. Fix. 2002. "The Health and Well-Being of Children in Immigrant Families." Policy Brief. New Federalism: National Survey of America's Families. Washington, DC: Urban Institute.

Rumbaut, R. G. 2002 (May). "Competing Futures: The Children of America's Newest Immigrants." Migration Information Source. Retrieved February 6, 2008, from www.migrationinformation.org/feature/display.cfm?ID=1.

Rumbaut, R. G., and W. A. Ewing. 2007 (Spring). "The Myth of Immigrant Criminality and the Paradox of Assimilation: Incarceration Rates among Native and Foreign-Born Men." Immigration Policy Center. Retrieved July 1, 2008, from www.immigrationpolicy.org/index.php?content=sr20070221.

Singh, G. K., and R. A. Hiatt. 2006. "Trends and Disparities in Socioeconomic and Behavioural Characteristics, Life Expectancy, and Cause-Specific Mortality of Native-Born and Foreign-Born Populations in the United States, 1979–2003." *International Journal of Epidemiology* 35: 903–919.

Sluzki, C. E. 1998. "Migration and the Disruption of the Social Network." In *Re-Visioning Family Therapy: Race, Culture, and Gender in Clinical Practice*, edited by M. McGoldrick. New York: Guilford Press.

Suárez-Orozco, C., and M. M. Suárez-Orozco. 2001. *Children of Immigration*. The Developing Child Series. Cambridge, MA: Harvard University Press.

Suárez-Orozco, C., M. M. Suárez-Orozco, and I. Todorova. 2008. *Learning a New Land: Immigrant Students in American Society*. Cambridge, MA: Belknap Press.

Trueba, H. T. 2002. "Multiple Ethnic, Racial and Cultural Identities in Action: From Marginality to a New Cultural Capital in Modern Society." *Journal of Latinos and Education* 1: 7–28.

Chapter 23: Beyond Family Structure: Family Process Studies Help to Reframe Debates about What's Good for Children, by Philip A. Cowan and Carolyn Pape Cowan

Ahrons, C. R. 2004. We're Still Family: What Grown Children Have to Say about Their Parents' Divorce. New York: HarperCollins.

Amato, P. R. 2000. "The Consequences of Divorce for Adults and Children." *Journal of Marriage and the Family* 62(4): 1269–1287.

——. 2001. "Children of Divorce in the 1990s: An Update of the Amato and Keith (1991) Meta-analysis." *Journal of Family Psychology* 15(3): 355–370.

Baumrind, D. 1980. "New Directions in Socialization Research." *American Psychologist* 35(7): 639–652.

Belsky, J., and N. Barends. 2002. *Personality and Parenting*. Mahwah, NJ: Lawrence Erlbaum Associates.

Blankenhorn, D. 1995. *Fatherless America: Confronting Our Most Urgent Social Problem*. New York: Basic Books.

Blankenhorn, D. G., S. Bayme, and J. B. Elshtain, eds. 1990. *Rebuilding the Nest: A New Commitment to the American Family*. Milwaukee, WI: Family Service America.

Brazelton, T. B., and J. D. Sparrow. 2001. *Touchpoints: Birth to Three*. Cambridge, MA: Perseus Books.

Bronfenbrenner, U., and S. J. Ceci. 1994. "Nature-Nurture in Developmental Perspective: A Bioecological Theory." *Psychological Review* 101: 568–586.

Caspi, A., and G. H. J. Elder. 1988. "Emergent Family Patterns: The Intergenerational Construction of Problem Behaviour and Relationships." Pp. 218–240 in *Relationships within Families: Mutual Influences*, edited by R. A. Hinde and J. Stevenson-Hinde. Oxford: Clarendon Press.

Cherlin, A. J. 2005. "American Marriage in the Early Twenty-first Century." *The Future of Children* 15(2): 33–55.

Cicchetti, D., S. L. Toth, and A. Maughan. 2000. "An Ecological-Transactional Model of Child Maltreatment." Pp. 689–722 in *Handbook of Developmental Psychopathology*, 2nd ed., edited by A. J. Sameroff, M. Lewis, and S. M. Miller. New York: Kluwer Academic/ Plenum Publishers.

Conger, R. D., G. H. Elder, Jr., F. O. Lorenz, R. L. Simons, and L. B. Whitbeck, eds. 1994. *Families in Troubled Times: Adapting to Change in Rural America*. New York: Aldine de Gruyter.

Cowan, C. P., and P. A. Cowan. 1995. "Interventions to Ease the Transition to Parenthood: Why They are Needed and What They Can Do." *Family Relations: Journal of Applied Family & Child Studies* 44(4): 412–423.

——. 2000. *When Partners Become Parents: The Big Life Change for Couples*. Mahwah, NJ: Lawrence Erlbaum Associates.

Cowan, C. P., P. A. Cowan, M. K. Pruett, and K. Pruett. 2007. "An Approach to Preventing Coparenting Conflict and Divorce in Low-Income Families: Strengthening Couple Relationships and Fostering Fathers' Involvement." *Family Process* 46(1): 109–121.

Cowan, P. A., and C. P. Cowan. 2002. "Interventions As Tests of Family Systems Theories: Marital and Family Relationships in Children's Development, and Psychopathology." *Development and Psychopathology*, Special Issue on Interventions As Tests of Theories, 14: 731–760.

———. 2006. "Developmental Psychopathology from a Family Systems and Family Risk Factors Perspective: Implications for Family Research, Practice, and Policy." Pp. 530–587 in *Developmental Psychopathology*, edited by D. Cicchetti and D. J. Cohen. Hoboken, NJ: Wiley.

Cowan, P. A., C. P. Cowan, J. Ablow, V. K. Johnson, and J. Measelle, eds. 2005. *The Family Context of Parenting in Children's Adaptation to Elementary School*. Mahwah, NJ: Lawrence Erlbaum Associates.

Cowan, P. A., C. P. Cowan, N. Cohen, M. K. Pruett, and K. Pruett. 2008. "Supporting Fathers' Engagement with Their Kids." Pp. 44–80 in *Raising Children: Emerging Needs, Modern Risks, and Social Responses*, edited by J. D. Berrick and N. Gilbert. New York: Oxford University Press.

Cowan, P. A., C. P. Cowan, and G. Heming. 2005. "Five-Domain Models: Putting It All Together." In *The Family Context of Parenting in Children's Adaptation to Elementary School*, edited by P. A. Cowan, C. P. Cowan, J. Ablow, V. K. Johnson, and J. Measelle. Mahwah, NJ: Lawrence Erlbaum Associates.

Cowan, P. A., D. Powell, and C. P. Cowan. 1998. "Parenting interventions: A family systems perspective." Pp. 3–72 in *Handbook of Child Psychology*, edited by W. Damon. New York: Wiley.

Cui, M., and R. Conger. 2008. "Parenting Behavior as Mediator and Moderator of the Association between Marital Problems and Adolescent Maladjustment." *Journal of Research on Adolescence* 18(2): 261–284.

Cummings, E. M., P. Davies, and S. B. Campbell. 2000. *Developmental Psychopathology and Family Process: Theory, Research, and Clinical Implications*. New York: Guilford Press.

Dadds, M. R., S. Schwartz, and M. R. Sanders. 1987. "Marital Discord and Treatment Outcome in Behavioral Treatment of Child Conduct Disorders." *Journal of Consulting & Clinical Psychology* 55(3): 396–403.

Davies, P. T., E. M. Cummings, and M. A. Winter. 2004. "Pathways between Profiles of Family Functioning, Child Security in the Interparental Subsystem, and Child Psychological Problems." *Development and Psychopathology* 16(3): 525–550.

Dion, M. R., S. A. Avellar, H. H. Zaveri, and A. M. Hershey. 2006. *Implementing Healthy Marriage Programs for Unmarried Couples with Children: Early Lessons from the Building Strong Families Project*. Washington, DC: Mathematica.

Durlak, J. A., and A. M. Wells. 1997. "Primary Prevention Mental Health Programs for Children and Adolescents: A Meta-analytic Review." *American Journal of Community Psychology* 25(2): 115–152.

Edin, K., and M. Kefalas. 2005. *Promises I Can Keep: Why Poor Women Put Motherhood before Marriage*. Berkeley, CA: University of California Press.

Faber, A., and E. Mazlish. 1995. *How to Talk So Your Kids Will Listen*. New York: Simon & Schuster/Fireside Books.

Fagan, P. F., R. W. Patterson, and R. E. Rector. 2002. "Marriage and Welfare Reform: The Overwhelming Evidence that Marriage Education Works." Backgrounder #1606. Washington, DC: Heritage Foundation.

Harknett, K., L. Hardman, I. Garfinkel, and S. S. McLanahan. 2001. "The Fragile Families Study: Social Policies and Labor Markets in Seven Cities." *Children & Youth Services Review* 23(6-7): 537–555.

Haskins, R., and I. Sawhill. 2003. *Work and Marriage: The Way to End Poverty and Welfare*. Washington, DC: Brookings.

Hetherington, E. M., and J. Kelly. 2002. *For Better or for Worse: Divorce Reconsidered*. New York: W. W. Norton.

Lamb, M. E. 2000. "The History of Research on Father Involvement: An Overview." *Marriage & Family Review* 29(2–3): 23–42.

Luchetti, V. I. 1999. "Perceptions of Fatherhood in Parenting Manuals: A Rhetorical Analysis." Ph.D. dissertation, University of the Pacific, Stockton, CA.

Marquardt, E. 2005. *Between Two Worlds: The Inner Lives of Children of Divorce*. New York: Crown Publishers.

McLanahan, S. S., I. Garfinkel, J. Brooks-Gunn, H. Zhao, W. Johnson, L. Rich, et al. 1998. *Unwed Fathers and Fragile Families*. Princeton, NJ: Center for Research on Child Wellbeing.

McLoyd, V. C. 1990. "The Impact of Economic Hardship on Black Families and Children: Psychological Distress, Parenting, and Socioemotional Development." *Child Development* 61(2): 311–346.

Mincy, R. B., and A. T. Dupree. 2001. "Welfare, Child Support and Family Formation." *Children & Youth Services Review* 23(6–7): 577–601.

Mincy, R., and H. Pouncy. 2002. "The Responsible Fatherhood Field: Evolution and Goals." Pp. 555–597 in *Handbook of Father Involvement: Multidisciplinary Perspectives*, edited by C. S. Tamis-LeMonda and N. J. Cabrera. Mahwah, NJ: Lawrence Erlbaum Associates.

Mistry, R. S., E. A. Vandewater, A. C. Huston, and V. C. McLoyd. 2002. "Economic Well-Being and Children's Social Adjustment: The Role of Family Process in an Ethnically Diverse Low-Income Sample." *Child Development* 73(3): 935–951.

Moore, K. A., S. Jekielek, and C. Emig. 2002. *Marriage from a Child's Perspective: How Does Family Structure Affect Children, and What Can We Do about It?* Washington, DC: Child Trends.

Parke, R. D. 1996. *Fatherhood*. Cambridge, MA: Harvard University Press.

Plomin, R. 2003. *Behavioral Genetics in the Postgenomic era*. Washington, DC: American Psychological Association.

Popenoe, D. 1996. *Life without Father: Compelling New Evidence That Fatherhood and Marriage Are Indispensable for the Good of Children and Society*. New York: Martin Kessler Books.

Powell, D. A. 2006. "Families and Early Childhood Interventions." Pp. 548–591 in *Handbook of Child Psychology*, vol. 4, 6th ed., edited by W. Damon, R. M. Lerner, K. Renninger and I. E. Sigel. Hoboken, NJ: Wiley.

Pruett, K. D. 2000. *Fatherneed: Why Father Care Is As Essential As Mother Care for Your Child*. New York: Free Press.

Pruett, M. K., and R. K. Barker. 2009. "Effectively Intervening with Divorcing Parents and Their Children: What Works and How It Works." In *Strengthening Couple Relationships for Optimal Child Development*, edited by M. S. Schulz, M. K. Pruett, P. K. Kerig, and R. D. Parke. Washington, DC: APA Books.

Rodgers, B., and J. Pryor. 1998. *The Development of Children from Separated Families: A Review of Research from the United Kingdom*. York, UK: Joseph Rowntree Foundation.

Seifer, R., and S. Dickstein. 2000. "Parental Mental Illness and Infant Development." Pp. 145–160 in *Handbook of Infant Mental Health*, 2nd ed., edited by C. H. Zoanah, Jr. New York: Guilford Press.

Silverstein, L. B., and C. F. Auerbach. 1999. "Deconstructing the Essential Father." *American Psychologist* 54(6): 397–407.

Stacey, J., and T. J. Biblarz. 2001. "(How) Does the Sexual Orientation of Parents Matter?" *American Sociological Review* 66(2): 159–183.

Tamis-LeMonda, C. S., and N. Cabrera (Eds.). 2002. *Handbook of Father Involvement: Multi-disciplinary Perspectives*. Mahwah, NJ: Lawrence Erlbaum Associates.

Tully, L. A., L. Arseneault, A. Caspi, T. E. Moffitt, and J. Morgan. 2004. "Does Maternal Warmth Moderate the Effects of Birth Weight on Twins' Attention-Deficit/Hyperactivity Disorder (ADHD) Symptoms and Low IQ?" *Journal of Consulting & Clinical Psychology* 72(2): 218–226.

Waite, L. J., and M. Gallagher. 2000. *The Case for Marriage: Why Married People Are Happier, Healthier, and Better off Financially*. New York: Doubleday.

Wallerstein, J. S., J. Lewis, and S. Blakeslee. 2000. *The Unexpected Legacy of Divorce: A 25 Year Landmark Study*. New York: Hyperion.

Chapter 25: Diverging Development: The Not-So-Invisible Hand of Social Class in the United States, by Frank F. Furstenberg, Jr.

Bendix, Reinhard, and Seymour Martin Lipset. 1966. *Class, Status, and Power*. New York: Free Press.

Bernstein, Basil. 1971. *Class, Codes and Control: Theoretical Studies towards a Sociology of Language*, vol. 1. London: Routledge & Kegan Paul.

Bernstein, Basil, and Dorothy Henderson. 1969. "Social Class Differences and the Relevance of Language to Socialization." *Sociology* 3(1): 1–20.

Blood, Robert O., and Donald M. Wolfe. 1960. *Husbands and Wives: The Dynamics of Married Living*. New York: Free Press.

Bourdieu, Pierre. 1973. "Cultural Reproduction and Social Reproduction." In *Knowledge, Education, and Cultural Change*, edited by Richard Brown. London: Tavistock.

———. 1986. "The Forms of Capital." In *Handbook of Theory and Research for the Sociology of Education*, edited by John G. Richardson. New York: Greenwood.

Bronfenbrenner, Urie. 1979. *The Ecology of Human Development: Experiments by Nature and Design*. Cambridge, MA: Harvard University Press.

Brown, Sarah S., and Leon Eisenberg, eds. 1995. *The Best Intentions: Unintended Pregnancy and the Well-Being of Children and Families*. Washington, DC: National Academy Press.

Buchmann, Marlis. 1989. *The Script of Life in Modern Society: Entry into Adulthood in a Changing World*. Chicago: University of Chicago Press.

Burton, Linda, and Carol Stack. 1993. "Conscripting Kin: Reflections on Family, Generation, and Culture." In *Family, Self, and Society: Toward a New Agenda for Family Research*, edited by Philip A. Cowan, Dorothy Field, Donald A. Hansen, Arlene Skolnick, and Guy E. Swanson. Hillsdale, NJ: Lawrence Erlbaum Associates.

Case, Anne, Angela Fertig, and Christine Paxton. 2005. "From Cradle to Grave? The Lasting Impact of Childhood Health and Circumstances." *Journal of Health Economics* 24: 265–389.

Chaudry, Ajay. 2004. *Putting Children First: How Low-Income Working Mothers Manage Child Care*. New York: Russell Sage Foundation.

Conley, Dalton, and Neil G. Bennett. 2000. "Is Biology Destiny? Birth Weight and Life Chances." *American Sociological Review* 65(3): 458–467.

Cook, Thomas D., Melissa R. Herman, Meredith Phillips, and Richard A. Settersten, Jr. 2002. "Some Ways in Which Neighborhoods, Nuclear Families, Friendship Groups, and Schools Jointly Affect Changes in Early Adolescent Development." *Child Development* 73(4): 1283–1309.

Cooley, Charles H. 1902. *Human Nature and the Social Order*. New York: Scribners.

Corsaro, William. 2005. *The Sociology of Childhood*, 2nd ed. Thousand Oaks, CA: Pine Forge Press.

Danziger, Sheldon H., and Peter Gottschalk. 1995. *America Unequal*. New York: Russell Sage Foundation.

Danziger, Sheldon H., and Jane Waldfogel. 2000. *Securing the Future: Investing in Children from Birth to College*. New York: Russell Sage Foundation.

Edin, Kathryn J., and Maria Kefalas. 2005. *Promises I Can Keep: Why Low-Income Women Put Motherhood Before Marriage*. Berkeley, CA: University of California Press.

Elder, Glen H., Jr. 1974. *Children of the Great Depression: Social Change in Life Experience*. Chicago: University of Chicago Press, (Reissued as 25th Anniversary Edition, Boulder, CO: Westview Press, 1999).

Ellwood, David T., and Christopher Jencks. 2001. "The Spread of Single-Parent Families in the United States since 1960." Cambridge, MA: John F. Kennedy School of Government, Harvard University, Working Paper RWP04-008.

Farkas, George, and Kurt Beron. 2004. "The Detailed Age Trajectory of Oral Vocabulary Knowledge: Differences by Class and Race." *Social Science Research* 33(3): 464–497.

Furstenberg, Jr., Frank F., Thomas D. Cook, Jacquelynne Eccles, Glen H. Edler, Jr., and Arnold Sameroff. 1999. *Managing to Make It: Urban Families and Adolescent Outcomes*. The John D. and Catherine T. MacArthur Foundation Series on Mental Health and Development. Chicago: University of Chicago Press.

Furstenberg, Frank F., Sheela Kennedy, Vonnie McLoyd, Ruben G. Rumbaut, and Richard A. Settersten, Jr. 2004. "Growing Up Is Harder To Do." *Contexts* 3(3): 42–47.

Gans, Herbert J. 1962. *The Urban Villagers*. New York: Free Press.

Garmezy, Norman. 1991. "Resilience and Vulnerability to Adverse Developmental Outcomes Associated with Poverty." *American Behavioral Scientist* 34(4): 416–430.

———. 1993. "Vulnerability and Resilience." In *Studying Lives through Time: Personality and Development*, edited by David C. Funder, Ross D. Parke, Carol Tomlinson-Keasey, and Keith Widaman. Washington, DC: American Psychological Association.

Goldstein, Joshua R., and Catherine T. Kenney. 2001. "Marriage Delayed or Marriage Forgone? New Cohort Forecasts of First Marriage for U.S. Women." *American Sociological Review* 66(4): 506–519.

Goldthorpe, John H., and Robert Erickson. 1993. *The Constant Flux: A Study of Class Mobility in Industrial Societies*. Oxford: Oxford University Press.

Haggerty, Robert J., Lonnie R. Sherrod, Norman Garmezy, and Michael Rutter. 1994. *Stress, Risk, and Resilience in Children and Adolescents*. New York: Cambridge University Press.

Hart, Betty, and Todd R. Risley. 1995. *Meaningful Differences in the Everyday Experiences of Young American Children*. Baltimore, MD: Paul H. Brookes Publishing.

Heinz, Walter R., and Victor W. Marshall, eds. 2003. *Social Dynamics of the Life Course: Transitions, Institutions and Interrelations*. Hawthorne, NY: Aldine De Gruyter.

Hertz, Tom. 2005. "Rags, Riches and Race: The Intergenerational Economic Mobility of Black and White Families in the United States." In *Unequal Chances: Family Background and Economic Success*, edited by Samuel Bowles, Herbert Gintis, and Melissa Osborne Groves. Princeton, NJ: Princeton University Press.

Hollingshead, A. de B. 1949. *Elmtown's Youth: The Impact of Social Classes on Adolescents.* New York: Wiley.

Inkeles, Alex. 1968. "Society, Social Structure, and Child Socialization." In *Socialization and Society*, edited by John A. Clausen. Boston: Little, Brown.

Joyce, Theodore J., Robert Kaestner, and Sanders Korenman. 2000. "The Effect of Pregnancy Intention and Child Development." *Demography* 37(1): 83–94.

Kefalas, Maria. 2003. *Working Class Heroes: Protecting Home, Community and Nation in a Chicago Neighborhood.* Berkeley, CA: University of California Press.

Kluckhohn, Clyde, and Alexander Murray, eds. 1948. "Personality." In *Nature, Society, and Culture.* New York: Knopf.

Komarovsky, Mira. 1987. *Blue-Collar Marriage*, 2nd ed. New Haven, CT: Yale University Press.

Lamont, Michele. 2000. *The Dignity of Working Men: Morality and the Boundaries of Race, Class and Immigration.* Cambridge, MA: Harvard University Press.

Lareau, Annette. 1989. *Home Advantage: Social Class and Parental Intervention in Elementary Education.* New York: Falmer Press.

———. 2003. *Unequal Childhoods: Race, Class and Family Life.* Berkeley, CA: University of California Press.

Levy, Frank. 1999. *The New Dollars and Dreams.* New York: Russell Sage Foundation.

Lynd, Robert S., and Helen M. Lynd. 1929. *Middletown: A Study in Contemporary American Culture.* New York: Harcourt Brace & Company.

Magnuson, Katherine A., and Jane Waldfogel. 2005. "Early Childhood Care and Education: Effects on Ethnic and Racial Gaps in School Readiness." *Future of Children* 15(1): 169–196.

McLanahan, Sara. 2004. "Diverging Destinies: How Children Fare Under the Second Demographic Transition." *Demography* 41(4): 607–627.

Mead, George Herbert. 1934. *Mind, Self, and Society: From the Standpoint of a Social Behaviorist.* Chicago: University of Chicago Press.

Mead, Margaret, and Martha Wolfenstein, eds. 1955. *Childhood in Contemporary Cultures.* Chicago: University of Chicago Press.

Medrich, Elliott, Judith Roizen, Victor Rubin, with Stuart Buckley. 1982. *The Serious Business of Growing Up: A Study of Children's Lives Outside of School.* Berkeley: University of California Press.

Miller, Daniel R., and Guy E. Swanson. 1958. *The Changing American Parent.* New York: Wiley.

Mortimer, Jeylan, ed. 2008. "Social Class and Transitions to Adulthood." *New Directions for Child and Adolescent Development* 119 (Spring). San Francisco, CA: Jossey-Bass.

Nelson, Charles A. 2000. "Neural Plasticity and Human Development: The Role of Early Experience in Sculpting Memory Systems." *Developmental Science* 3: 115–130.

Nelson, Charles A., Susan W. Parker, et al. 2005. "The Impact of Early Institutional Rearing on the Ability to Discriminate Facial Expressions of Emotion: An Event-Related Potential Study." *Child Development* 76(1): 54–72.

Newman, Katherine S. 1993. *Declining Fortunes: The Withering of the American Dream.* New York: Basic Books.

Noble, Kimberly G., M. Frank Norman, and Martha J. Farah. 2005. "Neurocognitive Correlates of Socioeconomic Status in Kindergarten Children." *Developmental Science* 8(1): 74–87.

Rhodes, Jean. 2002. *Stand By Me: The Risks and Rewards of Mentoring Today's Youth.* Cambridge, MA: Harvard University Press.

Rouse, Cecilia E. 2004. "Low Income Students and College Attendance: An Exploration of Income Expectations." *Social Science Quarterly* 85(5): 1299–1317.

Rutter, Michael. 1985. "Resilience in the Face of Adversity: Protective Factors and Resistance to Psychiatric Disorder." *British Journal of Psychiatry* 147: 598–611.

——. 2000. "Resilience Reconsidered: Conceptual Considerations, Empirical Findings and Policy Implications." In *Handbook of Early Childhood Intervention*, 2nd ed., edited by Jack P. Shonkoff and Samuel J. Meisels. New York: Cambridge University Press.

Settersten, Richard A., Jr, Frank F. Furstenberg, and Ruben G. Rumbaut, eds. 2005. *On the Frontier of Adulthood: Theory, Research, and Public Policy.* Chicago: University of Chicago Press.

Shonkoff, Jack P., and Deborah Phillips. 2000. *From Neurons to Neighborhoods: The Science of Early Childhood Development.* Washington, DC: National Academy Press.

Smyke, Anna. T., Sebastion F. Koga, et al. 2007. "The Caregiving Context in Institution-Reared and Family-Reared Infants and Toddlers in Romania." *Journal of Child Psychology and Psychiatry* 48(2): 210–218.

Tocqueville, Alexis de. 1835. *Democracy in America.* New York: Knopf.

Wagmiller, Robert L., Jr., Mary Clare Lennon, Li Kuang, Philip M. Alberti, and J. Lawrence Aber. 2006. "The Dynamics of Economic Disadvantage and Children's Life Chances." *American Sociological Review* 71: 847–866.

Warner, William Lloyd. 1949. *Social Class in America.* Chicago: Science Research Associates.

Weber, Max. 1949. *The Methodology of the Social Sciences.* New York: Free Press.

Werner, Emmy. 1995. "Resilience in Development." *Current Directions in Psychological Science.* 4(3): 81–85.

Whiting, Beatrice. 1963. *Six Cultures: Studies of Child Rearing.* New York: Wiley.

Wolff, Edward N. 2002. *Top Heavy: A Study of Increasing Inequality of Wealth in America.* New York: New Press.

——. 2004. "Changes in Household Wealth in the 1980s and 1990s in the U.S." The Levy Economics Institute at Bard College, Working Paper No. 407.

Wu, Lawrence, and Barbara Wolfe, eds. 2001. *Out of Wedlock: Causes and Consequences of Nonmarital Fertility.* New York: Russell Sage Foundation.

Chapter 27: Not Just Provide and Reside: Engaged Fathers in Low-Income Families, by Kevin Roy and Natasha Cabrera

Allen, Sarah, and Alan Hawkins. 1999. "Maternal Gatekeeping: Mothers' Beliefs and Behaviors That Inhibit Greater Father Involvement in Family Work." *Journal of Marriage and Family* 61: 199–212.

Allen, W., and M. Conner. 1997. "An African American Perspective on Generative Fathering." Pp. 52–70 in *Generative Fathering: Beyond Deficit Perspectives*, edited by A. J. Hawkins and D. C. Dollahite. Newbury Park, CA: Sage.

Black, Maureen, Howard Dubowitz, and Raymond Starr. 1999. "African American Fathers in Low-Income, Urban Families: Development, Behavior, and Home Environment of Their Three-Year-Olds." *Child Development* 70: 967–978.

Bronfenbrenner, Urie. 1979. *The Ecology of Human Development: Experiments by Nature and Design*. Cambridge, MA: Harvard University Press.

Cabrera, Natasha, Jeanne Brooks-Gunn, Kristin Moore, J. West, K. Boller, and C. S. Tamis-LeMonda. 2002. "Bridging Research and Policy: Including Fathers of Young Children in National Studies." Pp. 489–524 in *Handbook of Father Involvement: Multidisciplinary Perspectives*, edited by Catherine Tamis-LeMonda and Natasha Cabrera. Mahwah, NJ: Lawrence Erlbaum Associates.

Cabrera, Natasha, Hiram Fitzgerald, R. Bradley, and L. Roggman. 2007. "Modeling the Dynamics of Paternal Influence on Children over the Life Course." *Applied Developmental Science* 11(4): 185–190.

Cabrera, Natasha, and Cynthia Garcia Coll. 2004. "Latino Fathers: Uncharted Territory in Need of Much Exploration." Pp. 98–120 in *The Role of the Father in Child Development*, 4th ed., edited by Michael Lamb. New York: Wiley.

Cabrera, Natasha, Rebecca Ryan, Jacqueline Shannon, Jeanne Brooks-Gunn, Cheri Vogel, Helen Raikes, Catherine Tamis-LeMonda, and Rachel Cohen. 2004. "Low-Income Fathers' Involvement in Their Toddlers' Lives: Biological Fathers from the Early Head Start Research and Evaluation Study." *Fathering: A Journal of Theory, Research, and Practice about Men As Fathers* 2: 5–30.

Cabrera, Natasha, Jacqueline Shannon, and Catherine Tamis-LeMonda. 2007. "Fathers' Influence on Their Children's Cognitive and Emotional Development: From Toddlers to Pre-K." *Applied Developmental Science* 11(4): 208–213.

Carlson, Marcia, and Frank Furstenberg. 2006. "The Prevalence and Correlates of Multipartnered Fertility among Urban U.S. Parents." *Journal of Marriage and Family* 68: 718–732.

Carlson, Marcia, and Sara McLanahan. 2002. "Fragile Families, Father Involvement and Public Policy." Pp. 461–488 in *Handbook of Father Involvement: Multidisciplinary Perspectives*, edited by Catherine Tamis-LeMonda and Natasha Cabrera. Mahwah, NJ: Lawrence Erlbaum Associates.

———. 2004. "Early Father Involvement in Fragile Families." Pp. 241–271 in *Conceptualizing and Measuring Father Involvement*, edited by Randal Day and Michael Lamb. Mahwah, NJ: Lawrence Erlbaum Associates.

Coley, Rebekah Levine. 2001. "(In)visible Men: Emerging Research on Low-Income, Unmarried, and Minority Fathers." *American Psychologist* 56: 743–753.

Doherty, William, Edward Kouneski, and Martha Erickson. 1998. "Responsible Fathering: An Overview and Conceptual Framework." *Journal of Marriage and Family* 60: 277–292.

Eggebeen, David. 2002a. "The Changing Course of Fatherhood: Men's Experiences with Children from a Demographic Perspective." *Journal of Family Issues* 23: 486–506.

———. 2002b. "Sociological Perspectives on Fatherhood: What Do We Know about Fathers from Social Surveys?" Pp. 189–209 in *Handbook of Father Involvement: Multidisciplinary Perspectives*, edited by Catherine Tamis-LeMonda and Natasha Cabrera. Mahwah, NJ: Lawrence Erlbaum Associates.

Eggebeen, David, and Peter Uhlenberg. 1985. "Changes in the Organization of Men's Lives: 1960–1980." *Family Relations*, 34: 251–257.

Fagan, Jay, Rob Palkovitz, Kevin Roy, and Danielle Farrie. In press. "Pathways to Paternal Engagement: Longitudinal Effects of Cumulative Risk and Resilience on Nonresident Fathers." *Developmental Psychology*.

Hansen, Karen. 2005. *Not-So-Nuclear Families: Class, Gender, and Networks of Care*. New Brunswick, NJ: Rutgers University Press.

Hofferth, Sandra. 2003. "Race/Ethnic Differences in Father Involvement in Two-Parent Families: Culture, Context, or Economy." *Journal of Family Issues* 24: 185–216.

Hofferth, Sandra, Colleen Vesely, Natasha Cabrera, Frances Goldscheider, Jaslean LaTaillade, and Joseph Pleck. Under review. "The Transmission of Parenting from Fathers and Mothers to Sons."

Hogan, Dennis. 1981. *Transitions and Social Change: The Early Lives of American Men.* New York: Academic Press.

Jarrett, Robin, Kevin Roy, and Linda Burton. 2002. "Fathers in the 'Hood: Qualitative Research on African American Men." Pp. 211–248 in *Handbook of Father Involvement: Multidisciplinary Perspectives,* edited by Catherine Tamis-LeMonda and Natasha Cabrera. Mahwah, NJ: Lawrence Erlbaum Associates.

Kwon, Young In, and Kevin Roy. 2007. "Changing Social Expectations and Paternal Caregiving Experiences for Working Class and Middle Class Korean Fathers." *Journal of Comparative Family Studies* 38: 285–305.

Lamb, Michael. 1975. "Fathers: Forgotten Contributors to Children's Development." *Human Development* 18: 245–266.

———. 1997. "Fathers and Child Development: An Introductory Overview." Pp. 1–18 in *The Role of the Father in Child Development,* 3rd ed., edited by Michael Lamb. New York: Wiley.

———. 2004. *The Role of the Father in Child Development,* 4th ed. Hoboken, NJ: Wiley.

LaRossa, Ralph. 1997. *The Modernization of Fatherhood.* Chicago, IL: University of Chicago Press.

Mott, Frank. 1990. "When Is a Father Really Gone? Paternal-Child Contact in Father-Absent Homes." *Demography* 27: 499–517.

Nelson, Margaret. 2005. *The Social Economy of Single Motherhood: Raising Children in Rural America.* New York: Routledge.

Palkovitz, Rob. 2002a. "Involved Fathering and Child Development: Advancing Our Understanding of Good Fathering." Pp. 119–140 in *Handbook of Father Involvement: Multidisciplinary Perspectives,* edited by Catherine Tamis-LeMonda and Natasha Cabrera. Mahwah, NJ: Lawrence Erlbaum Associates.

———. 2002b. *Involved Fathering and Men's Adult Development: Provisional Balances.* Mahwah, NJ: Lawrence Erlbaum Associates.

Pleck, Joseph, and Brian Masciadrelli. 2004. "Paternal Involvement by U.S. Residential Fathers: Levels, Sources, and Consequences." Pp. 222–270 in *The Role of the Father in Child Development,* 4th ed., edited by Michael Lamb. New York: Wiley.

Roopnarine, Jaipaul. 2004. "African American and African Caribbean Fathers: Level, Quality, and Meaning of Involvement." Pp. 58–97 in *The Role of the Father in Child Development,* 4th ed., edited by Michael Lamb. New York: Wiley.

Roy, Kevin. 2005. "Transitions on the Margins of Work and Family for Low-Income African American Fathers." *Journal of Family and Economic Issues* 26: 77–100.

———. 2006. "Father Stories: A Life Course Examination of Paternal Identity among Low-Income African American Men." *Journal of Family Issues* 27: 31–54.

Roy, Kevin, and Linda Burton. 2007. "Mothering through Recruitment: Kinscription of Non-Residential Fathers and Father Figures in Low-Income Families." *Family Relations* 56: 24–39.

Roy, Kevin, and Omari Dyson. 2005. "Gatekeeping in Context: Babymamadrama and the Involvement of Incarcerated Fathers." *Fathering: A Journal of Theory, Research, and Practice about Men As Fathers* 3: 289–310.

Roy, Kevin, Omari Dyson, and Ja-Nee Jackson. Forthcoming. "Intergenerational Support and Reciprocity between Low-Income African American Fathers and Their Aging Mothers." In *Social Work Interventions for Young African American Men*, edited by Waldo Johnson and Earl Johnson. New York: Oxford University Press.

Roy, Kevin, Sarah Kaye, and Megan Fitzgerald. Under review. "Swap Reconsidered: Transitions in Paternal Involvement across Multiple Family Systems."

Roy, Kevin, Rob Palkovitz, and Jay Fagan. 2007. "Down But Not Out: Strategies for Stabilizing Involvement of Low-Income Fathers and Families." Paper presentation at National Poverty Center, Small Grants Program Conference, Ann Arbor, MI.

Shannon, Jacqueline, Catherine Tamis-LeMonda, and Natasha Cabrera. 2006. "Fathering in Infancy: Mutuality and Stability between 8 and 16 Months." *Parenting: Science and Practice* 6(2): 167–188.

Shannon, Jacqueline, Catherine Tamis-LeMonda, K. London, and Natasha Cabrera. 2002. "Beyond Rough and Tumble: Low-Income Fathers' Interactions and Children's Cognitive Development at 24 Months." *Parenting: Science and Practice* 2: 77–104.

Shwalb, D., J. Nakawaza, T. Yamamoto, and J. Hyun. 2004. "Fathering in Japanese, Chinese, and Korean Cultures: A Review of the Research Literature." Pp. 146–181 in *The Role of the Father in Child Development*, 4th ed., edited by Michael Lamb. New York: Wiley.

Sobolewski, Julie, and Valarie King. 2005. "The Importance of the Coparental Relationship for Nonresident Fathers' Ties to Children." *Journal of Marriage and Family* 67: 1196–1212.

Tamis-LeMonda, Catherine, Jacqueline Shannon, Natasha Cabrera, and Michael Lamb. 2004. "Resident Fathers and Mothers at Play with Their 2- and 3-Year-Olds: Contributions to Language and Cognitive Development." *Child Development* 75: 1806–1820.

Toth, J. and X. Xu. 1999. "Ethnic and Cultural Diversity in Fathers' Involvement: A Racial/Ethnic Comparison of African American, Hispanic, and White Fathers." *Youth & Society* 31: 76–99.

Townsend, Nicholas. 2002. *The Package Deal: Marriage, Work and Fatherhood in Men's Lives.* Philadelphia: Temple University Press.

Waller, Maureen. 2002. *My Baby's Father: Unmarried Parents and Paternal Responsibility.* Ithaca, NY: Cornell University Press.

Waller, Maureen, and Sara McLanahan. 2005. "'His' and 'Her' Marriage Expectations: Determinants and Consequences." *Journal of Marriage and Family* 67: 53–67.

Walker, Alexis, and Lori McGraw. 2000. "Who Is Responsible for Responsible Fathering?" *Journal of Marriage and Family* 62: 563–569.

Chapter 28: Briefing Paper: Unmarried Couples with Children: Why Don't They Marry? How Can Policy Makers Promote More Stable Relationships?

England, Paula, and Kathryn Edin, eds. 2007. *Unmarried Couples with Children.* New York: Russell Sage Foundation.

Chapter 29: Rituals As Tools of Resistance: From Survival to Liberation, by Andraé L. Brown, Melina Dimitriou, and Lisa Dressner

Almeida, R. V., K. Dolan-Del Vecchio, and L. Parker. 2008. *Transformative Family Therapy: Just Families in a Just Society.* Boston: Pearson.

Bennett, L. A., S. J. Wolin, and K. J. McCavity. 1988. "Family Identity, Ritual, and Myth: A Cultural Perspective on Life Cycle Transition." Pp. 211–234 in *Family Transitions: Continuity, and Change over Life Cycle*, edited by C. J. Falicov. New York: Guilford Press.

Bjork, C. 2002. "Reconstructing Rituals: Expressions of Autonomy and Resistance in a Sino-Indonesian School." *Anthropology and Education Quarterly* 33: 465–491.

Brown, A. L. 2004. "Exploring Blackness As a Site of Resilience for Street Life Oriented Young Black Men Living in the Inner-City." Ph.D. dissertation, Seton Hall University, South Orange, NJ.

Children's Defense Fund. 2007. *America's Cradle to Prison Pipeline*. Washington, DC: Children's Defense Furd.

Clothlesline Project. 2008. Retrieved September 10, 2008, from http://clotheslineproject.org.

Cohen, A. 2002. "They're Playing Your Song." Retrieved August 25, 2008, from www.alancohen.com/articles/Perennial/They'rePlayingYourSong.htm.

Cronin, D. 1997. "Be Who You Must Be." Retrieved August 25, 2008, from www.heartnsouls.com/stories/i/s887.shtml.

De Silva, C., ed. 1996. *In Memory's Kitchen: A Legacy from the Women of Terezin*. New York: Jason Aronson.

DMX. 2001. "The Prayer IV." *On The Great Depression* (CD). New York: Ruff Ryders Records.

Dundes, A. 1996. "'Jumping the Broom': On the Origin and the Meaning of an African American Wedding Custom." *Journal of American Folklore Society* 109: 324–329.

Fiese, B. H. 2007. "Routines and Rituals: Opportunities for Participation in Family Health." *OTJR: Occupation, Participation and Health* 27: 415–424.

Fiese, B. H., T. J. Tomcho, M. Douglas, K. Josephs, S. Poltrock, and T. Baker. 2002. "Fifty Years of Research on Naturally Occurring Family Routines and Rituals: Cause of Celebration?" *Journal of Family Psychology* 16: 381–390.

Fiese, B. H., and K. A. T. Marjinsky. 1999. "Dinnertime Stories: Connecting Relationship Beliefs and Child Behavior." In *The Stories that Families Tell: Narrative Coherence, Narrative Interaction, and Relationship Beliefs*, edited by B. H. Fiese, A. J. Sameroff, H. D. Grotevant, F. S. Wamboldt, S. Dickstein, and D. Fravel. *Monographs of the Society for Research in Child Development* 64 (2, Serial No. 257: 52–68) Malden, MA: Blackwell.

Giroux, H. A. 1988. *Schooling and the Struggle of Public Life*. Minneapolis, MN: University of Minnesota Press.

Imber-Black, E. 1999. "Creating Meaningful Rituals for New Life Cycle Transitions. Pp. 202–214 in *The Expanded Family Life Cycle: Individual, Family and Social Perspective*, edited by B. Carter and M. McGeldrick. Needham Heights, MA: Allyn & Bacon.

———. 2002. "Family Rituals: From Research to the Counseling Room and Back Again: Comment on the Special Edition." *Journal of Family Psychology* 16: 445–446.

Karenga, M. 1998. *Kwanzaa: A Celebration for Family, Community and Culture*. Los Angeles: University of Sankore Press.

Laird, J. 1984. "Sorcerers, Shamans, and Social Workers: The Use of Rituals in Social Work Practice." *Social Work* 29: 123–129.

Mackey, J., and G. Grief. 1994. "Using Rituals to Help Parents in the School Setting: Lessons from Family Therapy." *Social Work in Education* 16: 171–178.

Mbiti, J. S. 1969. *African Religions and Philosophy*. Johannesburg, South Africa: Heinemann Educational Botswana.

Meske, C., G. F. Sanders, W. H. Meredith, and D. A. Abbott. 1994. "Perceptions of Rituals and Traditions among Elderly Persons." *Activities, Adaptation and Aging: The Journal of Activities Management* 18(2): 13–26.

NAMES Project Foundation. 2008. Retrieved August 29, 2008, from www.aidsquilt.org.

Payne, Y. A. 2008. "StreetLife' as a Site of Resiliency: How Street Life Oriented, Black Men Frame Opportunity in the United States." *Journal of Black Psychology* 34(3): 3–31.

Pewewardy, N., and M. J. D. Severson. 2003. "A Threat to Liberty: White Privilege and Disproportionate Minority Incarceration." *Journal of Progressive Human Services* 14(2): 53–74.

Quantz, R. A. 1999. "School Ritual as Performance: A Reconstruction of Durkheim's and Turner's Uses of Ritual." *Educational Theory* 49: 493–513.

Roberts, J. 1988. "Setting the Frame: Definition, Functions, and Typology of Rituals." Pp. 3–46 in *Rituals in Families and Family Therapy*, edited by E. Imber-Black, J. Roberts, and R. Whiting. New York: W. W. Norton.

Scott, J. C. (1990). *Domination and the Arts of Resistance*. New Haven, CT: Yale University Press.

Shakur, T. 1993. "Keep Your Head Up." On *Strictly 4 My N.I.G.G.A.Z.* (CD). Santa Monica, CA: Interscope Records.

van der Hart, O. 1983. *Rituals in Psychotherapy: Transition and Continuity*. New York: Irvington Publications.

Chapter 30: Betwixt and Be Tween: Gender Contradictions among Middle Schoolers, by Barbara J. Risman and Elizabeth Seale

Adams, Natalie, and Pamela Bettis. 2003. "Commanding the Room in Short Skirts: Cheering as the Embodiment of Ideal Girlhood." *Gender and Society* 17: 73–91.

Adams, Natalie, Alison Schmitke, and Amy Franklin. 2005. "Tomboys, Dykes, and Girly Girls: Interrogating the Subjectivities of Adolescent Female Athletes." *Women's Studies Quarterly* 33: 17–34.

Adler, Patricia A., and Peter Adler. 1995. "Dynamics of Inclusion and Exclusion in Preadolescent Cliques." *Social Psychology Quarterly* 58(3): 145–162.

Adler, Patricia A., and Peter Adler. 1998. *Peer Power: Preadolescent Culture and Identity*. New Brunswick, NJ: Rutgers University Press.

Allison, M. T. 1991. "Role Conflict and the Female Athlete: Preoccupations with Little Grounding." *Journal of Applied Sport Psychology* 3: 49–60.

Bettie, Julie. 2003. *Women Without Class: Girls, Race, and Identity*. Berkeley, CA: University of California Press.

Broad, K. L. 2001. "The Gendered Unapologetic: Queer Resistance in Women's Sport." *Sociology of Sport Journal* 18(2): 181–204.

Burn, Shawn Meghan. 2000. "Heterosexuals' Use of 'Fag' and 'Queer' to Deride One Another: A Contributor to Heterosexism and Stigma." *Journal of Homosexuality* 40: 1–11.

Canada, Geoffrey. 1998. *Reaching Up for Manhood: Transforming the Lives of Boys in America*. Boston: Beacon Press.

Chambers, Deborah, Estella Tincknell, and Joost Van Loon. 2004. "Peer Regulation of Teenage Sexual Identities." *Gender and Education* 16: 397–415.

Cockburn, Cynthia, and Gill Clarke. 2002. "'Everybody's Looking at You!': Girls Negotiating the 'Femininity Deficit' They Incur in Physical Education." *Women's Studies International Forum* 25: 651–665.

Connell, R. W. 1987. *Gender and Power: Society, the Person, and Sexual Politics*. Stanford, CA: Stanford University Press.

Deutsch, Francine M. 2007. "Undoing Gender." *Gender & Society* 21(1): 106–127.

Eder, Donna, Catherine Colleen Evans, and Stephen Parker. 1995. *School Talk: Gender and Adolescent Culture*. New Brunswick, NJ: Rutgers University Press.

Enke, Janet. 2005. "Athleticism and Femininity on a High School Basketball Team: An Interpretive Approach." *Sociological Studies of Children and Youth* 11: 115–152.

Eitzen, D. S. 1990. *Fair and Foul: Beyond the Myths and Paradoxes of Sports*. Lanham, MD: Rowman & Littlefield.

Fine, Gary Alan. 2004. "Adolescence as Cultural Toolkit: High School Debate and the Repertoires of Childhood and Adulthood." *Sociological Quarterly* 45(1): 1–20.

Froyum, Carissa. 2007. "At Least I'm Not Gay: Heterosexual Identity Making among Poor Black Teens." *Sexualities* 10(5): 605–624.

Gerson, Kathleen. 2002. "Moral Dilemmas, Moral Strategies, and the Transformation of Gender." *Gender & Society* 16(1): 8–28.

Hurrelmann, Klaus, and Stephen F. Hamilton. 1996. *Social Problems and Social Contexts in Adolescence*. New York: Aldine de Gruyter.

Kehily, Mary Jane, and Anoop Nayak. 1997. "'Lads and Laughter': Humour and the Production of Heterosexual Hierarchies." *Gender & Education* 9: 69–88.

Kling, Kristen C., Janet Shibley Hyde, Carolin J. Showers, and Brenda N. Buswell. 1999. "Gender Differences in Self-Esteem: A Meta-Analysis." *Psychological Bulletin* 125(4): 470–500.

Klomsten, Anne Torhild, Herb W. Marsh, and Einar M. Skaalvik. 2005. "Adolescents' Perceptions of Masculine and Feminine Values in Sport and Physical Education: A Study of Gender Differences." *Sex Roles: A Journal of Research* 52: 625–636.

Krane, Vikki. 2001. "We Can Be Athletic and Feminine, But Do We Want To? Challenging Hegemonic Femininity in Women's Sport." *Quest* 53: 115–133.

Krane, Vikki, Precilla Y. L. Choi, Shannon M. Baird, Christine M. Aimar, and Kerrie J. Kauer. 2004. "Living the Paradox: Female Athletes Negotiate Femininity and Muscularity." *Sex Roles: A Journal of Research* 50: 315–329.

Lemish, Dafna. 1998. "Spice Girls' Talk: A Case Study in the Development of Gendered Identity." Pp. 145–167 in *Millennium Girls: Today's Girls around the World*, edited by Sherri A. Inness. Lanham, MD: Rowman & Littlefield.

Mahaffy, Kimberly A. 2004. "Girls' Low Self-Esteem: How Is It Related to Later Socioeconomic Achievements?" *Gender & Society* 18(3): 309–327.

Malcom, Nancy L. 2003. "Constructing Female Athleticism: A Study of Girls' Recreational Softball." *American Behavioral Scientist* 46(10): 1387–1404.

Nayak, Anoop, and Mary Jane Kehily. 1996. "Playing It Straight: Masculinities, Homophobias and Schooling." *Journal of Gender Studies* 5: 211–231.

Pascoe, C. J. 2003. "Multiple Masculinities? Teenage Boys Talk about Jocks and Gender." *American Behavioral Scientist* 46: 1423–1438.

——. 2005. "'Dude, You're a Fag': Adolescent Masculinity and the Fag Discourse." *Sexualities* 8(3): 329–346.

——. 2007. *Dude, You're a Fag: Masculinity and Sexuality in High School*. Berkeley, CA: University of California Press.

Peterson, Anne, Rainer K. Silbereisen, and Silvia Sorenson. 1996. "Adolescent Development: A Global Perspective." Chapter 1 in *Social Problems and Social Contexts in Adolescence*, edited by K. Hurrelmann and S. F. Hamilton. New York: Aldine de Gruyter.

Phoenix, Ann, Stephen Frosh, and Rob Pattman. 2003. "Producing Contradictory Masculine Subject Positions: Narratives of Threat, Homophobia and Bullying in 11–14 Year Old Boys." *Journal of Social Issues* 59(1): 179–195.

Plummer, David C. 2001. "The Quest for Modern Manhood: Masculine Stereotypes, Peer Cultures and the Social Significance of Homophobia." *Journal of Adolescence* 24: 15–23.

Sutton-Smith, Brian. 1982. "A Performance Theory of Peer Relations." Pp. 65–77 in *The Social Life of Children in a Changing Society*, edited by K. Borman. Hillsdale, NJ: Lawrence Erlbum Associates.

Swidler, Ann. 1986. "Culture in Action: Symbols and Strategies." *American Sociological Review* 51(2): 273–286.

Talbani, Aziz. 2003. "Keeping Up Appearances: Multicultural Education in Postmodern Society." *Education and Society* 21(2): 5–18.

Thorne, Barrie. 1993. *Gender Play: Girls and Boys in School*. New Brunswick, NJ: Rutgers University Press.

Visser, Irene. 1996. "The Prototypicality of Gender: Contemporary Notions of Masculine and Feminine." *Women's Studies International Forum* 19(6): 589–600.

Wellman, David T. 1993. *Portraits of White Racism*, 2nd ed. New York: Cambridge University Press.

West, Candace, and Donald Zimmerman. 1987. "Doing Gender." *Gender & Society* 1: 125–151.

Chapter 31: Orgasm in College Hookups and Relationships, by Elizabeth A. Armstrong, Paula England, and Alison C. K. Fogarty

Anonymous, M. D. 2006. *Unprotected: A Campus Psychiatrist Reveals How Political Correctness in Her Profession Endangers Every Student*. New York: Sentinel HC.

Bailey, Beth L. 1989. *From Front Porch to Back Seat: Courtship in Twentieth-Century America*. Baltimore, MD: Johns Hopkins University Press.

Bogle, Kathleen A. 2007. "The Shift from Dating to Hooking Up in College: What Scholars Have Missed." *Sociology Compass* 1/2: 775–788.

———. 2008. *Hooking Up: Sex, Dating, and Relationships on Campus*. New York: New York University Press.

Boswell, A. Ayers, and Joan Z. Spade. 1996. "Fraternities and Collegiate Rape Culture: Why Are Some Fraternities More Dangerous Places for Women?" *Gender & Society* 10: 133–147.

Braun, Virginia, Nicola Gavey, and Kathryn McPhillips. 2003. "The 'Fair Deal?' Unpacking Accounts of Reciprocity in Heterosex." *Sexualities* 6: 237–261.

Buss, David M. 1994. *The Evolution of Human Desire: Strategies of Human Mating*. New York: Basic Books.

Chodorow, Nancy. 1978. *The Reproduction of Mothering: Psychoanalysis and the Sociology of Gender*. Berkeley, CA: University of California Press.

Crawford, Mary, and Danielle Popp. 2003. "Sexual Double Standards: A Review and Methodological Critique of Two Decades of Research." *Journal of Sex Research* 40: 13–27.

Darling, C. A., J. K. Davidson, Sr., and D. A. Jennings. 1991. "The Female Sexual Response Revisited: Understanding the Multiorgasmic Experience in Women." *Archives of Sexual Behavior* 20: 527–540.

Denizet-Lewis, Benoit. 2004. "Friends, Friends with Benefits and the Benefits of the Local Mall." *New York Times*, May 30.

England, Paula, Emily Fitzgibbons Shafer, and Alison C. K. Fogarty. 2007. "Hooking Up and Forming Romantic Relationships on Today's College Campuses." In *The Gendered Society Reader*, 3rd ed., edited by Michael S. Kimmel and Amy Aronson. New York: Oxford University Press.

Fisher, Seymour. 1973. *The Female Orgasm*. New York: Basic Books.

Freitas, Donna. 2008. *Sex and the Soul: Juggling Sexuality, Spirituality, Romance and Religion on America's College Campuses*. New York: Oxford University Press.

Gagnon, John H., and William Simon. 1974. *Sexual Conduct: The Social Sources of Human Sexuality*. London: Aldine Transaction.

Gilmartin, Shannon K. 2005. "The Centrality and Costs of Heterosexual Romantic Love among First-Year College Women." *Journal of Higher Education* 76: 609–634.

Glenn, Norval, and Elizabeth Marquardt. 2001. *Hooking Up, Hanging Out, and Hoping for Mr. Right: College Women on Mating and Dating Today*. A report conducted by the Institute for American Values for the Independent Women's Forum, New York, NY.

González-López, Gloria. 2005. *Erotic Journeys: Mexican Immigrants and Their Sex Lives*. Berkeley, CA: University of California Press.

Hamilton, Laura, and Elizabeth A. Armstrong. 2008. "Gendered Sexuality in Emerging Adulthood: Double Binds and Flawed Options." Paper presented at the annual meeting of the American Sociological Association Annual Meeting, Boston, MA.

Hite, Shere. 1976. *The Hite Report: A Nationwide Study of Female Sexuality*. New York: Seven Stories Press.

Holland, Dorothy C., and Margaret A. Eisenhart. 1990. *Educated in Romance: Women, Achievement and College Culture*. Chicago: University of Chicago Press.

Kasic, Allison. 2008. "Take Back the Date." Independent Women's Forum. Available at www.iwf.org/campus/show/20122.html.

Kass, Leon R. 1997. "The End of Courtship." *Public Interest* 126: 39–63.

Laumann, Edward O., John H. Gagnon, Robert T. Michael, and Stuart Michaels. 1994. *The Social Organization of Sexuality: Sexual Practices in the United States*. Chicago: University of Chicago Press.

Mah, Kenneth, and Yitzchak M. Binik. 2001. "The Nature of Human Orgasm: A Critical Review of Major Trends." *Clinical Psychology Review* 21: 823–856.

Martin, Karin. 1996. *Puberty, Sexuality, and the Self: Boys and Girls at Adolescence*. New York: Routledge.

Paul, Elizabeth L., Brian McManus, and Elizabeth Hayes. 2000. "'Hookups': Characteristics and Correlates of College Students' Spontaneous and Anonymous Sexual Experiences." *Journal of Sex Research* 37: 76–88.

Popenoe, David, and Barbara Defoe Whitehead. 2000. *The State of Our Unions, 2000: The Social Health of Marriage in America*. New Brunswick, NJ: National Marriage Project.

Richters, Juliet, Richard de Vissar, Chris Rissel, and Anthony Smith. 2006. "Sexual Practices at Last Heterosexual Encounter and Occurrence of Orgasm in a National Survey." *Journal of Sex Research* 43: 217–226.

Schalet, Amy. 2004. "Must We Fear Adolescent Sexuality." *Medscape General Medicine* 6: 44.

———. Forthcoming. "Subjectivity, Intimacy, and the Empowerment Paradigm of Adolescent Sexuality." *Feminist Studies*.

Schwartz, Pepper, and Virginia Rutter. 2000. *The Gender of Sexuality*. Lanham, MD: AltaMira Press.

Sessions Stepp, Laura. 2007. *Unhooked: How Young Women Pursue Sex, Delay Love, and Lose at Both*. New York: Riverhead Books.

Stombler, Mindy. 1994. "'Buddies' or 'Slutties': The Collective Sexual Reputation of Fraternity Little Sisters." *Gender & Society* 8: 297–323.

Tanenbaum, Leora. 1999. *Slut! Growing Up Female With a Bad Reputation*. New York: Seven Stories Press.

Tolman, Deborah L. 2002. *Dilemmas of Desire: Teenage Girls Talk about Sexuality*. Cambridge, MA: Harvard University Press.

Townsend, J. M. 1995. "Sex without Emotional Involvement: An Evolutionary Interpretation of Sex Differences." *Archives of Sexual Behavior* 24: 173–206.

Waite, Linda J., and Maggie Gallagher. 2000. *The Case for Marriage: Why Married People Are Happier, Healthier, and Better Off Financially*. New York: Doubleday.

Waite, Linda J., and Kara Joyner. 2001. "Emotional Satisfaction and Physical Pleasure in Sexual Unions: Time Horizon, Sexual Behavior, and Sexual Exclusivity." *Journal of Marriage and Family* 63: 247–264.

White, Emily. 2001. *Fast Girls: Teenage Tribes and the Myth of the Slut*. New York: Simon and Schuster.

Yancey Martin, Patricia, and Robert A. Hummer. 1989. "Fraternities and Rape on Campus." *Gender & Society* 3: 457–473.

Chapter 32: Falling Back on Plan B: The Children of the Gender Revolution Face Uncharted Territory, by Kathleen Gerson

Acock, Alan C., and David H. Demo. 1994. *Family Diversity and Well-Being*. Thousand Oaks, CA: Sage.

Amato, Paul R., and Alan Booth. 1997. *A Generation at Risk: Growing Up in an Era of Family Upheaval*. Cambridge, MA: Harvard University Press.

Amato, Paul R., and Bryndl Hohmann-Marriott. 2007. "A Comparison of High- and Low-Distress Marriages That End in Divorce." *Journal of Marriage and Family* 69(3): 621–638.

Barnett, Rosalind C., and Caryl Rivers. 1996. *She Works/He Works: How Two-Income Families Are Happier, Healthier, and Better-Off*. San Francisco: Harper.

Belkin, Lisa. 2003. "The Opt-Out Revolution." *New York Times Magazine*, October 26.

Bengtson, Vern L., Timothy J. Biblarz, and Robert E. L. Roberts. 2002. *How Families Still Matter: A Longitudinal Study of Youth in Two Generations*. New York: Cambridge University Press.

Bennetts, Leslie. 2007. *The Feminine Mistake: Are We Giving Up Too Much?* New York: Voice/Hyperion.

Bianchi, Suzanne M., John P. Robinson, and Melissa A. Milkie. 2006. *Changing Rhythms of American Family Life*. New York: Russell Sage Foundation.

Blankenhorn, David. 1995. *Fatherless America: Confronting Our Most Urgent Social Problem*. New York: Basic Books.

Booth, Alan, and Paul R. Amato. 2001. "Parental Predivorce Relations and Offspring Post-Divorce Well-Being." *Journal of Marriage and Family* 63(1): 197–212.

Boushey, Heather. 2008. "'Opting out?' The Effect of Children on Women's Employment in the United States." *Feminist Economics* 14(1): 1–36.

Coontz, Stephanie. 2005. *Marriage, a History: From Obedience to Intimacy, or How Love Conquered Marriage*. New York: Viking.

Furstenberg, Frank F., and Andrew J. Cherlin. 1991. *Divided Families: What Happens to Children When Parents Part*. Cambridge, MA: Harvard University Press.

Galinsky, Ellen. 1999. *Ask the Children: What America's Children Really Think about Working Parents*. New York: Morrow.

Gerson, Kathleen. 2006. "Families As Trajectories: Children's Views of Family Life in Contemporary America." In *Families between Flexibility and Dependability: Perspectives for a Life Cycle Family Policy*, edited by Hans Bertram, Helga Kruger, and Katarina Spiel. Farmington Hills, MI: Verlag Barbara Budrich.

———. Forthcoming. *Blurring Boundaries: How the Children of the Gender Revolution Are Remaking Family and Work*. New York: Oxford University Press.

Harvey, Lisa. 1999. "Short-Term and Long-Term Effects of Early Parental Employment on Children of the National Longitudinal Study of Youth." *Developmental Psychology* 35(2): 445–459.

Hetherington, E. M. 1999. *Coping with Divorce, Single Parenting, and Remarriage: A Risk and Resiliency Perspective*. Mahwah, NJ: Lawrence Erlbaum Associates.

Hirshman, Linda. 2006. *Get to Work*. New York: Viking.

Hochschild, Arlie R. 1989. *The Second Shift: Working Parents and the Revolution at Home*. New York: Viking.

Hoffman, Lois. 1987. "The Effects on Children of Maternal and Paternal Employment." Pp. 362–395, in *Families and Work*, edited by N. Gerstel and H. E. Gross. Philadelphia: Temple University Press.

Hoffman, Lois, Norma Wladis, and Lise M. Youngblade. 1999. *Mothers at Work: Effects on Children's Well-Being*. New York: Cambridge University Press.

Li, Allen J. 2007. "The Kids are OK: Divorce and Children's Behavior Problems." Santa Monica, CA: Rand Working Paper WR 489.

Lorber, Judith. 1994. *Paradoxes of Gender*. New Haven, CT: Yale University Press.

McLanahan, Sara, and Gary D. Sandefur. 1994. *Growing Up with a Single Parent: What Hurts, What Helps*. Cambridge, MA: Harvard University Press.

Moen, Phyllis and Patricia Roehling. 2005. *The Career Mystique: Cracks in the American Dream*. Lanham, MD: Rowman & Littlefield Publishers.

Moore, Kristin A., Rosemary Chalk, Juliet Scarpa, and Sharon Vandivere. 2002. *Family Strengths: Often Overlooked, But Real*. Washington, DC: Child Trends.

Parcel, Toby L., and Elizabeth G. Menaghan. 1994. *Parents' Jobs and Children's Lives*. New York: Aldine de Gruyter.

Pew Research Center. 2007a. "As Marriage and Parenthood Drift Apart, Public Is Concerned about Social Impact." Retrieved June 19, 2008, from http://pewresearch.org/pubs/526/marriage-parenthood.

———. 2007b. "How Young People View Their Lives, Futures and Politics: A Portrait of the "'Generation Next.'" Retrieved June 19, 2008, from http://people-press.org/reports/pdf/300.pdf.

Popenoe, David. 1988. *Disturbing the Nest: Family Change and Decline in Modern Societies*. New York: Aldine de Gruyter.

———. 1996. *Life without Father: Compelling New Evidence That Fatherhood and Marriage Are Indispensable for the Good of Children and Society*. New York: Martin Kessler Books.

Popenoe, David, Jean B. Elshtain, and David Blankenhorn. 1996. *Promises to Keep: Decline and Renewal of Marriage in America*. Lanham, MD: Rowman & Littlefield Publishers.

Risman, Barbara J. 1998. *Gender Vertigo: American Families in Transition*. New Haven, CT: Yale University Press.

Roberts, Sam. 2007. "Fifty-one percent of Women Are Now Living without Spouse." *New York Times*, January 16.

Skolnick, Arlene, and Stacey Rosencrantz. 1994. "The New Crusade for the Old Family." *American Prospect*, 18 (Summer): 59–65.

Springer, Kristen W. 2007. "Research or Rhetoric? A Response to Wilcox and Nock." *Sociological Forum* 22(1): 111–116.

Stacey, Judith. 1996. *In the Name of the Family: Rethinking Family Values in the Postmodern Age*. Boston: Beacon Press.

Stone, Pamela. 2007. *Opting Out? Why Women Really Quit Careers and Head Home*. Berkeley, CA: University of California Press.

Waite, Linda J., and Maggie Gallagher. 2000. *The Case for Marriage: Why Married People Are Happier, Healthier, and Better Off Financially*. New York: Doubleday.

West, Candace, and Don H. Zimmerman. 1987. "Doing Gender." *Gender & Society* 1(2): 125–151.

Whitehead, Barbara D. 1997. *The Divorce Culture*. New York: Knopf.

Williams, Joan. 2000. *Unbending Gender: Why Family and Work Conflict and What to Do About It*. New York: Oxford University Press.

———. 2007. "The Opt-Out Revolution Revisited." *American Prospect* (March): A12–A15.

Zerubavel, Eviatar. 1991. *The Fine Line: Making Distinctions in Everyday Life*. Chicago: University of Chicago Press.

Chapter 33: Men's Changing Contribution to Family Work, by Oriel Sullivan

Beck, Ulrich, and E. Beck-Gernsheim. 1995. *The Normal Chaos of Love*. Cambridge, UK: Polity Press.

Benjamin, Orly, and Oriel Sullivan. 1999. "Relational Resources, Gender Consciousness and Possibilities of Change in Marital Relationships." *Sociological Review* 47(4): 794–820.

Bianchi, Suzanne M., John P. Robinson, and Melissa A. Milkie. 2006. *Changing Rhythms of American Family Life* (Rose Series in Sociology). New York: Russell Sage Foundation.

Connell, R. W. 2000. *The Men and the Boys*. Cambridge, UK: Polity Press.

Coltrane, Scott. 1998. *Gender and Families*. Thousand Oaks, CA: Pine Forge Press.

———. 2004. "Fathering: Paradoxes, Contradictions and Dilemmas." Pp. 224–243 in *Handbook of Contemporary Families: Considering the Past, Contemplating the Future*, edited by Marilyn Coleman and Lawrence Ganong. Thousand Oaks, CA: Sage Publications.

Deutsch, Francine M. 1999. *Halving It All: How Equally Shared Parenting Works*. Cambridge, MA: Harvard University Press.

Ferree, Myra Marx. 1990. "Beyond Separate Spheres: Feminism and Family Research." *Journal of Marriage and Family* 52: 866–884.

Fisher, Kimberley, Muriel Egerton, Jonathan I. Gershuny, and John P. Robinson. 2007. "Gender Convergence in the American Heritage Time Use Study (AHTUS)." *Social Indicators Research*. 82(1): 1–33.

Gershuny, Jonathan. 2000. *Changing Times: Work and Leisure in Postindustrial Society*. Oxford, UK: Oxford University Press.

Gerson, J. M., and K. Peiss. 1985. "Boundaries, Negotiation, Consciousness: Reconceptualizing Gender Relations." *Social Problems* 32: 317–331.

Gerson, Kathleen. 2001. "Dilemmas of Involved Fatherhood." In *Shifting the Center: Understanding Contemporary Families*, edited by Susan J. Ferguson. California Mountain View, CA: Mayfield Publishing.

Giddens, Anthony. 1992. *The Transformation of Intimacy*. Cambridge, UK: Polity Press.

Goldscheider, Frances K., and Linda J. Waite. 1991. *New Families, No Families? The Transformation of the American Home*. Berkeley, CA: University of California Press.

Hochschild, Arlie Russell. 1995. "Understanding the Future of Fatherhood." In *Changing Fatherhood: An Interdisciplinary Perspective*, edited by M. C. P. van Dougen, G. A. Frinking, and M. J. Jacobs. Amsterdam: Thesis Publishers.

Hook, Jennifer L. 2006. "Care in Context: Men's Unpaid Work in 20 Countries, 1965–2003." *American Sociological Review* 71(4): 639–660.

Knijn, T. 1995. "Towards Post-Paternalism?" In *Changing Fatherhood: An Interdisciplinary Perspective*, edited by M. C. van Dougen, G. A. Frinking, and M. J. Jacobs. Amsterdam: Thesis Publishers.

Pew Research Center. 2007. "As Marriage and Parenthood Drift Apart, Public Is Concerned about Social Impact: Generation Gap in Values, Behavior." Social and Demographic Trends Report. Available at http://pewresearch.org/pubs/526/marriage-parenthood.

Pleck, Joseph H., and Brian P. Masciadrelli. 2003. "Paternal Involvement: Levels, Sources, and Consequences." In *The Role of the Father in Child Development*, 4th ed., edited by Michael E. Lamb. New York: Wiley.

Risman, Barbara. 1998. *Gender Vertigo*. New Haven, CT: Yale University Press.

———. 2004. "Gender As Social Structure: Theory Wrestling with Activism." *Gender & Society* 18(4): 429–450.

Robinson, John. P., and Geoffrey Godbey. 1999. *Time for Life: The Surprising Ways Americans Use Their Time*, 2nd ed. University Park, PA: Penn State University Press.

Scott, Jackie, D. F. Alwin, and M. Brown. 1996. "Changing Sex-Role Attitudes." *Sociology* 30(3): 427–445, 489.

Smart, Carol, and Bren Neale. 1999. *Family Fragments?* Cambridge, UK: Polity Press.

Sullivan, Oriel. 2006. *Changing Gender Relations, Changing Families: Tracing the Pace of Change over Time* (Gender Lens Series). Lanham, MD: Rowman & Littlefield.

Sullivan, Oriel, and Jonathan I. Gershuny. 2001. "Cross-National Changes in Time-Use: Some Sociological (Hi)stories Re-examined." *British Journal of Sociology* 52(4): 331–347.

Thompson, Linda. 1993. "Conceptualising Gender in Marriage: The Case of Marital Care." *Journal of Marriage and Family* 55: 557–569.

West, C., and D. H. Zimmerman. 1987. Doing Gender. *Gender & Society* 1: 125–151.

Chapter 34: Briefing Paper: Men's Changing Contribution to Housework and Child Care, by Oriel Sullivan and Scott Coltrane

Bianchi, Suzanne M., John P. Robinson, and Melissa A. Milkie. 2006. *Changing Rhythms of American Family Life* (Rose Series in Sociology). New York: Russell Sage Foundation.

Coltrane, Scott. 1996. *Family Man: Fatherhood, Housework and Gender Equity*. New York: Oxford University Press.

———. 2000. "Research on Household Labor: Modeling and Measuring the Social Embeddedness of Routine Family Work." *Journal of Marriage and Family*, 62: 1209–1233.

———. 2004. "Fathering: Paradoxes, Contradictions and Dilemmas." Pp. 224–243 in *Handbook of Contemporary Families: Considering the Past, Contemplating the Future*, edited by Marilyn Coleman and Lawrence Ganong. Thousand Oaks, CA: Sage Publications.

Cooke, Lynn P. 2006. "'Doing' Gender in Context: Household Bargaining and Risk of Divorce in Germany and the United States." *American Journal of Sociology* 112(2): 442–472.

Fisher, Kimberley, Muriel Egerton, Jonathan I. Gershuny, and John P. Robinson. 2006. "Gender Convergence in the American Heritage Time Use Study (AHTUS)." *Social Indicators Research*, 82(1): 1–33.

Gershuny, Jonathan I. 2000. *Changing Times: Work and Leisure in Postindustrial Society.* Oxford: Oxford University Press.

Gershuny, Jonathan I., Michael Bittman, and John Brice. 2005. "Exit, Voice, and Suffering: Do Couples Adapt to Changing Employment Patterns?" *Journal of Marriage and Family,* 67: 656–665.

Hook, Jennifer L. 2006. "Care in Context: Men's Unpaid Work in 20 Countries, 1965–2003." *American Sociological Review,* 71(4): 639–660.

Jacobs, Jerry A., and Kathleen Gerson. 2004. *The Time Divide: Work, Family and Gender Inequality.* Cambridge, MA: Harvard University Press.

Pleck, Joseph H., and Brian P. Masciadrelli. 2003. "Paternal Involvement: Levels, Sources, and Consequences." In *The Role of the Father in Child Development,* 4th ed., edited by Michael E. Lamb. New York: Wiley.

Robinson, John P., and Geoffrey Godbey. 1999. *Time for Life: The Surprising Ways Americans Use Their Time,* 2nd ed. University Park, PA: Penn State University Press.

Sullivan, Oriel. 2006. *Changing Gender Relations, Changing Families: Tracing the Pace of Change over Time* (Gender Lens Series). Lanham, MD: Rowman & Littlefield.

Sullivan, Oriel, and Jonathan I. Gershuny. 2001. Cross-National Changes in Time-Use: Some Sociological (Hi)stories Re-examined. *British Journal of Sociology,* 52(4): 331–347.

Chapter 36: Briefing Paper: Moms and Jobs: Trends in Mothers' Employment and Which Mothers Stay Home, by David Cotter, Paula England, and Joan Hermsen

Bergmann, Barbara. 2005. *The Economic Emergence of Women,* 2nd ed. New York: Basic Books.

Bianchi, Suzanne, John P. Robinson, and Melissa A. Milkie. 2006. *Changing Rhythms of American Family Life.* New York: Russell Sage Foundation.

Cotter, David A., Joan M. Hermsen, and Reeve Vanneman. 2004. *Gender Inequality at Work.* New York: Russell Sage Foundation and Population Reference Bureau.

Gornick, Janet, and Marcia K. Meyers. 2005. *Families That Work: Policies for Reconciling Parenthood and Employment.* New York, Russell Sage Foundation.

Juhn, Chinhui, and Kevin M. Murphy. 1997. "Wage Inequality and Family Labor Supply." *Journal of Labor Economics* 15: 72–79.

Mare, Robert D. 1991. "Five Decades of Educational Assortative Mating." *American Sociological Review* 56: 15–32.

Williams, Joan. 2006. "'Opt Out' or Pushed Out? How the Press Covers Work/Family Conflict." Center on Work Life Law, University of California Hastings School of the Law, available at www.uchastings.edu/site_files/WLL/OptOutPushedOut.pdf.

Chapter 37: Briefing Paper: Women's Money Matters: Earnings and Housework in Dual Earner Families, by Sanjiv Gupta

Bianchi, Suzanne, M., Melissa A. Milkie, Liana C. Sayer, and John P. Robinson. 2000. "Is Anyone Doing the Housework? Trends in the Gender Division of Household Labor." *Social Forces,* 79(1): 191–228.

U.S. Department of Commerce, Bureau of the Census. 1998. Statistical Abstract of the United States. Washington, DC: US Government Printing Office.

Chapter 39: Domestic Violence in Heterosexual Relationships, by Rhea V. Almeida

Almeida, R. 1993. "Unexamined Assumptions and Service Delivery Systems: Feminist Theory and Racial Exclusions." *Journal of Feminist Family Therapy* 5: 3–23.

Almeida, R. 1996. "Hindus, Muslims, Christians." In *Ethnicity and Family Therapy*, 2nd ed., edited by Monica McGoldrick, Joe Giordano, and Nydia Garcia-Preto. New York: Guilford Press.

Almeida, R., and M. Bograd. 1990. "Sponsorship: Men Holding Men Accountable for Domestic Violence." *Journal of Feminist Family Therapy* 2: 243–256.

Almeida, Rhea V., Ken Dolan-Del Vecchio, and Lynn Parker. 2007. *Transformative Family Therapy: Just Families in a Just Society*. Boston: Allyn & Bacon.

Almeida, R., and R. Durkin. 1999. "The Cultural Context Model: Therapy for Couples with Domestic Violence." *Journal of Marital and Family Therapy* 25(3): 313–324.

Almeida, R., and J. Hudak. 2002. "The Cultural Context Model." Pp. 1–26 in *Programs for Men Who Batter: Interventions and Prevention Strategies in a Diverse Society*, edited by Etiony Aldarondo and Fernando Mederos. Kingston, NJ: Civic Research Institute.

Almeida, R., and J. Lockard. 2005. "The Cultural Context Model." Pp. 301–19 in *Domestic Violence at the Margins: Readings on Race, Class, Gender, and Culture*, edited by Natalie Sokolov. New Brunswick, NJ: Rutgers University Press.

Avis, J. M. 1992a. "Current Trends in Feminist Thought and Therapy: Perspectives on Sexual Abuse and Violence Within Families in North America." *Journal of Marital and Family Therapy* 4: 874–900.

———. 1992b. "Where Are All the Family Therapists? Abuse and Violence Within Families and Family Therapy's Response." *Journal of Marital and Family Therapy* 18: 225–233.

Bograd, M. 1984. "Family Systems Approaches to Wife Battering: A Feminist Critique." *American Journal of Orthopsychiatry* 54: 558–568.

———. 1986. "Holding the Line: Confronting the Abusive Partner." *Family Therapy Networker* 10(3): 44–47.

———. 1988. "How Battered Women and Abusive Men Account for Domestic Violence: Excuses, Justifications or Explanations?" In *Coping with Family Violence*, edited by T. Hotaling, D. Finkelhor, J. Kirkpatrick, and M. Straus. Newbury Park, CA: Sage Publications.

Collins, Patricia H. 1989. "The Social Construction of Black Feminist Thought." *Signs: Journal of Women in Culture and Society* 14(4): 745–773.

Coontz, S. 2006. *Marriage, A History: How Love Conquered Marriage*. New York: Penguin Books.

Crenshaw, K. 1994. "Mapping the Margins: Intersectionality, Identity, Politics, and Violence Against Women of Color." In *The Public Nature of Private Violence*, edited by M. A. Fineman and R. Mykitiuk. New York: Routledge.

Dobash, R. E., and R. P. Dobash. 1979. *Violence Against Wives: A Case Against the Patriarchy*. New York: Free Press.

Duneier, M. 1992. *Slim's Table: Race, Respectability, and Masculinity*. Chicago: University of Chicago Press.

Farley, N. 1992. "Same Sex Domestic Violence." In *Counseling Gay Men and Lesbians: Journey to the End of the Rainbow*, edited by Sari H. Dworkin and Fernando J. Gutierrez. Alexandria, VA: American Counseling Association.

Freire, P., and M. B. Ramos. 1982. *The Pedagogy of the Oppressed*. New York: Continuum.

Kivel, P. 1992. *Men's Work: How to Stop the Violence That Tears Our Lives Apart*. New York: Ballantine Books.

Lui, Meizhu, Barbara Robles, Betsy Leondar-Wright, Rose Brewer, and Rebecca Adamson. 2006. *The Color of Wealth: The Story Behind the U.S. Racial Divide*. New York: New Press.

Narayan, Uma. 1995. "'Male-Order' Brides: Immigrant Women, Domestic Violence, and Immigration Law." *Hypatia* 10: 104–20.

Sokolov, Natalie, ed. 2005 *Domestic Violence at the Margins: Readings on Race, Class, Gender, and Culture*. New Brunswick, NJ: Rutgers University Press.

U.S. Department of Justice. 2005. Bureau of Justice Statistics. National Coalition Against Domestic Violence www.ncadv.org/files/DV_Facts.pdf

Weissman, Deborah M. 2007. "The Personal Is Political—and Economic: Rethinking Domestic Violence." *Brigham Young University Law Review* 2: 387–443.

Credits

Index